D1603669

SPANISH SEA

SPANISH SEA

The Gulf of Mexico
in North American Discovery
1500–1685

by

ROBERT S. WEDDLE

Texas A&M University Press

COLLEGE STATION

Copyright © 1985 by Robert S. Weddle

All rights reserved

Library of Congress Cataloging in Publication Data

Weddle, Robert S.
  Spanish Sea: the Gulf of Mexico in North American discovery, 1500–1685.

    Bibliography: p.
    Includes index.
    1. Mexico, Gulf of—History. 2. Gulf States—History—
To 1803. 3. America—Discovery and exploration—Span-
ish. 4. Mexico—History—To 1810. I. Title.
F296.W43 1985   970.01'6   84-40554
ISBN 0-89096-211-1

Manufactured in the United States of America

FIRST EDITION

In memory of
Charles Leonard Weddle, Senior,
whose legacy was an inquiring mind

Contents

List of Illustrations

Acknowledgments

This work was made possible through the assistance of a research grant from the National Endowment for the Humanities. During one of the two years' study supported by the grant, I was privileged to have David Block, then a Ph.D. candidate at the University of Texas at Austin, as my research associate. He has earned my eternal gratitude for wading through the Spanish archives with me, serving as my personal guide and, at times, interpreter, then putting in long hours at the microfilm reader, transcribing documents. His assistance in bibliographical matters was invaluable. Thanks also are due his wife, Peggy Robinson, not only for her forbearance but also for her expert assistance with travel arrangements.

Many are those who have contributed to this work, in many different ways. The sine qua non of the entire effort was the Nettie Lee Benson Latin American Collection at the University of Texas at Austin, and its courteous and helpful staff. Texas friends who helped in the planning or execution of the project include Elizabeth A. H. John, Chester V. Kielman, T. N. Campbell, G. Douglas Inglis, and Nancy Troike, all of Austin; David McDonald and the Reverend Father Benedict Leutenegger of San Antonio; Sister Mary Christine Morkovsky of San Antonio and Ogdensburg, New York; D. E. Kilgore of Corpus Christi; Donald E. Chipman of Denton; Light Cummins of Sherman; and H. G. Dulaney, director of the Sam Rayburn Memorial Library, Bonham.

From Texas to Florida, helping hands were extended by Glenn R. Conrad and Carl Brasseaux, University of Southwestern Louisiana, Lafayette; Paul E. Hoffman, Louisiana State University; John R. Kemp and Rose Lambert, Louisiana State Museum Library, New Orleans; Bobs M. Tusa, Loyola University; Robert D. Bush, Historic New Orleans Collection; Jay Higginbotham, Mobile Public Library; Caldwell Delaney and Roy V. Tallon, Jr., Mobile City Museum; William S. Coker, University of West Florida, and A. B. Thomas, Pensacola; Elizabeth Alexander and Samuel Proctor, University of Florida, Gainesville; Jack D. L. Holmes, Birmingham, Alabama; and Doris L. Olds of Santa Rosa Beach, Florida.

Fondly, I recall the spirit of friendly helpfulness that greeted us at the various archives visited in Seville, Moguer, Madrid, and Simancas. I am especially grateful for my association with Don Roberto Barreiro-Meiro, subdirector of the Museo Naval, Madrid, and for our subsequent correspondence that helped to tie up loose ends.

I retain fond memories also of fellow researchers met in Spain. To all of them, thanks for shared thoughts and fellowship. Thanks also to my wife, Nan Avis Weddle, for her patience and companionship on our various travels; to my brother-in-law James T. Young, companion and chauffeur on our long automobile trip covering almost all the Mexican Gulf coast; and to all those not mentioned by name who have listened, suggested, or contributed in other ways to keeping the challenge alive.

Preface

Eₐʀʟʏ in the twentieth century, New World discovery and exploration ceased to be popular subjects for historical study. The reasons are a bit obscure, for the task was not nearly complete. Many of the works most relied upon are marked by confused facts, unclear focus, and uncertain conclusions. The vital conduit for the first real European access to the North American mainland—the Gulf of Mexico—has been grossly neglected, never having been treated as the distinct entity that it is.

Following Columbus's initial discovery of the fringe islands, the Andalusian voyagers groped their way through the maze, seeking a continent. Running uphill, as it were, they found Central and South America. Not for sixteen years did the first navigator find the crucial passage into the Gulf of Mexico. Another decade passed before the discoverers realized that a second continent lay beyond the Gulf. Only then could the actual discovery of mainland North America begin. Through this "Spanish Sea"—which the Gulf remained for almost two centuries after the first known European entry—the discoverers and explorers advanced onto the continent. The Gulf and its environs were the theater for the earliest and most determined efforts to conquer the natives and explore and settle the interior.

In the present volume, I have knowingly attempted to serve two masters. The general reader—if my intention has been translated successfully—will find in the successive accounts of the various discovery episodes a lively series of related adventures, unencumbered by scholarly documentation until he comes to the "Sources and Notes" at the end of each chapter. He may skip over these if he finds them tedious. The specialist, on the other hand, will perceive from these bibliographical essays the depth of research supporting the challenge here offered to some longstanding concepts. If so inclined, he may pursue the sources himself.

It is not my purpose to dispute previous interpretations merely for the sake of being different or to justify my work by offering a spurious new twist. No disrespect toward those historians who established the basic framework is intended. In many respects their work remains solid—so solid, in fact, that no one has dared offer serious challenge. But no work stands forever, and the time has come to reassess; to take advantage of the more facile means of accessing archival material; to embrace the inevitable expansion of knowledge and the enhanced capacity for critical analysis that have occurred in the interim.

The sources of error in the various attempts to track the early explorers really are quite basic: (1) an anachronistic assumption of accuracy in latitudes, directions, and distances appearing in their accounts, which often were thrown askew by inadequate navigational instruments or tenuous guesswork; (2) a failure to consider how far a ship under sail, feeling her way along an uncharted, shoal-studded coast, might travel in one daylight span; (3) too-literal interpretations of primitive maps that were often speculative or schematic to start with; and (4) a failure to understand, or to keep in mind, that some geographical designations initially had different meanings from the ones attached at present.

Concerning the last point, it has been well established that Florida in its original context embraced a much broader territory than the present state. Yet our historical interpreters have had difficulty remembering that "Florida" in a sixteenth century document might actually mean Texas or the modern Mexican state of Tamaulipas.

Similarly, the Río de las Palmas, designating the river now called Soto la Marina in Tamaulipas, has been taken for the Río Grande. The name for the Gulf itself, Seno Mexicano, has been misapplied to the eighteenth-century colony of Nuevo Santander, as an abbreviation of "Costa del Seno Mexicano," which means "Gulf coast." Indications are found also that some Indian and very early colonial place names still in use have been shuffled about: Tampa, for example.

Writers of state and regional histories have been prone to error because of their inability to transcend political boundaries; the historians of Texas and Florida have had as much difficulty bridging the gap between them as the Spaniards had establishing a trail to link the two provinces. Greater still has been the dichotomy between the United States and Mexico.

Often overlooked in attempts at a comprehensive discovery narrative have been the relationship of the major expeditions with one another and the shading contributed by the minor episodes. A series of these lesser events, for example, reveals Tristán de Luna's Florida entry as a follow-up to Hernando de Soto's. Pedro Menéndez in peninsular Florida and Luis de Carvajal in Nuevo León espoused a common objective; the failure of one inspired the efforts of the other.

I make no claim of having completed in this one volume the ultimate reappraisal of all the discovery and exploration episodes herein recounted. Rather, my purpose has been to offer the *basis* for a long-overdue reassessment which, when it is made, should suggest a new starting place for the study of United States history. That place should be the Gulf of Mexico, through which the discoverers, explorers, and colonizers of North America moved for almost a century before there was a lasting European settlement on the Atlantic seaboard.

And what better time to speak of reexamination and reorientation? In less than a decade, the five-hundredth anniversary of Columbus's discovery will be celebrated throughout the Americas. Already at hand is another milestone marking the entry three hundred years ago of the Frenchman La Salle to plant a colony on the northern Gulf shore. La Salle's breach of the Spanish Sea, 1685, heralded the end of the Gulf's exclusively Spanish era. It brought a renewed burst of Spanish exploration and made the French partners in the enterprise. That effort, extending to 1803, when the United States acquired the Louisiana Territory, will be the subject of a later volume.

This work on discovery and exploration has involved several reconnaissance journeys of my own, extending around the Gulf from Fort Myers, Florida (where foul weather cut short the trip), to Río Lagartos, Yucatán, and thence down the Caribbean coast to Chetumal, Quintana Roo. With the exception of one short voyage along the Texas coast, all this coastal reconnaissance was by automobile. How I would like to examine the entire shoreline from the air and to view it from the sea! Nevertheless, two major expeditions and several lesser ones—plus travel in Spain and, over a period of years, to other parts of Mexico—provided unforgettable experiences, a large collection of photographs, and invaluable background for the narrative.

In the course of this travel and study, the extent to which Spanish surnames have been consistently mangled by writers in English was repeatedly impressed upon me. A special effort has been made, therefore, to use the proper form. If the reader finds himself confused by the use of Soto and León where he is used to seeing De Soto and De León, or Vázquez de Coronado and Alvarez de Pineda where he is accustomed to Coronado and Pineda, I offer apologies.

In Spanish, "De" does not ordinarily precede the surname when it is used alone. The compound *apellido*, consisting of the patronymic followed by the matronymic, takes three forms: the two may be joined by "de," "y," or neither. Although it is usually considered preferable to use the full compound form of the surname, dropping the matronymic in succeeding mentions is permissible. It is not always easy, however, to ascertain from appearance alone at just what point the given name ends and the surname begins.

Bibliographers and indexers in the United States, unfortunately, have not held strictly to correct Spanish form but have followed a convention of their own. The confusion that has arisen will not be easily overcome, but the effort at least seems overdue.

Abbreviations Used in Notes

AGI   Archivo General de Indias, Seville

AHN   Archivo Histórico Nacional, Madrid

APS   Archivos Protocolos de Sevilla, Seville

BN   Biblioteca Nacional, Madrid

BRP   Biblioteca del Real Palacio, Madrid

CDI   *Collección de documentos inéditos relativos al descubrimiento, conquista y organización de las antiguas posesiones españolas en América y Oceanía,* 42 vols. (Madrid, 1864–84)

CDIE   *Collección de documentos inéditos para la historia de España,* 112 vols. (Madrid, 1842–95)

CDI-IA   *Colección de documentos inéditos para la historia de Ibero-América,* 14 vols. (Madrid, 1927–35)

CDU   *Colección de documentos inéditos relativos al descubrimiento, conquista y organización de las antiguas posesiones españolas de ultramar,* 25 vols. (Madrid, 1885–1932), the succeeding series of *CDI*

MN   Museo Naval, Madrid

RAH   Real Academia de Historia, Madrid

SPANISH SEA

In the Beginning . . .

THE earth, whatever part of it lay beyond the Ocean Sea, was without form and void, and darkness was upon the face of the deep. Then came the Discovery, and the embodiment of God's spirit moved across the face of the waters. The sixteenth-century Catholic Spaniard, in his own mind, brought the light to this New World. Separating the light from the darkness, he sought the firmament in the midst of the waters.

In Triana, across the Río Guadalquivir from Seville, there stands a statue of an obscure sailor named Rodrigo, his likeness transfixed in time at the moment of the new beginning. The inscription contains but a single word, a word significant only for the time and place in which it was uttered:

¡Tierra!

Contemplating the marble figure upon its pedestal, the imaginative mind sees more than actually is present. Barefoot, his tattered pantaloons rolled up on lank shins, Rodrigo grips in one hand a bobbing mast while pointing afar with the other. Upon his face he wears an expression of unspeakable awe. The gently rolling deck of *Pinta* takes shape around him, her billowing sails catching the moonlight, her bow dipping into the swells to stir a phosphorescent glow. A split second of electrifying stillness follows Rodrigo's cry as its significance sinks in: Land ho! Then the shouts of triumph and a cannon shot, followed by brisk orders and a bustle of activity to shorten sail and await the arrival of *Niña* and *Santa María*.

Rodrigo de Triana, a simple seaman, may never have felt himself a harbinger of fortune for his mere utterance of such a common word. His excitement at the moment perhaps was born more of sea-weariness, of consuming stale bread and fetid water, than of any sense of destiny. Yet he marks the instant beyond which the world—particularly the sea-going world to which he himself belonged—would never be the same again.

The transformation boded by the Discovery was far reaching. Fifteenth-century Spain, just emerging from almost eight centuries of Moorish occupation, was scarcely prepared. Yet in a sense the knowledge that there was land beyond the Ocean Sea—whether the true Indies or some new world previously unknown to Europeans—came at a propitious time. With the final defeat of the Moors that same year, the Iberian nation needed a new sense of mission, a new challenge, to take the place of those now fulfilled. Challenge, opportunity, destiny; she found them all in the discovery of the myriad islands projecting from the American continents.

As a matter of convenience, swashbuckling Spaniards who had fought the Moorish "infidels" gained a new outlet for their restless energies. The impoverished kingdom of Castile, so recently united with Aragón through the marriage of Isabella and Ferdinand, owned a potentially opulent source of renewal. And the consolidated nation, long possessed of a sense of religious mission for conquering the heathen, might look toward the spiritual conquest of countless nations of *gentiles*. The American natives mistakenly called Indians must be won by the light of the gospel or slaughtered and enslaved by the might of Spanish arms.

It was a golden opportunity, in the dual sense of the term. Yet Spain was unprepared for the sudden turn of events signified by Rodrigo de Triana's excited cry during the moonlit midwatch of October 12, 1492. Whence would come the ships for carrying men and supplies across the Ocean Sea and bringing home the wealth on which Castile must depend for her revival? the seamen willing to subsist on meager rations and to hazard corsairs, scurvy, and hurricane?

Although Spain was a maritime nation, few of her captains had ventured farther from the mainland shores of Europe and Africa than the Canary Islands. Her ships were designed more for coastal sailing in known waters than for crossing the great ocean expanse separating Iberia from the new-found island possessions. Trained pilots, all too few for the imminent navigation explosion, were better versed in guiding themselves by coastal landmarks than by celestial observations.

In short, the age of discovery, exploration, and worldwide commercial development produced a need for knowledge and skills that greatly surpassed the resources for providing them. The sixteenth-century mariner often lacked the background for grasping all that he needed to know. The instruments on which he had to depend were far from adequate. The compass, hardly more than a magnetized wire pivoted beneath a circular card, provided directions that were often imprecise. Latitude computation was less accurate still. Effective use of the mariner's astrolabe, quadrant, and cross-staff—to observe the altitude of Polaris or the sun at its meridian—depended greatly on the user's skill and the calmness of the sea. No means but guesswork existed for determining longitude and hence the coordinates requisite to fixing a ship's true position. Obstacles to accurate instrument navigation were compounded by deficiencies in chartmaking. While geographers and cartographers had long understood that the world was round, they continued to make maps as though it were flat.

In view of such inadequacies, one must understand that the mariners of the continuing Discovery at times imparted more confusion than they dispelled. Yet they were charged with building the store of knowledge required by the navigational revolution; with transforming the science from purely coastal applications to one of global capabilities; with assessing natural phenomena such as winds and currents, as well as developing the technology of sailing the ocean deeps.

The extension of discovery and commerce beyond the Antilles called for larger ships; developments in tackle for handling them often failed to keep pace. Anchors, still made of brittle wrought iron, were likely to snap under strain, spelling disaster when the ship lay on a lee shore. The lack of an efficient steering mechanism made heavy ships difficult to manage in a beam or following sea, especially when running before a storm with reduced canvas or bare poles.

Such obstacles, however, could not be permitted to alter Spain's obvious destiny; of such enormous challenge great progress is born. Yet as the navigation explosion exceeded the pace of education and surpassed existing technology, it imposed a heavy toll in human suffering and in lost ships, cargoes, and lives.

To cope with the burgeoning maritime activity, the Spanish Crown prescribed an entirely new administrative apparatus. The Casa de Contratación in Seville served as a nerve center where geographical information about the New World was collected and analyzed. It was charged also with developing the basis for safe navigation and well-ordered commerce with "the Indies"—the commerce that was to revolutionize the economy of Europe.

As is almost always the case with tremendous government undertakings, the effort was mismanaged. Fraud and callous disregard of human life were its concomitants, as were hypocrisy and deceit. But no one has dared suggest that such abuses were confined to the great Spanish adventure, or to the colonial period.

The medieval seafaring man at best was inclined to be a rowdy individual, regarded with distaste in the port towns where he vented his pent-up passions after months at sea. As a result of the Discovery, he may have been accorded a new but fleeting respectability. In any event—hardships, dangers, and questionable social status notwithstanding—Spanish adventurers of all classes seized with alacrity the opportunity opened by Columbus. As the Discovery was extended, horizons expanded rapidly in some areas, at a snail's pace in others. It was sixteen years after Rodrigo de Triana's great moment in history that a fugitive from the death sentence in Spain sailed his caravel through the Straits of Florida into the Gulf of Mexico, thus fully opening the door to the North American mainland.

Considering Spain's—indeed, the world's—unpreparedness for the Discovery, it is scarcely remarkable that the process advanced so slowly. Three hundred years after Columbus, coastlines of the New World were often known only vaguely and mapped sketchily or inaccurately. But expanding scientific interest and accelerating technical developments were occurring to dispel the darkness that for so long had shrouded America's more remote regions. In the interim, one of the world's greatest dramas had occurred; one of history's most compelling challenges had been met. Confronted suddenly with half a world not previously known, Western man had probed its secrets, conquered its peoples, and appropriated its wealth.

Imagine the odds the explorers faced as they sailed their frail wooden ships, guided by crude and primitive instruments, into the uncharted sea, where shoals were unmarked and shifting currents a perpetual mystery. Conjure the challenge, the excitement, and the danger they experienced in confronting peoples who practiced human sacrifice amid great stone temples and an advanced culture that belied such barbarity; or wild cannibals, the most adept archers in the world. Picture, too, the deadly inland marches through untracked wilderness, with survival odds often reduced to nil.

Much has been written concerning the motivation for risking such hazard and hardship: lust for gold and glory; missionary zeal for converting the savage; or merely the restless conquistador spirit, the Ulyssian itching foot, that caused the hardy Extremadurans to forsake the connubial bed for a life of wandering. But there was another, perhaps allied, factor that has been given less consideration, one often expressed in royal orders and in the letters and reports of the *conquista-dores* themselves in reference to exploring the unknown land: "To know its secrets."

Such a quest has propelled man into the unknown since his very beginning. The discoverers, the explorers, and the conquerors, then, came for multiple reasons: for glory, God, and gold, yes—but also for knowledge.

In a sense, they found them all within the Spanish Sea.

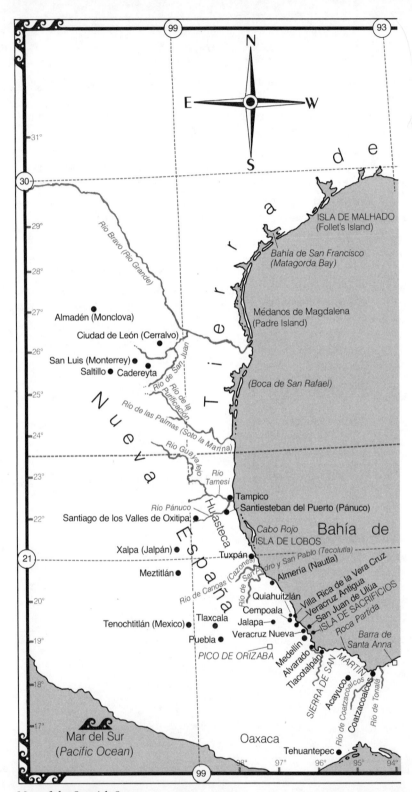

Map of the Spanish Sea

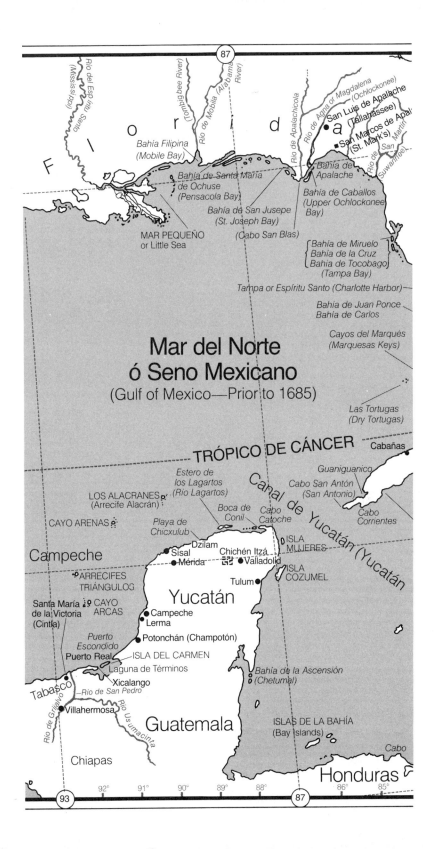

Río del Espíritu Santo
(Mississippi)

Río de Mobila (Alabama River)

(Tombigbee River)

Río de Apalachicola

Río de Agna or Magdalena
(Ochlockonee)

San Luis de Apalache
(Tallahassee)

San Marcos de Apal·
(St. Mark's)

Río de San Martín

Río de San Suwannee

F l o r i d a

Bahía Filipina
(Mobile Bay)

Bahía de Santa María
de Ochuse
(Pensacola Bay)

Bahía de San Jusepe
(St. Joseph Bay)

(Cabo San Blas)

MAR PEQUEÑO
or Little Sea

Bahía de
Apalache

Bahía de Caballos
(Upper Ochlockonee
Bay)

Bahía de Miruelo
Bahía de la Cruz
Bahía de Tocobago
(Tampa Bay)

Tampa or Espíritu Santo (Charlotte Harbor)—

Bahía de Juan Ponce
Bahía de Carlos

Cayos del Marqués
(Marquesas Keys)

Mar del Norte
ó Seno Mexicano
(Gulf of Mexico—Prior to 1685)

Las Tortugas
(Dry Tortugas)

TRÓPICO DE CÁNCER

Cabañas

Estero de
los Lagartos
(Río Lagartos)

LOS ALACRANES
(Arrecife Alacrán)

CAYO ARENAS

Playa de
Chicxulub

Campeche

ARRECIFES
TRIÁNGULOS

Santa María
de la Victoria
(Cintla)

CAYO
ARCAS

Puerto
Escondido
Puerto Real

Guaniguanico

Cabo San Antón
(San Antonio)

Canal de Yucatán (Yucatán)

Boca de
Conil

Cabo
Catoche

Cabo
Corrientes

Cabo

Dzilam

Sisal

Mérida

Chichén Itzá

Valladolid

ISLA
MUJERES

ISLA
COZUMEL

Tulum

Yucatán

Campeche
Lerma

Potonchán (Champotón)

ISLA DEL CARMEN

Laguna de Términos

Tabasco

Xicalango

Río de San Pedro

Río de Grijalva

Villahermosa

Río Usumacinta

Guatemala

Bahía de la Ascensión
(Chetumal)

ISLAS DE LA BAHÍA
(Bay Islands)

Cabo

Chiapas

Honduras

92° 91° 90° 89° 88°   86° 85°

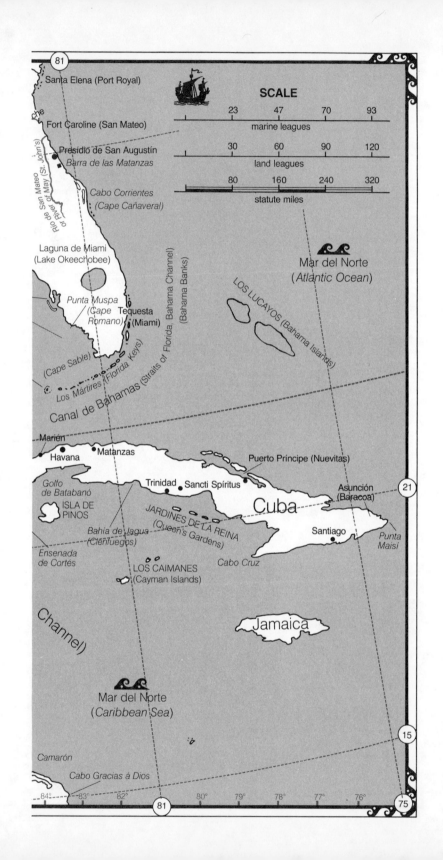

SCALE

	23	47	70	93

marine leagues

	30	60	90	120

land leagues

	80	160	240	320

statute miles

Santa Elena (Port Royal)

Fort Caroline (San Mateo)

Presidio de San Augustín
Barra de las Matanzas

Cabo Corrientes
(Cape Cañaveral)

Laguna de Miami
(Lake Okeechobee)

Punta Muspa
(Cape Tequesta
Romano) (Miami)

(Cape Sable)

Los Mártires (Florida Keys)

Rio de San Mateo
or River of May (St. John's)

che

(Bahama Banks)

(Straits of Florida, Bahama Channel)

Canal de Bahamas

LOS LUCAYOS (Bahama Islands)

Mar del Norte
(*Atlantic Ocean*)

Marien

Havana • Matanzas

Golfo
de Batabanó

ISLA DE
PINOS

Trinidad • Sancti Spíritus

Puerto Príncipe (Nuevitas)

Asunción
(Baracoa)

Cuba

JARDINES DE LA REINA
(Queen's Gardens)

Bahía de Jagua
(Cienfuegos)

Ensenada
de Cortés

LOS CAIMANES
(Cayman Islands)

Cabo Cruz

Santiago

Punta
Maisí

Channel)

Jamaica

Mar del Norte
(*Caribbean Sea*)

Camarón

Cabo Gracias á Dios

84°	83°	82°	80°	79°	78°	77°	76°

81

21

15

75

81

PART I

West from the Islands

Cuba and the Hidden Sea:
Discovery and Conquest, 1500–14

Beyond the extenuated finger of land thought certainly to be an Asian peninsula lay the hidden sea, unvisited and unknown by Europeans. Christopher Columbus, intimidated by "seas rushing westward like torrents from the mountains," had turned away from its discovery on the second voyage, June 13, 1494. He demanded that each of his followers affirm his belief—under penalty of having his tongue cut out—that Cuba, the land they had been coasting, was a peninsula rather than an island.

Not all the affiants clung to that notion the rest of their lives, but Columbus did; the Admiral went to his grave 12 years later without having seen the Gulf of Mexico or even suspecting that it existed. His time and energies had been used up probing the Caribbean perimeter. As for North America, he had discovered only the fringe islands that would serve his host of successors as springboards to the yet unknown wonders west of Cuba.

That island, especially, was the keystone. Long misunderstood, it lay like a loose-fitting bottle cork in the Gulf's mouth, with a navigable passage on either side. Cuba's western tip, inclining southwest, is washed on one side by the Caribbean Sea, on the other by the Gulf, the existence of which remained a matter of speculation for sixteen years after the first voyage. The island's other two-thirds, jutting eastward, divide the Caribbean from the western Atlantic.

Even after the Gulf of Mexico was discovered and explorers began gradually to probe its recesses, it had no name apart from the one given the Atlantic. In Columbus's time, all the earth's great waters were considered to be a single body—el Mar Océano, or "the Ocean Sea." The Admiral's initial insular discoveries came to be called "the

Indies of the Ocean Sea" to distinguish them from the East Indies, but
the name usually was abridged as simply "the Indies." Cuba, though at
first called Isla Juana, became Isla Fernandina of the Ocean Sea. "Tierra
Firme of the Ocean Sea" designated the mainland of South and Central
America discovered by the early Andalusian voyagers. When Vasco
Núñez de Balboa crossed the Isthmus of Darién and looked southward
upon a second ocean, new terminology was called for. Thus, the Atlantic, of which both the Gulf and the Caribbean were part, became the
North Sea; the Pacific, the South Sea.

The Gulf of Mexico was nameless until the early 1540s. For more
than a century after its discovery, it remained a sacrosanct Spanish sea,
forbidden to other nations. None dared violate the prohibition except
as a premeditated act of war or piracy, or when driven by storm. The
Spanish name most often applied to the Gulf was Seno Mexicano—the
Mexican gulf or pocket—although it occasionally was called Golfo de
Mexico, Golfo de Nueva España, or some other variant.

The primary entrance, or front door, to the Gulf in the age of sail
was through the Yucatán Channel, some 125 miles wide, between
Cuba and Yucatán. Ships left the Caribbean and entered the Gulf as
they passed between Cuba's western cape, Cabo San Antón (or San Antonio), and Yucatán's Cabo Catoche. They usually left it, on the homeward course for Spain, through the Straits of Florida; arbitrarily, the
eighty-first meridian may be considered to mark the end of the Gulf
and the beginning of the Atlantic. From Cabo Catoche clockwise to
Florida's Cape Sable, the Gulf is bordered by almost three thousand
miles of mainland coast, shortcutting the scores of bays and inlets that
punctuate the littoral.

Through this enclosed sea lay the initial approach to the North
American mainland. It served as the avenue for discovery, exploration,
and settlement of southern and western sectors of the present-day
United States as well as Mexico—well before anything was done by
the English on the Atlantic seaboard.

Cuba's strategic position was more than symbolic. On one hand
the Straits of Florida formed a major cultural divide; in an ethnic sense,
they delineated North America from South. On the Cuban side of the
straits the pacific Arawaks, of South American origin, cultivated small
plots and lived in multifamily *bohíos*. They differed in physique, language, and habits from Florida's natives, who were warlike and hunted

with bows and arrows. Yet there must have been some mixing of the cultures, for native canoemen crossed the waters from time to time.

The Yucatán Channel may also be viewed as a cultural divide of sorts, for beyond it dwelt the temple-building Mayas, in their descendancy at the time of the Discovery. Around the Gulf a variety of native cultures comprised an ethnic diversity that included the wealthy and culturally advanced Mejicas, or Aztecs, who offered the first real motivation for serious exploration inside the hidden sea.

Columbus's assertion that Cuba was a peninsula evoked doubts from the start; hence, the actual circumnavigation of the island and the discovery of the Gulf of Mexico came as something of an anticlimax. Several maps dated prior to the event, though doubtless hypothetical, showed the territory as an island, occasionally projecting a gulf beyond. Attempts to explain these maps have brought forth countless theories, the net result of which has been nearly hopeless confusion.

The first map to show an insular Cuba was Juan de la Cosa's, dated 1500 at Puerto de Santa María (near Cádiz). La Cosa, a noted pilot and

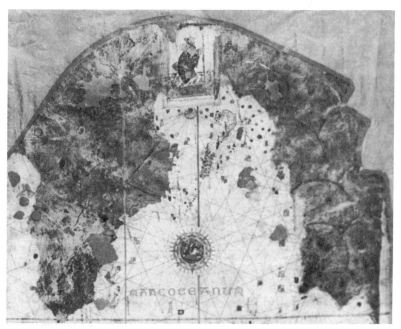

Fig. 1. La Cosa's map, New World portion, 1500. Courtesy Museo Naval.

master, and owner of Columbus's ill-fated flagship, *Santa María*, on the first voyage, was one of those who had taken the oath required by the Admiral at Cuba's Ensenada de Cortés on the second voyage. Significantly, he had signed on for the Cuban exploration as *maestre de hacer cartas*—master of chartmaking. Did La Cosa falsify the date of 1500 on his world map? If not, where might he have obtained such information eight years before it was proved?

The mapmaker's activities at this time provide a partial answer. About June, 1500, he returned from a voyage with Alonso de Ojeda and Amerigo Vespucci to the coast of South America. In October of the same year he sailed again, with Rodrigo de Bastidas, for the Gulf of Urabá. The discoveries of the Ojeda voyage are noted on his map; those of the voyage with Bastidas, including the Río de Magdalena and the Gulf of Urabá, are not. A reasonable inference, therefore, is that the map was drawn between the two voyages.

It has been suggested here and there that the date on the map represents merely its beginning, that it was completed after Cuba was circumnavigated in 1508–1509. By the time the feat was accomplished, however, La Cosa was on his way to South America again with Ojeda. He might have heard of it when they stopped en route at Santo Domingo, but he would have had no opportunity to incorporate the information on his map; he died of a poisoned arrow on February 28, 1510, while on a slave raid up the Magdalena River of Colombia, without having returned to Puerto de Santa María.

Theories concerning the origin of La Cosa's data on Cuba and the body of water beyond may be similarly put to rest. Speculation that Vicente Yáñez Pinzón (*Niña*'s captain on Columbus's first voyage) circumnavigated the island in 1499 stems from a confusion of two of Pinzón's voyages. This stalwart navigator did sail from his native Palos that year to make first American landfall on the Brazilian coast south of the equator. From the Gulf of Paria he returned directly to Santo Domingo and thence to Spain, in September, 1500. There is no likelihood that he entered the Gulf of Mexico.

Then there is the matter of Amerigo Vespucci, the Florentine ship chandler in Seville—he for whom the western hemisphere is named. Vespucci sailed in 1499 with La Cosa and Ojeda, but that is not the issue. He claimed, besides the two voyages he made for Portugal, another for Spain in 1497. It appears that he merely antedated the 1499 voyage to claim for himself the South American discovery credited to it. Yet some interpreters consider the Vespucci account to be of a voyage around the Gulf of Mexico and up the Atlantic seaboard as far as Chesapeake Bay. No documentation for such a voyage has come forth except Vespucci's own questionable letters to an old school friend and his former employer in Florence, and evidence has been adduced that in 1497 and 1498 he was occupied in Spain.

Vespucci, by royal decree, became a naturalized citizen of Castile and León in 1506. In 1508 he was elevated to the new post of pilot major in the Casa de Contratación, the government agency set up in 1503 to manage Spain's commerce with her overseas possessions. He evidently served honorably in that capacity until his death in 1512. But he should be denied the honor his most ardent advocates would bestow upon him, of sailing the Gulf of Mexico before other Europeans. Rather than being the Gulf's first discoverer, it seems more likely that he was America's first public-relations con man, and that the naming of the continents in his honor represents a grave injustice to Columbus.

La Cosa, in fact, did not need Vespucci's help in conjuring a New World map that was years ahead of its time; his own explorations were ample for the purpose. With Columbus, he had visited the Bahamas and coasted Cuba on the north and south. With Ojeda he had explored the northern coast of South America, east to west, to Cabo de la Vela, before 1500. He may have had data on the northern regions of North America from reports of the Cabots' voyages for England. On his map he affixed the appropriate national flag to each discovered area and used place names profusely. On the conjectural part, however, there are neither flags nor toponyms, and what might be taken for the western shore of the Gulf of Mexico is obscured by a vignette of Saint Christopher. If the facts of La Cosa's career are considered, the map quite simply explains itself.

That particular cartographic work, evidently hidden away in royal archives, exerted little influence on other mapmakers. The configuration given Cuba, however, does show up on an anonymous map drawn about 1509–10. Of greater influence on the geographical notions of the times was the work of an anonymous Portuguese cartographer that emerged two years after La Cosa's. It depicts not only an insular Cuba but also a peninsula that is alternately taken for Cuba, Yucatán, or Asia. This is the so-called Cantino map, named for Alberto Cantino, an Italian agent for Ercole d'Este, Duke of Ferrara, who obtained it for his employer in Lisbon in 1502.

As with the La Cosa map, there is no dearth of hypotheses concerning Cantino's, and some of them border on the farfetched. The map is clearly oriented by the meridional line separating Spanish and Portuguese territories that was established by a 1494 papal bull. A compass rose and the Tropic of Capricorn confirm the orientation. The "Ilhas Antilhas del rey de Castella" and the "Oceanus Occiditales," plainly labeled, define the locale. Were all these indicators added to the original sketch by someone other than its author? And is there room for supposing, as a number of interpreters have done, that the subject is Asia? Without these embellishments, might not the peninsula usually identified with Florida just as well be taken for Yucatán?

To bring "Yucatán" into its correct position, a 90° counterclockwise rotation of the map from its customary orientation is necessary; then the supposed island of Cuba—labeled Ysabella on the map—is 90° out of kilter. But such difficulties are met head-on by a Netherlands geographer who thinks the map may be the product of a European voyage—probably Portuguese—in the spring of 1502. Entering the Gulf through the Straits of Florida—by far the least likely and most difficult way—it is suggested, the exploration made first landfall at Punta Arenas, the northwestern promontory of Yucatán; thence east and south into the Caribbean to a point between Cabo Camarón and Cabo Gracias á Dios, Honduras.

That the explorer's field sketch might have been given the draftsman without directional indicators, as the geographer suggests, is by no means implausible. In this case the thesis is supported by the identification of place names on the 1502 map with present-day toponymy of the Yucatán coast. By interesting coincidence, the Río Lagartos on the north end of the peninsula, supposedly named by Francisco Hernández de Córdoba in 1517, corresponds with the location of Río de los Lagartos on the reoriented Cantino map. Other map names are associated with holy days or other dates to reconstruct the supposed course. Caninor (Cananor), the Thursday following the first Sunday of Lent, is said to indicate a river on the north Yucatán coast just east of Silam; Cabo Santo, or Holy Cape, some 30 miles east of Río Lagartos, to mark Holy Week; Cabo do Fim do Abril, or End of April Cape, to place the expedition's arrival at the end of the peninsula (Cabo Catoche) on April 30.

While this hypothetical reconstruction is interesting, if not convincing, the geographer's proclamation that "there can be no reasonable doubt" is a bit hard to swallow. There have been many other interpreters just as certain that the continental land mass pointing toward Ysabella (from northwest, in the usual orientation) was intended to represent either Florida or Cuba itself.

The various attempts to explain the Cantino map range widely. It has been suggested that the portrayal of Florida derived from the Cabot or Vespucci voyages (neither of which reached Florida); from unreported forays of Spanish slave hunters in Florida or the Bahamas; from some unknown Spanish or Portuguese voyage; or from information supplied by the natives of the Bahamas, Hispaniola, or Cuba. All these are possibilities; none, unfortunately, can be proved.

The La Cosa and Cantino maps represent the two original cartographic works that anticipated proof of an insular Cuba and discovery of the Gulf of Mexico. La Cosa's influence on later maps was limited. The coastal configurations and toponymy of the Cantino specimen were soon repeated by numerous mapmakers, although the map itself remained hidden away in Italy and was not available for copying. The original still in Portugal must have been the prototype used repeatedly to supply Europe's geographical notions of the New World.

Among the first to borrow from this source was Nicolo Canerio, a Genoese whose 1504 map of the North Atlantic bears an undeniable resemblance to it. Extending the Cantino prototype beyond "Florida," Canerio shows an island-studded bay or gulf, but there is no Yucatán peninsula to enclose it on the southeast. Giovanni Matteo Contarini's world map, engraved in Florence in 1506, also gives the Cantino configuration to the "Tierra de Cuba." Some of Cantino's coastlines came to Martin Waldseemüller's 1507 world map via Canerio.

The Contarini map is the earliest printed specimen showing any part of the New World. Its chief interest otherwise lies in the confusion it reflects. The North American mainland extends in a great promontory from Asia. Such a concept, however, is hardly remarkable in view of the fact that both Columbus and Vespucci died believing the territories they had discovered and explored pertained to Asia. Confusion was to reign for many a year, but as the initial wave of the Discovery passed and another began, new doors opened; gradually the pieces began to fall into place.

At last Peter Martyr was able to write in 1510: "Cuba, that land so long believed a continent because of its great extension, has been proved an island." Martyr attributed the feat to Pinzón, but in 1508, not 1499. On his 1508 expedition with Juan Diaz de Solís, Pinzón sailed west along Cuba's south coast to the western cape. For reasons not told, he did not sail west into the unknown sea. From Cabo San Antón he "continued on and encountered other lands . . . already touched by the Admiral. Turning left, his ship coasted eastward, passing the bays of Veragua, Urabá, and Cuchibacoa and approached the land called Paria and Boca de Dragón."

This voyage had been planned in 1506, and it has often been claimed that it was made that year. Actually, the 1506 sailing was aborted by turmoil following the 1505 death of Queen Isabella. Ferdinand, forced to yield the Castilian throne to his daughter Juana and her husband, Philip, withdrew to his own kingdom of Aragón. Following Philip's death—arranged by Ferdinand, some believe—Juana was removed because of her mental instability. Ferdinand, upon returning to Castile, called a conference of prominent navigators to take up the matter of furthering exploration. Discussion centered on the possibility of finding a route through the West Indies to the far eastern Spice Islands and colonizing Tierra Firme. Thus was born the 1508–1509 voyage of Pinzón and Diaz de Solís, as well as the 1509 sailing of La Cosa and Ojeda. In the early summer of 1508, Pinzón and Solís put to sea with two vessels of fifty and sixty tons, *Isabelita* and *Magdalena*, each carrying a crew of fifty-two. Outbound, they reported to Governor Nicolás de Ovando at Santo Domingo, then sailed on west to Cabo San Antón before dropping off to the south.

Pinzón himself supports Martyr's version of the voyage in sworn testimony given in 1513. In the "Pleitos de Colon," the record of litigation contesting the hereditary rights of Columbus's descendants, he relates that he sailed east from Guanaja (Honduras) to the province of Camarón—evidently related to the cape of that name less than 100 miles east of Guanaja. Pedro de Ledesma, a pilot on the expedition, tells a different story but falls short of qualifying as an unbiased witness. His association with Columbus on the third and fourth voyages had ended in bitterness: he joined in the Porras brothers' mutiny against the Admiral at Jamaica. Apparently eager to discredit Columbus and negate the rights of his heirs, he related that Pinzón and Diaz de Solís had sailed north from Guanaja to 23.5°, a latitude that would have put them inside the Gulf of Mexico somewhat farther north than Tampico. The lack of any specific observation along such a route, such as Mayan temples on the eastern Yucatán coast—not to mention Pinzón's conflicting testimony—strongly suggests that Ledesma perjured himself.

While Pinzón and Diaz de Solís may have proved Cuba an island, they did not penetrate the Gulf. By the time they returned to Santo Domingo about a year after leaving it, another had sailed completely around Cuba, and his claim to proving its insularity took precedence. In the closing months of 1508, Governor Ovando of Hispaniola had sent Sebastián de Ocampo to follow Cuba's shore as far as he could and to determine once and for all whether it was island or mainland.

The early chroniclers describe Ocampo simply as a Galician hidalgo and former servant of Queen Isabella who had come to Hispaniola with Columbus on his second voyage and taken up land. To this meager sketch, new facts may now be added. Actually, Ocampo was a lifetime exile to Hispaniola, forbidden by royal decree ever to return to Spain or even to leave the island. For "differences he had with Juan de Velázquez of Jerez" in 1501, he had been condemned to death, a sentence commuted by royal intervention to perpetual exile: he was to leave Spain within 60 days, never to return; he must remain forever in Hispaniola.

In defiance of this decree, Ocampo left Hispaniola on numerous occasions, not only to circumnavigate Cuba but also to employ his ships in extensive trade across the Caribbean. He had important connections among the colonial officials, yet his status as an exile dictated silence concerning his most important service to the Crown. His leaving Hispaniola to explore Cuba, as well as his trading voyages, violated the royal order. Whether he was brought to task for it has yet to be proved. It is known only that he returned to Spain in 1514 and, in a manner suggesting that he expected an early demise, put his affairs in order.

That Governor Ovando regarded Ocampo as trustworthy is implicit in the assignment he gave him in 1508. Late in the year, after Pinzón and Diaz de Solís had left Hispaniola, Ocampo embarked on the eight-month voyage with two vessels, sailing west along Cuba's northern shore. Traversing the Old Bahama and Nicolás channels and edging into the Gulf, he passed up Matanzas Bay, as it afforded little protection. Farther up the island he put into "an excellent harbor, capable of accommodating many ships." Here he careened his own two vessels—which involved hauling them up on the beach, removing and washing the ballast, cleaning the bottom, and caulking the seams—and bestowed the name Puerto de Carenas. In time it became Havana.

Thence Ocampo proceeded west past the Archipélago de los Colorados and the Sierra de los Organos, doubtless hugging the shore when possible to avoid the current rushing into the Straits of Florida. Doubling Cabo San Antón and turning back eastward, he had the unequivocal proof of Cuba's insularity. Looking west, he had a full view of the open Gulf and must have felt the tug of challenge from the unbroken horizon spanning the water. What unheard-of wonders might lie in the distance yonder!

After groping his way among the shoals of the Gulf of Batabanó, Ocampo put into the bay the natives called Jagua (present Cienfuegos). With an entrance a crossbow shot in width, it was seen as "one of the best and largest harbors in the world." The Cuban Indians served the mariners partridge and mullet fish, which they took, as easily as from an aquarium, from sea corrals of woven reeds stuck in the bay's mud bottom.

Ocampo's return to Santo Domingo in the spring or summer of 1509 created little stir. Governor Ovando, lacking authority and mindful of his complicity in violating the terms of Ocampo's exile, made no move to occupy Cuba. He was recalled shortly in favor of Diego Columbus—the Admiral's son and heir to his titles—who ultimately was to undertake the Cuban conquest.

The circumnavigation of Cuba was hardly more than a baby's first step, but adult strides followed quickly under a twofold impetus: the prospect of new wealth, and the need for laborers to exploit it. The Spaniards had begun their New World colonization on Hispaniola amid a native population placed by Bartolomé de las Casas at three million. This gadfly of the conquistadors and the Indians' champion claims the figure was reduced to two hundred in the first fifty years of Spanish occupation as the invaders entered like "starving wolves, tigers, and lions" among these "gentle sheep." With the local Indian population

Cuba and the Hidden Sea   23

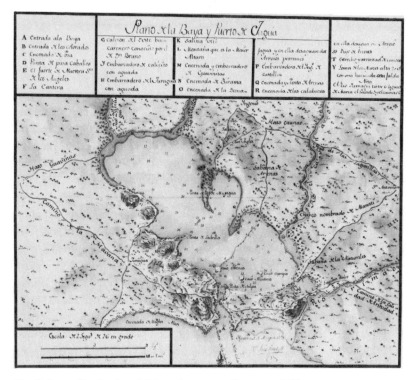

Fig. 2. Jagua Bay in the eighteenth century. Courtesy AGI.

dwindling, slave raids were made in the Lucayos (Bahamas), where half a million souls are said to have dwelt on the poorest of the more than sixty islands. The Lucayans endured slavery no better than the Hispaniola natives; by the middle of the sixteenth century, the island chain was depopulated.

This growing labor shortage, the increasing Spanish population, and diminishing gold mines had caused Governor Ovando to dispatch Ocampo to examine Cuba and assess its suitability for settlement, while Juan Ponce de León moved to conquer Puerto Rico. In 1509, Ovando was withdrawn, and Diego Columbus came to govern under the watchful eye of the royal treasurer, Miguel de Pasamonte. Diego sent Juan de Esquivel, seconded by Pánfilo de Narváez, to seize Jamaica before it was attached to the Tierra Firme colony. Alonso de Ojeda, supposedly sharing the Tierra Firme jurisdiction with Diego de

Nicuesa, was deeply resentful; if Esquivel carried out the assignment, he vowed, he personally would cut off his head. But those were words he would have the dubious pleasure of eating.

Cuba, meanwhile, was feeling the accidental impact of encroaching Europeans. On at least four occasions, vessels en route from Tierra Firme to Santo Domingo wrecked on the Cuban shore, casting their crews among the natives. The first instance involved Ojeda himself, who, seeking relief for his besieged and starving colony, had taken passage with Bernaldino de Talavera on a ship he had pirated from Santo Domingo. Ojeda left his settlement in the care of Francisco Pizarro, the future conqueror of Peru.

The voyage ended in shipwreck on Cuba's south shore at Jagua Bay. Ocampo's circumnavigation notwithstanding, the island still lay in primitive condition, relatively untouched by Europeans. As the seventy-odd castaways set out to march down the island, Ojeda made such a nuisance of himself that Talavera's pirates put him in irons. They freed him when they found themselves stalked by hostile natives, many of whom had fled Spanish atrocities on Hispaniola.

Cleaving to the coast, the Spaniards tramped a hundred leagues before finding their way blocked by a morass. Nevertheless, bogging to their knees in muck, they set out to wade across it, making scarcely a league per day and resting at night upon mangrove roots. Their travail endured for a month, during which time half the seventy died, before the remnant came to the Indian village of Cuiba and were guided thence to Macaca. At Macaca the chief provided a canoe and oarsmen to take a messenger across the Oriente Deep to Jamaica, twenty leagues distant, with a plea for Esquivel's help. Esquivel, still wearing his head, sent Narváez in a caravel. Despite Ojeda's threat, he and Esquivel became fast friends. Esquivel delivered the castaways safely to Santo Domingo, where Talavera was brought to trial and hanged for piracy. Ojeda, after bearing witness against him, withstood an assassination attempt by his erstwhile shipmates, Talavera's pirates.

The second shipwreck episode also had its beginning in the Tierra Firme colony on the Gulf of Urabá, where Ojeda had left Pizarro to deal with the dual problem of starvation and hostile Indians. With men dying daily, Pizarro decided to withdraw to Hispaniola. He boarded the survivors on two brigantines and set sail, himself and thirty-six men on one ship, twenty-seven men and two women on the other.

Pizarro's crew was suffering severely from hunger, and nine men died at sea. Then one night the two vessels became separated in darkness. Pizarro, sailing up the Colombian coast toward Cartagena, met the ships of his partner, Martín Fernández de Enciso, bringing fresh supplies and renewal for the colony.

The other brigantine, driven off course by contrary wind and current, ran northward into the Yucatán Channel and grounded near Cabo San Antón in the Cuban province of Guaniguanico. The castaways, like Ojeda and Talavera, set out to walk to Hispaniola. Following the north coast, they were set upon by natives as they tried to cross a large bay. The bloody affair, in which twenty-six Spaniards died, gave the place the name it carries today: Matanzas, or "massacres." Three of the castaways, two of them women, were spared to live among the Indians while awaiting rescue—which came three years later.

A third shipwrecked crew saved itself by walking the length of Cuba to reach Santo Domingo. These occurrences in 1510 contributed to the motivation for conquest. Yet another, just as the conquest began the following year, gave rise to its most tragic episode.

Diego Columbus, frustrated in his first plan for occupying Cuba, was forced to make a choice not to his liking. By the time King Ferdinand directed him to proceed, in 1510, it seemed that only Diego Velázquez de Cuéllar was available to lead the undertaking. And he, for pecuniary motives, had allied himself with an opposing clique. Velázquez had come out from Spain with the first Admiral on the second voyage, which also included such notable island conquistadors as Esquivel, Narváez, and Juan Ponce de León. He seems to have fit well into this cadre; his success against the natives was achieved by brutal massacre, enslavement, and exploitation. As Ovando's lieutenant over the area that now constitutes the Republic of Haiti, he employed tactics that caused many to flee across the Windward Passage to Cuba.

Yet a leading Spanish historian of his own century, Antonio de Herrera, describes Velázquez as "the wealthiest and best loved of all the first Spanish inhabitants of Hispaniola . . . a man of experience, of mild and affable temper, who knew how to maintain his authority." This writer is just as laudatory of his physique: "body well-shaped, of fair complexion, very discreet." Such an admirable personage was Velázquez, according to Herrera, that, when it became known that he was to lead the Cuban expedition, men flocked to his banner.

Herrera's generous appraisal has not been universally accepted. "Experienced in the shedding of Indian blood" in the assessment of his chaplain Las Casas, Velázquez was inclined to be verbally abusive and impulsive. Present-day historians occasionally have pegged him as "one of the most unsavory figures in the annals of the New World."

In any event, the natives who had fled Hispaniola for Cuba trembled at the thought of his pursuing them into their new lands. Hatuéy, one *cacique* who had fled Haiti, was moved to assemble his people near Punta Maisí before a basket of gold and jewels—objects, he said, of Spanish worship. Let the Indians dance before them to appease these "Christian gods." When it was done, the treasure was thrown into the river, lest the Spaniards kill them for its possession.

When Hatuéy was captured in the early stages of the conquest, Velázquez ordered him burned alive. While he was being tied to the stake, a Franciscan friar sought to impart Christian teachings, that the Indian might attain Heaven's glory rather than Hell's torment. Hatuéy was not impressed. If Heaven was where the Christians went, he responded, he would prefer the other place.

With Hatuéy gone, the Spaniards soon held the the entire Maisí province, and its people were distributed among Velázquez's soldiers and servants as slaves. The crash of arms reverberated across the Oriente Deep to Jamaica, where old warhorses—experienced, like Velázquez, in the shedding of Indian blood—thirsted for action. Narváez, who had served as Esquivel's second in command, gathered up thirty crossbowmen and sailed for Baracoa, where Velázquez was planting Cuba's first Spanish settlement, called Asunción. He became Velázquez's second also, tantamount to being placed in charge of the conquest.

Like Velázquez, to whom he bore a physical resemblance, Narváez came from Cuéllar. Las Casas, who served as the expeditionary chaplain for two years, described him as having an air of authority. He was tall, with fair hair tending toward red. He was honorable, had good habits, and had demonstrated valor in fighting the Indians. But he was not very prudent and had a marked tendency to carelessness. By less-tempered judgment, he was "the most incompetent of all who sailed for Spain in this era . . . [he was] both cruel and stupid." His later involvements bear out such an assessment. Yet Velázquez gave him a hearty welcome, assigned him Indians already captured, and made him his field commander.

It was just a few days later that Las Casas came from Hispaniola, summoned by Velázquez "out of past friendship" to serve as chaplain with Narváez's force. Las Casas, whose father and uncles had sailed with Columbus on the second voyage, had himself come with Ovando in 1502. For his part in quelling native uprisings, he was awarded an *encomienda* and willingly took his share of Indian slaves. Even after he became a priest in 1510, at age thirty-six, he held few religious scruples against oppression of the natives and remained a fast friend of Velázquez and Narváez; only later, after his true "conversion," did he recall their exploits with some bitterness. It is he who provides an eyewitness account of the Cuban conquest and sits in judgment thereof.

Another close companion of Narváez during the campaign was Velázquez's young protégé and nephew, Juan de Grijalva, destined to be the discoverer of New Spain. The task of making conversions among the Indians fell to a Franciscan friar, Juan de Tosín—perhaps the one who had attempted to instruct Hatuéy.

With thirty foot soldiers, Narváez, on his spirited mare, led the march to Bayamo, near the south coast of modern Oriente province. The natives came out to meet him bearing provisions, for they were much impressed by the strange animal managed so skillfully by the Spanish captain. Following this display of friendship, the Spaniards quartered themselves in an Indian village, a testimony to Narváez's lack of prudence and caution. During the night they awakened to find themselves surrounded by seven thousand naked natives gathered from all parts of the province, seemingly intent only on stealing the invaders' clothes. Barefoot and in his nightshirt, Narváez managed to mount his saddled mare; with hawkbells jingling on the crupper, he galloped about the village, frightening the Indians into flight.

Narváez, his warrior's blood stirred by the episode, tramped out the area but found it depopulated. He pursued the fleeing natives into Camagüey province, but the Indians, forewarned, had outdistanced him. "There was no conquest of Cuba other than by terrorizing the natives."

Ahead lay almost 300 leagues of virgin wilderness. The high ridges stretching westward 30 leagues from Punta Maisí gave way to a level, forested land of delightful rivers full of shad and mullet and occasionally glistening with gold. In a powerful river that the Indians called Cauto, pouring into the Caribbean from a range of low hills that girded the island's middle, was found "an infinite number of crocodiles" that would drag a man down and devour him.

The stagnant water between the coastal islands called the Queen's Gardens and the Camagüey sector was the breeding ground of sea turtles that grew "large as a buckler, or even a shield," to a weight of a hundred pounds. Here the female turtle each season would quit the sea to deposit some five hundred eggs in the sand, leaving them to hatch in the sun's warmth. When the young emerged, their instinct led them forthwith to the sea.

On several occasions, 300 to 400 Indians approached the Spanish camp laden with turtle meat or fish to appease the soldiers' ravenous appetites. The invaders found the turtle meat tasty and healthful, and the yellow fat, likened to molten gold, "good for clearing up leprosy, itch, and similar diseases." The natives used sucker fish (remora) to catch the turtles. Attached by the tail to a long line and cast into the sea, the fish would swim about until it found a turtle, then attach itself beneath the shell. The Indian then had but to pull in the prey. Live turtles were kept in underwater reed corrals built like those for mullet. Such a pen might contain as many as a thousand of the creatures, which would yield a quantity of meat equal to the beef from a hundred cows.

The abundance of native *yuca* plantings provided ample cassava bread, the island staple. "Never," concludes Las Casas, "was there a land discovered in these Indies which, in the abundance of food and of necessary things, would surpass Cuba."

Velázquez, for whatever reason, was content to leave field operations to Narváez. The governor himself sought to preserve the security of the conquered provinces by occupying them with almost three hundred men, who began dividing up the Indians in the system of slavery known as the *repartimiento*.

To their Spanish conquerors, there seemed little to set the Cuban natives apart from those of Hispaniola, who had learned to understand their language. The peoples of the two islands were hardly distinguishable in general appearance and customs. ("Their dress," says the royal chronicler Fernández de Oviedo, "is that with which they were born.") The principal distinction lay in marriage customs: when a Cuban man took a bride, he had to give her first to all the other men of his station, *cacique* or plebeian, to be "proved." After her sexual performance had been thoroughly tested, the *novia* would emerge with arm raised and fist clenched, shouting *"Manicato, manicato!"* thus indicating her vigor and spirit, drawing applause for her stamina.

As the conquerors entered village after village, Las Casas would gather all the children and, with the help of natives he had brought from Hispaniola, baptize them—opportunely, he allows, because almost none remained alive after a few months. The Cubans' pacific nature spared them few of the ravages of conquest: "The Spaniards did not fail to injure and scandalize them. Not content with what the Indians freely gave, they took their wretched subsistence, and some . . . chased after their wives and daughters."

Las Casas, to avoid the abuses he so vividly describes, had persuaded Narváez to let him go first into each village to gather all the inhabitants into half the houses, leaving the other half vacant for the Spaniards. The soldiers were forbidden to enter the Indian section. But then came the senseless massacre of Zucayo.

With the march in its early stages, Sebastián de Ocampo, who originally had no part in the conquest, suddenly reentered the picture to influence its course. Velázquez, learning from Indians that a Spanish ship had put into the port of Jagua, 200 leagues away, dispatched a native canoe with orders for the master to proceed to Asunción. The vessel, it developed, was Ocampo's; having taken a cargo of provisions to Núñez de Balboa at Darién, he was returning to Hispaniola when his ship was disabled by storm. The Indian canoe brought him and 15 sailors to Velázquez's capital.

A number of Ocampo's crewmen, however, had left the wreck site before help arrived, and started east along the shore. When Velázquez heard of them, he beefed up Narváez's forces from thirty to one hundred, plus a number of Hispaniolan and Jamaican Indians, and sent them marching into Camagüey province to look for the missing men. Reaching Cuiba, where Ojeda and his companions had found refuge after their miserable trek through the quagmire, the captain learned that the chief still venerated an image of the Virgin given him by the earlier castaways. Narváez also learned from the friendly natives that nine of Ocampo's sailors had been murdered in the large Caonao River town of Zucayo, nine leagues distant, on the south coast of Camagüey.

With this news, Velázquez sent from Asunción a force of forty foot and ten horse with provisions for the hundred men in the field. By the time these reinforcements overtook Narváez, the punishment of Zucayo was an accomplished fact.

In recounting this example of Narváez's brutality, Las Casas neglects to mention that it was motivated by the murder of Ocampo's nine sailors; still, that was only provocation, not justification. Approaching the town, the Spaniards stopped to breakfast in a dry stream bed strewn with stones suitable for whetting their blades. Their swords sharpened, they proceeded across a dry plain to arrive at the town in the early evening. A feast of cassava and fish had been spread for them by some two thousand natives, who sat on their haunches marveling at the horses the captains rode. Another 500 Indians, too fearful to come out, cowered in a nearby *bohío*.

No one could say who started it, or why—so says the venerable chaplain. Narváez still sat upon his horse, watching food being distributed to his men. Las Casas had withdrawn to the Spanish quarters. Suddenly a Spaniard "in whom the devil is thought to have clothed himself" drew his sword. The other soldiers did likewise, ripping open the bellies and slashing the throats of the men, women, and children who had fed them. Within two *credos* all were slain. Then the soldiers entered the building where the others were sequestered, and blood soon ran from the door as from a slaughter house. Only a few escaped by climbing the support poles.

Out of sight of the massacre, with Las Casas, were five Spaniards and about forty Indians who had served as porters on the march. When these soldiers heard the sounds of the slaughter, they drew their blades and would have killed the porters had not Las Casas intervened; they "went to kill where the others were killing."

Las Casas followed to look upon the horrible scene of piled-up bodies, the slaughter still going on. When Narváez saw him, he said, "How does Your Honor like what these our Spaniards have done?" Snapped the cleric, "I commend you and them to the devil!"

Narváez, unshaken, sat his horse like a block of marble, silently watching the bloody spectacle that he might easily have prevented. Las Casas went from soldier to soldier, trying to stop the killing. The Spaniards now were spreading themselves among the trees, seeking any helpless Indian into whom they might plunge a blade. The priest, in the midst of his rounds, went into the large house where most of the 500 were already dead. Seeing a number of natives cowering on the support poles, he told them to come down, assuring them that there would be no more killing. As one young man began to descend, the cleric went on to stop the butchery elsewhere. When the Indian reached the ground, weeping for the senseless slaughter of his people, a soldier standing there drew his cutlass and slashed him across the loins so that his intestines fell out. Holding himself in, the young man escaped from the house and encountered Las Casas outside. Awestruck, the priest hastily explained to him "some things about the faith" and offered to baptize him. The Indian consented and, the sacrament bestowed, fell to the ground dead.

As word of the massacre spread over the island, the natives fled, some to the Queen's Gardens, others into the mountains. Velázquez, on hearing the news, sent advice to Narváez that in the future no man should draw a sword unless the Indians attacked first. Little by little, largely through the chaplain's efforts, the natives were persuaded to come out of hiding.

The army then marched across the island to the north coast. In the level expanses the woods were so dense that one might walk the entire length of the island in their shade. Stately cedars with trunks as thick as stout oxen exuded a heady fragrance. From this red-hearted timber the Indians made their large canoes, capable of bearing seventy men and voyaging on the sea. The natives built their night fires of sweet gum, and the soldiers found the scent of the burning wood pleasing to the senses as the smoke ascended with the mist at sunrise. There also was the *jagua* tree, producing a honey-filled fruit, as large as a veal kidney, that ripened after picking and was more delicious than candied pears. Throughout the island, huge grape clusters dangled from vines thicker than a man's body.

Before reaching the north coast, Narváez's men heard of the three Spanish castaways who had come from Urabá three years previously and were living among the Indians of Havana province. Awaiting further word, the conquerors paused at a coastal town near Sagua la Grande, where the houses were built on poles above the water. There they found ample provisions of cassava and fish, and "a multitude" of parrots, of which it is said they consumed 10,000 in fifteen days. The parrots were green except for a tiny patch of red feathers on their foreheads. The young were delicious either boiled or roasted, and the ease with which they were caught accounts for the rapid decimation of their numbers. An Indian boy of ten to fifteen years would carry a live parrot into a tree and strike it a muffled blow on the head to make it cry out. All the other parrots, hearing the distress call, would come and light on the tree, and the boy would catch as many as desired. Using a stick with a loop at the end he would drop the loop over a bird's head, would draw it tight, pull in the bird, and wring its neck. The act would be repeated until the ground beneath the tree was covered with plumed carcasses.

The interlude by the sea, in the fall of 1513, ended when an Indian canoe appeared, bringing the two castaway Spanish women. About twenty and forty years old, they were naked but for leaves covering their privates and able to speak of their harrowing adventure only in babbling incoherency. Worse, they recalled having seen gold in certain streams but could not say where. At last they were able to tell of their shipwreck and the massacre at Matanzas Bay that had spared only themselves and a man named García Mexía.

In fifteen Indian canoes the soldiers proceeded up the coast to seek Mexía and the gold. On the way they came to the village of Chief Yacagüex, whom the women identified as the one responsible for the massacre. Narváez, stayed from his brutal instincts in this instance by Velázquez's order, advised the natives to take warning from the Zucayo affair; the Spaniards, after all, had come not to do them harm but to make peace and find gold. Yacagüex redeemed himself by revealing the river the women had mentioned, and a sample of its gold was sent to Velázquez.

In a village of modern Havana province ruled by Habagüanex, the troop found Mexía, his ability in his mother tongue, like that of the women, impaired by his years of captivity.

With the conquest in its final stages, the expeditionary force moved back and forth across the narrow western part of the island. Velázquez sent a brigantine to circumnavigate the island again, exploring the ports and bays. The campaign ended early in 1514 as Narváez's men reached the two native provinces of the western cape, Guaniguanico and Guanahacabibe. The two groups of inhabitants, evidently close kin, probably were the remnants of a culture that once extended to the islands farther east, having yielded ground to the invading Arawaks until driven to Cuba's tip. The Guanahacabibes, whose name survives in the peninsula forming the cape and the adjacent gulf on the north, were a small enclave living in caves and subsisting on meat from the hunt and fish and turtles from the sea; they had neither houses nor cultivated fields.

In his narration of the Cuban conquest, Las Casas may be accused of exaggeration or excessive dramatization, but other sources reveal that he spoke an essential truth. Francisco López de Gómara, some forty years later, wrote: "Cuba was densely populated by Indians; today there are only Spaniards."

On June 26, 1514, the discoverer of the Gulf of Mexico, Sebastián de Ocampo, appeared in Seville, making his last will and testament. Was he brought home to face the old death sentence, the result of having violated the terms of his exile? The record does not say. The will and various codicils bear out that Ocampo was a Galician, a native of Túy (on the Río Mino at Portugal's northwest border) and the son of Pedro Fernández de Túy. He named as his heir his own natural son, Simón de Ocampo, who was living on the island now called Puerto Rico, and he set out detailed instructions for his burial in the church of his native parish.

Otherwise, the notarial documents attest Ocampo's relationship with several important explorers and prominent figures in colonial administration. The will itself provided for payment of a debt for Diego de Nicuesa, the gentleman explorer who shared colonization rights on the Tierra Firme coast with Ojeda and was later expelled from the colony, by Vasco Núñez de Balboa, in a leaky brigantine that was lost at sea. Under authority given him in Tierra Firme, Ocampo named a proxy to clear up certain business matters for Núñez de Balboa (who had already discovered the Pacific Ocean) and further disclosed that he was a partner "in a certain company" with Miguel de Pasamonte, the king's treasurer at Santo Domingo, setting out sums due Pasamonte from his final estate settlement.

So ends the record of the Gulf's discoverer. Presumably, he died a short time later and was buried, as he requested, in the churchyard of his native Túy. His name, though little known today, deserves to be re-

membered, for it was Sebastián de Ocampo who pried open the door
to the hidden sea.

SOURCES AND NOTES

The Gulf and Its Name

Sixteenth-century descriptions of the Gulf of Mexico and its adjacent territories are provided by Francisco López de Gómara (*Historia general de las
Indias*, first published in 1552) and Juan López de Velasco (*Geografía y descripción universal de las Indias*, written in the 1570s but not published until
the late nineteenth century). Each of these discusses early names given the
Gulf. An anonymous map issued after 1541 mentioned by Justin Winsor (*Narrative and Critical History of America*, 2:222) may have been the first to
name the Gulf, calling it Seno Mejicano. Sebastian Cabot's 1544 map (ibid.,
p. 447) calls it Golfo de Nueva España. All references to the Gulf in the *fichero*
of the Museo Naval in Madrid are indexed under "Seno Mexicano." For a different construction of the name question, see Paul S. Galtsoff, "Historical
Sketch of the Explorations in the Gulf of Mexico," 3–36.

The description of the Straits of Florida as a major cultural divide is Carl
Ortwin Sauer's (*The Early Spanish Main*, 189).

La Cosa and His Mappemonde

The only known copy of the La Cosa map in its original form is in the
Museo Naval in Madrid. The New World portion is reproduced in color in W. P.
Cumming, R. A. Skelton, and D. B. Quinn, *The Discovery of North America*, 36;
also in Charles Bricker, *Landmarks of Mapmaking*, 199.

Martín Fernández de Navarrete (*Biblioteca Marítima Española*, 2:201)
in 1851 noted certain indications that the Juan de la Cosa of Columbus's second voyage might not have been the same man as *Santa María*'s master on the
first, who has been blamed for the loss of the vessel off Cape Haitien (Hispaniola). Others pounced on the idea and expanded it until Antonio Ballesteros Beretta (*La marina cántabra y Juan de La Cosa*, 129–31) sought to
put it to rest in 1954. Samuel Eliot Morison (*Admiral of the Ocean Sea* and
*The European Discovery of America: The Southern Voyages, A.D. 1492–
1616*), having maintained for years that there were two men of the same name,
finally equivocates; doing so must have been difficult, for he had been as vigorous in his praise of the mapmaker as in his denunciation of the supposedly
recalcitrant shipmaster. The two are merged with irrefutable citations by Roberto Barreiro-Meiro, subdirector of the Museo Naval (in *Juan de la Cosa y su
doble personalidad*), who concludes that the blot on La Cosa's record is
wholly a mistake: he deduces that La Cosa, never ostracized by Columbus, may

well have been master of the flagship, *Marigalante*, on the second voyage as far as Hispaniola.

La Cosa, a Basque from the seaside village of Santoña on the Bay of Biscay, was a well-established pilot and shipowner at Puerto de Santa María prior to the first voyage. Columbus chartered *Santa María* and engaged her owner as master and second in command. La Cosa afterward was offered perquisites by the Crown to compensate him for her loss.

Barreiro-Meiro ("Algo sobre la carta de Juan de la Cosa," in *Puerto Rico, La Aguada, Ponce de León, etc.*, 31) offers the facts concerning La Cosa's career that support the 1500 date on his mappemonde.

Concerning Vespucci, John Fiske (*Discovery of America*, 2:73), writing in 1892, places the Florentine on a voyage with Vicente Yáñez Pinzón and Juan Diaz de Solís in 1497–98, touching Honduras's Cape Gracias á Dios and proceeding thence around the Yucatán peninsula into the Gulf of Mexico. His thesis is based on the 1865 work of the Brazilian Adolpho de Varnhagen (*Amerigo Vespucci*) and is supported by the Argentinian Roberto Levillier (*América la bien llamada*, 1:100). Levillier contends that all the maps indicating an insular Cuba or a Gulf of Mexico prior to 1508 stem from the pretended 1497 Vespucci voyage. Barreiro-Meiro makes a penetrating assessment of Levillier's work and the Vespucci matter in general in his "Vespucio y Levillier."

Cantino and Others

Justin Winsor (*Narrative and Critical History*, 2:107) gives facts concerning Cantino and his map, the North American section of which is reproduced in Cumming, et al., *Discovery*, 57. The idea that the peninsula represents Yucatán rather than Florida is Edzer Roukema's ("A Discovery of Yucatán prior to 1503," 34).

The somewhat widespread earlier view that Cabot reached peninsular Florida probably stems from a failure to understand the term in its sixteenth-century context, a factor perhaps responsible for more historical error in this period than any other. The name "Florida" originally was applied to all the territory northward as far as 50°. Morison (*Portuguese Voyages to America in the Fifteenth Century*, 38) hypothesizes a 1498 voyage by Duarte Pacheco Pereira.

George E. Nunn (*Geographical Conceptions of Columbus*, 95) presents a facsimile of the Canerio map. Bricker (*Landmarks*, 195) and Cumming et al. (*Discovery*, 53) reproduce the Contarini and Waldseemüller maps. Henry Harrisse (*The Discovery of North America*, 93–94) presents a list of 14 maps from various countries dated to 1520 showing a "continental region," as well as Cuba, "akin to that of Cantino." Only two exclusively Spanish maps relating to the New World constructed before 1520 are known to exist: La Cosa's planisphere, and the one appearing with Peter Martyr's first decade.

Discovery of the Gulf

Peter Martyr (Pedro Mártir de Anglería, *Décadas del Nuevo Mundo*, p. 108) relates the proof of Cuba's insularity, which he attributes elsewhere (p. 172) to Diaz de Solís and Pinzón. Numerous writers, overlooking Martyr's own statement that he put aside his work for a number of years before completing book 10 and revising portions written earlier, in 1510, have mistakenly linked this event to the 1499 voyage (pp. 105–106). Instructions for the 1508 voyage are given in José Toribio Medina, *Juan Diaz de Solís*, 2:26–34; also in *CDI*, 22:5–13.

The "Pleitos de Colón" are printed in *CDU* 7 (the pertinent passages on pp. 266–70). Ledesma's adherents include Manuel de la Puente y Olea (*Los trabajos geográficas de la Casa de Contratación*, 80) and Sauer (*Early Spanish Main*, 167–68). Sauer's assessment is somewhat myopic, especially in his assertion that the Mexican Conquest "had no concern with finding a strait" because of the "negative results" obtained by Pinzón and Diaz de Solís. He assumes a copyist's error in Pinzón's direction to take him west instead of east from Guanaja, even though the names Pinzón gives (e.g., Camarón) show that he really did sail east from his Honduras landfall. Perhaps the most egregious non sequitur is Sauer's inference that Pinzón and Diaz de Solís took no notice of the rather striking Mayan ruins along the Yucatán coast because they were concerned with finding a strait.

Brief sketches of Ocampo are found in Bartolomé de las Casas, *History of the Indies*, 149, and Antonio de Herrera y Tordesillas, *Historia general de los hechos de los castellanos en las islas, y Tierra-firme de el Mar Occéano*, 2:94. The royal decree for his exile, long ignored by historians of Cuba and the Gulf, is printed in *CDI* 39:13–14. His will and codicils are in the notarial archives of Seville (APS, 1514, oficio 4, libro 2, *escribanía* Manuel Segura, ff. 693v, 681v, 686). Las Casas (*History*, 148–49) relates Ocampo's circumnavigation of Cuba and describes the principal bays, which he himself saw during the conquest. José Manuel Pérez Cabrera (*En torno del bojeo de Cuba*) discusses the voyage but is useful mainly in establishing its date (1508–1509).

The Conquest

Herrera and Las Casas both supply details on Cuba and its conquest. To Collard's translation of Las Casas's *History* should be added George Sanderlin's translations (*Bartolomé de las Casas: A Selection of His Writings*). The expeditionary chaplain frequently overstates his case; his account therefore should be balanced with other sources, such as Diego Velázquez's letter to the Crown of April 1, 1514. This document appears to have been little used, even though a somewhat flawed transcription is printed in *CDI* 11:412–29. The original in AGI, Patronato 178-1-1, is in a difficult hand even for that time, but with David Block's help I managed to compare the two. It gives a somewhat different version of the Zucayo affair, contrasting sharply with Las Casas's dramatized ac-

count of wholesale slaughter of the village's 27,500 inhabitants. Velázquez acknowledges only 100 victims.

The similarity of the Cuban natives to those of Hispaniola is discussed by
Gonzalo Fernández de Oviedo y Valdés (*Historia general y natural de las Indias, islas y Tierra-firme del Mar Océano*, 3:244–45) and López de Gómara
(*Historia*, 112). Las Casas, Peter Martyr, and Fernández de Oviedo constitute a
triad of *cronistas* who wrote of events immediately following the Discovery as
they happened.

For a survey of Cuba's history, see Willis Fletcher Johnson, *The History of
Cuba*.

CHAPTER 2

Florida and the Fountain:
Juan Ponce de León, 1513–21

Noʀᴛʜ of Cuba and Haiti lie the Bahama Islands, known to sixteenth-century Spaniards as the Lucayos. The natives, first contacted by Columbus on October 12, 1492, when he landed at Guanahaní, or San Salvador, were whiter and more graceful than the aborigines of either Cuba or Hispaniola. The women were so strikingly beautiful that men came from Florida, Yucatán, and even Tierra Firme to seek their favor and live among them; so wrote Francisco López de Gómara, circa 1550. These foreigners attracted by the island sirens contributed to a great diversity of language and an elevation of manners and culture: "It is from there," says the chronicler, "that the report comes of amazon women and a fountain that restores old men."

Such an account, in circulation in one form or another almost since the first Discovery, was a natural for stirring the fancy of an unemployed conquistador. In that circumstance in 1512 was Juan Ponce de León. That the Fountain of Youth legend influenced his discovery of Florida has long been accepted as fact.

The myths were by no means new, nor did they die with Ponce. López de Gómara merely provided embellishment for the tale recorded by Peter Martyr in 1516. Among the islands north of Hispaniola, says Martyr, was one called Boyuca, alias Ananéo, which had a notable fountain: "From the drinking of its water the aged are rejuvenated." The story was widely circulated in the Spanish court at Burgos, and no few noblemen "distinguished by virtue and fortune" had taken it as truth.

The fable of "the rejuvenating fountain that makes old men young," as Fernández de Oviedo tells it, came to light while Ponce was fitting out his ships to discover the island of Bímini. "It was so widely circulated and attested by the Indians of those parts" that Ponce made it an objective of his voyage. As for old men turning young, the *cronista* chuckles, he himself had seen it happen, without a fountain's help. It was evidenced by *el enflaquescimiento del sexo*—the loss of sexual powers—and by old men's childish behavior. For this, it seemed, the said Juan Ponce had gone searching at his own great cost, kept by vanity in a "natural state of credulity concerning this Indian nonsense."

Ponce's main concern, according to the royal *cronista* Herrera, writing somewhat later, was to make new discoveries; but he was also intent on finding the "Spring of Bímini" and a certain legendary river in Florida whose existence was rumored among the Indians of Cuba and Hispaniola. Herrera's account of the fountain comes from Hernando de Escalante Fontaneda, who was shipwrecked on the Florida Keys in 1551 and grew to young manhood among the Calusa Indians (see Chapter 17). It was the Jordan River, Escalante had said, for which Ponce went to search in Florida, "that he might have some enterprise on foot, earn greater fame . . . or become young from bathing in such a stream." In earlier times, the notable castaway continues, the Cubans had risked death at sea to come in great numbers to the "Province of Carlos" at the peninsula's southern end, seeking the magical waters. One named Senquene formed them into a settlement, and Escalante found their descendants still there, still seeking the restorative balm in every pond and creek. He himself, while a captive, had bathed in many a stream, he tells us tongue in cheek, without the good fortune of finding one that restored his youth. (He was hardly more than a youth at the time.)

Ponce was thirty-nine years old when he undertook the voyage on which he discovered "the island of Florida" and made the second recorded entry of the Gulf of Mexico. This fact gave rise to one elderly historian's wry observation that Ponce himself could scarcely have needed a cure for impotence. Not necessarily so, as modern sexologists will testify. Yet it is obvious that the explorer was not the decrepit oldster of gray hair, wrinkles, and faltering steps that romanticists have tended to portray. He was red-haired, robust, and full of vinegar. If the fountain myth excited his imagination, he cannot be faulted, for it has stirred the fancy of countless millions since.

Juan Ponce de León, born in 1474 in San Tervás del Campo, Valladolid province, was of distinguished noble parentage. He sailed with

Columbus on the second voyage at age nineteen, already a veteran of the Granada campaign that attained final victory over the Moors. Following his notable part in Hispaniola's Higüey war, Ponce was put in charge at the village of Salvaleón de Higüey, so named for his mother's native village in Spain. His interest in Boriquén, or Puerto Rico, directly across the Mona Passage, jumped into sharp focus when an Indian from that island brought him a gold nugget. With Governor Ovando's authority, he proceeded to conquer the island by terrorizing and enslaving the Indians. It was his ticket to fame and fortune—until it came to royal attention that his franchise as governor ran afoul of Diego Columbus's hereditary rights; with the second Admiral's arrival to govern the islands, Ponce's tenure was terminated. Don Diego's favorites, Juan Cerón and Miguel Díaz de Aux, whom Ponce had packed off to prison in Spain, were returned to govern Puerto Rico and avenge themselves. Ponce, in consequence, was unemployed.

Yet when he petitioned the king for the right to search for Bímini, he was granted a contract, under date of February 23, 1512. By that time slavers were making great strides toward depopulating the Lucayos, which appear to have been well known. Just what Ponce had in mind is not clear, unless it was to investigate reports of other islands beyond, hoping to extend the limits of slaving voyages. By terms of the royal concession, he was to equip his ships at his own cost, discover and settle "the island of Bininy," and aportion the Indians in *repartimiento*. Nothing was said about looking for a rejuvenating fountain.

A little over a year later, on March 4, 1513, Ponce sailed from Puerto Rico with three vessels: *Santiago*, a caravel of which Diego Bermúdez was master and Antón de Alaminos pilot; *San Cristóbal*, a brigantine with Juan Pérez de Ortubia as captain; and *Santa María de la Consolación*, Juan Bono de Quejo, captain. The ships carried several beeves on the hoof and Ponce's mare, which the voyage provided him little opportunity to use.

A key personage on this voyage was the pilot Alaminos, whose hydrographical observations were to affect the course of discovery. A native of Palos, whence Columbus departed on his first voyage, Alaminos is credited by Las Casas with having sailed with the Admiral as a ship's boy (*paje*) on his fourth. Recent efforts to place him on the Cuba exploration of the second voyage should be discounted, for his name does not appear on the sworn statement that Columbus required of his crew concerning Cuba as a peninsula. Nor could he have been a ship's boy on the fourth, for by then he was twenty years old. It seems likely that he was already on his way to becoming a pilot when he sailed with Columbus on his final voyage.

Alaminos is said to have been the most experienced pilot in the Indies of his time, but to judge him so in 1513, when he was thirty-one, is to anticipate the fact. His experience was to be broadened considerably on Ponce's voyage, even more so on the next three voyages of discovery into the Gulf of Mexico. From 1513 to 1520 he expanded his geographical and hydrographical knowledge and fine-tuned his perceptions with hard lessons from that expensive teacher, experience. His name should be remembered, for he truly was the Gulf's pilot of discovery.

Remember also the name of Juan Bono de Quejo. This doughty Basque, native of San Sebastián on the Bay of Biscay, was to be Ponce's companion for several years before involving himself in the Gulf's navigation and dabbling in the conquest of Mexico.

Ponce's three ships took their departure from Aguada, on Puerto Rico's northwest point, the afternoon of March 4. Standing away northwest by north during the night, they made eight leagues by sunrise. While it is needless to detail the voyage along the outer edge of the Bahamas, one pertinent fact emerges: the latitudes given are consistently more than a degree too much. Errors in latitudes computed from solar observations, especially at sea, were the rule during this period; Alaminos, however, exceeds the normal limits so regularly that the deviations cannot be written off as erratic observation. Rather, they must have been due to a constant factor, such as out-of-date tables or a faulty astrolabe. At San Salvador, the Guanahaní of Columbus's first discovery, for example, the latitude is given as 25°40'. San Salvador lies between 23°57' and 24°07', indicating an error of at least 1°33'. Other computations at points that can be identified with reasonable certainty reflect a margin somewhat greater than one degree—representing sixty nautical miles.

Leaving San Salvador about March 25, Ponce's three ships took a northwesterly course through "the windward gulf" outside the northern Bahamas. On March 27—Easter Sunday, *Pascua Florida* or *Pascua de Flores*—the explorers sighted an island (Great Abaco) they did not recognize. On Wednesday, foul weather brought a course change toward the west. The Florida coast was sighted the following Saturday, April 2. Ponce, believing it an island, named it Florida for the Easter festival.

The landfall is given as 30°08' in the only extant account of the voyage; allowing for error of at least one degree, it was perhaps near Ponce de Leon Inlet, just north of New Smyrna Beach on present-day maps. There is no accounting for the next five days. On Friday, April 8, the three ships sailed north briefly before turning back south; they ran south by east with the shore current until April 21. Then, in the mouth of the Bahama Channel, they felt the full force of the mighty Gulf Stream. Attempting to get underway that morning, the vessels "met with a current so strong that it drove them back, though they had a favorable wind." The two ships nearest shore dropped anchors, but the flow was so powerful that it strained the cables. The brigantine *San Cristóbal*, finding no bottom, was carried out of sight, even though the day was clear.

This incident occurred where the Gulf Stream, confined between the Florida coast and the Little Bahama Bank, gushes forth into open water. It was a high point of the voyage, for it enabled Alaminos eventually to establish the enduring course to Spain, using the strongest of ocean currents and the Bahama Channel.

On Sunday, May 8, the voyagers "doubled the Florida Cape, naming it Cabo de Corrientes, because here the water ran so strong that its force was greater than the wind." They anchored behind the cape near a native village called Abaiós, and Alaminos's noon sun shot showed a latitude of 28°15'. The pilot's error was 1°27'.

A league-long island, named Santa Marta (observed latitude, 27°), probably was Key Biscayne, in 25°44'. On Friday, May 13, running along a string of island reefs, the mariners came to another island, which they called Santa Pola. The bay sighted within the reefs doubtless was Biscayne. The latitude observed by Alaminos was 26.5°.

Pentecost Sunday, May 15—no mention of sailing on Saturday— took the voyagers ten leagues along a string of small islands that inspired the name Los Mártires. The rocks seen from a distance, it is said, resembled suffering men, and many a shipwrecked Spaniard was to suffer and die there in years to come. Assuming a 1.5° error in the observed latitude of 26°15', the ships could have been no farther west than the eighty-first meridian; probably closer to a longitude of 80.5°

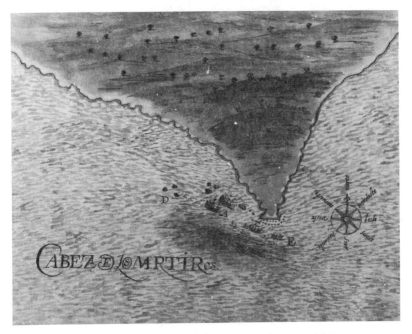

Fig. 3. Ponce's discovery: Florida and the Martyrs. Courtesy Biblioteca Nacional.

west, since they were only ten leagues—34 miles—from Pola. Some 48 hours' sailing time remained before they could pass the Marquesas Keys and turn north; three to four days of daylight sailing. At this unfortunate juncture, a hiatus occurs in the account, perhaps a line dropped from Herrera's narrative, presumably based on the original diary. With the ships not yet to Upper Matecumbe Key, the next sentence tells us, "they were sailing at times to the north and others to the northeast until May 23, and on the twenty-fourth they ran along the coast to the south (not observing that it was mainland) to some islands that ran out to sea." Something is missing.

The general tendency has been to ignore the hiatus, jump the ships over the keys, and take them up the west Florida coast as far as Charlotte Harbor, Tampa Bay, or even Pensacola. Yet to clear the reefs, they had still to travel a distance almost as great as that from Cabo de Corrientes, which had taken eight days.

The keys throughout history have been notorious traps for unwary navigators. Alaminos surely took every precaution, constantly heaving the sounding lead, and keeping a sharp lookout at the foretop to detect any change in water color that would warn of diminishing depth. The ships would have anchored from dusk to dawn to avoid slipping up on a hidden shoal in darkness.

There is no reason to doubt that the north and northeast navigation "until the twenty-third" did take the voyagers around the keys and to the mainland coast on the west side of the peninsula. The gap in the only available account has provided license for all kinds of wild guesses as to how and when they got there and how far they ascended. The bay of Ponce's brief sojourn on the west Florida coast has most often been identified with Charlotte Harbor, thought to be the same as Carlos Bay, which has been assumed to be in the vicinity of Charlotte Harbor or its offshoot, San Carlos Bay. The unfortunate result of this assumption has been to provide trackers of the voyage a destination to work toward, allowing them to make whatever adjustments were necessary to reach it. Reconsideration of the whole matter is in order.

Since Herrera provides no starting time or place for the northward navigation, let us assume that he should be amended to read something like this: "After finding their way around the reefs on the nineteenth[?], they were sailing at times north, others northeast, until May 23." Where could they have gone in the four days remaining before turning back south?

In forty leagues along the Martyrs, says Herrera, there was no passage to accommodate a ship, not even a brigantine; only canoes could pass through them. That distance, at 3.43 nautical miles per league, extends on a present-day chart from Biscayne Bay beyond the Marquesas Keys. Ponce's ships, therefore, must have passed the Marquesas before turning northward. Once clear of the keys they would have veered to starboard seeking the Florida coast and quickly come again within soundings, where it was necessary still to anchor at night. Progress during daylight hours would have been less than the ten leagues logged on May 15. It seems extremely doubtful, therefore, that in the four days remaining they would have come to Charlotte Harbor.

Any conclusion on the matter hinges on identification of the "islands tending out to sea" that were reached in one day's southward sailing or less on May 24. There are but two possibilities: those in the vicinity of Cape Romano and those near Cape Sable. One would indicate a mainland landfall between Charlotte Harbor and Cape Romano, the other between Romano and Cape Sable.

When the voyagers reached these islands, they found a passage between them and the mainland. The ships entered the channel to take on wood and water and anchored until June 3. During that time *San Cristóbal* was careened on one of the islands. At first the Indians, among them one who spoke Spanish, crossed the inlet in canoes to barter pelts and *guanín*, a low-grade gold. Then they turned hostile, seizing the anchor cables and trying to board the ships. The Spaniards captured four Indian women, who told them of a chieftain called Carlos who had some gold. Before the voyagers could get underway to look for Carlos, the ships were assaulted from twenty canoes. A number of Indians and one Spaniard were killed, and Ponce's men took four more captives.

Then came what seemed to be the break they were waiting for. While a boat crew was sounding to find a better anchorage, some natives approached to report that Carlos would come the next day to trade. But, instead of the *cacique*, there came eighty canoes filled with screeching warriors. In a day-long sham battle, they loosed harmless arrows from beyond the range of the Spaniards' guns and crossbows.

The ships moved to the new anchorage after the second attack and remained there nine days. On June 14 the Spaniards returned to the watering place (named Matanza for the Indians slain there), preparatory to returning to Hispaniola and Puerto Rico. After topping off the water casks, they set out to discover on the way the eleven islands that the Indian captives had told them lay farther west: the Dry Tortugas. Feeling their way cautiously along the lower part of the Martyrs and the Marquesas, the voyagers took until Thursday, June 21, to reach them. Lying some sixty-five miles beyond Key West, these islands were named by Ponce's men for the 160 giant sea turtles, each as big as a war shield, captured during a single evening. They also caught seals, or manatee, called *lobos marinos*, and killed thousands of gannets and other sea birds before sailing again on Friday, June 24.

Now arises an intriguing question. Leaving the Tortugas, Herrera says, Ponce's ships sailed not east but southwest by west; apparently they were seeking Cabo San Antón and passage through the Yucatán Channel to return to Puerto Rico by sailing south of Cuba and Hispaniola. But the cape failed to appear when expected. Holding course, they sailed 18 leagues farther before sighting land on Sunday, then followed the mysterious shore all day Monday. Nothing is said about Tuesday's occurrences, but on Wednesday the Spaniards put into an anchorage to repair yards and sails. The sailors were mystified by the strange country. None could recognize it as Cuba, although the shoreline ran east-west, as Cuba's did. Confronted with such strange circumstances, the mariners concluded that they had reached a new land.

From these facts the claim has arisen that Ponce's ships had crossed the Yucatán Channel, "sailing large before a brisk trade wind," to a discovery of Yucatán not previously credited. The supposed landfall has been placed between Cabo Catoche and Progreso. If they even raised Cabo Catoche in two days from the Tortugas, they were sailing large indeed. The distance is slightly greater than the first four full days' run at the start of the voyage, when they were sailing in blue water with favorable wind and current. Here, they would have had to buck the building Gulf Stream, flowing out of the Gulf of Mexico through the Straits of Florida toward the Bahama Channel. Because of it, the ships doubtless were set to larboard, striking Cuba much farther east than expected. Near the landing place the voyagers found some dogs, some iron tools, and other signs that Europeans had been here ahead of them—signs that in June, 1513, might have been encountered in western Cuba but hardly in Yucatán.

Alaminos chalked up a lesson on the Gulf's hydrography that would prove useful later. He certainly understood that the current had caused the confusion, for the following Friday, July 1, a week after leaving the Dry Tortugas, the ships sailed again for the Martyrs. Two days later—much too short a time for sailing from Yucatán—they picked up Matecumbe Key, called Achecambei by Herrera—then sailed on past Santa Pola and Santa Marta, which Ponce had named on May 12 and 13. Nearby, they came to Chequesca, or Tequesta (not mentioned previously in the Herrera account), the present site of Miami Beach. Proceeding thence toward the Lucayos, Ponce anchored on some shoals on the western side of the Bahama Banks on July 18. The latitude, given as 28°, was about 1°11′ less.

Reconnoitering Grand Bahama Island, Ponce encountered a Spanish pilot named Diego Miruelo from Hispaniola—either on a slaving expedition or sent by Diego Columbus to spy on Ponce. Miruelo has been credited, erroneously, with the next penetration of the Gulf of Mexico (more of him in due course).

The rest of the return voyage through the Bahamas is apart from our concern. *San Cristóbal*, in trouble almost from the start, was lost in her anchorage during a blow. Ponce could not forget the reports of Bímini's richness, "especially that celebrated fountain which the Indians said made old men young again." While he and Bono de Quejo returned to Puerto Rico with *Santiago*, Pérez de Ortubia and Alaminos sailed with *Santa María* on the mission of mercy for all men past their prime, to find Bímini and the magical waters.

Ponce, reaching Puerto Rico 21 days later, was eager to sail for Spain, lest his rivals claim his discovery before him. (Miruelo's unexplained appearance evidently had disturbed him.) Impatiently, he waited for *Santa María*'s return. She came in at last on February 20, 1514. Pérez de Ortubia, having found Bímini, described it as a large island with many trees and clear, fresh waters but no youth-restoring fountain.

In Spain, King Ferdinand readily accorded Ponce the title of *adelantado* of Bímini and "the island of Florida," and granted him license to settle and govern the territory. But first he must lead a campaign to curb the cannibalistic Carib Indians of the Lesser Antilles. Bono and Ponce bought three caravels for the new assignment and returned to the Indies to carry it out.

Details of that affair are of no concern here except to bring out the character of Juan Bono de Quejo, for he comes back into our narrative later. According to Las Casas, "Juan the Bad" did not confine his raids to the hostile Caribs but practiced betrayal on the peaceful natives of Trinidad, the Caribs' enemies. Herding 400 of them into a house the Indians had built for their Spanish guests, Bono and his men slaughtered those who resisted captivity—almost all—and sold the remnant into slavery at Hispaniola.

Alaminos had stayed behind when Ponce and Bono went to Spain. He is said variously to have joined Ponce later on the Carib campaign, and to have gone directly into Francisco de Garay's employ at Jamaica. He probably did neither. He next appears on a new voyage into the Gulf of Mexico in 1517, revisiting Florida ahead of Ponce.

To carry Ponce to the conclusion of his endeavors, it is necessary to forsake chronology. At the end of the Carib campaign, he was authorized to use the ships and men to conquer and settle Florida. By 1521, when he at last turned his attention to the matter, those vessels were no longer available, and he purchased two others at his own expense. Bono de Quejo already had involved himself in other affairs and could not be a part of the new undertaking.

Ponce wrote to the emperor, Charles V, from Puerto Rico on February 10 that year, declaring his intention of returning to "that island" and taking a number of people to settle. "I also intend to explore the coast of said island further, and see whether it is an island, or whether it connects with the land where Diego Velázquez is [meaning New Spain, that part of Mexico which by that time had been occupied by Cortés, discovery of which was claimed by Velázquez] or any other. . . . I shall set out in five or six days."

He sailed on February 26 with the two ships. Little is known of the expedition itself. Ponce is said to have taken secular priests to minister to the colonists and religious friars for establishing Indian missions. He also took horses, cattle, sheep, and swine. There is nothing to locate his landfall in Florida beyond the record of the previous voyage and some obscure references by writers of the same century. It has been generally assumed that his second landing, in 1521, was at or near the site of the first, in 1513. This assumption raises a question as to what Ponce saw in the Florida Everglades that caused him to believe this area a suitable place to settle. Was he motivated by the report he had heard that the *cacique* Carlos had gold? If so, it was a tragic mistake.

The colonists were attacked while attempting to erect buildings, and many were slain by Indians; others succumbed to illness. Ponce himself suffered a wound in the thigh, so painful that he decided to withdraw to Cuba. The company reached Puerto Príncipe, where he died in July, 1521, at the age of 47.

Like Columbus, Ponce de León came to his end without knowing the extent of his discovery. But where Columbus had assumed an island to be an Asian peninsula, the land Ponce took for an island proved to be the tip of a large new continent.

Aside from the Florida discovery, Ponce's greatest contribution is to hydrography. Yet his experience with the Gulf Stream, of such great importance later, for the moment served chiefly to confuse. "Everyone agrees," Peter Martyr comments, "that the seas run toward the west [through the Caribbean] like torrents from the mountains. For this reason I am confused concerning where these waters go. With continuous motion they run from the east, fleeing toward the west, from which they never return; yet the west is neither filled nor the east emptied. . . . Those who have sailed those coasts offer no explanation." The majority believed that vast gulfs lay at the extreme end of this "great territory west of the island of Cuba," and that they absorbed the ocean flow, discharging it to the west, whence it "returns to our east." Others held that the current flowed out of these gulfs through a northward passage that brought it back into the Ocean Sea; still others, that the gulf was closed, all the known coastlines actually being contiguous and extending northward past the shores of Cuba, where the current was narrowed and intensified.

Somewhere between the Cabots' land of Bacalaos (Newfoundland) and the Spaniards' Tierra Firme, Martyr reasoned, there must be "great apertures" to give passage to the waters ever running from east to west. "I think that the impulse of the heavens makes these waters flow in a circular pattern around the terrestrial globe, and no demogorgon with open mouth either expels or absorbs them."

Those returning to Spain from Hispaniola and Cuba, he learned, found the current not so strong, because in the open sea the flow was able to spread. It was strongest among the islands, as in the Gulf of Paria and among the Honduras Bay islands, where on Columbus's fourth voyage the flow had been so fierce that it carried the sounding lead. From these places it often was necessary for a ship to return to Hispaniola or Cuba and "take the wide sea by the northern route to get on the course to Spain."

One evening in 1515, Martyr—whose voluminous writings include much information derived from personal interviews with New World explorers—was host for a discussion of the matter in his home in Madrid. The other two participants also were men of prominence in compiling knowledge of the discoveries: the historian Gonzalo Fernández de Oviedo y Valdés and Andrés de Morales, noted pilot and hydrographer. Martyr himself fueled the conversation with questions. His two guests agreed that the Castilian lands of Tierra Firme must be joined without interruption to those lying north of Cuba, discovered for the English. Morales, who had been a pilot on Columbus's third voyage and later explored and mapped parts of the Antilles for Governor Ovando, maintained that the flow, encountering the continental shelf, was turned northward. Forced by the configuration of the coast to take a rotating course, he believed, it ran back along the north Cuban shore. There, as Ponce de León had discovered, it attained its maximum velocity, like water forced through a mill channel. Then, entering the open sea, the current became diffused and placid.

Both Martyr and Fernández de Oviedo held reservations regarding Morales's idea, but in time he was proved right. Eventually, he evolved a theory concerning currents of the Atlantic. In the meantime, Antón de Alaminos put the pieces together in his own mind and gave his own observations the stress test. On his next voyage, the current would play an important part. Silently, almost insidiously, it was leading—or pushing—the Spaniards toward further discovery in the Gulf of Mexico.

SOURCES AND NOTES

The Fountain of Youth

Almost all the major sixteenth-century Spanish historians of the Indies give some account of the Fountain of Youth, Las Casas being the notable exception. Peter Martyr, the first of this group to describe the fountain, does not relate it to Ponce de León. Fernández de Oviedo, writing some two decades later, does. One of the more interesting accounts comes from Hernando de Escalante Fontaneda, who had lived among the Calusa Indians—with whom Ponce did battle—for some 15 years. A Spanish manuscript copy of his memoir is in Martín Fernández de Navarrete, *Colección de documentos y manuscriptos compilados por Fernández de Navarrete*, 14:357–66. It has been translated into English by Buckingham Smith as *Memoir of D.° d'Escalante Fontaneda Respecting Florida* (1854) and reissued (1944) in an edition edited by David O. True.

Antonio de Herrera, whose *Historia* was first published in 1601, drew upon this account (2:212), giving rise to speculation by True—who obviously had not read Fernández de Oviedo's comments—that Escalante Fontaneda, through Herrera, was responsible for connecting Ponce's name with the fountain.

Juan Ponce de León

Biographical data on Ponce come from Samuel Eliot Morison, *The European Discovery of America: The Southern Voyages*, and Aurelio Tió, *Nuevas fuentes para la historia de Puerto Rico*. Fernández de Oviedo, in his *Historia* (vol. 3 of the 1944 edition), relates the difficulties in Puerto Rico that led to his seeking the royal concession, which is printed in *CDI* 22:26 and in Tió's *Nuevas fuentes*. See also Vicente Murga Sanz, *Juan Ponce de León*, especially concerning preparations for the 1513 voyage. Murga Sanz corrects Herrera and other earlier writers, who give the year of the voyage as 1512, rather than 1513.

Antón de Alaminos

Morison (*Southern Voyages*, 506, 532) places Alaminos on Columbus's second voyage. Roberto Barreiro-Meiro, subdirector of the Museo Naval, Madrid, takes issue. Barreiro-Meiro assisted me in establishing Alaminos's age, which appears as 47 in a published 1522 document ("Probanza sobre las causas que se dieron a la suplicación de las provisiones del veedor Cristóbal de Tapia," 230) but as forty in the original.

In June, 1979, David Block and I spent two days in Palos and nearby Moguer trying to fill some of the blanks concerning Alaminos and other early navigators from that area. Although there are many volumes of sixteenth-century records in the notarial archives at Moguer, the earliest is about 1535. We found no mention of Alaminos. We visited the parish church in Palos and La Rábida Monastery outside Palos, and heard again what the Moguer archivist had told us: that the ecclesiastical records were destroyed in the Spanish Civil War.

The 1513 Voyage

Herrera's account (*Historia*, 2:207–12, 1944 edition) is the only primary source on the voyage. It is generally believed that it is based on an actual log that has long since been lost and, in fact, has not been seen since Herrera used it. Writers have been much inclined, in relating Ponce's discovery, to go beyond what Herrera tells; hence the great confusion.

Various ideas have been put forth concerning the consistent error in latitudes given by Herrera. Henry Harrisse (*The Discovery of North America*) thought the latitudes might have been taken from a map drawn later, rather than from the original log. Doubtful. Morison (*Southern Voyages*, 531) quotes with skepticism a theory he attributes to Edward W. Lawson, *The First Landing Place of Juan Ponce de Leon*: that an obsolete edition of the Alphonsine Tables of Declination was responsible for the error.

Robert S. Chamberlain ("Discovery of the Bahama Channel," [1948], 109–16) gives the most adequate treatment of that subject. The evolution of Alaminos's career will be developed in succeeding chapters.

Where did Ponce go on the west Florida coast? Herrera has left room for guesswork, and guesswork is what has been applied to the question. Morison (*Southern Voyages*, 510) places the careening of *San Cristóbal* (after May 24) on the Marquesas Keys, then takes the ships north on June 3, in one day, "at least to the mouth of the Caloosahatchee River, or nearby Charlotte Harbor."

John Gilmary Shea ("Ancient Florida," in Justin Winsor, ed., *Narrative and Critical History*, 2:233) has them discover the Tortugas first, then sail "up the western shore of Florida to a bay, in 27°30′ [about the entrance of present Tampa Bay], which for centuries afterward bore the name of Juan Ponce." Woodbury Lowery (*The Spanish Settlements within the Present Limits of the United States, 1513–1561*, 141) takes Ponce up the peninsula directly from his May 15 position outside the Martyrs between that date and May 23, without concern for getting him through the reefs. Harrisse (*Discovery*, 153) concludes on the basis of the 1519 Alvarez de Pineda map (see my ch. 7) that Ponce "went further north-westward and westwardly in his first voyage to Florida, than the account of that expedition, as given by Herrera, would lead us to believe": to wit, latitude 30°. T. Frederick Davis ("Juan Ponce de León's Voyage to Florida," 39–40) has Ponce pass the Tortugas "about May 18" before turning north, and return to those islands after June 15. Edward Lawson (*The Discovery of Florida and Its Discoverer, Juan Ponce de León*, 25) speculates that Ponce sighted some of the Tortugas before turning north. The difficulty of seeing them has been commented upon by many observers, including Escalante Fontaneda.

Herrera's account seems to rule out the Charlotte Harbor vicinity as the location of the Indian battles. Additionally, official Spanish sailing instructions of 1583 place the Bahía de Juan Ponce in latitude 25°, about where Ponce de Leon Bay is shown on present-day maps. Juan López de Velasco, the royal Spanish geographer, seems to suggest the jumbled islands of the Cape Romano vicinity in his description of 1574 (*Geografía y descripción*), although his distances and latitudes cannot be reconciled with each other. Like Escalante Fontaneda, he indicates that the original Tampa was in the Charlotte Harbor vicinity, a concept that may alter a number of conclusions on Florida's historical geography.

Lowery appends to his *Spanish Settlements, U.S.* a study of 12 maps of the sixteenth and early seventeenth centuries in an effort to locate Bahía de Juan Ponce. He finds the choices almost equally divided among the first, second, third, and fourth bays that are depicted. Lowery concludes that no conclusion can be reached on the basis of the maps.

Lawson's tracking of Ponce (*Discovery*, 39) takes into consideration the effects of wind and current, factors that certainly weighed on the ship's course and progress. Yet he, too, becomes confused by the gap in Herrera's account and evidently yields to the temptation to take the generally accepted destination, near Charlotte Harbor, and work toward it.

"Discovery of Yucatán"

The claim that Ponce, after discovering Florida in 1513, went on to discover Yucatán (see Morison, *Southern Voyages*, 511) also is fraught with confusion. A 1519 petition of Diego Columbus that identifies Yucatán with Bímini (appearing in La Duquesa de Berwick y de Alba, *Autógrafos de Colon y pa-*

peles de América, 71–72) seems to lie at the roots of the problem. Therein the second Admiral urges the Crown not to grant Yucatán to Hernando Cortés or Diego Velázquez: "These lands now called Ulloa Yucatán," he says, were previously called Bímini among Christians. Aurelio Tió, a descendant of Ponce, first came up with the idea of a 1513 Yucatán discovery, in "Historia del descubrimiento de la Florida y Bímeni ó Yucatán," 141–43. For a counter view, see Roberto Barreiro-Meiro, *Puerto Rico, etc.,* 47–48.

Tió (*Nuevas fuentes,* 114, 361) also offers certain documents as proof that Ponce extended his 1516 Carib campaign to a discovery of both Yucatán and New Spain, in the vicinity of present-day Veracruz. The material consists largely of depositions taken by the Audiencia de Guatemala in 1606 pertaining to a petition by Ponce's great-grandson, Perafán de Rivera. The earliest evidence to support such a claim, however, is the 1571 declaration of one Juan Griego, then eighty-one years old, to the effect that Ponce had sailed from Puerto Rico in a single caravel with Alaminos as pilot and that he had discovered both Florida and New Spain. Support from any other contemporary source is conspicuously lacking. All known accounts that mention Alaminos on the expeditions discovering Yucatán and New Spain in 1517 and 1518 offer no hint that he was a part of any such prior discovery by Ponce de León.

Ponce's Second Voyage

Henry Harrisse (*Discovery,* 159–62) hypothesizes Ponce's itinerary on the second voyage. His basis is the reported arrival at Villa Rica de la Vera Cruz of one of Ponce's ships in October, 1521. He surmises that the expedition lasted at least five months, four of which were spent ranging the west coast of the Florida peninsula from Chatham Bay or Charlotte Harbor to Tampa or Wakasassee; finding no suitable place to settle, Ponce sailed on northward to the point shown on "the 1519 map of Garay"—i.e., Alvarez de Pineda—which Harrisse thinks he might have visited in 1513.

López de Velasco, however, in locating the Bahía de Carlos near the keys, says that Ponce disembarked there "in the year 15" and was fatally wounded. This is perhaps the only source for the site of Ponce's final disaster. Harrisse (*Discovery,* 143–44), quoting Las Casas, brings out the place of Ponce's death (Puerto Príncipe), usually given as Havana.

The Mysterious Current

Peter Martyr relates the discussion concerning the mysteries of ocean currents in the Indies in his *Décadas* (pp. 251–54, 299–300). For one treatment of the discussion with Morales and Fernández de Oviedo and of the topic generally, see Harold L. Burstyn, "Theories of Winds and Ocean Currents from the Discoveries to the End of the Seventeenth Century." The importance of Martyr's informants escapes that writer, who refers to them merely as "two experienced seamen."

The Lead Line

One device that Ponce's navigators doubtless put to good use while running the unknown Florida coast was the lead line, which has refused to be outmoded by technological advancements. The deep-sea lead line, 200 fathoms long and weighted with fourteen pounds, was used to determine the proximity of land before the actual sighting. In shoal water, a shorter line with a seven-pound weight was used, cast continuously from the bow in the direction of the ship's movement as a precaution against a sudden diminishing of depth that could put the ship aground. The sounding lead was hollowed at the lower end and the concavity filled with tallow that would bring up samples of the bottom material. It was the pilot's duty to keep a careful record of depths and a description of the bottom material "in soundings." The record was incorporated into sailing instructions to guide other navigators (J. H. Parry, *The Age of Reconnaissance*, 97–98).

An example of how this information was used is found in Francisco Manuel's 1583 summary of Urdaneta's instructions (British Museum, additional manuscript 28,189). Ships traveling from Veracruz to Havana took soundings at the Tortugas. If the lead brought up sand, the pilots were told, they would lie east-west with the islands; if conchite, northeast-southwest; black sand, north-south. Thus the course for Havana was determined.

Rewards of Discovery:
Hernández de Córdoba, 1517

Dᴵᴇɢᴏ VᴇʟᴀᴢQᴜᴇZ, married one week and widowed the next, mitigated his grief by throwing himself into the colonization of Cuba. On
completion of the conquest, Spanish villages were founded near the
Indian population centers: San Salvador de Bayamo, Trinidad, Sancti
Spíritus, and Santiago de Cuba, the capital. Gold was found close to
nearly all these towns, but in small quantities. To bolster the economy,
Velázquez sent to Hispaniola for seed, cattle, and horses, the foundation for the island's agriculture.

Cuba's principal crop in the early years was *yuca*, the manioc
plant whose roots provided the Indies staple, cassava (*casabí*). Mounds
in which the plant was grown were made of earth, three to four feet
square and just as high. The building of such mounds, with no implement but a cudgellike stick, was grueling work. Yet any Indian strong
enough to stand was sent to the task, often without proper nourish-
ment. Nursing mothers were not excluded; their milk dried in their
breasts from overwork on a starvation diet, and the infant mortality
rate soared. Gradually, the natives were exterminated by such harsh
treatment.

Scarcely a year after the conquest of the island, Cuba's native population had been reduced to the extent that Velázquez was looking elsewhere for a labor supply. In 1515 and 1516 he was sending ships to the
Honduras Bay Islands and the Lucayos on slave raids. One vessel,
loaded with 400 natives after raiding Guanaja, Roatán, and Barbareta,
returned in 1515 to Puerto de Carenas, future site of Havana. The slavers took their ease ashore, leaving only eight or nine men to guard the
Indians confined below decks. The captives—who were awaiting such
an opportunity—forced the hatch cover, killed the guards, and made

sail for home, 600 miles away. The Mayas of the Bay Islands evidently possessed seamanship abilities the Spaniards had not reckoned with. They made it home safely; remains of the ship, wrecked on a reef and burned, were found by Velázquez's next slaving expedition.

The motivation for slave raids increased with the Spanish population. In 1516, Bernal Díaz del Castillo, a Velázquez kinsman and historian-to-be of the Mexican Conquest, came to Cuba from the Isthmus of Darién with a hundred or so other soldiers, hoping for a share of the island's wealth and Indians. Finding that no unassigned natives remained, they proposed a voyage to "discover new lands." As Díaz del Castillo tells it, "One hundred ten of us got together, comrades who had come from Tierra Firme and others of Cuba who had no Indians. We made an agreement with Francisco Hernández de Córdoba [a wealthy planter of Sancti Spíritus] to be our captain." They purchased and outfitted two caravels and a brigantine, the latter on credit from Velázquez, who then attempted to attach strings: the voyage should be to the Honduras Bay Islands, its purpose to take slaves. Self-righteously, the conquistadors from Darién protested that such was in accord with the laws of neither God nor man (all this according to Díaz del Castillo).

Participants in the expedition who testified some years later in a hearing convened by Hernando Cortés gave a different version: it was a partnership venture of Hernández de Córdoba, Lope de Ochoa de Caezedo, and Cristóbal Morantes, who were among Cuba's oldest conquistadors and earliest settlers. Velázquez, most of them agree, got into the act later by fraud, claiming Hernández de Córdoba's discoveries as his own. Five of the six deponents, including the shipmaster Ginés Martín, said that the three vessels set out for the Lucayos but were carried off course by contrary winds, resulting in the accidental discovery of Yucatán—a version that seems highly unlikely from a hydrographical standpoint. The chief pilot, Antón de Alaminos, told it otherwise. After the vessels were fitted out for the Lucayos, he said, Hernández and his partners came to him with a proposal: since Alaminos had been on discovery voyages previously, he should go with this fleet in search of new lands. Thus, discovery is indicated as the purpose before the voyage began.

As Las Casas tells it, Hernández, Ochoa, and Morantes each put in 1,500 to 2,000 *castellanos* to provision the ships; Velázquez appointed Hernández captain because "he was very able at kidnaping and killing

Indians." He was the only one of the partners actually to sail. Each soldier and sailor "would have a share in the Indians they should kidnap or the gold . . . they might obtain."

The ships were two caravels and a brigantine; little else is known of them. They were outfitted at Santiago de Cuba with cassava and live swine. Besides the 110 soldiers said to have organized the undertaking, there was a number of Levantine sailors. Hernández de Córdoba, as expedition captain, may also have commanded one of the caravels. The other sailed under Bernaldino Iñíguez de la Calzada, a Galician who also served as *veedor*, to see that the king got his rightful share of any loot. The skipper of the brigantine was probably Ginés Martín.

There were a cleric named Alonso González and three pilots: Juan Alvarez, Pedro Camacho, and Alaminos, who had sailed with Juan Ponce de León on the 1513 discovery of Florida and was the only pilot available who had ventured into the Gulf of Mexico. Just how and when Alaminos had come to Cuba is not known. Andrés Duero, a rather prominent figure in Cuba, testified in October 1519 that he had known the pilot only since he embarked on this voyage. By that time it was well known that he was experienced and capable, "adept in the art of navigation."

Alaminos seems certain to have diverted the expedition from a slaving voyage to one of discovery, whether after the ships had sailed for the Lucayos or before. According to Las Casas, the pilot confided to Hernández his feelings concerning the unknown sea west of Cuba: with Columbus in 1502, he had observed that the Admiral was much inclined to sail in that direction, believing that he would find a rich and settled country, but for want of better ships, he had turned east toward Veragua instead. Thus Hernández was persuaded to alter the course and purpose of the voyage. There appears no hint that Alaminos, in Ponce's service, had visited Yucatán previously. If Alaminos had ever seen the lands he mentioned, he kept it a close secret from his shipmates and the expedition's chroniclers.

Leaving Santiago around February 8, 1517, the three vessels sailed along the north Cuba shore to Puerto Príncipe (present-day Nuevitas) and thence west to Cabo San Antón. About February 20 they doubled the cape and stood off into the Yucatán Channel. Thenceforth, they sailed only by day, lying to at night lest they run on some shoal. "We sailed . . . toward the west," says Díaz del Castillo, "without knowing of shoals, currents, or the winds that usually blow at that latitude." Out in the channel, noted for rough weather as well as swift current, a storm struck with such fury that the ships were judged at the point of being lost. It lasted two days and nights.

Eight days from Cabo San Antón, the voyagers sighted a shore that Díaz affirms had never been discovered before and was totally unknown. The landfall was Cabo Catoche, on an island eight miles long at the northeastern point of the Yucatán peninsula—itself taken for an island by Alaminos.

From the anchorage off the cape, Hernández de Córdoba's men saw a large town, doubtless marked by a pyramidal Mayan temple, for the voyagers named it Gran Cairo. Three days later, three large canoes hollowed from heavy tree trunks approached under oar and sail, each carrying forty natives. As more than thirty Mayas came aboard the flagship, each group eyed the other with equal amazement. The natives wore cotton shirts and a sort of sash around the waist that covered the private parts. The Spaniards, therefore, credited these Indians with more intelligence than those of Cuba, who went about with their privates showing. The chief responded to a gift of green beads with an invitation, conveyed by signs, for the Spaniards to visit him.

In a dozen dugout canoes and the ship's boats, the captains and all the soldiers were conducted to the shore, which was lined with curious natives exuding friendliness. On the beach, the chief led them toward the town—and into an ambush. Squads of Indians, wearing colorful war plumes and quilted cotton armor reaching to the knees, burst from the brush. As 15 soldiers fell, wounded by arrows, the attackers pressed forward with lances and shields, stone slings, and bows and arrows.

Hernández, wisely, had brought 25 crossbowmen and musketeers; their missiles put the natives to flight, leaving a dead Indian for each wounded Spaniard. Two cross-eyed Indian boys were taken captive with the hope of using them as interpreters. They were given Christian names: Julián and Melchior.

During the fighting, the cleric Alonso González took from a native shrine a number of clay idols, "some like faces of devils, some of women, and others of evil figures that appeared to be Indians practicing sodomy with each other." Pendants, medallions, and idols of alloyed copper and gold were taken to the ship "as evidence of the discovery."

Withdrawing, the Spaniards patched up their wounded and weighed anchor. For 15 days they groped along the Yucatán coast, west, then south, still believing it a large island. Anchoring at night, they navigated with extreme caution by day, heaving the sounding lead and keeping a sharp lookout. Along the way they cast into the sea the bodies of two men who had died of wounds received at Catoche.

On Lazarus Sunday, March 29, the explorers anchored and went ashore at a considerable town, which they named Lázaro for the feast day. A variant of the native name, Campeche, was to prove more lasting. After filling the water casks, they found themselves confronted by fifty Indians demanding by signs to know the reason for the intrusion and whether the Spaniards came from the direction of the sunrise. The Mayas repeated a word that sounded like "Castilan." Not until later did the visitors realize that they were trying to say Castillano—"Castilian"—indicating previous contact with Spaniards.

The Indians, like those of Cabo Catoche, invited the explorers to their town. The experience that followed was eerie: "They took us to some large buildings, which were the temples of their idols, well built of masonry," relates Díaz del Castillo. "On the walls were serpents and large snakes . . . and other evil-looking figures." There was a sort of altar, splattered with fresh blood—from a human sacrifice made to assure victory over the invaders. Ten "priests of the idols," wearing ankle-length white cotton mantles, their hair matted with blood, emerged from the temple to perfume the Spaniards with copal heated over clay braziers. While a ceremonial fire was being laid, hordes of Indians gathered. Two squads of archers, wearing cotton armor and carrying shields, lances, and slings, stood guard. The priests signaled a warning to their visitors: leave before the fire burned out or be slain. As the flame was lighted, the Spaniards retreated amid a terrible din of whistling, clanking shells, and beating drums. Returning safely to their ships, they carried away descriptions to defy the imagination: brick-and-lime houses with towers; well-ordered, paved streets; squares and marketplaces; magnificent temples that resembled fortresses; and elaborate raised courts accessible by long stairways and roofed over with palm thatch. The natives' cotton garments were of many colors. The women were clothed from waist to heels, with various kinds of veils over their faces and breasts.

Hardly anything is said about the evidence of decay that lay at every hand. After attaining a high cultural level, built upon a millennium of development, the Mayan civilization in the ninth century had plunged suddenly into decline. Scholars have been wont to attribute the dramatic collapse to some unknown ecological disaster, causing heavy population loss. More recently, social factors have been suggested: a breakdown of the class structure through which the aristocracy maintained its authority. Whatever the reason, the magnificent temples and cities built before the collapse were already in ruins when the Spaniards first saw them.

The cause of the natives' hostility evidently eluded the explorers. While their demands seemed simple, they required the one thing the Mayas could ill spare: water. Spring is the dry season in Yucatán. Not until the summer months do rains come to replenish the *cenotes*, the natural sinks providing access to underground reservoirs. In most parts of the peninsula, there are no continuous streams.

As the Spaniards sailed away from Campeche, their casks, dry too long, were leaking the precious fluid at an alarming rate, compounding the potential for disaster. For six days they sailed south with good weather before a norther drove them into a cove where parting cables and dragging anchors posed the dire threat of shipwreck. Underway again, they sighted a town about April 10 and anchored a league offshore, lest the ships be stranded at ebb tide. The brigantine and the shallops proceeded into the inlet, and crews went ashore to fill the casks from wells. As the Spaniards started to depart, they found their way blocked by a line of plumed warriors, their faces painted black and white or ruddled with ocher.

The Indians paused to parley—inquiring, as had the people of Lázaro, whether the visitors had come from where the sun rises—and then withdrew. The Spaniards posted sentinels and set up camp for the night. It was a foolish, tragic mistake. In darkness they heard Indians gathering in the adjacent cornfields, but disagreement stalled action. With daybreak, they could see many more warriors marching along the coast to a drumbeat, plumes and war banners flying; there were about two hundred Indians for each Spaniard. After loosing a shower of arrows, darts, and stones, the natives closed quickly to assault the

Spaniards with lances and obsidian-edged *macanas*, wounding more than eighty of the soldiers.

The Spaniards counterattacked with crossbows and muskets. The natives dispersed, then mounted a new assault aimed at killing the white captain. Hernández took ten arrow wounds. All but one of the soldiers were injured; two were carried away alive by the natives; more than fifty lay dead. In desperation, the survivors broke through the Indian line to gain the beach, almost swamping the boats in their haste. Those who could not get on board clung to the gunwales, paddling alongside, the salt water smarting their lesions. The Mayas waded into the water, still hurling lances and shooting arrows, inflicting further injury.

The venturers lacked ablebodied men for hauling the rigging of three ships, for most of the sailors as well as the soldiers were wounded. After clawing off the shore, they removed the brigantine's gear and crew, dividing the able sailors between the other two vessels, and set her afire. Sailing northward, they cast five more bodies into the sea.

The place they left, called Potonchán by the Indians, is marked on present-day maps as Champotón. To the survivors of this fierce battle, which had reduced the Spaniards' numbers by more than half in no more than an hour, it had another name: Costa de Mala Pelea—"Coast of the Bad Fight."

Cruising northward without water, the voyagers still suffered severely from thirst. After three days they put into an inlet with many alligators (accordingly naming it Estero de los Lagartos) near the present-day village of Río Lagartos, eighty miles west of Cabo Catoche. The shore detail found only brackish water, even in wells dug in the sand. A storm that caused the ships to drag anchor toward the beach cut short the search.

Some of the soldiers were blaming Alaminos for bringing them to such a wretched "island," but it was this veteran navigator who devised the means of their deliverance. They should sail for Florida, the pilot advised, "because he found from his chart and the latitude that it was only some seventy leagues, and that route was better and shorter than the one by which we had come." Alaminos put to use the knowledge of the Gulf's hydrography gleaned from the 1513 voyage with Ponce de León. Four days later, about April 18, the ships anchored in the Florida bay that he had seen four years previously. Recalling the

Indian attacks on that occasion, he put the company on guard. The pilot and Díaz del Castillo went ashore with 20 soldiers whose wounds had largely healed, carrying crossbows, muskets, and water casks.

Digging wells, they found good water, filled their vessels, and washed out clothing for the wounded men. Then came the alarm from one of the sentries: Indians were approaching both on foot and in canoes, large men dressed in deerskins, carrying long bows and lances. "They came straight toward us shooting arrows," making to seize the Spaniards' boat. The soldiers, wading in waist-deep water, fought back with swords and crossbows. When the fight was over, they had half a dozen wounded, including Alaminos. A sentry, the only soldier who had escaped the Potonchán disaster without injury, was taken alive by the Indians, thirty-two of whom lay dead along the shore and in the shallows.

Alaminos had a painful arrow wound in the throat. He and the others nevertheless made it safely back to the ships with the filled water casks. Before they could get aboard, a thirst-crazed soldier jumped into the boat, grabbed a water bottle, and drank so much that he "swelled up and died within two days."

The account of this landing at Ponce's bay offers a clue to where the 1513 anchorage might or might not have been. Obviously well into the day, Hernández's ships got underway for Cuba. They "passed that day and night near some small islands called the Mártires." Less than a day's sail could not have brought them to the keys from as far up the coast as Charlotte Harbor or Estero Bay.

This time, with so many suffering men on board, Alaminos included, the pilot sought a shortcut. Instead of going around the Marquesas Keys, as Ponce had done, he found the shallow passage between the Marquesas and Key West. The deepest water was four fathoms, the same as it is today. Not surprisingly, the flagship scraped bottom and began making water. The soldiers, working the pumps furiously to little avail, called on the Levantine sailors for help. The Levantines, resentful at having no proceeds from the voyage, balked. Defiance of the conquistadors was ill-advised; Díaz records succinctly, "We made them help us, and, sick and wounded as we were, we managed the sails and worked at the pumps until our Lord carried us to the Puerto de Carenas."

From there, Díaz continues, Hernández de Córdoba went to his home at Sancti Spíritus, where he died of his wounds ten days after arriving; the ship was pumped out by a Portuguese diver, then taken to Santiago, where the relics and gold specimens from Yucatán created a stir that spread quickly among the islands and even to Castile. It was said that no better lands had ever been discovered. The two Mayan captives, Julián and Melchior, added to the excitement. When shown gold dust, they declared that there was much of the precious metal in their country—a report which, after much suffering, was to be proved false. The captives also were shown the plantings of *yuca*. Repeating the word, they added their own name for it: *yuca tlati*. Thus, it is said, the land that Hernández had named Santa María de los Remedios came to be known as Yucatán.

The captain spent his dying energies complaining of Velázquez's presumption in getting up a new voyage to the land he himself had discovered, with Juan de Grijalva at its head. Hernández was determined to go and present his case to the king when he was well enough—but his wounds proved fatal.

Velázquez, says Díaz del Castillo, wrote to Crown officials in Spain claiming the discovery as his own. The act occasioned some bitterness among the soldiers who had spent what little they had to make the voyage, and had returned wounded and in debt, leaving fifty-seven of their number dead among the Mayas. Such were the rewards for making a voyage of discovery.

"How difficult it is to go out and discover new lands," wrote Díaz, recalling the expedition's trials. "No one can imagine what we endured who has not experienced such excessive hardships."

SOURCES AND NOTES

Treatment of the Indians

Bartolomé de las Casas relates the abuse of the Cuban Indians following the conquest and the part it played in his own conversion, which launched him as the Indians' champion (see his *History*, 208, and *Selection of His Writings*, 87).

Both Antonio de Herrera (*Historia*, 2:342–44) and Peter Martyr (*Décadas*, 321–22) tell of the slaving voyages to the Lucayos and the Bay Islands, and of the Indians' seizure of a Spanish ship.

Origin of the 1517 Voyage

Bernal Díaz del Castillo, historian of the Mexican Conquest, was to some extent the historian of discovery in the Gulf, as well. He claims participation in three crucial voyages, of which the 1517 venture was the first. His version of the voyage's inception appears in his *Historia verdadera de la conquista de Nueva España*, 1:43 (1955 edition). In 1522, depositions were taken from a number of Cortés's adherents when Cristóbal de Tapia came to New Spain to delineate the various discoverers' claims. These appear in "Probanza sobre las causas que se dieron a la suplicación de las provisiones del veedor Cristóbal de Tapia," 183–235 (Alaminos's statement concerning the origin of the voyage is on p. 231).

Accounts of the Voyage

The various narratives of the Hernández de Córdoba voyage have been translated and brought together by Henry R. Wagner in *The Discovery of Yucatán by Francisco Hernández de Córdoba*, including those of Peter Martyr, Fernández de Oviedo, Alonso de Santa Cruz, López de Gómara, Las Casas, Francisco Cervantes de Salazar, and Díaz del Castillo. Díaz's is by far the most substantial, although the others add shading that is important to a reconstruction of the episode.

Andrés Duero's comment on Alaminos is from a document published in *CDI* 12:161.

Díaz del Castillo (*Historia verdadera*, 1:45–46) is the only one of the chroniclers to mention the Mayas' use of sail.

The Las Casas version of the fight at Cabo Catoche (in Wagner, *Discovery of Yucatán*, 46) contrasts sharply with that of Díaz del Castillo. The Indians were entirely friendly, says the cleric; on this occasion, as others, the Spaniards initiated the battle.

The Maya

Concerning the prevalence of crossed eyes among the Maya, see Alfred M. Tozzer, ed., *Landa's Relación de las Cosas de Yucatán*, 120, n. 547. Tozzer (p. 125) knew of no archeological finds at Mayan sites of figures of "Indians practicing sodomy on each other."

The inquiry concerning whether the Spaniards had come from the direction of the sunrise was a manifestation of a Mayan legend corresponding to that of the Mexican deity Quetzalcóatl, who the Aztecs believed would one day return from the east to rule over his people. Quetzalcóatl's counterpart in Mayan lore was Kukulcán.

At its zenith, the Mayan culture extended from Mexico to Honduras. It was marked by a turbulence that seems to contradict the cultural elegance manifest in the Mayas' amazing architectural and scientific achievement. Diego de Landa's *Relación* and the compilation of data offered by Tozzer with his translation of it are basic to serious study of the subject. As a brief introduction, Howard La Fay's "The Maya, Children of Time" will serve. See also Norman Hammond, "Unearthing the Oldest Known Maya."

End of the Voyage

Las Casas gives the voyage an ending different from the one described by Díaz del Castillo. The two caravels, he says, were in such poor condition on returning to Puerto de Carenas that they were left to sink; Hernández de Córdoba went by native canoe to Santiago, where he wrote to Las Casas in the royal court at Zaragoza.

CHAPTER 4

"A Luckless Man":
Juan de Grijalva, 1518

R<small>ETURN</small> of the Yucatán discoverers to Santiago de Cuba bore a resemblance to Columbus's visit to Seville following his first voyage. The two cross-eyed Indian boys, the copper-and-gold talismans of an alien religion, and accounts of the Mayas' elegant culture—unlike any other yet seen in the Indies—excited the fancy of the insular Spaniards. Diego Velázquez was moved to make instant plans for a second voyage.

By implication, at least, the governor claimed the recent discovery as his own. From the friars of San Jerónimo in Hispaniola—sent by the Crown a short while previously to direct Indies affairs—he obtained license for a new Yucatán expedition "to trade with the natives for gold, pearls, and precious stones." He also wanted authority to conquer and to that end sent his agent Gonzalo de Guzmán to Spain bearing a *relación* for the king.

Preparations for the new voyage advanced rapidly, as Velázquez named his twenty-eight-year-old nephew to head the venture. Juan de Grijalva, like Velázquez and Narváez, was a native of Cuéllar, residing at Trinidad, near Hernández de Córdoba's estate at Sancti Spíritus. While he is said to have played a prominent part in the Cuban conquest, no specifics are known. Las Casas, who served with him in that affair, speaks of his later misfortunes as just payment for "the damage he had caused the Indians." Yet he knew him as "a moderate and pious man."

Velázquez placed at the new captain-general's disposal a brigantine and four caravels—two of which, Díaz del Castillo says, had been on the previous voyage. Three prominent young *encomenderos* were assigned as their captains: Pedro de Alvarado commanded *Trinidad*; Alonso de Avila, *Santa María de los Remedios* (the same name that

Hernández had given to Yucatán); Francisco de Montejo, one of two ships called *San Sebastián*. All these captains are remembered better for their later exploits, but the Grijalva voyage was to shape their destiny. The second *San Sebastián* was Grijalva's flagship, with Graviel Bosque as master and pilot.

Bosque may have been an irritant for Antón de Alaminos, who again was designated chief pilot, "as there was no other so skilled as he." So crucial were Alaminos's services that departure was delayed to await the healing of the wounds he had received at Champotón and the Bay of Juan Ponce. Yet he was not assigned to the flagship. He probably was billeted on Avila's *Santa María*, which was smaller than the other caravels and therefore more useful for probing shallow bays, an essential part of the chief pilot's task. The other pilots, also veterans of Hernández's voyage, were Juan Alvarez and Pedro Camacho.

Antonio de Villafañe, destined to be hanged by Cortés, went along as treasurer; Diego de Godoy, notary; Francisco de Peñalosa, *veedor*, or Crown overseer; and Bernardino Vázquez de Tapia, chief ensign. All told, the company consisted of some two hundred Spaniards, including forty hidalgos seeking adventure and eight of the thirty known survivors of the previous voyage, plus some Cuban natives. Among the more noteworthy voyagers was Diego de Ordás who, like Alvarado, Avila, and Montejo, was to be one of Cortés's captains. And there was Julián, one of the two young Mayas Hernández had brought back; having learned a little Spanish, he was to serve as interpreter.

Velázquez enjoined Grijalva against settling land discovered by either Hernández or himself, yet he evidently intended such instructions as a mere formality, to be appropriately disregarded. On January 25, 1518, the four caravels sailed from Santiago and proceeded at a leisurely pace up Cuba's north shore, gathering men and supplies of cassava and live pigs at Boyúcar, Matanzas, and Puerto de Carenas. The brigantine had gone on ahead. By the time the other ships reached Cabo San Antón on May 1, she had used up her provisions and gone home. The four caravels set course immediately for Santa María de los Remedios, or Yucatán.

The weather was good, the wind on the quarter. The ships made landfall in forty-eight hours, not at Cabo Catoche but at Cozumel, seventy miles down the eastern shore. Since it was the feast day of the Finding of the Cross, the voyagers named the island Santa Cruz. In the days following, formal possession was taken in the name of "Doña Juana and Don Carlos, her son"; the latter, who had ascended to the Spanish throne as Charles I on Ferdinand's death two years previously, was soon to become Holy Roman Emperor Charles V. The chaplain, Juan Díaz, celebrated mass among the pagan idols of the Mayan temple. Friendly Indians brought gifts of honey and chickens, but in response to proposals to trade for gold, they produced only some dishes and ornaments of a *guanín* that was hardly more than gilded copper.

On May 7 the explorers crossed to "the island of Yucatán." Grijalva had laid down stringent rules beforehand to govern relations with the natives: only he should talk trade terms, and the men were not even to speak to the Indian women. Now he forbade the men to enter the three sizable mainland towns. The conquistadors, stirred up by the chaplain's wagging tongue, began to grumble.

Through Julián, Grijalva learned that one of Hernández de Córdoba's two men who had been taken captive the previous year was still alive. The ships searched south along the coast, hoping to rescue the man and put him to work as interpreter. At sunset on May 8 they sighted from far off the magnificent ruins of the ancient Mayan city of Tulum, high on a rock bluff overlooking the Caribbean. Chaplain Díaz, being from Seville, describes it in terms familiar to him: "so large that the city of Seville could not look larger or better." Indians were running along the shore with banners—signaling the ships to approach, Díaz thought, "but the captain was not willing."

On May 11, Alonso de Avila spied a lone figure waving from shore. Believing he had found the Spanish captive, he went in with *Santa María*, but it proved to be a Christian Jamaican woman, one of a fishing party whose canoe had been carried westward by the current. Her companions slain, she had managed to escape her Mayan captors.

During this leg of the voyage, Alaminos got his tail over the gate, as it were; he complained to Grijalva in writing that he was not being permitted to do his job and wished to be relieved of the chief pilot's duties. Whether his dissatisfaction stemmed from the fact that Bosque was piloting the flagship or that Avila had approached the shore without his say-so is not clear. Grijalva patiently reassured him, but in Fernández de Oviedo's eyes, it was a sorry spectacle; a person of such petulance, he avers, "might easily fall in with a captain who would hang him from a yardarm."

Sailing both day and night, the voyagers came on May 13 to a shallow bay, which they named Bahía de la Ascensión for the feast day. Taking the extensive body of water to mark the end of the "island," the voyagers hoped to sail through it into the Gulf of Mexico. Towed by the launches, the ships negotiated the entrance, but the lead line soon warned of dangerously shallow water. Without a shallow-draft vessel such as the brigantine that had defected, they must reverse course and sail around Yucatán on the north to reach the Gulf.

Approaching Cabo Catoche, the explorers saw many women coming to pray and offer sacrifices at a temple on the point of an island. The place, Juan Díaz concluded, was "inhabited by women who lived without men . . . a race of amazons." Thus it became Isla Mujeres.

Doubling the cape, the Spaniards sailed along the same coast Hernández de Córdoba had followed. As on the previous voyage, they were in desperate need of water on arriving at Campeche. Hostile demonstrations by natives who lined the shore, sounding drums and shell trumpets, caused Grijalva to hestitate. During the morning watch of May 26, he and his captains disembarked in the boats, each craft carrying a squad of soldiers and a falconet. They landed two hours before dawn, and all might have gone well had they taken only a little water and departed. But the rains had not yet started; the well near the beach was a poor one; and the detail of ship's boys and sailors, stopping their work repeatedly to allow the well to replenish itself, took two days to fill the casks.

During the first day the Mayas were alternately friendly and threatening. They paraded their armed might with menacing gestures, then sent emissaries with fruits and tortillas for the soldiers standing guard by the well, and accepted colored beads and baubles in return. When a soldier began playing a tambourine, some of the Indians danced to the rhythm.

Finding the uninvited guests still present next morning, the natives' mood changed. Armed and ready for battle, they placed a *guaymaro*, or incense burner, on a boulder near the Spanish camp. From Julián, the soldiers knew that it was both an offering to the Mayan idols for victory and a warning; when the *guaymaro* burned out, the Indians would attack.

Grijalva, attending to form, had Julián order the Mayas not to make war. He took testimony from his men that he was defending himself because he was being attacked without cause. Then he sent Julián away to the ships, lest he escape; the Indian boy wept at his lost opportunity. When the offering burned out, the natives sprang upon the invaders with yells, whistles, and deadly arrows. The falconets signaled the counterattack, and the Indians made for the woods, pursued by the Spaniards. Grijalva, leading his men, took an arrow in the mouth, shattering teeth. One soldier was killed and many others wounded, some to die later. Fighting a rearguard action, Grijalva removed the wounded men to the ships, leaving the water detail with an escort to finish filling the casks. Next day the ships weighed anchor and sailed down the coast.

Less than a day's sail south, they came to Champotón, or Potonchán, where the sight of Spanish sails aroused the Indians to instant fury. Warrior-laden canoes scurried back to shore under artillery fire. Juan Díaz, Grijalva's gadfly, complains again at the captain's refusal to land.

Monday, May 31, brought the voyagers to a large bay, the Laguna de Términos, a much-desired haven where the wounded could convalesce and a leaky ship be careened. Going ashore at this "Puerto Deseado," they built a brush arbor and dug wells for fresh water. While the caulkers worked on the ship, others gathered wood for the fireboxes and caught fish from the bay. Four Indian fishermen crossing the bay in a canoe were seized and divided among the four ships to be schooled as interpreters. Baptized by the chaplain, their leader was christened Pedro Barba for the hidalgo who stood as his godfather.

Alaminos, meanwhile, brought his navigational computations up to date. Having coasted Yucatán on three sides and believing he had found a water passage on the fourth, he remained convinced that it was an island. Viewing the upper end of the Laguna de Términos, at a pass called Puerto Escondido (long since closed), he saw an expanse of water that seemed endless. Surely, he reasoned, it must open into the Bahía de Ascensión at its far end. He reckoned the distance between the two mouths at twenty leagues. Puerto Deseado, he declared, marked the end of the land discovered by Hernández de Córdoba; beyond this "island" lay a new land, never before discovered or even seen by Christians, which Grijalva might claim. It was thus that the terminus of Hernández's claim became the Laguna de Términos.

On June 5 the caravels coasted westward along the "new land," which the recent captives said was called Colúa. Two days later they passed a large river, the San Pedro y San Pablo, one of the mouths of the mighty Usumacinta. Indians lined the coast, marveling at the strange ships, the likes of which they had never before seen. Five leagues farther on, the explorers anchored near the mouth of an even larger river, gushing forth with such force that they were hesitant to enter it. This was the Río de Tabasco—soon to be renamed the Grijalva—through which the Usumacinta's main stem discharges. The Indian Pedro Barba described the interior, through Julián: there were great mountains, a river where much gold was found, and—distant some fifty or sixty days' travel—the other ocean.

Next day the ships went half a league up the river against swift current. Indians armed with bows, shields, and lances lined both banks while a hundred canoes swarmed the water, boldly approaching the ship. The venturers, as much agog as the natives, observed that their leader carried a brightly plumed shield centered by a gold medallion. Through Julián and Pedro Barba, the captain-general managed to communicate to the chief his desire to trade in friendship.

In exchange for items of little worth to the Spaniards—glass beads, mirrors, scissors, knives, a pair of sandals—they obtained plumed or gilded masks, shields, knee guards, and helmets worked with gold, as well as gold earrings, pendants, and neck pieces. The captain and the chief each dressed the other in his own finery, so that the *cacique* came out looking like a Spanish lord and Grijalva like a Tabascoan chief.

As the ships sailed on west, the men began to murmur anew against Grijalva's strict adherence to his orders prohibiting settlement. The whole coast was covered with Indians waving their turtle-shell shields and mocking the strange ships. The vessels passed the Río Tonalá, or Pedregal—called San Antonio because it was St. Anthony's Day—then the Coatzacoalcos, followed by a range of volcanic mountains called San Martín. As Orizaba's snow-capped peak rose in the distance, Pedro de Alvarado put his ship *Trinidad* in jeopardy by entering the Río de Papaloapán. Grijalva watched and fumed. Alvarado succeeded in attaching his name to the river, but neither he nor the captain-general realized at the moment the great damage to Grijalva's fortunes that would result from his rash act, or the considerable influence it would have on Alvarado's own.

Grijalva had twice sent men ashore to capture groups of Indians, who in each case wept because they thought they were to be put to death. Hearing the natives' declaration that there was gold in the country, he kept two hostages and let the others go on their promise to bring him all of the precious metal they could. They never returned. The hostages' fate is not of record.

After the Río de Alvarado came the Río de Banderas—today's Jamapa—so named because a number of Indians waving banners from their lance shafts stood along the shore. Mistaking them for his released captives, Grijalva sent a boat, but the heavy surf prevented a landing. That evening the ships came to anchor between a small island and the mainland.

On the island next morning, Grijalva and some soldiers followed a tree-lined path to a lofty temple and ascended a stone staircase. At the top was a room with marble statuary and a bloody stone font flanked by a plumed idol. There were piles of severed human heads and the putrifying bodies of mere boys, their chests slashed open. With gestures, an Indian demonstrated how the heads were cut off, then the hearts removed with flint knives, burned with pine faggots, and offered to the idol. Grijalva's only recorded reaction was to bestow the name Isla de los Sacrificios—"Island of Sacrifices."

Later that day the Indians with the white banners appeared again on the mainland shore. They were messengers bearing gifts from the Aztec ruler Moctezuma, who somehow had heard of the Spaniards' coming. In the days following, the voyagers carried on extensive trade with the natives, exchanging goods of little value for gold ornaments and figurines. From the *cacique*, Grijalva received a special gift: nothing was wanted in return, the Indian told him; the nubile maiden, clad only in a thin cotton dress, was gratis.

But take heed, all those who might envy such trade, warns Fernández de Oviedo; the Spaniards' gain was not as great as it seemed. Consider where one must go to get it and "the hardships and dangers from which half those who undertake such business do not escape with their lives." It was not the stuff of which dreams were made. A part of the cost in this instance is spelled out by Díaz del Castillo: since the fight at Campeche, the Spaniards had buried at sea thirteen of their comrades.

Grijalva, with Alaminos's reassurance that the adjacent coast was mainland, went ashore at the site of the present city of Veracruz and took formal possession. On the feast day of St. John the Baptist, June 24, he named the province, combining the saint's name with a corrupt form of the native name for Mexico, Colúa; hence San Juan de Ulúa, the island in front of Veracruz harbor, which the natives called Chalchicueca.

That same day Pedro de Alvarado sailed for Cuba with his ship *Trinidad*, which was leaking badly since his ill-conceived sally up the Papaloapán. Seeing that the ship must be either careened or sent home, Grijalva had decided to dispatch her with the gold he had gathered and a report to Velázquez. He also sent the Indian girl given him by the *cacique* and the Jamaican woman found in Yucatán.

The captain-general, despite Alaminos's growing uneasiness, sailed north with the three remaining caravels. They could proceed on the current, the pilot warned, but getting back might be another matter. The crew's growing discontent compounded Grijalva's worries; the men were much put out by his refusal to settle. "A luckless man," Fernández de Oviedo calls him. Grijalva closed ears and mind to those who would divert him and thus, turning away from the opportunity of a millennium, embraced an alternate fate far less rewarding.

The ships ran north along the Veracruz coast, seeking proof that the land did not terminate at the end of the mountain range. Battling rough seas, they doubled Punta Delgada and found the mountains falling off in latitude 20°. From a seaside village at the present Nautla—named Almería for the Andalusian town on the Mediterranean—Indians paddled out to the lead ship, *Santa María*, in four canoes, urging the explorers to stop and visit. Sailing well ahead of the other ships, Alonso de Avila could not do so.

Another degree of latitude brought the three caravels to a large town of 5,000 stone houses, overlooking a river mouth. To Juan Díaz, the town seemed "no smaller than Seville." Twelve canoes came out boldly to attack the ships and prevent their anchoring. Showered with arrows, the Spaniards returned missiles from harquebuses, artillery, and crossbows, sinking one canoe and killing four Indians. The other natives scurried back to shore. The conquistador spirit favored laying waste to the town with fire and sword, but the captain-general forbade it. The river was named Río de Canoas, shortly corrupted to Río de Cazones, the name it still carries.

The weather worsened. Alaminos repeated his warning, expressing anxiety over winter's approach when it was not yet July. His greatest concern was the current, still running north and promising difficulty on the return. On June 28 the voyagers turned back at Cabo Rojo, the V-shaped sliver of land enclosing the Laguna de Tamiahua. Not until later did they perceive their error.

Retracing the course, they came back to the Río Coatzacoalcos, but the current and contrary winds forbade entering. The flagship, *San Sebastián*, was limping along with a broken mast, and water was running low. Putting into the Río Tonalá, recently named San Antonio, the voyagers waited out three days of bad weather, trading with the Indians for copper hatchets thought to contain a good measure of gold. On the way out of the river, *San Sebastián* missed the channel, bumped on shoals, and began making water. She had to be brought back into the river mouth under tow and careened.

At this awkward time, Indians appeared on the riverbank, giving signals. In the confusion of getting the ship into her berth and going to see what the natives wanted, the Mayan interpreter Julián and his friend Pedro Barba escaped—deceitful interpreters and faithless Christians, Fernández de Oviedo judges.

Repairs to the flagship took eleven days. During that time the mariners traded for pineapples, corn, turkeys, and objects of gold, with Indians who had their ears torn and blood running down their cheeks, the results of a religious rite to appease their deity and win protection against the strangers. In shallow graves the Spaniards found the headless bodies of three children, sacrificed out of fear of the intruders. Various gold objects, placed in the burials to aid the victims in the hereafter, aided the Spaniards instead.

On July 27 the three ships put out from the Tonalá to sail homeward. Seeking a direct route across the open Gulf, the voyagers found both wind and current against them. For almost a month they beat into the northeasterlies, their progress impeded by the Caribbean current coursing westward on its circuit of the Gulf before reversing itself to exit through the Straits of Florida. It was a hard lesson that Alaminos would not forget. Weighing the experience later, he realized that he had erred in not sailing on north from Cabo Rojo, keeping the advantage of wind and current. On his next voyage he would apply corrections.

After twenty-eight days, unable to make progress across the Gulf and again short of water, the ships fell back on Tabasco. The landfall, down the coast from Puerto Deseado, was at a more prominent pass into the Laguna de Términos, the site of the present ferry-crossing between Puerto Real and the lighthouse station of Isla de Aguada. In this wild and beautiful setting, plentiful in game and fresh water, they saw Indians crossing from Yucatán to "the other country" every day in canoes under sail. On shore, the Spaniards found a native shrine consisting of more than a dozen clay idols and braziers for perfuming them. One of the figures represented two persons engaged in sodomy and another masturbating. Such matters were better forgotten, Fernández de Oviedo opines, but he mentions them anyway, "to declare the crime for which God castigates these Indians, and for which they have been forgotten by His mercy for so many centuries."

Toward the end of August the mariners weighed anchor and sailed up the Yucatán coast. On September 1 they anchored off Potonchán. While the two larger ships held off in deeper water, *Santa María* approached to within half a league of the shore, to serve as the launching pad for an invasion. Even considering the magnitude of Hernández de Córdoba's defeat here the previous year, the rationale for this move defies understanding; a vengeance strike seems totally out of character for the cautious Grijalva.

Before nightfall the captain-general moved some of his men from the larger ships to the smaller one, anticipating a predawn landing on the tiny island before the town. The islet appeared unoccupied, but during the night Indians standing guard there made themselves known with martial drums. Before daybreak, Grijalva began landing artillery and infantry. When a fleet of canoes came out from the mainland, a cannon shot sank one of the craft and killed an Indian or two. The natives withdrew, but the fortified town, plainly visible from the island, came alive with martial activity. Shrieking horns and trumpets signaled the Mayas' readiness for battle.

Grijalva held council and found his men divided. When he had his ordinances read, some of the soldiers protested that they were not obliged to obey them; if they went ashore, they would avenge the Christians who had died there by burning the town and punishing the natives in a manner they would not forget. Seeing that he would lose control over his troops once they landed, the captain-general decided to withdraw.

The caravels weighed anchor and two days later stood before Campeche, scene of the battle that had cost Grijalva fourteen men and his front teeth on May 27. Armed with four artillery pieces, harquebuses, and crossbows, crewmen landed to take on water. Unarmed Indians, ostensibly pointing the way to the well, led them instead into an ambush of three hundred warriors. Artillery shots put the natives to flight, and Grijalva himself landed with reinforcements. The Spaniards then spent two nights unmolested, filling their water casks and taking corn from the fields.

From Campeche the ships tacked northward, away from shore. Four days later their traverse brought them at sunset to a low-lying "new land." Veering off for safety during the night, they returned next morning and found only shoals—Cayo Arenas, lying northwest of Mérida in latitude 22°13'. They fell back on Yucatán, sighting the coast near "el Palmar"—Punta de Palmas. After coasting the top of the peninsula for six days, they set course across the Yucatán Channel for Cuba.

Reaching Puerto de Carenas on September 30, Grijalva sought news of Alvarado and *Trinidad*. Had they made it home with the gold he had sent? He learned not only of Alvarado's safe return but a great many other happenings, not all of them to his benefit.

Velázquez, growing anxious as months passed without word, had dispatched a caravel and sixty men with Cristóbal de Olid to look for Grijalva. Sailing first to Cozumel, they coasted Yucatán to "land's end"—Laguna de Términos—without success. After losing anchors and cables in a squall, Olid returned to Cuba. Grijalva, proceeding along Cuba's north shore toward Santiago, heard this report from Olid himself at Matanzas on October 8, before Velázquez did.

Olid, having just returned, had not yet reported; Alvarado's arrival, with word that Olid had not overtaken Grijalva, compounded the governor's anxiety. News of Alvarado's difficulties in crossing the Gulf in the leaky caravel also intensified Velázquez's concern. Furthermore, while it appeared that Grijalva had found a rich native paradise, he had evidently been blinded by his sponsor's tongue-in-cheek orders and refused to settle. Velázquez was beside himself with frustration.

The source of his agitation, usually ascribed to simple greed, may well have been somewhat more complex. While the evidence so far is meager, it appears likely that Velázquez was more than a little in debt to the Genoese merchants who managed to lay hold of much of the

Indies' wealth during this period. It is known that he shared ownership of certain plots of land at Santiago with Juan Francisco de Grimaldo and Gaspar Centurión, members of that merchant-banker group. It may be that Velázquez felt himself dependent on a grand financial coup to retain his solvency.

In any event, without waiting for his nephew's return, he decided to send out a new trading expedition to exploit the wealth Grijalva had found. To head it he chose Hernando Cortés. The governor, issuing orders to his new agent on October 13, couched them in terms that seemed to justify his action. First, it was necessary to search for Grijalva and Olid, who were long overdue. Aside from that, he had heard from the Mayan boy Melchior, brought to Cuba by Hernández de Córdoba, that there were six Spanish castaways living in Yucatán. Believing them part of Diego de Nicuesa's crew, unheard from since Núñez de Balboa had expelled Nicuesa from Darién in a leaky brigantine half a dozen years previously, he hoped to effect rescue. Additionally, since Alvarado had demonstrated the wealth of the land Grijalva had discovered, it was incumbent upon him to "explore all the islands and lands to learn their secrets."

Grijalva's unexpected return posed a severe embarrassment for Velázquez. Cortés, having anticipated his orders, already had preparations well underway. How could the governor square himself with both Cortés and Grijalva? In desperation, he tried to withdraw his authority and support from Cortés, only to find that he had created a monster that could not be checked.

SOURCES AND NOTES

Primary accounts of the Grijalva voyage have been translated and published in a single volume by Henry R. Wagner (*The Discovery of New Spain in 1518 by Juan de Grijalva*). These include the writings of such early historians as Las Casas, Fernández de Oviedo, and Francisco Cervantes de Salazar, as well as those of participants like Juan Díaz and Díaz del Castillo, and several lesser accounts.

For the Hernández de Córdoba voyage, Díaz del Castillo's narrative surpasses all others in accuracy and detail. Not so with the Grijalva venture; he is so often at variance with others that Wagner expresses doubt that he even made the voyage. It may be, however, that his memory of it suffered from its being compressed between the earlier one and that of Cortés, the events of which were so much more spectacular.

The single most valuable source for the 1518 voyage is Fernández de Oviedo (*Historia*, 3:250–309 [bk. 17, chs. 8–18]). Wagner omits a key portion, (ch. 12, 275–77), in which Alaminos's navigational computations are discussed.

Juan Díaz's account, translated by Wagner from an Italian version (in RAH, A/103), is useful also, especially concerning the discontent with Grijalva. Wagner's translation of the Italian has been checked against "Diario del viaje que hizo la Armada del Rey Cathólico del cargo y mando del Capitán D. Juan de Grijalva acia la Isla de Yucatán en el año de 1515" (BRP, 2861).

A number of other documents and studies have been drawn upon, including the report of the *regimiento* of Villa Rica de la Vera Cruz, which has been treated as Cortés's first letter to the emperor in his *Cartas de relación*. Actually, Cortés's first letter has been lost. The *regimiento* recounts the Hernández and Grijalva voyages.

Antonio Velázquez de Bazán ("Probanza," Mexico, Jan. 14, 1590, AGI, Patronato 183-1-14), a grandson of Diego Velázquez's sister Isabel, gives Grijalva's relationship to the governor.

Concerning Graviel Bosque, the source is Juan Bosque Bacernada ("Probanza hecha en la ciudad de Antequera," March 9, 1558, AGI, Patronato 61-2-2). Bosque Bacernada says that his father, Graviel Bosque, sailed with Grijalva as "pilot and master of the said armada and the *nao capitana*." In 1520 he piloted Pánfilo de Narváez to New Spain for his confrontation with Cortés, as will be seen.

Las Casas's assessment of Grijalva is from his *History of the Indies*, bk. 3, ch. 114, p. 224.

Díaz del Castillo (*Historia verdadera* 1:70–75) and Francisco de Montejo ("Armas para Francisco de Montejo," Granada, Dec. 8, 1526, AGI, Indiferente General 421, libro 12) describe the mainland landing near the Isla de Sacrificios to meet Moctezuma's messengers, for both apparently took part. Montejo, unfortunately, eclipses the rest of the Grijalva voyage and proceeds to his service with Cortés.

On the location of Puerto Deseado, see José N. Rovirosa, *Ensayo histórico sobre el Río Grijalva*, 36.

Concerning the discovery of Cayo Arenas, see Juan Orozco y Berra, *Apuntes sobre Cayo Arenas*, 6–10.

The Mayas' Use of Sail

Two sightings of Mayan craft using sail as well as oars are mentioned in the accounts of the Hernández and Grijalva voyages. On the first, Díaz del Castillo tells of native vessels under sail near Cabo Catoche (*Historia verdadera*, 1:45–46). On the Grijalva voyage, Fernández de Oviedo (3:301) relates that Indian boats with sails were seen crossing the Laguna de Términos.

Ascensión Bay

The bay on the eastern Yucatán coast to which Grijalva gave this name has generally been identified with the one so known today, but there is evidence to the contrary. The distance from the vicinity of Cozumel is much too short, as Juan Díaz tells us that the ships were sailing past Tulum at sunset on May 8, and continued day and night until the thirteenth. The latitude of the bay attributed to Alaminos, 17°, is 2°40' too far south; it is much closer to Bahía de Chetumal. Fernández de Oviedo (5:65) says Ascensión was the nearest bay to the Gulf of Higueras. That would be Chetumal, in 17°50'. Alaminos reckoned Puerto Deseado, at the upper end of the Laguna de Términos, to be in 18°30'; actually, it is about 18°55'. His erroneous conclusion concerning a water passage from the Caribbean to the Gulf was the basis for a persistent cartographical error. The source of Fernández de Oviedo's dislike of the pilot is not known, but Alaminos's latitude observations, as well as his logic, were more accurate than the *cronista* gives him credit for.

Río de Canoas

The identification of Río de Canoas with Río de Cazones is my own, based on the various descriptions of the location in relation to other landmarks, plus the fact that Canoas seems to have disappeared from maps and written accounts of the coast about the time Cazones began to be used. The transition occurred by the middle of the sixteenth century. Either phonetic similarity or misreading may have been responsible. The question is addressed in a confused manner in "¿A que río dió Juan de Grijalva el nombre de Canoas?" 467–71. The anonymous author confuses the native province of Pánuco, reached by the explorers, with the Río Pánuco. He therefore concludes erroneously that the Canoas was the present-day Río Tamesí.

Prelude to Conquest: Cortés and Velázquez, 1518–19

CORTÉS. At the height of his glory, even the mention of his name created a stir of excitement. His heart harbored the darkest of human passions and the noblest of aspirations. His deeds reflected the best and the worst of which mankind is capable. In the end he was greatly honored by the king whose fortunes he had saved, then cast aside to die in obscurity.

In his native Medellín, Extremadura, Cortés had been a sickly child; a mischievous youth; then a restless, haughty, and lustful young man, a dropout from the study of law at Salamanca. His lust for women often overshadowed his other passions—for gold, glory, and power—and cost him his earliest opportunities to attain them. In 1504, after several false starts, he sailed to the Indies, blatantly announcing upon arrival that he had come for gold. He spent the next several years in relatively fruitless, frustrating pursuits, too time-consuming to satisfy his desire for instant gold and glory, adding little to the experience needed for grander schemes. He watched explorers come and go, and thirsted for their kind of adventure; yet when the opportunity came to sail for Darién with Diego de Nicuesa, he was thwarted by an abscess in his leg—the legacy, it is said, of venereal disease.

Cortés followed Diego Velázquez to Cuba but sat out the conquest as his secretary. At Santiago he had an affair with the poor but lovely Catalina Suárez, sister of Velázquez's mistress. The Suárez sisters had come to the Indies as ladies-in-waiting to Doña María de Cuéllar, Velázquez's bride of only a week before her death. Cortés's refusal to marry Catalina either caused or complicated his difficulties with Don Diego, who at one point imprisoned the brash young man and threatened to hang him. But Cortés at last took the maid to wife and thereby put matters aright; Velázquez witnessed the marriage ceremony and stood as godfather to Cortés's illegitimate daughter by a native woman.

That was in 1515. During the next three years, Cortés prospered in a trading partnership with Andrés Duero. Watching for still greater opportunity, he saw none in either Hernández de Córdoba's voyage or Grijalva's. But when Pedro de Alvarado brought home samples of gold, and Velázquez proposed sending an expedition to look for Grijalva and Olid, it was another matter. Cortés had but to wait for the governor to exhaust other possibilities in his quest for a leader, for he met the requirements: he had considerable wealth and a willingness to risk all for the sake of opportunity.

The events that followed have been greatly confused, although much is made clear by Velázquez's instructions to Cortés. Having heard nothing from either Grijalva or Olid, the governor was genuinely concerned that they had met with accident. His anxiety heightened when Alvarado returned not only with samples of Aztec gold but also bearing the distressing news that Olid had not overtaken Grijalva. Velázquez was concerned also for the lives of the six Christian Spaniards who the captive boy Melchior told him had shipwrecked on Yucatán several years previously and were being held as slaves by the Mayas. These castaways, Velázquez was convinced, might well be from Diego de Nicuesa's crew, who had sailed from Santa María la Antigua on the isthmus in 1511 and had not been heard from since. Obviously, a considerable force would be necessary to effect their rescue. And who knew what kind of difficulty Grijalva and Olid might have got themselves into? Velázquez, therefore, set about helping Cortés put together a strong and well-provisioned force of men and ships. From the St. Jerome friars at Santo Domingo, he obtained license to trade with the natives as a means of offsetting expenses.

The orders reflect Velázquez's confidence that the dealings between himself and Cortés would be nothing but honorable. They also indicate that his objectives, aside from finding the two missing expeditions and rescuing the castaways from heathendom, embraced the advancement of discovery and the establishment of a basis for a prosperous and lasting trade. The pilots, examining all rivers and ports, were to take soundings of key harbors and record their observations on the charts. Every effort was to be exerted "to know the secret of the said islands and lands": the manners and customs of the people; the kinds of trees, fruits, plants, and birds to be found; the existence of gold, pearls, precious stones, or spices, and their sources. The truth behind reports of people with enormous ears and others with faces like dogs should be determined, as well as the whereabouts of the amazons of whom the Indian captives had spoken.

Should Cortés, after landing at Cozumel, either rescue the captive Christians or find himself unable to do so, he was to follow the Gulf coast to San Juan de Ulúa in search of Grijalva and Olid. Once the expeditions were joined, each commander was to retain command of his own ships, abiding by the instructions Grijalva carried. While possession was to be taken of any islands on which they might land, nothing in the document could be construed as authorizing a settlement on the mainland.

Interpreters of the Conquest have often faulted the cynicism seemingly implicit in the customary form of such orders: what red-blooded conquistador would abide by the prohibition against courting the native women? Such a question reflects a lack of understanding of Spanish legalism and its built-in loopholes. Velázquez's instructions specified that "none of the Christian Spaniards of your company shall have carnal union with any woman outside our law." The rule no longer applied after the woman was baptized, and the expeditionary chaplain stood ever ready to remove the barrier. Similarly, Cortés— like Hernández and Grijalva—was enjoined against attacking the Indians without cause. But cause was easy to come by; an Indian's defiance of a Spanish order not even understood might be so construed.

When these instructions were issued, on October 13, 1518, Velázquez had no inkling that both Grijalva and Olid had returned to Cuba two weeks previously and were then at Matanzas. Indeed, he seems scarcely to have considered the dilemma he would face should his nephew appear. Not so Cortés, who had embarked with verve on the task of outfitting the expedition, moving as rapidly as possible to thwart the complications certain to arise.

Velázquez observed with misgivings that his commander-designate purchased all sorts of war materiel: firearms, powder, crossbows, and horses. What need had he of horses if he was not to penetrate the interior? The governor must have noticed also that Cortés walked with a new swagger, decked himself out in gold-trimmed finery, and began acting like a highborn Spanish lord instead of the son of an impoverished country squire. The new captain-general published his true intent in the legend on his banner: "Let us follow the sign of the holy Cross with true faith, and through it we shall conquer."

Grijalva, having heard of the new plans, hurried away from Matanzas on October 22. Foul weather impeded his voyage to Santiago, which consumed weeks. Just when he arrived, or at what point Velázquez learned of his return to Cuba, remains in doubt. When the governor did hear the news, he was somewhat discomfited and sought to discourage Cortés by withdrawing his financial support. But Velázquez, being miserly by nature or force of circumstance, had been too willing to let Cortés spend his own money; the conqueror-to-be already had a far greater investment in the voyage than Don Diego. Hearing of his sponsor's uncertainty, Cortés hastened preparations. On November 18—probably just a few days after Grijalva arrived at Santiago—he boarded men and supplies, and sailed up the island, leaving Velázquez to pacify Grijalva as best he could. The governor, to conceal his embarrassment, castigated his nephew for not having the good judgment to ignore his orders against settling when the time was right. Grijalva, from all accounts, did not accept the rebuke gracefully.

Pausing at various ports along Cuba's south coast, Cortés allowed time for Grijalva's men to come and join him. Most of them did so, including the three captains: Pedro de Alvarado, who brought his three brothers; Francisco de Montejo; and Alonso de Avila. Antón de Alaminos came also, to make his fourth discovery voyage into the Gulf of Mexico as chief pilot. Most of the men, says Díaz del Castillo, would have preferred to sail again with Grijalva, "because he was a good captain and had no fault in his person or in knowing how to command." But Grijalva would have no part of it.

Cortés's force, comprising Cuba's best, soon was superior to any Velázquez could muster; as the effort to call off the venture intensified, Cortés was able to ignore it. Velázquez's messengers, bearing revocation of the commission and, finally, orders for his arrest, joined the now illicit captain-general, who went merrily about his business of overseeing final preparations. On February 10, 1519, the voyagers attended mass, and the fleet sailed for the rendezvous at Cabo San Antón.

There were eleven ships and close to 600 Spaniards, heavily flavored with Grijalva's men plus a sprinkling of Hernández de Córdoba's. The number from Grijalva's expedition is variously placed at 100 to 200; for a certainty, 45 of the 60 who have been identified sailed also with Cortés. Eleven of the 30 known survivors from Hernández's crew appear also. Through various circumstances, a number of others from both groups would join the conquerer-to-be later.

Of great significance to the maritime aspect of the venture was the presence of Grijalva's three ship captains—Alvarado, Montejo, and Avila—among those who commanded Cortés's vessels; and the three pilots, Alaminos, Juan Alvarez of Huelva, and Pedro Camacho of Triana, who had sailed with both Hernández and Grijalva.

Besides the Spaniards, there were 200 Cuban natives, including a few women, to serve as servants and porters, and the Mayan captive Melchior as interpreter. But most important, according to Díaz del Castillo, were 16 horses and several Negroes, by all counts worth their weight in gold.

Of the ships, little is known except that they were taken wherever they could be obtained and were totally lacking in uniformity. Most European naval commanders, had they been ordered to invade a continental empire with such a fleet, would have cried out in dismay. Bearing the flag and lantern was a 100-ton *nao, Santa María de la Concepción*, commanded by Cortés himself. Behind the flagship sailed three caravels of 70 to 80 tons' burden. The other seven were "small open vessels or brigantines," as diverse in size, appearance, and seaworthiness as in previous service; one piloted by Ginés Nortes was hardly more than a launch. Yet they followed the flag with its flaming blue and white cross and its confident motto.

Years later Cortés recited for his biographer, López de Gómara, the speech he made to his assembled troops before embarking on this "great and beautiful enterprise," which he promised would be famous "because . . . we shall take vast and wealthy lands, peoples such as have never before been seen, and kingdoms greater than those of our monarchs . . . pleasing to God Our Lord, for love of whom I have willingly offered my toil and my estate." A just and good war would be waged in God's name; "I offer you great rewards, although they will be wrapped about with great hardships. . . . I shall make you in a very short time the richest of all men who have crossed the seas." The extent to which his eloquence was enhanced by the intervening years cannot be known.

After mass was celebrated and prayers said on February 18, the ships caught a fair wind for Cozumel. A bit of unpleasantness attended the crossing: a fierce northwesterly scattered the ships, and one failed to make the rendezvous. Gnawed by uneasiness over the missing vessel, Cortés was further irritated that Pedro de Alvarado had sailed ahead and, on reaching Cozumel, sacked a village and terrorized the natives. The captain-general rebuked Alvarado, clapped the pilot Camacho in irons, and set about wooing the Indians back and restoring their property. Then he undertook to give them the Spaniards' great gift, supplanting their ancient religion with Catholicism, breaking up their pagan idols and substituting the cross and images of the Virgin.

Through Melchior, Cortés inquired about the six Spanish castaways said to be in the country and was told that several Spaniards were kept as slaves by a *cacique* living two days' travel inland. While eager to obtain interpreters, Cortés also must have relished the thought of rescuing Diego de Nicuesa, with whom he once had arranged to sail. He enlisted three Indians to carry his message to the captives, and sent the brigantine and caravel of Juan de Escalante and Diego de Ordás to put the couriers ashore at Cabo Catoche. The ships waited out the allotted six days and stayed one more, but neither the messengers nor the Spaniards appeared. Suspecting that the report of castaways was false to start with, they returned to Cozumel.

The captain-general's letter, however, had been placed in the hands of a Spanish captive in two days—not Nicuesa but Jerónimo de Aguilar, who had endured slavery among the Mayas for eight years. Trembling as he read the message, Aguilar took the ransom of beads to his master and begged leave to depart.

Complex and bizarre circumstances had brought Aguilar to Mayan captivity. In 1511 he had left the Spanish colony of Santa María la Antigua del Darién, on the isthmus. Sailing for Hispaniola with Juan de Valdivia, his purpose was to acquaint Diego Columbus with the ambience of deceit in the colony since Vasco Núñez de Balboa had deposed Fernández de Enciso and Nicuesa; Valdivia's, to win support for Núñez de Balboa's march for "the other ocean" and dispatch to Spain the samples of gold that would impress the king. But at this juncture the course of history was scrambled by a caprice of fate.

At Darién, the months dragged by without word from Valdivia. Suspecting desertion or disaster, Núñez de Balboa sent a second vessel with Rodrigo Colmenares and Juan de Caezedo. Shipwrecked on Cuba's western cape—one of the four such disasters on Cuba's shores just before the island's conquest—they found on the beach the wreckage of a ship presumed to be Valdivia's. From the Indians they heard of the massacre at Matanzas Bay, related by García Mexía and the two women, and concluded that Valdivia and his crew had been the victims. Colmenares, Caezedo, and company trekked the length of Cuba before finally reaching Hispaniola.

Valdivia's fate, in fact, was not so different from the one ascribed to him. His caravel, within sight of Jamaica, encountered a hurricane that drove her back upon the shoals called Las Víboras, southwest of Jamaica, where the vessel broke up on the reef. Valdivia and his seventeen shipmates—including two women—set out in the ship's boat, hoping to reach Cuba or Jamaica, but they were powerless against the current. For thirteen days they drifted westward without food or water. Seven of the fourteen crewmen died of hunger and thirst and were cast overboard to appease the sharks.

The others at last ran up on the shore near Yucatán's Cabo Catoche. They were met by fiercely hostile Indians, who sacrificed Valdivia and some others to their pagan idols and feasted on their flesh. Anticipating a similar fate, Aguilar and the rest escaped to the woods, were captured by different *caciques*, and became slaves.

One by one, the captives died of disease or overwork. The two women, outlasting most of the men, lived several years in this cruel captivity, but finally only Aguilar and Gonzalo Guerrero, a sailor from Palos, remained. Guerrero became completely Indianized: he married a native woman and had three Indian sons; his face was tattooed, and his ears and lower lip were pierced after the Indian fashion. Losing all hope, even all desire, of ever returning to civilization, he became a war chief of his *cacique*, Nachancán, lord of Chetumal.

Aguilar, having taken religious vows, is said to have resisted efforts by his *cacique*, Taxmar, to persuade him to take a wife or violate his oath of chastity. Having withstood a carefully laid plot to seduce him, according to one romanticized version, he was entrusted with the keeping of the chief's wives. Indeed, that makes a better story than the harsh truth: he labored constantly at carrying burdens and cultivating the cornfields.

After half a dozen years of captivity, Aguilar's hopes were heightened by news that three ships stood off Cabo Catoche. While he struggled to conceal his yearning, Guerrero entertained quite different thoughts: he counseled the Maya to war. He has been blamed for the ambush laid for Hernández de Córdoba at his first Yucatán landing site.

Aguilar, upon receiving Cortés's message, felt impelled to make the opportunity known to Guerrero, who lived five leagues distant. Guerrero spurned the offer; he had his Indian family. Furthermore, with his face tattooed and his ears pierced, he dared not dwell on what civilized Spaniards might think of him. Sadly, Aguilar left him to his Indian life and went with the messengers to the rendezvous. Finding that the ships had departed, he despaired, fearing that his only chance of rescue had slipped away.

By the time Ordás and Escalante returned to Cozumel, the storm-damaged ships had been repaired, and Cortés, anxious for the still-missing vessel, was ready to sail. About March 1 a fair wind beckoned them to sea. The hand of God was seen in the events that followed. First, a leaking ship forced the fleet to return to port; then foul weather kept it there. At last a large native canoe came from the mainland with four passengers who looked like Indians. When Andrés de Tapia went to investigate, one of them spoke to him in Spanish. Jerónimo de Aguilar at last had ended his exile.

On such fortuity hinged Cortés's mission: a little-known but highly memorable shipwreck provided the interpreter who opened the door to conquest. Yet for the moment, Cortés was more concerned with the lost than the found. Informed that Guerrero had encouraged the natives' attack on Hernández de Córdoba's men at Cabo Catoche, he exclaimed, "Truly, I wish I had my hands on him, for no good will come of this."

From Cozumel the Cortés fleet followed Grijalva's route around Yucatán into the Gulf of Mexico. At Puerto Deseado—now called Puerto Escondido—the missing ship was found. The crew had been attracted to the place by a dog running along the shore, and someone recognized a greyhound bitch left behind by Grijalva's ships. She, like Aguilar, paid for her rescue; she caught rabbits for the ship's larder.

At the Río de Grijalva, where the previous voyage had engaged in friendly trading, the Tabascoans had turned hostile. Since yielding their gold for Grijalva's trinkets, they had found themselves ridiculed by the Mayas of Campeche and Champotón, as cowards too faint-hearted to fight. In attempting to vindicate themselves, they incurred disaster. After the initial attack, the Mayan captive Melchior found occasion to escape, leaving his Spanish clothes hanging on a tree. Cortés countered the preliminary skirmish by putting ashore the cavalry mounts—the first landing of horses on the North American continent, with the possible exception of Ponce's mare. On a marshy plain near the town of Cintla, now a ferryboat landing on the Río de Grijalva's left bank, the greatly outnumbered Spanish troops met the Indian hordes with harquebuses, crossbows, and artillery, but it was the sixteen horsemen and their mounts that carried the battle. In commemoration of his first military triumph, Cortés renamed the town Santa María de la Victoria.

The vanquished natives brought presents of cotton cloth and gold. Yet the most valuable gift of all stood unnoticed among the twenty young women presented to the soldiers for their pleasure. By birthright, she was a Mexican princess, sold into slavery in Tabasco by her own mother. When the women were preached to and baptized by Father Bartolomé de Olmedo, the chaplain—requisite to becoming the mistresses of Christians—she was christened Doña Marina and given for the time being to Alonso Hernández de Puertocarrero. In time, she became Cortés's interpreter, confidante, and mistress. She, like Aguilar, was a keystone to the Conquest; Aguilar, conversant in the Mayan dialect, could communicate through her with the Mexicans, or Aztecs.

With information that the Tabascoans' gold came from the west, the Spaniards turned their vessels up the coast toward the Isla de Sacrificios. On Good Friday, Cortés went ashore at the island of San Juan de Ulúa, followed by the horses and all the soldiers and servants. His dealings with Moctezuma's messengers brought forth gifts to astound even the most opulent European ruler: cotton cloth, colorful plumes woven into intricate patterns, and gold and silver disks as big as cartwheels. But in announcing his religious intentions—of putting an end to human sacrifice and supplanting the Aztecs' pagan idols with the cross and the image of the Virgin—Cortés committed a tactical error that ended his welcome and called for a change of strategy. Then came the Totonac visitors from Cempoala and the revelation that Moctezuma was surrounded by enemies who needed only an organizing force to unite them against him.

Already, Francisco de Montejo had sailed north with two brigantines, piloted by Alaminos and Juan Alvarez, to look for a better place to settle, away from this unhealthful site, where thirty-five men already had died "from wounds inflicted at Tabasco and from sickness and hunger." Having examined the coast as far north as Cabo Rojo, the explorers returned to report on the one protected anchorage they had found. It was thirty-five miles up the coast, within view of a fortified Indian town that looked down upon it from the mountain slope.

The events that followed constitute a study in manipulative power. Cortés's first moves were designed to overcome the division in his own ranks, to win over or emasculate the Velázquez adherents among his men. He calculated each step to conform with a convoluted legalism that would square him with the Crown. First, he formed the organization of a town, appointing his strongest allies to positions of authority. Next, he declared fulfilled the mission on which Velázquez had sent him and resigned as commander, leaving all his powers in the hands of the new town council. His own appointees then elected him governor and captain-general of the new colony.

Sending the ships to await him at the new anchorage, Cortés and the soldiers started overland for the Totonac village seen from the sea, called Quiahuitzlán. Marching by way of Cempoala, they found it to be the largest town yet discovered in the New World. Enormous white-washed buildings, landscaped with luxuriant vegetation, glimmered like burnished silver in the sunlight. Curious men and women crowded the wide streets as the troop marched to the court for their formal reception. The head chief—of such great proportions that he is known to history as the Fat Cacique—exchanged embraces with Cortés and presented the captain-general with gifts of textiles, gold, and jewels. Offering his services in the emperor's name, Cortés gave an ear to the Fat Cacique's complaints against Moctezuma, whose demands for tribute included not only goods but also the Totonacs' sons and daughters for slavery or sacrifice. Cortés promised relief, after he had established his headquarters near Quiahuitzlán.

As Díaz del Castillo describes it, Quiahuitzlán stood on the mountainside "amid great rocks and lofty cliffs." Today, its ruins are found in just such a place, at the base of a spirelike peak called Bernal Grande—known locally as Cerro de los Metates—with a commanding view of the cove that served as the Spanish anchorage. On its unsuspecting people, Cortés worked the strategy that forced them into irrevocable commitment as his allies. With bland promises he persuaded them to arrest the Aztec tribute collectors, an effective pronouncement against Moctezuma. Then he secretly had the Aztecs set free, an act calculated to erase Moctezuma's suspicions of the Spaniards and cause the ruler to drop his guard. The Aztec leader thus was convinced that the visitors were the fulfillment of ancient prophecy, that Quetzalcóatl had come back across the eastern waters to establish his kingdom anew. Moctezuma lavished more gifts on the strangers, and Cortés pressed his advantage. To Moctezuma he sent word that he and his company were on their way to Tenochtitlán for a visit.

Too late, the Fat Cacique realized the vulnerability of his position. In an effort to assure himself the continued protection of the Spaniards, he offered the sojourners eight of the fairest Totonac maidens, that they might have children by them and thus join the two peoples. Cortés, recognizing the ploy, imposed harsh conditions: before the damsels could be accepted, they must become Christians; moreover, the Totonacs must cease the human sacrifices by which they offered their pagan idols the hearts of four or five victims each day. In the tense moment that followed these demands, each side squared off for battle. Cortés had Doña Marina explain the dire consequences the Cempoalans faced, including the ravages of Moctezuma's armies. Checkmated, the Fat Cacique stood abjectly aside. While the soldiers ascended the temples and smashed the idols, the Totonacs prayed and wept.

The priests of the sacrifices were commanded to cut off their blood-matted hair. The encrustation of human gore was scrubbed from the temple walls, and the Virgin's image supplanted the pagan idols. Mass was celebrated; the damsels were baptized and distributed among the ranking captains. Cortés took as his mistress the Fat Cacique's ugly niece, who was christened with his wife's name, Doña Catalina.

While messages passed to and from Mexico, Cortés had begun the building of Villa Rica de la Vera Cruz, first European settlement on the North American mainland. It rose on the sandy beach near his anchorage, within view of Quiahuitzlán. The arrival of Francisco de Salcedo on a ship from Cuba—with a horse, a mare, and ten soldiers under Captain Luis Marín—seemed a good omen at first. But then Salcedo revealed the news that Velázquez had been accorded royal appointment as *adelantado* of Cuba with authority to trade and found settlements in the mainland territory discovered by Grijalva. Cortés stood in jeopardy, unless he could prove himself more valuable to the Crown than Velázquez. While Francisco de Montejo and Diego de Ordás persuaded the men to give up their share of the gold thus far accumulated, in order that a significant gift might be sent the king, the flagship, *Santa María de la Concepción*, was made ready for sea.

Chosen proctors to carry the gold and reports to the monarch were Montejo and Hernández de Puertocarrero, who would leave his most prized possession with Cortés: Doña Marina. Juan Bautista was master of the vessel, with Alaminos and Alvarez as pilots. Alaminos was about to make his crowning contribution to Indies navigation. Although on previous voyages the vagaries of wind and current had at times perplexed him, he sorted out the phenomena and settled on a course for Spain—through the Straits of Florida and the Bahama Channel—that would frustrate any pursuit by Velázquez.

Before the ship was ready, new problems arose. Velázquez supporters plotted to seize another vessel and make for Cuba to put the governor on notice. Cortés got wind of the plot and dealt summarily with the perpetrators: the pilots Juan Cermeño and Pedro Escudero—who as chief constable at Santiago had once imprisoned Cortés—were hanged; Fray Juan Díaz, Grijalva's erstwhile chaplain, escaped a like fate only by virtue of his holy orders; others got 200 lashes; and the pilot Gonzalo de Umbria had one of his feet cut off. Then, to end the threat of defection once and for all, Cortés had his ships destroyed. First, they were stripped of gear and rigging (which would serve later to fit out the brigantines constructed for the 1521 inland naval operation on Lake Texcoco, the means of the final defeat of the Aztecs); then the sounder craft were hauled up on the beach, and the rest were scuttled in the anchorage.

With all possibility of retreat cut off, Cortés left Juan de Escalante in command at Villa Rica and moved most of his force to Cempoala to prepare for a march on Mexico. But as the march was about to begin, distressing news came from Escalante: four ships sent out on a voyage of discovery by Governor Francisco de Garay of Jamaica had anchored off Villa Rica. To the domain the captain-general had come to think of as his own, it was a threat he could not tolerate.

SOURCES AND NOTES

The Life of Cortés

Francisco López de Gómara, who served Cortés as secretary following the conqueror's return to Spain, became his biographer. Translated and edited by Lesley Byrd Simpson, the biography is readily available in English as *Cortés: The Life of the Conqueror*. The writer never saw the New World, and he therefore has been accused of writing only what Cortés told him. It was such a judgment, in fact, that caused Bernal Díaz del Castillo, desirous of setting the record straight, to write his *Historia verdadera*, or "True History," of the Conquest in which he himself participated. Díaz is not without bias; he both criticizes and venerates his former leader, but for the most part his criticism bespeaks no more than the dissatisfaction with officers of any rear-rank soldier. Haven't military officers *always* taken the best for themselves?

Bartolomé de las Casas, in his *History*, is at odds with both López de Gómara and Díaz del Castillo in his treatment of certain matters relating to Cortés, and writes of the conqueror with his customary lack of objectivity.

William Hickling Prescott's *History of the Conquest of Mexico*, first published in 1843, still heads the list of comprehensive accounts of Cortés and the Conquest, which are inseparable. Not to be overlooked in any serious study of those subjects is Henry R. Wagner, *The Rise of Fernando Cortés*. A recent (1975) biography of Cortés, concisely written, is William Weber Johnson, *Cortés*.

Cortés and Velázquez

Grave injustice has been done Diego Velázquez, by almost all who have written of Cortés and the Conquest, in the failure to assess properly the reasons for his attempted withdrawal of Cortés's commission. Cuba's governor did not act merely on jealous whim. Grijalva and Olid unreported, he ordered Cortés to find them; when they appeared, the situation changed appreciably. Not only was one of the principal reasons for the voyage abrogated, but Grijalva had earned the right to conduct any follow-up that was to be made. Yet from study of the Grijalva voyage and of Velázquez's orders to Cortés (in *CDI* 34:516–44 and *CDIE*, 1:385–406), the true genesis of Cortés's voyage becomes obvious. The search for Nicuesa was perceived by Prescott as one of Velázquez's motives for sending Cortés but has been largely ignored by writers since.

It is worthy of note that one of those whom Velázquez sought to interest in commanding the voyage was Vasco Porcallo de Figueroa. Porcallo, neighbor and friend of Grijalva, was to play a prominent role in outfitting subsequent voyages of discovery in the Gulf of Mexico. See Díaz del Castillo, *Historia verdadera*, 1:81, 88.

Concerning Grijalva's return, Wagner (*Discovery of New Spain*, 48) quotes Juan Diaz de Solís as saying he reached Santiago on November 15, three days before Cortés sailed.

Makeup of the Voyage

C. Harvey Gardiner (*Naval Power in the Conquest of Mexico*) and Henry R. Wagner (*Discovery of Yucatán* and *Discovery of New Spain*) have compiled lists of known participants in the Hernández and Grijalva voyages who later joined Cortés. From various documents in AGI, I have been able to make several additions to those lists. More intensive study doubtless would reveal that the number of Grijalva's men accompanying Cortés was indeed somewhat greater than 45.

The Yucatán Castaways

Concerning the shipwreck that put Jerónimo Aguilar and Gonzalo Guerrero in Yucatán, see Díaz del Castillo, *Historia verdadera*, 1:103; López de Gómara, *Cortés*, 32; and Las Casas, *History*, 231. Concerning the Mayan practice of cannibalism, see Tozzer, *Landa's Relación*, 120, n. 547. Prescott, in his history of the Conquest, and Washington Irving (*The Life and Voyages of Christopher Columbus*, 3:251) are among those reciting the fanciful tale of the attempted seduction of Aguilar, which originated with Francisco Cervantes de Salazar (*Crónica de la Nueva España*). The pertinent passage is translated by Tozzer, in *Landa's Relación*, 237. The story falls apart with knowledge that Aguilar later sired two illegitimate children by an Indian woman and is said to have contracted syphilis. See "Información sobre la que dió Luisa Aguilar . . . hija de Gerónimo Aguilar," AGI, Patronato 78A-1-7; also Baltasar Dorantes de Carranza, *Sumaria relación de las cosas de Nueva España*, 200.

Edward Gross, *Warrior of the Sun*, is a recent paperback novel built around the adventures of Gonzalo Guerrero.

For Doña Marina's story, see Mariano G. Samonte, *Doña Marina, "La Malinche."*

The Totonac Towns and Villa Rica

When the Comisión de Cempoala visited the site in 1890, it found the rubble mounds overgrown with trees estimated to be 350 years old. Six months of constant labor were required to remove the growth preparatory to beginning excavation (Francisco del Paso y Troncoso, *Las Ruinas de Cempoala y del templo del Tajín*, cxii). Today the visitor sees a well-ordered compound of restored or rebuilt Totonac edifices.

Quiahuitzlán is a national archeological site and may be visited by anyone with stamina for the half-hour climb from the El Cerro bus stop on Highway 180. Nine small structures stand upon a mound that may well hide the real archaeological treasures. The Comisión de Cempoala, which explored the surroundings fairly thoroughly otherwise, evidently did not visit Quiahuitzlán.

A jolty drive over a dirt road through a sugarcane field took me to Villa Rica, where fishermen labored at mending their nets and an elderly gentleman proudly recited the history of the place. He gave me present-day local names for the landmarks, including Cerro de los Coyotes for Punta de Villa Rica (Punta de Bernal or Cerro de la Cantera), which protected the anchorage; Cerro del Metate for Bernal Grande or Cerro de Quiahuitzlán. Paso y Troncoso (*Las ruinas*, cvi–cvii) describes the cove where Cortés's ships anchored after passing between the point and a rocky islet, Bernal Chico. Three natural lakes lie along the shore: Laguna del Viejón, Laguna Verde, and Laguna del Farallón. The 1890 commission found a copper coin minted during the reign of Ferdinand and Isabella and a dagger blade from the period of the Conquest, but the place today offers poor prospects for artifact hunters.

Destruction of the Ships

Gardiner (*Naval Power*, 28–31) discusses Cortés's destruction of his ships at length, opting for beaching as the probable means of disposal. See also Díaz del Castillo, *Historia verdadera*, 1:175–76; Hernán Cortés, *Cartas de relación*, 32 (second letter). The chronology is confused among the various accounts, but Montejo and Hernández shed light in their joint deposition given at La Coruña (published in CDI 11:435–39); they show clearly that at least some of the ships were disposed of before they sailed for Spain.

The Name "Mexico"

Mexico takes its name from the Mexica, the people popularly known as Aztec ever since Prescott called them that because of their Uto-Aztecan language. At the time of the Conquest, the name referred to the Valley of Mexico, the focus of the so-called Aztec culture since the thirteenth century. See T. R. Fehrenbach, *Fire and Blood: A History of Mexico*, 55–56. Throughout colonial times, the name Mexico was used principally to designate the capital city and its environs, the country as a whole being referred to as New Spain, which was a viceroyalty, with boundaries that were subject to change from time to time.

Amichel:
Alvarez de Pineda, 1519–20

It was an awkward moment for Cortés, about to begin his conquest of the Aztec empire. In view of the magnitude of the task, help from almost any quarter would have been welcome, but he could brook no meddlesome intrusion. Such, he feared, was what these four vessels of Garay's represented. Receiving the news at Cempoala, Cortés at first supposed that the ships had been sent by Velázquez to arrest him. He therefore set march immediately for Villa Rica, where he had left Juan de Escalante in charge. Escalante, not waiting for the captain-general, went out to the anchorage a league distant and learned the ships' true identity. It was not Garay himself who commanded them but Alonso Alvarez de Pineda, who comes to us as a man of mystery mentioned by name only by Bernal Díaz del Castillo.

Escalante, informing Alvarez de Pineda that Cortés already had founded a town, offered to guide the ships into the harbor, where the visitors' intentions might be discussed. Alvarez agreed; however, instead of following Escalante's boat, he proceeded to an anchorage three leagues away, leaving Escalante mystified.

Cortés, considerably agitated when he reached Villa Rica, refused to rest. With a few men he marched for the coast near the ships, hoping to speak with the intruders. A league from the anchorage he and his companions met four men who had come ashore. The notary Guillén de la Loa carried a document putting Cortés on notice that Alvarez de Pineda's company intended to settle the region north of Nautla, or Almería, which they had discovered. The others were to have been witnesses: Andrés Núñez, ship's carpenter; Pedro de la Arpa, a shipmaster from Valencia; and one other. Besides Alvarez himself, only these three participants in his voyage have been identified. Their part in it ended abruptly.

Cortés, by his own account, bade the men bring their captain to Villa Rica, where he would see to their needs and do all within his power to aid them in the king's service. The offer was spurned. Under no circumstance, he was told, would the captain or any of his men meet with Cortés on shore. Thus Cortés justified his action to thwart the visitors; since they obviously were up to no good, he seized the messengers, took their clothing, and had four of his own men put it on. On signal from the Cortés men in disguise, a boat came ashore with a dozen occupants. Two of them landed and were promptly surrounded. Cortés claims that one of them, a ship's captain, aimed his harquebus at Escalante, but the weapon misfired. The boat shoved off, leaving half a dozen men in Cortés's clutches. By the time the craft reached the ships, they already were making sail.

Cortés, interrogating the prisoners as to Alvarez's intentions, learned that the ships had anchored previously in a river mouth thirty leagues beyond Almería. There, on the Río Pánuco, the natives had given them a friendly welcome. The Spaniards had traded for food and gold valued at 3,000 *castellanos*, and from their ships had observed populous villages of straw houses near the shore.

It was not a matter to Cortés's liking; still he must chance the possibility that Alvarez de Pineda, on Garay's behalf, would settle on the Río Pánuco, thereby restricting the empire he himself hoped to build. With his forces augmented by six men, he turned his attention again to the Conquest.

The Alvarez voyage is generally said to have had its inception in a conversation between Governor Garay and the pilot Alaminos, following the voyages of Hernández de Córdoba and Grijalva. Alaminos and the other pilots who sailed with Grijalva in 1518, says Díaz del Castillo, discussed with Garay the voyage they had made to the southern Gulf. They offered the suggestion that a broad expanse of promising territory lay on the northern Gulf shore, between the discoveries of Grijalva and Juan Ponce de León. The terminus of the reconnaissance made for Velázquez, Garay was told, was the Río San Pedro y San Pablo—the present-day Tecolutla. The territory north of that river had yet to be claimed.

When Alaminos imparted this information, he was about to sail with Cortés. When Cortés found out about it, much later, he was quite put out with Alaminos. Although the pilot could not have known it at the time, he had placed Garay and Cortés on a collision course.

In truth, Garay had been planning a discovery voyage of his own for several years, under the impulse of circumstances that have never really been assessed. Since coming to the Indies with Columbus on the second voyage, 1493, Garay had been both blessed with good fortune and plagued with setbacks. Always loyal to the first Admiral, he was related to Diego Columbus's wife, María de Toledo, who was a relative of King Ferdinand. He therefore stood opposite the Ponce de León–Bono de Quejo clique, which resisted the second Admiral's authority. In fact, he was a business partner of Miguel Díaz de Aux, Ponce's rival for control of Puerto Rico. This factional division had far-reaching implications, extending well beyond the Antilles islands where it began.

Garay, as a Hispaniola settler, proved himself more a businesman than a conquistador. Christopher Columbus appointed him notary of Santo Domingo in 1499. He took his allotment of Indians and became engaged in stockraising and mining. With Díaz as his partner, he operated the Minas Nuevas, across the Hayna River 20 odd miles from Santo Domingo, and there met his first stroke of good fortune. An Indian girl, idly poking the ground with a stick, uncovered a gleaming object that proved to be a 35-pound gold nugget valued at 36,000 *pesos de oro*—the equivalent of almost 60,000 standard one-ounce silver pesos.

This find in 1502 supposedly launched Garay on the road to wealth and power; he reportedly employed 5,000 natives in tending his farms and livestock. Perhaps the taste of riches gave rise to a thirst for more, for it seems that Garay, within the next few years, seriously overextended himself. By 1508 he and Díaz had begun a long series of transactions with the Genoese merchant-bankers, an indication that they already were in financial difficulty. Garay's indebtedness to these loan sharks may well have become the driving force behind his attempts to discover new lands and new wealth, for indeed he seems to have become a soul possessed.

Despite his proven ineptitude at conquest, he attempted to conquer the island of Guadalupe in 1511 and failed. By 1512 he was serving as *alguacil mayor*, or chief constable, of Hispaniola and soon thereafter as *alcaide* of the fort of Yáquimo. In 1514 he voyaged to

Spain, supposedly to petition the Crown concerning extension of *encomendero* rights. Whatever his purpose, it was an opportune time for him to appear at court. Juan de Esquivel, Jamaica's conqueror and first governor, had died, and two successors had been tried without satisfaction. Ferdinand chose Garay to manage the royal estates in Jamaica. Diego Columbus gladly obliged the king by making him his lieutenant in charge of the island.

Garay, however, had other business in Spain. He arrived early in the year; the royal appointment did not come through until September. In the meantime, on February 25 in Puerto de Santa María, he purchased from Portuguese owners two lateen-rigged caravels of forty- and forty-five-ton capacity "for the service of the island of Jamaica": *Santa María la Antigua* (Hernando Chamorro, master) and *La Concepción* (master, Diego de la Mezquita).

The purchases evidently were in anticipation of Garay's appointment as governor of Jamaica and manager of the royal estates on that island. The vessels may have been intended for trade purposes, but several aspects of the transaction indicate that they were part of a plan, perhaps originating with Ferdinand himself, to seek new lands. The vessels are described as ships of the king, although the *alcabala*, or sales tax, was paid. The extensive purchases of rigging, tools, and spare gear suggest some intended use besides transporting cargo on short hauls between islands. Arms purchases—lances, cannon (bombards), and powder—strengthen the suggestion. Moreover, a royal pilot, Basco Gallego, was assigned.

All this in 1514. Why would such elaborate preparations have been made five years before the voyage was to take place? The answer lies in developments that prevented Garay from carrying out his design as soon as he intended. He did not reach Jamaica until May, 1515, and conditions there were far short of his expectations. With the Indian population already diminished, there was a serious shortage of labor for tending the island's vast herds of cattle and swine. The livestock itself was a liability, for the market on the other islands was already glutted. The loans Garay had been able to obtain in Seville were but a token of his needs, and the twelve slaves he had contracted to purchase not nearly enough to meet the labor shortage.

Garay seems to have spent the next year and a half trying to improve the island economy, building a sugarcane mill and turning available native labor to weaving cloth from the island cotton. When he heard of Hernández de Córdoba's impending venture, he doubtless chose to await the result before launching one of his own. Hernández's tragic outcome and Diego Velázquez's immediate follow-up with the Grijalva voyage might have caused him to wait still longer.

At last moved by information from Alaminos and the other Hernández and Grijalva pilots, Garay sent to Santo Domingo for permission from the priors of San Jerónimo, the Crown's West Indies administrators since 1517. Hoping to redeem his flagging fortunes, he received authority to arm, man, and provision four ships for probing the mainland coast. His stated purpose was to search between Juan Ponce de León's discoveries and the far limits of those made for Diego Velázquez for a strait connecting the Gulf of Mexico with the "South Sea" discovered by Núñez de Balboa. Such a passage, indeed, might lead to discoveries as great as Columbus's own.

No more is known of the four ships placed in Alvarez de Pineda's charge than of their captain-general. They are described simply as *navíos armados*, or ships equipped for war. They may have included the lateen-rigged Portuguese caravels Garay had purchased in Puerto de Santa María in 1514, but the number of men—given as 270 by Díaz del Castillo—indicates larger vessels.

No account of the voyage survives, not even the report that Garay sent to the king. Garay did petition afterward for the right to settle the region discovered, and the royal *cédula* issued in response contains a summary of his *relación*, dated before the end of 1519. There is no mention of Alvarez de Pineda. Garay, says the *cédula*, had armed four ships and sent them, well provisioned and with adequate crews and good pilots, to discover any gulf or strait in the mainland.

Alvarez set sail, probably from the principal Jamaican town of Sevilla on the north coast, at least by the end of March, 1519—five or six weeks after Cortés departed Cabo San Antón for Yucatán and San Juan de Ulúa. Proceeding through the Yucatán Channel, he sailed north till he sighted the mainland coast near the western end of the present state of Florida. He then turned east along the coast, expecting to find the passage believed to separate the mainland from the "island" discovered by Juan Ponce de León. When the expected channel failed to appear, he followed the coast to the Florida cape, where "the land left him by the prow in the direction of the sunrise." The pilots, according to the *cédula*, "wanted to run the coast to pass beyond [the peninsula] but could not because . . . the wind was constantly against them and because the strong current forced them to go back." The ships therefore turned west again and ran along the coast "until they encountered Hernando Cortés and the Spaniards who were with him on the same coast," a distance of "more than 300 leagues."

Along the way, Alvarez de Pineda registered, on the feast day of Espíritu Santo (June 2, in 1519), the mighty discharge of the Mississippi River, which is noted on the map sketch found attached to the royal *cédula* as Río del Espíritu Santo.

All along the coast Alvarez de Pineda discovered, he found land, ports, and rivers pleasing to the eye. This "very good land" was peaceful and healthful, offering a variety of fruits and other means of sustenance. The rivers yielded "fine gold," as evidenced by the specimens the Indians displayed and by the gold jewelry they wore "in their nostrils, on their ear lobes, and on other parts of the body." The people were affectionate by nature, indicating that "much success could be attained in their conversion and indoctrination to our Holy Catholic Faith." Some of the people, we are told in a somewhat doubtful passage, were giants more than seven feet tall, while others were dwarfs growing to no more than four feet.

Alvarez de Pineda, after the encounter with Cortés that cost him six of his men, sailed north along the Veracruz coast, in late July or early August, 1519. There is every indication that he returned to the Río Pánuco, that river "thirty leagues" up the coast from Almería, or Nautla, where Díaz del Castillo and Cortés indicate he already had begun a settlement. The *cédula* relates that on the return voyage he took his ships up a "very large and fluent river" with a sizable village at its mouth. Sailing up the river six leagues (about twenty miles), the voyagers observed forty Indian villages on one bank or the other. They remained on the river more than forty days, careening the ships. This river, it can now be said with certainty, was not the Río Grande or the Mississippi; it was the Pánuco.

In late fall 1519, Alvarez's ships returned to Jamaica, where the pilots laid before the governor a map showing the character of the Gulf in more or less accurate proportions. Alvarez de Pineda had discovered more of the Gulf littoral than any previous navigator—from the Florida peninsula to Cabo Rojo—and his map was a landmark. Ad-

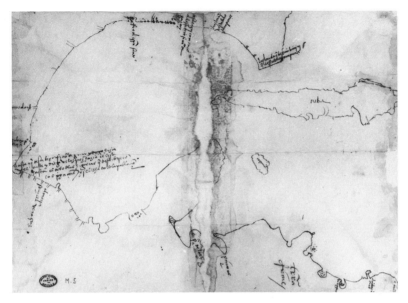

Fig. 4. The first Gulf map, Alvarez de Pineda. Courtesy AGI.

ditionally, he had proved Florida not an island and had discovered the continent's greatest river.

Garay's *relación*, written before the end of the year, was taken to Spain by some of the pilots from Alvarez's voyage. An important part of the presentation, the *cédula* acknowledges, was "a drawing, which you had brought before us by the pilots who went in said armada." It was the so-called "Pineda" map.

The royal officials acting for Charles V, then in Flanders, exulted that Garay, Velázquez, and Ponce de León had discovered the entire Gulf coast, proving it to be contiguous mainland. Garay's expedition, they noted, had shown the new lands to be "very suitable for settlement," as attested by the desire of the voyagers to return there. They therefore favored his plan to send a colonizing expedition. The land recently discovered, it was noted, "is called the province of Amichel, and it is so named." With the royal *cédula* issued at Burgos on June 4, 1521, they granted him authority to settle it at his own expense, with title of *adelantado*.

Noting the impossibility of fixing the boundaries of the various discoveries, the Crown officials advised Garay that Cristóbal de Tapia was being sent from Santo Domingo to mark the limits. That complications could arise from misunderstandings over each *adelantado*'s rights already had been demonstrated by Cortés's seizure of Alvarez's men at Villa Rica. In response to that bit of chicanery, Garay caused charges to be filed against Cortés in Santo Domingo, on December 24, 1519.

As for settling "Amichel," Garay was not disposed to await the ponderous turning of official wheels. In fact, there is room to suspect that Alvarez de Pineda did not return from his voyage of discovery but remained on the Río Pánuco to establish a settlement; if not, he was sent back there almost immediately. As Bernal Díaz del Castillo tells it, Garay "then sent three ships with up to 240 soldiers, musketeers and crossbowmen, and many horses, and Alonso Alvarez de Pineda as captain."

The command of this new expedition has often been ascribed to Diego de Camargo, an unheralded sailor on the 1518 Grijalva voyage and, according to Díaz, a Dominican friar. Camargo did sail for the Pánuco, as some of his crewmen later recalled, two months before Pánfilo de Narváez sailed for Mexico with orders to arrest Cortés—in other words, early in January, 1520. Testimony given in the 1562 *probanza* of Alonso García Bravo, who sailed with Camargo, offers a hint that the settlement seven leagues up the Pánuco already was underway when Camargo arrived. However, shortly after his coming the friendly Huastec Indians turned hostile, "killing all the horses and soldiers except sixty who came to the Port of Villa Rica on a ship with Camargo as their captain." Alvarez de Pineda, says Díaz, died with his men at the hands of the Huasteca.

As Camargo undertook the evacuation, nearly all the people were wounded, including himself. With the two leaky caravels that escaped burning, he was able to elude pursuit by a fleet of war canoes and get out of the river mouth, but with scarcely any provisions. Many men, unable to get on board, fled on foot, most of them to be overtaken and slain. After a few days a number of the men with Camargo elected to be put ashore to forage, rather than face the certainty of starvation on the ships. Natives from Nautla fed them and guided them on to Villa Rica, while Camargo coaxed his troubled vessels toward the same port. Four leagues short of his destination, one of the caravels, leaking badly, was beached. The other sank in the anchorage a few days after reaching Villa Rica.

Camargo arrived just a few days after Narváez's forces had been defeated by Cortés at Cempoala. Most of the vanquished joined the victor. Camargo and his "green bellies" were spared for the moment, for these bloated, emaciated men were in no condition to fight. Indeed, a good many—Camargo included—never made it into Cortés's army, for their wounds from the Pánuco uprising proved fatal.

Garay had no word of the Pánuco disaster. At intervals, he dispatched two more ships carrying provisions. The first was commanded by Miguel Díaz de Aux, Ponce de León's old rival for Puerto Rico, who, as Garay's partner, shared his precarious financial plight. Díaz, finding no sign of Spaniards or their ships on the Pánuco, sailed down the coast looking for Camargo and Alvarez de Pineda. His ship was caught in a squall and began leaking so badly she had to be beached. His fifty-three men and seven horses, like Camargo's survivors, joined Cortés's army of conquest and there encountered an old enemy: Juan Bono de Quejo, who once had taken Díaz to Spain in irons. Bono had come with Narváez.

The next ship from Jamaica was commanded by "Ramírez *el viejo*." Finding the Pánuco settlement abandoned, he brought to Villa Rica his forty men clad in cotton armor, ten horses, and some crossbows. Cortés, in the midst of regrouping after initial setback, welcomed these gratuitous reinforcements obtained at the expense of his rivals. Garay, on the other hand, could not tolerate this pirating of his vessels and proselyting of his men. With what seemed like unequivocal authority from the king, he determined to renew the colonization effort on the Pánuco himself.

SOURCES AND NOTES

The Alvarez de Pineda Map Sketch

The map sketch attributed to Alvarez de Pineda reflects the extent of Garay's territorial claims by right of discovery. A notation near the top of the Florida peninsula credits Ponce de León with discovery to that point, and a little farther west another marks the starting point of Alvarez's discoveries in Garay's name. On the west side of the Gulf, the end of Alvarez's reconnaissance is indicated between "Tamahox Puerto"—Tamiahua—and Villa Rica.

"To this point," reads the notation, "Francisco de Garay discovered toward the west and Diego Velázquez toward the east as far as Cabo de las Higueras, which was discovered by the Pinzons."

Justin Winsor (*Narrative and Critical History*, 2:285 n.) believed the map was prepared by Tapia in the performance of the duty assigned him, by the royal *cédula*, of marking off the boundaries of each discovery. Actually, Tapia did not arrive in New Spain until December, 1521, six months after the date of the decree that mentions the map, and then was unable to carry out the assignment. Whether or not the drawing actually was prepared by Alvarez de Pineda, the *cédula* seems definitely to link it to his voyage.

The map is often cited as the basis for fixing the northernmost point on the west Florida coast reached by Ponce de León in 1513. Yet the accuracy of the statement that "Juan Ponce discovered to this point" is by no means assured. As for the discoveries made for Velázquez, the evidence is strong that Grijalva sailed farther north than the map indicates. If the Crown had been willing to accept these designations, certainly, it would not have been necessary to send Tapia to mark the boundaries.

Sources for the map's portrayal of the southern Gulf and the Yucatán peninsula are not known. The Alvarez voyage did not extend to those areas, and Grijalva's chief pilot, Alaminos, was convinced that Yucatán was an island. Yet the sketch shows Yucatán in its proper peninsular form and links it quite accurately to Honduras. In that respect it was years ahead of its time.

Although the map is almost devoid of place names, there appears at the Gulf's northern apex the Río del Espíritu Santo, usually taken for the Mississippi and misjudged by many to be the "large and fluent river" of Alvarez's 40-day sojourn. It seems rather obvious that no prudent captain discovering for the first time that maze of channels, choked with logs and ringed by mud lumps, would go sailing up it unless he were truly desperate. The shape of the river mouth on the map indicates that the explorers observed no more of the river than its powerful discharge, probably perceived from some distance offshore. The Spanish custom of naming geographical features for the feast day of their discovery must also be considered. The Pascua del Espíritu Santo—Festival of the Holy Ghost, or Pentecost—coming seven weeks after Easter, fell on June 2 in 1519 by the Julian calendar. The royal *cédula* makes it clear that the lengthy pause for careening the ships did not occur until after the encounter with Cortés, in late July or early August.

While eastern provincialism is responsible for this error, myopia on the part of southwestern writers has given it a different twist. The river of "Pineda's" careening, they often claim, was really the Río Grande. The author of this latter interpretation has not been established, but his logic was convoluted indeed. When Garay himself voyaged into the Gulf in 1523, he landed not at the Pánuco but at a river farther north, which he named Río de las Palmas. Ignoring the reasons for this landing place, this misguided historian concluded that Garay certainly would have landed at the same river on which Alvarez careened his ships; therefore, Alvarez must have spent the forty days at the Río de las Palmas, and surely the river north of the Pánuco large enough to accommodate Garay's ships must be the Río Grande. Between the Pánuco and the Río Grande, however, is the Río Soto la Marina, which was known until the middle of the eighteenth century as the Río de las Palmas; in fact, a southern tributary still is. Countless maps and documents bear out this identification.

Another point long in controversy is whether the Río del Espíritu Santo on the map sketch really represents the Mississippi. Jean Delanglez (*El Río del Espíritu Santo*, 132, 145) thinks it might have been Galveston Bay. Peter Joseph Hamilton ("Was Mobile Bay the Bay of Spiritu Santo?") has a different idea. Both Hamilton and Delanglez argue that none of the chroniclers of Hernando de Soto's expedition identified the Mississippi as the Espíritu Santo, simply calling it *río grande*. Indeed, the authors of the three principal narratives may have overlooked the connection, but Luis de Moscoso, who led the expedition out of the wilderness, did not. His letter to the Crown of Oct. 17, 1743 (AGI, Mexico 95, ramo 3) definitely identifies the *río grande* that Soto's survivors descended to the Gulf as the Río del Espíritu Santo.

A document related to Garay's 1523 expedition locates the Río del Espíritu Santo 200 leagues from the Pánuco—close to the actual distance between the Pánuco and the Mississippi ("Provisión del Adelantado Francisco de Garay," in Manuel Toussaint, *La conquista de Pánuco*, 219).

The Encounter with Cortés

This episode is described by both Díaz del Castillo and Cortés himself, in his second letter. There are discrepancies as to the number of men captured (four or six) as well as the number of ships that actually appeared before Villa Rica (one or four). The royal *cédula* fixes the number of vessels on the voyage as four. Cortés, to whom is attributed a map of the Gulf oriented with south at the top, consistently uses "down" to indicate north, and Díaz seems to do the same. When Cortés says that the captives "told me how they had come to a river that is thirty leagues down the coast beyond Almería," it is evident that he means north, because that is the direction of Almería. Díaz, saying Alvarez de Pineda went to an anchorage three leagues "down the coast," must mean north also, for there is no indication that the ships sailed farther south than Villa Rica. They probably lay in the lee of Punta Delgada, to the north.

The captives from Alvarez's ships took active parts in the Conquest. Guillén de la Loa's daughter later married Gómez de Alvarado, Pedro's brother; their son, while serving as *corregidor* of Tlayacapa in 1585, petitioned for his grandfather Loa's *encomienda* rights at Guayacoctla and for a subsistence grant on the basis of Guillén's service. He says nothing of Loa's having sailed with Alvarez de Pineda (Domingo de Orive to the Crown on behalf of Guillén de la Loa Alvarado, 1585, AGI, Mexico 110, ramo 5). Guillén de la Loa died of a reed thrust in a jousting match in Mexico, says Díaz del Castillo.

Andrés Nuñez was one of two men chiefly responsible for building the brigantines to negotiate Lake Texcoco for the final assault on Tenochtitlán.

According to Cortés's second letter, the captives from Alvarez's ships included an Indian from the Río Pánuco, whom Cortés himself used to establish contact with the natives of that region. The voyagers took other Pánuco natives back to Jamaica, where they learned Spanish, then embarked on Garay's 1523 expedition as interpreters.

Río de San Pedro y San Pablo

The first application of this name to a river north of San Juan de Ulúa has not been pinned down; nor has the reason for using it to mark the limit of unexplored or undiscovered territory. At least two sixteenth-century sources place it in latitude 20° north, 20 leagues north of Vera Cruz (Antigua), between the Río de Almería and the Río de Cazones. This description corresponds to the Río de Tecolutla in 20°28'. (Juan López de Velasco, *Geografía y descripción*, 116; "Relación de los puertos que hay en esta Nueva España," 1576, in Fernández de Navarrete, *Colección de documentos*, 13 :f. 341, doc. 75.)

Francisco de Garay

Las Casas (*History*, 85–86) tells of the gold nugget that supposedly launched Garay on the road to riches. Other facts concerning him come from Joaquín Meade, "El adelantado Francisco de Garay."

As many as 28 references to transactions of Garay and Díaz de Aux, pointing to their involvement with the Genoese merchant-bankers, are found in APS for the years 1508–14 (principally in oficio 1, escribanía Mateo de la Cuadra; and oficio 15, escribanía Bernal González Vallesillo). The partners incurred a debt to "Jácome de Grimaldo, *genovés*" of 336,000 *maravedís* in 1508. In 1510, when Díaz and Juan Cerón were imprisoned by Ponce de León and taken to Spain by Juan Bono de Quejo, Díaz, after winning his release, spent a year negotiating various business deals, borrowing from Nicolao Grimaldo four times. (See also Francisco de Paso y Troncoso, comp., *Epistolario de Nueva España*, 1 : doc. 10, pp. 7–8.) In 1511 the partners were being pressed for various debts.

Concerning the Genoese merchant-bankers and their stranglehold on the Spanish economy, see Ruth Pike, *Enterprise and Adventure*.

Garay's purchase of the two Portuguese caravels in 1514 is detailed in "Relación del costo de las dos caravelas latinas de su alteza que francisco de garay alguacil mayor de la ysla española conpró en el puerto de Santa María," Feb., 1514, MN, ms. 1764, doc. 21, f. 89. Concerning his arrival in Jamaica, see Pedro de Marcielo to the king, Jamaica, Dec. 10, 1536 (AGI, Santo Domingo 177, ramo 3, no. 52, ff. 2–3); also Francisco de Garay, "Relación de las cosas de Francisco de Garay," Jamaica, June 11, 1515 (AGI, Patronato 179-1-2).

Alaminos, Garay, and Cortés

Antón de Alaminos, according to Díaz del Castillo, had a son by the same name. They and the other pilots of Cortés's following, says Díaz, were "not on good terms" with the conqueror as a result of their having given information to Garay. The others were Camacho, Cárdenas, Juan Alvarez ("the cripple") of Huelva, and Gonzalo de Umbria, who, as one of the plotters against Cortés had had one of his feet cut off. Díaz relates that this group, on parting with Cortés, went to Cuba, Jamaica, and Castile seeking employment as pilots. He fails to say when the breach occurred. Alaminos, his son, Cárdenas, and Umbria made complaints to the Crown, which ordered them compensated in New Spain with 1,000 pesos each. Only Cárdenas went to New Spain to claim the money.

Alonso Alvarez de Pineda

His surname properly is Alvarez, or Alvarez de Pineda, not Pineda or "Piñeda." Wherever the name Alonso Alvarez or Alonso de Pineda cropped up during our search of Spanish archives, my associate David Block or I pursued it until it became evident that this was not our man. Our best hope seemed to be a guide reference to a document in BN concerning "Alonso Alvarez, Portuguese," who was imprisoned in Santo Domingo about 1513. But, alas, the document contained no more information than the reference. And so it went through several men called either Alonso Alvarez or Alonso de Pineda. The sole fruit of our search, therefore, is a shaky conjecture that our explorer was either of foreign birth or an exile (like Sebastián de Ocampo). How else can the dearth of information about him be accounted for?

Nevertheless, the city of Corpus Christi, Texas, has created a "Plaza de Pineda" and is erecting a statue of the explorer, in flowing cape and gauntlets, brandishing a sword. The subject, of course, is deserving of the honor; it is too bad they failed to get the name right.

In 1974 amateur diggers found a broken fired-clay tablet beneath several feet of river silt at the mouth of the Río Grande. The plaque, in lettering that paleographers say is decidedly not of sixteenth-century vintage, relates that Alonso Alvarez de Piñeda (*sic*), with his four ships and 270 men, reached this point in 1519, sailing under Garay's orders. Attempts to explain it so far have been fruitless, but it seems clear that it was not left by Alvarez de Pineda.

The Alvarez Voyage

The royal *cédula* that summarizes the voyage, issued June 4, 1521, is fully described as "Real cédula dando facultad á Francisco de Garay para poblar la provincia de Amichel, en la costa firme que con navíos armados por su cuenta para buscar un estrecho habia reconocido." It is published in Martín Fernández de Navarrete, *Colección de los viages y descubrimientos que hicieron por mar los españoles*, 3:147–53. Fernández de Navarrete found attached to the copy of this document in the AGI, Seville, the Alvarez de Pineda map of the Gulf entitled "Traza de las costas de Tierra Firme y de las Tierras Nuevas."

The Pánuco Settlement

Díaz del Castillo (*Historia verdadera*, 2:104) identifies Alvarez de Pineda as the officer in charge of the settlement and goes on to tell of his death there. By far the most comprehensive account of this enterprise available is Alonso García Bravo's "Probanza de méritos y servicios" (AGI, Patronato 83-4-5), compiled in 1561.

Camargo's escape from the ravaged colony is told by Antonio de Herrera y Tordesillas (*Historia*, 3:372–73).

PART II

Amazing Mexico

New Spain of the Ocean Sea:
Conquest and Confrontation, 1519–22

To Cortés belongs the Gulf's greatest discovery episode and one of the most remarkable in the history of the New World. So astounding was the Mexican Conquest that it has become the central focus of the European entry into the Gulf. Much as Cortés usurped his adversaries' territorial rights, he tends to hog the historical spotlight. So complex were his personality and performance, so involved the events of the Conquest—not to be detailed here—that even his own considerable contributions to discovery and exploration have been obscured. In the act of conquering, he was concerned with exploring the land, a prerequisite to its development.

On the march to central Mexico, for example, the Spaniards sighted the towering peaks of Popocatépetl and Ixtacíhuatl, the Smoking Mountain and White Woman of Mexican folklore. Cortés marveled that even at the end of August they were covered with snow. From the taller—16,000-foot Popocatépetl—there often rose a column of smoke like that from the chimney of a large house, so strong that even the violent winds of the high altitude did not alter its direction. "Because I have always desired to give Your Highness a special account of all the things of this land," Cortés wrote to Charles V, "I wished to know its secret." He sent ten men with native guides to scale its heights, but deep snow and severe cold turned them back short of the summit.

Much of the land Cortés and his companions marched over remains little changed after four and a half centuries, though the native civilizations they encountered vanished with the Conquest. Beholding new wonders at every turn of the mountain trail, the conquistadors proceeded to destroy them, that no one might ever see them again.

Leaving Juan de Escalante and 150 men at Villa Rica, Cortés began the march on Mexico on August 16, 1519—a week or two after Alvarez de Pineda sailed away toward Pánuco—with 400 Spaniards, 300 Indians, and fifteen horses. On November 18 they entered the capital, Tenochtitlán, situated on an island in the middle of Lake Texcoco and accessible only over long causeways. There they were welcomed as Moctezuma's guests. Such wonders had seldom greeted a conquering army. Accorded a royal reception, Cortés gradually maneuvered the supersititious and confused Moctezuma into his clutches.

There was trouble, meanwhile, at Villa Rica, where Escalante received friendly overtures from Cualpopoca, the native chieftain of Nautla—some sixty miles north—and an invitation to visit him. Escalante sent four men. Cualpopoca, after receiving them into his home, revealed his murderous intent. Two of the soldiers escaped, and Escalante marched against the double-dealing *cacique* with fifty Spaniards and an army of Totonacs from Cempoala. Cualpopoca fled, but his people were defeated. Nevertheless, Escalante and six other Spaniards were slain, and Spanish prestige suffered. The mountain peoples and the Totonac towns subject to Cempoala revolted, cutting off Villa Rica's food supply. The Nautla prisoners revealed that Cualpopoca's treachery had been perpetrated on Moctezuma's orders, a fact that boded ill for Cortés and his troops, as well as the feeble coastal settlement.

Cortés used the episode as an excuse for arresting Moctezuma. He thus tightened his control over the emperor, who continued to exercise his powers only in accord with Cortés's wishes. Cualpopoca and 16 followers were brought to Mexico and publicly burned. Yet Cortés was vulnerable and knew it. Should the natives decide to cut the causeways leading to the city, his own men would become prisoners. He therefore had sloops built by the carpenter Andrés Núñez, late of Alvarez de Pineda's crew, and Martín López, the master shipbuilder. Then he went about acquiring an understanding of his surroundings, sending out several exploratory expeditions with Moctezuma's cooperation. The first such ventures were directed at finding mines, for Cortés wisely discerned that gold was the key to the emperor's support. On this quest he sent eight Spaniards in teams of two, each accompanied by two of Moctezuma's Mexicans, to explore rivers and mines in four native provinces, up to 300 miles from the capital. Near the South Sea, gold was found in the stream beds at Tututepec (Tuxtepec in modern Oaxaca). Spanish workmen were sent to begin a settlement.

The captain-general then turned his attention to finding a suitable port. He had not been favorably impressed with San Juan de Ulúa, destined for prominence as a harbor only after a number of others had been tried. Villa Rica's cove, while partially shielded from northers, was dangerously exposed to offshore winds and heavy seas. Cortés therefore asked Moctezuma for information about rivers and bays along the Gulf coast that might offer a more secure harbor. The emperor had his artists paint on cotton canvas a map of the coast, which showed a river flowing into the sea between the sierras of San Martín and San Antonio with a bay so wide that the Spanish pilots thought it might be the long-sought strait to the South Sea. Cortés sent ten men, including some pilots, with Moctezuma's guides to reconnoiter the coast southeast from San Juan de Ulúa. In seventy leagues they found the only promising harbor to be the one shown on the native map: the Río Coatzacoalcos.

Tuchintecla, lord of Coatzacoalcos and Moctezuma's enemy, provided boats for sounding the river. It had two and a half fathoms over the bar and five or six inside. Ascending the stream twelve leagues, the explorers found the depth constant, the banks heavily populated, the land fertile and productive. They returned to Mexico with the *cacique*'s gifts of gold, cotton, plumed ornaments, and jaguar skins, as well as his pledge of tribute to the Spanish king if Cortés would but keep the Mexicans out of his territory. Cortés sent Juan Velázquez de León with 150 men to erect a fortress and lay out a village at Coatzacoalcos, though unforeseen developments soon forced his recall.

This period of exploration lasted from November, 1519, to early May, 1520, a time of relative tranquility in Mexico. Reconnaissance groups were sent to "many and diverse areas, pacifying and settling this land."

But Cortés had overstepped himself in dealing with Moctezuma's people. The major clash of wills occurred over religion; the Spaniards were determined to erect their own spiritual symbols and to extirpate human sacrifice and other practices. Dire warnings came from Moctezuma. At this crucial time word reached Mexico that a fleet had dropped anchor at San Juan de Ulúa. The native ruler received the news first, in the form of a drawing showing eighteen ships riding at anchor behind the island dunes. He informed Cortés with ill-concealed relish; now the interlopers had vessels, and all of them could leave together.

The captain-general would have liked to believe that the ships brought him reinforcements, but he considered it more likely that they had come to carry him away in irons. Diego Velázquez's rancor had been building ever since Cortés's sly departure from Cuba. It multiplied with the latter's failure to send him a report, while dispatching news of his discoveries and a gift of Aztec treasure directly to the king.

Cortés's flagship, having sailed from Villa Rica on July 16, 1519, had had orders not to stop at Cuba. Crossing the Gulf, however, proved more difficult than expected, despite Alaminos's previous experience with its contrary wind and current. Before the voyagers sighted "Isla Fernandina," provisions were running low, and Hernández de Puerto-carrero was ill. On August 23, thirty-eight days after sailing, Montejo directed that *Santa María de la Concepción* put into Marién to reprovision from his nearby hacienda. During the three days spent taking on water, live swine, and bread, the mission's secrecy was compromised.

Montejo took what he wanted from his hacienda without contacting his overseer, Juan de Rojas, a Velázquez loyalist, but left him a letter. On reading it, Rojas searched out one of the Indians who had helped load the ship and informed Velázquez. Thus, the governor learned the identity of the ship and the principal officers; that many provisions had been taken on board; and that the vessel, bound for Spain, carried a considerable quantity of gold.

If Velázquez had held doubts concerning Cortés's disloyalty, they now evaporated. The governor claimed ownership of the ship *Santa María* and the gold she carried, which by royal regulation should have been registered in Cuba before being sent to Spain. He claimed also that Alaminos, whom he respected as the most knowledgeable pilot of the Gulf, was in his personal employ, having received 400 *pesos de oro* for his services on the two previous voyages; his most trusted servant had done him falsely.

Assuming that the ship would take the old Bahama and Nicolás channels to get on the standard course for Spain, Velázquez hastily dispatched Gonzalo de Guzmán with two caravels from Santiago. Proceeding through the Windward Channel, Guzmán never got a glimpse of his quarry; instead of taking the expected route, *Santa María* had turned north with the Gulf Stream, reversing the course Alaminos had sailed with Ponce de León in 1513 when he first discovered the Bahama Channel. With Guzmán's report, Velázquez was seized by grave suspicions: that course, untried and potentially dangerous, he believed, bespoke desperation; it appeared that Cortés's proctors were headed not for Spain but for some foreign kingdom where they might trade their gold at greater profit, and Velázquez so reported to the king.

At this stage Don Diego stood in high favor with Juan Rodríguez de Fonseca, bishop of Burgos, who had kept Indies affairs under his personal control almost from the beginning. By the influential cleric's grace, Velázquez had received the title of governor and *adelantado* of the mainland territory discovered by Hernández de Córdoba and Grijalva. His cohorts, Guzmán and Narváez, were named treasurer and royal accountant of the new territory. Velázquez was granted authority for building ten ships of no more than 100-ton capacity for use in the island trade and for making further discovery.

That Rodríguez de Fonseca had sided with Velázquez in his row with Cortés appeared obvious to Montejo and Hernández on their arrival at Seville near the end of 1519; the treasure sent by Cortés, even the gift for his father, was confiscated by the Casa de Contratación. The young king, having been named Holy Roman Emperor the previous summer, was about to depart for the empire. The proctors, overtaking the court at La Coruña, learned that Rodríguez de Fonseca had informed the monarch of Cortés's rebellion against Velázquez and suggested that his envoys be hanged. But Charles V, who was to prove himself a profligate spender, already stood at the brink of financial disaster. Cortés's gift temporarily restored his solvency, and the royal tide began to turn in his favor.

In Coruña, on April 29 and 30, 1520, Montejo and Hernández were interrogated separately, by Lorenzo Galíndez de Carbajal of the royal council and Juan de Sámano, the royal secretary. Their testimony was well rehearsed. Pleading ignorance of the administrative nuances that placed Cortés under Velázquez's authority, they claimed that Cortés had borne at least two-thirds of the cost of outfitting the Mexican expedition, to Velázquez's one-third. Cortés, they related, had yielded to the insistence of his followers to settle in Mexico only because there were not sufficient provisions for returning to Cuba and the ships no longer were seaworthy; after some of the vessels had sunk in the anchorage, all the others except three were scuttled.

Hernández, insisting that he be permitted to visit the emperor in Flanders, was instead thrown into prison and died there.

Just what Alaminos was doing during this time is not known. Probably after a visit to his native Palos, he embarked for New Spain and was back in Mexico before Montejo. The ship *Santa María*, meanwhile, rode at anchor in the Puerto de las Muelas at Seville, in the care of Master Juan Bautista. Evidently expecting to sail her again to the Gulf of Mexico, Bautista spent almost 7,000 *maravedís* on supplies and provisions on March 20, 1520. On June 24, however, Cortés's father, Martín, named an agent to sell the vessel. She was purchased the following September 15 by Pedro de Soria, Seville merchant, for 30,000 *maravedís*.

The ponderous grinding of the royal mills was not immediately felt in the Indies. Velázquez proceeded with plans to bring Cortés to heel, unaware that matters were turning against him; he had been named *adelantado* and governor of Yucatán, and that seemed to be all the license he needed. In the latter part of 1519, he occupied himself with preparations for sending a flotilla to New Spain to arrest Cortés. To command the operation, he chose Pánfilo de Narváez, the aggressive and brutal, as well as impulsive and stupid, leader of the Cuban conquest.

When word of the projected voyage reached Santo Domingo, it provoked consternation. The *audiencia*, abhorring the prospect of Spaniards shedding Spanish blood, delegated one of its members to stop the operation or divert it to more constructive ends. This official was the licentiate Lucas Vázquez de Ayllón, the same who later lost his life in an attempt to settle the Carolina coast. Vázquez embarked from Santo Domingo early in January, 1520, for Santiago de Cuba, hoping to dissuade Velázquez. The *adelantado*, devoting great personal effort to the preparations, already had departed for Trinidad, collecting all the men and ships he could find. Vázquez followed in his own vessel, finally overtaking him at Guaniguanico, where he had gone to witness Narváez's departure.

Vázquez, as he proceeded westward, noticed that the island was almost empty of Spaniards. Velázquez had gathered the strongest army possible, leaving only the ailing—a circumstance in which the licentiate saw imminent danger: the native population, few of whom had experienced kind treatment at the hands of the Spanish conquerors, might well seize the opportunity for insurrection.

At Guaniguanico on February 23, 1520, Vázquez de Ayllón urged on Velázquez his plan for averting disaster, suggesting several alternatives to making war on Cortés: Velázquez might reap greater profit in Aztec gold by supplying the Conquest; if that were not to his liking, there were still plenty of other lands to conquer. Why not leave Mexico to Cortés and take Yucatán, or even "pass beyond" Cortés and make other discoveries? Vázquez painted a grim picture of the consequences should Velázquez persist in his plan of seeking retribution.

Velázquez at first seemed to see the wisdom of the licentiate's reasoning, but by the next day he had suffered a change of heart. What business had the Audiencia de Santo Domingo to interfere? Was it not obvious that he was right and Cortés wrong? And so Velázquez, like prideful, avaricious men since the dawn of history, insisted on risking more in the fortunes of war than he stood to gain.

Vázquez, seeing himself unable to stop the voyage, decided to join it, in the futile hope of averting the tragic outcome that seemed imminent. His ship brought to nineteen the number in the fleet. There were six hundred Spaniards and eighty horses; a considerable number of Cubans; and several Spanish women who would suffer cruel death in Mexico.

Early in March, Velázquez himself returned to Santiago de Cuba, and Narváez's armada—of which Graviel Bosque, late of the Grijalva voyage, was pilot—set sail for Yucatán. The fleet first touched at Cozumel. There, declares López de Gómara, the voyagers were greeted by natives shouting and singing "Cortés, Cortés! María, María!" Vázquez de Ayllón, however, relates that a different sort of Spanish legacy was evident at Cozumel: the island had been virtually depopulated by smallpox. From Cozumel the fleet followed Grijalva's route to Tabasco, where the natives of Cintla—renamed Santa María de la Victoria by Cortés—fled at the sight of so many sail. Reassured by Narváez's messengers, they returned, bringing the captain gifts of corn, game birds, and nubile maidens.

Four days after the voyagers left the Río de Grijalva, with the Sierra de San Martín in view, they were overtaken by a storm that scattered the ships and occasioned the first known shipwreck in the Gulf. Some of the ships, including Vázquez de Ayllon's, reached San Juan de Ulúa a day ahead of Narváez, who paused at the Río de Alvarado to put ashore sixty ailing men and women. These unfortunates found temporary refuge at Tuxtepec pueblo, only to be massacred by their hosts sometime later.

By the time Narváez put into the anchorage around April 23, Vázquez already had talked with a young soldier from one of Cortés's exploring expeditions, who had come to his ship in a canoe. Thus he learned of Cortés's precarious situation at Tenochtitlán and of the post of Villa Rica twenty leagues up the coast. He also got a description of the Mexican culture, including the cotton clothing, the colorful plumed ornamentation, and the jewelry of precious stones and finely worked gold. Cortés, the visitor revealed, was of no mind to heed Diego Velázquez or anyone whom he might send here; the conqueror had instructed his native allies that any Spaniards who came to the coast were out to do him harm and should be denied welcome.

Narváez, on learning that Cortés and most of his army were sixty leagues inland, decided over Vázquez's protests to establish his base on shore. To silence the licentiate once and for all, the captain-general made him a prisoner on his own ship, which then was dispatched for Cuba with a substitute master and crew to serve as guards. After a three-month voyage, Vázquez was left near Isla de Lobos, off Cuba's north shore, and returned thence to Santo Domingo. The *audiencia*'s intervention in the matter, in sum, would accrue to Cortés's benefit.

Narváez and Cortés, meanwhile, each tried to seduce the other's troops. Cortés was the more successful, for he had gold; while Narváez hesitated, Cortés smuggled expensive gifts into his adversary's camp to win away some of the most trusted leaders.

Narváez, finally advancing to Cempoala, confiscated Cortés's possessions, including the Totonac women and a stash of gold. He dealt high-handedly with the Fat Cacique's people. Cortés, with Narváez at his back and Moctezuma's warriors all around him, felt compelled to take the bait. Arranging as best he could for the security of his position in Mexico, he left the Spanish island in Moctezuma's sea in the charge of Pedro de Alvarado, a valiant soldier noted for rashness. The result was disaster.

Approaching Cempoala, Cortés contacted his former business

partner, Andrés Duero, and other friends in the opposing faction, thus weaving a web of deceit about Narváez. In the end, Narváez was trapped by his own cockiness. His force was vastly superior in numbers; he had eighty horsemen to Cortés's five; and it was simply incredible, to his mind, that Cortés was not coming humbly to surrender rather than to give battle. On a night march in driving rain, the Cortesian army advanced to the stream where Narváez's sentries were posted. One of the guards escaped to Cempoala to sound the alarm, but Narváez had waited in camp a bit too long. His artillerymen had time to get off only four shots, killing three of Cortés's men, before pikemen—among them Bernal Díaz del Castillo—were upon them.

The men from Villa Rica, led by Gonzalo de Sandoval, rushed Narváez's quarters and were being resisted stoutly when Narváez himself uttered a cry of pain; with one of his eyes put out, he believed himself dying. Cortés's followers sent up a victory chorus.

Cortés, coming to terms with Narváez's soldiers, returned their arms and horses so that they might serve in his army. The ships were brought from San Juan de Ulúa to the Villa Rica anchorage and stripped of their rigging so that none might sail away. Narváez himself and the *veedor* Salvatierra were imprisoned in the Villa Rica fortress, there to remain for two and a half years.

The army of conquest, more than doubled in manpower, also had the advantage of Narváez's eighty horses. A few days later Diego de Camargo's ship arrived, bringing news of the Pánuco disaster. The time seemed ripe to nail down the Pánuco region against further intrusion and to renew the settlement on the Río Coatzacoalcos. To those ends Cortés dispatched expeditions led by Diego de Ordás and Juan Velázquez de León. Twelve days later he had to call them back because of distressing news from Mexico. Pedro de Alvarado, with questionable provocation, had marched his soldiers from their fortress to fire into the midst of natives dancing in religious celebration. Tenochtitlán was in revolt.

There followed a nightmarish forced march, begun on June 24, 1520; the death of Moctezuma from stones hurled by his own people; and, on July 20, *la noche triste*, the Spaniards' night of sorrow. Cortés, as his forces fled the capital over broken causeways and under attack from swarms of war canoes, lost as many men as he had gained from Narváez, many of the horses, and much of the Aztec treasure.

The shattered remnants withdrew to Tlaxcala to heal their wounds and plan for a future that appeared all too grim. With 4,000 Tlaxcalan warriors as allies, they set about conquering the surrounding Aztec towns. The first was Tepeaca, on the road to Villa Rica, where a Spanish town called Segura de la Frontera was founded.

The Narváez invasion, meanwhile, was having an effect not foreseen. Among those who had come with Diego Velázquez's lieutenant was a black man who, at the time of the Cempoala occupation, was covered with smallpox sores. Thus was introduced a force that would prove disastrous indeed for the American natives, who had never known the disease previously and therefore had no immunity. Like wildfire the deadly malady swept the land. Streets were filled with rotting corpses, emitting such stench that no one would bury them. López de Gómara rationalizes that the Indians were repaid in this manner for having introduced syphilis among the Spaniards. The epidemic brought to power the great Mexican chieftain Cuauhtémoc, for Cuitlahuac, Moctezuma's immediate successor, was one of its victims. The new ruler mobilized his people to renewed resistance.

With the invading forces at a numerical nadir, their fortunes began a gradual turn. Pedro Barba, who had been with Grijalva, sailed a small ship to Villa Rica with orders for Narváez to send Cortés as a prisoner to Cuba, if he was still alive. Barba and his 13 soldiers and two horses were promptly "captured" and sent to Cortés at Segura de la Frontera. A few days later Captain Rodrigo Morejón de Lobera brought another small vessel carrying 8 soldiers, six crossbows, and a supply of bowstring, all meant for Narváez. Cortés, rebuilding his forces at the expense of his rivals, got them instead. Garay's contributions, by way of Pánuco, amounted to twenty horses and 150 men. All the way from Spain came Juan de Burgos with his shipload of horses, munitions, and merchandise. Cortés purchased the lot; Burgos, his master, and his crew joined the conquistadors. Burgos deserves credit for inaugurating the thriving commerce that was to operate between New Spain and Seville. From the men he brought came four captains for the 13 brigantines being built to conquer the Mexican lake, the key to the new effort.

Malcontents among the new troops were dispatched on one of Narváez's ships to Cuba. One of this group was Juan Ponce de León's old ally, Juan Bono de Quejo, who had come with Narváez as sailing master. Bono's dissatisfaction perhaps stemmed from finding himself in the same army with Díaz de Aux, whom he once had taken to Spain in irons. Díaz, it seems, had a way of disquieting his enemies.

Over date of October 30, 1520, Cortés wrote his second *carta de relación* to Charles V, but severe weather that destroyed three vessels in the anchorage prevented the sailing for Spain. Not until May 5, 1521, were Diego de Ordás and Alonso de Mendoza able to sail. It was in this second letter that Cortés suggested the name for the country he was attempting to conquer. Because of its similarity to Spain—its vastness and the coldness of its heights—it seemed the most appropriate name was La Nueva España del Mar Océano, "New Spain of the Ocean Sea."

Two days after Christmas of 1520, Cortés reviewed his troops at Tlaxcala. With 40 horses, 550 foot soldiers and thousands of native allies, 9 cannon, and the 13 brigantines—rigged with gear stripped from the original fleet at Villa Rica—the Spaniards marched back to Tenochtitlán, where they demolished the capital and with it the Mexican civilization. Cuauhtémoc surrendered on August 3, 1521.

Thus ended the phase of the Conquest that customarily draws the focus of the historical spotlight. Less attention has been paid to the difficult and crucial task the conquerors faced of exploring, subduing, and settling the rest of the country. About the time of Cuauhtémoc's capitulation, his allies at Tuxtepec killed the 60 Spaniards left on the Gulf coast by Narváez. Toward the end of October, 1521, Cortés sent Gonzalo de Sandoval with 200 foot and 35 horse soldiers to that trouble spot, on the Papaloapán River headwaters some distance from the coast. Sandoval seized the cheftain responsible and burned him alive, then laid out the town that Cortés had decreed should be named Medellín for his birthplace in Extremadura.

From Medellín, Sandoval moved to pacify the surrounding coastal country. The former brigantine captain Briones took 100 soldiers against the hostile Zapotecs of Tiltepec, ten leagues distant. He found the steep trails of the rugged country slippery from constant mist, and the Indians armed with long lances with six feet of stone cutting edge, sharper than the Spaniards' swords. Protected by shields that covered the whole body, they shot arrows and hurled javelins and stones, while emitting a weird whistle or cry that reverberated among the hills. In this eerie setting Briones met defeat, and most of his men were wounded.

From another Zapotec province, Jaltepec, twenty chieftains came to Sandoval in peace. Clothed in heavily embroidered cotton robes that reached to the feet, like Moorish burnouses, they bore gifts of gold and asked Spanish help in their war with the Mijes. Sandoval sent ten men to reconnoiter the mountain passes and examine the mines. They found washing troughs on three rivers, all yielding considerable gold.

He then proceeded to the Río Coatzacoalcos, whence Juan Velázquez de León—since a victim of *la noche triste*—had been withdrawn upon the coming of Narváez. On the festival of Espíritu Santo in May, 1522, he began crossing men and horses over the stream in a hundred Indian canoes tied in pairs. The Spanish settlement in the native village was named Espíritu Santo for the festival. It was there that Sandoval received news of the arrival of a ship from Cuba in the Río de Agualulco, fifteen leagues distant. Among the several married women on board was Doña Catalina Suárez la Marcaída, wife of Cortés, accompanied by her brother, Juan Suárez. Sandoval conducted them to Mexico, and in his absence the natives rose against the settlers and killed several.

While Sandoval was at Medellín, another distraction presented itself to Cortés: the arrival of Cristóbal de Tapia, overseer of the gold smelter at Hispaniola, who carried a royal commission as governor and *juez pesquisidor* (magistrate) of New Spain.

Tapia, it will be remembered, had been given special instructions to determine boundaries between the territories discovered by Alvarez de Pineda in Garay's behalf and those discovered for Diego Velázquez. His instructions called for investigating and informing the Crown of certain other matters relating to the Conquest. His ship dropped anchor at Villa Rica about December 2, 1521, just a few months after the fall of Tenochtitlán. He wrote forthwith to Cortés at Coyoacán, stating his purpose and asking for an early meeting. Cortés could not be bothered. In an elaborate legal document drawn up by his officers, he gave his reasons: the country was so recently conquered, his forces so widely dispersed in pacifying and exploring other provinces, that it would be both unwise and contrary to His Majesty's interests for him to leave the capital. (He admitted no thought of letting Tapia see the devastated city.) Certain officials were empowered to act in his stead.

While awaiting this reply, Tapia visited at Villa Rica with Pánfilo de Narváez, still a prisoner, and received some advice: Cortés's luck had not yet run out, and Tapia was treading dangerous ground; he had best depart quickly and silently to Spain, report what he had observed, and await developments. Soon after Tapia's departure, Narváez was hustled off to Mexico to avoid such blabbing in the future.

On December 24, Tapia's royal provision was presented to the junta convened on Cortés's orders at Cempoala. The gathering comprised the *cabildo* of Villa Rica—Francisco Alvarez *chico*, Bernardino Vázquez de Tapia, Jorge de Alvarado (Pedro's brother), and Ramón de Cuenca; also Pedro de Alvarado, *alcalde* of Tenochtitlán; Cristóbal Corral, *regidor* of Segura de la Frontera, and Andrés de Monjaraz, *alcalde* of Medellín—all present in official capacity; and Cortés's special representatives, Gonzalo de Sandoval, Diego de Soto, and Diego de Baldenebro.

Tapia's charge called for a three-fold investigation. First there was the matter of Diego Velázquez's discoveries under the authority of the father priors of San Jerónimo, and Cortés's insurbordination after having sailed under Velázquez's orders. Also of concern was the armed conflict between forces of Narváez and Cortés, and the uncivil treatment accorded Lucas Vázquez de Ayllón, who had come to keep the peace. The third matter was the imprisonment of Narváez and some of his followers and the confiscation of their property. Tapia was empowered, on paper at least, to command the presence and testimony of any of the principals or their agents and to assess penalties on their persons or property for failure to comply. But in New Spain his written authority had all the impact of a lost poodle barking up a hollow log.

The governor-designate found himself surrounded by a battery of hostile witnesses. He was, says López de Gómara, insulted, threatened, and "possibly bribed." But he refused to back off from their bullying tactics.

After time out to celebrate the Feast of the Nativity, the hearing resumed on December 28. Cortés's delegates were ready. They began with the assertion that the very presence of "the overseer"—the only title conceded Tapia in the proceedings recorded by Cortés's own scribes—posed a grave danger, running the risk of serious scandal by which Their Majesties' service would be severely damaged. Then they attacked the validity of his commission: while the document bore the signatures of the regent Cardinal Adrian of Utrecht (later pope), Bishop Rodríguez de Fonseca, and royal secretary Juan de Sámano, it was "not properly countersigned by a royal secretary."

Proceeding to the questions raised in the charge, the junta claimed that whatever Diego Velázquez or the father priors had done, New Spain lay beyond their insular authority; Hernández de Córdoba had claimed all the new territory in the name of the king, not for Velázquez; the only commission Cortés had from Velázquez was to find Grijalva, and Cortés himself had borne the cost of the fleet, Velázquez's claim to the Crown notwithstanding. Instead of being motivated by covetousness and ambition, as the charge alleged, Cortés had been solely concerned with serving his king and lord, whose loyal servant he was by nature. Having undertaken trade with the natives, as Velázquez had asked him to do, he had encountered the Mexicans' many barbarous practices. Their scandalous behavior and insults made it obvious that the only adequate means for Cortés to serve Their Majesties lay in forming a settlement.

As for the imprisonment of Vázquez de Ayllón, that was the doing of Narváez, who remained a prisoner in New Spain as punishment for the offense. The original proceedings had been sent to the emperor, and there were no copies.

No indication is found that Narváez, though still in Villa Rica, was permitted to testify at the hearing, or that Tapia requested his appearance.

Tapia recognized the cover-up and spelled it out in his written replication of December 30. Any scandal that might arise, he said, would not be his doing but that of the witnesses who refused to honor his commission as governor and denied the validity of his royal provision, tactics that were both false and ridiculous. The evasive and obfuscatory answers made all the witnesses subject to the penalties prescribed in the royal document.

The Cortés crowd fired one parting shot the following day: they had responded adequately to the provision and would make no further reply except to point out that the *veedor* was in no position to impose penalties; they would submit neither to that nor to other points of his complaint. On January 6, 1522, the scribe granted Tapia's request for a transcript of the proceedings, and he shortly sailed for Hispaniola. The transcript represents the only apparent concession made him, but that was enough to cause uneasiness among the Cortés faction. Out of fear of the effect this document would have when Tapia took it to Spain, a hearing was convened at Coyoacán the following April, its purpose to compile proof of the testimony given Tapia.

Presiding over the hearing was Alonso de Avila, "*alcalde mayor* in this New Spain of the Ocean Sea," who had captained a vessel on the Grijalva voyage of 1518. He soon would sail for Spain with Cortés's third letter and the Aztec treasure. Fifteen questions were submitted to eleven witnesses from April 20 to May 5, 1522. Among them were six who had sailed with Hernández de Córdoba: Ginés Martín, Pedro Prieto, Benito de Béjar, Cristóbal Hernández de Alaniz, Diego de Porras, and our old friend the pilot, Antón de Alaminos, who only recently had returned from Spain. He gave his age as forty. Béjar, like Alaminos, had sailed with both Hernández and Grijalva. Two other witnesses, Bernardino Vázquez de Tapia and Bernardino López, had made the Grijalva voyage. López and Juan Rico had been on expeditions sent by Cortés to discover the South Sea, while Vázquez de Tapia, with Diego de Baldenebro and Andrés de Monjaraz, had been present at the sessions with Cristóbal de Tapia in Cempoala. Ginés Martín, who had been a shipmaster with Hernández de Córdoba, and Diego de Porras had come to the Cortés camp from Narváez's forces.

The fifteen questions put to the witnesses were designed to elicit testimony upholding the case presented to Tapia at Cempoala. Specifically, they sought to show that any claim Velázquez had to the discovery of Yucatán or New Spain was fraudulent; to emphasize Cortés's contributions in the royal service, including the fitting-out of his fleet at his own expense; and to underscore Tapia's lack of fitness for governing New Spain under the existing circumstances. This group of witnesses could hardly be considered unbiased. Most of them acknowledged the statement of facts contained in the questions, with only an occasional tendency to elucidate. Yet they put an interesting light on Hernández de Córdoba's voyage of discovery and the Conquest itself, while somewhat clarifying Velázquez's role in both.

It seems unjust that the only assessments of Tapia at hand are those of Cortés and his adherents, Díaz del Castillo and López de Gómara. While López de Gómara suggests that Tapia was bribed, Diaz tells how: Cortés sent gold to buy from Tapia some Negroes, a few horses, and a ship. Some of Tapia's crew, Díaz adds, joined Cortés's army, as did others who had lately served with Vázquez de Ayllón at Chicora or Juan Ponce de León in Florida. Whatever Tapia's shortcomings, he succeeded in taking the pulse of New Spain; it was no mean accomplishment to confront Cortés's rowdies and be able to sail away with the information he had come for. However, he had done nothing toward establishing boundaries between the claims of Velázquez (or Cortés) and Garay. He therefore failed to head off the next confrontational disaster.

Tapia was about to depart when the ubiquitous Juan Bono de Quejo put into the Río Coatzacoalcos and proceeded to the village of Espíritu Santo. He was bearing "dispatches from Spain," which turned out to be letters in blank signed by Bishop Juan Rodríguez de Fonseca, promising perquisites for any of Cortés's officers who would accept Tapia as governor. Finding Tapia already gone, Bono went to Villa Rica and thence to Mexico, whence Cortés sent him packing. Although a defector himself, Cortés had little liking for those of similar inclination; Bono could go elsewhere to stir up trouble.

As Tapia sailed away with information valuable to his own cause, he may have left behind information equally vital to Cortés. The conqueror somehow managed to get wind of the royal grant awarded Francisco de Garay for the settlement of Amichel. News of the royal *cédula* issued at Burgos the previous June must have come to New Spain with either Tapia or Alaminos. It signified that Garay was preparing to carry out his commission, taking up where Alvarez de Pineda and Camargo had left off when the Huastécs ravaged the Pánuco settlement. Cortés again must devise a strategy for dealing with an unwelcome intruder.

SOURCES AND NOTES

Cortés the Explorer

The conqueror's concern with discovery and exploration is revealed in his letters to Emperor Charles V (*Cartas de relación*). There are English translations available, but some of them (e.g., Bayard Morris, trans., *Hernando Cortés: Five Letters, 1519–1526*) are abridged, and the deleted portions often are significant to persons with a specialized interest. Díaz del Castillo's *Historia verdadera* and López de Gómara's *Cortés* are invaluable supplements to the Cortés letters. Díaz's work has been fully translated into English by Alfred P. Maudslay (1912) and published in five volumes by the Hakluyt Society as *The True History of the Conquest of New Spain*. This work has been abridged as *The Discovery and Conquest of Mexico* (New York: Farrar, Straus and Girroux, 1956), which ends with the fall of Mexico. I have used the 1955 Spanish edition of Díaz, in two volumes, issued by Editorial Porrúa, Mexico.

The Voyage to Spain

Several documents published in Spanish reveal events of the proctors' voyage, including the stop in Cuba: "Información recibida ante el gobernador y adelantado Diego Velázquez sobre una espedición sospechada emprendida desde la Habana," Santiago de Cuba, Oct. 7, 1519 (*CDI*, 12:155–60); Velázquez to the Crown, Santiago, Oct. 12, 1519 (*CDIE*, 1:437–74); and Francisco de Montejo and Alonso Hernández de Puertocarrero, "Declaración," La Coruña, April 29, 1520 (*CDIE*, 1:486–95).

Notarial documents in APS (1520, oficio 4, escribanía Manuel Segura: libro 1, f. 805; libro 3, f. 1943; libro 4, f. 2984) discuss disposition of "a caravel called *Santa María de la Concepción* of sixty *toneladas*, of which Juan Batista, *vecino* of the Island of Cuba, is master, being the same that was sent from the Indies to this city [Seville] by Fernando [*sic*] Cortés, son of the said Martín Cortés." *Tonelada* corresponds to a wine tun; a ship's size during this period usually was expressed in terms of its carrying capacity, or the number of wine tuns it would hold.

Concerning Bautista, see APS 1516 (oficio 1, libro 2; escribanía Mateo de la Cuadra, f. 793); 1518 (oficio 4, libro 3; escribanía Manuel Segura, f. 75); and 1525 (oficio 5, libro 3; escribanía Francisco de Castellanos, f. 75). A member of the Grijalva expedition, Bautista had taken ships to the Indies in 1516 and 1518, evidently arriving just before Grijalva sailed. He was still a shipmaster in 1525, when he again sailed for the New World. Henry Harrisse (*Discovery*, 705) speculates that he is the Juan Battista Ginovés who took part in the conquest of Yucatán and died there in 1554.

The Narváez Affair

This episode has been treated previously from the accounts of Díaz del Castillo and López de Gómara. Documents emanating from Vázquez de Ayllón and the Audiencia de Santo Domingo broaden the picture: Lucas Vázquez de Ayllón to the king, Santo Domingo, Jan. 8, 1520 (*CDIE*, 1:481–83), and "Paracer" (ibid., 476–80); Audiencia de Santo Domingo to the Crown, Santo Domingo, Aug. 30, 1520 (ibid., 499–500); Vázquez de Ayllón, "Relación," included in Audiencia to Crown, 500.

Among the witnesses to the "Paracer," which Vázquez presented to Velázquez at Guaniguanico, was the discoverer of the territory in dispute, Juan de
Grijalva. Another was Vasco Porcallo de Figueroa, Grijalva's friend and neighbor at Trinidad and a prominent supplier of discovery expeditions. Since neither is mentioned elsewhere in connection with the Narváez voyage, it is assumed that they withdrew when Velázquez did. Porcallo came to Cuba from
Tierra Firme, where he had served in the army of Pedro Arías de Avila (Pedrarias Dávila), in company with Francisco de Montejo and other conquistadors
(see testimony of Alonso Alvarez Gallote in "Ynformación de los méritos y servicios de Alonso Ortiz de Zúñiga," AGI, Patronato 60-1-2).

Vázquez de Ayllón seems to have recorded an exaggerated report of the
loss of ships and lives in the storm near Sierra de San Martín, as he says six
ships and 50 men were lost, while Díaz del Castillo credits the loss of only one
ship and her crew. Díaz also seems to set Cortés straight on the number of men
left with Alvarado in Mexico when the captain-general departed to deal with
Narváez: where Cortés says 500 remained, Díaz claims there were only 80 soldiers, all those with suspected loyalties to Velázquez among them.

While Cortés claims that he had Narváez's ships stripped of their rigging,
there is evidence that he took one further step. Diego Suárez, a pilot from Triana, testifies in "Ynformación" given in Seville on June 18, 1528, in behalf of
Pedro González de Nájera, that González was among the shipmasters who lost
a ship at Villa Rica "because Hernando Cortés ordered them sunk so that the
people would go with him into the interior." González is described as "a pilot
on ships that discovered New Spain of the Ocean Sea or Yucatán" (AGI, Patronato 54-2-1).

The Conquistadors

Concerning the character of Miguel Díaz de Aux, see Díaz del Castillo
(*Historia verdadera*, 1:421–22), and Baltasar Dorantes de Carranza (*Sumaria relación*, 216–17).

Diego de Ordás, who sailed for Spain with Cortés's second letter on May
5, 1521, gave a "Testimonio" in Santo Domingo less than four months later, on
Sept. 14, 1521 (AGI, Santo Domingo 9, ramo 1, doc. 5).

Juan de Burgos ("Información," Tenuxtitán [Tenochtitlán], Oct. 10, 1536,
AGI, Patronato 55-3-3, f. 1) reflects no awareness of the historic role he played
in opening the commerce between New Spain and Seville; he mentions only
having served in the Conquest with his arms and horses.

Díaz del Castillo (*Historia verdadera* 1:485) gives the names of the Lake
Texcoco brigantine captains. The four who came with Burgos were Jerónimo
Ruiz de la Mota, Antonio de Carbajal, Portillo, and Briones. Additionally, there
were Pedro Barba, Díaz de Aux, García Holguín, Juan Jaramillo, Zamora, Col-
menero, Lema (Juan de Lerma?), and Ginés Nortes.

Cristóbal de Tapia

Besides the fragmentary information given by López de Gómara and Díaz del Castillo, the sources on the Tapia visit include two documents published in *CDI* 26: Hernán Sánchez de Aguilar (notary), "Requerimiento hecho a don Hernando Cortés, sobre la venida de Cristóbal de Tapia," Coyoacán, Dec. 12, 1521 (pp. 30–36); "Provisión de Cristóbal de Tapia" (pp. 36–43). There is also the highly important "Probanza," Coyoacán, April 20, 1522 (in *Boletín del Archivo General de la Nación*). Henry R. Wagner (*Discovery of Yucatán*, 31) takes note of this document but glosses over its importance as "an investigation about the alleged taking of possession of Yucatán by Hernández de Córdoba."

Source of Reinforcements

Henry Harrisse (*Discovery*, 159–60), citing Juan de Torquemada (*Monarquía indiana*, 1:614), posits that Díaz confuses the names of Vázquez and Ponce de León. Instead of coming from Chicora, he offers, perhaps the ship came directly from Florida, where it had taken part in the second Florida expedition with Ponce. If that could be proved, it might have implications for the restructuring of Ponce's 1521 voyage, as Harrisse attempts to do.

Victoria Garayana:
Garay and Pánuco, 1523

ON June 14, 1523, Francisco de Garay, governor of Jamaica and *adelantado* of Amichel, sailed with 11 ships from Jamaica's north coast. Among the vessels, with an aggregate capacity of almost 800 *toneladas*, were two caravels, and two brigantines equipped with oars for negotiating shallow coves. The rest were heavier *naos*, carrying horses and artillery. By Garay's own count there were "600 men, including 150 horsemen." Their ultimate destination was the Río Pánuco, where Garay hoped to pacify the Indians and establish a colony in compliance with his royal commission.

The captain of the fleet was Juan de Grijalva, the same who had coasted Yucatán and discovered New Spain in 1518. Chief pilot was Diego Morillo, occasionally taken for Diego Miruelo and said to be the nephew of the pilot of that name who has been mistakenly credited with visiting the Florida Gulf coast in 1516. Shipmasters included Diego de la Serpa, Juan del Huerto, Gonzalo Gómez, Juan Martín, and Pedro Díaz de Castromocho. Juan el Griego was the chief boatswain. Captains of horse and foot were Diego de Figueroa, Gonzalo Dovalle, Gonzalo de Figueroa, and Gil González. There was also Gonzalo de Ocampo, who was Garay's brother-in-law, and a Huastec Indian who had evidently been brought home by Alvarez de Pineda and had learned Spanish well enough to serve as interpreter. One whose presence on the expedition becomes important only in the light of his later exploits was Angel de Villafañe, age 19. Years later, he was to have a part in picking up the pieces of Tristán de Luna's Florida enterprise.

Two years had elapsed since the issuance of the *cédula* authorizing Garay's venture. During that time Cortés had drained the resources of Cuba and Jamaica to support his conquest, weakening his adversaries in the process. Ships as well as men and horses had become scarce in the islands. Garay himself had sent out perhaps half a dozen vessels that failed to return, lost in the Huastec uprising or to Cortés. In Cuba, Narváez's ill-fated voyage had cost Velázquez almost all the eighteen vessels taking part.

Garay's fleet, having sailed from Jamaica, dropped anchor at the Cuban port of Jagua (Cienfuegos) to top off with fresh water, firewood, and hay for the horses. There the *adelantado* gleaned news brought by Juan Bono de Quejo that Cortés already had conquered Pánuco and established a settlement called Santiesteban del Puerto. (Bono seemed always to be turning up with bad news, or where he could stir up trouble. There is room to suspect that he may have played the role of troublemaker to some considerable degree in the Garay-Cortés confrontation.)

In response to this intelligence, Garay sought to enlist Alonso de Zuazo, an attorney in Cuba, to accompany him and serve as mediator with the Cortés faction. Zuazo, being otherwise engaged at the time, agreed to go to Mexico later and treat directly with Cortés. As it turned out, he was detained overlong in Cuba; his arrival in Mexico was delayed further by shipwreck, and he was too late to do Garay any good.

Bono de Quejo's news created division in Garay's camp. Calling his captains to council, the *adelantado* found that the majority favored continuing the voyage. He therefore named officers for his town and extracted from each an oath of fealty in opposing Cortés by whatever means necessary—a pledge given all too lightly. Yet Garay, as he issued sailing orders, happily rolled in his mind the name he had chosen for his new colony: Victoria Garayana. It had a pleasant ring.

The *adelantado* felt secure in the royal authority he carried, so explicit that not even Cortés seemed likely to contest it. But he failed to reckon with his adversary's newly won power and influence. More than a year previously, May 30, 1522, Cortés's third letter had been sent to the emperor. With the *procuradores* (proxies), Antonio de Quiñones and Alonso de Avila, went Juan de Rivera, Cortés's secretary, who knew of Garay's commission for settling Amichel; Rivera's job was to get the commission revoked. The three caravels also carried "many things rich and strange" to please His Majesty—curiosities to amuse him, as well as gold and silver idols and images to a total value of 150,000 ducats (207,000 pesos).

The ships stopped at Terceira in the Azores, where Quiñones, brawling over a woman, was done in by a stab wound. As they left the islands, French corsairs led by the notorious Jean Florin of La Rochelle fell into their wake; ten leagues short of Cape St. Vincent, the freebooters captured two of the caravels, and Avila was packed off to a French jail. Rivera, however, did reach Spain; shortly thereafter, Charles V appointed a commission to investigate the differences between Cortés and Velázquez, and Cortés emerged the clear winner. A royal *cédula* dated October 15, 1522, named Cortés governor and captain-general of New Spain. Then, on April 24, 1523, the monarch issued a "Provision of His Majesty ordering Francisco de Garay not to intrude . . . in the jurisdiction of Hernando Cortés, subject to severe penalties." The document cites statements by Rivera that Cortés had pacified eleven Huastec villages since the disaster resulting from the first attempt by Garay's designates to settle the province. It was information given before the fact, but it achieved its purpose: effective abrogation of Garay's rights in Pánuco. But while the new *cédula* was being dispatched to Cortés, Garay was on his way to that region without knowing that the document existed.

On St. John's Day, June 24, 1523, Garay's ships hoisted sail and doubled Cabo San Antón into the Gulf of Mexico, aided by the Caribbean current and a brisk southerly wind. The *adelantado* paced the rolling deck with visions of glory to be won at Victoria Garayana. Not until July 25, feast day of Spain's patron St. James, did the ships make landfall on the western Gulf shore. The southerly wind and current had carried them farther north than expected; they landed not at the Río Pánuco but at the river presently known as the Soto la Marina, some ninety nautical miles up the coast. Safely anchored in the river mouth, Garay would have chosen to settle there, but he let himself be overruled by his officers, who preferred the Pánuco. The *adelantado* was to pay a dear price for his lack of firmness.

After naming the river Río de las Palmas, Garay sent his brother-in-law, Gonzalo de Ocampo, to explore it. Ocampo, in his shallow-draft brigantine carrying both oars and sail, ascended the stream 15 leagues in three days—almost to the present Soto la Marina townsite. He saw it as a wild, unpopulated land, inhospitable for settlement.

Other exploring parties went out into the country to find many strange phenomena but little of real importance. Most impressive was "a quadruped a little larger than a cat, with the face of a wolf, silver colored, scaly, and caparisoned as the armed cuirassier going into battle caparisons his horse. A sluggish creature, it folded itself up like a hedgehog or a tortoise on seeing a man at a distance and allowed itself to be caught." The captured armadillo was taken to one of the ships, where, unattended, it died of starvation.

Upon Ocampo's return, preparations were made for proceeding to the Pánuco. Provisions were running low, and Garay decided to take the horses, already weak from the voyage, and march overland while Grijalva sailed the ships along the coast. All those who recalled this march in later years spoke of it in terms of severe hardship and hunger.

"We have come to the land of misery," one man wrote to a friend in Spain, "where there is no order whatsoever but everlasting toil and all the calamities that treat us so cruelly: hunger, the heat, malignant mosquitoes, foul bedbugs, vicious bats, arrows, vines that encircle, mudholes and swamps that swallow us."

It was a grueling trek through marshlands, the troop constantly on guard against Indian attack. In the first three days the soldiers saw no human sign. After crossing the Río de Montalto (present-day Carrizal) by swimming and on driftwood rafts, they frightened a village of Indians to flight. From the meager stores left by the natives, they fed themselves on corn and prickly-pear tunas, described as "fragrant apples" with a bittersweet taste, useful in treating the flux. During a seemingly endless march along a coastal lagoon—the Laguna de San Andrés—they treated through their Huastec interpreter with the natives of another squalid village for rations of corn, fruits, and game birds. A flooding river swept away eight horses during the crossing; then they slogged in waist-deep water through a maze of tidal sloughs swarming with mosquitoes, the banks overgrown with snaring vines.

Arriving at the Pánuco in a bad hour, Garay called a halt to await the ships, which meanwhile had incurred disaster. Caught in a storm, four of the eleven had been lost. With nothing to eat for man or beast, Garay suspected Cortés of having stripped the country to reduce his men to helplessness. The soldiers scattered to seek sustenance in the Indian camps and villages.

Feeling Cortés's evil eye upon him, Garay sent his brother-in-law to test the spirit in his adversary's colony. Ocampo was either seduced or deceived, as other messengers to Cortés had been before him; he returned to report, falsely, that all was well and the people favorably disposed to Garay. With such words, Peter Martyr relates with characteristic eloquence, the evil star that attended the expedition descended on the Pánuco.

To get at the truth concerning Cortés's conquest of Pánuco, it is necessary to examine his letters to the emperor and sift fact from fabrication. The conqueror claims that following his first entry of Tenochtitlán, he sent the Huastec Indian taken from Alvarez de Pineda's ships to treat with the lord of Pánuco and as a result won the loyalty of the Pánuco chiefs. All would have been well, he maintains, had not Garay's expeditions (led by Alvarez) come along and disturbed the Indians. Cruel treatment of the natives caused the 1520 massacre, creating a situation that Cortés was compelled to face up to. He was prevented from doing so immediately by those misbegotten intrusions of Narváez and Tapia. Or so he tells it.

The purpose of sending his agent Rivera to Spain, Cortés explains, was to inform the emperor of his plan to pacify Pánuco, although Rivera had presented the matter as an accomplished fact. The need had been emphasized not only by the massacre of Garay's first settlers but also by the slaying of an entire ship's crew wrecked on the Huasteca coast— not to mention the fact that one of the best ports on the entire Gulf coast lay within the mouth of the Pánuco. The killings, Cortés would have us believe, were all a mistake. The Indians had acted on knowledge that the intruders were not of his company; if Cortés would send his own people, the natives would gladly serve them.

Again Cortés readied an expedition. Again his plans changed when a ship from Cuba—Juan Bono de Quejo again?—brought word that Garay had joined forces with Velázquez and Diego Columbus with purposes inimical to him. Fearing another attempt on his domain like that made by Narváez in 1520, he decided to take to Pánuco an even larger force under his personal command.

Cortés's story of having received an oath of fealty from the Pánuco natives prior to this time is doubtful. In all likelihood this was to be his first real contact with the Huastecs. Its motivation was greed; its objective, to usurp Garay's claim, which was legitimately based on Alvarez de Pineda's discovery.

Not long after the death of his wife in November 1522 (he would later be accused of her murder), Cortés marched from the capital with a force given as 120 horse, 300 foot, some artillery, and up to 40,000 native warriors from the environs of Mexico. The army descended the Moctezuma River, a drainage of the Valley of Mexico flowing northeastward to the Pánuco. At Coxcatlán, 20 leagues from Tampico, it first encountered resistance. Confronted by a sizable Huastec force, Cortés called for peaceful submission. Jeers, then a vigorous attack, came in answer. But the Huastecs had chosen their battlefield unwisely; it was a level plain, and the Spanish cavalry quickly put them to rout. The army moved on to Chila, a charred ruin that marked the fatal encounter of Alvarez de Pineda and his companions with the Huastecs.

Cortés ferried men and horses across the river at night to engage the Indians and deal them their first defeat. Other battles followed, with similar results, until the natives sued for peace. At an abandoned town three leagues down the river from Chila, the soldiers came upon a gruesome sight. Displayed on native oratories were the skins of "the shameless Spaniards" who had died with Alvarez de Pineda, preserved with hair and beards intact. Some were even recognizable to those who had known them in the islands.

With the province finally at peace, Cortés sent soldiers to explore every part of it. Unfortunately, he neglects to pass along their reports. Santiesteban del Puerto was founded near the present town of Pánuco, Veracruz; municipal officers were named, and the native villages assigned to the 130 men who wished to settle.

By the time Garay arrived in August, 1523, Cortés had long since returned to the capital. Pedro de Vallejo, in charge at Santiesteban del Puerto, hastily sent a messenger to Mexico. What happened next is recorded in a mass of juristic documents calculated not so much to satisfy the notorious Spanish concern for legal form as to bamboozle and frustrate Garay. The first of these, entitled "Notification made in the Villa de Santiesteban del Puerto to Francisco de Garay," reveals the happenings of August 22.

The public notary of Santiesteban, Cristóbal Ortega, presented allegations against Garay to the Council of Justice and the magistrates: Garay's men had stationed themselves at the Pánuco pueblo and were making sallies throughout the territory conquered by Cortés a year previously ("more or less"), stirring up the natives and inciting them to rebellion. Since Garay had ignored every summons to appear in San-tiesteban, it was necessary to proceed against him at his headquarters in the Pánuco pueblo.

Garay, as "*adelantado*, governor, and captain-general of this prov-ince of Victoria Garayana and other territories discovered by him," re-sponded the same day. The summons, he said, lacked effect and value, as it was made by persons without due authority; it therefore was not necessary to account to them for his coming to these regions, which had been discovered by him in the name of Their Majesties. He never-theless explained that, with His Majesty's license and at his own cost, he had sent four ships to discover them. On this voyage (Alvarez de Pineda's) no one had gone ashore on land claimed by someone else. Thus his ships had discovered from the other side of the Río del Es-píritu Santo to the Río de San Pedro y San Pablo. Beyond the latter river he had recognized the discoveries of Diego Velázquez, as shown on the chart that had been made following the voyage. This discovery, he continued, had been recognized by His Majesty in making him *ade-lantado* and granting him the lands discovered, as shown by the royal order he carried.

Since coming overland from the Río de las Palmas, Garay said, he had merely been awaiting the arrival of his ships and in no manner had he been disturbing the land and inciting the natives. He had obeyed the royal stipulations given him, treating with them in peace and love. They had remained tranquil in their villages, informing him that they wished to be His Majesty's vassals, voluntarily sharing their sustenance with his men. On the other hand, he had found some pueblos already burned, the Indians already stirred up; they had come to him com-plaining of the damage done them by other Spaniards.

Garay's error was the same as Velázquez had made: as a gentleman himself, he relied on gentlemanly conduct from his adversary, unaware that such was not in the nature of Hernando Cortés. Admitting none of the charges leveled against him, the *adelantado* stood on his rights under his royal commission. He had no way of knowing that that par-ticular royal rug had been royally yanked from under him.

When the news of Garay's arrival at Pánuco reached Cortés, the supreme conqueror took it as confirmation of the report he had re-ceived from Cuba: Garay indeed had formed an alliance with Veláz-quez and Diego Columbus. Vallejo's messenger informed him that several days after Garay's arrival, a caravel had come from Cuba with certain "friends and servants" of Velázquez and the second Admiral, as well as one lackey of the bishop of Burgos, Rodríguez de Fonseca. The bishop's representative, it was said, claimed a commission as agent for Yucatán—a threat to another of the territories on which Cortés had designs; indeed, he was already preparing expeditions under Cristóbal de Olid and Pedro de Alvarado to Chiapas, Honduras, and Guatemala, of which Yucatán seemed but an island adjunct. Peeved at the necessity of canceling those plans, the conqueror sent Alvarado marching for Pánuco instead.

Cortés himself, nursing a broken arm received in a fall from his horse, planned to follow shortly and in fact did begin the march two days later. He had gone but ten leagues when he learned of the opportune arrival of important documents from Spain, the fruit of Juan de Rivera's lobbying with the Crown. One was the royal *cédula* of October 15, 1522, naming Cortés governor and captain-general of New Spain; another, the royal provision of April 24, 1523, enjoining Garay against interfering in Cortés's territory—of which Garay at this point had no knowledge.

With such authority, it no longer seemed necessary to undertake the journey himself; instead, Cortés sent Diego de Ocampo to present a copy of the royal provision to Garay. While Ocampo held the office of *alcalde mayor* at Tenochtitlán, it hardly seems likely that Cortés was unmindful of his relationship to Garay's brother-in-law; Diego and Gonzalo de Ocampo were brothers. Diego, Cortés further claims, also carried instructions for Alvarado not to approach Garay's camp and risk provoking an incident. If so, the order arrived a bit late; Alvarado had come upon Captain Gonzalo Dovalle's cavalry company encamped at an Indian village. Dovalle's men, taken by surprise, laid down their arms. In true form, Cortés made much of the incident, alleging that the Garay forces were using their Huastec interpreter to incite the Indians against him by spreading the word that they had come to drive the Cortés forces out.

Garay's ships, meanwhile, had stood at the mouth of the river some two months, hesitant to enter for fear of being seized. By Cortés's version, they were poised like pirates, ready to strike Santiesteban. When Vallejo ordered them into the port, only those of masters Martín and Díaz de Castromocho responded. Going in those vessels to persuade the others, Vallejo was fired on by Grijalva, who doubtless regarded Cortés much as Cortés regarded Velázquez. The fleet commander, unsupported by the other ships, relented and was jailed for his impudence. All the ships sailed up the river to Santiesteban, where their crews went ashore. The net tightened about Garay.

Cortés's men, now armed with their leader's new authority, used it to bully Garay. Upon his arrival, September 23, Diego de Ocampo had a transcript of the royal provision. On October 4 he called on the *adelantado* at the pueblo of Chiachacata and had it read to him by the notary Francisco de Orduña. Garay then was made to take the instrument in his hands, kiss it, place it on his head, and swear to abide by it. All Garay's men were ordered to bring their arms and horses, join their leader, and leave the country. They might settle, if they liked, on the Río del Espíritu Santo.

Garay, however, proved more than a little stubborn. He had come in all good faith, he informed Ocampo, to settle in the king's name, with what he had believed to be good and legal authority. Then came Pedro de Alvarado, acting on Cortés's behalf, to seize his ships, arrest their captain, and disperse their crews, with the result that the ships' stores were pillaged and the vessels themselves destroyed. Alvarado further had kept Dovalle's men at Santiesteban without sustenance, forcing them to trade their horses and arms for food to avoid starvation. The rest of his men, Garay claimed, had scattered for fear of similar arrest and could no longer be assembled. For such abuse he blamed the imagined but baseless alliance with Velázquez. Since he had been treated so badly by the king's subjects, in a land that he had legitimately discovered and come to settle on His Majesty's own authority, the royal provision could have no effect unless his people, ships, arms, and provisions were restored.

Ocampo delegated Rodrigo Rangel, the chief constable, to gather up Garay's men, return the horses and arms taken in trade, and provision the ships so that the *adelantado* and his men might be gone from Pánuco as quickly as possible. Seeing the emaciated condition of the men as they began to appear, Garay appealed to Rangel to feed them until they could leave. Rangel arranged meals and lodging at the pueblo of Tocalula, held in *encomienda* by Juan de Busto, but admonished them against molesting the Indians.

Then came a petition from eleven of Garay's men, protesting the order by which all who had come with the *adelantado* "must again embark with him, to go and settle at the Espíritu Santo, which they say is two hundred leagues from here," and setting forth serious grievances against their leader. The origin of this document is gravely suspicious. Doubtless there were men among Garay's force who had nourished misgivings that they might be called upon to fight Spaniards rather than Indians; on the other hand, Garay's complement surely included some who craved the opportunity to join Cortés and share the riches of New Spain. Whatever the petition's motivation, it is shot with doubtful claims and, in certain passages, precisely echoes the Cortés party line. There is reason to believe, at worst, that the deponents were solicited, the petitioners seduced with gold or gilded promises; at best, that it was a somewhat contrived gesture, of questionable value in gauging either Garay's character or his judgment.

In the dozen or more points, the soldiers protested their failure to receive pay, the condition of the ships, and the lack of provisions for the proposed new voyage. They had fulfilled their obligation by coming to the Pánuco, and Garay had no authority to take them anywhere else. There were not, they claimed, enough people or horses to undertake a new settlement; many had died of hunger, and most of those remaining were hiding out to avoid sailing again with Garay, so bad was the treatment the *adelantado* had accorded them from the beginning. So skimpily had the voyage been provisioned that it seemed Garay's purpose to see them die of starvation rather than settle, in fulfillment of the promises he had made the Crown. In recompense for their hardships, their leader had accorded them verbal abuse, calling them vulgar names customarily spoken only "to slaves and Negroes." When on the march from Las Palmas the Indians had brought guavas to relieve their hunger, Garay had tossed the fruit into the air and let it fall to the ground before his starving men—this to make them grovel before the Indians to show his power. Through the interpreter, he had represented himself as the lord, the other Spaniards as his slaves.

The protestors on the one hand complained of Garay's pacific approach to the Indians and his refusal to let the men pillage the native villages and cornfields to feed themselves; on the other they faulted his refusal to consider that "if the Indians had not been at peace, having been pacified as they were [by Cortés], they would have killed us all." The soldiers had been reduced to such a state by hunger and rendered so vulnerable in crossing the marshes that a hundred warriors might easily have wiped them out. In that sense they owed their lives to the Lord Governor Cortés, who had pacified the province and established a Spanish settlement to keep it safe.

Cortés himself could not have said it better.

Garay, knowing their feelings, the soldiers feared, would lead them all to their deaths and die with them for the sake of vengeance. Even if the *adelantado* had a willing and able force, he could not succeed, they maintained, for he was totally inept at waging war in these regions, failing to perceive the difference between the Huastecs and the island Arawaks.

Whether or not the petitioners were suborned, it is evident that they were well informed on what their judges wanted to hear. Certain passages, hollow echoes of Cortés, cast doubt upon the entire document. Assuredly, Garay was not in Cortés's league; he was not a soldier. Rather, he seems to have been an honest man who was driven out of his element by ambition beyond his abilities, or by financial necessity.

Faced with the petition, Garay conceived a new plan. First, he went to Santiesteban to inspect his ships. He found them by no means ready for sea. In addition to the four vessels lost on the voyage from the Río de las Palmas, another had sunk in the port; the rest were making water badly, and the provisions they had brought had long since been used up or stolen. Not for many days could the ships be put in condition to sail. The pilot Morillo and several of the shipmasters supported his appraisal: the ships lacked proper caulking as well as sails and rigging, had foul bottoms, and were otherwise in bad repair. By no means could they carry horses; it was doubtful, even, that they could make it out of the river mouth to the Gulf. To assuage his mutinous men while avoiding the risk of going to sea in leaky ships, Garay proposed marching back to the Río de las Palmas to settle there.

The plan struck no favor with either Rangel or Ocampo. At the least, Cortés must be consulted first. Ocampo sent a messenger to advise the governor and captain-general that he was bringing Garay to Mexico. Cortés's reply exuded hospitality. As they proceeded toward the capital, Ocampo served as tour guide to impress the wonders of New Spain on his guest. Garay beheld the sights with appropriate awe at Huachinango, Otumba, and Texcoco, marveling at the magnificent buildings and other sights "impossible to believe if one had not seen them."

In Mexico, Garay was hospitably treated while he negotiated with Cortés for colonization rights on the Río de las Palmas. They came to an agreement and, in the manner of royalty, sealed it by betrothing Cortés's illegitimate *mestiza* daughter (yet a child) to Garay's son. Garay found in the capital an old friend whose fortunes had suffered of late: Pánfilo de Narváez, who had been Cortés's prisoner for some two and a half years. Don Pánfilo had heard of Garay's boast that he would never be taken as Narváez had been, goading his men to show more courage than had Velázquez's lieutenant. But now the two were in much the same plight. Garay interceded with Cortés for Narváez's release, and the latter returned to Cuba, probably early in 1524. In that, he came off better than Garay.

Cortés, meanwhile, was asked to decide the disposition of certain suspicious persons of Garay's company still in Pánuco. These "friends and servants of Diego Velázquez" continued to stir up trouble by their intemperate remarks. The governor found authority in his royal orders to expel them from the province as "scandalous persons." In this class were Gonzalo de Figueroa, Alonso de Mendoza, Antonio de la Cerda, Juan de Avila, Lorenzo de Ullóa, Juan de Medina, and Juan de Grijalva. They were rounded up and put on a ship for Cuba. Only Grijalva, it seems, was given an alternative: he was to receive 2,000 pesos for his return to Cuba; or, if he wished to remain in New Spain, he would be provided everything necessary for him to come to Mexico. He chose to return to Cuba. Thus ended Grijalva's involvement in discovery and exploration in the Gulf of Mexico. Not content to stay in Cuba, he soon went to Honduras, where in 1526 he was slain in a native uprising at the pueblo of Olancho. (Las Casas calls it the valley of Ulanche and mistakenly puts it in Nicaragua.)

Following Garay's departure from Pánuco for Mexico in late October, a major Indian uprising occurred. Cortés, in characteristic form, blamed the disaster on Garay's followers: having scattered in the wilds to avoid going with their leader on a new venture, he says, they committed intolerable atrocities on the natives. One source claims that Cortés ordered the Huastecs to kill Garay's men. For whatever reason, the natives began waylaying the roving bands of Spaniards, and emboldened by success, they decided to rid the province of intruders altogether. From 250 to 500 Spaniards, including many of Cortés's own men, are said to have been sacrificed and eaten.

With the colony in danger of being wiped out, Cortés sent Gonzalo de Sandoval with 50 horsemen, 100 crossbowmen and musketeers, four fieldpieces, and several thousand Mexican and Tlaxcalan allies. Sandoval reached Santiesteban just in time to save the beleaguered garrison of 122 men from annihilation. Joining his force with the defenders, he waged brutal war on the Huastecs. Some 400 captured chiefs and principal warriors, having confessed their part in the revolt, were burned alive with their sons as witnesses.

In Mexico, meanwhile, Garay and Cortés attended midnight mass on Christmas Eve, then breakfasted together in Cortés's home. Shortly afterward, Garay became violently ill and took to his bed. Within three days he was dead.

Quite naturally, Cortés was suspected of having poisoned his adversary; in truth, however, he no longer had reason to wish Garay dead. Cortés himself attributes Garay's death to grief and guilt brought on by news of the bloody uprising in Pánuco, where his son remained. Cristóbal Pérez, Garay's friend from Jamaica who attended him on his deathbed, exonerates Cortés but disputes his diagnosis; the cause of death, he says, was *enfermedad de costado*, which the medics called pleurisy—doubtless pneumonia.

With both Narváez and Garay out of the way, Cortés ruled the field. Velázquez was past contending with him, for he had been leashed by order of King Carlos himself. He had not yielded easily. On receiving news of Narváez's defeat at Cempoala, he resolved to go to New Spain and deal with Cortés personally. To that end he armed and manned seven or eight ships and set sail along the south Cuban shore, but arriving in sight of Yucatán, he decided to heed the counsel of the licentiate Alonso de Parada and return to Cuba. He remained deeply grieved by the wrongs Cortés had done him. His suffering reached a peak when in May, 1523, the royal *cédula* naming Cortés governor and captain-general of New Spain was publicly proclaimed in Santiago de Cuba; Velázquez was forbidden either to go or to send people or ships to the territory he had claimed as his own discovery. The proclamation was "a manifest beginning, yet a final conclusion," of Velázquez's total perdition. He obeyed the royal command, but sent Manuel de Rojas to

Spain to seek redress. He determined to go himself to the royal court the following year to give the emperor his own version of the Cortés affair and to relate to the Crown his own services, which he had rendered at great cost. But like Garay's final plans to establish his colony of Victoria Garayana on the Río de las Palmas, Velázquez's last strategy was overruled by death; it was a strange parallel to the bitter end of Hernández de Córdoba, in which Velázquez had played a part.

Of all the island conquistadors who had helped to carry discovery and exploration into the Gulf of Mexico, only Narváez was left. Soon he, too, would embark on one last disastrous fling to the North American mainland. The efforts of these ambitious men bred results far different from their visions.

NOTES AND SOURCES

Garay's Voyage

Peter Martyr (Anglería, *Décadas*, 523–27, 569–83) gives the most comprehensive account of Garay's voyage to Las Palmas and his march thence to Pánuco. His source is Cristóbal Pérez, who was Garay's close companion during the journey and the subsequent trip to Mexico.

Garay's own accounting of the makeup of his fleet is in *CDI*, 28:501.

Martyr and Manuel Toussaint (*La conquista*) provide the names of expedition personnel, and Toussaint appends to his work a number of documents dealing with the episode.

Donald E. Chipman (*Nuño de Guzmán and the Province of Pánuco in New Spain, 1518–1533*) treats the Garay expedition in his discussion (ch. 2) of the discovery and conquest of Pánuco.

The Huastecs and Pánuco Province

At the time of the Conquest, says Gordon F. Ekholm (*Excavations at Tampico and Pánuco in the Huasteca, Mexico*, 329), the Huastecs "lived in that pocket of warm lowlands formed by the lower valley of the Pánuco and its tributaries which extends inland slightly more than 100 km." They spoke a Mayan dialect, although they were separated from the Maya by the Totonacs of central Veracruz and various Nahuatl-speaking peoples of southern Veracruz, Tabasco, and Chiapas. Noting an absence of typical Mayan remains in Huasteca, Ekholm concludes that the relationship between the two existed before development of the typical Mayan culture.

Chipman (*Nuño de Guzmán*, 19) observes that the boundaries of Pánuco (or Huasteca) are somewhat vaguely described in sixteenth-century documentation. To compound this uncertainty, it should be added, latter-day interpreters have tended to confuse the Pánuco River with the border of Pánuco province, somewhat farther south; for example, the Grijalva voyage of 1518 and Montejo's the following year reached the borders of Pánuco (meaning the southern boundary of the province); it has often been assumed that they reached the Pánuco River.

Alonso de Zuazo

Both López de Gómara and Díaz del Castillo tell of Zuazo's shipwreck on the voyage to New Spain to represent Garay with Cortés. The two differ somewhat in the details. The ship struck a reef on the Campeche Bank, which Juan Orozco y Berra (*Apuntes*, 9–10) identifies as the Triángulos, rather than the Alacrán reefs indicated by Díaz. The ship broke up, and crewmen constructed a boat of her timbers. Four men then sailed to Medellín, which had been relocated near the mouth of the Jamapa River to serve as New Spain's principal port. When Zuazo at last reached Mexico, he was courted and bribed by Cortés until he succumbed to his blandishments and joined his camp.

Rivera's Mission

The Cortés letters, López de Gómara, and Díaz del Castillo discuss various aspects of the Avila-Quiñones-Rivera voyage. Two live jaguars among the curiosities being sent to the king seem to have provided forebodings of the disasters that befell Quiñones and Avila: they broke out of their cage, and one was shot; the other sprang among the crew and slashed two men fatally before leaping to its own death in the ocean.

Avila wrote to the Crown from his prison cell in La Rochelle, June 16, 1523 (AGI, Patronato 267-1-1, ff. 1–2). López de Gómara chronicles the results of Rivera's lobbying with the Crown (*Cortés*, 328–29), supported by various documents; see especially the "Provision" ordering Garay not to intrude upon Cortés, published by Toussaint (*La conquista*, 203–205).

The Garay-Cortés Confrontation

The "Provision" set the stage for Cortés to badger Garay. When the Crown learned that Garay had been permitted to sail, it addressed a sharp rebuke, dated Dec. 27, 1523, to the Audiencia de Santo Domingo, ordering restraints on both Garay and Cortés (royal *cédula* to the Audiencia of Santo Domingo, *CDI*, 13:494–501). But the confrontation had already occurred, and Garay had met his destiny.

The "Notifications," or *requerimiento*, of Aug. 22, 1523, and Garay's reply are in *CDI*, 28:497–504.

Cortés's allegation that a representative of Bishop Rodríguez de Fonseca claimed a commission as agent for Yucatán refers to Bernaldino Iñíguez, late of the Hernández de Cordoba voyage, who, having first been assigned as *veedor* of Yucatán only to be frustrated by Cortés, was appointed treasurer of Pánuco in May, 1523 (*CDI*, 12:204–13; Chipman, *Nuño de Guzmán*, 98).

The series of documents in Toussaint's appendices (pp. 203–36), plus Cortés's letters, Díaz del Castillo, and López de Gómara tell of Garay's difficulties with Cortés's representatives and his own men.

Cortés's claims concerning his early contact with the Huastec Indians of Pánuco province have been gleaned from his letters; the final act of conquest occurred soon after the death of his wife. Doña Catalina's mother and her brother, Juan Suárez, brought charges against Cortés for her murder (see *CDI*, 26:298).

The letters also tell of the second Huastec uprising, which Cortés blames on atrocities committed by Garay's men against the natives. It was Juan de Burgos who claimed Cortés incited the Huastecs to kill Garay's men. Burgos, after joining the Conquest, became Cortés's bitter enemy. He made this and various other charges against the conqueror in Cortés's *residencia* some years later (see *CDI*, 26:503–507; 27:294). Martyr (*Décadas*, 577); López de Gomara (*Cortés*, 312); and Díaz del Castillo (*Historia verdadera*, 2:113) all discuss the uprising, variously placing the number of Spaniards slain at 250 to 500.

Other documentation on this affair and various matters related to the Garay expedition includes Juan de Ojeda, "Probanza" (Compostela de la Nueva Galicia, June 26, 1557, AGI, Patronato 61-1-3), and Blas Pérez, "Ynformación de los servicios hechos por Blas Pérez" (Mexico [City], 1536, AGI, Patronato 55-3-5). Ojeda tells of the landing at the Río de las Palmas in "unsettled, deserted land" and of the overland march to Pánuco, during which the soldiers "suffered very great labors and hunger because the coast was full of rivers and swamps and lacking food and all necessary things." He relates that "more than three hundred Spaniards" were killed in the uprising. Pérez echoes Ojeda concerning the hardships and tells of a five-day siege the Indians laid to Santiesteban del Puerto. He describes the suffering and hunger but gives no casualty figure.

Juan de Grijalva

D. I. Garcia Icazbalceta (*Obras*, 4:318), while denying Grijalva's kinship to Diego Velázquez, credits his participation in the Garay affair and fixes the time and place of his death. There are numerous indications of Grijalva's presence in Cuba following his 1518 voyage, including his witnessing of Vázquez de Ayllón's dealings with Velázquez over the Narváez voyage early in 1520. Like Vasco Porcallo de Figueroa, our Grijalva was a citizen of Trinidad de Cuba. Early in 1522, Porcallo—as lieutenant chief justice of Trinidad, Sancti Spíritus, and Havana—took twenty armed and mounted men to Sancti Spíritus "sworn to do what they were ordered . . . to quell the uprising and scandals occurring there in imitation of the *comunidades* rebellion in Spain." Grijalva was one of the group (Vasco Porcallo de Figueroa, "Declaración," Santiago de

Cuba, Feb. 28, 1522, in Buckingham Smith, ed., *Colección de varios documentos para la historia de la Florida y tierras adyacentes*, 45–46; "Juramento de Basco Porcallo de Figueroa," Trinidad, Dec. 28, 1522, AGI, Santo Domingo 77, ramo 2, no. 35.) Las Casas (*History*, 224) saw Grijalva in Santo Domingo in 1523, probably at the conclusion of the Garay affair, "a needy and broken man." Afterward, he entered the service of Pedrarias Dávila and lost his life in Honduras (or Guatemala, as is often stated). Díaz del Castillo (*Historia verdadera*, 2:206), who claims to have served with Grijalva in 1518, refers to Garay's captain as "a captain called Grijalva"—hardly the way he would be expected to describe his own former leader.

—◄{ CHAPTER 9 }►—

Learning the Secrets:
Honduras to Nueva Galicia, 1521–35

Dᴜʀɪɴɢ four centuries of Spanish presence in the New World, the continuing process of exploration had four basic kinds of motivation: scientific, military, economic, and religious. All four were in operation to greater or lesser degree from the first Discovery throughout the colonial period, often in combination. Not until the late eighteenth century did purely scientific expeditions become popular. Yet hardly any exploratory endeavor was devoid of scientific concerns, for science almost always figured into both economic and defensive, or military, considerations, as well as the religious *entradas* aimed at rescuing "lost souls." In short, the key to successful occupation of conquered territory lay in "learning its secrets," as the explorers so often expressed it in their *relaciónes*. They acquired knowledge while seeking material riches.

Whenever there was a lull in the Conquest, Cortés sent soldiers into the hinterlands to seek the mines whence came the Aztec treasure, and along the seacoast to look for a suitable port. Always, they were instructed to observe the country's nature and resources: mineral wealth, building materials, soil fertility, and flora and fauna. In his *Cartas de relación*, the conqueror included descriptions of the new land. With one of his letters he is said to have sent a map of the Gulf of Mexico showing the entire coastline, second in this regard only to the Alvarez de Pineda sketch.

Cortés's dreams embraced not only his immediate continental environs but also the vast unknown territory to the north; not only the western Gulf shore but also that northern segment which—to his great irritation—was wont to appear on maps as Tierra de Garay, and even the eastern Florida shore reaching northward as far as the Baca-

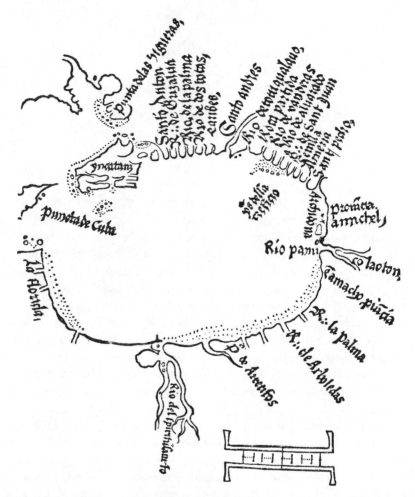

Fig. 5. Map attributed to Cortés. Reprinted from Winsor, *Narrative and Critical History.*

laos of the Cabots' discoveries; not only the North Sea but the South Sea as well. His plans were enough to stagger the wildest imagination. But he was a rare individual, in whom the elements of great vision were combined with the dauntless energy and unwavering ruthlessness required for fulfillment. Seldom has the human race produced his equal in genius, drive, and avarice.

A motivation for the conqueror's exploration arose from Diego Velázquez's influence with the royal adviser Juan Rodríguez de Fonseca, who had been known to undercut those not in his favor. On several occasions Cortés sent money to Spain to pay for arms that never came. He suspected intervention by the venal bishop with the Casa de Contratación in Seville. Not to be outdone by bureaucrats, he sent men into the country to look for copper for making bronze artillery. A small quantity of tin was discovered at Taxco, and when it was mined, significant iron deposits were found. The next problem was to locate powder ingredients. With saltpeter abundantly available, an anonymous daredevil was lowered more than 400 feet into Popocatépetl's smoking crater to bring out a quantity of sulfur. Considering the danger involved, Cortés hoped that the imperious bishop would be restrained from obstructing his shipments in the future.

Returning to Mexico from the Pánuco conquest, Cortés proceeded south along the coast, hoping to find a solution to a persistent problem: the lack of suitable port facilities. After visiting Villa Rica—where many ships had been lost in the exposed anchorage—Cortés spent several days tramping out the shifting dunes around San Juan de Ulúa. He then moved on down the coast two leagues to a narrow bay fed by the Jamapa and Atoyac rivers, where he discovered "a very good site, with all the qualities required for settling." Exploring the estuary at present Boca del Río, Veracruz, Cortés found little more than a fathom of water over the bar, the pass choked with driftwood. Yet, with removal of the drift and cleaning of the channel, barges could traverse it to discharge cargo at the projected town's portals. Here, he believed, was the remedy for the continuing problem of servicing the ever-increasing fleets plying between Spain and New Spain of the Ocean Sea.

Villa de Medellín had been founded hardly a year previously in the native province of Tuxtepec, twenty leagues inland on the headwaters of the Río Papaloapán. Its future in that isolated location seemed far from bright. Cortés therefore ordered it moved to the estuary of the Río Jamapa, and nearly all the inhabitants moved with the town. By October, 1524, their houses were completed, and Cortés had given orders for cleaning the barge channel and building a house of trade. He also had a house built for himself.

The port was not ideal, for the unloading of ships was slowed by the necessity of transshipping merchandise on barges to the site two leagues up the river; but the ships themselves enjoyed a safe harbor, secure from the sudden northers that had occasioned losses at Villa Rica. "I am certain," said the town's founder and principal booster, "that it must be the best that could be had in New Spain."

Mounting restlessness and boredom with administrative affairs caused the governor to conceive new projects and plan new conquests. He longed "to know the secrets of the coast . . . between the Río Pánuco and Florida, the discovery of Juan Ponce de León, and beyond that region north as far as Bacalaos, because in that coast it is certain there is a strait to the South Sea." Whether or not the strait was found, he reasoned, the reconnaissance was bound to discover fertile lands to enrich the Crown. Cortés planned to send a fleet to search the Atlantic coast while another sought the strait from the Pacific. From one side of Mexico or the other, his men could not fail "to know the secret."

In late 1523 and early 1524, several expeditions were sent out. Pedro de Alvarado left Mexico with a force of 450 foot and horse to follow the Pacific shore to Guatemala. Another captain took 130 men to Espíritu Santo on the Coatzacoalcos to put down an Indian rebellion. Rodrigo Rangel, an *alcalde* of Mexico, waged a futile two-month campaign to subdue the Zapotecs and Mijes on the Isthmus of Tehuántepec. Cristóbal de Olid, leaving San Juan de Ulúa on January 11, 1524, with six vessels, proceeded to Havana to pick up supplies, then sailed for Cape Higueras to establish a colony. Once having landed in Honduras, Olid was to send Diego de Hurtado, his chief pilot, to run the coast south from Bahía de Ascensión looking for the sea-to-sea passage also being sought from the south by Pedrarias Dávila and Gil González de Avila. Hurtado's voyage, however, fell victim to one last devastating stroke by Diego Velázquez.

Though ailing and not far from death, Velázquez succeeded in bringing Olid into a conspiracy that would repay Cortés in some measure for his defection. Olid was persuaded to cut himself loose from the conqueror, as Cortés had done from Velázquez, and establish Honduras as his own colony. On reaching Higueras, Olid imprisoned González de Avila, who was penetrating Honduras from the south, and expelled his forces. When word of these doings reached Cortés, he sent his cousin Francisco de las Casas to arrest Olid, but Las Casas's ships, rendered helpless by storm, were blown upon the Honduras coast. He and his men were seized by Olid.

Cortés, in the absence of news, became uneasy and finally resolved to go to Honduras himself. It was an ill-considered decision that might well have cost him the Conquest if not his life. The governor put together a sizable force, consisting of 130 horsemen, plus musketeers and crossbowmen, and 3,000 Mexican Indians. Among the troop was Gonzalo de Sandoval, who recently had led the reconquest of Pánuco; the chronicler Bernal Díaz del Castillo; young Francisco de Montejo, who was to acquire experience that would prove invaluable when he joined his father in the conquest of Yucatán; and Doña Marina, to serve as interpreter. Almost two years would elapse before Cortés returned to Mexico. During that time Marina, who had borne Cortés a son and who had proved the key to the Conquest, was to marry Juan de Jaramillo and bear him a daughter.

This expedition, added to those of Olid, Alvarado, and Las Casas, left Mexico drained of manpower; hardly 200 Spaniards remained in the capital. To guard against rebellion in his absence, Cortés took with him the displaced emperor, Cuauhtémoc, and a number of his lords.

Two brigantines commanded by Simón de Cuenca were provisioned at Medellín or Villa Rica to rendezvous with the troop on the Tabasco coast. To feed the army during its march, the Indians drove a herd of swine. The entourage marched from Mexico in October, 1524, to pursue a difficult and largely unexplored land route to Cape Higueras. It proceeded via the pueblo of Orizaba, where Doña Marina's marriage to Jaramillo took place, and thence to Villa del Espíritu Santo on the Río Coatzacoalcos.

At Espíritu Santo, Cortés received word of trouble in Mexico, where mutiny threatened those left in charge. There was little he could do short of turning back. In a feeble gesture, he sent two other lieutenants with authority to deal with the matter, thereby compounding the difficulty.

At the Coatzacoalcos, Cortés sent to Tabasco and Xicalango for guides. Some wandering traders came, bringing a map painted on henequen cloth showing the route with its rivers, mountains, and towns. Unfortunately, the native mapmakers had no understanding of the difficulties of crossing horses over bogs, flooding rivers, and steep mountains. Cortés had chosen the worst route possible. A sea voyage would have been easier; so would the way of Alvarado's march down the Pacific coast. But the choice, it seems, had stemmed from Cortés's desire to explore this lush tropical country, as wild as it was beautiful.

A few leagues beyond the Coatzacoalcos, the Tonalá and Agualulco rivers were crossed in canoes, the horses and swine swimming. Such crossings robbed the expedition of the pigs, which fell prey to alligators and sharks. Then began the real travail. Adhering to the marshy coast through an area that even yet is barely accessible by automobile, the marchers found their way blocked half a league from the Gulf by a lagoon, evidently an arm of the Laguna del Carmen. Since it was too wide for the horses to swim, the Indians from Mexico built a wooden bridge close to half a mile long—"a marvelous thing to see," but the labor had exhausted the Indians. It was but a small initiation to what lay ahead.

In the next twenty leagues, the Indian workmen had to build fifty bridges over rivers and sloughs. Had it been the rainy season, Cortés observed, the route would have been impassable except in canoes. The country, though swampy, was densely populated and productive of cacao, corn, fruit, and fish. The natives, who paid tribute to the Spaniards at Espíritu Santo, were friendly.

Some distance beyond the Río de dos Bocas (San Bernabé), the expeditionists came to the populous town of Copilco. The inhabitants were not familiar with the land route the Spaniards now chose to follow, since the natives traded only by canoe. Turning away from the marshy coast, the troop went toward the mountains but still had to cross numerous swamps and streams, the horses standing precariously in canoes lashed together. Men were drowned and gear was lost. The entourage held the southward course for 125 miles, through Teapa to Ixtapa, whence the frightened natives fled. Cortés wooed them back, only to have one of the Mexican Indians threaten the peace by killing and eating an Ixtapan. He had the Mexican burned alive.

This great detour, designed to circumvent the coastal marsh, led only to greater hardship. Bent on reaching Acalán province (southwestern Campeche state), Cortés learned that the only direct route traversed more rivers and swamps. Without competent guides, the travelers marched northeast across the central lowlands of Chiapas, through forest so dense they could see only the sky immediately above them and the ground at their feet. In this dark jungle they would have become hopelessly lost but for a mariner's compass Cortés had brought and a marine pilot named Pedro López who could follow the Tabascoans' map. Hacking their way through the tangled growth to a village indicated on the map, they found it deserted. A dozen soldiers and many of the Mexicans succumbed to the hardship or, driven by hunger, were lost in the wilderness.

Crossing the Usumacinta River in canoes, the marchers lost a horse and some baggage. Then came the Río San Pedro Mártir, a seemingly impassable barrier 500 paces wide and flanked by marshes. Heavy rains pouring down on the already sodden country made retreat out of the question; the river must be crossed. From rafts, the Indian workmen managed to sink pilings in the mud. In six days they built a bridge, and the troop crossed into Maya Chontal country. In the Acalán capital of Izancanoc, whispers were heard that Cuauhtémoc and his followers were plotting to kill their captors. Cortés, already threatened with destruction by the wilderness, could not run additional risk. He ordered the emperor and two of his lords put to death.

Disaster, meanwhile, had befallen the ships, which Simón de Cuenca had brought to the port of Xicalango, near the present Zacatal ferry-crossing on the Laguna de Términos. Cortés had sent word by river for the vessels to proceed to Bahía de la Ascensión on the Caribbean coast and to send canoes thence up the estuary to Acalán with provisions. The captains of the two vessels had differences that led to a bloody encounter between their respective crews. Witnessing the event, the Indians of Xicalango and Gueyatasta finished the slaughter, then burned the ships.

Hardships still dogged Cortés's troop as it crossed the base of the Yucatán peninsula. At last reaching the Montagua River, the soldiers met Spaniards from Gil González's company and learned the result of Las Casas's confrontation with Olid: as Olid's captive, Las Casas had joined with González de Avila to overpower Olid and kill him; then Las Casas and González had marched for Mexico through southern Guatemala, by that time under Alvarado's control.

There was news also that troubles in the capital persisted. Las Casas and González, in fact, had run headlong into the turmoil there. With Cortés absent and believed dead, they were arrested on charges of murdering Olid and were conducted as prisoners to Spain by that old gadabout with an affinity for dirty work, Juan Bono de Quejo.

To deal with the unrest in Mexico, Cortés sent Sandoval and his company back over Alvarado's route. After settling matters in Honduras, he himself embarked in a brigantine which, following a storm-tossed voyage, came to anchor two leagues off San Juan de Ulúa at nightfall on May 24, 1526. Cortés went ashore in the ship's boat and walked the four leagues to Medellín alone. "Without being detected by anyone in the village," he relates, "I went to the church to give thanks to Our Lord." There he was found at daybreak by townspeople who scarcely recognized him, so harsh was the mark of hardship upon him.

The Honduras expedition marked the beginning of the end of Cortés's dominance in the land he had conquered. Hardly had he returned to Mexico when word came that Luis Ponce de León had arrived from Spain to take his *residencia*—a trial or investigation into the official conduct of royal servants, wherein all with grievances against the subject might give testimony. Cortés sent instructions to officials at Medellín, where Ponce had landed, to quarter the judge in his own house. Ponce, wary of compromising his position, declined. His coming heralded the fall of Cortés's fortunes, for the conqueror was promptly stripped of his authority as governor.

Hardly was the investigation underway when the judge became ill and died amid rumors that Cortés had poisoned him. In truth, he succumbed to a contagion that already had claimed at Medellín the lives of many who had come on his ship. The *residencia* nevertheless went on, in the hands of Alonso de Estrada, the storm center in Mexico during Cortés's absence.

Cortés continued his active interest in discovery and exploration, though largely beyond the Gulf region. In 1527 he sent Alvaro de Saavedra Cerón and three ships across the Pacific to assist the expedition of García Jofre de Loaysa, retracing Magellan's route to the Spice Islands. Cortés also explored the western coast of Mexico as far north as the Gulf of California, called Cortés's Sea. In this effort Saavedra's brother, Jorge Cerón—to appear later in connection with Luna's Florida fiasco—had a significant part. In the meantime, the territory claimed by Cortés was being diminished. Honduras, Yucatán, and Pánuco fell away.

Repeated massacres of shipwreck victims, plus Simón de Cuenca's disaster, caused Cortés to plan the conquest of the Río de Grijalva region. Another expedition also was projected to subdue the Zapotecs on the Isthmus of Tehuántepec. In September, 1526, Cortés claims to have ordered a settlement on the Río de las Palmas, north of the Pánuco "in the direction of Florida," and people were gathered for the enterprise. "I have information," he said, "that the land and port are very good." Additionally, he was sending 60 horsemen and 200 *peones* with native allies into the country of the hostile Chichimecs, between the Gulf coast and the province of Michoacán. The captains of all these expeditions were prepared to depart at about the same time, wrote Cortés in his fifth letter, dated September 3, 1526.

Before either letters or expeditions were dispatched, however, the royal quietus was put on further exploration by the conqueror. Juan de Rivera, who had been Cortés's agent to the Crown, brought the royal mandate: not only did His Majesty not require such activity, but it was contrary to his wishes. The captain-general wrote his feelings on the matter in a shorter letter dated September 11. From the thoughts expressed therein, it is evident that the great conqueror was wounded and bleeding.

Already stripped of his civil powers, Cortés felt compelled to go to Spain to exercise with the Crown whatever influence he had left. He took with him Gonzalo de Sandoval, Andrés de Tapia, and a number of other renowned conquistadors; a son of Moctezuma and a number of other lords of Mexico and Tlaxcala; "several very white Indian men and women, and dwarfs and monsters." He arrived at Palos toward the end of 1528. "The whole kingdom," says López de Gómara, "was agog with his fame and the news of his coming."

He was honored by the Crown with the title of Marqués del Valle de Oaxaca and grants of territory of his own choosing in New Spain, but his title of governor was not restored. He was, however, assured of liberty to explore the South Sea and to serve as governor of any islands and westward lands he might discover. Just before sailing, Cortés learned that a new *audiencia* had been named for Mexico. He embarked just ahead of a royal order that would have prevented his going, to reach Veracruz on July 15, 1530.

Cortés, launching his plans to explore the Pacific coast, found his efforts blocked at every turn. The new *audiencia* forbade his use of Indian labor to build ships at Tehuántepec and Acapulco. Nuño de Guzmán, who had taken over Pánuco and conquered Nueva Galicia, obstructed the ports and seized his vessels. Then the viceroy, Antonio de Mendoza, arrived in 1535 and eventually put an end to his explorations for good. Cortés again went to Spain in 1540 to plead his interests with the Crown. He never again returned to his New Spain of the Ocean Sea.

For the most part, the job still to be done there—apart from religious conversion, a concern of both church and state—was administrative. The heart of the territory had been discovered, conquered, and explored. The nature of the remaining task was spelled out to the emperor in a 1532 letter of Bishop Sebastián Ramírez de Fuenleal, president of the Audiencia de Mexico. Ramírez recorded that many opulent gold and silver mines had been discovered, and more were being revealed daily; yet much was being lost for want of craftsmen to refine the ore. Mineral salts, various drugs, and resins, all to be taken with little labor, had also been found. The need was for capable men to bring their families to settle, develop these natural resources, and become established. The whole land was pacified, from the *gobernación* of Nuño de Guzmán in Nueva Galicia to that of Alvarado in Guatemala.

True, much work remained in pushing back the frontiers and opening new areas, and in that Cortés might have made a contribution; but the Crown had long since become suspicious of his motives and doubtful of his methods. His job of conquest and exploration was finished.

There was more than a little connection between the sending of Luis Ponce de León to conduct Cortés's *residencia* and the assignment of Nuño de Guzmán as governor of Pánuco. The two sets of orders issued the same day (November 4, 1525) "were jointly to buttress crown policy in New Spain." Various cross-references between the two documents affirm the close relationship intended by the Crown.

Guzmán purchased three ships at Seville and sailed on May 14, 1526, from Sanlúcar de Barrameda. Detained at Hispaniola and Cuba by illness or intrigue, he was more than a year in reaching Pánuco. Ponce had died in the interim.

Motivated in part by his royal instructions and in part by his hatred for Cortés, Guzmán promptly revoked the *encomiendas* of the conqueror's followers. There followed a mass exodus of the earlier settlers, and the few Cortés supporters who stayed found themselves unreasonably persecuted.

Guzmán quickly became disillusioned with Pánuco, which he found impoverished for want of gold and silver, livestock, and other resources, with only the one settlement at Santiesteban del Puerto. Yet the province had one marketable commodity—Indians. Guzmán wasted little time in exploiting the natives to alleviate other economic problems. On July 8, 1527—hardly more than six weeks after his arrival—the town crier of Santiesteban pronounced the new governor's proclamation concerning the first slaving expedition, to the Río de las Palmas region. Each mounted soldier taking part would be entitled to twenty slaves; a foot soldier, to fifteen. License to export the slaves could be obtained by agreeing to exchange them for livestock.

The expedition, led by Sancho de Caniego, who had come with Guzmán from Spain, got underway shortly after the proclamation was read. It lasted four or five months. Guzmán, quite likely, knew that Pánfilo de Narváez had received royal authority the previous November for colonizing the region called Florida, encompassing all the territory above Las Palmas. Cortés-like, he may have planned a little claim-jumping before Narváez's arrival.

Caniego, after the manner of Guzmán himself, proved a cruel and heartless commander, adept at dishing out brutal treatment to his men as well as to Indian foes. Sick or injured soldiers were left to die, while Indian captives occasionally were beaten to death or shot full of arrows. Pedro de Vallejo, who had been in charge at Santiesteban del Puerto when Garay arrived there in 1523, made no secret of his loyalty to Cortés. Caniego clapped him in irons. The man was kicked and beaten by the captain until his body, black with bruises, was lifeless. The expedition itself was a signal failure. The Palmas country was deserted—just as Gonzalo de Ocampo had reported it, after his reconnaissance for Garay four years previously.

This initial disappointment notwithstanding, Guzmán was able to build a considerable slave trade. Ships plying between Pánuco and the Antilles carried Huastec slaves to exchange for the livestock needed to build an economic base for the province. The Pánuco natives thus were used in the islands to fill the void left by the Arawaks' extinction. By Guzmán's rationale, the trade benefited both his province and the Indians, who were removed from their native overlords and offered the benefits of Christianity; Pánuco needed livestock more than it needed Indians.

The provincial governor granted to certain settlers license to collect slaves, including *indios de rescate*—natives who had been enslaved by other Indians—and prisoners taken in war. The slaves, including men, women, and children over the age of six or seven, were branded on the face with a hot iron. The Río de las Palmas affair is the only known instance of an actual raid in the Pánuco region, and it netted only 300 captives. Yet from August 20, 1527, to September 6, 1529, 3,441 Indians were loaded on ships at Santiesteban. While the average slave ship carried 220 slaves, the actual cargo ranged from as low as 130 to as high as 400. Several ships sank in the mouth of the Pánuco with heavy loss of life, and many of the Indians died en route to the Antilles.

Probably in early December, 1528, Guzmán left Santiesteban for Mexico, where he was to serve as the first president of the Audiencia de Mexico. In military charge of Pánuco he left Juan de Cervantes, with specific instructions concerning the conquest of the region called Valles de Oxitipa. A year later Guzmán set out from Mexico to conquer the area that became known as Nueva Galicia. Guzmán's campaigns along the western shore and his founding the towns of Guadalajara, Compostela, Culiacán, and others lie beyond the scope of our narrative.

After winning appointment as governor of Nueva Galicia early in 1531, Guzmán moved to implement his original plan of linking that province with Pánuco. He appointed Lope de Mendoza as military commandant and governor of Pánuco, and Mendoza organized an expedition to the Valles area. Guzmán himself left the Pacific coastal region with thirty horsemen early in 1533 to search for a road through the Sierra Madre Occidental to connect the two provinces. Traversing 200 leagues, the troop was beset by countless dangers, including rain-swollen rivers; horses, mules, and Negroes were lost by drowning. Reaching his destination, Guzmán founded the town of Santiago de los Valles with twenty settlers, in the area already conquered by Mendoza. It was decreed a part of Nueva Galicia.

Guzmán returned to Santiesteban late in July, 1533. Later that year he was removed as governor of Pánuco, which reverted to the Audiencia de Mexico; his sphere was limited to Nueva Galicia. After withdrawing to Valles and thence to Compostela, he was summoned back to Mexico late in 1536 by Viceroy Mendoza, who had news that Pérez de la Torre was coming from Spain to conduct Guzmán's *residencia*.

Birthplace of discoverers. Palos de la Frontera was the hometown of the Pinzón brothers, Martín Alonso and Vicente Yáñez, captains of *Pinta* and *Niña* on Columbus's first voyage, and of Antón de Alaminos, the Gulf's pilot of discovery.

Grandeur of the Mayas. The impressive remains of the ancient city of Uxmal suggest the awe with which the first Spanish visitors to Yucatán must have viewed the decaying Mayan civilization in 1517.

Scene of the bad fight. After the conquest, Spanish fortifications replaced the Mayan at Champotón, where disaster befell Hernández de Córdoba's men in 1517.

"As grand as Seville." Thus the chaplain of the Juan de Grijalva voyage described the Mayan city of Tulum, which the voyagers saw from the sea at sunset on May 8, 1518.

Laguna de Términos. At Puerto Real, the scene is still "wild and beautiful," as it was in Grijalva's day.

Cempoala. The Totonac capital, where Cortés first allied himself with Moctezuma's enemies, today is a well-ordered compound of restored and rebuilt edifices, where local children still unearth fragments of pre-Columbian figurines.

Quiahuitzlan and Villa Rica Cove. Today a national archaeological site, the Totonac townsite overlooks the anchorage where Cortés scuttled his ships to close all roads but that of conquest.

Río Jamapa at Medellín. During the brief period that Medellín, Veracruz, served as New Spain's principal port, ships were unloaded at the mouth of the river, and the cargo taken upstream by barge. This view is downstream from ruins said to be of Cortés's house.

Nerve center. Throughout the sixteenth century, Seville, on the Río Guadalquivir, was the nerve center of Spain's commerce with the Americas. Both of
these prominent edifices, the Torre del Oro (Golden Tower) and the cathedral, were standing when Columbus discovered America.

Temple in the wilderness. This scene at Cobá, Quintana Roo, with its overgrown temple mound, typifies sights that greeted Francisco de Montejo when
he marched across the Yucatán peninsula in 1527–28.

Symbol of oppression. The conquistador on the façade of the Montejo house in Mérida, Yucatán, standing upon the heads of Indians, suggests the oppression suffered by the Mayas at the hands of the early Spaniards.

Left: Chichén Itzá. In the ruins of ancient temples was a ready supply of building stone for the Spanish conquerors. *Right*: Dominican shrine. In the Convento de San Pablo in Seville, Bartolomé de las Casas, protector of the Indians and gadfly of the conquistadores, was consecrated bishop of Chiapas in 1544.

Mission to the Maya. The ruins of this old mission at Kikil bespeak the work of the church-building Franciscans across northern Yucatán. Many of the colonial mission churches are still in use as centers of worship.

Old Tampico. Tampico Alto, eight miles south of modern Tampico, was one of several early sites of the town, which moved about because of Indian attacks and pirate raids.

When Torre arrived, he placed Guzmán in prison, to remain there until the Crown ordered his return to Castile eighteen months later.

While Guzmán stands condemned in history for inhuman brutality and venality, he made important contributions to discovery and conquest. The road he opened to connect Pánuco and Nueva Galicia was vital to the country's development. Yet he made no inroads in exploring and conquering the coastal wilderness north of Pánuco; there was to be no territorial dispute between him and Narváez over the Río de las Palmas, for that region would remain untamed for another two hundred years.

SOURCES AND NOTES

The "Cortés Map"

The map published with the August, 1524, Nuremberg edition of Cortés's second letter was the first specifically of the Gulf of Mexico to appear in print, and the first printed map to use the names of Florida and Yucatán. Questions have arisen as to whether the map actually pertained to the second letter; it could have just as well accompanied the third—or neither, for Cortés himself makes no mention of it in his reports to the Crown.

Indeed, the origin of the map data seems more definite than the map's authorship. The insular Yucatán reflects the error of the pilot Alaminos on the 1518 Grijalva voyage, which also provided most of the Spanish names along the Tabasco-Veracruz coast. Strangely, Sevilla—the name given by Cortés to Cempoala—appears, but Villa Rica de la Vera Cruz does not. Farther north, some of the features appear also on the Alvarez de Pineda map: the Río Pánuco, and the Río del Espíritu Santo in the approximate position of the Mississippi. The Florida peninsula is joined to the mainland, as Alvarez had proved it actually to be. There are a Río de Arboledas and a Punta de Arrecifes not shown on the Alvarez sketch, but there is no other known voyage prior to 1524 that might have provided them. And the Provincia Amichel, although it does not appear on the Alvarez map, is pretty certain to have originated with his voyage and was later confirmed by the Crown as the name of the region that Alvarez discovered for Garay.

Conceivably, Cortés could have heard all these names from Alvarez's men captured at Villa Rica in July or August 1519, yet it seems rather unlikely that these men would have carried around in their heads more place names than were consigned to the Alvarez de Pineda map. While the notary Guillén de la Loa took to Cortés written notification of Garay's plans to settle the region north of Villa Rica, it is doubtful that the document would have named the region's rivers and other coastal features.

Peter Martyr tells us that the name Río de las Palmas was given (to the river now known as Soto la Marina) by Garay himself in 1523. Martyr could have been wrong; Alvarez himself might have named the stream—even though he did not put it on his map—and it could have come to Cortés through the captives.

But the greatest doubts concerning the conqueror's authorship of this map are raised by the use of the name Amichel. As reluctant as he was to credit Garay's discovery, why would he acknowledge it by using on his map a name that does not appear in any of his letters?

If the map did not originate with Cortés, who then? Any answer would be only a guess—perhaps one of the proctors, excluding the first two, who left New Spain before Alvarez de Pineda arrived; perhaps Alaminos or one of the other pilots who were deposed by Cortés following the Conquest. Regardless of authorship, however, the linkage of the "Cortés Map" to that of Alvarez de Pineda is sufficiently clear to shed light on Alvarez's voyage. The Cortés map, unlike its predecessor, indicates shoals or islands extending from the Pánuco to the Río del Espíritu Santo. This representation of the barrier islands of the Texas-Tamaulipas shore and the Tiger and Trinity shoals on the Louisiana shore suggests that Alvarez viewed this sector rather closely. The absence of the Alabama-Mississippi sea islands and the failure of both maps to show the Mississippi Delta projecting into the Gulf hints that this part of the coast was seen only from afar, the Mississippi River or Río del Espíritu Santo perceived from its great discharge rather than observed close at hand. Along the Florida peninsula, on the other hand, the representation of shoals and islands, even to the Florida Keys, indicates close observation.

The publication history of the Cortés map—which we must continue to call it for want of another name—is given in Winsor, *Narrative and Critical History*, 2:403; Jean Delanglez, *El Rio del Espíritu Santo*, 14; and Cumming, et al., *Discovery*, 67.

Campaigns and Explorations

Deployment of forces to subjugate various native groups and to explore and pacify the country is discussed in Cortés's fourth letter (*Cartas de relación*, 175–206, Editorial Porrúa edition). Concerning plans to seek the strait from both oceans, Cortés neglects to reveal the extent to which the search was carried out. López de Gómara (*Cortés*, 322) says that at the same time Olid departed for Honduras in January, 1524, two ships went "to explore the coast between Pánuco and Florida" to look for a strait. At least until 1565, the Río de las Palmas marked the beginning of Florida. The area explored, therefore, might have been rather narrow, depending on López de Gómara's construction of the term.

Olid and Honduras

López de Gómara (*Cortés*, 335–77) and Díaz del Castillo (*Historia verdadera*, vol. 2) supplement Cortés's own account of Olid's betrayal and the resulting march to Honduras. Díaz relates that Doña Marina went along as interpreter because Jerónimo de Aguilar had died. In this he errs, for Aguilar gave testimony in Cortés's *residencia* in 1529 (*CDI*, 27:16, 153, 154, 224, 225, 441, 457, 567; 28:226).

Concerning Doña Marina and Jaramillo, see Mariano G. Samonte, *Doña Marina*, 81; López de Gómara, *Cortés*, 346.

The Mayas' oral history of the execution of Cuauhtémoc and the other Mexican lords, recited in 1612, is given in the Paxbolon-Maldonado Papers in France V. Scholes and Ralph L. Roys, *The Maya Chontal Indians of Acalán-Tixchel*, 391–92. The Mayas say Cuauhtémoc was beheaded rather than hanged, as López de Gómara says he was (*Cortés*, 356).

Díaz del Castillo (*Historia verdadera*, 2:199) recounts Simón de Cuenca's disaster. The plan for provisioning the march was based on the belief that the Bahía de la Ascensión or Chetumal Bay joined the Laguna de Términos to form a water passage between Yucatán and Honduras (see my ch. 4).

Villa Rica, Antigua, and Medellín

In the village of Antigua, the second site of Veracruz, is a little old chapel dating from the sixteenth century. Local legend has it that Cortés gave his thanksgiving prayer there on returning from his hazardous journey. His own account, in the fifth letter, tells it otherwise. Villa Rica de la Vera Cruz was moved from its original site to the Río Veracruz (now Río Antigua) shortly after Medellín was brought to the Río Jamapa from Tuxtepec. For several years Medellín was the principal harbor of New Spain. When Antonio de Mendoza came as the first viceroy in 1535, it was still of sufficient importance for that official to begin the building of a breakwater at the river mouth—an "expensive but necessary" project, in López de Gómara's view (*Cortés*, 406). Yet within a few years, Medellín declined. Shipping records of the 1550s accord it no mention, although a proposal was heard to relocate Veracruz at that site (García de Escalante Alvarado to the Crown, May 12, 1553, RAH, Colección Muñoz A/113, f. 270r). As traffic mounted and ships increased in size, vessels began loading and discharging cargo at San Juan de Ulúa, and lighters transported merchandise to and from Veracruz (Antigua), fifteen miles up the coast. Medellín faded.

In 1599 Veracruz was moved again, to the site adjacent to San Juan de Ulúa, where it has remained since. There it was referred to for many years as Nueva Veracruz, while the previous site was called Veracruz Antigua. Besides the colonial chapel, Antigua, as it is now called, has the ruin of an elaborate building extolled by tourist guides as the house of Cortés, although Cortés's house was at Medellín rather than Antigua. Angel de Altolaguirre y Duvale (*Descubrimiento y conquista de Mexico*, 135) nevertheless captions a photo, "Ruinas del palacio de Hernán Cortés en la Antigua Veracruz." Medellín residents have only foundation stones and the remains of a fireplace to point to as the ruins of Cortés's house.

Nuño de Guzmán

The definitive work on Guzmán in Pánuco is Donald E. Chipman, *Nuño de Guzmán*. It is Chipman who assesses the relationship of Luis Ponce de León's orders to those of Guzmán. The orders themselves are in *CDI*, 23:368, 412.

The founding of Santiago de los Valles is related in Nuño de Guzmán to the emperor, *CDI*, 13:437. See also "Relación hecha por Pedro de Carranza," 1531, *CDI*, 14:347. Guzmán's "Memoria de los servicios que había hecho Nuño de Guzmán desde que fue nombrado gobernador de Pánuco en 1525" (in *Crónica de la conquista del Reino de Nueva Galicia*, 1:189–90) tells of the march across the sierra and the founding of Valles.

An interesting sidelight on Guzmán's stopover in Hispaniola is given in a letter from the bishop-elect of Mexico, Fray Juan de Zumárraga, to the emperor (Mexico, Aug. 27, 1529, AGI, Patronato 184-1-7, f. 4v.). Guzmán, says Zumárraga, was closely allied to the Diego Velázquez faction in Cuba and in fact spent "many days" in Santiago de Cuba "in conversation and great friendship" with his kinsman Gonzalo de Guzmán, who had been Velázquez's loyal servant and now was governing the island. He was, the bishop declared, the staunch enemy of Cortés.

During his stay in the islands, Guzmán may also have laid the groundwork for trading the slaves he was to send from Pánuco.

CHAPTER 10

Grijalva's Captains:
Montejo and Avila in Yucatán, 1527–42

As Nuño de Guzmán arrived on May 24, 1527, to take charge of Pánuco, the Spanish port at Seville bustled with the activity of launching two new voyages. Pánfilo de Narváez, freed at last by Cortés, was about to undertake the exploration and conquest of the extensive territory "from the Río de las Palmas to the Island of Florida." Francisco de Montejo was fitting out for the "pacification" of Cozumel and Yucatán.

Implicit in these two expeditions was the Crown's desire to nail down its claim to the entire Gulf of Mexico perimeter. So far, only that portion between Tabasco and the Río Pánuco had been brought under any semblance of control. Little notice had been accorded the northern shore since Alvarez de Pineda had established its outline eight years previously. Yucatán, though coasted many times after Hernández de Córdoba's 1517 voyage, languished in the backwater of more momentous discovery. The two enterprises about to embark might be likened to sending a bucket of water to quench the fires of Hell.

Previous discovery voyages into the Gulf had originated in the Antilles islands, a trend now temporarily reversed. It had become necessary to go to Spain to win Crown approval, and the fitting out of a voyage there stood a better chance of escaping Cortés's ever watchful eye. Additionally, resources of the islands—Cuba, Jamaica, and Hispaniola—had been siphoned off by other conquests.

Narváez, after losing an eye and seemingly his honor in the clash with Cortés, had returned to Spain in 1525. In audiences with royal officials, he complained loudly of his treatment at the conqueror's hands—a procedure that had become quite popular among disenfranchised conquistadors. Cristóbal de Tapia was there for the same reason; so were countless others.

Montejo, after bringing the first offering of Mexican treasure to the king, had returned to New Spain in 1522 to become a citizen of the new city of Mexico. In 1524 he went again to Spain to lobby first for Cortés's interests, then his own. Just how it was that he and Narváez got together and the precise nature of their symbiotic relationship are not known. It is known that Diego Velázquez's old lieutenant added his voice to those supporting the Yucatán concession for the conqueror's erstwhile captain, and Montejo quite likely returned the favor. The Crown issued both contracts the same day, November 17, 1526, couching them in almost identical terms.

Each was to undertake his venture at his own cost. In exchange, he was to be governor, captain-general, and *adelantado* of the conquered territory for life. Arms, horses, and other needs for the colony were exempted from royal export duties, and each *adelantado* was to pay the Crown only a tenth of gold and silver found, instead of the usual fifth. He was authorized to enslave natives who rebelled against Spanish authority, as well as those held in slavery by other Indians, as *indios de rescate*. The royal purpose was to make Christians and useful citizens of the New World denizens rather than slaves. An elaborate set of regulations designed to avoid repetition of past abuses and establish the Indians' civil rights was affixed to each set of instructions, which specified that at least two clerics were to accompany each expedition. The general rules governing all future *entradas* were thus established, but sufficient reason and latitude could always be found for disregarding them.

Narváez, armed with the contract, put together an armada of five ships and 600 men, most notable of whom was his treasurer and *alguacil mayor*. This mild-mannered and enduring man, remembered for his chronicle of the epitome of all colonial disasters, was Alvar Núñez Cabeza de Vaca—more of him later.

Montejo gathered 257 officers and men, and fitted out four vessels. He chose as his chief lieutenant Alonso de Avila, who like himself had captained a ship on the 1518 Grijalva voyage, then served as one of Cortés's stalwarts. Only recently had he been released from prison at La Rochelle, following his seizure by French pirates in 1522. Named chief pilot was Antón Sánchez Calabrés, who had served Montejo as boatswain during the Grijalva voyage and again on the noted 1519 voyage to Spain.

In June, 1527, Narváez's and Montejo's fleets sailed down the Guadalquivir River to Sanlúcar de Barrameda. The two fleets probably sailed together. Both made port at Santo Domingo, where they must have found themselves in competition for men, mounts, and supplies. While Montejo recruited additional men and bought horses, Narváez spent forty-five days trying to buy steeds without finding enough to satisfy his needs. With desertion reducing his ranks, he proceeded to Cuba and was still there when Montejo founded the first settlement on mainland Yucatán. Let us forsake Narváez for the moment and follow Montejo.

The latter captain-general sailed west along Cuba's south shore, crossed the Yucatán Channel, and dropped down to Cozumel, landing place of Grijalva, Cortés, and Narváez, 1518–20. The natives of this independent Mayan *cacicazgo* were friendly. Their chief, Naum Pat, pledged allegiance to the Spaniards. Montejo, after four days, moved his ships across the channel to anchor near Xelha, not far from the ancient ruins of Tulum, where he took possession for the Crown and unloaded the ships. Relations were established with the *caciques* of Xelha and the nearby village of Zama, who contributed provisions and labor for the building of a Spanish town adjacent to the harbor half a league from Xelha. At this Salamanca, established before the end of October, 1527, and named for Montejo's birthplace in Spain, temporary dwellings of palm thatch and a headquarters and supply building went up.

Despite previous coastal voyages, the Spaniards knew no more of the Yucatán interior than Jerónimo de Aguilar had related. The townsite—hot, humid, and in close proximity to disease-breeding swamps and lagoons—proved to be the worst possible. The entire company fell ill, and forty died. Supplies dwindled rapidly, a fact that alienated not only the Spanish merchants, whose stores had to be confiscated, but also the Indians. The natives' resources were too skimpy to nurture the Spaniards indefinitely. They offered passive resistance, then open hostility, as Montejo sent armed men to seize whatever food they could find. The caravel *Nicolasa* went to New Spain for food and other needs, but the master died at Veracruz and the vessel sailed for Cuba. Montejo, like Cortés at Villa Rica, got wind of a desertion plot and, also like Cortés, destroyed the ships to forestall it and impressed the crews into his land forces. All doors were closed but that of conquest.

Leaving at Salamanca forty soldiers too ill to march, Montejo and ninety Spaniards slogged northward through swampland, hacking a path through dense brush. Disease and hunger stalked. More men died, and Montejo himself fell gravely ill. The Indians, though more populous in this region, remained invisible. They might easily have destroyed the invaders at a blow; that they did not was credited to the Mayas' fear of horses. Twenty men too ill to travel stayed at the native port town of Pole. Events of the advance might have portended a disaster like those awaiting Narváez and Hernando de Soto in Florida. But then Montejo's difficulties were mitigated by the friendly lord of Cozumel, Naum Pat. On a visit to the mainland, the *cacique* relieved the Spaniards' plight by sharing his provisions and treated with other *caciques* in their behalf for peace.

The way prepared, the Spaniards advanced to Moc-hi, farther up the coast, where they found a hundred well-built houses, and temples and shrines of carved stone. For the moment, they were welcomed. The natives provided an abundance of fowls, tortillas, and *posol*, a corn gruel flavored with honey. Moc-hi's friendly people cleared the road, and the Spaniards entered a still more populous country to reach the capital and trade center of Ecab, on an eminence high above the sea near Cabo Catoche—the Gran Cairo of the Hernández de Córdoba expedition.

Montejo made the most of the friendly reception. The native lords summoned *caciques* of other districts to visit the Christians and see them perform feats of horsemanship, carefully calculated in the Spanish mind to strike terror into their souls. Montejo and Pedro de Añasco, already with considerable knowledge of the native language, received gifts of jeweled gold necklaces. Thus were born visions of great wealth, just as a golden rattle in a native village of Florida would stir the gold lust of Narváez and spur him on to tragedy.

During two months at Ecab, Montejo established friendly relations with neighboring *caciques* while his ailing men recovered. He kept his soldiers in close discipline, and the only instance of unpleasantness did not involve the Indians. The *alguacil mayor*, Hernando Palomino, flew into a rage and killed one of his own servants. He was tried and executed.

From Ecab the Spaniards marched for Conil, eight leagues west on a large bay. The first part of the trek lay through a rich agricultural area, with tree-lined paths, populous towns, and friendly people. Then came a five-league stretch of barren, uninhabited country. But the hospitable people of Conil, advised of the Spaniards' coming, had provided sustenance in an unusual manner: at half-league intervals they had placed food caches and canoes converted to watering troughs, from which both men and horses drank. Basking in such friendliness, Montejo kept his force at Conil two months while exploring adjacent territory.

Conil, with 5,000 houses, was one of the principal towns of Ecab province, supported by a prosperous agriculture and fronting the best harbor yet seen in Yucatán. Fresh water gurgled to the surface of the bay just off shore. In disbelief, the Spaniards rode their horses out into the saltwater cove, and the animals drank from the amazing fresh current.

Ending this pleasant sojourn toward spring 1528, the Spaniards skirted the large inlet and traveled west to Cachí, a seat of justice with a plaza-centered marketplace offering a variety of goods. A large pole in the middle of the plaza resembled the gibbet of Spanish towns, but with a difference: thieves and adulterers were nailed to the post alive. After two days the march was resumed, into Chikinchel province, through well-tended fields and lush savannas studded with trees that yielded copal, the fragrance burned before Mayan idols. At the first town, Sinsimato, the ominous scent hung heavy in the air. The Spaniards passed an uneasy night and hastened away at daybreak.

Two or three leagues farther on, they came to Chauaca, Chikinchel's principal town, so large that they spent most of the afternoon getting from the outskirts to the *cacique*'s palace. Chauaca was situated on a large freshwater lake—Laguna de Lagartos—just west of Conil Bay. It had an abundance of freshwater ponds and watercourses, and large buildings of carved stone. Its people had reason for holding themselves superior to other Mayas in culture and intelligence, yet while receiving the Spaniards with outward friendliness and hospitality, they secretly plotted war.

Montejo, having approached other native towns with needless caution, dropped his guard and permitted his men to be scattered about the city. The following morning he awoke to find that the Indians had evacuated their city. By midmorning, while the Spaniards were preparing defenses, the Mayas returned to attack in overwhelming numbers with long lances, *macanas*, and deadly flights of arrows. With some of the soldiers cut off, Montejo mustered available men and horses for a mounted counterattack. The Spanish victory was decisive but hardly affordable; a dozen soldiers died. Behind the Chikinchel lords' bid for peace lay further deceit.

From Chauaca, Montejo turned south into the interior. His destination was Aké, an independent city-state long at odds with Chikinchel. The Chauaca lords saw their chance to work vengeance on foreign and domestic enemies alike: they provided porters, who warned the *adelantado* of an ambush waiting at Aké; at the same time they sent messengers to Aké with advice that the Spaniards were coming to make war and take the women.

On guard, the Spaniards entered the town and found it abandoned. They erected fortifications while the bearers from Chauaca looted the deserted city and fled. The attack next day culminated in a decisive Spanish victory: in the slaying of many of Aké's warriors, not one Spaniard was lost. As the news spread, other *caciques* sent envoys seeking peace.

Consolidating the victory, Montejo marched inland, to Zizha and Loche. Instead of the fluent streams hoped for, he found severe water scarcity and the spring dry season at hand. His mind much on the men left at Salamanca and Pole, he turned east at Loche, toward the Caribbean coast. The route is nowhere described, despite its importance from an exploration standpoint.

At Salamanca, sad news awaited: of the forty ailing soldiers he had left, no more than twelve remained alive. It was disease that had taken the frightful toll. Not so at Pole; there, all the twenty soldiers had been killed by the natives.

His hopes devastated, Montejo felt himself robbed, his costly efforts devoid of benefit. He must have reinforcements to continue. Like an answered prayer, the brigantine *Gavarra*, which he had left at Santo Domingo, arrived with fresh supplies and men. While sagging morale was boosted, the most basic problems remained.

Looking for a better port and townsite, Montejo sailed *Gavarra* down the east coast. Avila, intending to march along the beach with the soldiers, turned inland to avoid marshes and lagoons, and lost contact with the ship. At Chetumal Bay, Montejo learned from captured Indians that Gonzalo Guerrero, cast away with Jerónimo de Aguilar in 1511, was a chief military leader of the local lord. The *adelantado*, remembering Aguilar's valuable service as Cortés's interpreter, sent word to Guerrero, urging him to join the Spanish expedition. Guerrero's answer was recognized as false. He was a slave, he said, and could not escape the Indians. In truth, he was embittered and dangerous, at that moment plotting to keep Avila and Montejo from uniting, hoping to destroy them. Well-concealed pits were dug around Chetumal to entrap Avila's horses. Canoe-borne warriors attacked Montejo's brigantines. Through native messengers, Guerrero managed to convince each of the Spanish leaders that the other had perished.

Avila, thinking that command of the colony had fallen on him, took his company back to Salamanca and soon moved to a better location at Xamanhá. Montejo explored the coast south as far as Río de Ulúa of Honduras and thus disproved the long-prevalent idea that Yucatán was an island.

Returning to Cozumel, the *adelantado* learned that Avila was safe at Salamanca de Xamanhá, across the channel. After a joyful reunion, he resolved to sail *Gavarra* to New Spain for reinforcements. Leaving Avila in charge, he departed for Veracruz late in the summer of 1528 to seek the means of bolstering the conquest.

Proceeding from Veracruz to the capital, Montejo found his natural son, Francisco, who had accompanied Cortés as a page on the march to Honduras, collected rents from Montejo's property, and recruited reinforcements. Back in the port town with his son, Montejo wrote to the king his first report on Yucatán—with restrained candor. He had lost some men and horses in battle, he related, though disease had taken a greater toll. In the rocky though rich and fruitful territory, he had found signs of gold but had not learned its source. The lack of a suitable port was the greatest drawback, having resulted in the loss of all his ships except the brigantine *Gavarra*. He had bought another brigantine and a larger vessel in Veracruz and was fitting them out for renewing the conquest.

Influenced by several factors, the *adelantado* had decided to shift his Yucatán approach to the Gulf coast. One consideration was his son's knowledge (acquired from the march with Cortés) of Tabasco and Acalán, the southwesternmost *cacicazgo* of Yucatán. Another was the frustration attending efforts thus far to establish a permanent

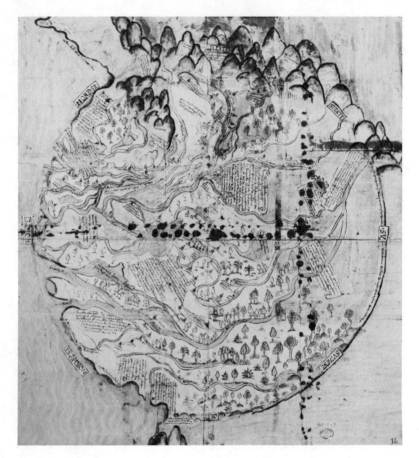

Fig. 6. Tabasco in 1579, Melchor de Alfaro Santa Cruz. Courtesy AGI.

colony at Santa María de la Victoria at the mouth of the Río de Grijalva. Baltasar de Gallegos had just come from the outpost, bearing the colonists' threat to abandon the project for want of support. Gallegos urged Montejo to take over the enterprise. Opportunely, Nuño de Guzmán arrived from Pánuco to assume the presidency of the new Audiencia de Mexico; eager to strip the absent Cortés of as much of his territory and power as possible, Guzmán readily granted Montejo authority over Tabasco as *alcalde mayor*.

With temporary authority from the *audiencia*, Montejo proceeded to annex Tabasco and establish his supply base and port at the Río de Grijalva. His son, with the stalwart Gonzalo Nieto at his side, took the three ships to Santa María de la Victoria to relieve the suffering colonists. The *adelantado* himself marched overland with twenty-five men, driving herds of livestock. Thus Santa María, beset by hostile natives and rent with dissension, was saved from destruction. While the Montejos moved against the rebellious natives, Nieto took the ships to Salamanca de Xamanhá for Avila and his men. The eastern Yucatán coast was abandoned, not to be reoccupied for more than a decade.

A key part of the entire effort was Juan de Lerma, veteran of the Mexican Conquest and well-established merchant-shipowner, whom Montejo had found in Mexico. While the exact nature of their agreement is elusive, it has been suggested that Lerma took on the job of supplying Montejo's forces for a share in the proceeds from slaves sold in the West Indies. Lerma freighted horses and cattle, men, and arms to Montejo for at least five years. Yet his involvement was greater than that of a mere contract supplier; interested in all aspects of the conquest, he received royal appointment in 1533 as treasurer of Yucatán. His supply operation was not always to his advantage: when a ship was lost, it had to be replaced at his own expense, and his absence from Mexico provided an excuse for the *audiencia* to deprive him of his allotment of Indians. By 1535 he was in such dire financial straits that he was imprisoned in Cuba for debt.

When Nieto arrived at Salamanca de Xamanhá, he found Lerma's ships in the anchorage. He and Lerma, returning to Tabasco with Avila's men, ran into a storm in the Bay of Campeche and lost one of the ships with all its horses and equipment. To make room for the rescued men, more horses had to be thrown into the sea. Badly battered, the two remaining vessels at last made port in the Laguna de Términos, where Nieto found a contingent of Montejo's soldiers at Xicalango, the new base camp for the Yucatán invasion. Lerma unloaded his ships, patched them up, and sailed again to the West Indies for more men, horses, and supplies.

The Montejos by this time had subdued the Indians from Xicalango to Copilco, west of the Río de Grijalva. The *adelantado*, joined by Avila, took a hundred men and thirty horses, and followed the Grijalva and its tributaries. Transporting the horses on rafts until they reached the high country, they encountered much the same sort of obstacles as had Cortés on the Honduras march. Fierce native resistance at Amatlán, Cimatán, and Zoque compounded the hardships and occasioned desertion. Battle and disease each took its toll; hardly a man escaped bone-wracking illness, and the losses totaled more than thirty of the hundred men. Nevertheless, by the end of 1529, the conquest of Tabasco was a reality.

The end of the campaign found the Spaniards at Teapa, near the Chiapas border. Here Montejo got word that Juan Enríquez de Guzmán, by authority of his kinsman, the president of the *audiencia*, was campaigning through Chiapas, and a meeting was arranged. Considering the jealousy with which conquistadors customarily guarded their conquests, a jursidictional dispute might have been expected. Instead, the two leaders resolved to help each other, as befitted the service of God and king. Both companies were hungry, worn out, and disease ridden, but each shared what it had with the other.

Informed of Montejo's plan to make Acalán his Yucatán capital, Enríquez advised proceeding by way of his own headquarters at San Cristóbal de Chiapas. The *adelantado*, however, was so severely ill that he had to turn over full command to Avila and descend by canoe to Santa María. Avila set out for San Cristóbal, thirty leagues distant, through rugged mountains that sapped the strength of man and beast. Horses were crippled on the rocky road or plunged over precipices to their death. Hardly any were fit for service by the time they reached San Cristóbal. But Enríquez de Guzmán made good his promise of aid, which was vital for Avila to continue; he supplied horses, arms, and quilted cotton armor of the type adopted from the natives.

Thirty leagues on the road to Acalán, Avila, like Cortés before him, discovered that his native guides no longer knew the route. The trail became rough, and men had to walk to spare their mounts. Descending out of the mountains, they came upon a large lake, swam the horses over to an island village, and succeeded in capturing Indians who knew the road.

Advancing thirty leagues farther through swampy country, the Spaniards came to the Usumacinta River, where they obtained guides and canoes in a friendly hamlet. Using vines to bind the canoes in pairs, they transported the horses downstream, standing awkwardly with hind legs in one section, forelegs in the other. For three leagues the double canoes surged along on the treacherous current to reach the pueblo of Tanoche (modern Tenosique), whose hundred houses stood deserted and silent. Some Indians taken in a night raid placed the Spaniards on Cortés's old road toward Acalán—el Camino de Malinche—near the most difficult part of the conqueror's passage. Following the brushy trail fifteen leagues, they came to the estuary that had given Cortés so much difficulty, the Río de San Pedro Mártir. Cortés had found the river 500 paces wide; with recent rains, the opposite bank now was lost to view. A three-day reconnaissance revealed only more impenetrable swampland. Finally, the captain learned from the Indians of Cortés's mammoth bridge-building effort, and his scout located some of the pilings. Work was begun to rebuild the span, but the weary men, hampered by a constant downpour, found the task too arduous. Canoes were the only answer. Avila backtracked for three days, won the friendship of some Indians near Tanoche, and persuaded them to carry canoes to the swollen river. The Spaniards then crossed without further difficulty to the opposite bank, two leagues distant.

Beyond the San Pedro, Cortés's road was overgrown, the country closed in by unbroken forest. After thirty leagues the soldiers came to the first pueblos of Acalán province. Avila sent messengers to the nearby city of a thousand thatched and whitewashed stone buildings, on a stream flowing northwest to the Laguna de Términos. The Maya Chontal, remembering that Cortés had taken away the lord of the province and hundreds of burden-bearers who never returned, were not disposed to trust him; they fled, leaving most of their possessions. Next morning, Acalán's *cacique*, presenting himself and a following of 400, pledged fealty to the Spanish leader. Avila, despite his promises, seized the *cacique* and his lords, put them in chains, and held them hostage until the townspeople returned to their homes.

The captain went through the motions of founding a town, but it was not a suitable location for the capital of Spanish Yucatán. Acalán, the only town in its region, offered no great abundance of agricultural produce and no gold at all. With the help of the Chontal, Avila explored northeast through country so swampy and wet that it was not possible even to build a fire. At the *cacicazgo* of Cehache the natives, so long accustomed to intertribal warfare, had constructed covered pits concealing sharp-pointed stakes designed to impale men and horses. The Spaniards eluded the trap and entered the town. Avila assigned a number of pueblos in *encomienda* and claimed to have pacified the region. But he had not found a site for the Yucatán capital.

Turning the march toward the coastal town of Champotón, site of Hernández de Córdoba's 1517 fiasco, he pursued a grueling thirty-league march through swamps and dense brush, losing a number of soldiers on the way. A band of itinerant Mayan salt merchants pointed out the trail, and the troop finally was accorded an overwhelming reception at Champotón by a crowd estimated at fifteen thousand persons. Montejo, it seems, already had opened diplomatic relations.

The city, claiming eight thousand stone houses, was surrounded by a dry rock wall and moats. Each day the native men went out in a fleet of two thousand canoes to fish in the Gulf. On an island a quarter league offshore—the one on which Grijalva had landed briefly in 1518—a high stone tower rose from a platform with ten or twelve steps. Filled with idols, this was the temple in which the anglers made offerings to their god of fishing.

Montejo, having heard nothing from Avila since their parting at Teapa, again had given him up for dead. He rejoiced at the news from Champotón, but political developments in Tabasco presented new difficulties. Baltasar de Osorio, whom he had displaced as *alcalde mayor*, had managed to get himself reinstated. Under Osorio's vengeful harassment, Montejo withdrew from Santa María de la Victoria to establish a permanent base at Xicalango. His troops, poorly fed and in rags, were prone to desertion. Just as the *adelantado* was feeling himself at rock bottom, Juan de Lerma's ships appeared, as they did on many opportune occasions, with supplies of fresh food and clothing. Again, the tide turned. Montejo took half a hundred men up the coast in native canoes to establish a town from which to advance inland. The choice, ultimately, was Campeche, seat of the *cacicazgo* of Canpech, where both Montejo and Avila, as Grijalva's captains in 1518, had twice felt the sting of Mayan hostility. This time, however, the *cacique* was ready to pledge fealty to the Spaniards; so were the lords of the northern province of Ah Canul. Early in 1531 the town of Salamanca de Campeche was founded, and villages of the district were assigned to Montejo's followers in *encomienda*.

Montejo intended to colonize the entire peninsula. He therefore gathered data on the geography, the native peoples, and their political relationships. Avila, with fifty men, explored across Yucatán, through territory previously unknown to the Spaniards, looking for gold. They traversed the provinces of Maní, Cochúa, and Uamil-Chetumal without opposition, but that circumstance proved deceptive. The renegade Gonzalo Guerrero still held sway over the Chetumal natives. Avila soon found himself beset by hostile forces on all sides. For a time he was able to elude their ambushes and win battles, but the small Spanish force gradually wore itself out against the overwhelming odds. Six men sent to carry specimens of gold and turquoise to Montejo were ambushed and slain. A dozen others fell victim to disease and battle. The Spaniards had waited too long to extricate themselves; no longer was the force strong enough to march back to Campeche. The only exit was by sea, in native canoes. In desperation, they paddled south in March, 1532, to reach Honduras, where they engaged a brigantine.

Montejo, meanwhile, had withstood the St. Barnaby's Day rebellion, June 11, 1531. With only forty-five men and just nine horsemen among them, he put to flight a horde of Mayan warriors estimated at twenty thousand. He then embarked on the second phase of the occupation. The younger Francisco came up from Tabasco to lead it, with authority as lieutenant governor and captain-general.

With several large ships and two hundred men, he felt his way north along the coast. Doubling Punta Nimún, he anchored off Ceh Pech province and marched inland. The Ceh Pech and Ah Kin Chel Maya, long at outs with their neighbors, promptly pledged fealty. The younger Montejo established a base in the Ah Kin Chel capital near the coast, southeast of Dzilam. With Pech and Chel auxiliaries, he marched inland to the massive ruins of Chichén Itzá, exploring various provinces and subjugating natives along the way.

Nacon Cupul, chief of the adjacent pueblo, manifested friendliness and quartered young Montejo in his own dwelling. The village, though only a shadow of the once great city of Chichén, seemed a suitable place for the Yucatán capital. It had two abundant *cenotes*, the natural sinks from which the natives drew their water supply; the ruins of ancient temples offered a ready supply of building stone. Montejo began the town, called Ciudad Real for Alonso de Avila's birthplace in Castile, and received tribute in local produce, including textiles and pottery. But he was mistaken in the assumption that the Cupul and their neighbors would submit indefinitely to such overlordship. It was a miscalculation that almost cost him his life.

One day when his back was turned, Nacon Cupul seized the captain-general's sword and tried to kill him. A watchful soldier drew his own blade and severed the *cacique*'s arm. The incident marked the beginning of a general uprising. Driven back in heavy fighting, the Indians laid starving siege. The Spanish force dwindled from ambuscades and lost heavily in bloody battle. Reduced to less than half their original two hundred, the defenders at last slipped past the Mayan blockade at night to reach the friendly provinces of Ceh Pech and Ah Kin Chel.

At Campeche, meanwhile, the *adelantado* recounted his accomplishments in a letter to the king, still pressing his claim to Tabasco. With Avila's recent report on Honduras, he moved to extend Yucatán limits in that direction, fitting out two of Lerma's ships for the purpose. Montejo's letter and one from Lerma were dispatched on Alonso López's ship for Spain on June 12, 1533.

With Lerma's ships about to sail for Honduras, friendly natives brought news of the Ciudad Real siege. The voyage was canceled. Avila marched inland with all the Spaniards he could muster and a sizable force of native auxiliaries—a Trojan horse. These Mayan allies, swept up in the spirit of revolt, suddenly turned on the Spaniards; the soldiers, caught off guard, were badly cut up. Avila turned back to Salamanca. Montejo, joined by Lerma, took charge of the campaign. In Chakán province, near the ruins of T-hó, the present site of Mérida, he heard of the Ciudad Real evacuation and soon was joined by his son and his remnant.

In a six-month war, the two Montejos restored order to a number of Mayan provinces and reestablished Ciudad Real near the native port of Dzilam, with the younger in charge. The threat of a general uprising in 1534, however, caused it to be abandoned. A factor in the withdrawal was the conquest of Peru and the discovery of the immense mineral wealth there, the likes of which Montejo's soldiers had only dreamed of. It had become obvious that this wild country of tangled brush and stony ground had no gold, no compensation for their arduous labor, hardship, and constant danger. The impact of the news from Peru, consequently, was immediate. Montejo's private army, enlisted with the promise of sharing the spoils of conquest, rapidly disintegrated.

Lerma, who claims to have explored the entire peninsula by both land and sea, assesses its situation in graphic terms: although the peoples were racially and culturally homogeneous, they were bound by no centralized government but divided into a large number of independent *cacicazgos*; nevertheless, they stood united against the Spanish invaders. Not only was the country rough, rocky, and short of water, but it had no gold, either above ground or below. The seven-year effort at conquest seemed largely wasted.

When Montejo's forces withdrew to Santa María de la Victoria near the end of 1534, not a Spaniard remained in Yucatán—save one. The renegade Gonzalo Guerrero, whose potential for causing disaster was foreseen by Cortés, had had much to do with the failure. In 1535, Guerrero led a force of canoe-borne Mayan warriors across the Gulf of Honduras to block colonization by the acting Honduras governor, Andrés de Cereceda. Pedro de Alvarado, another of Grijalva's captains, came to Cereceda's aid from Guatemala, assaulting Mayan fortifications in the Ulúa river valley. When the battle was over, Guerrero was found among the Indian dead.

Montejo disbanded his remaining forces in Tabasco, where his son remained, and went to Mexico with Avila, who died there in 1538. The *adelantado*, while not forgetting Yucatán, became involved in governing Chiapas and Honduras. In 1537 the conquest was renewed by the son and yet a third Francisco Montejo, the *adelantado*'s nephew, who that year occupied Champotón. This tenuous foothold withstood disease and Indian hostility until it was moved to Campeche, forty miles up the coast, late in 1540.

Out of previous failures now came a new strategy, devised by the *adelantado* himself. The campaign, he advised his son, should concentrate on the major population centers. The younger Francisco moved first to occupy the ruins of the ancient Mayan city of T-hó. Subduing native opposition, he founded Mérida as his administrative capital in January, 1542. Thence the Spaniards advanced in two columns, led by the *adelantado*'s son and nephew, to subjugate the eastern provinces of Ecab, Tazes, and Chikinchel. The nephew's conquests brought forth the new Spanish town of Valladolid on May 24, 1543.

In 1544, Melchor Pacheco carried out the concluding episode with the bloody subjugation of Chetumal. The great Mayan revolt of 1546–47 posed a serious challenge, but it was quickly suppressed. The conquest was essentially complete. This last phase, unlike the first, carried no illusions. Yucatán's wealth lay not in gold but in its soil and its people, to be exploited by a second generation of Montejos in the long-term enterprise of occupation. Yucatán, in the final analysis, was conquered and settled "for what it was and what it was known to be."

In viewing the Yucatán struggle from afar, one can see a paradox typical of the Conquest as a whole. On the façade of the Montejo house on Mérida's plaza, the site of ancient T-hó, two Spanish conquistadors in bas-relief stand with their feet on Indians' heads. Yet all across the peninsula, in virtually every village and hamlet there is an old church, dating from colonial times and likely still in use—testimony of a different aspect of the Spanish occupation. But then, since the beginning, man's best has often stood side by side with his worst.

SOURCES AND NOTES

The definitive study of Montejo in Yucatán is Robert S. Chamberlain, *The Conquest and Colonization of Yucatán, 1517–1550*. Fernández de Oviedo (*Historia*, 8:172–209) is an indispensable primary source but, for serious study, must be taken with a number of documents, some of which are cited by Chamberlain.

Narváez and Montejo in Spain

Bernal Díaz del Castillo (*Historia verdadera*, vol. 2) devotes his chapter 168 to complaints brought against Cortés by Narváez, Tapia, and others and the answers given by Cortés's *procuradores*—Diego de Ordás and Francisco Núñez—and his father, Martín Cortés. When the outcome favoring Cortés was proclaimed in Santiago de Cuba with a herald of trumpets, he says (p. 162), Diego Velázquez took to his bed and died within a few months, impoverished and grief stricken.

In a letter to the Crown dated Ciudad Rodrigo, Nov. 15, 1526 (AGI, Indiferente General 421, lib. 12, f. 14v), Narváez complains of having been falsely accused by Lucas Vázquez de Ayllón and asks that his fine of 600 pesos be returned.

See also López de Gómara, *Cortés*, 392.

Montejo ("Armas para Francisco de Montejo," Granada, Dec. 8, 1526, AGI, Indiferente General 421, lib. 12) recites his three years of service with Pedrarias Dávila in "Tierra Firme called Castilla del Oro"; his service as a ship captain on the Grijalva voyage; his coastal reconnaissance for Cortés, during which he discovered the Villa Rica site and the ports of Almería and San Pedro (Río Tecolutla); and the 1519 voyage to Spain, claiming for himself the discovery of the homeward passage through the Bahama Channel (actually based on the observations of the pilot Alaminos).

The contracts ("Capitulación que se tomó con Francisco de Montejo

[Pánifilo de Narváez] para la conquista de Yucatán [del Río de las Palmas]"), both dated Granada, Nov. 17, 1526, are printed in *CDI*, 22:221–23, 224–25. Montejo's muster list, compiled prior to his sailing, is published in José de Rújula y de Ochotorena and Antonio del Solar y Taboada, *Francisco de Montejo y los adelantados de Yucatán*, 379–97; also in Francisco del Paso y Troncoso, *Epistolario*, 1:104–20. Part of the date is left blank, in a manner indicating that his departure was later than June 20.

The sailing date is not definite for either Montejo or Narváez. Both June 17 and June 27 appear in various editions of Alvar Nuñez Cabeza de Vaca's *Relación de los naufragios y comentarios* for Narváez's departure, probably the result of some editor's attempt to convert the Julian calendar to the Gregorian. Certain it is that the two *adelantados* sailed within a few days of each other. Considering the practice of dispatching fleets together for their mutual protection during this period, it is my conclusion that they sailed at the same time.

Concerning Avila's imprisonment in France, see Alonso de Avila to the Crown, La Rochelle, June 16, 1523 (AGI, Patronato 267-1-1); Díaz del Castillo, *Historia verdadera*, 2:334–35 n.

The Conquest

By Fernández de Oviedo's account (*Historia*, 8:183), only 72 of the 380 men who had left Spain remained alive at the end of the conquest's first phase. He overlooks in the computation a number of ailing men left at Santo Domingo to come later with the brigantine *Gavarra*. Yet the fact that discovery and conquest were an extremely hazardous business is clearly emphasized.

Concerning Gonzalo de Guerrero, see ibid., 186.

Montejo's first report to the Crown on Yucatán, dated Veracruz, April 20, 1529, is printed in *CDI*, 13:86–87.

Little information is found on the Spanish effort at Santa María de la Victoria and its Tabasco environs. Antonio de Herrera y Tordesillas (*Historia* 4:352) credits a Captain Vallesillo and seventy soldiers with the initial effort, which was attended by considerable difficulty; Gallegos was sent to complete the "pacification," effect the *repartimiento*, and found the village of "Nuestra Señora de la Victoria [*sic*]" on a branch of the Río de Grijalva a league from its mouth in latitude 17.5°.

Juan de Lerma

Chamberlain (*Conquest*, 19), having speculated that Lerma's services to the conquest were paid for with a share of Mayan slaves sold, suggests that Avila's absence from Salamanca de Xamanhá when Nieto and Lerma arrived there was to supply Lerma with slaves. If that was the purpose, however, it seems that the Mayas were not being sold in Cuba; in 1534, Manuel de Rojas, the governor of Cuba, sought royal permission to import slaves from Yucatán

180   *Amazing Mexico*

(Rojas to Crown, Santiago de Cuba, Nov. 10, 1534, AGI, Santo Domingo 77, ramo 4, no. 81).

Various facts concerning Lerma not found in Chamberlain emerge from "Carta de Juan de Lerma," June 1, 1534 (*CDI-IA*, 1:67–70); "Ynformación a pedimiento a Juan de Lerma," Santiago de Cuba, May 5, 1531 (AGI, Santo Domingo 9, ramo 3, no. 39); Lerma to Crown, Santiago de Cuba, Oct. 20, 1535 (AGI, Santo Domingo 9, ramo 124, no. 19). See also Montejo to Crown, Aug. 10, 1533 (AGI, Patronato 184-1-44). The "Carta de Juan de Lerma" is especially important, as it recounts events of the conquest and gives Lerma's view of the Yucatán enterprise.

Avila's March to Acalán

Fernández de Oviedo is the basic source here. He gives a vivid description (8:190) of the manner of transporting horses in two canoes lashed together. The oral tradition of Avila's visit was recited in 1612 by descendants of the Acalán ruler (Paxbolon-Maldonado papers in Scholes and Roys, *Maya Chontal Indians*, 393). The description of Champotón is also Fernández de Oviedo's (8:205).

Avila's Chetumal Campaign

Avila's own account ("Relación de lo sucedido á Alonso Dávila," June, 1533, *CDI*, 14:99) is supplemented by Fernández de Oviedo (8:209) and the "Carta de Juan de Lerma" cited above. Avila relates that a mining expert named Francisco Vázquez went along, with the promise of a bonus from the Salamanca *cabildo* if he should discover gold.

Montejo the Younger

Diego de Landa discusses young Montejo's march to Chichén Itzá. For an English translation and detailed analysis, see Tozzer, *Landa's Relación*. Cf. Chamberlain, *Conquest*, 132–39.

Chichén Itzá was the worship center for the deified Kukulcán who, according to Mayan legend, would return from the east bringing a new religion. The ancient prophecy paralleled that of Quezalcóatl among the Mexicans.

The six-month campaign to restore peace following the escape from Ciudad Real is told in the "Carta de Juan de Lerma," 69–70.

Montejo's Crowning Disaster

In 1550 the aging *adelantado*, having been suspended from office in Yucatán, set out to appeal to the Crown for reinstatement. With viceregal appointment as captain-general of the New Spain fleet as far as Havana, he sailed in March, 1551, from San Juan de Ulúa aboard the galleon *San Miguel*. The ship carried gold and silver and many passengers, including women and children. Unable to enter Havana harbor because of contrary winds, she sailed on through the Bahama Channel and encountered a full-blown hurricane in which she lost masts and rudder. Limping toward Hispaniola, the crippled vessel received a fatal blow and went to her grave on a reef off the Hispaniola shore. All the passengers and crew made it safely to Puerto de Plata, and a caravel was sent to salvage the cargo. See Luis de Velasco, "Nombramiento de capitán de los navíos y comisión para llevar a la Habana el oro, la plata y monedas de S.M., a favor del adelantado don Francisco de Montejo," Mexico, Oct. 1550, in J. Ignacio Rubio Mañé, ed., *Archivo de la historia de Yucatán, Campeche y Tabasco*, 1:105–13; Robert S. Chamberlain, "The Spanish Treasure Fleet of 1551," 243; Montejo's report of the voyage in Rújula y de Ochotorena and Solar y Taboada, *Francisco de Montejo*, 371–77.

The Mapping of Yucatán

Yucatán in many respects has a cartographic history even more interesting than Florida's. It will be remembered that after the pilot Alaminos had proclaimed this peninsula an island during the Grijalva voyage of 1518, the Alvarez de Pineda sketch a year later described a peninsular Yucatán. Then the "Cortés map," said by some authorities to have been sent to Spain with the second letter in 1520, made it an island.

About 1525, both the "Castiglioni" and the "Salviati" maps pictured Yucatán as an island. The following year, Juan Vespucci, Amerigo's nephew, rendered it as a fat jug linked to the mainland by a skinny neck (in Cumming, et al., 74, 72, 86–87). The "Maiollo" map of 1527 not only makes it an island again but, with a highly speculative touch, shows a passage called Streito Cubitoso through the continent to the South Sea. The same year Nuño García de Toreno expressed his uncertainty by first drawing Yucatán as a somewhat round island and then, as an afterthought, linking it to the mainland with a narrow land bridge, neglecting to erase his earlier mark at the outer end (Winsor, *Narrative and Critical History*, 2:219–20).

That was the year also that Montejo began his Yucatán conquest and *proved* it a peninsula, but the old misconception did not die easily. Diogo Ribeiro, the Portuguese cosmographer serving as Spain's royal hydrographer, sought to record the latest discoveries on his 1529 world map. He showed Tierra de Ayllón on the Atlantic coast and attached a historical note concerning Vázquez de Ayllón's colonization attempt. He still showed Tierra de Garay on the U.S. mainland and drew a channel across the bottom of Yucatán connecting the Gulf of Mexico and the Caribbean. Ribeiro's conceptualization held even in the face of the *adelantado*'s explorations. Yucatán was shown as an island as late as 1544 and was given only a tenuous connection to the mainland on the south well into the next century.

No sixteenth-century map has surfaced to support or refute my conclusion that the bay called Ascensión on the Grijalva voyage was different from the one by that name on present-day maps. Guillaume Delisle's "Carte du Mexique et de la Floride" of 1703, however, shows Ascensión at the upper end of the Gulf of Honduras, approximating Chetumal. Another French map of Yucatán that first appeared in Prevost's *Voyages* in 1754 shows "Baye de Chetumal ou de Ascensión" in the location of the present-day Bahía de Chetumal (the Historic New Orleans Collection, *Degrees of Discovery*, 16; Winsor, *Narrative and Critical History*, 8:262).

Actually, the old maps are of limited value in tracking the early explorers—especially if taken without critical analysis. They often create more confusion than they dispel. The best mapmakers were concerned with the truth and exercised every diligence to find it, but there were many who sought to capitalize, at the expense of accuracy, on the popular thirst for something new and different. It is possible to find among these primitive maps of America support for almost any geographical theory one might choose to espouse.

The 1579 Tabasco Map

A copy of the map attributed to Melchor de Alfaro Santa Cruz of Santa María de la Victoria is reproduced, with captions translated into English, in Scholes and Roy, *Maya Chontal Indians* (Map 2). Dated April 26, 1579, it was part of a report on the history, geography, and resources of Tabasco, prepared in response to royal instructions.

"The highly conventionalized circular form," the authors note, "resembles two colonial Yucatecan Indian maps." The suggestion is offered that Alfaro either had a native map before him as he worked or used an Indian collaborator familiar with the Mayan convention. The authors conclude that the result, despite the distortion due to the design, "portrays in a remarkably accurate manner the principal features of Tabasco hydrography."

PART III

The Continent of Florida

Survival:
Cabeza de Vaca, 1527–36

W<small>HEN</small> Nuño de Guzmán's slave raiders rode north from Pánuco for
the Río de las Palmas in 1527, they half expected to meet Pánfilo de
Narváez, sent that year to explore the region between Las Palmas and
the Florida cape. Guzmán's men would, in time, encounter Narváez's
remnants, but in a locality and under circumstances quite different
from the expected.

Narváez's misfortunes were augured even before he left Spain,
again in Cuba, and as he disembarked on the Florida shore. But Don
Pánfilo had given up neither the brutality nor the stupidity that marked
his previous ventures. Both traits figured in the ensuing disaster. The
historian Fernández de Oviedo, who was his friend, tried to dissuade
him. Perceiving that Narváez was motivated more by sentiment than
by reason, the chronicler urged him to count his blessings. Narváez's
wife, María de Valenzuela, had endured stoically the long separation
during his imprisonment in Mexico. She had kept a vigil as faithful as
Penelope's for Ulysses. Furthermore, Fernández de Oviedo argued,
Narváez owned ample material wealth and had reached the time of life
at which one should seek repose with his family, rather than marching
off to new conquests. But Narváez was not of a mind to listen: "Although he thanked me for the advice, I saw that it did not set well with
him."

Narváez's fleet, presumably accompanied by Francisco de Montejo's, followed the standard course to the Indies, bought horses and
provisions during 45 days at Santo Domingo, then proceeded to Cuba
to buy more. From Cabo Cruz the *adelantado* sent Captain Pantoja
and Cabeza de Vaca ahead with two ships to Trinidad to load supplies
offered by Vasco Porcallo de Figueroa. Porcallo's brother, Sotomayor,

was to sail with Narváez as *maestre de campo*, or camp master. Cabeza must have reflected later on the Trinidad episode. The meeting of Pantoja and Sotomayor, seemingly insignificant at the time, represented the casting of characters for the major tragedy in which they were minor actors.

The dramatis personae included Andrés Dorantes de Carranza, captain of infantry, native of Béjar del Castañar, Extremadura; Dorantes's black slave, Estebanico, from the west coast of Morocco; and Captain Alonso del Castillo Maldonado of Salamanca. Cabeza de Vaca himself is the narrator and the protagonist in their eight-year struggle against Indians and wilderness. But for the strength he drew from his enduring faith, they would have shared the fate of their companions.

Alvar Núñez Cabeza de Vaca was born about 1490 at Jerez de la Frontera, near Cádiz, the son of Francisco de Vera and Teresa Cabeza de Vaca. His mother's unusual name, meaning "Cow's Head," derived from an ancestor who enabled the Spanish victory over the Moors in the great battle of Las Navas de Toloso in the year 1212. His valorous deed consisted of directing the king's forces to a strategic mountain pass by marking it with a cow's skull. Alvar Núñez took the name of this distinguished ancestor as his own surname. Alvar was inspired by his paternal grandfather, Pedro de Vera, conqueror of the Canary Islands, to seek the military career that took him in 1511 to Italy against the French; he was in the bloody rout at Ravenna on April 11, 1512, when 20,000 died. Somewhat broken by that experience, he served the Duke of Medina Sidonia, the overload of Niebla, in putting down the 1520 Comunero uprising. Prior to his appointment on February 15, 1527, as royal treasurer for the Narváez expedition, his career was unmarked by any real distinction. In the new venture his mettle was to be severely tested.

On reaching Trinidad de Cuba, Cabeza and Pantoja, with thirty men, went ashore to arrange the loading of supplies. Then came a hurricane that all but leveled the village and dashed the two ships to pieces on the rocks. With the vessels went twenty horses and sixty men. Some days later, on November 5, Narváez limped into port at Trinidad with the other four ships, all badly battered in the storm. With winter at hand, he went ashore and sent Cabeza de Vaca to secure the ships in the safer harbor at Jagua, whence the treasurer wrote a report to the Crown. In response, Francisco de los Cobos of the royal court urged Cabeza to continue writing of the expedition's occurrences. The Crown official could hardly have expected an account such as Cabeza later produced.

Narváez, reaching Jagua on February 20, 1528, brought the pilot Diego de Miruelo. This man is said to have been a nephew of Vázquez de Ayllón's pilot on voyages to the Atlantic coast in 1520 and 1523, to whom has been credited a 1516 landing in Florida, where he was blown by storm. Historians have tended to justify the appearance of "Miruelo Bay" on early maps, in the vicinity of Apalache, by taking the elder Miruelo to that place, although the sources do not specify on what part of Florida he is supposed to have landed. Florida's Miruelo Bay is almost certain to have been named for the nephew and not the uncle, the name stemming from the Narváez voyage. The nephew, on the basis of his claim to have visited the Río de las Palmas, has often been confused with Garay's pilot, Diego Morillo. Yet his claim to knowledge of the entire northern Gulf shore indicates a different voyage: that of Alvarez de Pineda.

Two days after Narváez's arrival, the expedition sailed with five vessels, eighty horses, and four hundred persons, including ten women, wives of some of the voyagers. The first mainland destination was a bay on the Florida peninsula that Miruelo claimed to know. Hardly were the sails filled when the pilot committed his first blunder. Taking the ships through the Gulf of Batabanó, he got them entrapped among the Canarreo Shoals and spent fifteen days trying to get them out. Following rough weather in the Yucatán Channel, a new tempest arose on the approach to Havana, preventing rendezvous with Alvaro de la Cerda, who was waiting there with another ship. Borne by the southerly gale, the voyagers sighted Florida on Tuesday, April 7, 1528, and ran the coast two more days before dropping anchor in the mouth of a shallow bay.

Narváez, prowling about the huts of an abandoned Indian village on a nearby promontory, found a golden rattle, which raised hopes out of all proportion to its value. After taking possession of the territory and naming the bay Bahía de la Cruz, the captain-general on Good Friday disembarked the people and the sea-weary horses, half of which had died during the voyage. On Sunday—fittingly, another Pascua Florida, the Easter festival from which Florida had taken its name—the Indians returned to their village, but communication efforts proved fruitless.

On Monday, Narváez and Cabeza de Vaca took six mounted men and forty foot soldiers to explore the country north or northeast of the landing. After a full day's march they came to a large bay sweeping inland—Old Tampa Bay by popular assessment, but more likely Tampa Bay proper. Returning to the anchorage two days later, Narváez sent the brigantine to look for the bay Miruelo claimed to know. If it was not found, the vessel was to proceed to Havana, load up with provisions, and return with Cerda's ship.

Narváez, meanwhile, resumed the exploration, tramping out the bay shore. His soldiers captured four Timucua Indians, who conducted them to their village on a promontory of the bay. There the leader saw a sight that triggered his vindictiveness: several Castilian merchandise crates, each containing the corpse of a Christian shrouded in painted deerskins—evidently victims of a Spanish shipwreck. Cabeza de Vaca tells only that the commissary, Fray Juan Suárez, had the bodies burned. From other sources it appears that Narváez released his innate brutality in a way that engendered lasting hostility; it is said that he cut off the chief's nose and cast his mother to the dogs. The Timucuas had several pieces of gold, which they said had come from a distant place called Apalache. Thus, the unwelcome guests were urged onward, out of the Indians' way.

No news came from the brigantine looking for Miruelo's bay. Narváez decided to send the other ships to find the harbor and there await the soldiers marching overland. Cabeza de Vaca's opposition to the plan provoked a row with the captain-general, who, implying cowardice, ordered him to take charge of the vessels. Cabeza refused: "I told him that I was certain he would never see the ships again. . . . I would prefer to share the dangers that he and the others faced . . . than to have it said that I held back out of fear, to risk my life than leave my honor open to question." In this clash of wills the expeditionists were launched irrevocably on their tragic course. A lieutenant named Caravallo was left in charge of the ships and, as Cabeza prophesied, Narváez never saw them again.

The treasurer was not alone in his prophecy. Still on board the ships were the ten women, about to see their husbands—seduced by false promises of gold—march off into a trackless wilderness among unknown Indians. One of these distraught wives prophesied much as Cabeza did: neither Narváez nor any of his company would return; if any should come back, God would work miracles through him. Narváez scoffed. Some would die in the conquest, he agreed, but the rest would win great wealth. The woman then turned to her sisters. Their husbands were going to certain death, she told them; they should not waste time in finding new ones. As for herself, she would be no Penelope, waiting long years for a man who never came.

The ships sailed along the coast in the direction of Pánuco, looking for Miruelo's bay. Not finding it, they turned back. "Five leagues below where we had disembarked they found the port, extending seven or eight leagues inland," Cabeza relates, "and it was the same one we had already discovered." For a year the ships searched for Narváez's men, inside the bay, then along the coast west. At last they gave up the quest and sailed for New Spain.

Cabeza's description indicates that the bay was Tampa: "This port . . . is the best in the world and enters upon the land seven or eight leagues and has six fathoms at the entrance, five near shore. The bottom is ooze. No sea or wild storm breaks within, and it can hold many ships. It is a hundred leagues from Havana . . . and is north-south with that port . . . four days from one to the other with the wind on the quarter."

The brigantine first sent to look for Miruelo's bay had proceeded to Cuba as ordered. By the time it returned to Florida, the other ships had departed. Looking for some sign, four sailors went ashore and soon found themselves surrounded by menacing natives. The brigantine, hopeless of effecting rescue, sailed away without them. Only one of the captives survived the Timucuas' torture, an eighteen-year-old lad named Juan Ortiz. Spared by the Pochahontas-style intercession of the chief's wife and daughters, Ortiz became a slave. He was rescued eleven years later.

Narváez, on leaving the ships at Bahía de la Cruz—in the vicinity of Tampa Bay—about May 1, 1528, marched north toward Apalache with three hundred men, forty of them mounted. Each carried his own meager rations of hardtack and salt pork. Fifteen days later, the marchers built rafts to cross the unfordable Withlacoochee River and on the other side met two hundred Indians drawn up in threatening posture.

In a skirmish not detailed, the Spaniards took half a dozen captives, who led them to a nearby village and assuaged their growling stomachs with fresh corn. Amid growing uneasiness for the ships, scouts waded the marsh to the river mouth but found only a shallow cove without a harbor. No sails marked the horizon.

Guided by their captives, the Spaniards resumed the march toward Apalache. Travel was through sloughs and marshes punctuated with patches of quicksand, then loose sand and pine forests with tangled windfalls. On one occasion they were astounded by a weird music coming out of the woods. A band of natives playing reed flutes appeared, followed by their chieftain, clad in a painted deerskin and borne on the shoulders of another man. Thus, the explorers were privileged to glimpse the "cultural elegance" for which the Timucua were noted. Conversing with the chief by signs, Narváez learned that the Apalache Indians were his enemies.

Twenty-seven days from the Withlacoochee, the travelers, having turned inland, came to a wide, swift river generally identified as the Suwannee. It was remembered for a soldier who, impatient at the crossing, plunged his horse into the current and was drowned with his mount. Outwardly friendly Indians fed the visitors corn, then slunk away to shoot arrows out of the darkness whenever a soldier ventured away from camp.

Beyond the Suwannee the road traversed country "difficult to travel but marvelous to see," through stands of tall pines devastated by wind or lightning. Another week brought the marchers to Apalache, "that thing they most desired in all the world," with promise of both food and gold. Cabeza de Vaca led an assault force into the village of 40 straw huts. There was no one to oppose him but a handful of women and children, who were seized as the Spaniards helped themselves to corn from the fields. When the Indian men returned, Narváez took the chief as hostage. Angered by such high-handed treatment, the Apalachinos set fire to the houses in which their uninvited guests had lodged themselves and began shooting arrows at horses and men at the water holes. An Aztec chieftain who had been brought from New Spain by Fray Juan Suárez was killed.

Scouring the country in three expeditions, the Spaniards found it filled with lakes. This area northeast of present Tallahassee was thinly populated and primitive, the lakes aswarm with waterfowl, the woods filled with animals, including bears and lions. For Narváez's purposes, the land offered little promise. There was no gold; the cornfields and cribs were being depleted, the Indians increasingly hostile. This forty-hut village was said to be Apalache's finest, the rest of the country poorer still. Farther south, near the sea, said the natives, was a prosperous village called Aute that offered greater abundance. To Aute, then, the Spaniards must go.

They started about July 20, picking their way among lakes and swamps. The second day they waded breast-deep water among floating and submerged logs and huge cypress trees, each, it seemed, shielding a lurking Apalachino warrior, ready to loose an arrow. So swift were they that the soldiers found their own weapons ineffective. "There were men this day," Cabeza relates, "who swore that they had seen two oaks, each as thick as the lower leg, pierced by the Indians' arrows."

That same day the Spaniards discovered a large river and named it Río de Magdalena for the July 22 feast day. This was the Ochlockonee, which our travelers evidently crossed to follow its right bank, as closely as possible, into the present-day Apalachicola National Forest.

Just before they reached Aute—nine days' travel from the Apalache village—an arrow shot from ambush struck an hidalgo named Avellaneda just above the cuirass, piercing his neck. He died instantly. Aute was found abandoned and in ashes.

At Narváez's urging, Cabeza de Vaca went looking for the sea, with Castillo, Dorantes, and Suárez among seven other horsemen and fifty foot soldiers. They came to an arm of the Gulf that yielded oysters in abundance—probably upper Ochlockonee Bay—but twenty men who went on to seek the sea found only an impenetrable maze of creeks and bays.

Back at Aute, the explorers found Narváez and several others wracked with malarial chills. In their quaking condition they had withstood a night attack, losing another horse. Narváez decided to move the troop to the explorers' camp on the bay. It seems a foolish move, for on arriving there they found themselves hemmed in: by the Ochlockonee Bay or River on the left, Crooked River in front, and the swamp all around. Their plight was desperate. Not only had they failed to find the ships; they could not even reach the sea. The horsemen plotted desertion, a threat that only the governor's rhetoric could counter; he shamed them into staying and called a council.

Only one course, the officers agreed, remained open: to build boats and put to sea. Yet so impossible it seemed that the idea fell upon the men like a pall. There was no pitch or oakum for caulking, no sails or rigging. But for a single carpenter, the Portuguese Alvaro Fernández, there were no craftsmen. They had no tools, no iron but their own weapons and stirrups, no forge, and, worst of all, no food to sustain them at such labor. The men dispersed in silence.

Next day a soldier came forth with inspiration: he could make wooden flues for the forge and a bellows from deerskin. Thus challenged, the others gave up their spurs, stirrups, and crossbow iron for the making of tools and nails. Palmetto fiber became oakum, and Doroteo Teodoro the Greek knew how to make pitch from the native pines. Hair from the horses' manes and tails were woven into ropes. Patchwork sails were fashioned from clothing. With homemade tools, planking was split from tree trunks, oars shaped from cypress logs. The near-stoneless country was scoured for rocks to serve as ballast and anchors. From desperation sprang remarkable enterprise.

It was agreed that a horse should be killed every third day to feed the workmen (the hide from the horses' legs was tanned and used for water bags). Raids on Aute's fields yielded corn, but then came harsh retribution: ten men gathering seafood in the cove within sight of the camp were slain in an arrow attack.

The work went on from August 4 until September 20, when five crude boats stood ready for launching. All the horses but one had been killed for food. The men, still numbering almost 250, were divided 48 or 50 to each boat, packed so tight they could hardly move. Fully loaded, the crude craft had scarcely nine inches of freeboard. No one in the company knew anything about navigation or managing a boat under sail. "From necessity," Cabeza says, "we ventured to place ourselves on such a troublous sea."

Narváez himself had charge of one boat; Dorantes and Castillo took another; Alonso Enríquez, the accountant, and Fray Juan Suárez commanded a third; Captains Telles and Peñalosa, the fourth; Alonso de Solís, *veedor*, and Cabeza de Vaca, the fifth. Thus they departed from Bahía de Caballos—the Bay of Horses—which Cabeza reckoned at a greatly exaggerated 280 leagues from Bahía de la Cruz. For a week they made difficult passage through coastal marshes no more than waist deep before reaching Dog Island, just off Carrabelle, Florida.

Two leagues farther on they perceived that the island marked the beginning of "a strait"—St. George Sound—which they named San Miguel for the feast day of St. Michael, September 27. Sailing within the sound through Apalachicola Bay, they emerged into the open sea beyond St. Vincent Island, near Cape San Blas.

Beyond the cape, the coast offered no barrier islands for protection. At intervals, the voyagers sought shelter in shoaly coves until, after many days' sailing, a storm marooned them on a waterless island near Santa Rosa Sound. Several men died there from drinking brackish water. Underway again before the storm had completely abated, the boats were tossed about for hours before at last finding shelter in Pensacola Bay. The Panzacola Indians, friendly at first, turned hostile; they killed three men, and all the fifty soldiers guarding the withdrawal were wounded.

Four days later, in an estuary near Mobile Bay, Teodoro the Greek and a Negro slave foolishly went with some Indians to get water and never returned. In 1540, when Soto's men were marching through the area, they heard from the Mobilas of the Christians who had lived among them and who were long since dead.

How the voyagers kept from getting lost along the ragged "trembling coast" of the Mississippi Delta is a marvel, yet no time was lost in reaching North Pass, where the first major Mississippi River distributary enters the Gulf on the east side of the delta. Narváez's and Cabeza's boats, attempting to enter the river to await the others, were driven out to sea by the swift current and a freshening wind. Half a league from shore, they could not find bottom at 30 fathoms.

For three days they sailed out of sight of land, struggling to turn shoreward. Then, after standing near the shore in three fathoms at dusk, they lost it again during the night. The boats, now well west of the Mississippi, were scattered. Cabeza and Solís adhered to a westerly course, while the coastline, running northwest, slanted away from them.

That evening Cabeza de Vaca, his boat having sailed alone all day, sighted two others and came within hailing distance of Narváez's craft to ask for instructions. The time for giving orders was past, the governor told him; each man should do what he could to save his own life. Unable to keep pace, Cabeza soon lost sight of the other boat. He never saw Narváez again, although he was to learn his fate from others who did.

For four days he followed Telles and Pañalosa's boat, then lost it in a squall. Daily rations were reduced to half a handful of raw corn per man. Despondency seized the crewmen, who, all but lifeless, lay upon each other in the crowded boat. Until after midnight Cabeza steered alone, thinking Solís near death. But then the *veedor* arose and took the tiller.

Cabeza de Vaca, sleepless, roused near dawn to the pounding of breakers. He sounded seven fathoms and, as the sky lightened, sighted land and steered toward it. Suddenly the nearly dead men were shocked to consciousness as a tremendous wave caught the boat and tossed it upon the beach. Crawling into the shelter of dunes, they built a fire to parch corn and drank from pools of rainwater.

Lope de Oviedo went to scout the island and returned, followed by three Indians armed with bows and arrows, soon joined by a hundred others. Resistance was out of the question, for hardly half a dozen of the forty-odd castaways were able to stand. Solís and Cabeza resorted to offerings of hawkbells and beads; the Indians responded by giving each an arrow in token of friendship. By signs, they promised to return with food.

The date was November 6, 1528. Historians, though inclined to identify the place as Galveston Island, still equivocate. A likely alternative is Follet's Island—now joined to the mainland—a little farther west.

With fish and roots dug from underwater by the Indians, the Spaniards provisioned the boat to renew their voyage. Stripped naked to keep their clothing dry, they launched the craft into the surf and climbed aboard. Two crossbow shots from shore, mountainous waves crashed upon them, capsizing the boat. Solís and two others who tried to cling to the craft for safety were drowned beneath it. The rest were cast half dead upon the beach, their wet, naked, and emaciated bodies pierced through by the chill November wind.

When the Indians saw the Spaniards' plight, they sat down among them and wept. Then, conducting the unfortunates to their dwellings, they lighted fires to warm them along the way. The natives danced that night in celebration, but the Spaniards were joyless—and sleepless—in anticipation of being sacrificed.

Next day the castaways were joined by Dorantes and Castillo's crew, who had landed a day earlier on another part of the same island. Together, they planned to refit the second boat, man it with the strongest, and send them in search of the "land of Christians," but the craft was too badly damaged to float. Believing Pánuco not far off, four men, accomanied by an Indian from the island, set out on foot: the Portuguese carpenter-sailor Alvaro Fernández, Méndez, Figueroa, and Astudillo. About eighty men were left at the place the Spaniards aptly called Isla de Malhado—"Island of Misfortune."

On the island, the winter turned bitter cold; the Indians could no longer pull roots, and the fish stopped running. The Spaniards were spread about the island to improve their chances of finding food, but by spring no more than fifteen of the eighty had survived. Five Christians encamped near the sea had slowly starved; when one died, the others cannibalized his body. The Indians were shocked and angered; although the natives of all that shore engaged in anthropophagy at a later time, to cannibalize their own people was unthinkable. The island natives represented two different tribes, Atákapan and Karankawan (called Capoques and Han by Cabeza de Vaca), and spoke different languages. The men of both groups were tall and well formed. Each had his lower lip and a nipple perforated, with reeds thrust through the holes. Their only arms were bows and arrows.

During that first winter Cabeza had ample opportunity to observe the Indians' death ritual. Starvation, combined with a deadly stomach malady, reduced their ranks by half. The natives, at first blaming the Spaniards, planned to kill them until one observed that the visitors were dying also. It was during this time that Cabeza and some of the others first were pressed into service as medicine men and began to work the "miracles" that had been prophesied for them. Under duress they devised their own healing ritual, which consisted of making the sign of the cross, reciting a Pater Noster, an Ave María, and a prayer to God to make the patient well. All those prayed for seemed to respond immediately.

Till the end of February, the castaways fed on the native fare of roots dug from under water and fish caught in cane weirs, tasks that fell to the women. When those sources failed, the Indians crossed the bay in dugout canoes to forage on the mainland. Cabeza, who had gone with the Han Indians to take oysters from the mainland bays, was not present when Dorantes and Castillo, with the Capoques, held muster early in April. There were on the island only fourteen Spaniards, all who had survived the winter except Cabeza. Twelve of these set out on a coastal march toward Pánuco, leaving only Lope de Oviedo and Jerónimo Alaniz, who were ill.

The Indians of Malhado, glad to see the Spaniards go, took them to the mainland in canoes from the lower end of Follet's Island, some ten miles east of present Freeport, Texas. Traveling west, they came in two leagues (five miles) to a flooding stream (Oyster Creek), which they crossed on rafts made on the spot. Three leagues farther on, they found the Brazos River and again built rafts, one of which was swept out to sea by the current. Two men drowned. On the west bank the survivors were joined by another Christian, not identified by name. At the San Bernard River, four leagues farther, they found the wreckage of Enríquez and Suárez's boat but no sign of the crew. At a fourth crossing six leagues beyond—on Caney Creek—they met the first of many Karankawan groups occupying the Matagorda Bay area. From the Indians who helped them across the stream in dugout canoes, they learned that Narváez's boat had passed along the shore. During a four-day march down the Matagorda Peninsula, two men died of hunger and exhaustion before they reached an inlet—Pass Cavallo—more than a league wide. On the side toward Pánuco they could see a point of land extending a quarter league out to sea, with dunes of white sand large enough to be visible far from shore. For some unknown reason, these features caused them to suppose this to be the Río del Espíritu Santo named by Alvarez de Pineda in 1519.

Finding a broken canoe, the marchers repaired it and crossed to Matagorda Island, then walked along it twelve leagues while suffering extreme hunger and stomach disorders from roots they had eaten. At Cedar Bayou, the pass between San José and Matagorda islands, an Indian came from the opposite bank bringing Figueroa, one of the four men who had left Isla de Malhado the previous November. Figueroa had news that confirmed their worst fears. His three traveling companions were dead, either of starvation or slain by Indians. Alonso Enríquez's men, after losing their boat (at the mouth of the San Bernard), he related, had followed the beach toward Pánuco until Narváez's boat overtook them. The governor sent his sea-weary crew ashore to walk with Enríquez's men and forage along the beach, while the boat sailed within sight and assisted the river crossings.

After transporting both crews over the "Río de Espíritu Santo," Narváez felt "very feeble, sick, and full of leprosy" and was quite irritable. In a falling-out with Enríquez over some trifle, the governor voided the *contador*'s commission and gave it to Pantoja; then, in a sulk, Narváez insisted on spending that night on the boat while the others slept on shore. Only the mate Antón Pérez and a page went with him. During the night a brisk norther arose; the boat dragged anchor, drifted out to sea, and was seen no more.

The rest of the two boat crews fared even worse, for death came slowly and painfully, by either starvation or exposure, during the winter of 1528–29. Those who lived longest fed on the bodies of their companions. Figueroa had heard the story from Hernando de Esquivel, the sole survivor, still living among some Indians not far away. These men had eaten crawfish and seafood for a while, but still their ranks dwindled. As with the La Salle expedition in the same area a century and a half later, internal dissensions worsened their plight. Pantoja, taking seriously the authority Narváez had given him, stirred resentment. Sotomayor (Vasco Porcallo's brother) clubbed him to death. "Thus they perished, one after another, the survivors slicing the dead for meat." Sotomayor was the last to die. Esquivel fed on his corpse until March, when he was taken in by the Mariames, the easternmost Coahuiltecan group. Figueroa had urged Esquivel to go on with him to Pánuco, but Esquivel refused, insisting that Pánuco now lay behind them.

The Indians who had brought Figueroa to Cedar Bayou would not permit him to stay with the Spaniards from Malhado. An Asturian priest and two others who could swim crossed the bayou and went after them, leaving the half-dozen nonswimmers marooned for a time on Matagorda Island. They never got to talk with Esquivel, who was slain a few weeks later because of a Mariam woman's dream that he had killed her son. Figueroa and the Asturian priest, it was learned, had escaped their captors and fled toward Pánuco.

The Dorantes-Castillo group soon was split up, as their ravenous appetites proved too much for their hosts. Castillo, Pedro de Valdivieso, and Diego de Huelva were taken by a native group living "six leagues forward," at Aransas Pass. Andrés Dorantes, his cousin Diego Dorantes, and his slave, Estebanico, remained together, enslaved by their Karankawan hosts. Despite their emaciated condition, the Indians forced them to carry heavy burdens and pull their dugout canoes through the shallows. They were constantly taunted in sport by the native boys, who pulled their beards, stoned them, and scratched them with long fingernails or knives until the blood ran. One day when gathering food, they came upon the bodies of two Spaniards; Valdivieso and Huelva, they later learned, had been killed for "going from one lodge to another."

In May, 1530, Dorantes escaped his hosts to cross to the mainland alone. Estebanico followed, but the two were kept by different Karankawan bands. When Castillo came to the mainland a year and a half later, he found Estebanico, but Dorantes had gone to the Mariames, on a river near the "Ancón del Espíritu Santo"—the Guadalupe. These were the Indians who had killed Esquivel because of a dream and treated Figueroa and the Asturian priest severely before their flight. Diego Dorantes had been similarly put to death. Only Andrés Dorantes, Castillo, and Estebanico, as far as any of them knew, remained alive. There had been no word from Cabeza de Vaca and the two men left on the Isla de Malhado. They had no reason to believe they still lived.

Cabeza de Vaca, however, had recovered from his illness. After a year of slavery among the island Indians, he fled to "those who live in the mainland woods," called Charrucos, an Atákapan tribe of the Texas Big Thicket region. Among the Charrucos his status improved, as they made him a trader with freedom to travel inland as far as he wished and along the coast forty or fifty leagues. Carrying shell knives and ornaments to the interior, he exchanged them for hides, red ochre, flint for arrow points, and hard canes suitable for making arrow shafts. He was occupied thus for nearly three years, all the time desiring to escape to Pánuco but unable to convince the lone Spaniard still on the island to go with him. Jerónimo de Alaniz had long since died, but Lope de Oviedo remained, unable to make up his mind.

At last Cabeza persuaded him to go, and they set out after the others, crossing the four rivers to reach Matagorda Bay at Pass Cavallo. Indians in canoes came from the other side to help them across and gave them the first dismal news of their companions: all were dead but three, and they were in bad shape from having been beaten and otherwise abused by their Indian masters. The natives proceeded to demonstrate by slapping and kicking the Spaniards, gesticulating with arrows, and threatening to kill them as their friends had been killed. It was too much for Oviedo. He recrossed the inlet and headed back to Isla de Malhado and an unknown fate.

Alone among these threatening Indians—the Guevenes—Cabeza went with them to the Guadalupe River where the Mariames, among whom the other Spaniards lived, were expected soon to gather pecans. The Indians who held Dorantes did appear shortly. He and Cabeza managed to meet, in the autumn of 1532, and Cabeza learned the details of the others' fate as it had been told by Esquivel and Figueroa.

Dorantes had long desired to travel toward "the land of Christians," but Castillo and Estebanico, who were with the Yguaces, were afraid to go because they could not swim. Dorantes and Cabeza devised a plan. In six months all the tribes would come together in the prickly-pear fields thirty leagues distant to feed on the ripe tunas. At the end of the season, the Spaniards could slip away together by joining a tribe returning to their homeland in the direction of Pánuco.

Cabeza, meanwhile, was taken as a slave to a Mariam family. All that remained was to await the next tuna season. But when the time came, in summer, 1533, the tribes had a falling-out that drove them apart before the plan could be effected. The Spaniards must wait another year.

When the 1534 tuna season arrived, the four castaways met and fixed the date of their escape once again, only to be separated by the Indians that very day. They nevertheless agreed on a rendezvous at the next full moon, and Cabeza de Vaca vowed that if the others did not come he would go alone.

The Indians at the prickly-pear fields, meanwhile, gave him sad news of the last of the five boats: that of Peñalosa and Telles. Having progressed farthest of all, it had crashed on the beach in the country of Indians called Camones. Too weak to defend themselves, the men had been promptly slain and stripped of their clothing and arms. These roving Indians displayed some of the garments and weapons. The boat, the natives said, still lay on the beach at the site of its misfortune— doubtless one of the Tamaulipas barrier islands between the Río Grande and the Río de las Palmas, or Soto la Marina.

On the appointed day, Dorantes and Estebanico joined Cabeza de Vaca. Castillo remained with the Anagado Indians, in whose direction the Mariames were traveling. Two days later the four survivors of the three hundred persons Narváez had brought ashore on the Florida peninsula six years previously began their journey from slavery toward the land of Christians. It was September, 1534.

Fearful of being overtaken, they fled toward smoke seen in the distance and at sunset came to the lodges of the Avavares. They were Coahuiltecans, like the Mariames and Yguaces, but spoke a different dialect. These bowmakers, on their way to trade with the Mariames, had heard of the bearded sojourners and "how we healed and the wonders our Lord worked through us." Castillo was pressed into service that very night to ease the headaches of several natives apparently suffering sinus congestion brought on by the coastal humidity. The visitors were well paid for their healing efforts, in venison and tunas.

The country ahead, they were told, was uninhabited and offered little sustenance now that the tuna season was over. Rather than traverse it in winter, the castaways decided to stay with the Avavares till spring. During that time they heard one final report of members of their expedition still alive. Sometime previously, the Avavares had seen the Asturian priest and Figueroa farther down the coast, still walking toward Pánuco. (It is thus made apparent that the Avavares ranged the coastal country rather than central Texas, as many have claimed.)

The Avavares were much on the move. First there was a five-day journey to a river where they found a tree yielding a pealike fruit suggesting the ebony bean that grows in Texas from Matagorda Bay to the lower Río Grande. Cabeza, while out looking for the beans, became lost in open prairie country cut by occasional stream courses. "Naked as I was born," he says, he carried wood on his back and a burning faggot in his hands to avoid being caught in the open at night without a fire. For cover he pulled the long grass and tied it into bundles, which he drew about him after building fires all around. One night the grass caught fire, and he was painfully burned. He at last found the Avavares, encamped on a different river. Then followed another journey southward to a place where, despite the lateness of the season, some tunas remained. Foraging for tunas over a wide area, the nomads encountered other Coahuiltecan bands: Cultalchuches, Coayos, Susolas, and Atayos, who monopolized the Spaniards' time with demands on their curative powers. It was among the Susolas that Cabeza performed his greatest "miracle"—restoring life to a "dead man."

In the spring of 1535, when fruit began to form again on the prickly pear, they took leave of the Avavares and went on to other tribes: the Maliacones, one day's travel from the Avavares; then the Arbadaos, whom they found at a plum thicket where the Maliacones had gone to feed on the half-ripened fruit until the tunas matured. Of the country, the chronicler tells only that it was overgrown with thorny vegetation that tore their naked bodies, and that water was scarce—an apt description of the land between the Nueces River and the Río Grande.

Cabeza, drawing on his experience as a trader for the Atákapas, made nets, combs, bows and arrows, and matting of the sort used to construct the native huts. He bartered these items for his sustenance. It was a time of severe hunger. The work of scraping hides assigned the Spaniards by the Arbadaos provided a "great luxury": they ate the parings. When by good fortune they were given a piece of meat, they ate it raw, lest some hungry Indian snatch it from the roasting spit before it was done and gobble it down. After leaving the Arbadaos, they ate—in the manner of the Indians they were with at the time—a "sweet and wholesome" mixture of ground mesquite beans and earth.

About the first of August, 1535, the castaways began their travels in earnest. Going from one tribe to another, they crossed the continent, finally to be rescued in April, 1536, by Nuño de Guzman's slave raiders on the Río Yaqui in the present Mexican state of Sonora. Only one point on that route has been established by other historical data: La Junta de los Ríos, the juncture of the Río Grande and the Río Conchos near present Ojinaga (in the state of Chihuahua) and Presidio, Texas. Antonio de Espejo, passing that way in 1582 en route to New Mexico, heard accounts from the natives "that three Christians and a negro had passed through here." How they got there has been the subject of widespread and diverse speculation; yet the indications are fairly clear. Only some days after crossing a breast-deep river "as wide as the one at Seville" was the decision made to turn inland to avoid the hostile Indians living near the Gulf. By that time the travelers had begun to see mountains that "ran from the direction of the North Sea"— meaning the Atlantic, which, in the nomenclature of that period, embraced the Gulf of Mexico. From what the Indians told them, they concluded that they were fifteen leagues (thirty-four miles) from the Gulf. The river was the Río Grande—not the Texas Colorado, as some have taken it to be—and the mountains were those of the present Mexican state of Nuevo León, forming a chain with the Sierra Madre Oriental and the Sierra de Tamaulipas and extending from the direction of the "North Sea."

Cabeza gives three reasons for the decision to turn inland: (1) the coastal Indians were extremely hostile, those of the interior friendly and hospitable; (2) the country, being more densely settled, offered better sustenance; and (3) the route would provide a better idea of the country as a whole. After years of hardships such as the four men had endured, exploration could scarcely have been a primary consideration; it was the hostility of the coastal Indians that forced the long detour. The fate suffered by travelers of the coastal route for two centuries more indicates that the decision saved their lives.

Turning west, they found the way blocked by the mountains that ran northwest from the Gulf. The terrain directed their course, among countless Coahuiltecan bands who honored them as healers, from the Sierra de Cerralvo to the Serranías del Burro. Thus, it took them back to the Río Grande, probably near the mouth of the Pecos River. Thence, the four castaways continued westward, across Trans-Pecos Texas to La Junta and through Mexico's Sierra Madre Occidental. By the time they met Guzmán's slave raiders on the Río Yaqui in the spring of 1536, they not only had explored more of the Gulf coast by land and sea than anyone before them, but they also had joined paths with other Spaniards crossing Mexico in the south and advancing up the Pacific coast.

Their tale of eight years' suffering in the wilderness served to stimulate, rather than discourage, the Spanish thirst for discovery and conquest.

SOURCES AND NOTES

The most comprehensive, accurate, and penetrating secondary treatment of the Narváez expedition is Morris Bishop's *Odyssey of Cabeza de Vaca*. There are several translations of Cabeza de Vaca's *Relación*. The best one is Fanny Bandelier, *The Journey of Alvar Nuñez Cabeza de Vaca*, first issued in 1905 but reprinted in 1964. There also are numerous editions in the original Spanish. All quotations used here from Cabeza's account either come directly from or have been checked against the 1906 Madrid edition entitled *Relación de los naufragios y comentarios de Alvar Núñez Cabeza de Vaca*. The entire narrative was written after Cabeza's return to Spain in 1536 and therefore is subject to errors of memory, especially as to dates and time segments, as well as Indian names.

Numerous books and articles have undertaken to establish the route of Cabeza and his companions across the continent, most of them based solely on the *Relación*. This account, however, does not stand alone. Cabeza and Dorantes, soon after their return to Mexico, wrote a joint account of their adventure that was forwarded to the Audiencia de Santo Domingo. It became the basis for the narrative published by Gonzalo Fernández de Oviedo y Valdés in his *Historia*, 10:190–252. Dorantes accounts for the trek down the Texas coast before Cabeza rejoined the main group, thus putting the route in an entirely different light. This substantive version has been translated into English by Bernardo Calero and Joseph K. Wells and edited by Harbert Davenport, with extensive annotation. Extracted from Fernández de Oviedo's commentary, it appears in its entirety as "The Expedition of Pánfilo de Narváez by Gonzalo Fernández Oviedo y Valdez," in the *Southwestern Historical Quarterly*.

Various interpreters of the route have led Cabeza all over the map. Buckingham Smith (*Relation of Alvar Núñez Cabeça de Vaca*, first published in 1851 and revised and reissued in 1871) contributed the greatest confusion by ending Narváez's voyage east of Mobile Bay and marching the castaways north through Tennessee and west through Arkansas and Oklahoma. More persistent, however, has been the inclination to take survivors inland across Texas rather than across the Río Grande, a matter that Fernández de Oviedo clarifies. Bishop's *Odyssey* is straight on this point, but the error lingers as persistently as the one that takes Alvarez de Pineda up the Río Grande (or the Mississippi). Even with Bishop's lucid account at hand, writers like Cleve Hallenbeck, (*Alvar Núñez Cabeza de Vaca: The Journey and Route of the First European to Cross the Continent of North America, 1534–1536*) manage to misinterpret and make ill-founded assumptions. Hallenbeck, for example, goes off course by assuming that Caney Creek (Matagorda County, Texas) then flowed into East Matagorda Bay as it does now. He therefore takes the castaways on an extended trek around the bay because, he says, their guides would not have followed such a difficult route as crossing Pass Cavallo. Many of his statements and conclusions are similarly ill-founded or poorly documented.

Cabeza's Background

Bishop's work is biographical and therefore provides the pertinent data on our hero. Having visited the castle at Niebla and puzzled over its origin, I came upon some interesting information in AHN, Madrid (sección Diversos, legajo 74). The Duque de Medina Sidonia, Juan de Guzmán, in 1493 also was the Conde de Niebla. It is therefore presumed that the Niebla castle, on the road from Seville to Moguer, was his, and either he or his successor was

Cabeza's employer in 1520. The duke-count in the late fifteenth and early sixteenth centuries was outstanding in his service to the Crown. In 1497 his fleet captured Melilla on the Morocco coast from the Barbaresques. The seventeenth-century heir to the titles was of a different hue; in 1665 the Duke of Medina Sidonia was the greatest landed proprietor in Andalucía and brother of the Queen of Portugal. When his plot to make himself king of that province, with Portuguese help, came to light, he was banished from Andalucía. The castle at Niebla, probably built after Alfonso X retook Niebla from the Moors in 1241, stands as a reminder of the feudal era to which Cabeza de Vaca belonged. (See Louis Bertrand and Charles Petrie, *The History of Spain from Musulmans to Franco*, 123, 220, 258–59.)

The Expedition in Cuba

Cabeza's report to the Crown from Cuba has not come to light but is mentioned in Francisco de los Cobos's letter to Cabeza de Vaca (AGI, Indiferente General 421, lib. 13, f. 298).

The Crown, in a letter dated June 12, 1527, at Valladolid, ordered officials of Española and Cuba to cooperate with Narváez, who was "acting under the king's banner," in outfitting his expedition to the provinces of "el Río de las Palmas e la Florida," indicating his need for "ships and other items" (AGI, Indiferente General 421, lib. 12, f. 71v).

The depopulated condition of Cuba and the "extreme necessity" resulting from loss of people to the Conquest by the time of Velázquez's death in 1524 is described by Manuel de Rojas to the Crown, Santiago de Cuba, May 5, 1532 (AGI, Santo Domingo 99, ramo 1, no. 15).

The exploits of both Diegos de Miruelo are vague and confused. The uncle, remember, was encountered in the Bahamas by Juan Ponce de León in 1513, under circumstances that remain unclear. The idea that he made a 1516 sally into the Gulf of Mexico and that Miruelo Bay was named for him has persisted beyond all reason (see Morison, *Southern Voyages*, 515). The basis is the mere statement by Garcilaso de la Vega (*The Florida of the Inca*, 9) that Miruelo's trading caravel from Santo Domingo "was blown by storm to the coast of Florida or some other region." There is no mention of the Gulf of Mexico.

Cabeza's account of efforts to find "Miruelo's bay" on the Narváez expedition seems to make it clear that the feature appearing later on maps derived its name from the second Miruelo, designated chief pilot by Narváez on the basis of his familiarity with the northern Gulf shore. His career is confused also. The notion that he had been with Garay at Pánuco stems from Andrés Barcia Carballido y Zúñiga (*Barcia's Chronological History of the Continent of Florida*, 9), who evidently confused the name with Morillo. He could not have claimed familiarity with the entire northern Gulf shore on the basis of Garay's 1523 voyage. He must, therefore, have sailed with Alvarez de Pineda (in Garay's behalf) in 1519.

The Florida Landing

Most interpreters have placed the Florida landing—Bahía de la Cruz—on the peninsula between Old Tampa Bay and the Gulf. There is really no sound basis for disputing this except that to get there the pilots would have had to overlook the Tampa Bay entrance from fairly close at hand. I prefer to believe that the landing was south of this entrance, perhaps around Sarasota Bay.

The choice of a site north of the bay entrance has been influenced largely by Cabeza's statement that "Miruelo's bay" was finally found "five leagues below [*mas abajo de*] where we had disembarked" and that it was the same bay already discovered by the land forces. Map orientation in that period, however, did not always fit the present-day convention of putting north at the top. Like Cortés, Cabeza may have considered it just the opposite. If so, Tampa Bay was north of the landing place, not south. Cabeza's description seems to fit Tampa Bay rather than Old Tampa Bay.

The Bay of Horses

Woodbury Lowery (*Spanish Settlements, U.S.*, 187) locates the shipbuilding at "one of the little harbours in Apalachee Bay," offering in a footnote a variety of choices by different interpreters, none of which seems as accurate as Davenport's ("Expedition of Pánfilo de Narvaez," 217 n). Davenport places the shipbuilding camp three leagues from the sea by a water route and three leagues from the entrance to Ochlockonee Bay. Narváez's men, he adds, navigated westward through an extension of Ochlockonee Bay that receives the Ochlockonee and New rivers and opens into St. George Channel near Carrabelle: i.e., Crooked River. Had they come from Apalache Bay to reach St. George Sound, they would have sailed in open water.

The Westward Voyage

From the dates given, we know that forty-four days elapsed from the embarkation at Bahía de Caballos to the landing on the Texas shore. Yet Cabeza distributes fifty-six days among the various stages of the voyage, and he allows but a single day from Mobile Bay to the first pass of the Mississippi River, which is all too short. Obviously, he could not have been completely accurate in recalling such details nine years later.

An oft-repeated error is that Narváez's boat perished when swept seaward at the mouth of the Mississippi (see John Gilmary Shea, "Ancient Florida," in Winsor, *Narrative and Critical History*, 2:243–44). Although Cabeza himself did not see the governor after becoming separated from him just west of the Mississippi, he learned from others that Narváez's boat, anchored at Matagorda Bay, drifted out to sea during the night while the *adelantado* slept.

Isle of Misfortune

Cabeza describes the island as being half a league wide and five long, about half Galveston Island's actual length; yet no other island or peninsula comes closer. There is mention, however, of "an island backward from where they lost the boats." Was the landing place farther west, perhaps on Follet's Island? Davenport suggests "the next island west of Galveston" as the likely place. I agree; the dimensions approximate those given by Cabeza.

The Coastal Trek

Davenport's copious expository notes offer one of the best route interpretations available on the castaways' march down the Texas coast. His identification of the rivers crossed is precise, although he is in error in stating that Caney Creek then was a main channel of the Colorado River, a condition that geological studies show to have ended several hundred years previously. Caney Creek at that time did flow directly into the Gulf rather than into East Matagorda Bay as it does at present. The Colorado River, on the other hand, flowed into Matagorda Bay until man-made works about 1929 caused it to flow into the Gulf (University of Texas Bureau of Economic Geology, oral information).

The mistaken conclusion that Matagorda Bay was the Río del Espíritu Santo, discovered by Alvarez de Pineda in 1519 and shown on several maps by 1528, is understandable. The north wind and powerful current at North Pass had prevented Narváez's people from getting a close look at the Mississippi, any more than Alvarez de Pineda had. Unfortunately, such a misinterpretation has contributed to the perpetual confusion surrounding application of the name Espíritu Santo. Hallenbeck (*Cabeza de Vaca*, 135) claims that "Pineda" gave the name Espíritu Santo to Matagorda Bay and asserts, without giving his reasons, "It is known that Pineda did not reach the delta of the Mississippi, and there is no question that his Espíritu Santo bay was Matagorda bay." Really!

Cabeza and the Indians

Cabeza de Vaca's descriptions of the various Indian groups with which he came in contact from the Florida peninsula to western Mexico have been of inestimable value to anthropologists and still make interesting reading. The weakness is that it is often difficult to tell whether his data are meant to be specific or general. Even so, he gives information on the Karankawas that corresponds with that derived from the La Salle expedition to the same area a century and a half later. On the Coahuiltecans, his descriptions fit those given by Alonso de León (*Historia de Nuevo León*) in the frontier soldier's history written in the middle seventeenth century, and by Isidro Félix de Espinosa (*Crónica de los colegios de propaganda fide de la Nueva España*). Espinosa, like other early chroniclers, places the large concentrations of mesquite below the Río Grande, with only patches between the Río Grande and Nueces River. Since the mesquite bean was an important Indian food item mentioned by Cabeza, this information indicates the area through which he traveled. Alonso de León was the first to ascribe a route to Cabeza across northern Nuevo León, "very close to the town of Cerralvo." His own experience on the frontier enabled him to compare Cabeza's description of the natives with his own observations.

Cabeza's memory probably failed him on many of the Indian names he attempted to call to mind in writing the *Relación*, but some are close enough to those learned later that conclusions as to their identity seem warranted. W. W. Newcomb, Jr., for example (*The Indians of Texas from Prehistoric to Modern Times*, 49), links the Mariames with the Aranames. He also notes (p. 60) a vague phonetic similarity between the Arbadaos and the Borados of the lower Río Grande and the Maliacones and the Malaguitas of Padre Island.

The Pelones or their kinsmen of the Tamaulipas coast are suggested as Telles and Peñalosa's slayers by the fact that they robbed their vitims of their clothing. Repeated instances of the natives' stripping of Spanish castaways are noted in that particular area over a period of two centuries.

The Search for Narváez

The full extent of the search for Narváez and his followers by the ships he left on the Florida peninsula has not emerged. One of the participants in the search, Hernando de Ceballos, was jailed in Cuba on charges by Narváez's widow, María de Valenzuela, long before the four survivors emerged from the wilderness. Ceballos appealed to the king for his release, claiming to have spent a sizable sum in provisioning the search voyage. Having sold Narváez two brigantines purchased in New Spain, he claims to have spent more than the amount Narváez paid him "in searching for the said Pánfilo de Narváez and in sustaining his wife, because I bought ten *botas* of wine and another ten of flour and thirty arrobas of oil, forty arrobas of vinegar, and a quarter *bota* of olives" for the rescue operation (Ceballos to the king, Cuba, March 16, 1531, AGI, Indiferente General 1203, no. 28).

One man from Narváez's ships was in Mexico when Cabeza de Vaca and his companions arrived in 1536. Alonso de la Barrera ("Información de Antonio [*sic*, for Alonso] del Castillo," Mexico, Nov. 23, 1547, AGI, Patronato 57-4-1) tells of their arrival at the principal church almost naked (*vestido de meros*)— as they had come from the land of Florida.

Wasted Conquest:
Soto and Moscoso, 1539–43

FROM the Río Yaqui, Cabeza de Vaca and his companions traveled southeast with Captain Diego de Alcaraz to Culiacán, San Miguel, and Compostela, the headquarters of Nuño de Guzmán. The Nueva Galicia governor provided clothing and beds, but the castaways, having gone naked and slept on the ground for eight years, took little comfort in either. Arriving in Mexico in time to observe the Feast of St. James, July 25, 1536, the weary wanderers were greeted by Cortés—now the Marqués del Valle—and Antonio de Mendoza, who had come the previous year to serve as New Spain's first viceroy.

Cabeza and Dorantes wrote a joint report on the Narváez expedition and their own travels, which was forwarded to the Audiencia de Santo Domingo. The two of them then embarked for Spain on different ships of the same fleet. While Dorantes's vessel sprang a leak and turned back before reaching Havana, Cabeza sailed on, still leading his charmed existence through a mid-ocean storm and a brush with French corsairs. Traveling part way with a Portuguese fleet from the Far East for protection, his ship made port at Lisbon on August 9, 1537—more than ten years after he had left Spain with Narváez.

Dorantes returned to Mexico, where the viceroy offered to outfit him "to search out the secret of those parts" through which the castaways had traveled. He withdrew from the project at the last minute, without explanation. Dorantes and Castillo settled down in Mexico and married prominent widows. The viceroy borrowed Dorantes's slave Estebanico to guide a reconnaissance mission preliminary to a major expedition. The venture was headed by Fray Marcos de Niza, agent for a 28-year-old protegé of Mendoza, just named Guzmán's successor as Nueva Galicia governor: Francisco Vázquez de Coronado.

It was not the castaways' account of the northern Gulf shore that stirred the viceroy's interest but their report of a fertile valley far up the Río Grande. After leaving the coast, they had visited, at La Junta de los Ríos and beyond, a people who lived in permanent houses, raising corn, pumpkins, and beans and weaving cotton blankets. They also had met Indians who traded for turquoise, emeralds, and buffalo robes with natives living farther north.

Early in March 1539, Estebanico departed with Fray Marcos, one other priest, and a number of Indians to investigate the rumored wealth. He was to lose his life in a Zuñi pueblo whose chieftains could not abide his haughty airs. Fray Marcos, supposedly versed in cosmography and navigation as well as theology, proved less than a competent observer. From a safe distance he looked upon an Indian town that he took for the first of Cíbola's fabled seven cities, of which the natives had told him. He decided that its people must use vessels of gold and silver because they had no other material for the purpose. The precious metals, he reported, were more abundant than in Peru. That was more than enough to send Vázquez de Coronado marching to find Cíbola, the figment of fertile imaginations combined with an old legend of the Seven Cities of Antillia.

Such was the genesis of the *entrada* inspired by Narváez's survivors. The participants would return more than two years later, stripped of their dreams. No settlement would rise from their efforts. Expeditions into New Mexico during the remainder of the century were made not because of this venture but in spite of it, harking back to the rumors of riches recited by Cabeza de Vaca. Yet its outcome was far less tragic than that of another follow-up to Narváez that had landed in Florida almost ten months before Vázquez de Coronado's departure from Compostela.

Cabeza de Vaca, on arriving in Spain, learned that Hernando de Soto had been named governor of Cuba and *adelantado* of Florida three months previously. Soto, native of Jerez de los Caballeros, had accompanied Pedrarias Dávila to Darién in 1514. In more than twenty years' service in the New World, he served Pedrarias in Nicaragua and Castillo del Oro, then followed the fortunes of Francisco Pizarro in Peru as a captain of dragoons. In the latter venture he attained wealth and distinction before discord between the Almagros and the Pizarros caused him to return to Spain in 1536, leaving castoff native mistresses and illegitimate children in his wake. He had a large retinue of young men, many of whom had come from Mexico with Pedro de Alvarado to serve in Peru. One of them was Luis de Moscoso Alvarado, a nephew of Don Pedro. On Moscoso ultimately would fall the burden of the Florida enterprise.

Upon returning to Spain, Soto set himself up in Seville as a gentleman, surrounded by all the servants requisite to the role, then went to the royal court. His first move was to request a councillor close to the king to seek for him a grant in South America or the governorship of Guatemala. When this approach failed, he drafted another appeal. In the meantime, he had found among the court ladies the daughter of his old commander, Pedrarias Dávila. His marriage to Doña Isabel de Bobadillo is signaled by a conveyance of dower signed by her mother on November 14, 1536. The following April 20, having made the Crown a sizable loan from his Peruvian wealth, Soto was granted a concession for "the government of Cuba and conquest of Florida with the title of *adelantado*." The nature of his second proposal is indicated by the Crown's reference to Soto's expressed "desire to return to those our Indies to conquer and settle the Province of Río de las Palmas to Florida, the government whereof was bestowed on Pánfilo de Narváez, and the Province of Tierra Nueva, the discovery and government of which were conferred on Lucas Vázquez de Ayllón."

By that time news had come to Spain of Narváez's four survivors. The king had doubtless had his fill of the bungling that seemed to mark all efforts to conquer the "Tierra de Garay" and Tierra Nueva. If the tide could be turned, surely Soto was the man to do it. The monarch therefore gave him authority as governor and captain-general over 200 leagues of coast of his own choosing, which he was to conquer at his own expense. His salary was to come from profits accruing to the Crown from the grant, and he was to embark within a year. Soto also was charged with responsibility for converting the natives and developing his territory with forts, hospitals, and harbors—provisions that seem rather beside the point, in view of the outcome.

Cabeza de Vaca, finding the matter already settled, took his written narration to the king but shrank from showing it to others. He spoke mostly of the country's poverty and hardships, intimating that some pact with Dorantes forbade his saying more. Soto was eager to enlist him, but Cabeza was having no part of it. Three years later he embarked on another tragic enterprise as governor of the Río de la Plata. But his kinsmen followed Soto.

Within the allotted year, on April 7, 1538, Soto embarked from Sanlúcar de Barrameda with seven ships. *San Cristóbal*, his flagship, or *capitana*—commanded by himself, assisted by the chief pilot, Alonso Martín—carried his entire household, including his recent bride. The *almiranta*, commanded by Nuño de Tobar (from Soto's hometown of Jerez de los Caballeros) as fleet admiral, was *Magdalena*. Both these vessels are described as being of 800-ton burden—enormous for that period. The next two were 500-ton galleons: *Concepción*, commanded by Luis de Moscoso Alvarado, native of Badajoz and citizen of Zafra; and *Buena Fortuna*, skippered by Andrés de Vasconcelos, one of a number of Portuguese volunteers from Elvas. Next in order of size was *San Juan*, captained by Diego García of Villanueva de Barcarroto, and *Santa Bárbara*, by Arías de Tinoco of Badajoz. A "smaller galleon," *San Antón*, had Alonso Romo de Cardeñosa, Tinoco's brother, as captain; he was accompanied by a third brother, Diego Tinoco. The ships carried more than 600 persons, including several priests and a number of women and children. They sailed in company with the New Spain fleet of twenty ships commanded by Gonzalo de Salazar, with Soto in overall command.

Reaching Gómera in the Canaries on Easter Sunday, April 21, the fleet topped off with bread, wine, and meat and sailed again within a week. The island governor, Doña Isabel's kinsman, entrusted to her his natural daughter, Leonor de Bobadilla, in hopes she would find a suitable husband in Cuba. The ships stood off Santiago de Cuba on Whitsunday, June 9. The townspeople, mistaking them for pirate vessels, by which they had been lately victimized, gave false signals that almost put the fleet on the rocks.

Soto promptly sent Juan de Añasco to Havana, a 300-league canoe trip, to make arrangements for the Florida venture. Añasco found that the town had been sacked by the French pirates who had failed to take Santiago. Soto, meanwhile, was visited by Vasco Porcallo de Figueroa of Trinidad, "a very rich and generous man who helped magnificently in the conquest of Florida." If generous, Porcallo had made generosity pay; his prosperity stemmed from provisioning fleets like Narváez's and Soto's. To Soto, he offered more than material goods; he proposed to join the expedition himself. The governor soon found a vacancy be-

Fig. 7. Havana harbor. Courtesy Biblioteca Nacional.

fitting Porcallo's age and stature. Nuño de Tobar, the fleet admiral, had put himself in disfavor by seducing the young lady from Gómera, Leonor de Bobadilla, who shortly turned up pregnant. Tobar mitigated the governor's wrath by marrying the girl, but Soto gave his position to Porcallo.

Soto, buying horses and swine for the expedition, gave Cuba's economy a spurt. Gonzalo de Guzmán, Diego Velázquez's old sidekick who had served as governor following Don Diego's demise, had little appreciation for the new governor's buying spree. It only inflamed the greed of the island residents, he complained to the king, causing them to sell livestock and seeds needed for breeding and planting. Sanctions should be imposed, he suggested, to prevent such rapacity by future expeditions of conquest.

Having devastated Santiago with his free spending, Soto sent the ships with the infantry and the dependents toward Havana, through the Yucatán Channel. The fleet, commanded by Carlos Enríquez, his niece's husband, was scattered by storm. Some of the ships, driven within sight of Yucatán, took forty days to reach Havana. The governor himself marched with the cavalry in August to reconnoiter the island before proceeding to Havana. He found the country little changed since Las Casas saw it during the conquest. Near Bayamo, on the south shore, the marchers observed a river "larger than the Guadiana," where monstrous alligators were wont to attack Indians and domestic animals at the fords. Snakes thick as a man's thigh lurked in the undergrowth, and wild dogs ran in packs, feeding on the swine herds. Crossing the island to Puerto Príncipe, the soldiers found the roads overgrown and had to hack their way through tangled brush while battling swarms of mosquitoes that gushed with their blood when swatted.

When the ships reached Havana, Añasco arranged quarters, then took a brigantine built in Havana and one of the fleet caravels to reconnoiter the Florida landing. His account of this voyage, though brief, cuts through the confusion in which others have shrouded it. He made one trip, not two; as winter was approaching, he encountered foul weather that put the ships in jeopardy, but he makes no mention of being marooned by shipwreck. He brought to Havana four Florida Indians to serve the forthcoming *entrada* as interpreters and found Soto waiting. Seventy-five to eighty leagues from Havana, he reported, he had located a port that was inhabited and secure. By the time the fleet was ready to sail, the captives already were learning Castilian.

In Havana, Soto heard news of the impending expedition by Vázquez de Coronado. To avoid a confrontation like the one he had witnessed in Peru or those involving Narváez, Garay, and Cortés in New Spain, he dispatched a messenger to Viceroy Mendoza. Assurances came back that there was no danger of the expeditions' crossing paths; Florida was large enough for both.

A favorable wind on May 18 caused Soto to take the ships to sea a week ahead of schedule. With provisions already on board, the 237 horses were loaded, then the 513 soldiers, plus sailors and servants. After a smooth voyage, land was sighted on Whitsunday—festival of the Holy Spirit, or Pascua del Espíritu Santo—and anchors were cast in four fathoms, two leagues from shore. Añasco, on his exploratory voyage, had neglected to sound the channel approaches. He and the chief pilot argued concerning the location. To resolve the difference, Soto took them both aboard a brigantine and sailed up the coast five leagues to find the bay. Then five days were spent sounding and marking the channel, with two brigantines anchored on either side. Even so, when the larger vessels were brought through the shoals, with constant heaving of the sounding lead, they scraped sand-and-mud bottom several times. "This day," says Rodrigo Ranjel, "there were hard words between the Governor and Johan de Añasco."

This landing, by age-old consensus, is said to have occurred at Tampa Bay, but there is considerable evidence to the contrary. The question rests in part on where the boundary lay between Calusa and Timucua territory, for the landing is generally conceded to have been among the Timucuas; indications—both archeological and historical—to support a more southern Timucuan range, and hence a more southern landing for Soto, cannot be ignored. Soto probably made port in the general vicinity of Charlotte Harbor. This "Bay of Espíritu Santo," says Ranjel, lay "due north of the Island of Tortuga, which is in the mouth of the Bahama Channel . . . ten leagues west of the Bay of Juan Ponce." These distances suggest a landing south of Charlotte Harbor proper. By Soto's description, the bay extended "a dozen leagues or more from the sea."

Men and horses were put ashore on Friday, May 30. Vasco Porcallo, eager to be off exploring, immediately encountered Indians and killed two of them. The episode boded ill for the enterprise. On Trinity Sunday the army marched to occupy the village of Chief Ucita and became lost for want of adequate communication with Añasco's captive guides, who shortly escaped. The abandoned village, found at last, consisted of only eight pole houses covered with palm fronds, including a temple adorned at the crest with a gilt-eyed wooden fowl. Setting up headquarters, the governor lodged himself with Moscoso and Porcallo in the chief's house and burned the others.

Scouts exploring the country became confused in the maze of sloughs or mired in mud flats. Juan Rodríguez de Lobillo, at the head of fifty infantrymen, was attacked by twenty warriors who wounded six men, one fatally. The bone-tipped arrows struck with such force that the soldiers' armor parted at the joints, and shirts of mail were pierced; the missiles penetrated as deep as would a crossbow bolt. Soto's men appraised these Timucua warriors in much the same terms as had Cabeza de Vaca: they were so fleet and agile that they had no fear at all of foot soldiers; so swiftly did they maneuver among the timbered marshes that neither musket nor crossbow could be aimed at them effectively.

Baltasar de Gallegos, leading a mounted reconnaissance, encountered a band of Indians in an open field a day's ride from camp. Alvaro Nieto rode with drawn blade upon a naked warrior but was stayed by an urgent plea in Castilian. Quivering before him stood Juan Ortiz of Seville, lost from one of Narváez's ships eleven years previously. Thus Soto acquired as interpreter a Spaniard who had lived years among the Timucua, much as Cortés had obtained Jerónimo de Aguilar from the Maya. Ortiz was naked, tattooed, armed with bow and arrows, and in all respects indistinguishable from the Indians.

Soto was eager for his knowledge of the country and its natives, but Ortiz, like Aguilar in Yucatán, had done little traveling. With his first captor he had been confined at hard labor; after escaping to Chief Mocozo's custody, he had not dared to venture far, out of fear of his former master's warriors. Ortiz knew of no gold or silver, but he had heard of a chief named Paracoxi, 30 leagues distant, to whom Mocozo, Ucita, and the other coastal peoples paid tribute. Soto "rejoiced no little over [Ortiz], for he speaks the language," even though he had almost forgotten his own. The governor promised to protect Mocozo from the other chieftains who had threatened him for giving up his captive to please the Christians.

Small wonder that the other chiefs were resentful; the Spaniards were roving over the countryside, terrorizing Indians wherever they found them. Savage dogs were used at times to tear a native to pieces. Añasco, sent by boat to disperse a gathering of natives on an island, bombarded them with artillery, killing ten. Porcallo, entering into the affair with forty horse, rounded up the Indian women and took them to camp. A quarrel arose between him and Soto, and it was agreed that Porcallo should return to Cuba.

Soto had sent Gallegos to Paracoxi on a scouting mission, asking about silver and gold. Farther on, at a place called Cale, he was told, there was so much of the precious metal that the warriors wore golden hats. With this word the governor left Captain Pedro Calderón with 100 men to guard the port and marched inland on July 15, driving a herd of swine to feed the troops. Joining Gallegos after six days, Soto proceeded north toward Cale, or Ocale, accompanied by a number of the Paracoxi Indians.

The marchers, after bridging a large river, often waded swamp water to their chins, carrying clothing and saddles on their heads. They were reduced at times to eating corncobs and boiling unknown roots; cabbage from the low palmetto was a rare delicacy.

Ocale, though deserted, had abundant corn, but the cost was high: three soldiers were slain from ambush. There were beans to eat, and some "little dogs"—opossums—but no gold. The governor loaded pack mules with food and sent them back to the rear guard. In a week at Ocale, several captives were taken to serve as guides to Apalache, which, they said, could be reached in seven days. They seemed to know nothing of the intervening country.

On August 11, with a vanguard of 50 horse and 100 foot, Soto took up the march in the direction of New Spain, keeping a dozen leagues from the coast. Moscoso and the rest remained at Ocale. A month after leaving the bay, the soldiers built a bridge of pine logs to cross a river and two days later they came to Caliquen (Aguacalequen, variant spelling among Soto chroniclers), where they fed from the natives' corn cribs for three weeks while hunting Indian guides. There they heard for the first time the natives' reports of the Narváez expedition and how its members had embarked in crude boats because they could find no land passage to take them forward. The effect on Soto's men was demoralizing. "Every mind was depressed," relates one chronicler, known only as "the Gentleman of Elvas." "All counseled the Governor to go back to the port, that they might not be lost, as Narváez had been, and to leave the land of Florida." But Soto was not inclined to act on rumors; he must see for himself what lay ahead. He sent messengers to order up the *maestre de campo*, Moscoso, from Ocale.

Caliquen lay between two rivers—the Santa Fe and the Suwannee, near the confluence—and it was necessary to bridge the second stream on leaving the town. The Spaniards departed on September 9, taking the Caliquen chieftain and his daughter and a lesser chief as guide. They were greeted daily by emissaries from Uzachile, a kinsman of the Caliquen chieftain, who lived farther on. The visitors played flutes and beseeched the governor to release his captives. At Napituca, Soto went to treat with such a group and found himself surrounded by threatening warriors with long bows. Moscoso, with a trumpet call and the battle cry "*¡Santiago!*" sent his lancers to the attack. Thirty natives "fell to the lance." The Indians took refuge in some ponds, which the horsemen surrounded. During the night, when an Indian camouflaged by a water lily or a branch approached the shore, a horseman would plunge in and force him to retreat. Most of the Indians—more than 100—gave up before dawn and were put in chains.

On September 25 the Spaniards crossed the Río de Venados— Deer River—so named for the venison provided by Uzachile's people. Beyond the Econfina they came to Agile (or Axille), phonetically linked to the Aucilla River, the Timucua-Apalache boundary. This village, subject to Apalache, was memorable for an incident involving a soldier named Herrera. While he was guarding some women captives, an agressive female seized him by the testicles. Rendered helpless, he would have been killed had not his companions come to his rescue.

Soto left Agile with his vanguard on October 1 and shortly came to a river or swamp that had to be bridged. Indians lying in ambush in the tall marsh grass beyond shot three Christians with arrows. The Spaniards found the nearby village, Vitachuco, was in flames; so was another, Iviahica, reached on October 5. Nevertheless, the country abounded in corn, beans, and pumpkins, as well as ripe persimmons; the Spaniards pitched camp about the town to stay the winter.

Añasco, reconnoitering toward the sea, eight leagues distant, found Narváez's boat-building camp near the mouth of the Ochlockonee River. Horse bones and other relics of the prior Spanish visit lay scattered among trees with crosses carved upon them. The captain observed the latitude with instruments so that he could find the place from the Gulf. On his return to camp, Soto sent him with thirty horsemen to the original landing place, Espíritu Santo Bay, 130 leagues back, to bring up Captain Calderón and the brigantines. In forty days Añasco made the journey, repaired the vessels, and sailed them to the Bay of Horses. Calderón came to the winter camp by land, losing two men and seven horses to Indians on the way.

During the winter at Apalache, the natives set an impressive example of boldness and courage. Many Christians were slain from ambush. Captured Indians, even while watching the burning of their comrades, showed no willingness for peace on Spanish terms. If their hands and noses were cut off, says Ranjel, they took no account of it.

While waiting for the brigantines, Soto had a *piragua* built for reaching the Gulf. The ships, on arriving, were put in the charge of Francisco Maldonado and directed to seek a harbor farther west, where Soto expected to take his army. Sixty leagues from Apalache, Maldonado found a province called Ochuse, on the shores of a deep and well protected bay: Pensacola. When he returned to Apalache, Soto sent him to Havana for provisions to be brought to Ochuse. Should Soto, marching overland, not reach that point by the following summer, Maldonado was to go back to Havana and come again the next season. And it was Soto who failed to keep the rendezvous.

From an Indian boy taken at Napituca came news that changed his plans: toward the rising sun lay a rich land ruled by a woman who received tribute in gold from neighboring lords. Departing from the Apalache camp on March 3, 1540, the Spaniards marched across Georgia, chasing the chimera. On this trek Soto fails to endear himself to the geographer by providing good descriptions. "The first idea in the minds of these cavaliers," says the Inca, Garcilaso de la Vega, "was to conquer that kingdom and seek gold and silver, and they paid no attention to anything that did not pertain to these metals."

Yet this leg of the journey was to influence the course of other explorations for years to come; expeditions attempting to link the Gulf with the Atlantic, or Florida with New Spain, would follow segments of Soto's trail and provide clues to his route. Traveling northeast, his troops passed unseeing over the riches they sought: the Georgia gold country. At the town of a female chief, Cofitachequi, on the Savannah River near present Augusta, they acquired a quantity of pearls damaged by fire—the result of the Indians' cooking their mollusks in the shell—the most exciting find of the march. Bending northwest through the edge of South Carolina, they doubled back through the Appalachian range, perhaps touching the corners of North Carolina and Tennessee. From Upper Creek territory Soto turned southeast toward Choctaw country, descending the Coosa River. Reaching the Alabama River, he believed it the Río del Espíritu Santo discovered in 1519 by Alvarez de Pineda. Seeking gold, he "failed to accomplish other things of more import such as tracing out the limits of the land."

At the province of Tascaluza on October 10, 1540, the Spaniards might have seen an omen in the haughtiness of the elaborately attired and plumed Mobila chieftain. This giant watched with disdain as the visitors performed feats of horsemanship and jousted with reeds. When he refused Soto's request for bearers, the governor took him prisoner, says Hernández de Biedma, "whence sprang the ruin that he afterwards wrought on us."

The day after leaving Tascaluza, the procession arrived at Piachi, a village overlooking the rockbound Alabama River gorge. The Piachi chief was ill-disposed. Two Spaniards were slain from ambush while building rafts to cross the river, a matter for which Soto held the Tascaluza chief responsible. It was here that Soto's men heard of Doroteo Teodoro the Greek and the black man with him, from Narváez's troop, who had gone ashore at Mobile Bay looking for water. The two men had been slain in this very village, said the Indians, laying out Teodoro's dagger as proof.

On Monday, October 18—St. Luke's day—at nine o'clock in the morning, Soto reached Mobila. Inside the pallisaded town with only two entrances, the villagers began to dance to chanting and flute music. Observing suspicious signs, Soto made inquiry of an Indian and was ignored. Captain Gallegos took hold of the man, who jerked away and gave the captain a shove. Gallegos drew his sword and severed the Indian's arm. Thus the melee began. With loud shouting and beating of drums, the natives loosed a swarm of arrows. As the Spaniards withdrew from the stockade, the Indians flung shut the gates. Soto divided his men into four squadrons to assault the enclosure from all sides. Dismounted soldiers fought their way back into the town and set fire to it, burning their own baggage with the town and its occupants. The Mobila fought bravely; there was no surrender. "We killed them all," says Hernández de Biedma, "either with fire or the sword."

Twenty Spaniards died. The rest remained at Mobila until November 14, treating the wounded men and horses. Pressed by his other priorities, Soto ignored his officers' urging to go to Ochuse, six days' travel, to meet Maldonado's ships. The pearls from Cofitachequi, which he had hoped to send to Cuba for show, were gone. He had nothing of value from this terrible land to compensate for the loss of the 102 Christians who had been claimed by Indians or disease since leaving Espíritu Santo Bay. He would send no news until he could report a rich discovery.

Renewing the quest, Soto marched northwest along the Tombigbee River and thence into the present state of Mississippi. Reaching a Chickasaw town on the Tombigbee headwaters in mid-December, the troop went into winter camp. It was a time of unmitigated hunger and hardship. At Christmastime a heavy snow fell; the ill-clad men shivered in bitter cold, likened in its severity to that of Burgos. As the Spaniards prepared to depart in early March, 1541, the Chickasaws' smoldering resentment at the imposition burst forth in roaring flames; the Indians set fire to the camp and devastated the horse herd. Twelve Christians died. Among them was Francisca de Hinestrosa, in the final stages of pregnancy; she perished in the blaze while her husband, Hernando Bautista, was out fighting.

Still, Soto must pursue his El Dorado. Reaching the Mississippi, near the mouth of Arkansas's White River, the Spaniards built barges, crossed men and horses on June 8, and marched on to new frustrations and disasters. Making a loop through Arkansas to the Ouachita Mountains, they turned back southeast to winter at Utiangue, on the Ouachita River of southern Arkansas. Here during the hard winter, Juan Ortiz succumbed to illness. His rescue from the Florida natives after 11 years of captivity had raised only false hopes that he again would see his native Seville.

The following spring saw the passing also of the expedition's leader. By then his losses had mounted to more than 200 men. Returning again to the Mississippi some distance above the Red River, he realized the Gulf of Mexico was nowhere near. Hardship and disappointment turned to despair; with a raging fever, he called his officers and designated Luis de Moscoso to succeed him as governor and lead them back to civilization. He died on May 21, 1542, at age forty-two, "the victim," in Woodbury Lowery's words, "of his own insatiable ambition and lust for gold." To prevent desecration of his body by the natives, it was removed from the initial burial place and sunk in the Mississippi, weighted down by a mantle filled with sand.

If Soto's flaming ambition ever burned in Moscoso, it had long been extinguished. He acceded readily to the desires of his men to withdraw. On June 5 they left the Mississippi and marched westward, hoping to reach New Spain. The course took them over 150 leagues through country determined by the Indian names to have belonged to Caddoan peoples. From Naguatex, in northwestern Louisiana, the route bent south into the land of the Ais (Eyeish) and Asinai, the focus a century and a half later of Franciscan missions in eastern Texas.

They traveled until October without word of any road to Mex-

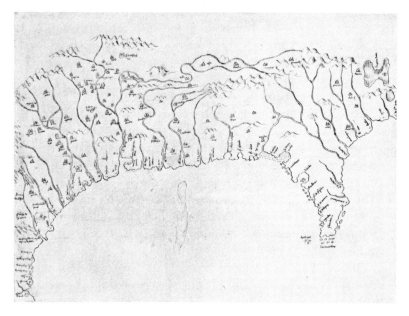

Fig. 8. The "Soto" map, Alonso de Santa Cruz. Courtesy J. P. Bryan Collection.

ico. They had no interpreter of the native languages, and beyond lay only the prospect of meeting the roving hunters and gatherers encountered by Cabeza de Vaca, with no crops to sustain them during the coming winter. Moscoso's officers favored turning back toward the Mississippi to undertake withdrawal by the river and the Gulf. In January, 1543, they went into winter camp at the pueblo of Aminoya, not far from where Soto had died, and there began construction of seven brigantines.

Despite the ravages of almost four years in the wilderness, the men were better equipped for the undertaking than Narváez had been. Carpentry tools had been brought in anticipation of the need. Among the craftsmen of diverse nationalities—Genoese, Portuguese, and Sardinian, as well as Spanish—were a shipbuilder, a cooper, carpenters, and caulkers. While virtually nothing but the length is known of Narváez's five vessels, the building of Moscoso's is rather fully described. The Vizcayan carpenters hewed planks and ribs to the specifications of the Genoese shipbuilder; the henequen plant furnished fiber for caulk-

ing. Yet it was considered a wonder that the craft floated, caulked as
they were without pitch. Neighboring Indians contributed robes for
sails and ropes for rigging. Cables were woven from mulberry bark.
Stirrup iron and the chains and shackles for Indian slaves were forged
into anchors and nails. Six months in the building, the ships at last
were finished. The planks were a bit thin because the nails were short.
There was no decking to shed water; planks were laid fore and aft
to accommodate the sailors who hauled the rigging. But they were
sturdy vessels, with rudders for steering, as opposed to the steering
oars Narváez's fleet had used. The cooper provided each vessel with
two half hogsheads, called *cuartos* to hold drinking water.

The voyage began on July 2, 1543. Into the seven craft went 322
of the 513 Spanish soldiers and unknown number of servants who had
embarked from Havana four years previously. Left behind were 500
Indian men and women whom the Spaniards had captured, enslaved,
removed from their own country, and taught a new language—only to
abandon them among a strange people. Small wonder that they wept
when their captors set sail. A hundred other natives went with the
Spaniards, in small canoes towed by the brigantines. A few of these
would return to Florida in later expeditions.

All but twenty-two of the best horses, plus the remaining hogs,
were butchered to provision the ships. The steeds were transported
down the river in Indian canoes bound in pairs.

On the seventeen-day voyage to the Gulf—the first by Europeans
on the Mississippi—the brigantines were constantly assailed by Indian
war canoes. Fifty such craft appeared the second day, each with eighty
warriors shooting arrows. Some of the soldiers cut loose the towed
canoes and went after the Indian fleet, but the natives surrounded and
upset them. Twelve Christians, weighted down by armor, drowned
while those aboard the cumbersome brigantines looked on helplessly.
Emboldened by this success, as well as by the fact that the Spaniards
had hardly a serviceable crossbow or harquebus among them, the Indians pursued the invaders down the river, inflicting many arrow
wounds.

The double canoes carrying the horses proved difficult to manage. They repeatedly fell behind, increasing the brigantines' vulnerability when they stopped to wait. Finally, the animals were butchered,
that the pace might be accelerated.

At last the fleet approached the sea—hundreds of miles, by the river's meanders, from the launching. The lower river divided into two arms, each a league and a half wide. The brigantines took the right-hand channel, pointing toward Pánuco. Half a league before reaching the Gulf, the Christians, worn out from two weeks of continuous rowing, anchored for two days. There was little rest; seven canoes of natives shortly appeared to attack the Indians in the towed canoes. As the Spaniards buckled on armor, other Indians appeared through the thicket and bog to fight dexterously with spears tipped with fishbone, as well as bows and arrows. When the Spaniards charged, they darted swiftly away, evading punishment for the wounds they had inflicted.

Exiting the Mississippi's Southwest Pass, the voyagers entered, as Hernández de Biedma describes it, "a very large bay . . . so extensive that we passed along it three days and three nights, with fair weather, in all that time not seeing land, so that it appeared to us we were at sea." Actually, they *were* at sea, the bay only assumed. Moscoso's brigantines, like Narváez's crude boats, were swept so far seaward by the river's discharge that it took them three days to come back within sight of land.

Before embarking from Aminoya, Juan de Añasco had charted the course for the sea voyage. He claims to have composed sailing instructions and a chart for reaching their destination at Pánuco, and had even fashioned an astrolabe and a cross-staff by which he could determine latitude. Añasco proposed setting a course directly across the Gulf. In this way, he believed, they could reach Pánuco in ten or twelve days; following the coast, they might be overtaken by winter first. His confidence in himself, however, was not shared by the others, who feared the open sea. They steered toward the shore and at last sighted some small islands to the west.

After anchoring for a night at the islands—the Timbaliers or Dernieres—Añasco won Moscoso's support for sailing out to sea. Two days later, they tried to regain the shore but could not because of an offshore wind. By the fourth day, water was giving out. The captains put Moscoso on notice that they would sail no farther to seaward. Then the wind changed to south, carrying them toward the shore.

While the open sea had its hazards, so did coastal sailing. Dragging anchors under force of galelike winds and heavy swells, the boats twice came close to crashing on the shore. All hands went into the surf to hold the craft off the beach with their bodies. On one occasion, twelve days after leaving the Mississippi, the battle lasted all night. Despite the wind, swarms of mosquitoes attacked the men; they could spare no hands to fight them off. Huge welts arose on faces and other exposed skin. Toward morning, the wind lulled, and the mosquitoes became even more vicious; the white sails were black with the insects. The crisis past, the men looked at each other and, seeing ludicrously swollen faces, roared with laughter.

In a nearby cove they found a natural resource they had lacked in building the brigantines: pitch for caulking. Seeping from underground reservoirs, this black tar still rolls up on beaches around the Gulf in lumps and blobs. After paying the bottoms of the boats, the voyagers went on; in two more days they came to a bay, the end of which was not found by six men who went up it in a canoe—probably Texas's Matagorda Bay. They left it sailing south with a headwind and two days later entered another, which was encircled by an island—a description fitting Corpus Christi Bay, accessible through Aransas Pass—where they were held up a fortnight by bad weather.

After sailing six more days within sight of the shore, the voyagers at daylight one morning saw palm trees rising along the coast; by midday they espied large mountains, the likes of which they had not seen in all their travels. They realized they had sailed past the Río de las Palmas during the night. As night came on again, Añasco, sighting Polaris, determined that the Pánuco was only eight leagues distant. Sails were reduced for fear of passing it in darkness. Two of the vessels, in fact, did overshoot the river mouth, thus delaying their arrival by eight days. Moscoso and the other five made it safely into the Pánuco on September 10, 1543—fifty-three days after sailing from the Mississippi. Thirty days were spent in sailing, twenty-three in various stops. More than four years had elapsed since they had left Havana. Of some six hundred soldiers and servants who had set out, hardly more than half had come out of Florida alive.

On reaching the town of Pánuco, they all went directly to the church to give thanks for their preservation. The *alcalde mayor*, who immediately sent a messenger to inform the viceroy, took the governor to his home, while the others were divided among the seventy households.

Although the Soto men were at first jubilant over their return to "civilization," their joy soon wore off. They saw around them "no more than a start at settling and miserably cultivating a land which, with its many fine qualities, was inferior to the one they themselves had forsaken." Thus, dissatisfaction set in among the returned explorers, and their ennui soon turned to ill-tempered factionalism; the former comrades-in-arms began fighting and killing each other. Their greatest anger was directed at the officers and soldiers of Seville, noble and otherwise, who had insisted that Florida be abandoned. The wasted conquest weighed heavily on all of them.

The viceroy, informed of this state of affairs, commanded that Moscoso's men be sent forthwith to Mexico in groups of ten and twenty; care should be taken to divide them according to their factions, lest they kill each other on the way. In Mexico, they were well received by royal officials and townspeople, but the trouble persisted until the soldiers divided: some to return to Spain hoping never again to see the Indies; others to seek the remedy for the wasted conquest in a new adventure; some, like Luis de Moscoso, to settle in New Spain. Most, according to the Inca, went to Peru, where "they ennobled themselves in the service of the Crown." Soto's secretary, Ranjel, settled in Pánuco. Some years later, he added his voice to those advocating a return to Florida, and a new chapter in the continuing tragedy unfolded.

Garcilaso de la Vega—son of an Inca woman and a Spanish soldier—carries Soto's ill-starred venture to a conclusion by following the ships with which Soto was supposed to rendezvous at Pensacola Bay. In October, 1543—about the time Moscoso wrote his report to the Crown from Mexico—Captains Francisco de Maldonado and Gómez Arías, still carrying on the search, sailed into Veracruz harbor and there had their grave suspicions confirmed. In keeping with Soto's orders, they had returned to Ochuse in the fall of 1540. When Soto failed to appear, the two captains parted to sail along the coast in opposite directions, seeking the governor and his army. Wherever they went ashore, they marked the trees and left written messages in hollow trunks. As winter came on, they returned to Havana, then took up the quest again in the spring of 1541, running the coast as far as Mexico and up the Atlantic side of Florida. They continued to search during the next two years before hearing the tragic news at Veracruz.

They returned to Havana to take the word to Doña Isabel de

Bobadilla, who gladly would have shared her husband's fate. Having lived in anxiety and anguish for three years, it is said, she soon died of grief. Such were the fruits of the wasted conquest.

SOURCES AND NOTES

Return of the Castaways

Alonso de la Barrera ("Información de Antonio [*sic* for Alonso] del Castillo," Mexico, Nov. 23, 1547, AGI, Patronato 57-4-1), who had served on one of Narváez's ships, was in Mexico when Cabeza de Vaca and his companions arrived. He tells of their arrival at the principal church, almost naked.

Concerning Viceroy Mendoza's offer to Dorantes, see his letter to the emperor in Fanny Bandelier's translation of Cabeza de Vaca's *Journey*, 199; also Dorantes de Carranza (son of Andrés Dorantes), *Sumaria relación*, 264–69, and Barrera in the aforementioned "Información."

Marcos de Niza's relation is translated in Bandelier, 228–29. Samuel Eliot Morison (*The European Discovery of America: The Northern Voyages*, 97–102) discusses the Antillia legend.

Vázquez de Coronado

For the "Coronado" expedition, see Herbert Eugene Bolton, *Coronado: Knight of Pueblos and Plains*. Among the cavalry captains was Tristán de Luna y Arellano, who will be heard from again in connection with a new Florida disaster. A ship captain under Hernando de Alarcón, who sailed up the Pacific shore in support of the army, was Bernaldino de Villagómez, who had served Francisco de Montejo in the conquest of Yucatán. Villagómez's "Memoria," dated Valladolid de Yucatán, Jan. 8, 1546, is in AGI, Patronato 57-3-2.

Soto and Moscoso

Biographical data on Soto are given in the United States De Soto Expedition Commission's *Final Report*, a tedious compilation largely from previously published material that fails to live up to its potential. No effort appears to have been made by the commission to obtain new information from Spanish archives. Soto's will and a number of other documents are translated in Buckingham Smith, *Narratives of De Soto in the Conquest of Florida*. Theodore Maynard (*De Soto and the Conquistadores*) offers a fairly good secondary account of Soto and his enterprise.

Moscoso (to the king, Mexico, Oct. 17, 1543, AGI, Mexico 95, ramo 3) refers to Pedro de Alvarado as his uncle. Dorantes de Carranza (*Sumaria relación*, 303) adds that Moscoso was the son of Alonso Hernández Diosdado Mosquera de Moscoso and Isabel de Figueroa, natives of Zafra, and that he married his first cousin, Leonor de Alvarado, widow of Gil González de Avila and daughter of Juan de Alvarado, Pedro's brother. Moscoso had two brothers on the expedition, another Juan de Alvarado and Cristóbal de Mosquera. In Mexico, Moscoso entered the service of Viceroy Mendoza and accompanied him to Peru in 1550. He died there the following year.

The Primary Accounts

Rodrigo Ranjel of Almendralejo, Soto's secretary, wrote the journal on which Fernández de Oviedo's account (*Historia*, 4:15–70) is based. It ends with Soto's death. No connection has been established between this Rodrigo Ranjel and the one who served Cortés during the Mexican Conquest; the latter, according to Díaz del Castillo (*Historia verdadera*, 2:34) died of syphilis. Both are alternately spelled Ranjel and Rangel; I use the different spellings to differentiate the two. The Ranjel–Fernández de Oviedo account is translated in Edward Gaylord Bourne, *Narratives of the Career of Hernando de Soto in the Conquest of Florida*, as an appendix.

Bourne's work also includes translations of the other two accounts by participants: that of the factor Luis Hernández de Biedma, which is rather brief and eclipses much; and a longer version by "the Gentleman of Elvas," one of eight Portuguese men from Elvas, whose precise identity is not known. Translations of these two appear also in Smith, *Narratives of De Soto*, and Smith's translation of Elvas is in F. W. Hodge and T. H. Lewis, eds., *Spanish Explorers in the Southern United States*.

Additionally, there is Garcilaso de la Vega's *Florida of the Inca*, completed in 1591 and based largely on interviews with participants. These and lesser sources are discussed by T. H. Lewis, "The Chroniclers of De Soto's Expedition," and "Route of De Soto's Expedition from Talipacana to Huhasene." See also Peter J. Hamilton, *Colonial Mobile*, 14–15.

Juan de Añasco

While Añasco's key role in the Soto *entrada* is known from various sources, I believe I am the first to use his "Probanza," dated at Pueblo de los Angeles, May 30, 1544 (AGI, Patronato 57-1-3). An aspirant's submission of his *probanza* to some ranking official was designed to put his services on record. Añasco's was presented to the *alcalde mayor* of Puebla in the hope of winning some perquisite to compensate him for his losses on the Soto expedition. Various members of the company give testimony in his behalf: Arías Tinoco, captain of the ship *Santa Bárbara* before the Florida landing; Diego García de León, captain of the ship *San Juan*; Fabián Rodríguez, García de Godoy, and Francisco de Reynoso, all of Medellín; Antonio Martínez, one of the Portuguese from Elvas; Miguel de Tiedra of Salamanca; and Alvaro Fernández. They bear out Añasco's claim of having taken to Florida five horses, two male slaves and one female slave, three sets of arms, clothing, provisions, and live swine, of which nothing was left but one male slave.

Añasco was an hidalgo from Seville. Although he had only recently joined Soto's retinue, he accompanied him to court, and served him as *contador* (or comptroller), navigator, and captain of cavalry. He evidently stood in high favor with the Crown, for he was granted special license to trade with the Florida Indians. The principal value of his account lies in correcting inaccuracies, chiefly those of Vega, and in clarifying details of his various feats: the preliminary voyage to Florida, his return to the landing place to bring forth the ships, and his navigation to bring the brigantines to Pánuco.

Other Archival Sources

Various other statements of services rendered by members of the Soto expedition were recorded and filed for years thereafter. Depositions like those compiled by Sebastián de Villegas Prieto of Zamora emphasize the incompleteness of the roll of Soto's men compiled in the *Final Report* (appendix G, 349–71), which is based largely on the list of Antonio del Solar y Taboada and José de Rújula y de Ochotorena, *El adelantado Hernando de Soto*, 275–334, and a partial list in Smith, *Narratives of De Soto*, 292–97. Villegas discloses the names of five expedition members (including himself) not registered by any of these sources, and mentions only one that is. Testifying for him were Juan de San Vicente, Francisco Lesondo, Hernán Vázquez (in *Final Report*), Lorenzo de Corana, and Alvaro Zambrano (Sebastián de Villegas Prieto, "Ynformación," Mexico, Feb. 17, 1569, AGI, Patronato 69-1-2).

Rodrigo Vázquez ("Ynformación," Mexico, Nov. 16, 1554, AGI, Patronato 60-5-7) is a brother of Alonso Vázquez, whose similar compilation is translated in Smith, *Narratives of De Soto*, 301–302. He doubtless is the same Rodrigo Vázquez who a few years later embarked again for Florida with Tristán de Luna y Arellano. His inquiry brings forth other unregistered expeditionists, including Lorenzo Carbajal, who gives a common soldier's view: the foot soldiers had to carry their own supplies on their backs; when Alonso Vázquez was wounded and could not walk, he says, Rodrigo carried loads of up to seventy-five pounds for himself and his brother.

One of the more interesting documents is Diego Méndez de Sotomayor's 1560 "Ynformación" (AGI, Patronato 63-1-10). One of the witnesses is Rodrigo Ranjel, who, having written an important letter to the king from Pánuco a few years earlier, at this time was a citizen of Mexico. Another witness is Juan de Moscoso, also a *vecino* of Mexico and obviously a kinsman of Luis de Moscoso Alvarado, for he emphasized the latter's role in bringing Soto's men out of Florida. He not only had known Méndez de Sotomayor for sixteen years, he testified, but had heard much of him from Governor Luis de Moscoso and the many *caballeros* of the expedition whom he quartered in his house upon their arrival in Mexico.

The two letters of Moscoso to the Crown, Oct. 16 and 17, 1543, are disappointingly brief and offer no substantiation for the claim by Andrés González Barcia Carballido y Zúñiga (*Chronological History*, 25) that Viceroy Mendoza tried in vain to persuade Moscoso and his companions to renew the Florida venture.

Moscoso does dispel the confusion as to whether or not the Soto expeditionists identified the Mississippi—most often called "río grande"—as the one to which the name Río del Espíritu Santo had been given by Alvarez de Pineda: "We decided to return to *un río grande* [a large river] that is in the land, called Río de Spíritu Santo, where two hundred leagues from the sea in a pueblo called Nuimoya [Aminoya] we built seven brigantines."

The Voyage

Soto's letter to the councillor and his contract with the Crown are translated in Smith, *Narratives of De Soto*, 263–64, 266.

Cabeza de Vaca's kinsmen on the expedition were Baltasar de Gallegos, captain of infantry and *maestre de campo* for a time, and Cristóbal de Espíndola, captain of the guard.

Gonzalo de Salazar, who conducted the New Spain fleet sailing under Soto's command, was one of those to whom Cortés entrusted the government of Mexico during his absence on the Honduras expedition.

The cause of pirate jitters at Santiago de Cuba is spelled out in two letters. On July 20, 1538, according to officials at Santo Domingo (AGI, Santo Domingo 49, ramo 2, no. 65), the French corsair, after evading the garrison and ships of that island, went on to raid Santiago and Havana, then to waylay ships from Tierra Firme and New Spain on the approaches to Havana. This is one of the earliest reports of such occurrences, which later became commonplace. About a year afterward, July 26, 1539, Santiago officials told of an artillery duel off that port between Captain Diego Pérez of Seville and a lone corsair; it lasted several days, claimed several lives, and ended when the corsair sailed away to sack and burn Havana (translation in Smith, *Narratives of De Soto*, 288–91).

Vasco Porcallo de Figueroa

Porcallo, now past fifty (the Inca tells us), "had suffered many hardships both in the Indies and in Spain and Italy, where in his youth he had been the victor in two duels." Porcallo, however, who was from Cáceres, declared himself 28 in February 1522 ("Declaración," in Buckingham Smith, ed., *Colección de documentos inéditos para la historia de la Florida y tierras adyacentes*, 45). He therefore was 45 in 1539.

Porcallo, in leaving Florida, became the expedition's only real winner. Shortly after his return to Cuba, he made a new discovery of gold and bluestone mines that promised great wealth ("Presidente e oydores de la Audiencia Real de la ysla de Española," Dec. 30, 1540, AGI, Santo Domingo 49, ramo 2, no. 86).

Women on the Expedition

Most of the women who had come from Spain stayed in Havana. An exception was Francisca de Hinestrosa, fated to die in the flames of the Chickasaw town. Añasco's female slave likewise failed to survive. Soto's two female slaves were inventoried with his property upon his death. Another woman who had survived the expedition gave testimony some years later in behalf of one of the soldiers. Ana Méndez by then was thirty-one, a serving woman of Doña Isabel de Soto, who had lost both her husband, Carlos Enríquez, and a brother on the Florida venture. Ana was only ten years old when she accompanied "Don Carlos my master" on the Soto *entrada*. She saw him killed by the Mobila Indians, endured all the hardships of the march, and reached Pánuco with the other survivors after four years in the wilderness. Nothing more is known of Ana except that her testimony, recorded by the official scribe, was not signed because she could not write. ("Ynformación de los méritos y servicios de Alonso Vázquez," Jerez, June 12, 1560, AGI, Patronato 51-3-2, translated in Smith, *Narratives of De Soto*, 301–302).

Provisions for Florida

Juan Gaytán, Juan de Añasco, and Luis Hernández de Biedma, in a letter to the Crown from Havana (published in Smith, 281–82) give the inventory of provisions taken to Florida: 3,000 *cargas* of cassava, 2,500 pork shoulders, and 3,500 *fanegas* of corn, as well as swine on the hoof for breeding and slaughter. There were 237 horses, of which about 20 died during the voyage. The 513 soldiers included 330 foot and 183 horse.

The Florida Landing Place

Cabeza de Vaca, remember, estimated the distance from Havana to Narváez's Florida landing place (Bahía de la Cruz) as 100 leagues. Añasco places Soto's at 75 to 80 leagues from Havana, about as much too far for Charlotte Harbor as Cabeza's estimate is for Tampa Bay. Obviously, no solid conclusion can be drawn from these tentative calculations, but they do suggest that the two landings may have been at different bays, separated by 70 to 85 nautical miles—within range of the distance from Charlotte Harbor to Tampa Bay.

The names of Indians encountered by Soto indicate that his landing was in or near Timucua territory. The question of the landing site, therefore, turns on the location of the border separating the Timucua of middle and upper Florida from the more southern Calusa. Escalante Fontaneda (*Memoir*, ch. 2) places the division at "Tanpa," which the sixteenth-century geographer Juan López de Velasco (*Geografía y descripción*, 82) locates not where Tampa is today but in the Charlotte Harbor vicinity.

Archeologists, long confounded by the historians' confusion, at last have begun to realize that the Timucua ranged much farther south than Tampa Bay, while "the Calusa never occupied any of the land north of the middle of Charlotte Harbor" (see Ripley P. Bullen, "The Southern Limit of Timucua Territory," 416). That conclusion stems from the study of ceramic remains of the two cultures. It would redraw the southern Timucua boundary at the north and northeast side of Charlotte Harbor.

First to deny a Tampa Bay landing was T. H. Lewis ("Route of De Soto's Expedition," 451). Rolfe F. Schell (*De Soto Didn't Land at Tampa*) has joined Lewis, and by his influence so have some others. Schell has augmented his life-long experience in sailing the waters in question by reading the extant reports in the original language. He brings Soto's ships to anchor inside the Caloosahatchee River above East Fort Myers.

Ranjel says the Bay of Espíritu Santo lay "due north of the island of Tortuga . . . ten leagues west of the Bay of Juan Ponce." Thus, if the landing was somewhere near the mouth of the Caloosahatchee, Ponce's bay would be in the Cape Romano area, in latitude 26°. Sailing instructions of 1583 ("Piloto Mayor Francisco Manuel, del derrotero del Padre Urdaneta," British Museum, additional manuscript 28,189) places Bahía de Juan Ponce in 25°.

Juan Ortiz and His Captors

Ortiz's first captor, the cruel chief whose wrath he was spared by intercession of the Indian women, evidently was Ucita (Ocita or Ecita), but Vega (*Florida*, 63, 71) confuses him with another chief of the region whom he calls Hirrihigua (rendered by Ranjel as Orriygua). These names, with the possible exception of Ucita, are Timucuan (*Final Report*, 47). Since it was Ucita's village that Soto occupied as his headquarters, the inference often has been drawn that Soto and Narváez landed on the same bay. Ortiz, however, was left by one of Narváez's ships that came from Cuba later and was searching the coast for sign of the *adelantado* at the time of the capture; the place of his capture was not necessarily the same as Narváez's landing.

The March Inland

Hernández de Biedma bespeaks the belief that the northeasterly trek reached the Santa Elena River discovered by Vázquez de Ayllón, and relates the finding of axes of Castilian make, a rosary of jet beads, and some false pearls (Spanish trade goods). On the basis of information from the Indians, he estimates the distance from the Atlantic Ocean as thirty leagues.

Of the Mobila conflagration, the Gentleman of Elvas relates, "Those who perished there were in all two thousand five hundred."

According to *Final Report*, Moscoso's trek west of the Mississippi crossed the Trinity River of Texas and may have approached the Navasota River some distance above its juncture with the Brazos, encountering natives of Bidai or Tonkawan affiliation.

The "Soto" Map

While the greater part of the map derives from the Soto expedition, it is hardly proper to call it the Soto map, for it includes information from several other sources. It begins at Punta de Santa Elena (South Carolina) in the territory discovered by Vázquez de Ayllón and describes the Atlantic coast south to the Florida cape and thence around the Gulf to Pánuco.

It is identified by Juan López de Velasco as the work of Alonso de Santa Cruz, cosmographer in the Casa de Contratación since 1530, and was found among his papers upon his death in 1572. When López de Velasco embarked on his landmark assessment of Spain's overseas possessions a year later, he found no better source on the northern Gulf shore.

Of some sixty Indian towns named on the map, fourteen correspond to those given in the three primary accounts of the Soto *entrada*. Much of the coastal toponymy comes from other maps and is traceable to no known expedition. There are clear indications that Santa Cruz's sources included not only the reports of Soto's men but also those of Ponce de León, Vázquez de Ayllón, Cabeza de Vaca, and the Vázquez de Coronado expeditions.

On the west Florida coast appeared Río de la Paz, brought forth from the Carta Universal or Hernando Colón map of 1527 and given elsewhere as Bahía de Juan Paz. The name probably stems from a misreading of "Juan Ponce" in its abbreviated form (Pōze, or Pōçe), but Santa Cruz also has Bahía de Juan Ponce farther up the peninsula. It is distinct from Bahía Honda, Hernández de Biedma's name for the bay of Soto's landing, and is far less prominent. Bahía Honda is one of two principal bays on the west side of the peninsula; the other is Bahía de Miruelo. It is my conclusion that the first represents Charlotte Harbor, the other Tampa Bay, the landing sites of Soto and Narváez.

Like virtually all the maps of this period, this one shows the Río del Espíritu Santo (the Mississippi) emptying into a large bay. Santa Cruz gives this body of water a double name: Mar Pequeña ("Little Sea"), a name that evidently originated with the Salviati map of 1525, and Bahía del Espíritu Santo.

Other place names on the map are also found on the Salviati map, on an anonymous one of 1540, on Jean Rotz's map of 1542, and on the so-called Harleian map, believed to have been drawn by either Rotz or Pierre Desceliers about 1544. See Cumming, et al. (*Discovery*, 72, 58–59, 151–52) for these maps and their background.

Santa Cruz, doubtful of the proper location of Río de las Palmas (Soto la Marina), uses the name twice. The first is about right for the Nueces River, just north of the Río Grande (Río Solo on the map), the other in its proper place. He thus helped to confuse historians, some of whom still identify Las Palmas with the Río Grande. (See, for example, Paul Horgan, *Great River: The Rio Grande in North American History*, 83–88, and W. Eugene Hollon, *The Southwest: Old and New*, 45).

The Río Solo is identifiable as the Río Grande by a notation on the left bank, some distance upstream from the mouth. From Quivira to this point, says the mapmaker, there were great herds of cattle—meaning the bison, or American buffalo, a creature seldom seen in large numbers below the Río Grande. Use of the name Quivira signifies that Santa Cruz had information from the Vázquez de Coronado expedition. His source might have been the Portuguese soldier and gardener Andrés do Campo, who had remained on the Kansas plains with Fray Juan de Padilla when the soldiers withdrew and who fled after Padilla's death "through the prickly pear country" to Pánuco and Mexico. (See Angelico Chavez, *Coronado's Friars*, 67–68, and Bolton, *Coronado*, 360).

Farther south, on the river's right bank, is another of the mapmaker's notes: "In these mountains there are silver mines." The first mountains south of the Río Grande, in the vicinity of Cerralvo, Nuevo León, are too far inland to be seen from the coast; Moscoso and his companions, sailing for Pánuco, could not have seen them. They *were* observed by Cabeza de Vaca shortly after his crossing of the river "as wide as the Guadalquivir at Seville," and by no other European prior to the drafting of the map, with the possible exception of Campo. That the mountains contained silver was proved before the end of the century, when Luis de Carvajal y de la Cueva founded a town and opened mines in the Sierra de San Gregorio, c. 1580 (see ch. 18).

Lewis gives a good assessment of the "Soto" map. While revealing "how little was known of the Gulf coast and its interior connections," it "supplies the best information of that day regarding the towns and rivers of the interior." It indicates the Appalachian mountain range with remarkable accuracy and shows the upper portions of the Tennessee, Coosa, Tallapoosa, Tombigbee, White, and Red rivers fairly well.

The Indian names warrant certain conclusions on the extent of Soto's and Moscoso's travels. Moscoso's western penetration is clearly indicated, for both the Ais (Eyeish) and Asinai of East Texas are shown. The map's value in this regard is emphasized by López de Velasco, who found that nothing was known of the native habitations along the northern Gulf shore beyond what had been described by Santa Cruz.

One Ship and the Cross:
The Dominican Martyrs, 1549 and 1554

"The more the conquerors discover new lands," wrote Bartolomé de las Casas in the early 1540s, "the more lands and peoples do they destroy and with ever greater iniquities against God and man." Into the mainland provinces of Florida, says this gadfly of the conquistadors, three tyrants had gone, each to attain new heights in "the nefarious acts that have been committed . . . in other parts of the Indies." Those "tyrants" were Juan Ponce de León, Pánfilo de Narváez, and Lucas Vázquez de Ayllón. Las Casas later added to the list the name of Hernando de Soto, whose "vile deeds were too many and too terrible to recount."

Florida's native population, says the venerable bishop, was "wise, well-disposed, politically well-organized." But such qualities did not deter the Spanish invaders from perpetrating massacres and spreading terror: "They afflicted, they killed the people, they took captives and compelled them to carry intolerable loads like beasts of burden. And when one of the burden-bearers sank under the load, they cut off his head at the neck-chain, so as not to interrupt the march of the others, since they were all chained together." A change in the approach to the settlement of Florida, in Las Casas's view, was long overdue. The instrument of the new undertaking was to be one of his own disciples, Fray Luis Cáncer de Barbastro.

Father Cáncer, born at Zaragoza, in Aragón, about 1500, entered the Dominican order at an early age. Before 1530 he came to Hispaniola and later founded a monastery in Puerto Rico. Frustrated in the island mission field because of the dwindling native population, he went with Las Casas to Guatemala about five years after leaving Spain. The Dominican missionaries there applied their conviction that the Indians should be civilized and converted by kindness and good example, rather than by force.

Cáncer twice voyaged to Spain with Las Casas, in 1539 and 1547, to enlist additional missionaries. During the second trip he discussed with his mentor his plan for a missionary *entrada* to Florida, where military conquest had signally failed. Aside from the disastrous outcome of the Narváez and Soto expeditions, a number of shipwrecks had occurred on the Florida peninsula, and castaways were treated harshly by the natives. While Spanish settlements had been formed along the Gulf shore from Yucatán to the Río Pánuco, no part of the vast region between the Pánuco and the Florida cape had yet been occupied successfully. The matter was viewed with grave concern by the Spanish Crown, which wished to gain a toehold on the Florida shore that would ease the hazards of shipwreck.

Cáncer was not the first Dominican religious to become interested in converting the Florida Indians. Soto's survivors had circulated descriptions of these peoples and their country, and some few of these natives had been brought to Mexico as slaves. In Mexico the previous year, Cáncer had talked with Fathers Juan García and Gregorio de Beteta, who had been moved by these accounts to undertake an overland journey from Nueva Galicia to Florida—in whatever context they understood the name—thinking the two territories adjacent. García and Beteta, finding the way unexpectedly long and difficult, were forced to turn back. They at last became a part of Cáncer's plan.

With Las Casas's support, the matter was presented to the Crown. On December 28, 1547, a royal *cédula* was issued ordering Mendoza, the viceroy of New Spain, to supply Fray Luis at royal expense with everything needed for the spiritual enterprise. Cáncer went immediately to Seville to begin preparations but there found his plan the object of ridicule, forestalled by bureaucratic heel-dragging.

Officials of the Casa de Contratación, finding in port no ship suitable for the voyage, sent to Huelva for a pilot named Juan López. López made no secret of his distaste. The king, he avowed, had surely not been well informed to order such a project with only religious; without soldiers to protect them, all would be killed the minute they set foot on shore. The Casa officials tended to agree, but Cáncer stood his ground, reciting the accomplishments of the religious colony in Guatemala. The Lord, wrote the padre to Bishop Las Casas, had provided such a special result in that instance that it had the effect of ending argument about the present enterprise. His audience in the Casa withdrew its criticism and conceded that the Florida project was commendable.

While acknowledging its worthiness, the Casa officials remained dilatory in attending to the matter. Forty days had passed since the priest had presented his authority—he wrote to Las Casas in late February 1548—but nothing had been done. Cáncer resorted to making a nuisance of himself: "Many times I went to their houses and to the Casa de Contratación twice a day and importuned and begged them to hurry it along. . . . God knows that, inasmuch as what I am about concerns the salvation of souls, I should have been even more persistent." The bishop's suggestion that the enterprise might be delayed a year did nothing to relieve Cáncer's urgency. "The devil would like nothing better," he replied, "for it would enable him to drag a few more hundred souls down to hell."

Cáncer had found no dearth of navigators knowledgeable of the west Florida coast. López claimed to have been one of Soto's pilots. There were four Florida Indians in Havana, he said, whom he had taken there on Soto's order; they could serve the missionary *entrada* as interpreters. Cáncer also consulted with Hernando Blas and a Captain Santana, each of whom had sailed in Florida waters. Francisco de Barrio, a pilot in Santo Domingo, he was told, had made several voyages to the Florida coast and knew it even better than López. But the pilot most familiar with Florida was Juan de Rentería, who could be found in either Santo Domingo or Mexico. His knowledge, however, was limited to the Florida coast and the route from Havana; he did not know the course from Veracruz. Cáncer, therefore, hoped on reaching the Indies to enlist both Rentería and Barrio for his expedition.

At last the fleet with which he was to sail was provisioned and ready for sea, but the matter of selecting religious personnel and naming the superior remained unresolved. There was no shortage of Dominican priests in Spain willing to undertake the venture, yet Cáncer took none of them. Quite likely the father provincial, anxious that Spanish monasteries were being depleted by New World spiritual conquests, prevented their going. On the other hand, it may be that the bureaucratic wheels simply could not turn fast enough to meet

Cáncer's demands. At any rate, the priest sailed for New Spain alone, determined to recruit his company in Mexico.

Reaching Veracruz by late summer 1548, Father Cáncer was frustrated in his desire to embark for Florida by the end of the year. In Mexico, he enlisted the two priests who had tried to reach Florida from Nueva Galicia, Beteta and García. To them were added Fray Diego de Tolosa and a lay brother named Fuentes. Viceroy Mendoza, in compliance with his royal orders, designated for the enterprise the ship *Santa María de la Encina,* Juan de Arana, captain and pilot. Whether or not Arana had been to Florida previously is not revealed.

Cáncer found the viceroy, though a realist, to be in accord with the enterprise "because it conforms to Christ's law." If it succeeded, the colonial official prophesied, it would be one of the greatest feats yet accomplished in the Indies; if it failed, it could be one of the worst, for the Indians, having killed the missionaries, would attack all comers and would be severely punished for doing so. Fray Luis recalled the conversation later, and the viceroy's words helped to decide his final course.

Plans were hastened by the decision to obtain provisions in Havana, but the search for the Florida Indians brought by Soto's men—to serve as interpreters—proved fruitless. Early in 1549 *Santa María de la Encina* set sail from San Juan de Ulúa. Emphasizing the peaceful intent of the voyage, she carried no arms.

In Havana, Cáncer at last enlisted a Florida Indian woman, Magdalena, as interpreter. The voyage then was entrusted to Captain Arana with but a single stipulation: all ports at which Spaniards had landed previously should be avoided. Arana ignored the request. Perhaps he had sailed up the west side of the peninsula previously and felt more secure in its navigation, or perhaps he considered the project only a token effort, to be discharged with all possible ease. Whatever his reasons, his cavalier decision bore the makings of disaster. On May 29, 1549, the eve of Ascension Day, the Florida coast was sighted in 28° north latitude—an area previously traversed by two of Las Casas's "nefarious tyrants," Narváez and Soto.

Not only was the captain ill-suited for the mission; so was the vessel. Despite the advice offered Cáncer in Seville, this was no shallow-draft sloop or brigantine, suited for operating in shallow coastal waters. Arana deemed it necessary to anchor in ten fathoms, miles from shore, while a boat crew went to take soundings and look for a harbor. His orders notwithstanding, the sailors, attracted by a beutiful tree-lined beach, went ashore. Hardly had they landed when they saw three Indians approaching and began to "flap their lips," crying, "Indians! Indians!" They scrambled back to the boat and shoved off into a freshening sea.

They had found no suitable port, although, as was later proved, they were near Tampa Bay. On the second day after the landfall, *Santa María* sailed north, thinking to reach either the bay of Miruelo or Apalache. She came to anchor in 28°30′, six leagues from land, and the shallop again was sent shoreward, this time with Fathers García and Cáncer in the boat. At Fray Luis's chosen landing place in a small bay, six Indian archers appeared out of the woods. The Spaniards therefore proceeded to a small island to spend the night and pulled the boat up on shore to prevent its being carried away in the flood tide. Cáncer felt a great uneasiness. "Only two canoes of Indians," he declared euphemistically, "might have done us great harm."

The following morning the boatmen rowed three leagues along the shore searching for a harbor. Finding none, they returned to the ship, which had advanced three leagues looking for them. Fray Luis, irked at Arana's refusal to follow more closely, curbed his tongue, lest the sailors refuse to take him in the boat.

The shore party back on board, *Santa María* came about to return to the first anchorage. Arana then went in the boat with the sailors to look for a harbor and reconnoiter the shore. With him went Cáncer, Tolosa, Fuentes, and the Indian woman Magdalena. Inside a bay they descried three or four fishing huts but no Indians.

Tolosa and Fuentes pressed Fray Luis for permission to go ashore, and Cáncer finally relented. Tolosa went first and climbed a tree for a better view. As one Indian after another came out of the woods, Cáncer sent Magdalena with Fuentes; Arana commanded Fray Luis himself to stay in the boat. Then a disturbing thought occurred to the priest: the Indians might kill the other religious before hearing the word they had brought. Heedless of the captain, Fray Luis plunged into waist-deep water, waded to the beach, and knelt to pray. He arose to walk toward the Indians, drawing gifts from his habit.

Embracing Fuentes "with great joy," he took out his prayer book to recite the holy word. The Indians fell to their knees. Afterward, the priests sat with the natives, partook of the proffered roasted meat, and learned that the port they were seeking was only a day and a half distant by land. No one seemed more delighted than Magdalena, although later developments bring her sincerity into question: she has been accused of grossly deceiving the trusting friars, in both the matter of her own religious conversion and the Indians' true attitude. Had she perhaps concealed a seething resentment in order to bring the padres to Florida and strike a blow of vengeance againt all Spaniards? Yet in fairness to Magdalena, it seems the priests saw the situation as they wanted to see it; if they were misled, it was at least partly their own doing.

"Our Lord knows how much we are pleased at seeing them in such peace as they have shown us . . . by their embraces," Fray Luis confided to his journal. He devised a test of the natives' good will, telling them through the woman that he had more gifts for them in the boat and was going to get them, when in truth all that he carried was in his sleeve. "I went and returned and found so many who had come to embrace me that I could not leave them."

Magdalena was busy interpreting: the Indians wanted beads, knives, and machetes, she said. The Spaniards had not brought these things, Fray Luis explained, offering all the goods he did have with him to the chief's brother, to be divided among his companions. But the Indian told him through Magdalena that he should make the division himself.

Fray Luis, meanwhile, was being importuned from two directions. The captain was shouting for him to return to the boat; Fray Diego was urging that he, Fuentes, and Magdalena be allowed to stay on shore: "I could not stop them, for another besides myself so ordered it." There seemed to be little danger, for all outward signs were friendly. One sailor twice came ashore and returned to the boat unchallenged; an Indian got into the boat and asked to be taken to the ship. Fray Luis took him and, after giving his guest some items of clothing, started back to the beach where Fray Diego, Fuentes, and Magdalena had been left.

Approaching the shore, he was disturbed by the emptiness of the beach. Then six Indians appeared with some fish and called to those in the boat to come and get them. The other Christians, they indicated, had gone into the huts with the chief. One of the sailors, thinking everything as peaceful as it had been earlier in the day, took it upon himself to wade ashore and get the fish. He was promptly seized. Held firmly by the arms, he called to the padre to come to him, that the Indians then would let him go. But Fray Luis recognized the plight more readily than he; the sailor, like Fray Diego and Fuentes, was a prisoner and in great danger of being put to death. As the sun faded from the sky, the shallop moved off the beach with its heavyhearted occupants.

The next day Fray Gregorio and Fray Luis went again to the beach but saw no sign of either their missing companions or the Indians. Returning to the ship, they set sail for the harbor the natives had spoken of, hoping to find them there.

The *relación* says nothing of the quarrel that occurred on June 3, the second day after the three Spaniards and Magdalena were left on the beach. The disagreement arose over whether or not the other religious should go ashore to rescue or join their companions. Beteta and García went to Captain Arana. The dissension among the priests was so great, they told him, that only the father provincial in Mexico could resolve it; the captain should return them there, for they knew that Father Tolosa would want it so.

Arana replied that he would do whatever the religious ordered, as long as they were in accord, but the ship was in hazardous waters, and they must decide where they wanted to go before the tide turned. García, whom the other priests had elected vicar, stood on that authority: he would go ashore with the others with nothing but a cross in his hand, if that was what they wanted, but to do so would mean certain death. The most they could do for Tolosa and Fuentes, he declared, was to return to New Spain and remain there until some means turned up by which they could make themselves useful.

When the sailors heard two of the friars arguing, matters came to a head. Fray Luis, taking it upon himself to speak for the absent Fray Diego, intervened resolutely. An undertaking of such great importance, he said, planned over a three-year period, should not be lightly abandoned. They were not far from Espíritu Santo Bay; they should proceed there with the hope that their companions on shore would appear. And so they embarked to look for the bay, believing it a voyage of only a day or so.

Father Cáncer, who wrote his record of the expedition's events as
they occurred, relates that it took eight days to reach the entrance,
another eight to enter the bay, which was six or seven leagues (15 to
18 miles) long. Yet starting from latitude 28°, they would have reached
the main entrance of Tampa Bay before sailing 30 nautical miles—less
than the distance covered in a single day on May 31, when *Santa
María* went north to look for "the bay of Miruelo or Apalache." Cáncer
makes no mention of calms, contrary winds, or other circumstances to
impede the southward voyage; the wind, by all odds, would have been
favorable. It therefore seems obvious that Tampa Bay was passed up,
possibly because the cautious Arana kept too far from shore to perceive the pass; the landing was farther south, in the Charlotte Harbor
vicinity.

On Corpus Christi Day, June 20, Fray Juan García and Fray Luis
went ashore to fill the water casks and celebrate mass. Seeing no native
dwellings, they became fearful that they had come to the wrong bay—
which indeed they had. Fray Gregorio and Fray Luis went again the
following day to look for some sign of the Indians and the missing
Spaniards. They came finally to a hut situated on a hillock, where a
single Indian stood in the doorway. They held up a shirt and gestured
to the native to come for it, but he stood motionless. Leaving the gar-
ment on a pole stuck in the sand at the water's edge, they rowed along
the shore to some huts a league away but found no one there.

Relaxing caution, they ate and rested. As they embarked again,
two Indians came running toward them, waving a white pennant of
palm fronds and calling, "Amigos, amigos, bueno, bueno," and other
Spanish words. At the beach, they urged the padres in Spanish to return ashore, saying they carried no weapons but came in peace. When
they declined the priests' invitation to come out to the boat, the two
religious waded ashore, presented them with a shirt, and told them in
signs and words that they should bring the two Christians and Magdalena; the Indians then should return to their huts and the Spaniards
to their ship. The natives, seeming to understand, agreed to bring the
others to the beach the following day. Fray Luis and Fray Gregorio
withdrew.

Next morning all three friars went in the boat, wary of ambush,
for eight or ten Indians were lined up near a pine grove that might
afford concealment for many others. As they approached the beach,

several natives came offering fish in exchange for garments. One of them asked Fray Luis for the wooden cross he carried. Cáncer hesitated but finally yielded. The Indian took the cross and kissed it, then held it out to a woman who did likewise. The object then was passed from Indian to Indian, each kissing it in turn.

The woman called in Spanish for the priests to come ashore, saying the natives were not armed. "It's Magdalena the interpreter," said one of the sailors. The priests did not believe him, for she was stark naked. But reaching the beach, they saw that it was indeed the woman they had brought from Cuba, and she had much to tell them.

Fray Diego de Tolosa and the other Christians, she said, were together in the chief's house, and she feared the chief might kill her for telling. All the natives were stirred up, thinking that an armada had arrived, and some fifty Indians had gathered, even though she had told them that they were only four priests who had come to preach to them of great things.

Magdalena's presence here is proof that some of the natives had followed the ship from the previous anchorage. These Indians, who were Timucuan, well knew the makeup of the expedition. The Spaniards, by proceeding to the wrong bay, had brought them to the border of Timucuan territory. The stirred-up natives may have been of a different Timucuan group, but it is not unlikely that they were the warlike Calusa, who ranged from the Florida Keys north to Charlotte Harbor. Magdalena and her people may after all have been well intentioned. The perpetrators—whoever they were—of the ensuing disaster, for which she has been blamed, had gained the upper hand.

As the friars pondered Magdalena's advice, the circumstances did appear suspicious. They could do nothing but return to the ship and hope that their companions would be surrendered the next day. Fray Gregorio wanted to remain with the Indians, but Fray Luis forbade it. The distressing news they received on board proved the wisdom of his judgment. A Spaniard from the Soto expedition, having fled his Indian captors of ten years, had reached the ship in a canoe, bringing word of the missing men that contrasted sharply with Magdalena's version.

This man was Juan Muñoz, captured at age fourteen from Captain Pedro Calderón's vessel in Soto's fleet, in which he had served as a ship's boy. Having been enslaved for a decade, he was scarcely able to speak his native tongue. After Soto's departure from Espíritu Santo Bay on his inland march in 1539, young Muñoz had gone with two other Spaniards in a canoe to fish. Twenty Indians approached them in two canoes with friendly words. But one of the Spaniards, Pedro López, responded with hostility, wounding one of the natives with his sword. Overwhelming the Spaniards with numbers, the Indians killed López on the spot and left Antón Galván for dead, his head laid open and his face a mass of lacerations. Muñoz was carried off to the native village. Galván was rescued and restored to health by some Spaniards encamped nearby.

The joy over Muñoz's rescue was offset by the news he brought of the three missing Spaniards. Fray Diego de Tolosa and the lay brother Fuentes had been killed, although the sailor who had accompanied them remained alive. Muñoz had been so informed by Indians who had witnessed the murders, and he had even held the priest's scalp in his hands.

For Fray Luis, the news came close to being "the worst possible in all the world," yet not the greatest evil that might befall the expedition; even worse would be the failure to make another attempt to win the natives to Christianity. Should he return to Mexico with reports only of death and failure, no further effort would be made to save the Indians' souls. Instead, the natives would be deemed deserving of death; war against them and confiscation of their lands would be considered justified. He recalled the words of Viceroy Mendoza, who had assessed the expedition's potential for becoming either the best or the worst that had ever occurred in the Indies.

In a world seething with cynicism, it is difficult to conceive of the dedication that caused Fray Luis Cáncer to risk his life to save the souls of the Florida Indians, who were in European eyes murderous and pagan savages. As he himself explains it, he had assumed an obligation at the outset; if he failed in fulfillment, not only would countless souls be lost, but these people might also be exterminated in a cruel conquest of the kind already seen too often in the New World. He had come to this wilderness to bring the Indians the gospel; as Viceroy Mendoza had told him, failure would not be benign but would sow among the natives a terrible malignancy that would destroy them and condemn their souls to Hell. Fray Luis's decision to put his life on the line had been made long before he reached Florida, long before the dreaded news of the deaths of his fellow religious. The decision was not reversible: "I do not lack reason for risking my life to save such a multitude of people but trust in our Lord and his great power to give me special help in preaching to them and in bringing these people light and understanding that they might hear and receive me in peace." He hoped not only that his life would be spared but also that the natives would receive him and hear with great desire the articles of "our holy Catholic faith"; if there were no possibility of achieving this, "then the whole world would not suffice to keep me here."

When Captain Arana and the other priests voiced their desires to return immediately to Mexico, Fray Luis had a ready answer: they should go if they wished, but he himself would remain, even if he must remain alone. The possibility of taking their spiritual conquest to another part of Florida was discussed among the priests. Arana's ship was too large to approach the shallow shores of this region; the ship's provisions had gone sour, and many of the sailors were ill of a fever; the rest had grown mutinous over being required to take the priests ashore each day in the shallop, not knowing when the natives might leap upon them from ambush. It was suggested, therefore, that Arana take the priests back to Havana or New Spain, where they might obtain a more suitable vessel with which to approach some part of Florida where the Indians were more receptive. Fray Luis was not taken with the idea. He preferred to remain here and work among the Indians who had shed his brothers' blood.

The next day was the feast of St. John the Baptist, June 24, 1549. *Santa María de la Encina* rode at anchor in the bay, and no boat was sent shoreward, for Fray Luis had certain preparations to make. The course he had decided upon would either leave him in self-imposed exile in the wilderness or bring him death. He gathered up the items he wished to take with him, then withdrew to spend the rest of the day writing. He added the final paragraphs to his account of the expedition and turned the manuscript over to Fray Gregorio, who was to relate the subsequent events.

On Tuesday, June 25, the three priests and Juan Muñoz boarded the boat to go ashore. They had sailed two leagues when a brisk offshore wind arose. Unable to reach land, they returned to the ship. This development, Muñoz asserted, was a manifestation of God's will: they should depart this land, taking Fray Luis with them. Yet Fray Luis remained firm in his resolve. On the following day, June 26, the boat was able to land.

Indians were spread out among the trees in ominous stance, their bows and lances in plain view. As the Spaniards approached, they withdrew to a thicket, refusing to come toward the boat. Fray Luis prepared to disembark while Fray Gregorio pleaded with him not to.

The Indians then called out to ask if the slave were with them. Muñoz stood up in the boat. "I am the one you want," he said. "You think to kill us as you killed the others, but you will not do so because we already know." The Indians appeared agitated. "Do not provoke them against me, brother," cautioned Fray Luis.

"You could not find anywhere in the world a people more provoked than these are already," said Fray Gregorio. "For the love of God, stay a while, do not go." But Fray Luis was heedless. He left the boat to wade ashore, toward the thicket where the Indians waited. As he reached the shore, he remembered a cross he had intended to take with him and called to Fray Gregorio to bring it. "Although there would have been no danger in taking it to him," says Beteta, "I told him, 'Father, for mercy's sake come for it yourself, for there is no one who will take it to you; these people are of very evil disposition.'"

Fray Luis walked on toward the thicket, the boat following along the shore until he waved it away, lest the occupants arouse the Indians further. As he approached the clump of trees, the danger signs pressed upon him. He fell to his knees briefly in prayer, than arose and went on. An Indian came out, embraced him, and led him onward by the arm, as others surrounded him, pushing him toward the wood. Then one of the natives snatched away his hat and felled him with a blow to the head. He uttered a muffled cry, clearly heard by the Spaniards in the boat, as other natives fell upon him to end his life. The Indians then gave a shout and ran toward the boat shooting arrows, but the sailors took it quickly out of range.

Fray Gregorio urged Arana to take them to another point on the Florida coast, but the captain refused, claiming the ship was unfit for a new voyage. On Friday, June 28, he set sail from the "Port of the Most Holy" and made for Havana on a southwesterly course. On July 2, a wind more favorable for New Spain than Havana arose, and course was changed for Veracruz. When land was sighted on July 14, Fray Gregorio thought it was the east coast of Yucatán; it turned out to be that of New Spain, in the vicinity of Almería (Nautla), north of Vercruz in latitude 20°. Five days later, on July 19, *Santa María de la Encina* made port at San Juan de Ulúa.

The cross, on this first attempt, had been no more successful than the sword in subduing the Florida Indians. The lives of three religious—Tolosa, Cáncer, and Fuentes—had been lost, and an unidentified sailor was either slain or enslaved by the natives. The climate for bringing the Indians to peace was no more favorable because of the attempt. Only Magdalena and Muñoz benefited, for they were returned to their own people.

Fray Gregorio de Beteta involved himself in a later attempt to settle Florida, but it was no more fruitful than the first. His return may have been influenced by disaster on another part of the Gulf five years after the Cáncer *entrada*: the wreck of three homeward-bound ships of the merchant fleet, which cast crew and passengers—five Dominicans among them—on a segment of the Gulf coast as yet scarcely trod by Europeans.

On April 9, 1554, the three ill-fated ships and one other sailed from Veracruz for Spain with the customary stop scheduled at Havana. By name they were *Santa María de Yciar*, Alonso Ojos, master; *San Esteban*, Francisco del Huerto, master; and *Espíritu Santo*, Damián Martín, master, and Miguel de Jáuregui, owner and pilot. The fourth vessel was *San Andrés*, whose master, Antonio Corzo, also served as captain-general of the small fleet. She was the only one to make port. Besides the barrels of cochineal, bales of cowhides, and other Indies produce, the four ships carried gold and silver worth 1.5 million pesos, and passengers and crew approximating 400 persons.

Among the five Dominican passengers was Fray Juan Ferrer, who had a reputation among his fellow clerics as something of a mystic. Attributed to him is a dockside prophecy that the fleet would never reach its destination; all but a few would perish, and they would experience great torment. Twenty days later the three ships were wrecked by storm "off the coast of Florida near the Río de las Palmas at 26.5°." The "coast of Florida" in this instance was Padre Island, one of the Texas barriers.

Recent research resulting from the discovery of the ships' remains has produced evidence that *San Esteban*'s master and about 30 others survived the disaster, probably by sailing one of the ships' boats to Pánuco or Veracruz. By far the greater number of the castaways, perhaps as many as 250, attempted to walk down the coat to Pánuco.

From available information, it appears that the castaways, while waiting for rescue, sought to move their camp from the island dunes and were cut off from the landing place by Indians. Thus, they undertook the march for Pánuco without food or adequate clothing. Constantly stalked by Indians, they crossed the Río Grande (Río Bravo, as it is known in Mexico) on a raft of driftwood, losing their crossbows in the river. The natives on the other side, perceiving that they were unarmed, pressed more closely, occasionally taking a captive whom they stripped of his clothing. Believing that clothing was the Indians' objective, the marchers cast off their garments and went naked.

The women and children walked ahead to lessen their shame. Suffering severe thirst, this strange vanguard reached the Río de las Palmas (present-day Soto la Marina) ahead of the men and fell down to drink. The Indians attacked; when the men arrived, not a woman or a child remained alive.

At "the last big river before the Pánuco," the surviving men saw a canoe full of Indians coming toward them and attempted to hide in the tall grass, only to be attacked by swarms of vicious ants. Throwing themselves into the river to escape the insects, they were assaulted by the natives and many of them were killed. Fray Marcos de Mena, a lay brother, had seven arrow wounds and was left for dead in the river's shallows. His blood brother, Fray Juan de Mena, died a short distance from the stream, an arrow in his back. Fray Marcos roused himself, plucked the arrows from his body, and went after his companions. They carried him across the river, but he had no strength to continue. Believing that he had but a short time to live, they buried him in the sand with his face exposed to allow him to breathe. The warm sand soothed his pain. As he slept, strength came back into his body. Throwing off his covering of sand, he arose and crept through the darkness. After walking only a short distance, he came upon the bodies of the last of his companions.

Finally reaching the Pánuco River, Fray Marcos was taken in an Indian canoe to the village of Tampico, where Fray Andrés de Olmos had founded a Franciscan mission a short time previously. After recuperating at the more populous village of Pánuco, he went on to Mexico.

The date of Fray Marcos's arrival at Tampico is not known, and the duration of the march is indefinite. But it appears that Master Huerto's boat had reached Veracruz long before the Dominican brother emerged from the wilderness. On June 4, 1554, the viceroy, Luis de Velasco, provided funds for a land expedition, headed by Angel de Villafañe, to search for the wrecks. By mid-June García de Escalante Alvarado, who, like Luis de Moscoso Alvarado, was Pedro de Alvarado's nephew, was fitting out six vessels at Veracruz to conduct a salvage operation.

Villafañe proceeded north from Mexico, probably on the road opened by Cortés in 1522, down the Río Moctezuma to Pánuco, which he had first seen as a member of Garay's 1523 expedition. There he learned that the *alcalde mayor*, Juan Jiménez, already had sent a salvage ship to the site and recovered more than four thousand marks of silver (equivalent to 32,000 pesos) from the largest of the three ships, Huerto's *San Esteban*, whose rigging was visible above the water. Villafañe, hiring a vessel at Pánuco, was on hand to greet Escalante when the latter arrived by sea on July 22. That was Magdalene's Day, and Escalante adhered to the old Spanish custom of naming geographical features for the religious occasion. Thus the Médanos de Magdalena—Magdalene's Dunes—found their way into the coastal toponymy and onto maps of the Gulf region.

Diving operations that lasted from July 23 to September 12 recovered less than half the silver and gold registered on the ships. As if jinxed, the recovered treasure was still stalked by disaster. One of the five ships on which it was loaded for Spain a second time went down in Veracruz harbor with the loss of eighty-five lives.

From such tragedy and failure came the inspiration for new effort.

SOURCES AND NOTES

The Cáncer expedition most often has been treated as church history, its significance for discovery and exploration ignored. V. F. O'Daniel (*Dominicans in Early Florida*), while presenting one of the most comprehensive and best-known secondary accounts of the episode, is typical in this regard. O'Daniel provides a brief biographical sketch of Cáncer and the background of the enterprise. Las Casas's review of Florida's previous history is from his *Devastation of the Indies: A Brief Account* (trans., Herma Briffault, 118–19). The primary sources on preparations for the undertaking are Cáncer's letters to Las Casas of February 6 and 24, 1548, in *CDIE*, 70:574, 580; on the voyage itself, the "Relación de la Florida," begun by Cáncer and completed by Beteta following Cáncer's death, in Smith, *Colección*. Unknown to either O'Daniel or Smith, the "Requerimientos repuestas que pasaron en la nao Santa María de la Encina de que era capitán, piloto y maestre Juan de Arana" (dated June 23, 1549; a copy is found in RAH, Colección Muñoz, A/112, f. 111) adds a new dimension, recounting the discord that influenced Cáncer's final decision.

Cáncer's Landing Place

The United States De Soto Expedition Commission (*Final Report*, 122) seizes upon the 28° latitude of the first landing as "proof" that the bay *Santa María* finally entered was Tampa. It ignores the eight days spent sailing south, as well as the difficulty encountered in finding a sufficiently deep anchorage. Both these factors suggest Charlotte Harbor or San Carlos Bay rather than Tampa Bay. The Cáncer-Beteta relation, instead of supporting Tampa Bay as Soto's Bahía del Espíritu Santo, does quite the opposite. The absence of the Indians when the ship arrived is further indication that the Spaniards had come to some bay besides Tampa, where the natives were expecting them.

The rescue of Juan Muñoz, lost from one of Soto's ships, does indicate that Cáncer's death occurred on the same bay at which Soto landed. While the "Relación" tells of his rescue, it does not indicate that he had a companion, as does Garcilaso de la Vega (*Florida*, 229–32), who gives Muñoz's Christian name as Diego, and says a sailor named Hernando Vintimilla also was rescued.

The Florida Pilots

The list of Soto's expeditionists in *Final Report* (359–60) contains five soldiers with the name Juan López, none of them from Huelva, as was the pilot with whom Cáncer talked in Seville. None of the other mariners he mentions appears in the records of the Soto *entrada*, but the list is far from complete, and little attention has been given the maritime phase of the operation. Cáncer gives no first name for Rentería; he is assumed to be Juan de Rentería, who explored the northern Gulf shore a few years later, preparatory to the launching of Tristán de Luna's colonization effort (see ch. 14).

The 1554 Shipwrecks

History and archeology related to the 1554 wrecks are presented in J. Barto Arnold and Robert S. Weddle, *The Nautical Archeology of Padre Island*. The history is drawn largely from original documents found in various archives in Spain. Antonio Rodríguez de Quesada (to the Crown, Mexico, July 15, 1554, AGI, Mexico 68) gives the location of the wreck in terms that reflect the sixteenth-century application of the name Florida to the territory adjacent to the Río de las Palmas of Mexico.

Fray Agustín Dávila Padilla (*Historia de la fundación y discurso de la provincia de Santiago de Mexico, de la Orden de Predicadores, por las vidas de sus varones insignes, y casos notables de Nueva España*, 275–90), mindless of his own lack of reportorial skills and geographical knowledge, published his version of Fray Marcos de Mena's account more than forty years after the occurrence. Despite these obvious shortcomings, he provides sufficient details to enable a reasonable reconstruction of the castaways' death march toward Pánuco.

The Indians of the Tamaulipas coast distinguished themselves over a period of two centuries by their practice of denuding their European captives. Cabeza de Vaca (see ch. 12) heard from South Texas natives that the Camon (Pelón) Indians, having killed the men in the boat captained by Peñalosa and Telles, stripped them of their clothing. A few years after the shipwreck episode, men put ashore near the Río de las Palmas by the Englishman John Hawkins were disrobed by the natives. So were other castaways up to the final conquest and settlement by José de Escandón in the mid-eighteenth century.

García de Escalante Alvarado served as "captain on land and sea" on the López de Villalobos expedition to the Far East and wrote an account of the voyage ("Relación del viaje que hizo Ruy López de Villalobos desde la Nueva España a las islas del poniente el año de 1542," AGI, Patronato 23-10-9). He and Moscoso were sons of Pedro de Alvarado's sisters. Angel de Villafañe was related to Alvarado by marriage.

The so-called Soto map of Alonso de Santa Cruz, dated as early as 1544, shows a Río de Magdalena situated about right for the Guadalupe River of Texas. This may be an indication that the map was drawn somewhat later than 1544. Herbert Eugene Bolton (*Spanish Exploration in the Southwest*, 224 n.) ascribes the application of the name Magdalena to a Texas stream to the naming of a river in the present state of Florida (the Ochlockonee) by the Narváez expedition of 1528. Santa Cruz, on his 1565 map, shows Escalante's Médanos de Magdalena but still places the Río de Magdalena farther up the Texas coast.

Genesis at Tampico:
The Staging of the Luna Expedition,
1555–59

FROM the ruins of the Soto and Cáncer expeditions, as from the 1554 Padre Island shipwrecks and a 1551 disaster in the Bahama Channel, there arose new fervor for the conquest of Florida. The advocates were many and varied, as were their approaches. Pedro Menéndez de Avilés, whose name was of rising importance in matters of Indies navigation, urged a fortress "where ships damaged by storm in the Bahama Channel might take refuge from the Indians." His suggestion stemmed from a succession of shipwrecks, especially that of *San Juan*, which in late 1551 left twenty-one persons marooned on the Florida peninsula to die at the hands of the natives. The emperor promised orders for Menéndez to explore the eastern Florida coast for a suitable location, but then the matter slipped his mind.

Voices from other quarters amounted to a clamor, among them those of representatives of various religious orders, as well as a noteworthy survivor of the Soto *entrada*. The clergy, especially, was sharply divided as to ideology and method. Some viewed the multiple tragedies as emphasizing the need to go and preach to the natives; others, as an excuse for subjugating them by military might. Both views were represented among the Dominicans, whose brothers had twice been victims of "the Indians of Florida" (they drew no distinction between the peninsular natives responsible for Cáncer's death and those on the Tamaulipas coast who had massacred the Padre Island castaways). In November, 1555, Fray Domingo de Santa María, provincial of the Dominican Order of Preachers in Mexico, urged the emperor "to provide and command . . . that Florida and her people come to the knowledge of their Creator." He wrote of the same concern to Philip II in June 1558, again citing the fate of the Cáncer expedition and the 1554 castaways.

To his voice was added that of Fray Diego Sarmiento, bishop of Cuba, whose ecclesiastical jurisdiction embraced Florida. Sarmiento seems to have been moved by practical, rather than spiritual, considerations. So many native women in Cuba had been wed to Spaniards and *mestizos*, he noted, that native men had difficulty finding wives. He proposed importing women from Florida to relieve this "thorn in the flesh" plaguing Cuban men. But the real impetus for the next move came not from the bishops and provincials but from the nascent settlement on the Río Pánuco.

Fray Marcos de Mena, escaping his wilderness nightmare in the summer of 1554, could have found at Tampico nothing more than a cluster of Indian huts about a crude mission. If there was that much, it was due to the efforts of a doughty Franciscan, Fray Andrés de Olmos, whose name more than any other is linked with Tampico's beginnings. Olmos is credited here and there with having led an exploratory expedition north from Tampico to the Florida peninsula, bringing back the Olive (Oliva) Indians to populate the Tamaholipa pueblo. Actually, this journey, as described by his contemporaries, was "to the *border* of Florida"—the Río de las Palmas. That region, not peninsular Florida, is known to have been the Olives' homeland.

Olmos, born near Oña, Tierra de Burgos, studied "the canons and laws" at nearby Valladolid and took the Franciscan habit at the age of twenty. Fray Juan de Zumárraga, guardian of the Convento del Abrojo, then chose him as a companion in carrying out a rather unusual royal commission: chastising the witches of Vizcaya. When Zumárraga was chosen as Mexico's first bishop, he asked Olmos to accompany him to New Spain. They arrived at Veracruz in November 1528. In Mexico, Fray Andrés habitually sought out the most desolate regions for spreading the faith. Remarkably adept at languages, he made vocabulary compilations that became basic texts for missionaries, and wrote extensively on native history and customs.

Advancing toward Huasteca, Olmos first penetrated the Sierras de Tuxpán, where he obtained many conversions and improved his knowledge of the Totonac language. Then, leaving ministers to carry on the work, he continued up the coast of Huasteca, eventually crossing the Río Pánuco into the land of the *chichimecos bravos*, adjoining Greater Florida.

Olmos's arrival at Tampico appears to have preceded an order issued by Viceroy Luis de Velasco on April 26, 1554—three days before the ill-fated fleet from Veracruz wrecked on Padre Island. Velasco had been informed, he says, of the great importance of establishing a house of worship and a monastery in the Tampico pueblo. He ordered the Franciscan provincial to see that it was done.

Velasco further ordered the *alcalde mayor* of Pánuco to see to the founding of a civil settlement at Tampico, allocating lands for settlers' houses and fields. The mission, if not already established when Velasco's order was issued, was begun shortly afterward. Olmos probably was on hand to greet Fray Marcos de Mena on his arrival in the summer of 1554 and must have witnessed the going and coming of the salvage ship from Pánuco, and of Villafañe. Twice during 1554, Olmos went among the "Chichimecas," whom he identifies as "those who say they killed, on the Río de Palmas, the Spaniards who escaped from the three ships and were coming toward Pánuco." The massacre of the castaways, he says by implication, was not so much the fault of the Indians as the lack of a settlement at Tampico that might have provided aid. Visiting two or three hours with these naked Indians, "who neither have houses nor plant crops," he gave them food and told them of the benevolence of God and the king. The natives kissed the cross and his hand, told him they desired peace, and gave him some arrows in token thereof.

These visits occurred shortly after the shipwrecks became known at Tampico and Pánuco, a fact that attests the padre's courage, for he evidently traveled alone. (It was not until 1555 that he was given a companion to assist him.) The second visit bore fruit almost two years afterward. "A squadron of Chichimecas from near the pueblo of Tamaholipa" (at the foot of the Sierra de Tamaulipas) came to see Olmos at Tampico, pledging peace and asking baptism. When urgent business called him to Mexico in November, 1556, many other natives from the Tanchipa vicinity, thirty leagues away near present Ciudad Mante, were awaiting the sacrament.

The Mexico trip was prompted by a royal order providing missionaries to assist him in Huasteca. While in the capital, Olmos presented to his prelates and the royal *audiencia* an additional four-point proposl. It called for still more ministers "to work in four pueblos extending to the border of the Chichimecas, including Tampico, Tamaholipa, Tanchipa, and Villa de los Valles." More important, the plan urged settlements on the Gulf coast at three locations: the Río de las Palmas, the Río Bravo, and Ochuse (Pensacola). That the proposal for settling the Río de las Palmas and the Río Bravo stemmed from the recent shipwrecks seems obvious. But what of Ochuse, half a continent away on a bay that Olmos had never seen? His concern for that location could have come only from members of the Soto expedition, of whom there were at least two living in Pánuco at the time.

As might be expected, the padre met with bureaucratic buck-passing, from viceroy to archbishop to Crown. Fray Andrés felt no reluctance to take the matter directly to the emperor. There were in the Indies, he wrote, plenty of Spaniards eating the king's bread who needed such a project to pay for their keep; at the very least, the Río de las Palmas and Ochuse should be settled, and such an extended coast surely required more than one port. Some were urging development of a harbor at the Isla de Lobos, said to offer a secure anchorage four leagues from the Río de Tuchipa (present Tamiahua) and the prospect of a good road thence to Mexico via Huachinango. But the Río Pánuco, adjacent to Tampico, seemed the more logical choice. It was deeper than four fathoms at low tide; the area had stone for ballast and building, good water, and an abundance of wood and salt, as well as fertile fields and a healthful climate. Ships of 300 *toneladas* could enter without difficulty, and the site offered greater security of lives and property than did San Juan de Ulúa.

Father Olmos envisioned development of the Gulf coast from the Río Pánuco to the Florida peninsula; like many another visionary, he outlined at a stroke the work of two centuries. But for his enlistment of important allies, his ideas might have come to naught. Shortly after his return to Tampico, his appeal was reinforced by Rodrigo Ranjel, Hernando de Soto's former secretary and the chronicler of his expedition, now serving as Pánuco's *alcalde mayor*. On April 25, 1557, Ranjel joined the vicar Pedro Fernández Canillas in advocating Olmos's plan to the Crown.

Fernández and Ranjel were attuned to the emperor's great desire to bring the Indians "to the knowledge of God our Lord and to Your Majesty's royal obedience." Having seen the royal order and letter to

Fray Andrés, they affirmed his zeal for the task; although illness had diminished his strength, he still worked diligently, and his labors had yielded fruit in conversions and baptisms and in the cause of peace among the infidels.

Father Olmos, the writers continued, manifested wisdom in advocating settlements on the Palmas and Bravo and at Ochuse. If it were not possible to settle all three locations, they urged, at least Ochuse should be settled to provide a haven for ships in distress. That it was the best approach to Florida, Ranjel asserted, he himself well knew, "for I traversed that country with Captain Don Hernando de Soto, who on Your Majesty's orders discovered the greater part of that province."

This letter, like Olmos's previous one, pointed toward the coming attempt of Tristán de Luna y Arellano to plant a settlement at Ochuse, or Pensacola Bay, and penetrate the land previously explored by Soto. The evolution of this venture is complex, but one conclusion now seems warranted: the Luna *entrada*, in both concept and execution, was more closely related to the Soto expedition than has been generally realized. While Ranjel counseled the new effort, a number of other Soto veterans wold join Luna's ranks and return to Florida. The prior episode is linked to Luna's enterprise by the events that intervened: particularly the 1554 shipwrecks, which heightened concern for taming the entire northern Gulf coast.

The shipping disaster was seized upon by both clerics and laymen in arguing the propriety and justice of making war on the Indians. Most prolix in his rhetoric was Doctor Pedro de Santander, who, as a royal overseer at Veracruz, had heard the first report of the tragedy and had witnessed the departure and return of Cáncer's ship. Having had the need thus impressed upon him, Santander submitted a proposal to the Crown on January 3, 1557, for occupying Florida. To emphasize the urgency of action, Santander cited the massacre of the castaways and the various attempts at conquest, of which the total result had been massive disaster. He recalled the experiences of Ponce de León, Vázquez de Ayllón, Narváez, and Soto, as well as Cáncer. The Florida Indians had provided ample justification for military conquest by maltreating the Spaniards sent to convert them, notwithstanding that they were "infidels, idolators, and sodomites." As Christ drove the money changers from the temple, he wrote, so should His Majesty take up the whip "to lash these rebels and cast them out of the land."

The 1554 massacre, Santander continued, emphasized the need to conquer and pacify the Gulf shore to make it secure for navigation, as well as to prevent encroachment by a foreign power. This was the promised land that had been usurped by idolators; God commanded that it be taken from them, "that for their sins and idolatry all should be put to the knife, leaving alive only maidens and children."

In this vein the good doctor went on and on; like Las Casas, he overstated his case before coming at last to the point: His Majesty should order Santander himself to undertake the pacification, conversion, and conquest of Florida. His plan called for constructing five vessels to patrol the Gulf coast from Veracruz to the Río Pánuco and thence along the entire Florida shore to Havana, to protect shipping, salvage lost vessels, rescue castaways, and supply the coastal garrisons. He proposed a fortified settlement on Miruelo Bay to make the Gulf coast secure for storm-driven ships. He asked for 500 horses and 1,500 Spaniards to pacify Ochuse, whence he would proceed to establish towns and villages at Tascaloosa, Talesi (Tallahassee), and Coosa, as well as an Atlantic port at San Jorge (South Carolina) to guard the Bahama Channel.

Santander proposed then to go by sea to the Río del Espíritu Santo—the Mississippi—which he describes as having "eight leagues of mouth" and flowing more than 500 leagues from its source to the Gulf. "It is fertile and luxuriant, and its banks twenty leagues upstream are well populated. There are many mulberry trees for silk, walnuts, grapes, and various other fruits. Down this river come many canoes manned by Indian archers, and the galleys will tame it completely and settle the people . . . in Your Majesty's name."

The great mistake of Florida's previous would-be conquerors, Santander maintained, was in seeking gold, silver, and pearls while ignoring all other possibilities; had they concerned themselves with the riches of the land itself, the region by this time would have been settled like New Spain. Yet he could not resist holding out the promise of great revenues for the Crown from precious metals.

If the Crown made any direct response, it has not come to notice. The plan has been obscured for historians by the writer's convoluted style and his profusion of ideas apart from the colonization scheme itself. Santander demonstrated a considerable knowledge of Florida history and geography, doubtless based on conversations with Soto's men or on their written reports. Yet he, like others now urging a re-entry, could not conceive of the vast territorial expanse separating the Magdalena Dunes from the Mississippi and from Ochuse and Miruelo bays, or the magnitude of the proposed task.

Santander was overlooked in the implementation of the new Florida settlement project, yet he may well have spurred the Crown to action. On December 29, 1557, Philip II, having succeeded his father on the Spanish throne, decreed the establishment of two colonies, one at Santa Elena on the Carolina coast, the other at a site to be chosen. The project was entrusted to Viceroy Velasco, who had proved himself an unwavering protector of the Indians. Since succeeding Mendoza in 1550, he had sought diligently to implement the New Laws promulgated in 1542 to assure just treatment of the Indians, a matter in which Mendoza had been remiss.

Velasco, realizing the need for further exploration prior to planting a colony, hastily outfitted three vessels to examine the Gulf coast from the Río de las Palmas to the Florida Keys. Command of the voyage went to Guido de Lavazares, a competent mariner who served the Spanish Crown on two trans-Pacific voyages, before and after his Gulf reconnaissance. A native of Seville, Lavazares had come to New Spain in the 1530s and served as comptroller of the 1542 López de Villalobos voyage to the Spice Islands.

On September 3, 1558, Lavazares put to sea from San Juan de Ulúa "to explore the ports and bays on the coast of Florida," preliminary to the new colonizing effort. His flagship was a large bark of which Hernán Pérez of Cartaya was master. The pilot was Bernaldo Peloso, like Rodrigo Ranjel a resident of Pánuco and a veteran of the Soto expedition, who has been credited with somehow saving the participants in that enterprise from total extinction.

Besides the flagship, Lavazares had a lateen rigged sloop and a shallop skippered by Constantino Oreja de San Remón and Juan Núñez. The three vessels, carrying 60 soldiers and sailors, were the smallest ships yet to undertake an extensive voyage of exploration in the Gulf of Mexico. If speed was the prime consideration, they were well chosen. Leaving San Juan de Ulúa on September 3, they entered the Río Pánuco two days later. On September 14 they sailed on north, apparently taking no pains to adhere to the coast until they reached 27°30'—approximately the latitude of present Kingsville, Texas. From that point they hugged the shore for another degree. In "28°30'" Lavazares discovered a bay, which he named San Francisco; the latitude indicates Matagorda Bay. The captain went ashore and took formal possession for the Spanish king, 127 years before the Sieur de La Salle, landing at this same bay, claimed the territory for France.

Lavazares, trying to sail eastward from Bahía de San Francisco, found himself buffeted by contrary winds. Falling back on the general sailing instructions, he set course for the "Alacranes"—the Arrecife de Alacrán off the Yucatán coast in latitude 22°35'—there to get on the course for the Florida peninsula. How far he progressed toward the Alacrán reef is not clear, but it became apparent that the weather would not permit him to carry out his plan. Well out into the Gulf, he turned north and struck an east-west coastline in "latitude 29°30'." Actually at one of the islands enclosing Mississippi Sound, he called the bay within Bahía de los Bajos, or "Bay of Shoals." After going ashore for another act of possession, he turned east ten leagues and came to Mobile Bay, to which he ascribes the same latitude. These 45-minute errors call to question the accuracy of his observations on the Texas coast. But there is no mistaking Mobile Bay, which he named Bahía Filipina and described as "the largest and most commodious" yet seen. Entering through a pass half a league wide, between Dauphin Island and Mobile Point, Lavazares claims to have sailed twelve leagues inside the bay, which extended three or four leagues farther (the distance is exaggerated). He gives the width as four leagues, somewhat too much for the inner bay but approximately correct for the wider part near the entrance. He found 3½ fathoms over the bar at low tide, almost a fathom more at flood tide, and a depth of 14 fathoms inside, with a good mud anchorage.

Lavazares was impressed by the stands of timber that began at the water's edge and extended inland. There were pine trees suitable for making masts and yards, live oak and other oak species, cedar, cypress, laurel, and chestnut, with an undergrowth of *palmitos* and grapevines climbing over the trees. Yet the forest was open enough to permit cavalry to skirmish, and there were grass and water for livestock. Several small streams of fresh water and what appeared to be a large river flowed into the bay. On the east side, somewhat higher than the west, red banks cut by ravines contained a ready supply of building stone, and soil judged suitable for making bricks. The yellow and gray clay on the west side would serve for making pottery. Eagles soared overhead, and geese and ducks inhabited the bay. Along the shores, deer and game birds, including partridges and doves, were plentiful.

Lavazares made no mention of direct contact with Indians, but natives in canoes sailed back and forth on the bay, running their fish traps. Their villages, surrounded by fields of corn, beans, and pumpkins, lined the shore. The captain computed the distance from San Juan de Ulúa as 270 leagues—about 925 nautical miles, which is remarkably close to the straight-line distance.

From Mobile Bay, Lavazares attempted twice to explore the coast eastward but was able only to reach the point where the shore began to turn southeast—east of Choctawhatchee Bay—before contrary winds forced him to turn back. The foul weather forestalled any effort to enter Pensacola Bay. The small, lateen-rigged craft, while affording advantages of speed with the wind on the quarter, were not suited for sailing close to the wind. At the turning point Lavazares again performed the act of possession and bestowed the name Ancón de Velasco to Choctawhatchee Bay.

Further exploration, Lavazares decided, was not worth the risk, for the winter winds showed no sign of letting up, and time was of the essence if the Luna expedition was to depart on schedule. On December 3, the three small vessels sailed from Mobile Bay for San Juan de Ulúa, setting another speed record to reach the home port a week later. The reconnaissance, extending from Veracruz to Choctawhatchee Bay and back between September 3 and December 10, was one of the speediest and most efficient of the colonial period. Yet—the standard histories notwithstanding—it was not this voyage that determined Luna's landing site but another that has passed unnoticed.

In 1564, Gonzalo Gayón—having served as chief pilot for Luna's supply operation—deposed in his *probanza* the only known record of this second preliminary voyage. "About six years ago," he says, he served as chief pilot of a single ship captained by Juan de Rentería. The purpose of the voyage was to discover the Florida ports in advance of the Luna expedition. It "discovered the port of Polonza [the name given to Pensacola Bay], the port of Filipina, the coast of Apalache, and the Costa de Médanos [the Médanos de Magdalena of Padre Island] in the land of Florida and the coast of New Spain." Departing from San Juan de Ulúa evidently after Lavazares's return, the ship proceeded to

Havana and thence sailed counterclockwise around the Gulf. It must have been fully as extensive a voyage as that of Lavazares.

Velasco, meanwhile, was carrying out other preparations. At the end of September, 1558, he reported to the king that six 100-ton barks were being built. They were of shallow draft, capable of sailing in four spans of water (about three feet), a necessity for entering shallow bays and eluding the canoes of hostile natives. Five hundred Spaniards— soldiers and artisans—were to sail in May, 1559. The people, he informed the Crown, would disembark at the port chosen by Lavazares to establish a town and a fort. From there they would proceed overland to Santa Elena. (The Rentería-Gayón voyage evidently altered the choice of sites from Mobile Bay to Pensacola.)

Both seamen who had sailed along the coast and soldiers who had served with Soto assured Velasco that it was better to approach Santa Elena by land; the overland route from the Gulf would preclude the long sea voyage around the keys and the risk of ship loss. Santa Elena's location was uncertain; Soto's men knew only what the Indians had told them, that it was three days' travel from their "River of Pearls" called Cofitachequi. Sailing charts of the region were said to be inaccurate, and there was no certainty of finding a suitable port.

The viceroy, in session with the royal *audiencia*, had conferred with the provincials of Dominican, Franciscan, and Augustinian orders on the religious aspects of the undertaking. It was agreed that only one order should be represented. The Franciscans and Augustinians yielded, and six Dominican priests were chosen.

On October 30, Velasco appointed Luna governor. While instructions were being drawn for the various contingents—governor, religious, and royal officials—the captains recruited soldiers from the provinces: Cristóbal Ramírez y Arellano, the governor's nephew, enlisted his cavalry in Oaxaca; Juan de Jaramillo raised his company in Zacatecas; Pedro de Acuña recruited in Puebla de los Angeles; Luna's own cavalry company came largely from Mexico. Infantry companies raised by captains Alvaro Nieto (late of the Soto *entrada*), Ladrón de Guevara, Antonio Ortiz de Matienzo, and Juan de Porras came from Puebla and Mexico. Instead of the 400 originally planned, the soldiers now numbered 500, half of them cavalry. Undisciplined and restless, they came close to rioting on March 8, when a constable in the capital attempted to deprive a disorderly soldier of his sword.

On March 30, 1559, the viceroy sent a copy of the royal decree to Luna and confirmed his appointment as civil and military governor. Luna was authorized to settle anywhere east of a line drawn northward from a point on the coast fifty leagues west of "the Río Grande de Espíritu Santo"—an interesting linkage of the names given the Mississippi by Soto's men and Alvarez de Pineda—which emptied into the Gulf at 29°. Aside from governing all the region's provinces, Luna was to see after "all that touches the service of God our Lord and our own," including conversion of the natives.

The troops marched from Mexico for San Juan de Ulúa late in April, their ranks swelled by servants, families, and camp followers to a total of 1,500. The viceroy himself departed the capital to accompany the procession as far as Tlaxcala. Luna left that point with his colonists and soldiers before May 12. At Jalapa he found Angel de Villafañe, whom Velasco had sent to draw up the muster roll of men and horses and take charge of the camp while the governor went on to San Juan de Ulúa to make arrangements for embarkation. At the port, stores of corn, hardtack, bacon, dried beef, cheese, oil, vinegar, and wine were being loaded, as well as cattle for breeding and tools for building, clearing the land, and working the fields.

Only with reluctance did the viceroy separate himself from the expedition, which he had fostered in every way possible. "I assure you," he told Luna, "that if I had license . . . I would go myself." Throughout the colony's unhappy life, he was never reluctant to give advice. Luna, in fact, developed an unreasonable dependency on his counsel, thus compounding his own difficulties. Even before leaving Tlaxcala, Velasco cautioned Luna about the makeup of the expedition, noting the great "multitude of mestizos, mulattoes, and Indians" being taken; Luna would see, he warned, that most of these would serve only to put the camp in confusion and to eat up the supplies.

Luna's instructions cautioned him to "take special care to punish public sins such as blasphemy, prohibited games, concubinage, witchcraft, soothsaying, and usury." Yet the viceroy had learned that the *alférez* Alonso de Castilla had taken with him a woman—a singer—a matter that demanded prompt remedy. "I charge you for the service of His Majesty not to permit an unmarried woman of suspicious character to embark, for you know how much she will offend. One public mortal sin is enough to cause the loss of an army." The viceroy in his righteous wisdom would find occasion later to recall having warned Luna against burdening the colony with useless people, and Luna would regret that in this one instance he had ignored Velasco's advice. On June 11 the governor sailed from San Juan de Ulúa with eleven vessels. The ships carried 500 soldiers, 1,000 serving people (including women, children, Negroes, and Indians), and 240 horses. It was a fair wind that bore them across the Gulf of Mexico, but it wafted forebodings of disaster.

SOURCES AND NOTES

Pedro Menéndez de Avilés first appealed to the Crown for a settlement on the Bahama Channel on August 31, 1555—ten years before he founded St. Augustine, Florida, as the first European settlement within the present limits of the United States. His letter to the emperor is in RAH, Colección Muñoz, A/114, f. 310r.

Fray Domingo de Santa María's concern is expressed in his letter to the emperor of Nov. 1, 1555, in *CDI*, 3:520–26; to the king (Philip II), June 15, 1558, in *Cartas de Indias* 1:134–37 (vol. 264, Biblioteca de autores españoles). See also "Capítulos de una carta de Fray Diego Sarmiento, obispo de Cuba," Bayamo, April 20, 1556, *CDI*, 5:553–55.

Andrés de Olmos and Tampico

Pedro Martínez de Loaysa, *alcalde mayor* of Pánuco about 1606, credits Olmos with founding the mission of San Luis de Tampico in 1532 ("Descripción de la villa de Tampico," extracted in Toussaint, *La conquista*, 291). This could not have been the case, however, for Olmos was active elsewhere until the early 1550s. A journey to the Florida peninsula in 1540 is credited by Vidal Covián Martínez (*Cronología histórica de Tampico, Ciudad Madero y Altamira, Tam. y de la expropiación petrolero*, 1:8). From there, says Covián, Olmos "would bring to the seno mexicano [a misapplication of the name for the Gulf of Mexico to the region later settled by José de Escandón] a numerous tribe of Olive Indians and with them would found in 1552 a pueblo called Tamaholipa." Fray Gerónimo de Mendieta (*Historia eclesiástica indiana*, 646) specifies that Olmos's journey was to the Florida border, which at that time was considered to be the Río de las Palmas, or Soto la Marina River. During Escandón's exploration and settlement of present Tamaulipas in the mid-eighteenth century, the colonizers were told by the Olives that their ancient homeland was on the Río de las Palmas. Pedro Martínez (in Toussaint, *La conquista*, 271–72) relates that "the natives of these pueblos speak the Huastec language, except those of Tamaholipa, who speak *oliva chichimeca*." The Olives evidently were related to the Chichimecs of Nueva Galicia.

Concerning Olmos's biography, see Mendieta (*Historia*, 644); Alfonso

Trueba (*Retablo franciscano*, 30); Toussaint (*La conquista*, 158). Mendieta (p. 606) relates that the Franciscan *custodio* commissioned Olmos to write on native history and customs. The resulting work, in which he collected drawings and accounts that had been handed down through succeeding native generations for centuries, has been lost, but the data are utilized by other Franciscan historians: Mendieta, Bernardo de Sahagún, and Juan de Torquemada. See Luis Velasco y Mendoza, *Repoblación de Tampico*, 122.

Having learned several languages—Mexican, Totonac, Tepehuán, and Huastecan—Olmos prepared his *Arte para aprender la lengua mexicana* and other language treatises to assist his fellow missionaries (Fray Diego Salada to the Crown, AGI, Indiferente General 1383B).

Viceroy Velasco's information on the Tampico pueblo that prompted his action probably came from Olmos himself. If not, the informant must have been Diego Ramírez, the king's inspector investigating abuses of the *encomienda* system. Concerning the Ramírez inspection, see Walter Vinton Scholes, *The Diego Ramírez Visita* (esp. 69–74); Diego Ramírez, "Relación duplicada de los puestos que Diego Ramírez visita en la provincia de Pánuco," Aug. 17, 1553 (AGI, Mexico 168).

The village of Tampico was established "one league from the bar of the sea, two crossbow shots from the river," about where the city stands today. "In colonial times," says Joaquín Meade (*Documentos inéditos para la historia de Tampico*, 11–12), "there were two Tampicos: the Huastec pueblo and the Spanish village of San Luis de Tampico, both north of the Río Pánuco, approximately where the city stands presently. It may be inferred that at some later time the Spanish settlement was moved to the south side of the Pánuco, perhaps where the Pueblo Viejo de Tampico is still found. . . . The repeated attacks of the Chichimecs from the north or the entry of the pirates must have motivated the move. Later [1754] it was moved to Tampico Alto." Dates of the various moves are not definitely established.

Olmos tells of his visits to the "Chichimecas"—a generic term applied to the more primitive, nomadic peoples—in his letter to the emperor of Nov. 25, 1556 (*Cartas de Indias*, 1:127). In the same letter he proposes the three settlements on the northern Gulf and development of a harbor at the mouth of the Pánuco. Fernández Canillas and Ranjel voiced their support in a letter dated Pánuco, April 25, 1557 (AGI, Mexico 168, printed in Herbert I. Priestley, ed., *The Luna Papers*, 2:264–65). A doubtful abbreviation in the signature gives the vicar's surname. Priestley read it as Rodríguez; I think it is Fernández.

Pedro de Santander

Santander's proposal (in *CDIE*, 26:340–65) gets a footnote in Francis Parkman (*Pioneers of France in the New World*, 13–14 n.). Lowery (*Spanish Settlements, U.S.*) briefly cites Parkman. Otherwise, the plan has escaped notice. Santander, despite his extended service in New Spain, was not highly regarded by some of the Spanish bureaucrats. Tello de Sandoval (to the Crown,

Mexico, March 27, 1545, AGI, Mexico 68, ramo 1) caustically announces the arrival of "one who is said to be the licentiate Santander, and he commenced to seek the office of physician in the city of Veracruz." When the Audiencia de Mexico called upon him to disclose his healing methods, "it seemed that although he was being called licensed that he was not." Santander showed a license signed by the king's physician that authorized him to seek the office in the islands and Tierra Firme, rather than in Mexico. That Santander returned to New Spain after writing his 1557 proposal (which he repeated after it was lost the first time) is revealed by his letter to the Crown, from Veracruz, of Oct. 15, 1559 (AGI, Mexico 168). Serving as the Crown's *veedor* and *denunciador* (informer) without pay, he performs the function of reporting ships suspected of carrying more precious metals than they have registered or evading the royal tax—a role that surely exacerbated his poor image. He requests appointment to remunerative office.

The Preliminary Voyages

Guido de Lavazares's voyage following Philip II's decree is well known from his "Declaración" (in RAH, Colección Muñoz, A/115, ff. 84–86, reproduced in Priestley, *Luna Papers*, 2:332–39). His name is signed "Lavazares," although the text gives it as Guido de Bazares, and it often is given as Guido de las Bazares. After serving as *contador* on the López de Villalobos voyage to the Spice Islands, he returned to New Spain and accumulated some wealth. He shipped 82 marks of silver to Spain with the ill-fated 1554 fleet, as shown by the register of *Santa María de Yciar*, one of the lost ships (AGI, Contratación 2490). Six years after his reconnaissance of the Gulf coast, he sailed with Miguel López de Legazpi from Puerto de la Navidad, on the west coast of Mexico, as treasurer of the expedition to conquer the Philippines and discover the eastward route across the Pacific. When López de Legazpi died in Manila in 1572, Lavazares, "man of great prudence and noble intention," became governor of those islands (Fernández de Navarrete, *Biblioteca*, 2:602–603). See also *Cartas de Indias*, 1:119, 328, and 3:782.

Priestley (*Luna Papers*, 1:262 n.) quotes the historian Icaza concerning Bernaldo Peloso's role in the Soto expedition.

The source on the Gayón-Rentería voyage, heretofore unknown, is Gonzalo Gayón ("Probanza," Havana, July 13, 1564, AGI, Santo Domingo 11, ramo 3).

Final Preparations

Viceroy Velasco relates plans for the expedition to the Crown in his letter of Sept. 30, 1558 (in AGI, Mexico 19, ramo 21). The letter is extracted in Priestley (*Luna Papers*, 2:256–61), but pertinent information is omitted. Other information on the preparations is from *Luna Papers*, vol. 1.

New Fiasco in Florida:
Luna and Villafañe, 1559–61

By all yardsticks, the Florida expedition of Tristán de Luna y Arellano should have been a rousing success. Never before had such an enterprise in the Gulf of Mexico drawn participants with such a wealth of experience. Its soldiers and sailors had served in diverse conquests: some in Italy and Africa, some in the conquests of Mexico and Peru, some with Soto and Cáncer in Florida. Luna himself had been a cavalry captain, then second in command, with Vázquez de Coronado on the march for Cíbola. Juan de Jaramillo, a nephew and namesake of Doña Marina's husband, also was a veteran of that venture and author of an important account of the episode.

Jorge Cerón Saavedra, Luna's *maestre de campo*, had sailed with Cortés on his voyage up the Pacific shore to Baja California, as captain at sea and *maestre de campo* on land. Mateo del Sauz, Luna's *sargento mayor*, had served in Peru. Like Guido de Lavazares, he was to sail to the Philippines in 1564. Fray Gregorio de Beteta, Fray Luis Cáncer's companion on the fateful Florida *entrada* of 1549, was to come from Spain to join the colony after it had reached Florida.

Even more important from the standpoint of experience were the men who had served with Soto. These included Luis Daza, who as factor commanded the supply ships operating between Florida and New Spain, and Bernaldo Peloso, a pilot in the fleet that took Luna to Florida, as he had been with Lavazares on the 1558 reconnaissance voyage. Rodrigo Ranjel, after advocating the Luna venture, did not join it himself, but he did recognize the contribution that Soto's erstwhile followers were making. In a 1560 legal proceeding, he was asked if the Soto *entrada* really had served the king in any significant manner. "Yes, and greatly," he replied. "Because of it, those who now have gone to settle [Florida] went well informed of the land and what it is necessary for them to do."

Probably the most important of Soto's men with Luna was Captain Alvaro Nieto, who on the previous expedition had found the Narváez castaway Juan Ortiz. With Mateo del Sauz, Nieto guided the march to the Coosa country of northeastern Alabama. On that trek as *alguacil mayor* went Rodrigo Vázquez, probably the same Rodrigo Vázquez who had marched with Soto. These two and Juan de Vargas—another name from the Soto expedition—stood fast with Luna when he was threatened with mutiny and excommunication.

Yet such an impressive array of conquistador talent was not enough to guarantee success, even with the other advantages that favored the enterprise. Never before had so much attention been given to provisioning such an undertaking. Velasco strained to keep the supply lines open, providing the best of men and ships. With Daza in command, the supply operation had as pilots Gonzalo Gayón and Hernán Pérez, both of whom had conducted exploratory voyages to the northern Gulf shore. When New Spain's resources failed, the ships went to Havana and Campeche, whence they brought all kinds of livestock. But even their efforts were not enough to stave off starvation.

Luna's age and service record reflect that he was a likely choice for the charge given him. The scion of a distinguished Aragonese family long conspicuous in the royal service, he had come to New Spain almost thirty years previously. His wife was Doña Isabel de Rojas, twice widowed, wealthy, and socially prominent. She had been married to Francisco Maldonado, who as a member of the Soto venture had discovered Ochuse, the bay to which Luna now sailed. Luna himself, having served Vázquez de Coronado with distinction, enhanced his prestige by quelling a native uprising in the Oaxacan provinces of Coatlán and Tetiepa in 1548. Yet there appears the suggestion that his appointment as Florida governor was influenced by friendship. Velasco accorded Luna a deference that was rare between a ranking official and his appointee; he even kept Luna's eldest son in his own household during the father's absence. While the viceroy was never sparing with advice, it was only advice—perhaps even beyond the point at which he should have issued stern commands. Even had Luna not been impaired by illness, the enterprise would have had problems enough. The penetrations of Florida by Narváez and Soto notwithstanding, there had yet been no effective conquest of the region to which Luna brought families to settle. These built-in handicaps were compounded by natural disaster on at least three occasions.

After leaving San Juan de Ulúa on June 11, the fleet of eleven vessels sailed with a fair wind for seventeen days. On June 28 its position was calculated as latitude 27°15', on the longitude of the Río del Espíritu Santo (Mississippi). From that point the voyagers sailed southeast with the current for six days to sight the Arrecife de Alacrán—the same maneuver attempted by Lavazares—there to take the wind for Florida. Then, sailing northeast for eight days, they sighted the mainland coast on July 12 in latitude 29°30', near Cape St. George or Cape San Blas. Anchored there five days, they took on wood, water, and hay before setting out on July 17 to look for Ochuse. A frigate scouted ahead, but the pilot, failing to recognize the landmarks, led the fleet instead to Lavazares's Bahía de Filipina—Mobile Bay.

Luna, acting on Gayón's information that Ochuse was the best and most secure port on the coast, sent the frigate back to search for it. It was found "twenty leagues" east of Filipina, 35 leagues "more or less" from Miruelo Bay. By the pilot's reckoning, Ochuse lay in 30°20', accurate within a few minutes for the present entrance to Pensacola Bay near Fort Pickens.

At Bahía Filipina the horses—of which more than a hundred had died—and some companies of soldiers were disembarked to proceed overland to Ochuse. Before the fleet was out of Filipina, the wind freshened, combining with the swift current and shallow bottom to make the passage difficult. The ships nevertheless got underway on the eve of the Assumption of the Virgin, August 14, and the next day reached Ochuse, which Gayón called Polonza. It was more commonly referred to as Santa María de Ochuse. Luna deemed it one of the best ports yet discovered in the Indies, "so secure that no wind could ever do any damage whatsoever"—a judgment soon proved tragically in error.

A few huts of Indian fishermen stood along the forested shore, with a cornfield nearby, but in the days following only a few natives were seen fishing on the bay.

On August 25 Luna dispatched Luis Daza with the galleon *San Juan* to carry news of his arrival to the viceroy. He picked out a townsite on an eminence sloping toward the anchorage, observing that the area's sandy soil promised no abundant crops, although there were many wild fruits, and game and fish abounded. He anticipated difficulty in provisioning the colony "until the port of Santa Elena is colonized and a road overland to New Spain is discovered."

About twelve days after arrival, Luna sent Captains Alvaro Nieto and Gonzalo Sánchez de Aguilar with 100 men to explore the Escambia River, flowing into Pensacola Bay. On this march Nieto, himself a Soto veteran, took as interpreter an Indian woman named Lacsohe, one of those whom Soto's force had captured in this region. In twenty days his company went 20 leagues up the river, which flowed swiftly in tortuous meanders and was not considered navigable. The explorers found only one small Indian village ten leagues from the landing. Returning to the base camp, Nieto and Sánchez learned that it had suffered the first in a series of disasters.

On Monday, September 19, a hurricane struck the fleet, still anchored in the bay and only partly unburdened. By the time the storm blew itself out twenty-four hours later, seven of the ten vessels lay in rubble on the beach, and many sailors and colonists still quartered on board had been drowned. With most of the provisions ruined, Luna's position at Bahía Santa María was rendered untenable at a stroke. His only hope for sustaining his people until Daza brought provisions from New Spain lay in finding well-stocked Indian villages.

With only a caravel and two barks spared by the storm, he had one of the vessels made seaworthy and sent Felipe Boquín to New Spain to carry the unhappy news. When Nieto and Sánchez returned, he sent them back with the *sargento mayor*, Sauz, and 150 soldiers to look for a native village with provisions. Traveling 40 leagues over wild and uninhabited land, they passed the head of the Escambia and found their way blocked by a large river known from the Soto *entrada* as the Piache—the Alabama. The marchers followed its banks to an abandoned Indian village which, though in ruins, still had supplies of corn and beans. At last finding some natives to regale with beads and ribbons, they learned that this was Nanipacana, not far from Soto's tragic encounter with the Mobila in October, 1540. Before these previous Spanish visitors had destroyed it, the natives said, Nanipacana had been large and populous.

As the expedition stretched past the allotted thirty days, the colonists at Santa María awaited news with mounting anxiety. About mid-

December the *alférez* Cristóbal Verdugo and twenty men reached the port with news from Sauz. Still at Nanipacana, the leader urged the governor to bring the camp up the Piache to partake of the natives' bounty. Luna, however, was severely ill and delirious. Months went by before he at last decided to make the move.

In his more rational moments, the governor wrote to Velasco of plans to move to Bahía Filipina because of Ochuse's unhealthfulness. He even had two brigantines built for transporting the colony and ascending the river from Filipina. To relieve the food shortage, he sent Alonso Velázquez and Sebastián Gamboa to Havana. Gamboa's vessel was lost during the voyage. After an exchange of messages with Sauz, Luna sent men to open a road to Nanipacana. Late in November the ships *San Juna* and *Francesillo* reached Santa María de Ochuse with welcome supplies from Veracruz, but the cargo provided only temporary relief. The vessels also brought the viceroy's reaction to news of the recent disaster.

Velasco, despite good intentions, was a master at second-guessing. The loss might have been avoided, he averred, if only the voyage had been conducted differently from the outset: "If you had not gone out toward the open sea as you did, you would have reached your destination some days sooner; if the pilots had been able to do so they would have saved time and labor and the loss of some of the horses and perhaps . . . some of the ships." He evidently referred to the long sweep southward from latitude 27°15′ to seek a favorable wind from the Alacrán reef—yet that was the course suggested by official instructions when the wind was northeasterly.

The viceroy manifested great concern for providing the colony's needs. In view of the shipping disaster, he turned his thoughts to the possibility of establishing an overland supply route through unknown country. If the Florida enterprise was to be promptly supplied with cattle and horses, he wrote in October, 1559, the animals should be taken overland. Yet the road was long and difficult, short of water in some parts, blocked by rivers and swamps in others. "God willing, I shall send out by December or January twenty-four or thirty horsemen with provisions for three or four months, to explore the land for two hundred leagues beyond Zacatecas." The explorers would return by an alternate route, between the valleys of Pánuco and Oxtipa (modern Valles), to determine which was better. Horses and cattle, meanwhile, would be gathered at Querétaro and San Miguel in the hope that the drive might begin within a year. But the plan depended on finding a road to the Río del Espíritu Santo and a suitable crossing.

To lead the exploration, Velasco proposed to enlist Juan de Busto (a Pánuco resident) or Lope Arellano, assisted by Alvaro Muñoz. He instructed Luna to give his precise location and the distance from the Espíritu Santo, or Mississippi. Would it be necessary for the drovers from New Spain to cross the livestock over the river? he queried. Or would Luna's men take charge there?

Before the letter was finished, Muñoz visited the viceroy and offered to go and find the road to the Espíritu Santo in late December or early January. Fray Andrés de Urdaneta was providing him directions. Five days later, on October 30, it was Busto, not Muñoz, who was to make the reconnaissance, setting out "the middle of December or the first of January" with forty horsemen. He was expected to return in four months, barring unforeseen difficulty. A description of the road then would be sent Luna by ship, that he might order a detail to meet the drovers and advise them on the route beyond the Espíritu Santo.

Whether or not Busto actually undertook the exploration, he never reached the Mississippi. Velasco wrote Luna on August 20, 1560, that he was sending Busto to visit the Florida colony and observe its situation firsthand. Six months later the viceroy blamed the breakdown of his plans on Luna's failure to explore westward. As for sending livestock overland, he wrote, "it will be very difficult until you have examined the land as far as the Río del Espíritu Santo and know where it is." Even so, Velasco planned to collect up to 3,000 cattle and 2,000 mares and start them up the road to Zacatecas and Valles. "I have had the road examined for seventy or ninety leagues from here. The country is rough, bad, and uninhabited. There is no one who dares believe it possible to go by this route, which is in part that which was followed by the Portuguese through the prickly-pear country and which they say belongs to the savage Chichimecas, thirty leagues beyond Zacatecas." Later that month (May, 1560) twenty horsemen and three hundred friendly Indians would probe even farther toward the Espíritu Santo. Whether or not any part of this plan was carried out is questionable. If any cattle or horses were started on such a drive, they did not reach their destination. The project was ahead of its time.

From the start it promised little timely relief for the colonists in their emergency.

Luna's move to Nanipacana (Monroe County, Alabama), via Bahía Filipina, began about mid-February, 1560. Part of the people went by land; the rest ascended the Alabama River in the brigantines. Both groups suffered severely from hunger during the journey, and Luna again became irrational. Jaramillo, with fifty men and some black slaves, stayed at Bahía de Santa María to hold the port and direct any supply ships to Filipina.

The governor set up camp on the Alabama, naming the new settlement Santa María de Nanipacana. The local natives by this time had fled, taking the food supply with them. There was a move afoot to get Jorge Cerón to take charge, but Luna rallied and sent Cerón, Sauz, Nieto, Castilla, and the comptroller, Alonso Pérez—possibly one of the Soto veterans—up the river with 100 men to look for Indian towns. During the first half of their journey of 70 leagues, they found abandoned houses and fields. The rest of the way was through unsettled country. They therefore retraced their course, returning to Nanipacana about the first of April.

Luna then decided to seek the fabled Coosa province, visited by Soto in 1540. To that end Sauz marched in mid-April with 100 foot soldiers and 50 horsemen. Servants completed the total of 200. Among the officers were Alvaro Nieto and Rodrigo Vázquez (Soto veterans), Cristóbal Ramírez y Arellano (the governor's nephew), Castilla, and Gonzalo Sánchez de Aguilar. Fathers Anunciación and Salazar rounded out the company.

Marching northeast through tangled forest marked by few trails, they ate herbs, berries, and acorns when they could find them. Six weeks after their departure, they received word from friendly Indians that the people at Santa María de Nanipacana were even worse off than they. Therefore, when they came upon an unexpected store of corn at the native village of Casiste, Tascaluza province, they sent it downriver in canoes and rafts manned by Juan de Porras and 12 companions. They hoped that Porras would bring back items they themselves needed, as both men and horses lacked shoes, clothing was threadbare, and there was no salt. Porras, reaching Nanipacana, found it abandoned. Not until mid-August did he reach the camp at Ochuse.

Sauz, meanwhile, took his men on up the Alabama to the Coosa River confluence and followed the latter stream to Onachiqui, the first town of Coosa province. Reaching that point ten days after Porras's departure, the travelers stayed a week, enjoying the food and rest.

Proceeding toward the main settlement of Coosa, they passed the native villages of Talpa, Ynicula, and Atache. Sauz noted that this was the best land for settling seen thus far, but it failed to please the friars, who were "inclined to have their own way." The march halted on July 6 at Apica, amid growing concern for Porras. Sauz began to think of sending a detail with Ramírez y Arellano to look for him, but was reluctant to diminish his force before reaching Coosa. He proceeded through a more densely settled country of friendly people who willingly provided native bearers and food. The dark forest, which had prevailed all the way from Nanipacana, now thinned slightly as the marchers traversed broken, stony hills. Sixteen days from Apica, they approached Coosa in humid late July. A range of fairly high, wooded mountains, running east-west, rose to the north, but they saw no mountains like those of Spain and New Spain. Except for the stony hills, the country was flat, cut by numerous creeks, rivers, and swamps.

Coosa, with thirty houses, stood at the juncture of two small rivers. It was surrounded by savannas where the Indians planted their crops, but dense forest of pine, oak, walnut, and chestnut trees enclosed the clearings. Blackberries and plums, as well as hazelnuts not yet ripe, were found in the woods, although the country as a whole offered few fruits of value. The people of Coosa were unafraid, making no effort to hide their food or their women. As Sauz and his men pitched camp on a small savanna a short distance from the town, the Indians brought corn, beans, and pumpkins.

Six or seven small villages, none with more than fifty houses, stood within two leagues of Coosa, some of them enclosed by six-foot walls. Each town had a plaza for sporting events; each plaza, a pole like a town gibbet. There were different dwellings for summer and winter, the winter quarters being earth-covered and overgrown with crawling vines. These natives, though seemingly inferior, culturally speaking, to denizens of the lower country, were more domestically inclined, suggesting that they might be more easily subjugated.

Such was the report signed on August 1 by Father Anunciación and all the officers, and sent to Luna with Ramírez y Arellano and twenty men. Nevertheless, it equivocated in its recommendation: better that Luna come and see the country for himself; while the region appeared well suited for settlement at first blush, it was found less so on closer examination. The men who had been with Soto said that all of Coosa province was the same. In reality, the Coosa Indians needed the Spaniards' friendship—more specifically, their crossbows and harquebuses, for they were beset by enemies who had interrupted trade and cut off communication with other villages. The country was so densely populated already that little room remained for a Spanish settlement. It was too poor to justify taking it by force, as Spanish settlers would be hard put to sustain themselves. On the way to Coosa, Sauz and his men, while exploring the rest of the province, hoped to go to Ulibahali, "the town mentioned so often by Soto's followers."

Luna was in no condition to travel to Coosa; he was hardly able to make a sound judgment. His state of mind had deteriorated to the point of dementia; the colony was rapidly disintegrating. The governor could not resolve a course of action, and the people, approaching starvation, could not endure with patience. Their cries of protest provoked irrational response. One by one, the various components of the enterprise became mutinous. Luna was beyond imposing reasonable discipline or rational persuasion.

Jorge Cerón, himself old and crotchety, became Luna's chief irritant. With the *maestre de campo*'s active leadership or implicit support, the company opposed the governor at every turn. The result was a malignant, defeating immobility. When Luna proposed sending a brigantine to Havana for food, the colonists protested that the vessel would be better used to remove them from Florida. When he proposed taking them to Coosa for sustenance, few were willing to go. Sapped by his illness, he lacked the resolve and energy to apply force. During the sweltering summer months of 1560, the enterprise swiftly and painfully fell apart in senseless bickering, retribution, and vituperation.

Acquiescing to his officers, Luna agreed to leave Nanipacana and withdraw to Filipina, that the people might sustain themselves on shellfish. They left toward the end of June, before Juan de Porras arrived with the corn from Casiste. Starvation and death stalked. Reaching Filipina, the colonists went on to Santa María de Ochuse, lest the fleet from New Spain fail to find them. Eight days after they reached

Santa María, the ships came with provisions, but they were all too mea-ger. Viceroy Velasco had grossly overestimated Florida's abundance, as the colonists saw it; as he tells it himself, he lacked ships with which to send more.

The fleet had come not, as many hoped, to deliver the people from their affliction but to charge them to further effort. It brought a royal order for Luna to occupy Santa Elena immediately because it was believed that Frenchmen, under pretext of going to Bacalaos (New-foundland), were planning to settle in Florida.

To support the new endeavor, Velasco had sent Captain Diego de Biedma, "an honest hidalgo and an old soldier," with 50 recruits from Campeche. In anticipation of going to Santa Elena, there came also an-other with previous experience in Florida. Fray Gregorio de Beteta, who had longed to return ever since the disastrous Cáncer expedition of 1549, had come from Spain to join Luna.

Juan de Jaramillo and some others had left Santa María in a brigan-tine three days before the fleet arrived. Captain Tomás Ortega's *Fran-cesillo* then returned to Veracruz, taking the father provincial, Fray Pedro Feria, and a number of children and ailing colonists. The ship carried Luna's letters, dated August 10, 1560, in which he revealed that there was yet no word of the expedition sent toward Coosa the previ-ous April. Even with these reports and those brought by Jaramillo, Velasco still failed to grasp the true situation in Florida. He continued to give advice that was wholly inappropriate for the circumstances.

Luna, nevertheless, acted promptly to dispatch three vessels for Santa Elena in compliance with the royal order. In command of two frigates and a small bark, he placed his young nephew, Martín de Hoz—another grave error in judgment, perpetuating the misfortune that had plagued the effort from the beginning. Biedma, as second in command, took the soldiers he had brought from Campeche. With them went Father Beteta, with high hopes of missionizing the Indians on the east coast, where he had wished to take the 1549 expedition following Cáncer's death.

The Santa Elena expedition sailed on August 10, in company with *San Juan* and the other supply ships bound for Havana to purchase provisions. As the fleet approached the Cuban port, a hurricane broke upon it. Hoz's vessels made port at Marién, then proceeded to San Juan de Ulúa, arriving with *San Juan* on September 5. Torrential rains resulting from the storm had drenched the Mexican coast, and it was ten days before the viceroy got the distressing news in letters from Hoz, Beteta, and Angel de Villafañe, commanding the San Juan de Ulúa garrison.

Velasco was greatly disturbed; not only had the Santa Elena enterprise aborted, but also the effort to provision Santa María de Ochuse from Cuba. Yet he would not be denied an expedition to Santa Elena. The fleet from Spain was then in port at San Juan de Ulúa, with Captain-General Pedro Menéndez de Avilés, who as early as 1555 had urged establishment of a fort on the Bahama Channel to protect Spanish shipping. The following January, when Menéndez was to sail for Spain, Velasco proposed to send two frigates with his fleet, carrying men, arms, and supplies for Santa Elena. Hoz and Biedma would remain at San Juan de Ulúa until time to renew the effort.

Luna's woes at Ochuse, meanwhile, continued unabated. Still ridden with mind-clouding illness, he was besieged with petitions expressing the mutinous sentiments of colonists, soldiers, and officers. In late August, Ramírez y Arellano arrived with the reports from Coosa. Luna presented Sauz's message to the council of officers with a proposal to march inland. Santa Elena, he suggested, might be reached from Coosa and the king's recent order thus fulfilled. The proposed move only intensified the row. The officers, demanding that Sauz be recalled, sent a letter to New Spain requesting permission to leave Florida.

Luna published a list of soldiers and officers whom he commanded to follow him to Coosa, but to no effect. Had he been a Cortés, ready to hang the first mutineer, or a Magellan, who could underscore the death sentence with drawing and quartering, he might have made his point. As it was, the argument fell into another pathetic round of charge and countercharge, demand and counterdemand. Luna, in H. I. Priestley's apt phrase, "was too close to the viceroy for independence, and too far away for help." At last, on September 2, Luna took the bold step of condemning to death the officers who had refused to follow him. But he nullified the sentence by admitting their appeals to authorities of New Spain.

On the same day, Cerón on his own authority ordered Juan de Porras, who had just come from Coosa, to return there to recall the soldiers. Porras and a company of 24 left Santa María on September 9.

Four days later, the sloop *Santiago*, Juan Alvarez, master, sailed for New Spain carrying a report to Velasco and about 100 persons, most of them ill or unfit. The number also included Captain Pedro de Acuña and some of his soldiers. Only about 400 persons, half of them still in the interior, remained in Florida.

In Mexico on September 22, the viceroy heard a firsthand report from Fathers Feria and Beteta on conditions at Santa María de Ochuse. A week later the high official learned of Alvarez's arrival at San Juan de Ulúa with Acuña's soldiers. He dispatched an order for their arrest on desertion charges. Yet he failed to get the full impact until October 2, when he received Luna's letter dated September 9, the day that Cerón had in effect seized control. "Never since I was born," wrote Velasco, "have I been so pained."

Still, the viceroy could not accept defeat; he must fulfill the king's order to occupy Santa Elena. He surely knew from that moment that Luna could not be salvaged as a leader, yet he proceeded deliberately, discussing the matter with the *audiencia*, the archbishop, and various lesser officials. Not until January 30, 1561, did he write Luna that Villafañe was being sent to replace him.

Sauz's company from Coosa, meanwhile, had rejoined the main camp at Ochuse in November, ending the one major exploratory thrust of the enterprise. The people, their number doubled with the expedition's return, suffered acutely from hunger. Before Villafañe arrived four months later, they were reduced to eating the hides of their cattle.

Coming early in March, 1561, Villafañe brought fifty men and fresh provisions. His purpose was not immediately apparent to the rank-and-file soldiers, because he paid Luna the respect due him as governor and captain-general, obeyed his commands, and addressed him as "Your Lordship." Then, in the presence of the entire camp, Luna announced plans to go to Spain and asked Villafañe to provide a frigate to take him to Havana. On April 9, Villafañe assumed authority as "governor of these provinces of La Florida and Punta de Santa Elena in His Majesty's name" and issued license for Luna to go and report to the Crown. Luna boarded the frigate, hoping to reach Havana in time to sail with Menéndez de Avilés. By the end of April, Villafañe himself was in Havana, en route to Santa Elena.

Despite Villafañe's active part in the affairs of New Spain and Florida, he has been little noted. Unwelcome attention had focused on him briefly in 1553, when, on orders of the Audiencia de Mexico, he arrested the king's inspector, Diego Ramírez. It was all a bad scene; Villafañe, caught between the viceroy and the *audiencia*, felt compelled to write directly to the emperor. The letter was dispatched on the only ship of the April, 1554, sailing to reach port. Villafañe shortly found himself marching north from Mexico to look for the three that had wrecked on Texas's Padre Island. A jealous contemporary, writing of Villafañe's part in salvaging the lost vessels, claims that Don Angel had become rich therefrom, while lawsuits by the rightful owners of the cargo to recover their property "were a sight to behold." When these events occurred, Villafañe claimed to have served in New Spain thirty-five years. Bit by bit, the pieces of his career have come together, beginning in 1513, when he sailed at age nine with his father, Captain Juan de Villafañe, in Pedrarias Dávila's Darién fleet.

The next notice is ten years later, when he came to Pánuco as a member of Francisco de Garay's force, fell in with the Cortés crowd, and went to Mexico to win a reputation—at least among his kinsmen—as "one of the principal *caballeros* of this city, of great quality and class." He married Doña Ynés de Caravajal, a relative of the Alvarados, and they were accepted in Mexico as "gentle people, hidalgos, and of great fortune." To earn such a billing, he served in the conquest of Michoacán and Colima and helped subdue the "Chontales, Zapotecas, and Mijes." He then took part in the pacification of Jalisco, and as a ship captain was associated with Jorge Céron in Cortés's exploration of the Pacific coast. When he assumed the Florida governorship, Villafañe was about fifty-six years old. The testimonial on his career ends here with the statement that he afterward returned to Mexico.

Villafañe, after revealing his commission to the Ochuse colonists, extracted fealty oaths and made ready for the voyage to Santa Elena. Leaving Diego de Biedma and Antonio Velázquez at Ochuse with fifty men, he sailed for Havana a few days after Luna's departure. A lateen-rigged caravel with Hernán Pérez as master served as his flagship. He also had the galleon *San Juan* and one frigate, to be joined at Havana by the one on which Luna had left Florida. Gonzalo Gayón was Villafañe's chief pilot, assisted by Juan Puerta; both were veterans of Luna's supply operation. Francisco de Aguilar, notary of the Florida colony, served in the same capacity for the Santa Elena undertaking and wrote a concise but lucid account of it. Aguilar, like Pérez, had sailed with Lavazares on the 1558 voyage.

Villafañe took about 230 persons from Florida. At Havana, he chose out 100 soldiers and released the rest. Cerón and some other officers embarked for Mexico to face the viceroy's wrath. Cuba's Governor Diego de Mazariego complained that more than 100 men were turned loose to live off the country—a noticeable switch, since previous officials had protested the taking of men from the island for discovery enterprises. A number of Villafañe's "carefully chosen" promptly deserted. By the time he sailed for Santa Elena he had only 60 soldiers besides the servants and sailors.

The four ships traversed the Bahama Channel in good weather to reach their destination within a month of their arrival in Havana. On May 27, 1561, Villafañe "entered the Río de Santa Elena in 33° with a frigate," sailed up the river five leagues, and went ashore to take possession. "He found no commodious port, no people, and no land suitable for settlement," says Aguilar. Returning to the sea, he ran the coast looking for a port, doubled Cape San Román in 34°, and went ashore on June 2. On a short march inland, Villafañe discovered the Jordán River (present Cape Fear River, North Carolina) and took the ships there. Still finding no suitable port, he coasted north with three vessels, while *San Juan*, having lost anchors and cables in a squall, stood out to sea. Near Cape Trafalgar (Hatteras) on June 14, a hurricane— the third such disaster experienced during the Florida–Santa Elena effort—blew down on the ships and sank the two frigates with a loss of twenty-five men. On Gayón's advice, Villafañe made for Hispaniola with the caravel, overtaking *San Juan* en route. Reaching Monte Cristi on the north side of the island, he spent a month repairing the two vessels, then took them to Havana.

Villafañe's extended stay in Cuba irritated Governor Mazariego, who claimed it lasted three months and twenty days. During that time, he says, the visiting governor treated his soldiers badly, taking away their food and arms and selling the supplies remaining from his abortive voyage. Most of the soldiers fled into the country or signed on other ships. At last Villafañe embarked, announcing that he was going to Polonza to retrieve the men left there with Biedma. Thus ended another attempt to occupy Florida without apparent benefit to God or king.

Mazariego, always ready to evaluate the effort for the king, blamed the failure on poor leadership, especially Luna's. Yet it was not that simple. The causes went beyond the lack of previous successful conquest and the obstacles imposed by the wilderness; beyond Luna's personal failure, which was at least partly attributable to illness; beyond the three hurricanes that wrecked the camp at Ochuse and aborted two attempts to occupy Santa Elena. All the participants shared responsibility for the failure, and the viceroy was due the largest portion. Unwilling to let go, Velasco attempted to keep tight rein despite the ponderous communications that forbade his effective control. Thus encumbered, Luna saw nullified the extraordinary benefits of extensive supply lines and experienced personnel.

If the expedition had any value at all, it was the advancement of geographical knowledge, not to be overlooked when Menéndez de Avilés a few years later established St. Augustine. Yet it fell far short of the need, as well as the hopes, of viceroy and king. Velasco had hoped that Luna, after building his brigantines, would explore and sound the rivers emptying into the Gulf as far west as the Mississippi. His aim was to provide a basis for future efforts, while linking the Luna colony with his overland expedition from Zacatecas. When the viceroy learned that Coosa had been reached, he expressed the hope that roads could be extended east and west, opening a route from the Atlantic to the Mississippi.

He had hoped also that Sebastián de Gamboa's frigate, lost on a voyage to Cuba, would "run the coast and discover the bays and ports." If Miruelo Bay were as good as reports indicated, he had said, Luna should have it inspected and sounded, "for some day it might be needed." One of the brigantines Luna built, Velasco suggested, might run the coast south as far as the Tortugas so that little by little all the ports in both directions would be discovered. Ships going back and forth from Cuba, he offered on another occasion, would do well to discover the ports between the bays of Juan Ponce and Juan Paz.

Nor had Velasco given up hope of discovering mines, despite the failure of Narváez and Soto to find gold. On one occasion he sent Luna a vial of mercury, with instructions for using it in the amalgamation of silver—the patio process developed in Mexico in 1554 by Bartolomé de Medina. Later, he sent by the factor Luis Daza instructions on the mining of mercury. If the metal that had become so vital to the silver industry should be found in Florida, he wrote, "it would be a great benefit for that land and this. Surely, God willing, it will be found, and also silver mines . . . for in such a big country it is not possible that there be none."

The failure of the Luna and Villafañe expeditions lies at the roots of other Spanish failures that came later. Not for another century would the several mouths of the Mississippi be probed by Spanish navigators, but by then it was too late, for the French also asserted a claim to that vital waterway. And the region of Punta de Santa Elena, difficult to control from Spanish St. Augustine, eventually would fall to English domination. Had Velasco's plans been realized, had Luna and Villafañe succeeded as the viceroy hoped they would, how different might be the map of North America.

On September 23, 1561, Philip II took note in a royal *cédula* to Viceroy Velasco of the recent failure in Florida, specifically, of the great cost and little effect of the effort. He had heard or read in reports of participants that the region was poor, offering less than satisfactory port facilities and little prospect for sustaining a Spanish settlement. The rumored French threat that had caused him to order the *entrada* in the first place seemed to have abated. Having consulted with Menéndez de Avilés, who had conducted two recent fleets to New Spain, the king was advised that, should the effort be renewed, it should be directed and supplied from Castile, not New Spain, where goods were scarce and prices high. Santa Elena itself, Menéndez believed, was not a suitable location because the river was shallow and the current swift; the coast from latitude 38° to Tierra Nueva should be explored for a better site.

Before the matter was shelved, the king ordered the viceroy to confer with participants in the Luna-Villafañe attempt on whether the settlement should be pursued or the Santa Elena region be abandoned altogether. In compliance, Velasco summoned Villafañe and Cerón; the captains Baltasar de Sotelo, the two Juans de Porras, and Biedma; the *sargento mayor* Sauz; the treasurer Alonso Velázquez; and the shipmaster Hernán Pérez. The secretary Jerónimo López registered the witnesses' unanimous opinion on March 12, 1562.

Sailing along the Gulf coast from the Río Bravo (modern Río Grande), in 25°30', they said, one came to the Río del Espíritu Santo; Bahía Filipina; Polonza, or Ochuse, Bay; and Miruelo Bay. These were the principal rivers and bays between New Spain and the Bahama Channel, which ended in latitude 28°. Beyond the channel mouth, in 33° (actually somewhat short of that) was the point and river of Santa Elena. Although the river was large and fluent, no ship of more than 50 tons could enter it because there were hardly six spans (about 4½ feet) of water. There were, the panel reported, no natives who could be settled and taught the Christian faith; the land was not well disposed, and there was no gold or silver. The coast beyond Hatteras, it was suggested, should be explored, but it could be done better and at less cost from Spain than from the colonies. Thus New Spain shucked responsibility for settling the Atlantic coast. The sour fruits of Villa- fañe's failure to occupy Punta de Santa Elena quickly ripened.

SOURCES AND NOTES

Thanks to Herbert Ingram Priestley's landmark compilation and translation (*Luna Papers*, first published in 1928 and reissued in 1971), the Luna- Villafañe episode is extraordinarily well documented. There is absolutely no basis for concluding, as one recent investigator has done, that "the de Luna expedition may never have disembarked in the nothern Gulf, but proceeded straightway to the vicinity of Santa Elena on the Atlantic coast." The National Park Service actually paid for a study that drew this conclusion while citing *The Luna Papers* in the bibliography (Coastal Environments, Inc., *Cultural Resources Evaluation of the Northern Gulf of Mexico Continental Shelf*, 2:29). Priestley's failure to arrange the documents chronologically poses an inconvenience, but the record is clear and as complete as any such compilation could be. Predictably (if not inevitably), there are some gaps, and there are shortcomings in the introductory summary; otherwise, there would be little point in the synthesis offered here. Yet Priestley's work is the basic source on the episode, and it is difficult indeed to expand upon it.

The Personnel

Juan de Jaramillo: the uncle for whom he was named, Doña Marina's husband, was one of Cortés's "old reliables." For the publication history of the younger Jaramillo's *relación* of the Vázquez de Coronado expedition, see Henry R. Wagner, *The Spanish Southwest, 1542–1794*, 1:106–107).

Jorge Cerón Saavedra: his brother was Alvaro de Saavedra Cerón, whom Cortés sent in 1526 with three ships to rescue the Loaysa expedition to the Spice Islands and who died at sea during the voyage. The discrepancy in the form of their surnames is not explained.

Mateo del Sauz: for brief mention of his service in Peru, see Garcilaso de la Vega, *Royal Commentaries of the Incas*, 2:1402.

Bernaldo Peloso: prior to the Soto expedition, Peloso took part in the conquest of Cartagena (Colombia) with Pedro de Heredia. After the Soto *entrada*, he, like Rodrigo Ranjel, settled at Pánuco and married a widow with two sons (*Luna Papers*, 1:262, 266). Priestley (ibid., xxi) credits "at least three" of Soto's men among Luna's but names only two. There probably were several more. At least thirty-three of the names on Luna's roster have identical counterparts on Soto's, though many are so common that they cannot be taken to indicate the same person. While Ranjel was Peloso's fellow townsman at Pánuco for several years, he was living in Mexico when he testified for Gonzalo Méndez de Sotomayor's "Ynformación" (AGI, Patronato 63-1-10), assessing Soto's contribution to the Luna affair.

Luis Daza: the only document at hand that pertains to him is dated prior to his participation in the Soto and Luna *entradas*. See "Relación de linaje de Luis Daza," Valladolid, Oct. 9, 1537 (AGI, Indiferente General 1205, no. 38).

Tristán de Luna y Arellano: aside from *Luna Papers* and Priestley's notes and introduction, see J. Ignacio Rubio Mañé, "Fin de los días de don Tristán de Luna y Arellano, genearca de los mariscales de Castilla en Mexico, año de 1573," 19.

Juan de Busto: See Priestley's note in *Luna Papers*, 1:262. Busto, a native of Cortés's hometown of Medellín in Extremadura, was a son of the first Count of Medellín. He was not the Juan de Busto of Soto's march. He had taken part in the conquest of Pánuco and native villages north of the Río Pánuco, and discovered the valleys of Oxtipa, or Oxitipa. In 1523, Francisco de Garay's men were fed and lodged at his *encomienda* village of Tocalula, which evidently was taken from him later by Nuño de Guzmán; in 1559 he held Tescuco, which was yielding scant revenue.

Fray Andrés de Urdaneta: he took the Augustinian habit after he had become a seasoned navigator on the voyage of Francisco García Jofre de Loaysa to the Spice Islands, 1525–36. Urdaneta is noted for his contribution to navigational science and the development of sailing instructions to assist mariners on voyages between Spain and the Indies. See Francisco Manuel, "Piloto Mayor Francisco Manuel, del derroto del Padre Urdaneta," April 1583, British Museum, additional manuscript 28,189. Biographical data are found in *Carta de Indias*, 3:851. At the time of the Luna *entrada*, Urdaneta was in Mexico preparing for another maritime venture as pilot with Miguel López de Legazpi. On that voyage he succeeded in finding the elusive eastward route across the Pacific from the Philippines, thus opening the enduring commerce between Manila and Acapulco. He was less successful in plotting a feasible route from Pánuco to the Mississippi.

The Supply Operation

Several documents not included in *Luna Papers* have been found that pertain to this phase of the colonization attempt. Velasco's numerous letters to the pilot Gonzalo Gayón provide a stronger indication of Gayón's importance to the enterprise than does the pilot himself. They are dated Oct. 7, 19, and 30, 1559; Jan. 7, 17, and 31, 1560. All are in AGI, Santo Domingo 11, ramo 3.

Additionally, there is the "Ynformación de los méritos y servicios de Alonso Velázquez Rodríguez," which tells of bringing two ships loaded with provisions and livestock—horses, mules, sheep, goats, and cattle—from Havana (AGI, Patronato 65-1-14). His ship, sailing with Hoz's fleet bound for Santa Elena, ran aground during the 1560 hurricane. After the storm, he righted his vessel and searched the coasts of Cuba, Yucatán, and Tabasco before finding the other ships at San Juan de Ulúa.

Place Names

Los Alacranes: this was the sixteenth-century name for the reefs presently known as the Arrecife de Alacrán, off the north coast of Yucatán. Because of the great distance traveled out of their way by both Lavazares and Luna to reach that point, I at first concluded that it meant something else, perhaps the Florida Keys. A renewed search of official sailing instructions (British Museum, additional manuscript 28,189; BN, manuscript 7119) set me straight. This example emphasizes the great detours that often were necessary for sailing vessels to get a favorable wind. Priestley (*Luna Papers*, 1:xxiv), not understanding this, contrived a storm to take Luna off his course.

Miruelo Bay: the initial sighting of the Florida coast is described ambiguously as being "eight leagues from Miruelo Bay on the west side" (*Luna Papers*, 2:272); then Miruelo Bay is said to be 35 leagues (east) from Pensacola. Velasco reflects the general confusion surrounding this feature. If indeed it was named for Diego Miruelo the nephew, Cabeza de Vaca (ch. 11) seems to make clear that the name originally designated Tampa Bay.

Nanipacana: the name is not used by any of the three major chroniclers of the Soto expedition. It evidently represents a different version of the place Ranjel calls Taliepacana. (See Priestley, n. 56 in *Luna Papers*, 1:xxxviii.)

Onachiqui: Lowery (*Spanish Settlements, U.S.*, 361 n.) places this Indian village in what is now Coosa County, Alabama.

"The Portuguese"

The man to whom Velasco refers (*Luna Papers*, 1:100) was Andrés do Campo, who had remained in "Quivira" with Fray Juan de Padilla when Vázquez de Coronado withdrew. Following Padilla's death at the hands of Indians, the man escaped and carried the news to Mexico, via Pánuco. Information emerging from his adventure is fragmentary and perhaps distorted, his route "through the prickly-pear country" left to conjecture. Luna, having served with Vázquez de Coronado, was naturally expected to understand the vague reference. (See discussion of the "Soto" map in ch. 12 notes.)

The Indian War

Priestley (*Luna Papers*, 1:xli–xliii) accepts Fray Agustín Dávila Padilla's account of the Spaniards' joining the Coosa Indians in war against another tribe called Napochies and pursuing the enemy nation across the Río del Espíritu Santo. Neither the joint letter (ibid., 1:230–32) nor other documents substantiate such a campaign, which would have been little short of ridiculous. By all accounts, Sauz's men were in no condition for such a march through unknown country over a distance greater than that from Nanipacana. Neither Cristóbal Velázquez nor Alonso de Montalván (ibid., 2:230, 288), Coosa soldiers who later made depositions at Hispaniola, even hints of such a campaign.

Diego de Mazariego

The Cuba governor Mazariego observed the Luna-Villafañe episode from his close vantage point and rendered accounts to the Crown. His letters are dated Havana, Aug. 28, 1560; June 29, 1561; and Feb. 21, 1562. All are in AGI, Santo Domingo 115.

Angel de Villafañe

Villafañe gave testimony for the "Ynformación de los méritos y servicios de Alonso Ortiz de Zúñiga," Mexico, May 19, 1553 (AGI, Patronato 60-1-2). He gives his age at the time as more than forty-eight.

Juan de Villafañe *el Mozo* (to the Crown, Mexico [1585], AGI, Mexico 108, ramo 3) details his father's career, and Alvaro de Ordaz gives testimony for "Ynformación de Juan de Villafañe," Mexico, Oct. 3, 1583, reciting additional facts. See also Diego Ramírez to the Crown, Mestitlán, Nov. 20, 1553, AGI, Mexico 168; Priestley, *Luna Papers*, 1:258 n, 264 n; Agustín Millares Carlo, *Indice y extractos de los protocolos del Archivo de Notarias de Mexico, D.F.*, 1:149.

"Testimonio de Francisco de Aguilar, escrivano que fue en la jornada a la Florida con Angel de Villafañe" (Puerto de Monte Cristi, July 10, 1561, RAH, Colección Muñoz, A/115, ff. 86–87) recounts the voyage to Santa Elena.

Philip II's royal *cédula* to Velasco commenting on the failure in Florida and ordering a conference with the participants is copied in the junta's report. The *cédula* is dated at Madrid, Sept., 1561; the junta's report, Mexico, March 12, 1562. Both are in AGI, Patronato 19-2-12.

Allegations that Villafañe enriched himself from treasure salvaged from the 1554 wrecks were made by Juan Suárez Peralta (*Tratado del descubrimiento de las Indias*). He was the son of Juan Suárez Marcaída, Cortés's brother-in-law, who brought charges agaist him in the death of the conqueror's wife, Doña Catalina Suárez. The *Tratado* as a whole is somewhat less than reliable.

PART IV

The Building Rivalry

St. Andrew's Cross:
Englishmen in the Gulf, 1556–86

W~HEN~ Angel de Villafañe took the last troops from Florida in late 1561, the North American coast from the Río Pánuco to the St. Lawrence was untenanted by Europeans. In all that region Spain had encountered no serious challenge to her territorial claims. Yet she had long been the object of envy for her New World treasure and the target of resentment for the vastness of her pretensions. Therein lay the seeds of conflict.

Such attitudes had surfaced first in 1521, when French corsairs, in wartime, seized a treasure-laden vessel being sent home by Cortés. Other European nations—often without regard for the status of diplomatic relations—also began licensing privateers to prowl the sealanes; they picked off stragglers from the treasure fleets and plundered ill-protected island ports. Confrontations, confined at first to the open sea and the Caribbean islands, extended eventually into the Gulf of Mexico.

The first warning of the threat to the inner Gulf came in July, 1558, while Viceroy Velasco was in the midst of preparations for dispatching Luna to Florida. Four French vessels, he learned, had entered Puerto de Caballos (in Honduras) and sacked the town and the church. Four or five persons, including a priest who made the mistake of guarding the church ornaments too zealously, were killed. Velasco received information that the pirates were guided by two Portuguese pilots and a Spaniard from Vizcaya, who boasted that they would proceed to Yucatán and even to San Juan de Ulúa itself. To forestall the threat, the viceroy made sure the port's defenses were in order, but all in all, he regarded the matter a bit smugly: "If they come they will not return to France with a prize, because the port has five well-armed

ships." He was more concerned for Havana, the gathering point of the
fleets from Veracruz and Nombre de Dios, and for the security of their
route, prescribed by wind and current, through the Yucatán Channel
and the Florida Straits.

Havana, long victimized by French raiders, did indeed stand in
danger. English freebooters were pestering the port when Pedro Menéndez de Avilés arrived there with the New Spain fleet on April 7,
1561—about the time Tristán de Luna left Florida. Menéndez delayed
his voyage long enough to chase off the pirates. But the really vulnerable point was Campeche, tucked away on the west side of the Yucatán Peninsula, too far from Veracruz to receive any timely assistance
therefrom. About February, 1560, the *flibustiers* landed on northwest
Yucatán to acquaint themselves with the region. Exploring along the
coast, they found themselves confronted by soldiers from Mérida. The
pirates regained their ships and made sail, only to encounter a storm
that drove them back upon the coast, into the hands of their pursuers.
Sent off to Mexico and Spain, the buccaneers spread abroad the entice-
ments of Mérida's more opulent households: the worked gold and silver with which the citizens adorned their serving tables and their persons. Inspired by these reports and guided by a Portuguese pilot who
lived in Triana and had a Spanish wife, French pirates appeared before
Campeche the evening of August 24, 1561.

The Campechanos saw the strange sloop standing offshore in the
gathering gloom but, taking her for a trading vessel from Veracruz or
Havana, paid her little mind. With no reason to expect French pirates,
since no Frenchman had ever landed at Campeche, they retired to
their homes and beds. But that Tuesday night changed everything. Not
for many a year would Campeche sleep so soundly again.

Dropping anchor in the bay, the Frenchmen waited until the town
was sleeping. Then they seized Master Juan Rodríguez de Noriega's
urca anchored nearby and, in sacking the ship, killed a Negro woman.
Two hours before dawn, twenty-two well-armed men stole ashore. Seizing storehouses and haciendas, they set fire to a number of houses in
the town and desecrated the church; they smashed the altar, the chal-
ices, and the image of the Christ child, "making it understood that they
were Lutherans and enemies of our holy Catholic faith." Strutting
about the town, terrorizing the people, the pirates demanded 1,500
pesos de oro as ransom for the 11 men and women they held captive.

When an angry citizen fired his harquebus from ambush and killed one of the pirates, the others fled to an unmanned ship anchored in the bay—a mistake, since the vessel had neither sails nor rudder. As the freebooters tried to maneuver her with oars toward the *urca*, a ship from Havana sailed into the bay, carrying fourteen of the soldiers Villafañe had left in the Cuban port at the conclusion of the Florida–Santa Elena affair. Taking in the situation at a glance, the soldiers joined the townspeople and, in a pair of rowboats, overtook the immobilized pirates. Boarding the frigate from port and starboard, they set upon the raiders with "stones and shouts" and the few arms they carried, killing nine and capturing five. The rest, most of them painfully wounded, fled in the frigate's lifeboat. A relief force from Mérida, led by Francisco Tamayo Pacheco, arrived in time only to take charge of the prisoners.

This episode was but a foretaste of the building rivalry that now threatened the Gulf, transgressing that inner sanctum which from its discovery had been exclusively a Spanish sea.

The rumored French designs on eastern Florida that had lent urgency to the Spaniards' Santa Elena attempt proved more than idle talk. Within two months after the Villafañe deposition denying the feasibility of that location, in early May, 1562, the Frenchman Jean Ribaut (or Ribault) garrisoned Charlesfort on nearby Port Royal Sound. That post, left without support because of the Huguenot-Catholic civil war in France, was soon abandoned. Ribaut then treated with the English in a colonization scheme and wound up in an English jail for his double-dealing.

Word of the settlement reached Cuba too late. On hearing the news, Governor Mazariego sent a ship commanded by Hernando Manrique, with Gonzalo Gayón as pilot, to investigate. Landing at the "Río de Mosquitoes," the voyagers learned from a native chief named Mayaca that the Frenchmen had departed. They found only one French lad who had remained among the Indians, and a pillar bearing the French coat of arms.

Shortly after the Spaniards departed, a new Huguenot company landed at the mouth of the St. John's River, which Ribaut had named the River of May. It was led by one of Ribaut's companions in the first endeavor, René de Laudonnière. In June 1564 he established Fort Caroline on a pleasant bluff overlooking the St. John's.

Laudonnière's men mutinied, made off with some of his ships, and proceeded to tweak the Spanish nose by various acts of piracy in the Straits of Florida and the Bahama Channel, and about the Caribbean islands. Made to suffer Spanish retribution, some of these freebooters retreated to Fort Caroline to ask and receive Laudonnière's forgiveness and protection. Thus the French post was placed squarely atop a fused powder keg. With the Spaniards' capture of some of the pirates, the fuse was lighted.

Laudonnière's settlement on the St. John's was still struggling with the effects of starvation, mutiny, and Indian hostility when, in late summer 1565, unexpected visitors arrived. With four sail sighted off the coast, the commander, fearing that they were Spanish, drew up for battle. When boats came ashore, however, the strangers proved to be English. Their commander was John Hawkins, fresh from a slaving voyage that provided the first substantial English account of the Gulf of Mexico, the Florida coast, and the Bahama Channel. Spain, having failed over half a century to gain a foothold on the Florida shore, was finding herself confronted with determined rivals at every turn.

John Hawkins, first and last, did his bit toward breaching the Spanish Sea and furthering the contest between Spain and England. A native of Plymouth, he was the son of William Hawkins, who had pioneered England's trade in African slaves, three times visiting Africa's west coast for Negroes to be sold in Brazil. John Hawkins was possessed of his father's adventurous spirit. Having spent several years in the British maritime service, he sailed on his first voyage as commander in 1562. Taking 300 slaves on the Guinea coast, he traded them in Hispaniola for hides, sugar, ginger, and pearls, then sailed homeward through the Windward Passage "without further entering into the Bay of Mexico."

Thus Hawkins became the prototype of the foreign merchant who, carrying black slaves needed for the mines and plantations or goods the colonial Spaniards could not obtain from their own fleets, induced them to violate the prohibitions of their king against trading with foreigners. Admitting the illicit trade opened a veritable Pandora's box for the insular Spaniards. Corsairs often entered the Indies ports disguised as traders, acquired a familiarity with harbors and sailing routes, and returned later to sack the settlements, sometimes with the complicity of renegade Spanish colonists.

With profits from the 1562 voyage, Hawkins fitted out another on a grander scale. It was this second voyage that brought him to Fort

Caroline in August, 1565, as Laudonnière's garrison struggled against overpowering adversity. He had sailed from Plymouth on October 18, 1564, with the 700-ton *Jesus of Lubeck*, 140-ton *Salomon*, and *Tiger* and *Swallow*, barks of 50 and 30 tons. As on the first voyage, the slavers made for the Guinea coast, loaded up with Negroes, then set course for the Antilles. After watering at Dominica, they crossed the Caribbean to the islands rimming the north shore of South America. They usually found the Spanish colonists willing enough to buy their wares, yet Hawkins was wont to use armed force to impose his own terms, then demand of the local governors testimonials of his good behavior. From Río de la Hacha, he sailed on May 31 for Hispaniola, but the current swept the ships off course; they came to Jamaica. Instead of sailing homeward through the Windward Passage, they doubled "Cape St. Anthony" and passed through the Yucatán Channel into the Gulf of Mexico and thence into the Bahama Channel. Years of probing and careful observation by the Spanish pilot Antón de Alaminos had been required to establish this route; it seems ironic that the most complete sixteenth-century description comes from an Englishman.

Hawkins's four ships, departing on June 17, 1565, from Jamaica, sighted Cabo San Antón, at Cuba's western tip, three days later. There, relates John Sparke the younger, "wee doubled along till wee came beyond the shoales, which are 20 leagues beyond S. Anthony." The prevailing wind, from the northeast, then filled the sails and carried them away from the Cuban shore, "and therefore we went to the Northwest to fetch wind, and also to the coast of Florida to have the help of the current, which was judged to have set to the Eastward."

Hawkins was exceptionally adept at reading the signs. He yielded to the natural forces and made a wide circuit of the Gulf, much as the Spanish fleet from Tierra Firme was accustomed to doing on approaching Havana, sailing with the current and keeping the wind on the larboard quarter as it neared the Florida Keys: "So the 29 wee found our selves in 27 degrees, and in the soundings of Florida, where we kept our selves the space of foure dayes, sailing along the coast as neere as we could, in tenne or twelve fadome water, having all the while no sight of land."

On July 5 they sighted the Tortugas and dropped anchor off the shoaly islands while the captain went ashore in his pinnace. Birds were so numerous that in half an hour they loaded the boat with them and might have done the same with ten boats more. Also present in large numbers were the giant sea turtles from which the islands derive their name. It was their breeding ground. They came up out of the sea, each female to lay 300 to 400 eggs, which she covered with sand and left to be hatched by the sun; "and by this means commeth the great increase. Of these we tooke very great ones, which have both backe and belly all of bone, of the thicknes of an inch, the flesh . . . eating much like veale." The Englishmen also found a number of turtle eggs, and "they did eat very sweetly."

After six hours a fair wind arose. The ships weighed anchor and made sail toward Cuba. On the sixth day they sighted a hill, which Hawkins took for the Mesa of Marién, and lay to during the night, hoping to take on water next day. But a Frenchman in Hawkins's crew (late of Ribaut's Charlesfort) had been to Havana and claimed to know the coastal landmark; he convinced Master John that he was mistaken, so they fell to leeward, back into the Gulf, to look for the mesa. By the time the Frenchman's error became apparent, they were beyond turning back without a grueling beat to windward and had missed their chance for a water haul. Hawkins then determined to seek the Río de los Puercos, taking pains to keep clear of the Florida Keys, "so dangerous that no ship escapeth which commeth thither, as the Spanyards have very wel proved the same."

When a westerly wind arose on July 8, the captain determined "not to refuse Gods gift." The ships ran eastward before the wind, again passed Marién Mesa, and overshot Havana during the night. By the time this error was discovered, they were 20 leagues past it, and no other watering place appeared. They dared not go farther, for dangerous shoals lay ahead and they were feeling the tug of the current to the northeast. So, turning away from the Cuban shore on the morning of July 12, "we fell with the Islands upon the cape of Florida." To this point the current had not been as strong as they had been led to believe it would be; "we felt little or none till we fell with the cape, and then felt such a current, that bearing all sailes against the same, yet were driven backe againe a great pace." The Englishmen's experience with the Gulf Stream was much the same as Juan Ponce de León's. It almost caused the loss of *Salomon*'s boat, which had gone to shore for water; only after an anxious night, during which the boatmen expected to be left among the Florida Indians, were they brought back aboard. Sailing thereafter only in daylight, the ships came to "the River of May" in "30°30'."

Fort Caroline, on the verge of being abandoned, already was dismantled. Laudonnière tried to conceal his true plight by making a feast of the sheep and poultry saved back for dire emergency. But Hawkins was not deceived. He offered to take the garrison on his vessels to France, but the innate mistrust between Frenchman and Englishman could not be overcome so easily. Laudonnière preferred to trade artillery and powder for provisions and one of Hawkins's small ships. He dared not reveal the silver he had gathered from the Indians, lest he be robbed. Actually, he had nothing to fear; Hawkins, though a rogue, held to a gentleman's code of sorts. He knew about the silver all along, deducing that it had come from Spanish wrecks on the keys.

The visitors learned that the Frenchmen, traveling toward "the cape," had found two Spanish castaways who had lived among the Indians for twelve and fourteen years and brought them to Fort Caroline. Their identity is not established, but their experiences must have paralleled those of Hernando de Escalante Fontaneda, who at this time had lived fourteen years in the Florida wilderness.

Sparke, during the two-week sojourn at Fort Caroline, July 14–28, gleaned information on the flora, fauna, and peoples of eastern Florida. His account assuredly helped stir among his countrymen a lust for both wealth and adventure. "The commodities of this land," he wrote, "are more than are yet knowen to any man . . . whereof there is more then any Christian king is able to inhabit." In short, the Spanish Crown had laid claim to more than its due. The time had come for Englishmen to cut themselves in for a share.

Fort Caroline, meanwhile, had not escaped Spanish notice. Twenty of the post's mutineers had been caught in Jamaica; three were spared hanging and sent to Spain for interrogation.

Jean Ribaut, having won his freedom from jail in England, learned just before sailing in late May, 1565, to relieve Laudonnière that Pedro Menéndez de Avilés was about to leave Spain for "New France." The French leader won the race, but it was his last victory. He had been at Fort Caroline hardly a week when, on September 4, 1565, Menéndez's six ships—sent by Philip II to drive him from Florida—appeared off the River of May.

Menéndez's founding of San Agustín, his destruction of Fort Caroline, and the massacre of his French captives are apart from our story of the Gulf of Mexico. Yet from its bloody beginning, San Agustín served as a base for converting the Indians and exploring the Florida peninsula; we shall return to its role in exploration affecting the Gulf.

With the ouster of Fort Caroline's defenders, the French threat in Florida was, for the moment, ended; that of the English, just beginning. Englishmen were finding their way into the Gulf of Mexico, the Spanish Sea, under various pretexts. One of those voyaging to New Spain was Master Roger Bodenham, who took the bark *Foxe*, of London registry, in the Spanish fleet from Cádiz to San Juan de Ulúa. England and Spain, it will be remembered, had become allied in 1554 with the marriage of Philip II to his cousin Mary Tudor, the English queen. The marriage, finally terminated by Mary's death in 1558, was not a happy one, but for a few years it enhanced trade relations between the two nations. A number of English tradesmen came to live in Spain, and many visited the Spanish colonies. Bodenham, at the time of his sailing with the Indies fleet in 1562, had lived a number of years in Seville and had taken a Spanish wife. The captain-general of the fleet that year was Pedro Menéndez de Avilés who, perhaps significantly, had accompanied Prince Philip to England for his wedding ceremony.

Bodenham discharged his cargo at Veracruz, sold it in Mexico, and loaded his ship for the return voyage with silver and other Indies produce. He sailed for Spain with the fleet nine months later and, on delivering the cargo to the Casa de Contratación in Seville, was 13,000 ducats richer. While he observed "many things" during his New Spain sojourn, he mentions only a few: the causeways and the churches and monasteries in Mexico, and the abundance of cochineal around Puebla de los Angeles. "Because the Spanish histories are full of those observations," he left off further description of the kind his native England was thirsting for. Apparently he honored the Spaniards' dislike for having reports of their colonial possessions blabbed abroad.

Bodenham was by no means the first Englishman to see New Spain, though he was perhaps one of the most fortunate. On more than one occasion, the Catholic Spaniards led an English sojourner into a theological discussion, as happened to Robert Tomson, then denounced him to the Inquisition for his "heretical" views. Tomson, native of Andover in Hampshire, went to Seville in 1553. He lived for a year with John Field, an English merchant who had resided in Spain eighteen or twenty years and had a Spanish wife and children. Tomson's purpose, as he tells it, was to learn the Castilian tongue and "see the orders of the countrey and the customes of the people." While at Seville he saw the going and coming of the Indies fleets, bringing home to Spain rich cargoes of gold, silver, pearls, sugar, hides, and ginger. He longed to see the country whence they came.

Field, at the same time, decided to emigrate to New Spain with his family and obtained the necessary royal license for himself and Tomson. Finding the Indies fleet held up at Sanlúcar de Barrameda, they booked passage in February, 1555, for the Canary Islands and, at Tenerife, joined the fleet from Cádiz the following October. This was the first Indies fleet in which Menéndez de Avilés sailed as captain-general. If Menéndez did not influence the relaxing of traditional prohibitions against admitting foreigners to the Indies trade, he certainly helped to implement the policy. Tomson and Field found among the ships a vessel belonging to one John Sweeting (who was married to a Spanish woman in Cádiz) and captained by his son-in-law, Leonard Chilton.

After a long layover at Santo Domingo, the fleet entered the "bay of newe Spaine" in February. Within 15 leagues of San Juan de Ulúa, a norther put the ships on a lee shore and caused them to turn seaward. One of them, *Carion*, held to her course and ran up on the beach. Seventy-five persons—men, women, and children—drowned.

The remaining seven ships were buffeted about the Gulf for ten days, lost in blinding rain, then in dense fog. As St. Elmo's fire danced on yards and masts, the Spanish sailors fell to their knees to pray to God and the patron of sailors for deliverance. A hole opened in Chilton's ship a fathom below the waterline. Bedding was stuffed into the opening while merchandise, personal belongings, and artillery were jettisoned to lighten the ship and bring the hole out of the water. The loss of ballast required cutting down the mainmast. With one piece of artillery kept on board, the mariners fired distress signals until one of the other vessels came to them out of the fog.

Chilton's passengers finally reached San Juan de Ulúa safely on April 16, 1556, though his ship and cargo were a total loss. As they walked along the beach to Veracruz, five leagues up the coast, they found it littered with huge trees—uprooted in Tierra Florida, the people said, and carried 300 leagues across the Gulf by the storm. At Veracruz (Antigua), Field met an old friend from Seville, Gonzalo Ruiz de Córdoba, who quartered the Field family and Tomson in his home for a month while outfitting the eight persons with new apparel, horses, and money for their trip to Mexico.

Two days on the road, Tomson became too ill to sit his horse and was carried on the backs of Indians. Then Field, one of his children, and two of his household servants fell sick; they died soon after reaching Mexico. Tomson, at the point of death for six months, finally recovered. Through a Scot named Thomas Blake, twenty years a resident of Mexico, he found employment with a first conqueror named Gonzalo Cerezo. A year later, he relates, "I was maliciously accused by the holy house for matters of religion," and spent seven months in a solitary prison cell. Then, in the company of another accused heretic, an Italian, he was garbed in a sanbenito—a yellow cloth fitted over the head and draped upon the shoulders, emblazoned with a red St. Andrew's cross—and made to stand on a scaffold in the church during high mass, while the priest delivered a sermon on the nature of their offense, and sentences were pronounced. Banished from the Indies, Tomson was to serve three years in prison at Seville, the Italian the rest of his life. Their sanbenitos, each inscribed with the name of the wearer, were put on display in the Mexican cathedral as a warning. Tomson's was seen there a few years later by other Englishmen: John Chilton and men from Hawkins's ships cast away on the Mexican shore.

A seemingly innocent dinner conversation among friends, Tomson relates, had brought him to such a plight. His companions, apparently out of benign curiosity, plied him with questions. Was it true that in England the churches had been overthrown, the images of the saints cast out, and allegiance to the pope disavowed? Yes, replied Tomson, they had put down the religious houses of friars and monks and removed the images, for they claimed they were contrary to God's express commandment: "Thou shalt not make to thy selfe any graven image, &c."

Whereupon one gentleman expostulated on the role of the saints as intercessors; as one who had offended his king must seek forgiveness through an intermediary, so must he who has sinned against God. Tomson lacked the good judgment to remain silent. Quite unlike kings—he responded—God had said, "Come unto me all ye that labour, and are ouer laden, and I wil refresh you," and had made a thousand other promises found in the holy Scriptures. Why, then, had men need of the saints, when the Lord so freely offered himself?

As is often the case when men discuss religion and politics, someone present took offense—and reported the conversation to the bishop of Mexico. Tomson was promptly arrested. After sentencing, he and the Italian were taken down to Veracruz and put on a ship for Spain. On reaching the Azores, the Italian, facing the certainty of life in prison if not death by burning, jumped overboard and swam to the island of Terceira; thence he escaped on a Portuguese ship to London. Tomson served out his three years in prison, was employed by an English merchant in Seville, and married María de la Barrera, who had inherited considerable wealth.

The era of good feeling between Englishman and Spaniard was— whether from encounters with the Inquisition like Tomson's, or Hawkins's practice of trading at gunpoint—doomed to early failure. On October 2, 1567, Hawkins sailed from Plymouth on his third voyage, adhering roughly to the pattern of the first two. The two flagships— *Jesus of Lubeck*, Robert Barrett, master; *Minion*, John Hampton, captain, and John Barrett, master—belonged to the queen. Hawkins, in company with some English merchants, equipped the others: *William and John* (Captain Thomas Bolton), *Judith* (Captain Francis Drake), *Angel*, and *Swallow*. Of the 400 soldiers and sailors aboard the six ships, those who saw England again could count themselves blessed by fortune. Bound for Guinea, they committed various acts of piracy, adding to the fleet a captured French trading vessel and its captain, whose name was Bland. In slave raids near Cape Verde and Sierra Leone, the Englishmen loaded up with 500 Negroes, while losing 25 of their own men to poisoned arrows.

Hawkins sailed with his slave cargo for the north coast of South America—Isla Margarita, Cabo de la Vela, Santa Marta, and Cartagena—where he bullied his way into advantageous trades. On June 24, 1568, with 100 Negroes still in the holds, he pointed the ships north into the Yucatán Channel. Doubling Cabo San Antón, they encountered a full-blown hurricane. *Jesus of Lubeck*, a dilapidated old tub, handled badly in the rough sea. Her high forecastle and sterncastle caused her to take dangerous rolls; she was shipping so much water that fish swam in her hold. In desperation, Hawkins had her buildings cut down and stood ready to abandon. Yet "hoping to bring all to a good pass," he sought "the Little Sea"—Mar Pequeña, near the Mississippi Delta—to make repairs but found no harbor deep enough. While *William and John* made for home alone, the other ships were caught in a new storm that drove them toward the reefs in the Bay of Campeche, well within the Spanish Sea.

The storm having abated, they came upon two ships near the Triángulos and took one captained by Francisco Maldonado. Advised that he might careen his ships at Campeche, Hawkins approached the port but found that he stood in danger of grounding a league from shore. Pirate watches now were posted along the Yucatán coast, and Campeche was forewarned that Hawkins might pay a visit. The people were under arms, the streets barricaded, "for which reason the said corsair could not carry out his design." Hence the decision to make port at San Juan de Ulúa, where no English fleet had ever been. On the way Hawkins's ships took another Spanish caravel, aboard which was Agustín de Villanueva, identified by the English captain as "the man that betrayed all the noblemen in the Indies and caused them to be beheaded."

The Spaniards at San Juan de Ulúa presumed the approaching ships to be the expected fleet from Spain. Like Campeche before the first French raid, they felt secure within the Spanish Sea, scarcely ever breached by foreign enemies. Hawkins seized the two port officials who came out to his ships, captured the unmanned shore battery, and sent the guards and workmen to the mainland.

Next day the Spanish fleet of thirteen sail, commanded by Captain-General Francisco de Luján, appeared out of the Gulf's blue haze. On board the flagship was Martín Enríquez de Almanza, coming to take charge as New Spain's viceroy. Hawkins, having fortified himself in the port, could have kept the Spaniards from entering, or thought so; but had the fleet been wrecked as a result, he would have faced his queen's certain wrath. Confident that he held the trump card, therefore, he set forth his conditions for allowing the Spanish ships to enter: that he be permitted to trade for provisions and the repairs needed by his ships, keeping the island in his possession while he did so. The agreement was to be bound by an exchange of 12 hostages. To those conditions Enríquez gave written acceptance, "signed with his hand and sealed with his seal," and the hostage exchange was effected.

After a four-day wait for the wind to change, the Spanish ships

Fig. 9. Fortress at San Juan de Ulúa. Courtesy Biblioteca Nacional.

came in and were situated apart from the English; all was accomplished in seeming good spirit. But Enríquez had no intention of keeping the agreement once his ships were inside. He felt no need to justify his deceit; Hawkins, after all, was a pirate and a heretic. Two days later, September 23, the English mariners began to notice suspicious signs, such as the arrival of great numbers of armed men and the shifting of ordnance on board the Spanish vessels. When Master Robert Barrett, a Spanish-speaking Catholic, went to ask Enríquez the meaning of this activity, the new viceroy had him seized. At dinnertime, trumpets sounded to signal the attack. Agustín de Villanueva, seated at table with Hawkins, had awaited this moment to kill the English general, but John Chamberlain spied the poniard in the Spaniard's sleeve in time to thwart the deed. The English-held shore battery quickly fell, with most of the artillerymen slain.

Hawkins had brought eight ships into the port, including the three caravels he had captured: the Frenchman Bland's, Maldonado's, and Villanueva's. Captain Bland, as the attack began, weighed anchor and tried to flee, but his vessel was disabled by the Spanish guns. He brought his men to *Jesus of Lubeck*, where Hawkins calmly drank beer from a silver cup while urging on his gunners. Three hundred men hidden on an old hulk that lay next to *Minion* tried to board her, but the English ship cut her lines and drifted out of reach. The English vessels turned their guns on the Spanish ships, disabling both the *capitana* and the *almiranta*, but the Spanish shore guns sank *Angel* and *Swallow*. *Jesus*, standing between *Minion* and the attackers, had to be abandoned when a Spanish fire ship came bearing down upon her. Her survivors, and those from the other lost ships, crowded aboard *Minion*.

Minion and *Judith* were the only English ships left afloat. For reasons unexplained, Francis Drake took the latter vessel to sea during the night and, as Hawkins puts it, "forsook us in our great misery." By morning light Hawkins brought *Minion* to the Isla de Sacrificios a league offshore, where a wild wind arose, and she lost cables and anchors.

The Spaniards, their cumbersome cargo ships not yet unburdened, did not pursue. The Spanish hostages, abandoned with *Jesus*, had been saved, as had the fifty Negroes in her hold, Hawkins's silver table service, and an undamaged caravel. And English pirates had been slain by the score.

Minion, short of food and water and still carrying fifty Negroes, "wandered in an unknown sea" for a fortnight. To her ravaged men, "hides were thought very good meat." Rats, mice, cats, and dogs were eaten, as well as monkeys and parrots that would have brought a fancy price in England. On October 8 they came to land in 23°30′, just north of the Río Pánuco, hoping to find a Spanish settlement and victuals. But having overshot the Pánuco, they found "neither people, victual, nor haven of relief." In this wilderness Hawkins left 114 sailors to fend for themselves against hostile Indians and jealous Spaniards.

The captain-general was criticized later for leaving Englishmen while keeping Negroes. Yet he might have traded the blacks among the islands for food to keep the rest of his men alive; he could not do so with Englishmen. Furthermore, it is said, the men were at the point of mutiny for want of food; some were clamoring to be put ashore to forage, and Hawkins agreed. So say his apologists. Others claim that he chose the castaways himself, ridding his vessel of undesirables. He promised to send a rescue ship the following year, but there is no record indicating that he made the effort. As the boat made for shore, a gathering storm prevented its landing. Officers of *Minion* and *Jesus* compelled the men to leave the craft more than a mile from the beach, to "sinke or swimme." Two of Captain Bland's men drowned.

On October 16, 1568, Hawkins sailed for England with eighty men and the fifty remaining Negroes via the Straits of Florida and the Bahama Channel. No effort was made to trade the Negroes in the islands. The westerlies carried *Minion* across the Atlantic to the Galician coast, where those not already dead of starvation sickened of "the excess of fresh meat" and many more died. They reached Mounts Bay in Cornwall on January 25, 1569.

The men who had been put ashore found themselves among untamed Indians with whom the Spaniards remained at war. These "Chichimecas," mistaking the castaways for their enemies, fell upon them with a terrifying shout and loosed a flight of arrows "as thicke as haile." Eight men were killed. The Englishmen had no armor or weapons with which to resist. On learning that these strangers were themselves enemies of the Spaniards, however, the natives called off the attack and treated them with kindness. Still, they followed the 200-year practice of the denizens of this coast in stripping those who wore brightly colored clothing. The Indians then pointed the unfortunates toward the south, explaining, "Tampeco, tampeco Christiano, tampeco Christiano."

The group split into two companies, and half the men, led by Anthony Goddard, went in the direction the Indians indicated; the others traveled north. Within two days the latter group again encountered hostile Indians. Their leader and two others were killed. This group then split again; twenty-five of them turned back to overtake Goddard's men four days after leaving them.

Among those who continued north was David Ingram of Barking, Essex County, whose account of the phenomena he observed on a year-long wilderness trek has left historians confused and frustrated. Ingram claims that he and two others, Richard Twide and Richard Browne, walked from the place Hawkins put them ashore to within 50 leagues of Cape Breton, Nova Scotia. As astounding as such a feat seems, there can be little doubt that they did it. The distance was somewhat greater than the 2,000 miles Ingram estimates; there are

302 The Building Rivalry

few clues to the itinerary. His description of the country and its resources, as of the people and their customs, cannot be reconciled with other accounts from that century or later. It is hardly more than the rambling of a demented man; his atrophied mind, unable to absorb what he saw, resorted to fancy. One may be fairly certain, for example, that he did not see Indian women wearing gold plates over their breasts, native banquet halls built on pillars of silver and crystal, or gold nuggets as big as his fist.

From a single indication, it may be deduced that the route was coastal; Ingram mentions the River of May, the St. John's of Florida, and uses it as a dividing point on his journey. (Seven of his 12 months of walking were spent north of that river.) Yet he obviously did not make contact with the Spaniards who had by this time settled at San Agustín and San Mateo, the former site of Fort Caroline. He makes cursory mention of Norumbega, which in the sixteenth century might have referred to the entire region between the Florida cape and Cape Breton or only the Penobscot River of Maine. Cannibals, says the chronicler, were found between Norumbega and Bariniah. Other towns mentioned are Gunda, Ochala (possibly the Ocala of the Florida peninsula visited by Soto), Balma—where he spent six or seven days, longer than at any other place—Bega, Saguanah, and Guinda. He offers scarcely a hint as to the location of any of these places and associates none of them with his various descriptions. The longer stay at Balma may have been in the vicinity of the River of May, an inference drawn from a second reference to that stream: "The ground and Country is most excellent, fertile and pleasant, and specially towards the River of May. For the grasse of ye rest is not so greene, as it is in these parts, for the other is burnt away with the heate of the Sunne."

Descriptions of certain tropical or West Indian products, such as cassava, are mixed with those indigenous to the northern mainland. Only with difficulty can the real be distinguished from the fanciful. It is doubtful in the extreme that he saw sheep or goats, even the wild native American species, and certainly not horses. He saw no elephants or penguins. If the "buffes" he describes were the American bison, he exaggerates the size of their bodies and especially their ears. "There is very great store of those Buffes, which are beasts as big as two Oxen, in length almost twentie foot, having long eares like a Blood hound, with long haires about their eares, their hornes be crooked like Rams hornes, their eyes blacke, their haires long, blacke, rough, and shagged as a Goat: The hides of these beasts are solde very deare, this Beast doeth keep companie onely by couples, male and female, and doeth alwayes fight with others of the same kinde when they do meete." Could he have mixed the features of the buffalo and the moose?

Beyond a doubt, Ingram includes descriptions of places seen while still with Hawkins's fleet; for example, an island called Corrasau—actually Curaçao, off the Venezuelan coast. He may also have added references to sights remembered from a previous voyage. Had he perchance sailed with Hawkins in 1564–65, stopping at Fort Caroline on the River of May?

Ingram, in typical confusion, relates that Hawkins left him and his companions "about four leagues west of the Río de Minas, which standeth about 140 leagues west and by North from the cape of Florida"—hardly recognizable as their actual landing place near the Río Pánuco. Thence, Browne, Ingram, and Twide walked north along the Tamaulipas coast, through the same country traversed by the 1554 shipwreck victims, the region Cabeza de Vaca in 1535 had sought desperately to avoid. After the exiles' several divisions, the three were in a group of 27. Miles Phillips, after talking with Ingram some years later, concluded that 23 of that number still were unaccounted for. "I doe thinke," he declares, "that there are some of them yet alive, and marryed in the sayd countrey, at Sibola."

A year after beginning their journey, the three reached the mouth of a river called Garinda—the St. John's of Newfoundland—60 leagues from Cape Breton. There they traded some pearls they had picked up in their travels for passage on a French ship. Reaching England by the end of 1569, they called on Master John Hawkins, "and unto eche of them he gave a reward."

Browne put to sea again and met his end aboard ship. Twide outlived him by two years and died at Ratcliffe. Nothing more is known of Ingram. Perhaps, as Morison has said, he engaged in "a profitable sort of pub crawling," telling his story in the taverns for pay. If so, he had earned the right.

All in all, these three were more fortunate than those they left in the wilds of Huasteca. From the seaside, Anthony Goddard's followers trudged toward Pánuco through coastal sloughs and tangled brush that tore their naked flesh. Voracious mosquitoes, an irritant they had

scarcely known before, sucked their blood and left their bodies covered with swollen red welts. Despite their nakedness, they did not suffer from the cold, "the countrey there is alwayes so warme." They fed
on roots and guavas, and wreathed themselves in green grass to keep
off the sun and "gnats of that country." In seven days they came to the
Tamesí River. Some Spaniards took them across in canoes on October
15. On the opposite bank a company of horsemen armed with lances
waited to arrest them and lodge them in the public jail at Tampico.
Thus the exiles came into the clutches of Luis de Carvajal y de la
Cueva, who would make capital of the incident to advance selfish
goals. As *alcalde ordinario*, Carvajal a week previously had received
official notice of the affair at San Juan de Ulúa and a warning to be on
the lookout for Hawkins's men.

Carvajal herded 77 unarmed, naked, and starving men into a little
house likened by Phillips to a hog sty. He fed them sodden corn, such
as the Spaniards gave their swine, and called them "English dogges"
and "Lutheran heretikes." Asked for a surgeon to treat the wounded,
the "governor" replied that the only surgeon they should have was the
hangman, who would remedy all their ills. (Carvajal was to be more
than repaid for such abuse when he himself fell into the hands of the
Inquisition some twenty years later.) All communication was through
a Portuguese captive, Antonio Tejeira, whom Hawkins had taken on
the African coast, and an Englishman named John Jones, the only ones
who could speak Castilian. Tejeira did not help the captives' cause by
reporting that Hawkins had intended taking provisions from Tampico
and planned to strike Campeche.

The Spaniards evidently enjoyed some sport at the prisoners' expense, for Job Hortop, with all credulity, relates, "In the river of Pánuco there is a fish like a calf, the Spaniards call it a mallatin; he hath a
stone in his head which the Indians use for the disease of the colic. In
the night he cometh on land and eateth grass. I have eaten of it and it
eateth not much unlike to bacon." Phillips was more impressed with
the salt taken from salines along the river and sent off in ships to Tamiahua, Tuxpán, and Veracruz.

For the journey to Mexico, the prisoners' hands were tied behind
them, and they were bound in pairs. Escorted by two Spaniards and a
large number of Indians, they walked over the now well-known road,
which ran through Meztitlán and Pachuca. Most of the men were sick

from wounds or malnourishment by the time they reached the capital. They were taken to a hospital, where several died and others remained as patients for as long as five months. There they met some of their comrades captured during the fight at San Juan de Ulúa. When they were well again, they were taken to prison at Texcoco, then assigned as slaves among various prominent Spaniards. Goddard and some others were sent to Spain on the fleet of Captain-General Luján, who had brought Viceroy Enríquez and fought Hawkins. Hortop and Robert Barrett (late the master of *Jesus of Lubeck*) were in another group dispatched two years later with Captain-General Juan de Velasco. The fleet, running the Bahama Channel, was saved from grounding on Cape Cañaveral by the alertness of Hortop and Barrett. But when these two were discovered in an escape plot at the Azores, the favor was quickly forgotten. Kept in stocks the remainder of the voyage, they were tried in the Casa de Contratación in Seville. John Gilbert and Barrett, the latter's claim to Catholicism notwithstanding, were sentenced to be burned. Hortop served twelve years in the galleys, then was turned over to the Inquisition for further punishment. After four years he borrowed 50 ducats to pay for having the St. Andrew's cross taken off his back and served his creditor three more years to repay him. He returned to England in December, 1590, twenty-three years after he had sailed with Hawkins.

Miles Phillips had returned to England seven or eight years previously but not without enduring equally harrowing experiences. The greater number of the Hawkins men had remained in Mexico, indentured to various grandees upon their release from prison. Some of these, including Phillips, were sent to the silver mines to oversee Indian and Negro slaves. Allowed up to 300 pesos per year, the Englishmen accumulated some wealth, which was augmented by small mining operations of their own.

When they had been in Mexico some five years, the Inquisition began to operate with greater vitality under the direction of the archbishop, Pedro Moya de Contreras (1573–86). Among the first targets were the Englishmen who had come to New Spain as enemies and been permitted to acquire wealth from the Spanish mines. Their property was appropriated to the Inquisition, and they were rounded up en masse and taken as prisoners to the capital. There they were confined in dark dungeons singly or in pairs, with no light but a candle. Over the space of a year, they were removed from their cells only to be interrogated anew by the inquisitors, who commanded them to recite the catechism in Latin. Few were able to do so. Eventually they "were all rackt, and some enforced to utter that against themselves which afterwards cost them their lives."

A platform was built in the marketplace; trumpets sounded to summon all who would come to hear the sentences "of the holy Inquisition against the English heretikes" and see them punished. On Maundy Thursday in 1575, the victims were draped with the traditional yellow "fool's coat" with the red cross of St. Andrew emblazoned front and back, then marched from the prison, "every man alone in his yellow coate, and a rope about his necke, and a great greene Waxe candle in his hand." Each man was conducted to the platform by a Spanish guard through hordes of curious onlookers who had to be separated by men on horseback. Seated on benches upon the platform, the victims saw first the inquisitors, then the viceroy and all the judges of the *audiencia* appear by different stairs. Then came as many as 300 friars, "white, blacke and gray." The religious took their appointed places, and the ceremony began. "¡*Oye, Oye!*" The assembly fell silent. Roger, the chief armorer of *Jesus of Lubeck*, was called and sentenced to receive "three hundred stripes on horseback, and after condemned to the gallies as a slave for 10 yeeres."

And so on, through the sentencing of seventy-one men, some assigned lesser punishment, some greater. By the time it was over, the day was almost gone, but the crowning event had been saved for last. George Rivelie, Peter Momfrie, and "Cornelius the Irishman" were condemned to be burned. They were taken immediately to the place of execution not far from the platform, where fires previously laid were lighted and "they were quickly burnt and consumed." The rest were taken back to their cells to await the start of their punishment the following morning, Good Friday, 1575. Sixty then were taken out to mount horses and receive their stripes on bare backs from long whips as they rode through the city's principal streets. This spectacle was heralded by criers and the inquisitors themselves, shouting, "Behold these English dogs, Lutherans, and enemies to God!" This phase of the punishment over, they were returned to prison to await transport to Spain and service in the galleys.

Miles Phillips was not among them; he and six others had been sentenced to serve in the monasteries from three to five years, still wearing their fool's coats. Phillips went to serve the "black friars," overseeing Indian workmen building a church. Learning the native language, he came to appreciate the "curteous and louing kind of people." He found the natives ingenious, possessed of great understanding, and owning such an intense hatred for the Spaniard for the cruelties visited upon them "that they and the Negroes also doe daily lie in waite to practise their deliverance out of that thraldome and bondage, that the Spaniards doe keepe them in."

It may have helped the Englishmen's feelings to learn that most of the friars and the Spaniards in general were not in sympathy with the Inquisition. While wearing their sanbenitos, they received kind and generous treatment. Yet the friars and citizens of New Spain dared not express their true feelings openly, lest they themselves be brought before the inquisitors.

When the sentences had been served, the Englishmen were taken once again before the chief inquisitor to have their fool's coats removed. These garments, each inscribed with the name of the wearer and his disposition, were hung permanently in the main church. The men then were permitted to seek employment, but they were not completely free. They well knew that the Inquisition had its spies. One by one, Phillips's companions married, some with Negro women, others with *mestizos* or Spanish widows. Phillips himself still longed for England and shunned the commitment that would keep him forever in New Spain. Fearful that returning to the mines would only bring him again before the Inquisition, he learned the weaver's trade, less subject to suspicion, while he sought opportunity for escape. The Inquisition, noting his reluctance to marry, issued a warning and forbade him to leave the city.

The prohibition was lifted in 1579 when the raids of Sir Frances Drake on the Pacific coast caused the viceroy to send troops to both coasts. Phillips went to Acapulco as an interpreter. But the wily Drake, having wrought vengeance for Enríquez de Almanza's deceit at San Juan de Ulúa, had finished his business and sailed away.

Phillips then was permitted to go with his master in the direction of Veracruz and, as the Inquisition had suspected he might, took the opportunity to flee to the port town in hopes of getting passage to Europe. He was arrested, not as an English fugitive but on suspicion of being the runaway son of a Spaniard. In shackles, he was sent away toward Mexico. Fearing the Inquisition's wrath, he managed to slip the shackles and traveled south, aided by sympathetic Indians. At Puerto de Caballos he passed as a Spaniard and took ship for Havana, where he signed on Captain-General Pedro de Guzmán's *capitana* as a soldier. His identity suspected during the crossing, he stole the ship's boat as the fleet neared Sanlúcar de Barrameda and made his escape.

Finding employment as a weaver in Seville, Phillips was careful to keep himself out of sight until the search had ceased. Then, hearing of English ships at Sanlúcar, he went there and told his story to an English shipmaster. The master wanted nothing to do with one of Hawkins's men, lest he jeopardize his port privileges. At Puerto de Santa María, Phillips signed as a soldier to go to Mallorca. Arriving at Christmastime in 1581, he found two English ships awaiting a fair wind. He boarded *Landret* and told the master that he had come to Spain two years previously to learn the language and was now ready to return home. Thus he was taken in February, 1582, to Poole, having been away from his native England almost fifteen years.

While Hawkins's men endured their sundry hardships and persecution in Mexico, another Englishman who had come to New Spain by a different route moved about the country at will. He was the merchant John Chilton, doubtless a kinsman of Leonard Chilton, the shipmaster who had brought Tomson and Field to Veracruz in 1556. Chilton, ironically, had come from Spain in General Luján's fleet and must have looked on with interest while Hawkins negotiated with the incoming Viceroy Enríquez for port privileges at San Juan de Ulúa, but his account makes no mention of the incident.

Chilton had left London in 1561, spent seven years in Spain, then sailed in March, 1568, for the New World and traveled over much of Mexico, Central America, and Peru before returning to London in 1586. He then composed his "notable discourse."

Going ashore at San Juan de Ulúa, he probably went on to Veracruz before the fireworks started between Hawkins and the Spanish fleet. He found it a town, of about 400 inhabitants, chiefly the factors of Spanish merchants, but they lived there only from the end of August until the first of April, while the ships were being unloaded and loaded again. During the remainder of the year they sought the more pleasant and healthful climate of Jalapa. Never, says Chilton, was a woman delivered of child in the port town; as soon as one perceived herself pregnant, she would be taken into the country to "avoid the perill of the infected aire," though stringent measures were taken daily to purify the place. (Two thousand cattle were driven through the town each morning, with the expectation that they would "take away the ill vapors of the earth.")

After moving on to spend six years in Mexico City, Chilton extended his trading operation north and west into the mining districts of Nueva Vizcaya, where jingling silver bought his merchandise; to the province of Colúa, where he converted his silver to cacao, the local medium of exchange; and to the port of Navidad where, in late 1569, he saw the ships that came from China and the Philippines, disgorging their cargoes of wonders from the Far East. Loading a mule train for Guatemala, he paused at Puebla de los Angeles and Oaxaca, where Indians paid tribute in "mantels of cotton wooll, and Cochonelio, whereof there groweth abundance throughout this Countrey." At Tehuántepec, a fortified port on the South Sea, he saw in 1572 "a peece of Ordnance of brasse, called a Demy culverin, which came out of a ship, called the *Jesus of Lubecke*, which Captaine Hawkins left in S. John de Ullua, being in fight with the Spaniards, in the yeere, 1568." The piece was being sent to the Philippines.

After his sweep southward, Chilton journeyed north to Pánuco, via Meztitlán—where lived twelve Spaniards and "thirty thousand" Indians—passing two Augustinian monasteries. At Tampico he found forty Christians, but while he was there the number was diminished by fourteen, the result of an Indian attack at the salines where they were gathering salt. "In those Countries," observed the Englishman, "they take neither golde, nor silver for exchange of any thing, but onely Salt, which they greatly esteeme, and use it as a principal medicine for certaine wormes which breede in their lippes, and in their gummes." Were it not for the bar at the mouth of the river, he hypothesized, ships up to 500 tons might ascend it more than 60 leagues.

At Pánuco, 14 leagues up the river, he found only a single priest and ten Christians. No longer was it "a goodly Citie," as it had been, for hostile natives had laid waste to it. There Chilton fell ill and remained six weeks before a companion came for him. Proceeding toward Santiago de los Valles, he became separated from his caravan, lost his way, and found himself among naked wild Indians who lived in straw houses. They brought a young girl who had lived in Mexico to interrogate him. It was good that he was lean, she told him; otherwise, he would be promptly eaten. When he asked for water, she brought him a gilded glass that provoked his curiosity. She readily supplied details of how it had been taken from an Augustinian monastery by this very chieftain, who had the monastery burned and all its occupants slain. But at last they put him on the road to Valles, where his companions waited in a mud-walled town of twenty-five Spaniards.

Convalescing there, Chilton met Captain Francisco de Puga, whom Viceroy Enríquez had sent to discover a route linking the Zacatecas mines with the sea. Joining this exploratory expedition of 40 soldiers and 500 Indians from the Tanchipa and Tamaholipa pueblos—"all good archers and naked men"—the adventurous Englishman penetrated the wilderness to "ye river de las Palmas . . . parting ye kingdome of nova Hispania, and Florida." Following the river three days without finding a crossing, the explorers cut timber to make a raft, which swimming Indians pushed to the other side. In thirty days' travel through woods and over mountains, they came, at Zacatecas, to "ye richest mines in all the Indies . . . thence they fetch most silver."

On a later trip to Yucatán, Chilton found a bishop and almost 100 Spaniards in Mérida, the Indians paying tribute in cotton mantles and cacao, with dyewoods, cochineal, hides, and honey being loaded on small frigates. (There was no port to accommodate larger vessels.) These small craft plied to San Juan de Ulúa with the produce for trade in Mexico.

Here, as elsewhere in Mexico, Chilton observed, "there groweth a certain plant called Nege [the maguay], which yeeldeth Wine, vineger, hony, and black Sugar, and of the leaves of it dried, they make hempe, ropes, shooes which they use, and tyles for their houses: and at the ende of every leafe, there groweth a sharpe point like an awle, wherewith they use to bore or pearce through any thing."

Before Chilton was out of Mexico, his interests were being impinged upon by his own countrymen. In April, 1579, when Sir Francis Drake was raiding the South Sea ports, the sum of 1,000 ducats belonging to Chilton was among the booty taken at Acapulco.

Chilton's account of sixteenth-century Mexico is amplified by that of another English merchant, Henry Hawkes. Living in New Spain from 1567 to 1572, Hawkes observed one effect of Hawkins's visit: an elaborate fortress was under construction at San Juan de Ulúa. New Spain's principal port, it was seen, had to be protected against future invaders. Of these there would be more in the years ahead.

SOURCES AND NOTES

The increasing pirate activity in the Gulf, as background to the growing rivalry, is drawn from a number of Spanish documents: Viceroy Luis de Velasco to the Crown, Mexico, Sept. 30, 1558 (AGI, Mexico 19, ramo 1, no. 21); Diego de Mazariego to the Crown, Havana, April 24, 1561 (AGI, Santo Domingo 15); Francisco Tamayo Pacheco, "Ynformación de servicios hechos en la provincia de Yucatán," Mérida, March 5, 1568 (AGI, Mexico 99, ramo 1); Hernando Manrique de Rojas, "Relación de los franceses que han de poblar la costa de la Florida," Havana, July 10, 1564 (ibid., no. 44); and the Gonzalo Gayón *probanza* cited in the previous chapter. Concerning the pirates from Fort Caroline, see "Confesión que se tomó a un hombre que vino de la ysla de Cuba lo tocante a la Florida," Seville, Sept. 15, 1565 (AGI, Patronato 19-1-5).

The English Voyagers

The world is indebted to Richard Hakluyt, who collected accounts from various participants and published them. *The Principall Navigations of the English Nation*—first published in 1589 and reissued in two volumes, facsimile, by Cambridge University Press in 1965—is the richest source. From this work and other Hakluyt compilations has come most of what has been written previously on the events treated here. The story is not complete, however, unless the English accounts are balanced with the Spanish. To achieve that, one turns to Irene A. Wright, ed., *Spanish Documents Concerning English Voyages to the Caribbean, 1527–1568*, and a number of unpublished documents from Spanish archives.

From Hakluyt, *Principall Navigations*, vol. 2, come the following accounts summarized in this chapter:

John Sparke the younger on the 1564–65 Hawkins voyage that visited Fort Caroline, the pertinent part of which is printed in Henry S. Burrage, ed., *Early English and French Voyages, Chiefly from Hakluyt, 1534–1608*. Hakluyt also includes the Laudonnière account of Hawkins's visit.

M. John Bodenham on his voyage to San Juan de Ulúa. He gives the year as 1564, but with Menéndez as captain-general, he must have sailed with the fleet of 1562–63.

Robert Tomson's narrative, which presents a different dimension of Menéndez's first voyage as captain-general, revealing that the voyage usually cited as a model of speed and efficiency actually incurred disaster. Tomson provides a description of San Juan de Ulúa and the town of Veracruz (Antigua) that parallels the one given later by John Chilton. He also describes sights he saw on the road to Mexico, including cochineal production, which he failed to understand. Cochineal, he allowed, was "not a worme, or a flye, as some say it is, but a berrie that groweth upon certain bushes in the wilde fields." Actually, it is a cactus-feeding insect that produces a red dye. John L. Stephens (*Incidents of Travel in Central America, Chiapas, and Yucatán*, 1:277) provides a classic description of cochineal culture.

Miles Phillips's chronicle of Hawkins's castaways, their encounter with the Indians, their trek to Pánuco, and their imprisonment by Carvajal. Phillips says 114 men were put ashore, but the figures he gives total 115: 11 slain by Indians, 27 marching north with Ingram, and 77 reaching Pánuco. Carvajal reported finding 12 bodies, which included one or both of Bland's men. Phillips relates the third recorded instance of the Tamaulipas Indians' stripping their European captives (see chs. 11 and 13).

David Ingram's tale, which is reproduced in facsimile from Hakluyt in Everette Lee DeGolyer, *Across Aboriginal America*. DeGolyer (p. 9) recites the publication history, including the fact that the story was omitted from Hakluyt's second edition because it seemed so improbable. Although it is clear from Miles Phillips's narrative that the landing was near the Pánuco, Samuel Eliot Morison (*Northern Voyages*, 467) says that Ingram and company were put ashore "on the gulf coast of Florida" and treats their march as though it began on the Florida peninsula. DeGolyer offers a map interpretation of the route: north from Tampico to the Río Grande, thence east some distance from the coast to Alabama and Georgia, and north to the St. John's of Newfoundland. Legend surrounding the village of Penitas (Hidalgo County), Texas—that six members of the 1520 Narváez expedition fleeing from Cortés settled at that site—perhaps should be related instead to the lost Englishmen from Hawkins's crew who started out with Ingram, Browne, and Twide. See Ben P. Bailey, Jr., *Border Lands Sketchbook / Libro de Bosquejos Fronterizos*, 120.

John Chilton's travelogue, which epitomizes the English exploration of New Spain in this period.

Published selections from Hakluyt besides that of Burrage include John Hampden, ed., *The Tudor Venturers*. Therein is found an anonymous account of Hawkins's first voyage to the Spanish Main and Hawkins's own "Battle of San Juan." Hawkins's ship, by his version, did not sail away from the Tamaulipas coast until after the castaways were arrested at Tampico. Hampden's selection also includes Henry Hawkes's "Traveling in New Spain" and Job Hortop's "A Powder-Maker's Adventures." Hortop accords Agustín Villanueva a significant role in the fracas at San Juan de Ulúa, but none of the Spanish sources mentions him. In a letter to the king (AGI, Mexico 101, ramo 4), Agustín Villanueva Cervantes claims that he and his brother, Alonso Villanueva Cervantes, sons of a first conqueror who came to New Spain with Narváez, notified the Audiencia de Mexico of a plot in the viceroyalty to rebel against the Crown; he had sailed for Havana with the intention of going to Spain to report. Villanueva refers to the alleged conspiracy to make Martín Cortés (the conqueror's son) ruler of

Mexico, the instigators of which were beheaded (see Winsor, *Narrative and Critical History*, 8:195).

The Spanish Documents

Wright's *Spanish Documents* comprises a valuable collection that counterbalances the English version of the San Juan de Ulúa incident. Here are found Martín Enríquez de Almanza's reply to Hawkins; a report to the *audiencia* from Veracruz by Luis Zegri; a statement by Enríquez with supporting depositions (including Francisco Maldonado's); the report of the viceroy and the *audiencia* to the Crown; and Robert Barrett's deposition, which contains an account of the entire Hawkins voyage.

Unpublished documents include the following:

Juan Céspedes to the Crown, Campeche, March 4, 1576 (AGI, Mexico 100, ramo 4), relates Hawkins's approach at Campeche.

A petition by Bartolomé García, Mérida, 1567 (AGI, Mexico 98, ramo 1), reveals that a pirate watch was posted on the Yucatán coast.

"Relación del sucesso entre Juan de Aquinas y la armada," San Juan de Ulúa, 1568 (AGI, Patronato 265-1-12), anonymous, summarizes the outcome of the San Juan affair from the Spanish point of view. See also Fernando de Portugal (royal treasurer) to the Crown, Mexico, April 3, 1569 (AGI, Mexico 323).

"Diligencias hechas por el muy magnífico Señor Luis de Carvajal sobre los yngleses," Tampico, Oct. 8, 1568 (AGI, Patronato 265-1-12), tells of the capture of the Englishmen at Tampico. Carvajal interrogated the prisoners on October 15, while Hawkins's ship was still on the coast.

Viceroy Enríquez to the Crown, Mexico, April 4, 1571 (AGI, Mexico 19, no. 65), relates: "To the Casa de Contratación I am sending some Englishmen and among them goes the master [Robert Barrett] who came with Juan Aquines. He is very knowledgeable of the sea and very well informed of all these coasts and of this land." In short, Barrett knew too much for the Spaniards ever to risk setting him free.

Viceroy Enríquez, as a result of the Hawkins affair, gives instructions for building fortifications at San Juan de Ulúa (Mexico, Aug. 7, 1570, AGI, Mexico 257). Progress was slow, and the building a continuing concern for the rest of the century. The engineer Juan Bautista Antonelli prosecuted the work in the 1590s, when the project moved forward in earnest (his reports are also found in AGI, Mexico 257).

--⊸{ C H A P T E R   17 }⊷--

Land of Angels:
Menéndez and Escalante, 1565–75

THE events of his forty-six years had directed Pedro Menéndez de Avilés toward the climax of his career, which came with his appointment as leader of the Florida venture. Born of lesser nobility in the Asturian seaport of Avilés on February 15, 1519, he ran away to sea at fourteen. His first voyage led to an encounter with French corsairs, and it was he who rallied the Spanish resistance that saved his vessel from being boarded. He fought the French in wartime and, with royal license, opposed French pirates with his own vessel in time of peace, a pursuit tantamount to privateering. After a period of chasing *flibustiers* in the Indies, he was named captain-general of the Indies fleet in 1555 and in that capacity made four voyages. The assignment represented his first emergence as man of the hour. Indies navigation, having suffered a string of disasters, was in trouble.

Financial havoc followed the 1554 wreck of three ships on the Texas coast, the crowning blow to a series of misfortunes that already had produced bankruptcies and bank failures; the Crown plunged deeper into the financial morass in which it was perpetually mired. Later that year the disastrous homeward voyage of Cosme Rodríguez Farfán left wrecks scattered across the Atlantic from the Bahama Channel to the Spanish coast with unthinkable loss of life and treasure. Charles V, facing financial ruin, stripped the Casa de Contratación of its traditional authority for naming the captain-general and made the appointment himself: Menéndez.

The new fleet commander set time and efficiency records for the two-way voyage, employing the talents of his two brothers as admirals. This phase of Menéndez's career culminated in personal tragedy that renewed his interest in a Florida colony. In 1563 his only son, Juan, was left in Veracruz to conduct the New Spain fleet to Seville. Juan's ship was lost in a hurricane in the Bahama Channel.

Since Menéndez had first proposed to Charles V a fort on the channel to protect Spanish shipping, the emperor had been succeeded by his son, Philip II; the Luna-Villafañe effort had failed; and the second Lucas Vázquez de Ayllón had defaulted (in August, 1564) on a contract to settle the Santa Elena region discovered by his father. When the king, on March 15, 1565, issued a contract whereby Menéndez would undertake the exploration, settlement, and religious conversion of Florida, the French reentry into that region was not yet known in Spain. In the midst of preparations, word came via the pirates captured at Jamaica of Laudonnière's fort on the St. John's River. The project was broadened, Crown support expanded, and preparations hastened. Menéndez once again became man of the hour. He sailed from Cádiz on June 29, 1565, on a race to reach Florida before Laudonnière was reinforced.

After sailing through an Atlantic hurricane, Menéndez was forced to leave Santo Domingo with only half his ten ships. On St. Augustine's Day, August 28, his five vessels dropped anchor in the inlet where soon would rise the settlement of San Agustín. A week later he sailed in search of Fort Caroline. Ribaut's ships, already on hand with reinforcements, eluded the Spaniards by cutting their own cables; Menéndez withdrew but soon returned by land to lay waste to the fort, with a vengeance born of religious intolerance and hatred of Huguenots. After the bloodletting, in which most of the Frenchmen were slain, 300 Spaniards garrisoned Fort Caroline. In commemoration of the St. Matthew's Day massacre, they called it San Mateo. When Ribaut's ships were driven by storm upon the coast, the crew members not drowned or killed by Indians surrendered to Menéndez in two groups, twelve days apart. With hands tied behind them, they were started along the beach toward San Agustín. By prearranged signal the Spanish soldiers fell upon the bound men, at the place since known as Matanzas, the massacre place, and cut off their heads. Only the sprinkling of Catholics among them was spared.

Besides driving the French Huguenots from Fort Caroline and forming a Spanish settlement, Menéndez's charge called for exploring Florida from St. Joseph's Bay on the Gulf of Mexico to the Martyrs and thence north as far as Newfoundland. With the first two tasks completed, he ran up the Atlantic coast to Santa Elena, where he founded a third settlement, San Felipe. He then set out to reconnoiter the 300 leagues of coastline on both sides of the peninsula, from the St. John's River to Tampa Bay, to discover harbors and establish forts.

These steps, carried out within 20 months of the *adelantado*'s first landing, began while the blood of Fort Caroline's martyrs was scarcely cold. In early November, 1565, Menéndez explored south along the Atlantic coast, established a garrison among the Ais Indians at St. Lucie, and proceeded to Havana. His nephew, Pedro Menéndez Márquez, and Francisco Genovés had just arrived with more ships and, by royal order, a welcome addition to Menéndez's staff: Gonzalo Gayón—who had explored these coasts with Juan de Rentería and piloted Tristán de Luna's supply fleet—to serve as chief pilot for the forthcoming exploration of the Florida Gulf coast.

Spending the winter in Havana, Menéndez heard reports of Christian men and women on the lower Florida peninsula whom the *cacique* Carlos had held captive for as long as twenty years. Doubtless with thoughts of his son, he had masses celebrated to his patron St. Anthony and embarked on February 10, 1566, for the Bay of Juan Ponce. He intended "to discover all the coast from the Bay of Filipina [Mobile] and the coves of San Jusepe [St. Joseph's Bay] to the Martyrs."

Putting Esteban de las Alas in charge of the five ships, Menéndez himself embarked with Diego de Amaya in the two brigantines, which drew only three feet. The fleet found ample passage between the Tortugas and the Marquesas Keys. While the larger ships stood off in deep water, Menéndez and Amaya followed the keys toward the mainland, where they probed bays and inlets, seeking contact with the people of Carlos.

On the fourth day out of Havana, as the brigantines sailed close to shore looking for the Bay of Juan Ponce, a canoe with a single occupant came out from shore and approached Amaya's vessel. The man in the canoe had the appearance of an Indian. His body, naked but for a deerskin breechclout, was smeared with paint. From beneath the deerskin, he produced a crucifix. Thus Menéndez met Hernando de Escalante Fontaneda, fifteen years a captive of the Calusa Indians since being left on the keys by shipwreck at the age of thirteen. Menéndez describes him as being "very good-looking, of noble parents, the son of the late García Descalante, a conquistador of Cartagena." Hernando himself says his father's name was Juan.

Born in Cartagena, he and his brother had been shipwrecked on the keys in 1551 while en route to Spain to attend school at Salamanca, aboard the ship of Master Juan Cristóbal. Most of the people from the ship reached the shore, Menéndez says, but forty-two of them, including Escalante's older brother, were killed by the father of the present chief Carlos.

Escalante had news of a number of other castaways; most important, Don Pedro's son, Juan Menéndez, not heard from since the 1563 hurricane. Having talked with a sailor from the same fleet, Escalante reported that Juan's ship had been lost on the east coast of Florida, and there was no likelihood that he survived. Don Pedro's search for his son had ended.

Escalante guided the brigantines into Carlos Bay, half a league from the village of the chief, of the same name as his ancestor who had opposed Juan Ponce de León. Carlos drew up 100 archers; Menéndez landed 30 harquebusiers. Carlos then invited Menéndez for a visit. There was a gift exchange, and Menéndez received from Carlos a silver bar and pieces of gold, plunder from some lost vessel. In touchy negotiations, Menéndez treated for the release of the white captives, said to have been 11 men and women. There was evidence of other castaways less fortunate: more than 50 human skulls piled up at the base of a tree testified to the natives' practice of killing their captives during fiestas, ceremonially placing the heads on pikes.

Carlos promised to deliver three other captives who were absent from the village, but those present told Menéndez that these people were on another bay 50 leagues up the coast. A bit of unpleasantness marked by a threat against Menéndez's life hastened his decision to go and look for them. It was Escalante who saved the day. As the contemporary historian Barrientos tells it, the chief had invited the governor to his house. When a large fleet of canoes gathered about, ostensibly to take him to the chief, Menéndez became suspicious. Just then "the Christian who had put out to sea bearing the Cross" arrived to warn the *adelantado* of a plot to kill him. Escalante himself mentions the incident, saying "the Vizcayan" (Pedro Vizcaino, one of the captives) would have sold Menéndez to the Indians "had it not been for me and a mulatto [Luis, another captive], who discovered the treachery; everyone would have been slain, and I among the rest, and Pedro Menéndez would not have died in Santander but in Florida in the Province of Carlos."

Menéndez took his people on board the brigantines and sailed up the coast "fifty leagues" (to Tampa Bay), looking for the other captives and the other ships, which had been driven offshore by a squall the day before the Carlos landing. Finding neither, he returned to Carlos Bay, where the other five vessels had come to anchor during his absence.

While waiting for Menéndez, Esteban de las Alas had gone ashore with 100 soldiers to begin trading. Carlos, in awe of the big ships and eager for more Spanish goods, had changed his attitude. He entertained Menéndez in his house with native singers and dancers, then served a banquet of oysters and fish. Menéndez had various delicacies brought from the ships and put on a show with a dancing dwarf, music by his trumpeters, and half a dozen singers. To cement their relationship, Carlos presented his sister to Menéndez to be his wife. When the *adelantado* objected on grounds that she was not a Christian, she agreed to go to the land of Christians and learn their religion. The governor sent the maiden, whom he named Doña Antonia, and her seven attendants to Havana with Alas. He himself sailed for San Agustín.

Escalante Fontaneda served Menéndez two years as an interpreter (as did some of the other released captives), evidently including this period in the seventeen years he claims to have spent among the Calusa. For that service he received only his keep. Escalante came and went among the Calusa with Menéndez and the other officers assigned there in connection with the abortive colony of San Antonio. The first occasion was in June, 1566, when Menéndez brought Doña Antonia back from Havana.

Relations between the *adelantado* and Carlos, uneasy from the beginning, were not helped by Menéndez's reluctance to consummate his marriage to the chief's sister. They were scarcely improved when Doña Antonia returned with only two of the several companions who had left with her, the others having died in Havana. Doña Antonia and one of her maids had been baptized. She begged Menéndez to go ashore immediately and begin building a Christian village, but he chose to wait for the wily Carlos to come to the ship. Carlos kept him waiting two hours. He and the other chiefs then dined with the Spanish leader and received gifts, but he was not ready to become a Christian.

When Carlos failed in his promise to deliver additional Christian captives, Menéndez resorted to threats. The chief became contrite, brought the captives, and permitted Menéndez to take his young cousin and heir, Don Pedro, and the lad's father, Sebastián, to Havana to be baptized. Escalante, having overheard the conversation among the Indians concerning the baptism, advised against it on grounds that their intentions were not proper and they were likely to apostatize. The validity of his admonition was later proved.

Leaving San Antonio a second time, Menéndez, accompanied by Escalante, proceeded to San Mateo at the mouth of the St. John's River (called Río de San Mateo), hoping to discover a water route across the peninsula to the Gulf. Escalante advised that such a route might utilize the waterways only part of the distance; it would be possible, he believed, to reach Tocobaga (present Tampa) by ascending the San Mateo 60 or 70 leagues, then going overland to the Cañogacola (a tribe subject to Tocobaga) and thence to the large river on which Tocobaga was situated. Menéndez still expected to ascend the St. John's until it joined with Lake Miami (Okeechobee) but could not because the channel became too narrow and the company was menaced by Chief Mocoya's archers. On returning to San Mateo, the *adelantado* left six men with Chief Carabay, who promised to guide them to the lake. That mission failed also, because of the threats from Chief Saturiba, who was constantly at war with San Mateo's garrison.

After visiting San Felipe at Punta de Santa Elena, Menéndez returned to San Agustín and thence embarked on a voyage to look for corsairs and fortify the ports of Puerto Rico, Hispaniola, and Cuba. Just before sailing from San Agustín, on October 20, 1566, he sent Francisco de Reynoso with thirty men, Escalante among them, to build a blockhouse at San Antonio. The captain was instructed to look in that region for a river that joined Lake Miami, thus forming the desired link between the coasts.

Reynoso, proceeding by way of Havana, returned Carlos's cousin and heir, Don Pedro, to San Antonio. Menéndez had great hopes for this young man. Expecting that he had by this time become a Christian, he hoped to wed Doña Antonia to him; the two of them then would inherit Carlos's rule. Menéndez would be rid of his Indian wife and also have the Calusa governed by Christians. Such hopes were doomed to disappointment.

On reaching Bahía de Carlos, Reynoso immediately detected hostility. He thwarted several plots to kill him. Menéndez, on receipt of such news in Havana, sailed at once for San Antonio with Juan Rogel, a Jesuit priest, and Francisco Villareal, a lay brother, to begin the religious instruction of the Calusa. By the time he arrived, Reynoso had disproved the hoped-for river link with Lake Miami. The passage he sought, Carlos advised, lay 50 leagues farther north, near Tocobaga. The chief's veracity was suspect, for he was Tocobaga's arch enemy. When an expedition was made, Carlos was permitted to join it only after a stern admonition.

Two days' sailing brought the six brigantines to Tocobaga's bay, "twenty leagues" from the entrance. Ordinarily, it would have been out of the question to enter an unknown bay on a moonless night with so many vessels. Yet Menéndez put his fleet in the hands of a native pilot, who, with a fair wind, guided it up the bay by the North Star to reach Tocobaga's village an hour before dawn. This location is generally conceded to be at the head of Old Tampa Bay.

The vessels came silently to anchor. Carlos was beside himself with his desire to leap ashore and put Tocobaga's village to the torch, but Menéndez would not allow it. When an interpreter hailed the chief's house and the Indians awoke to see the ships silhouetted against the sky, most of them fled. Only Chief Tocobaga and half a dozen others stood fast. The chief sent a Portuguese captive of six years to thank Menéndez for not attacking.

For several days Menéndez treated with Tocobaga for release of twelve Calusa captives, including a sister of Carlos and Doña Antonia. At one point more than fifteen hundred Indians armed with bows and arrows stood about watching the goings-on. Menéndez, growing uneasy, suggested that the negotiations be left to the leading chiefs; Tocobaga sent the others away. At last a peace treaty was effected between Tocobaga and Carlos, and Tocobaga asked Menéndez to leave Christians to teach him the Catholic faith. The *adelantado* left thirty soldiers commanded by García Martínez de Coz. The rest of the Spaniards returned to San Antonio with Carlos.

When Menéndez departed for San Augustín, he left fifty additional men with Captain Reynoso. Matters were far from settled with Carlos.

The *cacique* resented the enforced peace with Tocobaga, and the interpreters overheard threats he made against Menéndez and the other Christians. Some months later, probably in early spring 1567, the Spaniards at San Antonio suffered the last straw: Carlos sent out a fleet of war canoes with orders to seize an approaching supply ship before it came to land, and those on board were hard put to defend themselves. When Menéndez heard of this treachery, he sent his nephew Pedro Menéndez Márquez to mete justice. Menéndez Márquez testified to the result in a 1573 hearing in Madrid to determine future Indian policy: "This witness went, and beheaded the said *cacique* and twenty other Indians among the most guilty." Don Pedro then became chief, as Menéndez de Avilés had intended, but the change brought no improvement. There was a second round of executions, with the result that the Indians burned their buildings and fled. The settlement of San Antonio was abandoned.

The Spanish garrison at Tocobaga suffered an even worse fate. Menéndez Márquez, still at the Calusa settlement, heard the distressing news from a friendly native: Tocobaga's people, under pretext of arming for a deer hunt, had fallen upon the garrison. Going there, he found that all the soldiers had been slain.

Thus ended for a number of years any attempt to explore and settle on the Gulf coast; no other settlement of note was made on the west side of the peninsula for more than two centuries. With the *adelantado*'s departure for Spain in May 1567, the east-coast settlements hardly fared better. By the time the 1573 testimony was given, the natives all along the keys and the Bahama Channel were back at their old tricks of murdering shipwreck victims wholesale. While the Spanish occupation of Florida had resulted in the rescue of some castaways, it was largely ineffective; losses occasioned by the increased activity at times exceeded the gains.

Menéndez had sought by every means possible to make peace with the Indians of Ais, Jaega, Tequesta, Matecumbe, Carlos, and Tocobaga, Juan de Soto testified in the 1573 hearings. Still, they persisted in breaking the peace. An example was seen in the people of Matecumbe, living among the keys; seizing a shallop en route from Florida to Havana, they had slain eight soldiers and taken another as their slave.

Escalante Fontaneda ended his Florida sojourn in 1569. He may have gone to Spain; on October 20 of that year the Council of the Indies received his petition for Crown consideration. During his 17 years in Florida, he related, his parents had died in Cartagena. Since they had no known heirs, their *encomienda* in Nueva Granada and other property had been confiscated by the Crown. Consequently, he was a poor and unfortunate orphan and, because of his long captivity, had no one who might favor him. He asked the king's intercession to obtain property at Cartagena that might provide his livelihood. No record of the Crown's action, or the council's, appears.

The next word of the erstwhile Calusa captive is his memoir, written six years after he left Florida, judging from his reference to Menéndez's death in September, 1574. Despite the author's lack of formal education, the document offers a more comprehensive account of sixteenth-century Florida than does any other single source. Although Escalante's prose is difficult and provides less information than we wish it did, it bespeaks a keen intellect. At the time of his rescue, he had lived among the Indians more than half his life. Instead of taking his education at Salamanca, as his parents intended, he had taken it among the Florida natives. His observations were enhanced by his linguistic abilities: he learned to speak four native dialects.

His mastery of the Calusa tongue not only served Menéndez well but also benefited some of his fellow captives. Escalante and Juan Rodríguez—probably the shipmaster by that name whose vessel was lost from the 1549 fleet—saved the lives of some of these later castaways by teaching them the language. New arrivals among the Calusa, whom Escalante described as the meanest people of all Florida, were customarily ordered to dance and sing. The captives, not understanding, were considered rebellious when they failed to comply and were often put to death as a result—at least until Escalante found occasion to explain the matter to Carlos. Thus the chief came to understand the language barrier and instructed his people to use an interpreter when trying to communicate with new captives.

Calusa territory, Escalante says, began at the keys, where the towns of Chuchiyaga and Guarungube—one meaning "martyred place," the other "town of weeping"—were situated. Fifty other Calusa towns extended up the west coast and inland as far as Lake Miami (the earlier name for Lake Okeechobee), whence comes the name of the city of Miami. The first Calusa town—meaning the one farthest north—was called Tanpa, from which derives the name but not the site of the present city of Tampa.

The island people were large, the women well proportioned and of good countenance. They had "no gold, less silver, and [even] less clothing." The men went naked except for breechclouts of woven palm, while the women concealed their privates with a covering of Spanish moss. Their name signified a brave, fierce, and skillful people, "as in truth they are." The men were strong, skilled as archers, and understood Spanish tactics. Their food consisted of fish, turtles, snails, tuna, whalemeat, crayfish, knucklefish, and *lobos marinos* (manatee). The Spanish captives marveled at finding deer on the islands of Cuchiyaga, midway among the keys. On those nearer the mainland there were bear and also an unidentified foxlike animal that was fat and good to eat. The "fruit of many sorts" is not enumerated, but there was "the wood of many uses," which had medicinal applications—the lignum vitae, found on the higher points of the inner keys.

Subject to Carlos and paying tribute to him in food and deerskins were the people of Tequesta province, north of the head of the Martyrs on Lake Okeechobee and the Miami River. Their villages, of thirty to forty inhabitants each, surrounded the lake. The Tequesta Indians ate roots of many kinds, including one from which a bread was made and another, like the truffle, that was sweet. They preferred game, such as deer and birds, when it was available. The rivers offered abundant fish and an infinite number of eels, long as a man and thick as a man's thigh. The Indians also ate alligators, snakes, a ratlike animal (probably muskrat) that lived in the water, tortoises, "and many more disgusting reptiles." Their country was broken and marshy.

Escalante's mastery of four native dialects indicates that he was permitted to travel extensively. He tells of the time he spent among the tribes north of Calusa: "The Indians of Apalache are subject to those of Olagale [Ocale] and Mogoso [Mocoso] and others from the direction of the Sierra Aite, who are the richest of these regions and of greater valor." He spent two years among *them* (indefinite antecedent) looking for gold. Such wanderings enabled him to dispel the long-standing myth that precious metals could be mined in the peninsula. Gold, he says, was to be found only in the mines of the snowy mountains of Onagatano, "the farthest subject of Apalache"—a reference to the Georgia gold country. Repeatedly emphasizing the absence of native gold and silver, he says the only precious metals the Indians possessed had come from treasure ships wrecked on the coast from Calusa to San Mateo. The Apalache, however, collected tribute of base gold mixed with fine, many painted deerskins, and pearls from the people farther north. The pearls came from a river called Guasacaesgui, or "River of Canes," lying between Apalache and Olagale. The description indicates the Suwannee. The gems found their way thence to all the provinces and villages of Florida, but principally to Tocobaga, the nearest town.

The Apalache, in Escalante's estimation, were "the best Indians in Florida," being superior to those of Tocobaga, Carlos, Ais, and Tequesta. The men went naked; the women wore loincloths of the wool-like "straw that grows from trees." They ate deer, fox, and "woolly cattle"—the earliest known reference to bison in Florida. The Indians of the Apalache town, says Escalante, claimed that their chief had been hanged by Hernando de Soto's men because he wore around his neck some large pearls, the center one being about the size of a turtle-dove's egg.

The Tocobaga and Olagale, or Ocale, Indians mentioned by Escalante were Timucuan. Avowed enemies of the Apalache in Soto's time, they had been overcome since then and now paid tribute to Apalache. Tocobaga was named for its chieftain, who lived on a cape near a river mouth. The Indians of that town subsisted on corn and fish, supplemented by deer, antelope, and other wild game, as well as bread made from native roots. Their dress was like that of the Apalache, the men wearing loincloths and deerskins, the women draping themselves below the waist with Spanish moss. Escalante had only heard of the Cañogacola, who lived farther inland and were subject to Tocobaga. They were artists, as well as great warriors, painting colorful pictures of whatever they saw. Although they were skillful with the bow, the chronicler believed they could be overcome by Spanish arms.

All the Florida people from Tocobaga to Santa Elena, he says, were adept anglers and dexterous bowmen. "I am certain they will never be at peace, much less become Christians." They should be taken in hand, removed to the Antilles and even to Tierra Firme, and sold as slaves, he declares. Then the Spaniards could make stock farms in Florida, and people cast away by shipwreck could find a haven on shore.

Escalante and some other aides with experience in Florida are named on a list of "the old ones" prepared by Menéndez in October, 1566: Hernando de Escalante, and Luis the Mulatto, interpreters of the Calusa; Pedro de Bustinçuri, interpreter of the Ais, whom the French took to France and who went from there to the Spanish court—doubtless one of the two Spanish captives mentioned by John Sparke on Hawkins's visit to Fort Caroline; and "Don Luis the Indian," native of the region of Bacalaos, "in Tierra Nueva," who also had been to the Spanish court. It was Don Luis who later guided the exploration of Chesapeake Bay in the search for a strait and served the Spanish settlement in that region.

As for Escalante, nothing more is heard after his memorial addressed to some anonymous "Very Illustrious Lord." A good bet is that he returned to his native Cartagena.

Menéndez's search for a strait around Chesapeake Bay, held in abeyance several years, indicates his ambitions for exploring the continent. Of more direct concern here are the expeditions he sent from Santa Elena to "discover and conquer the interior from there to Mexico." While both religious and military efforts were being made to subdue the coastal Indians from Tocobaga to Santa Elena, the effort was launched from the latter point with expectations of approaching Mexico through country previously explored by Hernando de Soto.

Whether river courses directed the route or the expeditionists had a better conceptualization of Soto's route than one might expect, they soon hit Soto's trail. It seems more than coincidental that they traveled away from the Gulf of Mexico until they reached the point of Soto's easternmost penetration, then followed his path almost without deviation until it turned southwest toward the Gulf.

In the three extant accounts of the two journeys, there is no specific mention of the direction traveled. Both expeditions were led by Captain Juan Pardo, the first leaving Santa Elena about November 1, 1566, with 125 soldiers. Finding little of note in the marshy country covered in the first 40 leagues, the company came at last to a large river, probably the Savannah, and headed upstream, visiting the various native groups and treating for their fealty to pope and king. About a week later the group reached Juada—the Xuale visited by Soto in May, 1540—in northwestern South Carolina at the foot of the Blue Ridge. Pardo found there a large number of Indians willing to become vassals of both His Holiness and His Majesty. The Spaniards stayed fifteen days, building a fort called San Juan, which Pardo garrisoned with his sergeant, Boyano, and 30 soldiers.

From this point they explored up the river, then withdrew to Guatari, near the edge of the swamp, 40 leagues from Santa Elena. Finding many chiefs and Indians gathered, the Spaniards remained fifteen days before orders came to withdraw.

Thirty days after Pardo's return to Santa Elena, a dispatch came from Boyano reporting an outbreak of hostilities. Fifteen of Boyano's soldiers had killed more than 1,000 Indians and burned fifty of their *bohíos*, they themselves suffering only two minor wounds. While awaiting his captain's reply, Boyano was threatened by Chisca, a chief from the mountains. He seized the initiative, taking twenty of his thirty men to pursue Chisca and his people.

The small force marched for four days through the mountains, to find the enemy forted up behind a log stockade with parapets. There was no possible entry except by a single gate. The Spaniards made a large shield and, advancing behind it, took the fort and set fire to it, cremating 1,500 Indians.

On September 1, 1567, Pardo set out with new orders from Menéndez and proceeded over the same route. Before reaching Juada he came to a town called Quatariaatiqui, ruled over by a number of female chiefs—doubtless Soto's Cofitachequi. At Juada, he found Boyano still absent from Fort San Juan. He later turned up at another point visited by Soto: Chiaha, a stockaded town between two fluent rivers. Pardo rested his men there for ten or twelve days, learning meanwhile that Chisca had allied himself with other Creek chieftains. Having raised 7,000 warriors, he was preparing an ambush in case the Spaniards should press farther into the mountains. Instead, Pardo turned south "toward Zacatecas and the San Martín mines." Ignorant of the distance that separated him from those points deep within the Mexican interior, he followed Soto's line of march toward Coosa, on the Coosa River not far from Bynum, Alabama. The best description of the territory is given by Juan de la Vandera, who waxed eloquent in discussing Chiaha and the country beyond: "It is a very rich and extensive land, a great place surrounded by beautiful rivers. There are leagues of abundance, many very good grapes, and many medlars; in effect, it is a land of angels." In still higher mountains beyond Chiaha, the Spaniards observed signs of metallic ores, and Pardo believed there were both silver and gold.

In four days' travel from Chiaha, the Spaniards came to Satapo, where Pardo's interpreters picked up information that Chisca and the other Creek chiefs lay in wait a day's journey beyond. In council with his officers, he decided to turn back to Chiaha, convinced that Chisca's hostility was motivated by his enmity for "the Zacatecas" and a desire to keep them from uniting with the Spaniards.

Before departing, he received the report of his scouts who had gone on down the river: Coosa lay five or six days' journey beyond, through sparsely populated land with only three small villages to offer sustenance. The first of these was Tasqui, two days' travel, another of Soto's stops, near present Gadsden, Alabama. Not far from Tasqui was Tasquiqui, and, a day's journey beyond that, Olitifar. Coosa, two days from Olitifar, was described as a large pueblo, "the best this side of Santa Elena," with as many as 150 inhabitants. Seven days' march beyond was "Trascaluza, which is the end of the settlement of Florida." From there to the first settlement of New Spain, some said, was nine days' march; others said eleven, still others thirteen, but the majority thought nine. So said Juan de la Vandera. Narváez and Soto must have turned in their watery graves.

On the return journey, Pardo strengthened the fort Boyano had begun at Chiaha and left there a corporal and thirty men. Retreating toward Santa Elena, he built fortifications and placed small detachments at other key native villages, including Cauchi, Juada, and Guatari.

No account of the life of these outposts guarding "the road to New Spain" has come to light. Their end was reported in April, 1584, after the natives had risen in general rebellion and massacred the garrisons. Thus, it appears that one or more of the forts may have existed as long as sixteen years, extending well beyond Menéndez's lifetime.

There are also indications that Pardo's men discovered the Georgia gold deposits. When the first English settlers came in 1822 to the Nacoochee Valley of White County, Georgia—probable site of the Cauchi fort—they found parts of the area honeycombed with old mine shafts overgrown with trees and choked with debris. Ruins of houses and an old fortification, long covered over, and fragments of iron tools bespoke an early European settlement. In the absence of a written record, these remains provided the only testimony of the activity of the garrison Pardo had left there more than 250 years previously. Did they find gold? Quite likely, for the area of the diggings—the upper reaches of the Chattahoochee River—was the greatest gold-producing region of the United States prior to the 1848 discovery in California.

Pardo's trail from Santa Elena, on Port Royal Sound, connected with Soto's and approached that of Mateo del Sauz of the Luna *entrada*. Spanish explorers, therefore, had left their tracks from the South Carolina coast to Pensacola and Mobile bays and beyond the Mississippi to western Arkansas and eastern Texas. Yet the country traveled over was far from being well explored, still farther from being conquered and settled. Pardo's road to New Spain was only an illusion.

Menéndez coveted this "land of angels" that lay between the Florida settlements and those of New Spain. Probably on the basis of Pardo's explorations, he asked the Crown for permission to settle north of Pánuco, a region, he said, that was part of Florida and adjoined the region he had already conquered. The Crown, under date of July 31, 1568, sought the opinion of the Audiencia de Mexico on the matter, and that body quite naturally responded adversely. Pánuco, the *oidores* observed, was not 80 leagues from Santa Elena but 450—and more like 600 when all the detours for mountains, lakes, and rivers were considered. It was only 60 from Mexico. The plan was wholly unworkable.

Whether Menéndez's petition was based on an ignorance of geography or a deliberate distortion, the Crown eventually saw fit to grant it by royal *cédula* of February 23, 1573. The *asiento* of 1565, it was noted, granted the *adelantado* authority to discover, pacify, and settle the Gulf of Mexico territory from Bahía de San Joseppe (present St. Joseph's Bay) to the Martyrs, and thence up the Atlantic coast to Newfoundland. Efforts in that region would be facilitated, the Crown averred in one of the wildest of its uninformed judgments, if the area were extended westward to the Río Pánuco, "eighty leagues" from the boundary of his present jurisdiction, to join the territory discovered and settled from New Spain. Menéndez was given two years in which to establish a town. His instructions called for entering the region by way of the Pánuco to undertake pacification where the Indians were not already settled as a result of efforts from New Spain or Nueva Galicia.

Such an undertaking obviously lay beyond the abilities of one man. Menéndez, already overextended in Florida, sent Pedro Menéndez Márquez in 1573 to reconnoiter the Atlantic coast from the Martyrs to Chesapeake Bay (which was called Santa María), but there was no expedition into the Gulf of Mexico. In February, 1574, the *adelantado* was named captain-general of a large armada destined for Flanders. He died the following September 17. His right to the conquest north of Pánuco went to his nephew, Menéndez Márquez, who was no more able to carry it out than his uncle had been. After almost a century of effort, those Spanish officials in the best position to be informed remained thoroughly confused about much of the geography around the Spanish Sea.

A view of the discovery effort from afar reveals great ironies. The soldiers of Cauchi must have found the gold that Soto walked over but failed to see. It did not save them from the cruelty of fate. Could it have spared Soto?

There was irony indeed in Juan de la Vandera's choice of the term "land of angels," and it is manifest in his own destiny. Sailing from Santa Elena for Havana in 1571, his ship was wrecked on the keys. He and all his crew were killed and cut to pieces by the Indians.

SOURCES AND NOTES

A recent study of the early years of Florida settlement is Eugene Lyon, *The Enterprise of Florida*. See also Verne E. Chatelain, *Defenses of Spanish Florida: 1565–1763*. Published accounts by participants are the memorials of Francisco López de Mendoza Grajales, the expeditionary chaplain, and Gonzalo Solís de Merás in Eugenio Ruidíaz y Caravia, *La Florida* (Solís de Merás in vol. 1, López in vol. 2). An English translation (from a French translation) of López is in B. F. French, *Historical Collections of Louisiana and Florida*, second series, 191–234.

An important contemporary account is Bartolomé Barrientos, *Pedro Menéndez de Avilés, Founder of Florida*, translated by Anthony Kerrigan and published with a facsimile reproduction of the original Spanish work. Completed in 1567, Barrientos's narrative, which did not appear in print until Genaro García included it in his *Dos antiguas relaciones de la Florida*, 1902, reflects the vague geographical notions of the times. Barrientos says the chief Carlos took that name because the Christians told him of their king, "greatest lord of Christendom." More likely, it is a corruption of the name for his people, the Calusa. The writer's description of Carlos's territory—"between the head of the Martyrs and Bahía de Juan Ponce," directly west and on the opposite side of the peninsula—supports my conclusion that the Bay of Juan Ponce originally lay somewhat south of Charlotte Harbor, the Calusas' northern boundary. Barrientos also suggests that Ponce's bay (site of the 1513 battle) and the Bahía de Carlos where Menéndez landed were the same.

An indispensable tool for researchers of the Florida colony in its early years are the two volumes of documents translated and edited by Jeanette Thurber Connor: *Colonial Records of Spanish Florida*, covering the years 1570–80. This work (1:38–41) is the source for the information attributed to Pedro Menéndez Márquez, including his statement that on arriving at Carlos the *adelantado* obtained the release of 18 Spaniards, remnants of 250 taken by the Calusa from various shipwrecks; for Menéndez de Avilés's statement (p. 34) that 32 men and women, held captive for fifteen to twenty years, were rescued from the natives during the first year of the conquest; and for the depositions of Juan de Soto and Diego Ruiz at the 1573 hearings in Madrid.

Concerning the Chesapeake exploration, see ibid., 1:322–33. An interesting letter from Menéndez to the Crown (Havana, Jan. 30, 1566), concerning the motivation for this effort, is found in Ruidíaz (*La Florida*, 2:152–54): "With Padre Fray Andrés de Urdaneta, who arrived from China, I discussed the strait, which it is believed certainly exists in Florida, where goes the return from China . . . and the means that can be had for knowing its secret." Chesapeake Bay offered interesting possibilities.

Supplies from Cuba and Yucatán

The arrival of additional ships at Havana in November, 1565, enabled Menéndez to send his brother-in-law, Solís de Merás, to Campeche for provisions and to New Spain to enlist priests and soldiers. The *adelantado* appears to have had a close relationship with Fray Francisco de Toral, bishop of Yucatán, who had a hand in furnishing him supplies. At one point Toral, complaining of Yucatán's governor, Luis Céspedes de Oviedo, proposed to Philip II that Céspedes be replaced by Menéndez (Mérida de Yucatán, April 20, 1567, AHN, Diversos 203; also Toral to Menéndez, Mérida, April 5, 1567, ibid., 201). Yucatán during this period was beset by dissension between the governor, the missionaries, and Indians who alleged flagrant abuses by the ecclesiastics. Various letters concerning the difficulty are published in *Cartas de Indias* (vol. 1).

Menéndez obtained 4,000 arrobas (100,000 pounds) of meat from the hacienda of that veteran supplier of the conquest, Vasco Porcallo de Figueroa, at Trinidad, he reports to the Crown (Nov. 8, 1565, AGI, Santo Domingo 11, ramo 3, no. 54).

Concerning other preparations for the 1566 voyage into the Gulf, see Menéndez's letter to the Crown in Ruidíaz (2:146–47).

Hernando de Escalante Fontaneda

Lyon (*Enterprise*, 148) cites Menéndez's letter, which I have not seen, concerning the notable castaway. Escalante himself, in a letter to the Consejo de Indias (dated on receipt, Oct. 20, 1569, AGI, Indiferente General 1383A), gives his father's correct name. His "Descripción de las islas Lucayo, Achiti, Tortugas, Mártires, &c. y parte de la costa de la Florida con la Canal de Bahamas, y su navegación y de los costumbres y usas de sus naturales" is in Martín Fernández de Navarrete, *Colección de documentos*, 14:doc. 48. The description with the "Memorial" added is translated (with some questionable renditions) by Buckingham Smith as *Memoir of D.° [sic] d'Escalante Fontaneda, Respecting Florida*, first published in 1854. The 1944 edition has annotations by a number of authorities (including David O. True and John R. Swanton) whose interpretations often are doubtful. The letter to the Consejo de Indias includes Escalante's petition for Crown relief.

Escalante's "Memoria de los caciques de la Florida," slightly altered, is included in Smith's translation as "Memoranda"; the original is in AGI, Patronato 19-1-32, without a heading, and unsigned. The title here given appears on the second folio, followed by a listing of the Florida chieftains. The first part evidently was intended as a preface. A vertical line is drawn through the first two paragraphs, but the most curious feature is the tentative scribbling at the top of the first folio:

Florida   Chicora   1551

It seems fairly certain that 1551 marks the beginning of Escalante's captivity, a matter that was long in doubt. Then comes a sentence that has puzzled scholars perusing the Juan Bautista Muñoz copy in the Obadiah Rich Collection of the New York Public Library, from which Smith made his translation, for it seems to say that Columbus discovered part of Florida: "Colon descubrio las yslas yucayos i de Achiti y parte de la florida con otros vs.° [vecinos] de Santo Domingo. . . ." But bracketed on the next line in a different hand, as if Escalante were filling in blanks left for him by a copyist, are the names that complete the sentence: Juan Ponce, Lucas Vázquez. Thus we have a sentence that typifies Escalante's awkward construction but one in which the meaning is clear: "Columbus discovered the Lucayo Islands; and of Achiti and part of Florida, with other *vecinos* of Santo Domingo, Juan Ponce and Lucas Vázquez [were the discoverers]." Cf. *Memoir*, 23 and 62, n. 47E.

Menéndez's list of "old hands," naming Escalante and other Florida captives, is entitled "Lista de la gente de guerra y otras q sirvieron con el dho Adelantado antes de la armada de socorro q se llaman los viejos" (AGI, Contaduría 941).

Pardo and the Road to New Spain

The three accounts of Pardo's two expeditions are by Francisco Martínez, Pardo himself, and Juan de la Vandera. All are printed in Ruidíaz, *La Florida*, vol. 2. Their intent is revealed by Martínez (p. 477) and Pardo (p. 471). Vandera's "land of angels" description, with its mention of gold and silver, is encompassed in pages 481–86.

J. G. Johnson ("The Spaniards in Northern Georgia during the Sixteenth Century") summarizes the accounts and adds the observations by early English settlers of ruins and old mine shafts. Johnson places Chiaha near the confluence of the Etowah and Oostanaula rivers, at present-day Rome, Georgia. The United States De Soto Expedition Commission (*Final Report*, map 10) has it in southern Tennessee, just above the Alabama-Georgia line.

Only a fifer, his wife, and daughter escaped the general massacre, according to Woodbury Lowery (*The Spanish Settlements within the Present Limits of Florida, 1562–1574*, 296–97) and Johnson ("Spaniards in Northern Georgia," 167).

Concerning Menéndez's move to annex the region between Pánuco and his Florida concession, see Audiencia de Mexico to the Crown, 1569, in Fernández de Navarrete, *Colección de documentos*, 14:doc. 42; also the royal *cédula* to Menéndez, Madrid, July 31, 1568 (AGI, Patronato 19-1-25).

Pedro de Ribadeneyra (in Rubén Vargas Ugarte, *Los Mártires de la Florida, 1566–1572*, 93) tells of Vandera's fate. He says that 211 soldiers were killed by Florida Indians during the first eight years of Menéndez's colony—almost as many as were taken by the Calusa from shipwrecks previously.

The "Tragic Quadrate":
Carvajal and the New Kingdom of León,
1567–90

Two royal *cédulas* had gone out ordering the *audiencias* of Mexico and Nueva Galicia to mark their borders confronting the Pánuco-to-Atlantic jurisdiction conceded Pedro Menéndez de Avilés, but there the matter rested. Menéndez assigned his nephew Lope de Estrada to perfect his claim, but Estrada could do nothing without boundaries. The Florida *adelantado* had heard that the New Spain officials were trying to put the border at the Río de las Palmas instead of the Pánuco, in detriment to his interests; the Palmas, lacking a suitable port, lay in country inhabited by Indians noted for their hostility. This shuffling of the boundary, as he saw it, represented a 40-league intrusion into his territory. Yet he was willing to concede the area adjacent to the Pánuco if he might use the stream to reach, via the Tamesí and Guayalejo rivers, his projected settlement between the Pánuco and the Palmas. From this first settlement he proposed to explore, settle, and pacify all the vast territory of Florida in its broader sense. He asked another royal decree to specify his authority; Estrada had twelve Franciscan missionaries and a hundred Canary Island families standing by, and delay would prove costly. This was in 1570, four years before Menéndez's death.

Menéndez's urgency may have been influenced by the arrival on the Pánuco scene of an ambitious schemer with grand designs of his own: Luis de Carvajal y de la Cueva, already introduced in connection with the arrest of John Hawkins's castaways.

Carvajal has long posed an enigma for historians, who have little understood what he was about, or why. Those to whom he has been a concern at all have been more interested in his tragic and seemingly unjust ending than in his motivation or attainments. In truth, he accomplished little of what he promised. His rich opportunity was dissipated by his insatiable greed, which fed jealous enmities. With such difficulties compounded by the Inquisition, his career was cut short at age fifty.

One must admire him for his daring. A highly perceptive man, he recognized that the vast stretch of coastal territory known as Tierra de Florida lay virtually untouched by Europeans. He saw therein the greatest of opportunities. Like Menéndez, he proposed closing that wide gap between the San Agustín colony and the tenuous Spanish settlement on the Río Pánuco, a feat that would have made him the greatest explorer and colonizer of them all. His record, however, suggests that the plan he put forth was mere rhetoric, that he never had any real intention of carrying it out.

Carvajal, an hidalgo from the Spanish village of San Luis Varlos, was of Portuguese ancestry and Jewish heritage, the son of "new Christians." That term usually was applied to persons who themselves had been converted. Carvajal's parents, however, seem to have been steeped in Catholicism; one of his two brothers was a priest. A son of Gaspar de Carvajal and Francisca de León, Luis was born at Mogodorio, Portugal, and lived there until he was eight years old. Under the aegis of an uncle, Duarte de León, he trained briefly in Lisbon, then went to Cape Verde for three years as the king's accountant and treasurer in the black slave trade. He then went to Seville, where he traded in grain and wines, and married Doña Guiomar de Ribera, also a Lisbon native and daughter of Miguel Núñez, "factor in the Negro trade into Santo Domingo for the king of Portugal." The couple lived together only two years before he, driven by heavy losses in wheat trading—and, it has been suggested, by marital discord resulting from religious differences—sailed at age twenty-eight for New Spain, leaving his wife behind. He was to return but once, for a few months, before her death fifteen years later.

Either the slaving business or his other trading operations must have given Carvajal considerable maritime experience. He sailed as admiral of an Indies fleet organized by Crown permission in the Canaries, with his own ship, provisioned and armed at his own cost. He filled the billet well. On approaching a Jamaican port, the fleet found three corsair vessels anchored inside. While the captain-general remained with the fleet, Carvajal took two boats and "half the people," entered the port, and captured the three corsair ships, which he delivered to the island governor.

Carvajal undoubtedly came to New Spain with some introduction to the viceroy, Marqués de Falces; his capture of the freebooters did not damage his cause. He promptly received appointment as *alcalde ordinario* at Tampico. It was in that capacity, a little more than a year later, that he seized Hawkins's men, the sort of deed of which he could make considerable capital. Like a fisherman's tale, the exploit grew with each telling, until his capture of the unarmed, naked, and wounded men became by implication an armed assault in which he, with twenty Spaniards, subdued and captured a vastly superior force. In this and other matters, great discrepancies appear between what Carvajal claims for himself and what others attribute to him. After sending the Englishmen to Mexico to face the Inquisition, Carvajal and his company rode north along the Gulf Coast, looking for stragglers from the group. Three days' ride from Tampico they found the landing place and, not far away, the bodies of twelve of the castaways. His prompt dispatch of the English "threat" doubtless impressed Viceroy Enríquez, who, on arriving to succeed Falces, had directed the attack on Hawkins at San Juan de Ulúa. Another opportunity for strengthening his position presented itself to Carvajal shortly, when a ship from Spain, with a cargo of wine, wrecked "on the coast of Florida at the Río de las Palmas, the land of war." On board was Luis de Villanueva, coming to New Spain to take office as a judge of the royal *audiencia*. By the time Carvajal heard of the disaster and marched to the rescue, the survivors had wandered eleven days in the wilderness, trying to reach Tampico, with nothing to eat but wild herbs. For drinking water, they had only what seeped into holes dug in the sandy beach. They had been attacked by the "*indios chichimecos*," and one Spaniard was slain. The thirty-three others were near collapse from hunger and fatigue when Carvajal's men appeared with rations and spare mounts to take them to the settlement. Thanks to this episode, Villanueva became Carvajal's staunch supporter. After rescuing the people, the *alcalde* sent workmen to redeem the cargo of wine. They were attacked by the Salinero Indians, who killed "three men and three Negro slaves."

Viceroy Enríquez, impressed by Carvajal's capabilities, commissioned him a captain in 1572 and sent him to open a road between the province of Pánuco and the mines of Mazapil, Nueva Galicia. Enríquez treated the matter as though it were designed merely to pacify the natives and open trade between provinces, but Carvajal saw it as much more. Tampico, he pointed out, could serve as the port for the northern mining districts; it was 100 leagues closer than Veracruz, which had to be reached via Mexico.

The viceroy's commission, revealing that Carvajal then was serving as *corregidor* of Guaxutla pueblo (present Huejutla, Hidalgo state), was two-pronged. First he was to explore the road to Mazapil, northwest of Tampico in the northern tip of present Zacatecas state, then return by "the coastal route" to chastise the hostile Indians. Specifically, he was to proceed to the mouth of the Río Bravo, or Río Grande, and march southward along the coast. For many years, Enríquez observed, "the Indians of that coast have committed many murders, robberies, and other crimes on ships that have wrecked there," as well as on other Spanish subjects. Carvajal was to punish them. The guilty ones might be taken captive and sold into slavery for ten years.

Carvajal began his march in late May or early June, 1572. He took 40 mounted soldiers, 180 Indian auxiliaries, and 65 servants, with a drove of 230 cavalry mounts and 120 pack horses. Delay, waiting for a missionary priest who failed to come, had cost him the advantage of the season, and summer rains added to the hardship of crossing the rugged Sierra Madre Oriental. He encountered numerous unconquered Indian bands, with whom he claims to have made peace, and established a cart road. By this route, he says, only 60 leagues separated Mazapil from Tampico, only 40 from the mouth of the Río de las Palmas. Thus he had opened the way for the mining towns of Zacatecas, Mazapil, San Martín, Sombrerete, and Santa Bárbara to obtain Spanish goods at less cost. The greater convenience would result in increased silver production and accretion of Crown revenues.

Carvajal spent ten months in the exploration. Returning along the headwaters of the Río de la Purificación, which fed the Río de las Palmas, he turned north along the coast to carry out the second point of his commission. He proceeded to the Río Bravo and, according to the deposition of one of his soldiers, crossed that stream; if so, he must have been the first Spaniard to cross the lower Río Grande into present Texas. He sought "the Indians who had slain four hundred Spaniards going to Spain on three ships that went down between the Río Bravo and that of Palmas and robbed them of the gold and silver." The three ships appear to have been those of the 1554 fleet wrecked on Padre Island; the coastal Indians had waited eighteen years for their punishment. "To carry out the commission with all fidelity," says Carvajal, "I had the guilty punished, the chiefs hanged, the daring of that barbarous people repressed." From such punishment there was little lasting benefit.

At the conclusion of the coastal campaign, Carvajal visited the pueblos of Tamaholipa and Tanchipa, on the lower slopes of the Sierra de Tamaulipas, and learned there of the rebellion of some neighboring Indians called Capunoques and Palaluques. With new orders, he proceeded to pacify these groups, who previously had not been subject to the Spaniards. As a result, he claims, more than 400 were baptized by the Franciscan missionaries.

Carvajal spent the next several months among various Indian pueblos of Huasteca, attempting to establish a lasting peace. Early in 1576 the Indians of Xalpa pueblo rebelled, burned the monastery, and put the missionaries to flight. Rebellious natives terrorized the villages of Xilitla and Chapuluacán and demolished the churches. Viceroy Enríquez, seeing that Carvajal was fighting a brush fire, sent Francisco de Puga as his own special deputy with twenty-four soldiers to deal with the disturbance at its source.

On his way to Xalpa in the spring of 1576, Puga found Carvajal at Xilitla building a palisade to protect the missionaries. Carvajal withdrew toward Pánuco, while Puga proceeded to Xalpa. Two months later new orders came from Enríquez: Puga was to explore the route to Zacatecas—evidently the expedition by way of the Río de las Palmas on which he was accompanied by John Chilton (see Ch. 16). "As he [Puga] had accomplished nothing worthwhile," Carvajal recalled some years later, "he committed me to that war with no more than ten soldiers, with whom I brought [the rebels] to subjection, surrender, and peace within ten months, with great risk to my person. I reduced them to the knowledge of God Our Lord, from whose law they had apostatized, and rebuilt the pueblo of Xalpa anew." On a special order from the viceroy, he built at his own cost a stone-and-mortar fort, placing the church and monastery within its protective walls. It was to guard the mission villages as far south as Meztitlán.

This work, begun in the spring of 1576, extended well into 1577.

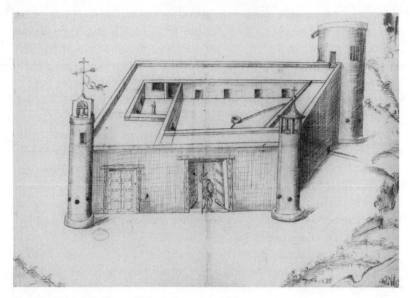

Fig. 10. Carvajal's fort at Xalpa. Courtesy AGI.

When the opportunity arose, Carvajal began laying the groundwork for the proposal he planned to make to the king. Menéndez de Avilés's heirs had done nothing to perfect his claim to the great expanse of territory that would link New Spain with Florida. Carvajal himself, while soldiering in Huasteca as far south as central Hidalgo, had ranged west to Mazapil and north beyond the Río Grande. His accomplishments, with some artistic embellishment, might well impress the Crown.

As he pondered the matter, a circumstance arose that lent urgency to his plan. In January, 1578, he was summoned to Mexico City to face accusations that he had deliberately falsified—to say the least, exaggerated—his own record, which was said to be less than honorable. After Carvajal made his own declaration, Viceroy Enríquez ordered testimony taken in the presence of a judge of the royal *audiencia*. The questions put to the various witnesses sought to establish whether or not his exploration to Mazapil, and the other marches he had made, were of any true benefit. Were they not carried out according to Carvajal's own private interests, such as discovering mines and taking Indian captives to be sold as slaves? And the capture of Hawkins's men— was this arrest of unarmed and helpless castaways, with no potential whatsoever for doing harm, of any real moment? As for his claim that he had spent 10,000 pesos of his own money to erect the fort at Xalpa, was it not true that this action was supported by His Excellency the viceroy in His Majesty's name?

The witnesses, most of whom had served in the Pánuco jurisdiction, generally upheld Carvajal's claims, as well as his character. No one came forth to denounce him for slaving or for acting according to his own interests, opposed to the Crown's. If the investigation bore any immediate deleterious result for Carvajal, the record is yet to emerge. In the absence of hard testimony against him, it seems the episode may have been politically inspired harassment. His advocacy of a port at Tampico would not have been popular with the vested interests at Veracruz. Those interests always could be depended upon to oppose any plan that would reduce the importance of Veracruz as a port, and official fears of contraband trade and unregulated commerce were in their favor.

A few months after the hearing, Carvajal embarked for Spain in the fleet of Captain-General Diego de Maldonado to lay his plan before the Council of the Indies and Philip II. If he was discredited in the eyes of royal officials in Mexico, it was not so with the *cabildos* and missionary priests in Huasteca. From the governing bodies of Pánuco and Tampico he carried written authority to represent them in the royal court, tantamount to endorsement of his petition. From Fray Pedro de San Luis, the Franciscan commissary at Tampico, he bore a petition for Crown support of additional missionaries to extend the religious effort into Greater Florida, a document that praises Carvajal highly.

Carvajal, on arriving in Spain, took care of his own business first. On March 28, 1579, he presented his petition to the Council of the Indies, with a summary of his service in Huasteca similar to the one he had offered at the hearing in Mexico—with certain embellishments. It was the most sweeping proposal the council had ever seen, but that august body, in its profound ignorance of New World geography, failed to perceive either its flaws or the insincerity of the supplicant.

"That Your Majesty might be informed of the relationship and distances," he offered a "painting"—evidently an illustrated map—and a written description of the jurisdictions of Mexico, Pánuco, and Nueva Galicia.

The petitioner astutely emphasized two crucial points: the great waste of Crown revenues spent in servicing the northern mining districts over the long road from Veracruz; and the unprotected status of the entire Gulf coast from Pánuco to the Florida Keys. He focused the council's attention on the fact that Menéndez's death and the default of his heirs had left the matter dangling. Carvajal proposed settling all the ports from Pánuco to Santa Elena, on the Atlantic coast, in a manner that would make the entire Gulf coast not only self-supporting but also safe from intrusion by any foreign aggressor; in short, he would fill in all the blanks on the coastal map. He further offered to settle the area between Tampico and the mines of Mazapil and Zacatecas, and to extend exploration and settlement across Mexico "from sea to sea," establishing a province to be called the New Kingdom of León.

The council was profoundly impressed. Carvajal's plan was immediately recommended to the king. Philip II also perceived merit in the proposal but, conscious of the chain of command, felt that it should be referred to the viceroy, to whom he would recommend that Carvajal receive an assignment in keeping with his station and his quite impressive accomplishments. Undaunted, Carvajal made a new appeal and received the immediate backing of the council. If the petitioner had to take the plan to the viceroy in Mexico, the councillors observed, he then must return to Spain to gather the colonists, ships, and supplies needed for the enterprise. Three years would pass, during which time nothing would be accomplished toward the actual settlement; this energetic royal servant would expend most of the resources needed for the enterprise itself; plunder and murder by the *indios chichimecos*, which had forced the frontier to retreat more than 30 leagues during the last twenty years, would continue; so would the shipwrecks, casting Spaniards on the hostile shore to be massacred by the natives; so would the Indian raids on the road between Mexico and Zacatecas. It seemed certain that the viceroy would agree to the proposal and grant the authority Carvajal asked in His Majesty's name. Why should the king himself not do so to eliminate the great loss of time and expense?

The red tape was cut, the wheels greased. At the end of May, 1579, at Aranjuez, the royal *capitulación y título* were issued, granting Carvajal authority for "discovery, pacification, and settlement" of the Nuevo Reyno de León with title of governor and captain-general, for his lifetime and that of his heir. The jurisdiction was defined as extending westward from the port of Tampico to the borders of Nueva Galicia and Nueva Vizcaya and northward into the vast expanse of undiscovered lands. Within five years Carvajal was to extend discovery 200 leagues into the interior, convert the Indians, and settle all the ports from Tampico to St. Joseph's Bay, "which you say is where the Florida jurisdiction begins." Thus, communication links were to be established between the Florida colony and Nueva Galicia and New Spain. North of Nueva Galicia and Nueva Vizcaya, Carvajal was to explore from sea to sea, but he should not exceed the 200-league limit.

Two hundred leagues north from Tampico would be almost to Austin, Texas. The same distance west would extend to the Pacific Ocean, embracing the mines of Zacatecas, Mazapil, Sombrerete, and Santa Bárbara. The late Mexican historian Vito Alessio Robles, presenting a map with that area delineated, calls it *el cuadrado trágico*—"the tragic quadrate," or "square." The Carvajal concession was not actually a quadrate, but it was indeed to prove tragic. It was intended to encompass the unsettled territory, whatever its configuration, extending no farther than 200 leagues either north or west from Tampico. There was no thought of granting Carvajal rights to rich mining properties already proved.

The grant did not begin to reach St. Joseph's Bay, the western boundary of Menéndez's Florida jurisdiction. The distance limit probably was imposed to avoid overlap, for the royal advisers still had little idea of the extent of the unsettled lands on the northern Gulf shore. In any event, the grant was far more than any one man could hope to explore, conquer, and settle in a lifetime.

His *título* in hand, Carvajal set to work to outfit his own ship, *Nuestra Señora de la Luz*. He took possession of her in the Gibralter anchorage on January 2, 1580, and began recruiting his 100 families. Many were his own relatives or his wife's—a matter that was to heap grief upon his head. In June he embarked from Sanlúcar de Barrameda to join the fleet from Cádiz under Captain-General Francisco de Luján— the same who had been kept outside San Juan de Ulúa by Hawkins a dozen years previously. Having carried Viceroy Martín Enríquez to his post in 1568, Luján now transported his replacement, Lorenzo Suárez de Mendoza, Conde de la Coruña.

At Gómera, in the Canaries, a number of ships, including Carvajal's *urca*, made port on June 19 to take on wood and water. As Luján's flagship and five other vessels waited offshore, the wind stiffened and carried them away from the islands. Luján dropped anchor in Ocoa Bay, Hispaniola, on July 20. Carvajal's ship and five others came in the next morning, followed by the remaining six the day after that. Leaving Ocoa on July 27, the fleet reached Cabo San Antón on August 11 and parted with the vessels bound for Havana. Becalmed inside the Gulf, it was carried by the current upon the reefs of Cayo Arenas and Isla Bermeja, off the northwest point of Yucatán. One ship ran aground in the night; there was time to save the passengers and crew and the vials of quicksilver, but nothing more. The fleet made San Juan de Ulúa on August 25.

Carvajal took his ship directly to Tampico, arriving in mid-September, to disembark his settlers. After the people were ashore but before the ship was fully unloaded, a hurricane struck Tampico, uprooting trees and leveling most of the houses in the village. The ship sank in the anchorage, a loss placed by Carvajal at 12,000 pesos.

The governor himself was already on his way to Mexico to present his dispatches to the viceroy. Only upon arrival did he learn that Enríquez was being succeeded by the Conde de la Coruña, who had come with Luján's fleet. Carvajal saw in the circumstance a great inconvenience, which he made known to the Crown. The letter provides the first real indication that he took too much for granted: the fate of the kingdom, in the Crown's view, did not hinge on the conquest of Nuevo León, and Carvajal's status did not equal that of the crown prince.

The governor, characteristically failing to keep a low profile, complained that Coruña already had begun giving him orders that interfered with his plans; the new viceroy, having just arrived, did not yet have his priorities straight. Carvajal had taken his first strike at a fast ball, outside.

He went on to inform the Crown of his plans to fortify the port of Tampico, playing over his arrest of Hawkins's men like a broken record. He asked that 100 settlers for Nuevo León be sent him with each fleet, with prohibitions against their settling anywhere else; he also requested license to import 100 black slaves, free of duty, to work the mines.

Carvajal began the exploration of his jurisdiction shortly after returning from Mexico. There are few details. One source, however, relates that he first sent a company of soldiers north from Tampico to punish the hostiles. The soldiers took seventy-two prisoners, one of whom wore a silver ornament about his neck. Eager to find the source of the metal, the Spaniards took the Indian as guide and tramped out the coastal salt marshes, lagoons, and jungle for five days before the guide escaped. In the meantime, the six soldiers left guarding the other captives and the horse herd were attacked and slain, and the horses scattered. Only a boy escaped on horseback to carry the word to the main troop, which he found lost and suffering from hunger. The company returned to the camp and buried the six men who had died for their foolishness.

There is ample indication that Carvajal was in trouble long before he was brought before the Inquisition. His difficulties stemmed from two sources: his refusal to bow to viceregal authority, and his repeated infringement on territory already claimed. A haughty spirit goeth before destruction.

The first to complain of the governor's attempts at usurpation was Francisco Guerrero, *alcalde mayor* of Santiago de los Valles. The matter created considerable stir. Guerrero, alleging that Carvajal threatened to take over his jurisdiction by force of arms, compiled written testimony against him and complained long and loud to the Audiencia de Mexico. When the royal *fiscal*, Eugenio de Salazar, informed the Crown, Carvajal received a stern reprimand. He was advised that he must adhere to the laws of the Indies, and threatened with dire punishment for failure to do so.

By Carvajal's own account, he carried out the reconnaissance of the 200 leagues of territory described in his concession. There appears no detailed report of the course of his travels. "Sixty leagues" northwest of Tampico—actually about twice that distance—he discovered silver mines in the Sierra de San Gregorio, near present Cerralvo, and founded there a village called Ciudad de León. Establishing ore mills, he mined a considerable amount of silver. Finding difficulty in bringing in enough provisions for the settlement, he had fields laid out and began growing wheat. Nearby, he established a second settlement, Villa de la Cueva, where he claims to have brought to peace more than 4,000 natives and organized a missionary church. "From there," he says, "by my commission, the provinces called New Mexico were discovered. Antonio de Espejo did it, with my commission, all of which is shown by the information given in [the Audiencia of] Guadalajara."

After establishing the mining settlement and the mission village, Carvajal withdrew southward to deal with Indian difficulties. If what he says is true, that he pacified the pueblos of Tamapache, Tamotela, Tampaschin, and San Miguel, he was operating well outside his own jurisdiction, in lower Huasteca. He returned northward to extend his operations west from Ciudad de León. Alonso de León, Nuevo León's first historian, relates that he left Diego de Montemayor (the elder) in charge of the mining settlement and went to Saltillo, which he found already occupied. He then withdrew to settle a village called San Luis "just north of the springs" at Monterrey. Later, he formed a settlement at present Monclova, which he called Almadén.

Litigation in the next century appears to discredit many of Carvajal's claims, establishing that virtually all the places he occupied had been settled previously, including the mines of San Gregorio, under authority of the governor of Nueva Vizcaya. Carvajal, however, had more immediate problems. Charges of usurpation against him persisted. The *fiscal* Salazar saw that the *audiencia* and Alvaro Manrique de Zúñiga (Marqués de Villamanrique), taking office as viceroy in 1585, were fully informed, adding charges that the governor was selling hundreds of Indian captives into slavery. Carvajal was hauled before the Audiencia de Mexico, in January, 1587, and subjected to an inquiry aimed at proving his malfeasance. Taking all too lightly the reprimand received previously, he complained at length to the Crown; he sent a transcript of the proceeding to the king, asking for a royal *cédula* enjoining the viceroy and the *audiencia* against meddling in his affairs. But the king and his council had already had their fill of Carvajal; a royal order recalling him to Spain had been dispatched some months previously, designating the *alcalde mayor* of Tampico to keep the peace during Carvajal's absence. Carvajal at this point became hard to find, flouting Manrique's order not to leave the capital without the viceroy's specific permission.

With a company of soldiers made up of fugitives from justice, it was charged, Carvajal had made a habit of slave raiding in the vicinity of the Río de las Palmas and the Río Bravo. There, according to Manrique, "the Indians had never seen Spaniards or committed any offense"—a somewhat dubious description of the natives who had massacred the castaways from countless shipwrecks. "Like those going to hunt hares or deer, they [Carvajal's men] captured each time eight hundred to a thousand of them and brought them to Mexico to sell." The Indians as a result were incited to war.

Having ignored the viceroy's order to keep himself within reach, Carvajal resumed his slaving, even daring to send one of his captains, Cristóbal de Heredia, to Mexico to sell a large number of Indian captives. Manrique, stripping Carvajal of his civil authority and putting Pedro de Salazar de Martel in temporary charge, sent Alonso López to find the recalcitrant governor. Tramping out the pretended Nuevo León jurisdiction with twenty soldiers, López compiled a report to the viceroy that reflects its true condition. From Tamaholipa to Mazapil, he found not a single settlement. In the whole region there were only two villages, if they could be called that, each comprising four or five houses of sticks, where Carvajal pretentiously had named municipal officials. These were distant from each other by some fifteen to twenty days' march.

López at last found Carvajal at the site of present-day Monclova, where he had established the Villa de Almadén, with a company of "more than fifty outlaw soldiers, criminals and murderers, who held neither law nor creed, renegades who acknowledged neither God nor king." They were going into the interior to capture peaceful Indians to be sold in Mazapil, Saltillo, Sombrerete, or wherever.

Arrested and taken to Mexico, Carvajal left Gaspar Castaño de Sosa in charge of the Almadén settlement. It was the appointee's great misfortune, for he was to be adjudged guilty by association. Finding the mines of Almadén unproductive, and perhaps fearing political repercussions, Castaño embarked on a new discovery. On July 27, 1590, he packed up the colony and set forth on a grueling march to northern New Mexico. With men, women, and children, their possessions tied on oxcarts, he marched north to the Río Grande and thence up the Pecos River through hundreds of miles of barren and hostile territory.

Carvajal's worst troubles were yet to come. While he was imprisoned in Mexico to await disposition of the viceroy's charges, he was accused by the Holy Office—the Inquisition—of heresy. He was a devout Catholic, and nothing in his conduct, by the standards of that day, indicated otherwise. But certain members of his extended family, whom he had brought from Spain to settle his Nuevo Reyno de León, had reverted to Judaism.

It was the governor's niece, Isabel Rodríguez, who brought him to grief. A widow, she had been courted by one of the governor's captains, Felipe Núñez, whom she attempted to reconvert. He denounced her to the Inquisition, and her testimony implicated her close relatives. Although she did not name Carvajal himself, it became evident that the governor was surrounded by Judaists, a fact of which he must surely have been aware. It was clear that he had known of Isabel's leanings, and it was said that she had tried to convert him. Why had he not fulfilled his obligation to denounce her? In his deposition of October 6, 1589, he pleaded that his absence on various expeditions to subdue hostile natives and form settlements had prevented it; but in view of the charges brought against him by the Marqués de Villamanrique, such a claim could hardly be honored. On February 23, 1590, he was sentenced to exile from New Spain for six years.

The final notice of Carvajal is found in a letter of Viceroy Velasco to the king dated October, 1590. By then the discredited governor reposed in prison, awaiting exile. Velasco, wrestling with the turmoil Carvajal had created, gives sum and substance to his conduct as governor: by his slaving operations, he had created Indian hostilities that would not soon be assuaged. His discoveries of mines and other resources had proved of little value, and he had soon deserted them to invade jurisdictions to which he had no right.

Appalled at the idea of leaving any of Carvajal's followers loose in the uninhabited country, where they might continue to terrorize the natives and take slaves, the viceroy was overwhelmed by a feeling of helplessness: the country was so vast and the dependable men he might send to round up the miscreants were so few. Yet there was one task he knew he must carry out: the arrest of Castaño de Sosa, in far-off New Mexico. A squad of soldiers was sent to bring back Carvajal's erstwhile associate, and Castaño was exiled to the Far East. By the time his appeal brought reversal by the royal council, he had been slain in a slave rebellion on a ship in the South China Sea.

Carvajal thwarted his own sentence of exile; before the year was out he died in prison in Mexico, by all accounts a discredited, broken man who felt that he had done no wrong. In the years that followed, the web of the Inquisition fell about other members of his family. Charges were instituted in 1596 against Luis de Carvajal *el mozo*, the governor's nephew who had taken his name and would have been his heir. Luis broke under torture and implicated up to 120 other practicing Judaists, including his mother, brothers and sisters. Many of them, after being placed on the torture rack, were condemned to burn. The sentences were carried out on Mexico's main plaza on December 8, 1596. Viceroy Velasco's successor, the Conde de Monterrey, and other members of the royal *audiencia* were witnesses. Luis's sister Mariana suffered the worst fate of all: madness. She was kept in prison until 1601 when, at the age of twenty-nine, she was put to death by the garrote and her body burned.

Luis de Carvajal y de la Cueva indeed was a tragic figure. The punishment inflicted upon him and his family, by present-day standards, may be judged cruel and unwarranted. Yet he might well have avoided it had he been inclined to explore and settle the territory the Crown had awarded him rather than trespassing upon the rights of others. In his wake he left problems that would not be settled for a century and a half. The Indians he had terrorized, the denizens of the Gulf shore encompassing the present Mexican state of Tamaulipas, withstood the encroaching Spaniards until the middle of the eighteenth century.

SOURCES AND NOTES

No comprehensive account of Carvajal's exploring and colonizing efforts is available in English and hardly any in Spanish. Despite his substantial influence on the settlement of northern Mexico, and therefore the American Southwest, North American historians have taken little note of him. Mexican writers have accorded him considerable verbiage but on the whole have fallen short of treating him definitively. The secondary accounts in Spanish include Candelario Reyes Flores, *Apuntes para la historia de Tamaulipas en los siglos XVI y XVII*, 33–55; Vito Alessio Robles, *Coahuila y Texas en la época colonial*, 89–95; Eugenio del Hoyo, *Historia del Nuevo Reino de León (1577–1723)*, 1:82–83. Seymour B. Liebman, ed., *The Enlightened: The Writings of Luis de Carvajal, el Mozo*, focuses on our subject's nephew but contains some information on the elder Carvajal and especially his family. See also Carl L. Duaine, *Caverns of Oblivion*, 54–58; Alfonso Toro, *La familia Carvajal*.

Published documents, also in Spanish, include Carvajal's own appeal for justice, written while he was in prison, in "Los Judíos en la Nueva España," and his "Capitulación y título" in Santiago Roel, *Nuevo León—Apuntes históricos*, 1:155–58. Also pertinent are Viceroy Enríquez de Almanza's "Instrucción" to his successor (*CDI*, 3:491), in which he praises Carvajal's accomplishments and recommends him to the Conde de la Coruña; and "Advertimientos generales que el Marqués de Villamanrique dió al Virrey Don Luis de Velasco en el gobierno de la Nueva España," Texcoco, Feb. 14, 1590 (in France V. Scholes and Eleanor B. Adams, eds., *Documentos para la historia del Mexico colonial*, 29–31).

Of somewhat greater importance is the volume of material in AGI, especially the Carvajal *expediente* (Mexico 103, ramo 2). These documents include the "Comisión del virrey al D. Luis de Carabajal," given in Mexico by Viceroy Enríquez de Almanza on April 11, 1572; "Comisión del virrey a Francisco de Puga," issued by Enríquez in Mexico, April 9, 1576; "Poder de la Villa de Tampico para el Señor Capitán Luis de Carvajal," San Luis de Tampico, June 4, 1577; Carvajal, "Declaración," Mexico, Jan. 15, 1578 (including testimony of Nicolás Hernández, Sebastián Gijón, Luis de Villanueva, Diego García, and Juan Delgado); "Poder de la villa de Pánuco para el Señor Capitán Luis Carabajal," Pánuco, Feb. 3, 1578; Fray Pedro de San Luis, "Carta," Tampico, March 12, 1578; Carvajal, "Declaración," Spain, 1579, and the Council of the Indies' summary for the king, March 28, 1579; and numerous letters from Enríquez to Carvajal concerning the building of the Xalpa fort and other matters.

Other documents are found in AGI, Mexico 104, ramo 3: Carvajal to the Crown, Oct. 15, 1580; Francisco Luján to the Crown, San Juan de Ulua, Nov. 20, 1580; Francisco de Guerrero, "Declaración," Santiago de los Valles, Aug. 25, 1584; Carvajal, "Declaración," 1584; and Philip II to Carvajal, Sept. 4, 1584.

Also in AGI, Mexico 110: Philip II's royal *cédula* giving "Título de gobernación" to Carvajal (ramo 5; this document, issued at Toledo, summarizes the 1579 "Capitulación" and prescribes administrative procedure for the Nuevo Reyno de León); and Carvajal to the king, Jan. 30, 1587 (ramo 1).

Menéndez and Carvajal

Pedro Menéndez de Avilés expressed his concern for the Pánuco-to-Florida settlement project in his 1570 letter to the Crown (AGI, Indiferente General 1384). Previously, in petitioning for the authority, he had estimated the distance from the Pánuco to St. Joseph's Bay—the western limit of his original Florida jurisdiction—as 80 leagues. In this letter, he indicated the distance from the Pánuco to the Río de las Palmas as half that, or 40 leagues. He obviously had little idea of the proportions of the area he sought to assume responsibility for.

The extent to which Menéndez's concession influenced Carvajal's design is not known. The fact that Menéndez and his heirs had defaulted, however, was noted in his declaration given in Spain in 1579.

The "Tragic Quadrate"

Area of Carvajal's Operations

The Huasteca Indian villages on which Carvajal's peacemaking efforts centered in 1576 are identifiable on a present-day map: Xalpa, Jalpán, northern Querétaro state; Xilitla, some 40 miles southeast in southern San Luis Potosí; Chapuluacán, northern Hidalgo. Situated where the three states corner, they are in what was known as Huasteca Baja, or lower Huasteca.

Proof of Carvajal's claim that he commissioned Antonio de Espejo to make his 1582 journey to New Mexico has been elusive. Two versions of Espejo's relation appear in *CDI*, 15:101–26, 163–189. See also Bolton, *Spanish Exploration in the Southwest*, 166, 168–94; and Diego Pérez de Luxán, *Expedition into New Mexico Made by Antonio de Espejo, 1582–1583*.

Carvajal's westward extension of his operations to Almadén (Monclova) is related by Alonso de León (*Historia de Nuevo León*), the frontier soldier who based his account on his own experiences and the reports of first settlers.

Concerning litigation in which Carvajal was accused of claim-jumping, see Hoyo, *Historia*, 1:82–83.

A Family Enterprise

Notarial documents in APS shed light on Carvajal's family and his enterprise. One of these (1580, oficio 13, libro 3; escribania, Alonso de Cívico, f. 267) reveals that Carvajal's father-in-law, Miguel Núñez, had died recently. The widow, Blanca Rodríguez, and her daughters, Doña Guiomar de Ribera (Carvajal's wife) and Doña Isabel de Ribera, residents of Seville, authorized their son and brother, Nuño Alvarez de Ribera, to collect the inheritance. He was empowered to receive from the Casa de Contratación "the shipments of gold, silver, merchandise, etc.," that had been sent from the Indies to the decedent's account.

The previous May, Doña Blanca had cosigned a note with her daughter and son-in-law in the amount of 1,100 *reales* to provision Don Luis's ship (1580, oficio 19, libro 4; escribanía, Gaspar de León, f. 119).

In other transactions of Carvajal before his departure in June (1580, oficio 21, libro 1; escribanía, Juan Bernal de Heredia, ff. 208, 815, 819, 1001, 1005, 1019, 1164), the surname Rodríguez pops up frequently. It may be inferred that several members of Doña Blanca's family (or that of Carvajal's sister, who had married a Rodríguez) had a part in the Nuevo León colony. On January 10, Carvajal posted bail for one Agustín Rodríguez. Carvajal authorized Alonso Rodríguez to contract with married farmers to go as settlers. Pedro Rodríguez, native of Espinosa de los Monteros, enlisted as a settler with three of his fellow townsmen. He also named Diego Ruiz de Ribera (a brother-in-law?), *regidor* of the Villa de Timena, as his captain and authorized him to recruit settlers.

Tierra Incógnita:
The Northern Gulf in the "Forgotten Century"

AT the end of the sixteenth century, the Gulf of Mexico littoral from Yucatán to the Río Pánuco had been explored and to some extent settled. As the Spanish occupation advanced northward through Nuevo León, it left unconquered and only partially explored a thin stretch of coast between the Pánuco and the Río Grande. Beyond, from the Río Grande to the Florida cape, lay extensive shoreline as yet touched only by a few abortive expeditions, the records of which were inadequate and confusing. Neither Pedro Menéndez de Avilés nor Luis de Carvajal had made good his promise to pacify and settle it.

During the first three-quarters of the seventeenth century, no singular expedition extended the conquest or broadened geographical concepts in the Gulf region. Rather, the period was marked by a gradual advance of the frontiers with few decisive thrusts into the unknown. The march of discovery had slowed to a crawl, impeded by Spain's mounting colonial rivalry with other European powers, the record of consecutive disasters in Tierra de Florida, and the ever precarious plight of the Spanish treasury. Yet the quest would be renewed toward the end of the "Forgotten Century" under impetus of a foreign threat of unprecedented boldness.

Carvajal's efforts in his "tragic quadrate" had provided a negative lesson for would-be discoverers. In many ways his undertaking had been cast in the image of Cortés's: his grand design for controlling the continent from sea to sea; his usurpation of prior rights; and his abuse of the natives without regard for royal regulations. The result served notice that the freebooting era of Cortés and Pedrarias Dávila had passed. Totally out of step with the times, Carvajal's bad example served to underscore the recodified ordinances governing "discovery, settlement, and pacification of new territories" issued by Philip II in 1573. These regulations sought to avoid repetition of old abuses, such as slaving and scandalous jurisdictional disputes. Carvajal's refusal to heed them brought him to ruin.

Despite the negative aspects of the Nuevo León enterprise, however, it did have a positive effect. Although proof of Carvajal's claim of sending Antonio de Espejo into New Mexico in 1582 is lacking, he did influence Castaño de Sosa's entry there in 1590. This unauthorized venture and others like it hastened the formal occupation of that territory while the frontier in other areas remained static.

The tenuous Carvajal settlements in the Nuevo Reyno de León quickly fell apart following his arrest. The settlers at Ciudad de León were forced to flee as the result of the hostility aroused by their slave raids. San Francisco, identified with the present village of Apodaca, was wiped out by Indian attack. The inhabitants of Villa de San Luis (Monterrey), like those of Ciudad de León, withdrew to Saltillo. About 1596 the two Diegos de Montemayor, father and son, undertook the unauthorized reestablishment of San Luis and called it Nuestra Señora de Monterrey. An effort to revive León, 1610–11, failed because of Indian resistance.

The Nuevo León pioneers had their fair share of Indian trouble, much of it their own doing. In the fashion of Guzmán and Carvajal, they raided the rancherías of docile tribes and sold the captives into slavery to work the mines and haciendas. No one knows how many slave raids there were or how far they penetrated. Extant records indicate that it was not till after the mid-seventeenth century that further Nuevo León Indian campaigns crossed the Río Grande into present Texas.

As Nuevo León became populated, the hostile Indian groups and mission apostates crowded into the unsettled coastal strip between the Pánuco and the Río Grande. Instead of eliminating the threat from this wilderness salt marsh, Carvajal had only exacerbated native hostility. As the settlement line advanced through Nuevo León, Coahuila, and eventually Texas, it folded itself around this *tierra despoblada*. The unsettled strip of land was left vacant and untamed for another century and a half, penetrated only by an occasional Indian campaign or exploring party.

The early trail linking Ciudad de León and San Luis with the port of Tampico fell into disuse with Carvajal's departure. While Monterrey maintained communication with the inland towns of Zacatecas, San Luis Potosí, and Durango, it had little with Pánuco or Huasteca. During the next half-century there is mention of only three trips from Nuevo León to Tampico. The first two, trade ventures from Monterrey in 1600 and 1609, were attacked by Indians with loss of life at a narrow defile near "the Estero," 14 leagues from the Tamaholipa mission. After a twenty-four-year lapse, an attempt was made from Cerralvo in 1633 to reopen the faded trail, but it fared no better than the previous efforts.

The first known penetration of the uninhabited coastal strip after Carvajal's time came in 1638, when the Camalucano Indians sighted foreign ships off the Tamaulipas shore. The news spread through various tribal groups—the Caranas, the Amapaules, and the Cataaras—until it reached the Spaniards at Cerralvo. As the story survived the telling, the vessels—carrying great guns that belched clouds of smoke and were capable of killing at great distances—were manned by blond, bearded men wearing red sashes, and jackets and hats of iron. These strangers had come ashore to offer the Indians gifts.

Governor Martín de Zavala, having just arrived at Cerralvo on an inspection tour, concluded that the intruders had landed at the mouth of the Río de las Palmas. Informing the viceroy, he sent forty soldiers toward the coast with Jacinto García de Sepúlveda. Four days after their departure, word came back that García's soldiers were surrounded by hordes of hostile Camulcano Indians. The governor sent a relief force of friendly natives, but the flooding Río de San Fernando blocked their way.

The soldiers' difficulties in fact differed from the reports. They were 30 leagues from Cerralvo when the weather closed in, obscuring the sun. Without a compass, the men became lost and wandered for twenty days through the flat coastal expanse that offered no distinguishing landmark. Arriving finally at the mouth of the Río Bravo, they saw no ships. Weak and starving, they turned toward the settlement, stalked by natives intent on picking up their possessions as they died.

A few days after the soldiers reached Cerralvo, news came from Mexico that Captain-General Carlos de Ibarra's fleet, recently arrived at Veracruz, had sighted enemy vessels in the western Gulf. The Indians' report, indeed, had some basis in fact. The story had a sequel in the fleet's bloody encounter with Dutch raiders on its homeward voyage (more of that in due course).

Nuevo León's early history was written by Alonso de León, who relates his own experiences on Indian campaigns and explorations, as well as eyewitness accounts gleaned from first settlers. Having come to Monterrey in 1636, he ended his chronicle a dozen years later. In August, 1643, as one of the founders of Cerralvo, he left that community with a company of explorers going toward the coast to look for salt deposits. Beyond the Río de San Juan, they found the salines on the eve of the feast day of St. Lawrence and named them San Lorenzo. The name survives in a nearby river. From the salines, they made a wide exploratory sweep through the coastal country but failed to find a bottomless spring of which their Cataara guide had told them.

By 1645, Indian hostilities had temporarily subsided, and the effort to open communications with Huasteca and the port of Tampico was renewed. León was put in charge of twenty-five soldiers from Cadereyta escorting a thirty-mule packtrain laden with flour for trade. At the same narrow pass near the Estero where previous expeditions had been waylaid, the Janambre Indians attacked, killing and wounding several horses.

Accorded a hospitable reception at Tampico, the visitors stayed a month. The local merchants were so receptive that plans were made for an annual trade fair at which the silver, lead, and produce of Nuevo León would be exchanged for the goods of Tampico. There was talk of establishing a settlement on the road between Tampico and Monterrey to facilitate trade, and delegations from the two towns agreed to meet at the mouth of the Río de las Palmas the following May to plan development of a port.

Governor Zavala, pleased with the outcome, approved the arrangement, but as León was getting ready to depart for the Río de las Palmas, the plans were suddenly changed: a member of the Tampico expedition charged him with treating there for his own personal gain. The meeting at Las Palmas was canceled, and the port opening delayed by more than a century.

León did lead an expedition to the Río de las Palmas eight years later, but it lacked the specific thrust of the one planned in 1645. Its purpose was to "discover the lands and know the routes," for whatever use that knowledge might be put to. The captain took thirty men from Cadereyta and marched over a fertile land to reach the mouth of the river in three days. He found numerous docile Indian tribes settled along the stream, which offered an abundance of fish. These natives had not inherited "the evil ways of their ancestors who killed many Spaniards who went to settle in those regions." The chronicler reinforces that statement with a recitation from Francisco López de Gómara's *Historia General de las Indias*, then in print for more than a century, concerning the vicissitudes of Garay and Narváez.

León's Palmas expedition enabled Zavala to claim some progress toward exploring the coast. The governor's memorial to the king, designed to win him certain royal perquisites, was carried to Spain by León himself. It recites the governor's claim as follows: "He has begun the discovery of that part of the north, in which he has explored more than fifty leagues, in order to pursue communication with the Spaniards in Florida." The old rhetoric refused to die.

Twenty years later, a petition filed by Alonso de León II recited several of his father's accomplishments as his own: discovery of the salines of San Lorenzo, opening of the road to Huasteca, and an exploration of the seacoast for 50 leagues that led to discovery of two promising ports, one of them at the Río de las Palmas.

Whether or not the younger León had accompanied his father on those endeavors, he did go with him to Spain to carry the governor's memorial. The voyage was entirely successful for Zavala's purposes and bore somewhat unexpected results for young Alonso, who had not yet reached his seventeenth birthday. About to embark at Cádiz for New Spain, the Leóns found the Spanish merchant fleet bottled up in the bay by eighty English warships. Young Alonso, with his father's permission, enlisted in the armada being organized to counter the threat. Thus began his many years of royal service, which included leading important expeditions from Nuevo León and Coahuila beyond the Río Grande.

At the start of the seventeenth century, the great expanse of unconquered wilderness on the northern Gulf shore was anchored on either end by the settlements of eastern Florida and New Mexico. Between the two lay the *tierra incógnita*, which was penetrated in the next half-century only around the fringes. From the settlements that bordered it on east and west, occasional expeditions of priests and soldiers advanced into the unknown land, gradually extending their influence over neighboring Indian tribes, making tentative missionary thrusts from the established settlements. Franciscan friars in both provinces looked longingly toward this hinterland, populated, as they were wont to say, by so many thousands of pagan souls living in darkness, their lives untouched by the light of the gospel. By flickering candles in lonely mission outposts, they pondered ways to elicit Crown support for spiritual conquests. They badgered the local military commanders and wrote letters to the king, often painting pictures that were less than objective. To augment these efforts, they recited long and fervent prayers to a Higher Authority, their zeal unaltered by the blood of their martyred brothers.

Many wore their lives away on these missionary frontiers, to die in painful solitude far from their native land. Even the more fortunate ones could not erase from memory the opportunity they had seen for a great harvest of souls. Beseeching the Crown for additional missionaries and royal funds for new foundations, they urged ingenious plans based not only on their own frontier experience but also on concentrated study that enabled an appeal to the king's own deepest desires. Such proposals were likely to be marked by a limited knowledge of geography. In some respects they bore a similarity to those seeking license for discovery and military conquest.

Such was the 1630 memorial that Fray Alonso de Benavides, retiring guardian of New Mexico missions, offered the Crown on his return to Spain. Native ambassadors had come to Santa Fé from Quivira and Aixaos, he related, asking that priests be sent to their country to instruct and baptize their people; they had been told to come by the same mysterious lady in blue who had visited the Jumanos of western Texas. Quivira, said Benavides, lay 150 leagues east of Santa Fé in latitude 37°; Aixaos was 30 or 40 leagues east of Quivira. These two native kingdoms were known "from evidence and from personal inspection" to contain "a very large quantity of gold," proof of which was provided by the Flemish and the English who lived near them along the Florida border and bartered with them for gold ore. What a shame, said the padre, "that heretics enjoy those great treasurers which the Catholic Church, in the name of God, conceded to Your Majesty, and they make use of it to wage war upon us."

That situation might be remedied, he added, by settling Aixaos and Quivira, and helping the Indians to embrace Christianity; then the riches could be enjoyed by His Majesty Philip IV, rather than by foreign Protestants. He went on to propose the means: "Looking from this site of Quivira toward the point closest to the sea, which is eastward, there is indicated on the sea charts a bay called Espíritu Santo. It is situated at 29°, between the Cape of Apalache and the coast of Tampico, which is the northern coast of New Spain, within the gulf." From Quivira to the Gulf, the chart indicated, was less than 100 leagues, and from Espíritu Santo Bay to Havana was a coastal voyage of five or six days.

Persons traveling to New Mexico from Spain normally sailed to Veracruz, then proceeded overland by way of Mexico City, through Nueva Galicia and Nueva Vizcaya. The trip took more than a year, and 400 leagues of the march was through hostile and dangerous territory. If the port of Espíritu Santo were opened, and a road thence to New Mexico through Quivira, Benavides suggested, the route could be shortened by 800 leagues. From Espíritu Santo to Quivira, he claimed, the entire 100 leagues of road lay through friendly country.

As added incentive, Benavides postulated, a profitable trade could be had at Havana with the hide and wool of the buffalo. From Cuba, shipments could be made to Tampico, San Juan de Ulúa, Campeche, and Florida, on vessels sailing in view of the shore. With this produce from the plains, plus pearls and amber from the coastal region, he prophesied, the ports surely would develop and become prosperous; new coastal settlements would eliminate the havens found by the "many unfriendly Hollanders" who were plundering ships all across the Gulf.

The "sea chart" on which Benavides based his geographical assessment has not been identified. The mouth of the Mississippi, named Espíritu Santo by Alvarez de Pineda, was not the closest segment of the Gulf coast to Quivira, which the priest seems to place in the Texas panhandle. He may possibly have seen a map showing Espíritu Santo in the position he describes, or, like a great many others, he may have been guilty of distorting geography to suit his own purposes. In either case, Benavides offered a plan the Crown might have done well to follow, for it could have secured the Spanish claim to the continent's midsection and its most vital waterway. Instead, the Crown held to a short-sighted policy that caused it to fear contraband trade in uncontrolled ports more than invasion of the Spanish Sea by the French, English, and Dutch.

While the Spaniards in New Mexico wrestled with their task of conquering such great distances, those in Florida struggled to expand their toehold on the eastern seaboard. In the main, it was Father Benavides's fellow Franciscans who bore the brunt of the effort. With military support—often meager, misguided, and unwelcome—they hacked out a trail across the peninsula to establish a chain of missions that eventually reached beyond the Apalachicola River.

Besides this missionary effort, occasional coastal voyages were made around the peninsula, for various reasons. In 1603 the old idea of a strait through the Florida peninsula that Menéndez had sought still remained alive in the minds of Crown officials. A royal *cédula* directed Governor Pedro de Ibarra to explore the Río de San Mateo (St. John's River) to determine whether it emerged on the Gulf coast. In January, 1604, the governor sent twenty men under Captain Francisco Fernández de Ecija from San Agustín. In a small ship they proceeded to the "Bahía de Carlos," by which he seems to have meant Charlotte Harbor, to look for Spanish captives among the Calusa. Finding none, they explored toward the Laguna de Maymi (present Lake Okeechobee), hoping that the lake might prove the key to linking the Gulf and the ocean. Two small streams flowing into the Bahía de Carlos from the lake were found. Fernández later explored from the territory of Ais, on the east coast, and found the headwaters of San Mateo—not in the lake but in a swamp. His efforts put to rest the persistent hope of an inland passage that would circumvent the Straits of Florida and the hazardous keys.

That same year, Governor Pedro de Valdés of Cuba, hearing reports of foreigners prowling about the west side of the peninsula, sent his son Fernando to run up the Gulf coast to "latitude 30°." The voyagers, failing to find the invaders, provoked an incident with friendly Indians at Acuera, a large town midway up the peninsula. When three natives came aboard the frigate, thinking it was from San Agustín, the Spaniards sought to restrain them and take them to Havana. When

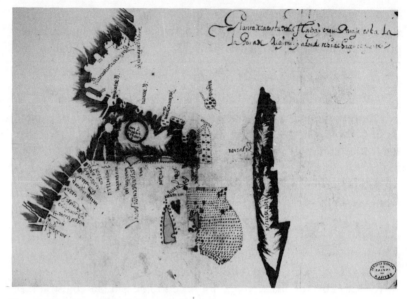

Fig. 11. Florida, 1604. Courtesy AGI.

the natives jumped overboard and swam for shore, one of them was slain by fire from the vessel. Governor Ibarra at San Agustín was hard put to soothe the Indians' resentment.

The Franciscan missionaries, who had replaced the Jesuits in 1573, began their advance across the Florida peninsula early in 1597. The principal chief of Timucua had come personally to ask for a priest. Fray Baltasar López, who claims to have spent seventeen years among the Timucua, returned with him to his village and remained three months instructing the natives, who perceived readily "the doctrine and law of God and some premises by which they might become Christians." His visit came to an end when news reached him of the Guale revolt, a tragic affair that began at the Tolomato mission on September 13, 1597. Starting with the murder of Fray Pedro de Corpa over his reprimand of a warrior for practicing bigamy, it claimed the lives of seventeen priests and lay brothers.

It was during his 1597 journey that Father López was first contacted by the chief from the Potano region of Timucua, immediately west of the St. John's River, asking for a priest. López had none to send. He did visit Potano's main village prior to the Guale uprising, and the chief came to San Agustín afterward, asking insistently for baptism. By 1602 the principal Potano village, eight miles north of present Gainesville, Florida, was a *visita*. Without a priest of their own, the ten Christians were served from the Mission San Pedro, near the mouth of the St. John's, by Father López. López made numerous journeys to familiarize himself with the interior but neglected to detail his travels. He was more concerned with the number of conversions and the shortage of ministers.

In April, 1606, Father Martín Prieto and another priest began work at San Francisco de Potano, whence Fray Martín went to visit other pueblos in the vicinity. His companion became so intimidated by the resistance of his subjects that he was sent back to San Agustín. Prieto, too, encountered hostility, especially at a village called Santa Ana, where the aged chief remembered having been held captive by Soto sixty-seven years previously. When the priest went to call on the chief, the ancient one ordered him thrown out of his hut and beaten. Only by the timely intervention of a storm that leveled all the structures in the village except the church and the cross that stood beside it was Prieto spared. The chief forthwith asked Fray Martín for Christian instruction. When he was baptized, four hundred others followed his example.

When Fray Juan de las Cabezas Altamirano, bishop of Cuba, visited the Potano villages in June, 1606, he did not journey as far west as San Francisco. First inspecting the Guale missions along the Georgia coast, the bishop left San Agustín on the westward swing after heavy spring rains had converted the road into a quagmire. At Tocoi, the site of San Diego Salamototo on the St. John's, he confirmed 90 professed Christians. On foot, he proceeded to Atonico, on a large lake 20 leagues farther on, and thence through the lake country northeast of present Gainesville. He visited half a dozen poor villages and confirmed 225 Christians before turning back to San Agustín.

In 1608, Father Prieto, after baptizing the principal chief of Timucua, set out for Apalache, west of the Aucilla River. He was accompanied by the Timucua chieftain and 150 of his warriors. The priest was cast in the role of peacemaker, for Timucua and Apalache were at war. At the principal Apalache town, Juitachuco, 70 chiefs gathered with their people, whom Prieto estimated at 30,000. It was the first time the Indians had seen a Spaniard in their land "in these times." Although the natives were "naked as the day they were born," their hospitality would have done justice to the royal court. So impressed was the principal Apalache *cacique* by his erstwhile enemies' manifestation of peace and friendship that he wept openly. A delegate was sent to San Agustín to render the Apalachinos' obedience to the governor. It was several years before ministers were available for Apalache. To keep in touch, Prieto and his fellow missionaries made several visits.

The westward push toward Timucua's outer regions was just beginning when Fray Luis Jerónimo de Oré, the Franciscan commissary-general, made his first formal visit, compiling an invaluable record in statements taken from missionaries. As visitor-general, Father Oré returned in 1616 to travel on foot and by canoe throughout the Florida mission system. Proceeding west from Tocoi and San Antonio de Enacape, he crossed the St. John's and traversed pine-studded, marshy flatlands to the Potano missions of San Francisco and San Martín, and thence to nearby Santa Fé de Toloca. On the Suwannee River above its confluence with the Santa Fé, he visited Santa Cruz de Tarihica and San Juan de Guacara, eight leagues apart. Turning north toward Guale, he traveled 50 leagues through woods with dense undergrowth, sparsely inhabited by pagan Indians. Food ran low, and endless rain soaked him to the skin and damaged his papers. After crossing deep rivers on footlogs so shaky that the priest was moved to make his confession, he descended the St. Mary's River into Guale. Vastly different were his experiences from those of the New Mexico friars who traversed the dry and dusty buffalo plains in search of spiritual conquests.

While the Timucua missions by this time had been extended to the Suwannee, Apalache remained without priests. Father Oré urged that more missionaries be sent because "entire provinces" were asking for baptism. The missionary priests themselves reported to the Crown that there still were no *doctrinas* in Apalache, Tama, Santa Elena, or Carlos. That was in 1617. Not until after 1633 did Apalache get its first full-time resident missionary.

Through the years the priests had to combat the Crown's lack of commitment to the Florida enterprise. Following the Guale revolt especially, there was considerable sentiment for withdrawal. Even before the first actual mission came to Apalache, the forces of ultimate destruction were at work. While Father Prieto was trying to negate the lingering hostility from Soto's *entrada*, the English planted their first permanent American colony at Jamestown in 1607. By 1633 the "Golden Age" of the Florida missions was just beginning, but already the English traders loomed on the horizon, ready to sow seeds of discontent among the Indians. For Spain and the mission system, the harvest was bitter fruit.

By 1627 both the English and the Dutch were attempting to move into the vacuum that existed along the Gulf coast and on the northern border. Governor Luis de Rojas y Borja, hearing reports of mounted white men among the natives, ordered a reconnaissance. Pedro de Torres, a veteran of many years in Florida, took twenty soldiers and sixty friendly Indians on a four-month march over difficult terrain cut by numerous rivers. Torres found no trace of the invaders, but Rojas was not satisfied. On a second journey, Torres penetrated the interior "two hundred leagues" to "Cofatachiqui," Soto's turning point on his northeastward march eighty-two years previously; it had not—Rojas reported with doubtful accuracy—been visited by Spaniards since.

Torres, like Soto, found lake-fed rivers that contained a great quantity of pearls, specimens of which the Indians wore around their necks or arms. The pearls, just as Soto's men had described them, were damaged by fire because the Indians cooked their mollusks in the shell. Torres sent some Indians to look for the pearl-bearing shells, but they were able to recover only a few because the water was so cold. Rojas sought royal license for taking a sizable force to exploit the find, but the king regarded the proposal as a matter that could wait.

Governor Luis de Horruytiner (1633–38), who fostered the Apalache missions, was also responsible for sending the first ships to Apalache. Sensitive to the difficulty of supplying the new *doctrinas* from San Agustín, whence Indians carried cargoes on their backs, he sent two marine pilots to the province. They made celestial observations to determine the latitude, sounded the port at the mouth of the St. Mark's and Wakulla rivers, and marked the channel. After returning to San Agustín, the pilot Miguel Alvarez sailed for Havana in a frigate, loaded up with supplies, and proceeded to Apalache. The voyage from Havana took only eight days. Horruytiner expected the port to serve as a refuge on the Veracruz-Havana run, from both foul weather and pirates; thenceforth, he believed, ships could supply both Apalache and Timucua.

Two years later Horruytiner's successor, Damián de Vega Castro y Pardo, expanded on the accomplishment, bypassing Havana. "I sent a frigate along the coast for the province of Apalache," he reported, "a voyage never made before because it seemed so difficult." Apalache was sighted "in less than thirteen days." Navigation between Apalache and Havana, 100 leagues, thereafter would be as easy as from San Agustín, Vega Castro averred. But the voyage was not always as easy or as safe as he pictured it. In 1668, Ignacio de Losa, on a supply run, lost his ship off Carlos Bay in a storm.

Even after the opening of the Apalache port, Indians continued to transport the produce of Apalache and Timucua on their backs along the overland trail. This and other services required by the military occasioned bloody uprisings in 1647 and 1656. In the first instance the Apalachinos rebelled over personal demands by the garrison. Three priests were slain before Francisco Menéndez Márquez subdued the natives with executions and sentences to hard labor on San Agustín's fortifications.

The causes of the Timucua rebellion, which spread into Apalache, were somewhat more complex. Governor Diego de Rebolledo, who had taken office in 1655, received news the following April that the English were planning to invade Florida. With orders to prepare his defenses, he sought to raise 500 Timucuans for service at San Agustín until the emergency was past. The Indians rebelled. Occupants of some Spanish ranches were killed, as were Francisco Menéndez and some of his soldiers. Rebolledo rounded up the principal chiefs and executed 11 by the garrote.

After suppressing the rebellion, the governor proceeded with a personal inspection of the Apalache and Timucua mission chain, begun January 16, 1657, at San Damián Cupaica, one of the westernmost missions of Apalache. Interrogating the various chieftains, he probed for the sources of dissatisfaction. The Indians complained of having to carry burdens for priests and soldiers; of being required to go beyond the Ochlockonee River to bring peltry obtained from the Chatot, in the course of which some of the Apalachinos were slain by other natives; of being forced to load the frigates from San Agustín and Havana and to carry corn across the peninsula to San Agustín.

Additionally, the Indians resented the priests' prohibition of the native dances and ballgames, their only recreation. The friars also forbade their trade with the San Agustín soldiers and the Havana frigates. The missionaries, in all justice, had reason for imposing such rules: the ballgames were brutal, often resulting in grave injury; the natives, naive in matters of trade with Europeans, were likely to be cheated.

From San Damián, Rebolledo went on to visit ten other Apalache pueblos, extending from a tight cluster in the Tallahassee vicinity east to the Aucilla River, and met the assembled Timucua chiefs at San Pedro. His objectivity is left open to question by his claim that the Apalachinos expressed complete satisfaction with the presidial garrison of San Luis de Apalache, established at present Tallahassee after 1645.

Withdrawing from Apalache, the governor left a set of instructions designed to eliminate the alleged abuses. Compensation was to be paid for native labor, and the priests were enjoined not to interfere with the natives' games and dances or with their trading privileges. The missionaries, in the face of such meddling, were not disposed to turn the other cheek. Before Rebolledo's notary at San Agustín had reduced the instructions to writing, the padres had their chance at rebuttal and used it to full effectiveness by pressing charges against him before the Council of the Indies, which resulted in his condemnation.

It was all part of a longstanding feud between the missionaries, who seem to have pinned no hopes on inheriting the earth through meekness, and the provincial governor, whoever that happened to be. Rebolledo was seen as one of the worst. His war with the friars bore disastrous results for both factions. Eleven of the religious, disgruntled at the harshness with which the 1656 rebellion was suppressed, took ship for Havana. The vessel perished in a storm. Rebolledo was ordered to Spain to face trial but cheated the order by dying at his post in 1659.

Rebolledo, during his inspection, had heard Indians' reports of English intruders on the Gulf coast. Various succeeding governors, viewing the foreign threat, urged fortification of the Apalache port, but the matter dragged on until Governor Pablo de Hita Salazar reopened the question in 1675. The Florida coast south from San Agustín and up the west side of the peninsula to Apalache Bay, he observed, remained in the hands of *indios infieles*, a constant threat to shipwreck victims. The English traders pressing the northern borders and pirates penetrating the Gulf in ever-increasing numbers posed additional hazards. The king at last responded with a royal *cédula* instructing Hita to erect a fort at the most suitable site. The governor occupied San Marcos de Apalache the following year, but several years passed before significant fortifications were completed.

Bishop Gabriel Díaz Vara Calderón, meanwhile, had come and gone, leaving for posterity his description of Florida and its missions toward the end of their Golden Age. The bishop of Cuba, whose jurisdiction embraced Florida, spent ten months on the mainland, from August of 1674 to June of 1675. For eight months he traveled among the missions, now extended to the province of Apalachicola and beyond the Apalachicola River. In Guale, Timucua, Apalache, and Apalachicola, he found 13,152 Christianized natives ministered to in thirty-six *doctrinas*.

Progressing through the Timucua and Apalache mission chain, the bishop came to the Agna (Ochlockonee) River, which divided Apalache from Apalachicola. Twelve leagues beyond, on the Apalchicola River near the junction of the Flint and Chattahoochee, he founded the mission of La Encarnación de la Santa Cruz de Sabacola. Nine and 12 leagues beyond, he visited the two Chatot missions, San Nicolás and San Carlos, founded the previous June. In the vicinity, he says, lived 4,000 "heathen" Chiscas; 70 leagues west lay the extensive Chacta (Choctaw) province; and on an island near the "harbor of Espíritu Santo" lived the Mobila, "barbarous heathens" like the Choctaws.

In all the native provinces, the bishop found the Indians to be large and heavy, adept at artistry but weak and sluggish when it came to work. As to weaponry and dress, his observations parallel those of Hernando de Escalante Fontaneda, conjuring an image with his account of finding in the villages 4,081 women "naked from the waist up and the knees down."

For food the natives made a "porridge" of corn and ashes—lye hominy—and had pumpkins, beans, game, and fish. They drank no wine or rum but made a hot drink called *cazina* from a weed. It was considered a great delicacy but was not intoxicating. The native houses were round grass huts without windows and only crawl holes for doorways. The people slept inside on reed frames covered with bearskins, building fires in the middle of the huts instead of using blankets. On one side of each hut was an elevated bin for storing grain.

Preparation of the fields for April planting began each year in January with the burning of grass and weeds. As this chore was carried out, the plot was surrounded by people ready to spring on wild animals fleeing from the fire. The Indians hunted bears, bison, and lions with bows and arrows; the kill would be taken to the principal *cacique* for equitable division. The best parts of the carcass were given as a church offering, which served to support the missionary.

Each village had a council house consisting of a wooden frame covered with straw. As many as 3,000 persons could crowd into these structures, where dances and festivals were held around a great central fire—the missionary standing by to reprimand any lewd conduct.

The bishop's description of the coast from San Agustín around the peninsula to the Apalachicola River cannot be reconciled with present-day maps. On the west coast he lists Carlos Bay, with Tampa Bay four leagues distant and Tocobago apparently 12 leagues above Tampa. His "Gauza," three leagues from San Martín, seems to identify with the Waccasassa River. "Twenty leagues" separated San Martín (the Suwannee River) and San Marcos de Apalache. "From there one goes by an inlet of 18 leagues to Matacojo where, they say, Fernando de Soto built ships to navigate it. At 3 leagues from there the river of Agna disembogues, and rounding the point of the cape which some call Apalache and others Hibineza, one comes to the inlet of Taxaquachile where the great river Apalachocoli empties."

Fernández de Florencia two years later sent a largely Indian force of 190 on a campaign into unexplored territory west of the Apalachicola River to punish the Chiscas who had been harassing the Apalache missions. Besides the Apalachinos gathered from seven missions and villages, the force included ten Chacatos. Led by Juan Mendoza with Mateo Chubas as *maestre de campo*, they marched from San Luis on September 2, 1677, following the established road to Santa Cruz de Sabacola on the Apalachicola River. After camping on the "Río Lagino" and creeks called Lapache and Ytaechato, they reached the Apalachicola (which they called Río de Santa Cruz) on the fourth day and crossed in canoes provided by the Sabacola chief Baltasar, who had 20 warriors eager to join the force.

Scouts having reconnoitered the territory ahead, the troop marched for the deserted mission of San Nicolás, ten leagues from the river, and San Carlos, four leagues beyond San Nicolás. Four leagues from Santa Cruz, the expeditionists camped on a lake, probably the marsh near Grand Ridge, then at a spring that formed the head of a river flowing south—quite likely Blue Springs, a few miles east of Marianna, Florida. The name of the wood in which they slept, Chapole, seems to identify with the Chipola River, which these waters join. San Nicolás and San Carlos, reached the next day, stood near the Chipola, not far from Marianna.

From San Carlos, the force traveled west into Chisca country, then turned south through wilderness that was unmarked except for an Indian trail linking the coast and the Chisca villages. Traveling south along this trace, they lost it on the tenth day of the campaign and turned west across narrow but deep and boggy arroyos surrounded by canebrakes. Descending out of the hills to the border of the coastal marshes, the scouts found bison trails. The Chiscas were temporarily forgotten while the Chacato auxiliaries went hunting and killed a buffalo.

Two days later the troop came to a large river called the Napa Ubab, on a course that suggests Econfina Creek, flowing into St. Andrew Bay from the northeast. There were rumblings among the Chacatos who, fearful that the unwarlike Apalachinos might flee in the heat of battle, were threatening to desert. Mendoza scolded them: either they could continue the march willingly or be taken by force; if, when the moment came, they refused to fight, they would be left to whatever fate might befall them. "In effect," says the report, "that is the way it turned out, for only three of them fought with us."

At a small, reddish stream called Ocalcasquis, tracks of men and buffalo were found. Twelve scouts were sent out, became lost, and failed to return that night. While the troop waited for them next morning, the pickets flushed two Chisca hunters, smoking meat from their hunt. The troop, not able to move swiftly enough to take them alive, had to kill them. A signal shot from the lost scouts was heard, and the troop marched on westward in search of the Chiscas' main camp. Cutting the enemy trail, the expeditionists followed it till sunset, the vespers of St. Matthew. The religious occasion boded well for battle; the pursuit was continued during the night until huge fires were sighted. The sound of drums and shouts rose from a large palisade near the sea (or bay) in which Chacatos, Panzacolas, and Chiscas, estimated at 300, were joined in an all-night festival.

As the force prepared for attack at three o'clock in the morning, a mysterious fire with a blue cast—doubtless the figment of superstitious imaginations—burst suddenly behind it. An Indian sentry shouted a warning to the celebrants. The Spaniards and their allies attacked from all sides with harquebuses and arrows. The Chiscas responded with a flight of arrows so thick that in the dim light it looked like smoke. Many of the Chiscas, dead or dying, fled to the river, while the attackers broke through the palisade to shoot into the houses and set fire to the buildings. The contents of the buildings burned with a green flame that frightened the villagers, causing men and women with babes at the breast to leap into the river and drown. Women and children, climbing the scaffolds to escape, were trapped by the flames. The punitive force had five dead and forty wounded. Poking through the smoking ruins, the Spaniards found nineteen charred Indian corpses.

Morning light revealed the Chisca survivors on the opposite bank of the narrow river, shouting threats and occasionally shooting arrows. While some of Mendoza's men treated the wounded, others began building a small palisade to protect them from counterattack. Mendoza took thirty men to forage, and one man was slain from ambush. Remaining in the village two days, the captain had the drum sounded morning and evening to signal the posting of the guard.

On the third day the village ruins were burned, and the withdrawal began. Harassing the retreat, the Chiscas wounded two men with arrows. Two of the auxiliaries each killed a stalker with a harquebus shot, and the enemy withdrew.

Carrying the wounded on litters, the force reached the abandoned missions of the Chacatos in eight days. The following day a relief party from Apalache arrived with provisions. The troop returned to San Luis on October 5 to end the month-long campaign.

Such tentative and tenuous thrusts along the fringes of the *tierra incógnita*, which make up the story of discovery and exploration around the Gulf during most of the seventeenth century, occurred against a backdrop of other troubles in Spanish Florida that boded imminent change. In 1670, 150 English colonists had landed at the mouth of the Ashley River in the territory the Spaniards called San Jorge—South Carolina. They presented a growing menace to Spanish control over the southeastern Indians and the Gulf of Mexico, challenging its integrity as a Spanish sea. The threat from the sea, manifest in other parts of the Gulf during this period, now pressed upon western Florida. In the gathering light of a June dawn in 1677, a pirate ship stole into the yet unfortified port of San Marcos de Apalache. Implicit in the sudden attack was a forecast of momentous events of the next decade.

SOURCES AND NOTES

Nuevo León

Alonso de León's account (*Historia de Nuevo León*) of the explorations he himself conducted is an indispensable source, especially since documentary material for the region and period of which he wrote is meager. The narrative is taken beyond León's ending in 1648 by Juan Bautista Chapa, also a participant in the events he reported, in the same volume. Chapa relates the expeditions made by Alonso de León *el mozo* toward the end of the century.

Eugenio del Hoyo's *Historia* is a recent history of Nuevo León that delves into the various exploratory endeavors.

Reyes Flores (*Apuntes*, 44–47) hypothesizes the route from Tampico toward Monterrey as extending from the Tamaholipa mission at the foot of the Sierra de Tamaulipas; thence to Los Esteros (present El Estero), 31 miles northwest of present Tampico by present-day highway; to Tonchoy, near Bernal de Horcasitas; to Tanchipa, near El Limón; and to the sites of Llera, Ciudad Victoria, Caballeros, Santa Engracia, Hidalgo, Villagrán, and Guadalupe Mainero. Hoyo (*Historia*, 1:119), projecting the route into Nuevo León, suggests as points on the way Linares, Congregación de Santa Engracia, and Los Ramones.

Alonso de León *el mozo*'s petition is in AGI, Mexico 616 (University of Texas transcripts). See Robert S. Weddle, *Wilderness Manhunt*, 55.

The royal dictum that Luis de Carvajal chose to ignore is the "Ordenanzas para el descubrimiento, población, y pacificación de nuevos territorios," Segovia, July 13, 1573 (AGI, Indiferente General 1378).

Descendants of the seventeenth-century León family still live in Cadereyta, Nuevo León, where in 1975 I met a namesake of the frontier soldier-historian. This gracious gentleman, keenly aware of his heritage, then operated a store on the main plaza.

The Benavides Memorial

There are two published translations of Fray Alonso de Benavides's work: *Benavides' Memorial of 1630*, translated by Peter P. Forrestal, with historical introduction and notes by Cyprian J. Lynch; and *The Memorial of Fray*

Alonso de Benavides, 1630, translated by Mrs. Edward E. Ayer and annotated by Frederick Webb Hodge and Charles Fletcher Lummis.

Between 1621 and 1629 the Jumano Indians of West Texas repeatedly brought to Benavides, in New Mexico, reports of a woman dressed in blue having appeared to them, teaching them the Christian faith. When Benavides returned to Spain in 1631, he heard the claims of María Jesús de Agreda, a nun born in 1602, that her spirit had left her Spanish convent on numerous occasions to go among the Indians in the American Southwest, taking them the divine message. After visiting her, the priest was convinced that it was she whom the Indians had seen. See Carlos Eduardo Castañeda, *Our Catholic Heritage in Texas*, 1:195–98.

Because the Mississippi (Río del Espíritu Santo) is not situated as Benavides describes it, various interpreters have concluded that he meant some other Espíritu Santo Bay. Lynch (in *Benavides' Memorial*, 64 n.) and Charles Wilson Hackett (in José Antonio Pichardo, *Pichardo's Treatise on the Limits of Louisiana and Texas*, 1:35 n.) opt for Matagorda Bay, which was called Espíritu Santo only after La Salle mistook it for the mouth of the Mississippi in 1685. Pichardo's early nineteenth-century attempt to establish the identity of Benavides's Espíritu Santo Bay (*Treatise*, 1:35) notes Cabeza de Vaca's conclusion that Matagorda Bay actually was the Espíritu Santo. All these interpreters, however, take an anachronistic view of the geographical understanding that Cabeza or Benavides might have had.

Westward Movement in Florida

There is a considerable amount of published material dealing with the Florida missions and other aspects of the westward thrust from San Agustín, including synthesized narratives (books and articles) and printed documents. Whether all this material adds up to a definitive assessment of the subject, however, is questionable. Concerning the missions, see Maynard Geiger, *The Franciscan Conquest of Florida (1573–1618)*, and Michael Gannon, *The Cross in the Sand*. Charles W. Arnade (*Florida on Trial, 1593–1602*) deals with the movement for abandoning the Florida enterprise. John Tate Lanning (*The Spanish Missions of Georgia*) treats the region as a whole, including the Anglo Hispanic conflict, in his discussion.

Both Lanning and Gannon describe Diego de Rebolledo as the worst of the Florida governors, but neither takes note of his "Testimonio de la visita que se hizo en la provincia de Apalache y Timucua," San Agustín, 1657 (microfilm from AGI, Escribanía de Cámara 155, in Stetson Collection, University of Florida), recounting his 1656–57 inspection.

Rebolledo's order against interfering with the Indian ball games was followed by a ten-year campaign to do away with the brutal sport (Amy Bushnell, "'That Demonic Game': The Campaign to Stop Indian *Pelota* Playing in Spanish Florida, 1675–1684," 1–19). A description of the game by Fray Juan de

Paiva is encompassed in an *expediente* on the *visita* to Timucua and Apalache ordered by Governor Pablo de Hita Salazar and carried out in 1677–78 by Domingo Leturiondo (Stetson Collection microfilm from AGI, Escribanía de Cámara 156). Hita's inspection followed closely that of the Bishop of Cuba. See Lucy L. Wenhold, trans., "A 17th Century Letter of Gabriel Díaz Vara Calderón, Bishop of Cuba, Describing the Indians and Indian Missions of Florida." New to his jurisdiction in 1675, Hita had sent two of his officers, Juan Fernández de Florencia of San Luis de Apalache and Pedro de Arcos, to make an enumeration of the missions the same year as the bishop's inspection. The list, attached to his letter to the queen of August 24, 1675, is translated by Mark F. Boyd ("Enumeration of Florida Spanish Missions in 1675," 181–85). The inventory was preliminary to the Leturiondo inspection begun in December, 1677.

Whatever the value of the Díaz Vara Calderón geographical description, it is not in fixing the location of Narváez's and Soto's boat-building operations, as John R. Swanton attempts to do in his introduction to Wenhold's translation. There is little justification in the bishop's letter for identifying Pine (Piney) Island as the place Soto had his vessel built for reaching the coast or the location of Narváez's boat-building camp.

The reports of the Florida missionaries gathered by Father Luis Jerónimo Oré (Atanasio López, ed., *Relación histórica de la Florida, escrita en el siglo XVII*, vol. 2) include Fray Baltasar López's "Declaración"; "Carta de los religiosas de la Florida dando quenta del alzamiento de los yndios" (1617); and Oré's own memorial to the Crown.

Some highly pertinent documents are printed in Manuel Serrano y Saenz, ed., *Documentos históricos de la Florida y la Luisiana, siglos XVI al XVIII*. These include Damián de la Vega Castro y Pardo's report to the Crown, San Agustín, Aug. 22, 1639, on the opening of the Apalache port; Rebolledo's letter to the Crown, San Agustín, Sept. 18, 1657; and Juan Fernández de Florencia, "Batalla que tubieron y vencieron la nación de yndios Apalachinos con los de los Chiscas," San Luis de Talimali, Aug. 30, 1678. The record of this campaign, as well as the Fernández mission list, indicates that the missions of San Nicolás and San Carlos are mislocated on the map in Gannon (*Cross in the Sand*, 65) and Charlton W. Tebeau (*A History of Florida*, 51).

Unpublished documents that enhance the picture offered by the published material include Pedro de Ibarra's two 1604 letters to the Crown and that of Pedro de Valdés of March 30, 1604 (all in AGI, Santo Domingo 232, no. 28); Valdés to the Crown, Havana, May 15, 1604 (ibid., 129, ramo 3); Fray Juan de las Cabezas Altamirano's report of *visita*, June 24, 1606 (Stetson Collection, microfilm reel 10); Luis de Rojas y Borja to the Crown (ibid.) on the Torres explorations; Luis de Horruytiner to the Crown, June 24, 1637 (AGI, Santo Domingo 225, no. 44), on the opening of the Apalache port; Rebolledo's "Testimonio," previously mentioned; Pablo de Hita Salazar to the queen, Aug. 24, 1675, and royal *cédulas* of June 20, 1676, and Nov. 5, 1677, and Hita to the king, Sept. 6, 1677 (all in Stetson Collection, reel 14).

Katherine Reding's "Plans for the Colonization and Defense of Apalache, 1675" comprises additional documents in translation relating to Hita's efforts to fortify the Apalache port.

Map of Florida, 1604

Our copy from AGI shows that the caption on the back has soaked through the paper and appears backwards on the print. It reads, "Map of the coast of Florida in which region is the Laguna Maymi and where the fort is to be made." Ron L. Seckinger discusses the map and its origin in "Observations on the Origin and Date of a Seventeenth-Century Florida Map," 385–87. He relates the map to the 1604 exploration by Francisco Fernández de Ecija. Governor Ibarra submitted it to the Crown in February, 1605, and indicated thereon a location he proposed for a fort, at the Bocas de Miguel Mora, on the Atlantic side of the peninsula at the southern tip.

The map shows the Bahía de Carlos where Charlotte Harbor is today; it also shows "Ensenada de Carlos" in the position of Apalache Bay. Fernández de Ecija claimed to have found a river link between his Carlos Bay and Lake Miami, or Okeechobee, while Francisco de Reynoso, exploring for Menéndez de Avilés in 1566–67, reportedly disproved such a link. The chief Carlos had told Reynoso the passage lay 50 leagues farther north, in the vicinity of Tocobaga (see ch. 17).

CHAPTER 20

The Gulf's New Explorers:
The English, the French, and the Dutch

WHILE Spanish soldiers and missionaries pushed west through the Florida swamps and forests, the course of the colonies' future was being fixed in the Caribbean. Insidious influences were rooted in the rise of corsairing, or privateering, distinguishable by the finest of lines from piracy. French corsairs, preying first on Spanish shipping along the sea-lanes to the Indies, made a major strike inside the Gulf of Mexico in 1558, as Charles V's war with Henry II of France was winding down. Returning from a raid on Nombre de Dios, the *flibustiers*, entering the Spanish Sea through the Yucatán Channel, overtook one or more vessels of the New Spain fleet making for Havana, then ransacked the Cuban port. Within two years the freebooters were making landings on the west Yucatán coast with an eye to raiding Mérida and Campeche.

John Hawkins's assault on Spanish trade restrictions, climaxed by the episode at San Juan de Ulúa in 1568, set the stage for worsening relations between Spain and England. Spanish treachery in the 1568 affair provoked Francis Drake to personal vendetta. Backed by Hawkins, he embarked on his course of vengeance, striking Nombre de Dios and Cartagena in 1571. In 1577 he ran Magellan's strait to surprise settlements on the Peruvian coast. He returned home, by crossing the Pacific and rounding the Cape of Good Hope, with half a million pounds in Spanish booty—and was knighted by his queen.

Hawkins's practice of trading with the Spanish colonials at gunpoint and Drake's audacious raids with the queen's obvious blessing did not stand alone as irritants to Anglo-Hispanic relations. There was also the difference over religion. Elizabethan Protestantism was aggravation enough for the Spanish "guardians of the faith"; even more offensive were the aid and comfort the English queen accorded Protestant rebels in the Netherlands, where Spain was struggling to establish domination. The two major powers drifted toward open war. In May, 1585, Spain widened the breech by seizing English vessels in Spanish ports, jailing crews, and confiscating cargoes. In response to the outcry from English merchants, Queen Elizabeth's lord high admiral was authorized to examine claims and issue letters of reprisal to those who proved their losses. Sir Richard Grenville, under Sir Walter Raleigh's aegis, already had sailed from England to plant a colony at Roanoke Island (in present North Carolina). The move had a definite place in the looming maritime war; a settlement on the eastern coast of North America would serve well as a base for privateering.

For Spain, the war that lasted until 1604 opened a Pandora's box, signaling the contest for domination of the seas. It initiated a shift in the economic hegemony of Europe. English as well as Dutch maritime interests, after eighteen years of feeding at will on the Spanish Indies fleets, would find it difficult to sit home with folded hands. The sea war sparked their exploration of the Gulf of Mexico, its shipping routes, and its ports and settlements.

It was well known that the treasure fleets from both Tierra Firme and Campeche gathered at Havana for the voyage to Spain. Along the northwest Cuban shore, from Cabo San Antón to Havana, the ships might be waylaid as they approached the required port. Drake himself passed that way in 1586, after sacking Santo Domingo and Cartagena. He passed up Havana but burned San Agustín, allegedly to safeguard the new English colony at Roanoke. Correspondence from Havana during the next several years is filled with accounts of corsairs lurking about the coast, so numerous that ships leaving the port ran serious risk of capture.

The doings of 1588 intensified an already deplorable situation. Philip II sent his "invincible armada" to teach the English a lesson; to chastise Elizabeth I for the privateering, as well as for the execution of the Catholic Mary Queen of Scots. Thanks to the wily Drake and his fire ships let loose in the English Channel, the Spanish fleet was forced to flee into the North Sea and thence came onto the rugged west coast of Ireland. A dozen ships went on the rocks. No more than half their original number made it back to Spain.

It was a serious setback to Spain's might, but she was far from having her stinger removed. Immediate steps were taken to forestall the impact on the Indies fleets and the colonies. In 1589 the fast-sailing *galizabras* came into use to transport the Crown's treasures. Fortresses were built to guard the Indies ports, and armed ships were sent to patrol the approaches. Such measures, however, were able only to impede the ravages of the privateers, not to prevent them. During the eighteen years of the maritime war, hundreds of Spanish and Portuguese merchantmen surrendered to English privateers.

Attacks were concentrated in the Caribbean and on the approach to Havana, just inside the Gulf. For a time the Gulf constituted a barrier to strikes on the Mexican mainland. Aside from Veracruz, New Spain's coast offered few settlements worth risking the Gulf's uncertain winds, currents, and shoals. Yet the Spanish Sea was not to remain inviolate. The more adventurous privateers first made tentative thrusts into the Bay of Campeche, building their own store of knowledge, for which some of them paid dearly.

Still, in the late sixteenth and early seventeenth centuries, the fleets approaching Havana bore the brunt of privateer attacks. The trouble spots were around Cabo San Antón, where the Tierra Firme fleet entered the Gulf, and the Sonda de las Tortugas, where ships took soundings just before beginning the final approach to the intermediary port.

Christopher Newport—best remembered as admiral of the Virginia Company fleets in that colony's early years—has been suggested as the prototype of the English merchant mariners who went in for privateering. A shipmaster at least by age twenty-two, Newport was mate of a ship in Drake's fleet that raided Cádiz in 1587, delaying the Armada's sailing for a year. He had his right arm shot off two years later while attempting to capture two of New Spain's treasure ships in the critical waters off northern Cuba, yet he averaged a voyage a year to the West Indies during the next four years. The record of one of these, when he came again to the crucial corner of the Gulf, is provided by John Twitt of Harwich, corporal on Newport's flagship, *Golden Dragon*.

Newport cleared Dover Road on February 12, 1591, with *Dragon*, two other ships, and a pinnace. At Dominica, he overhauled a Portuguese slaver and went on to sack four Caribbean towns before his ships were scattered by storm in the Yucatán Channel in June. The Tortugas had been designated as rendezvous, but *Dragon* and *Pru-*

dence dropped off to leeward so that "wee fell with certeine islands within the point of Florida." Newport sent his pinnace for water and found the Indians "very courteous." The natives, doubtless Calusa, waded breast-deep into the water, bringing a line with which to haul in the boat and pointing the way north to both fresh water and gold. "These Savages were farre more civill than those of Dominica: for besides their courtesie, they covered their privities with a platted mat of greene straw, about three handfulls deep, which came round about their waste, with the bush hanging down behind."

Next day the Englishmen sighted a Spanish frigate of 30 tons and came within range after a lively chase. "After a shot or two made at her, shee yeelded unto us: wee hoisted out our boat, and went aboard, where we found some five Spanyards, five and fifty hogges, and about some two hundred weight of excellent tabacco rolled up in seynes. We lightened them of their hogges and tabacco, and sent the men away with their frigat."

At times the privateers all but stumbled over each other along the Cuban shore and in the Straits of Florida. Such was the case in 1592, when four fleets—an aggregate of thirteen vessels sent out by London and Bristol merchants—vied with each other for prizes in the crucial waters. That summer, though one of the busiest for the privateer fleets, offers but a small sample of their total activity before peace was made in 1604. English raiders penetrated the Gulf's inner waters to sack Campeche in grim foreboding of the pirate raids of the next century. The leader in the first such instance was William Parker of Plymouth. Like Newport, he had been with Drake on the Cádiz expedition of 1587, and also with Robert Devereaux, Earl of Essex, who sacked the Spanish port again in 1596. In November of the latter year, Parker embarked for the Caribbean and the Gulf of Mexico.

Parker's men launched the first assault on Campeche at ten o'clock in the morning. The Spanish forces promptly withdrew but, as Parker later learned, only to form for a furious counterattack. Parker lost six men and was himself shot through the breast, "which bullet lieth still in the chine of my backe." Having taken a number of Spanish captives, the Englishmen formed them into a live barricade as they rowed shoreward from their ships anchored six leagues out. They managed to take a small ship containing some silver and other valuables. But as the English vessels sought to sail away, they were pursued by two war

Fig. 12. Vulnerable Campeche. Courtesy Biblioteca Nacional.

frigates, to which the bark *Adventure*, with her captain and thirteen men, fell prey. The booty taken was purchased at a dear price.

In 1599, Newport sailed into the Gulf with three ships and captured the "town of Tabasco." He brought away 888 ounces of silver, coinage valued at 200 pounds, 14 ounces of gold and pearls, 41 hides, and the church bells.

Before war's end the Spanish king Philip II died, on September 13, 1598. By most measurements he is judged a capable ruler. Yet he passed on to his son and heir almost as many problems as he had inherited from his own father, Charles V, and left them in much less capable hands. The young Philip III, taking the throne at age twenty-one, was ill-suited for governing the world's most powerful and complex empire: "His mind was empty, his will suppine."

Aside from difficulties with England and the Netherlands, Spain faced problems that defied solution. From 1596 to 1602 a plague epidemic—reminiscent of the Black Death of the fourteenth century—swept the peninsula, devastating the population. Philip III compounded this loss of people by expelling the Moorish remnants, bringing on what historian John Lynch calls "a century of demographic recession."

New Spain was suffering similar woes. During the sixteenth century, that colonial jurisdiction had lost an estimated three-fourths of its native population. Deep depression resulted, as virtually all enterprises—agriculture, mining, manufactures, and commerce—suffered for want of laborers. The impact of the white man's culture and his diseases, for which the Indians had no immunity, was severe.

Historians have assessed their own neglect of the seventeenth century, noting the scarcity of studies dealing with this period in the Spanish colonies, while recognizing that momentous events and trends continued. There is no dearth of history, no hiatus of human endeavor, to justify such neglect. Yet the faltering pace of Spanish discovery and exploration is not imaginary. The Spaniards, who to this juncture had held the Gulf of Mexico as their private domain, did little toward extending their discoveries in this Spanish Sea until late in the century. Exploration advanced, for the most part, only on the fringes of earlier settlements. Colonial officials were preoccupied with holding back foreign rivals and shoring up coastal defenses. It took the news that a foreign settlement (La Salle's) had been attempted in the Gulf, late in the century, to spur them to new exploratory endeavors. In the meantime, exploration fell to those very aggressors whom the Spaniards wanted most to thwart, as they sought a still greater share of Spain's colonial wealth. Compounding the dilemma, Spain found herself mired not only in demographic recession but also in the problems of dwindling resources and inept leadership.

If Philip III's will was "suppine," it inclined him more to peace than to war. Following the Treaty of Virvins with France in 1598, peace was made with England by means of the Treaty of London in 1604; with the Netherlands, the 1609 Truce of Antwerp. These agreements promised amicable relations with all three of Spain's major adversaries, seemingly a propitious sign for the coming decades. Yet all was not as rosy as it seemed. This was the century of the Thirty Years' War, which Philip IV, following his father's death in 1621, managed to stretch to forty years. Only sixteen years old when he assumed the crown, he abdicated his authority to Gaspar de Guzmán, Conde de Olivares, and, in Lynch's words, proved himself to be "a king who preferred private pleasure to public duty."

Spain's involvement with the Austrian Hapsburgs had expanded after the war began in 1618, and young Philip's government soon was warring again with the Low Countries, England, France, and, eventually, Sweden. With the 1648 Peace of Westphalia—marking the so-called end of the Thirty Years' War—Spain abandoned her conflict with the Dutch, conceding all the American territory the Netherlands then held. She thus was able to concentrate on the contest with France, at least until France was joined by England six years later.

The concomitants of this prolonged warfare were many. In essence, Spain bled herself white to sustain it, draining off both Crown revenue and private treasure from the Indies faster than it accrued. Both economic and military supremacy evaporated. As had been the case in the reign of Charles V, the treasure shipments failed when needed most. The 1622 Tierra Firme fleet was lost on the Florida Keys during a hurricane. The Dutch, seizing a base in Portuguese Brazil and others on Caribbean islands, afflicted Spanish shipping throughout the Indies. In 1627 alone, fifty-five Spanish vessels were seized. Then Piet Heyn, with thirty-one ships armed with seven hundred cannon and four thousand soldiers in the service of the Dutch West India Company, waylaid the New Spain fleet on the north coast of Cuba. On September 8, 1628, he sighted fifteen large vessels near Cabo San Antón and engaged the Spaniards in a running fight. His shallops swarmed around the huge galleons like sparrows chasing eagles. Some of the ships hove to and were boarded, while the rest put into Matanzas Bay and were taken there. The cargo of silver, gold, pearls, indigo, sugar, and "Campeche wood" was sold in the Netherlands for 15 million guilders, and the company declared an unprecedented 50 percent dividend.

For the Spanish Indies, it was by far the most devastating blow ever suffered from enemy action. The captain-general, Juan de Benavides, was brought to trial for dereliction of duty and was beheaded. The "infamous defeat, caused as it was by fear and cowardice," was a painful subject with King Philip, who acknowledged that at the thought, "the blood runs cold in my veins."

Fortunately for Spain, Heyn's great coup was "a happy accident," never to be repeated.

All in all, the Dutch harassment of Spanish shipping was more intense and better organized than the English. The West India Company, from its inception in 1621, perceived Havana as the jugular and directed its cutting edge accordingly. Considering that point too well fortified to be seized directly, it planned to take Matanzas Bay and establish there a permanent colony from which to operate against Havana. By the time such plans came to the attention of the Spanish Crown, the company already had provided itself with maps and intelligence. Playing catch-up, the Crown instructed the governor of Cuba to map Matanzas and prepare its defenses. Yet the plethora of navigable bays on the island raised doubts as to the efficacy of protecting a single sector. The threat, however, did not materialize, as the Netherlanders fixed their sights on Brazil.

Even so, the Dutch caused trouble all around the Caribbean and, as the English had done, found their way around Yucatán to the inner Gulf. Campeche was sacked in 1632, when five ships sailed into the lagoon and anchored boldly within sight of the town, obviously secure in the knowledge that it was defenseless. The invaders burned the ships in the harbor and new ones being built on the beach. Spreading over the countryside, they laid waste to haciendas and terrorized the natives, taking prisoners to be sold into slavery in the Bahamas or the non-Spanish islands of the Caribbean. With the need for improved defenses thus emphasized, Captain Joseph Brenan de Bertiz offered the Crown a fortification plan. There was news, he claimed, that a company was being raised in Holland to occupy Grand Cayman, just a hundred leagues east of Cozumel and the Yucatán Channel, as a base for raiding in the Gulf of Mexico. In an impassioned plea for relief, the Crown was charged with neglecting Campeche because of its remoteness. Never a year passed, the letter claims, without an enemy raid. The Armada de Barlovento, spread too thin over the Caribbean as well as the Gulf, offered no protection; the highly mobile privateers easily eluded it. All the other Indies ports, the petition claims, had defenses to discourage the pirates; of all the Seno Mexicano, only Campeche was the victim of such gross neglect.

Campeche, as future decades proved, claimed an exclusiveness not altogether its due. While it suffered more often than other Gulf coastal settlements, it owned no monopoly of either pirate raids or Crown neglect. Before the end of the century, almost all the coastal towns and villages around the Gulf sustained enemy raids, from Tabasco to Florida. Call these raiders privateers, for the moment, as that term is apropos for wartime; but they were the forerunners of savage pirates who recognized no government's authority and served no interests but their own. The Spanish fleets and coastal towns were not always the helpless victims; they often gave as good as they received.

In 1633 a Spanish squadron fought off a Dutch fleet near Cabo San Antón, losing its commandant, Miguel Redín, in the fight. Mention was made in the preceding chapter of Captain-General Carlos de Ibarra's sighting of a Dutch fleet in the western Gulf of Mexico in 1638, while Nuevo León settlers responded to reports of such from Indians. Now the sequel. Ibarra, on leaving Spain with the Indies fleet, had been forewarned that the noted Dutch freebooter Cornelis Corneliszoon Jol—known as Pie de Palo, or "Peg Leg"—was sailing for the New World. It was suspected that he intended waylaying Ibarra's fleet on its homeward course. Ibarra was instructed to avoid the encounter if possible; if not, to give good account of himself.

In August he set sail from Veracruz with seven ships laden with silver. Approaching the Cuban coast, he found Peg Leg lying in wait with fourteen vessels. As the Dutchmen came on in pursuit, the galleon *Carmen*, commanded by Sánchez de Urdanivia, fought a rearguard action. The enemy's *capitana* bore down on Ibarra's, while the Dutch *almiranta* took on her Spanish counterpart, swapping artillery and musket fire with Urdanivia on the way. *Carmen* stood off three other ships attempting to zero in on the Spanish admiral's ship, fighting them for three hours so close that she tangled rigging with the enemy. The Dutch then fell away. When they returned two days later, *Carmen* found herself engaging twelve of the enemy vessels alone. Only after she was dismasted did the other armada ships come to her aid, forcing the Dutch to withdraw.

The rest of the story was heard later that year in Sanlúcar de Barrameda, where an English captain related a bizarre occurrence in the English Channel. The captain told of having encountered a Dutch ship so broken up that she was barely afloat, steadily losing freeboard despite constant pumping. He took on board some three hundred mangled men, many with arms or legs shot off. There was just enough time to rescue the survivors and the artillery before the ship sank. While taking the suffering Dutch sailors to an English port, the captain heard their account of the battle: "The Spaniards sank seven of our ships, our admiral's ship among them. Our *capitana* is missing, and they killed our general." The Spanish fleet, while suffering some damage, they said, had not lost a vessel, but all entered Havana safely.

That report was not entirely correct. The silver fleet had reached Havana, but the valiant *Carmen*, damaged beyond repair, had to be beached and burned. The Dutch general reported killed was not Peg Leg; he lived to make an abortive raid on Matanzas in September, 1640, when a hurricane scattered his thirty-six ships and spared the Cubans the full impact of his atrocities.

Dutch ships, meanwhile, found their way to the far reaches of the Spanish Sea. In 1642, Antonio de la Plaza, admiral of the newly revived Armada de Barlovento (Windward Fleet), discovered four enemy vessels in the mouth of the Río de Alvarado, bent on destroying two galleons being built there. After seizing three of the ships, La Plaza reconnoitered the coast toward the Sierra de San Martín. Near Roca Partida he engaged three more enemy vessels. While suffering some casualties (one man killed and several wounded), the armada captured one of the foreign ships and killed the enemy captain and twenty-two of his men: just punishment, the admiral allowed, for the pirates who infested the coast of the Seno Mexicano.

The plethora of European enemies severely taxed Spain's ability to guard her extensive American possessions. England, having established the Jamestown colony in Virginia in 1607 and the Massachusetts colony in 1620, extended her American interests by taking up vacant islands in the Antilles: St. Kitts, later divided with the French; Barbados; Santa Cruz, shared with the Dutch; Nevis and Barbuda; Antigua and Montserrat. The French at St. Kitts formed a West Indies company that occupied Guadaloupe, Martinique, and other Windward Islands. The Dutch held trading stations on St. Eustatius in the north and Tobago and Curaçao off the South American mainland. Those island bases enhanced the spread of privateering and piracy.

The spirit of the age, perhaps, is summed up by the disenchanted English priest Thomas Gage, who went to New Spain in 1624 as one of a company of Dominicans: "Since that God hath given the earth to the sons of men to inhabit, and that there are many vast countries [in the Spanish Indies] not yet inhabited either by Spaniard or Indian, why should my countrymen the English be debarred from making use of that which God from all beginning no question did ordain for the benefit of mankind?" Such a view made no concession to the idea of an exclusively Spanish sea.

In the face of repeated depredations, various efforts were made to fortify the Gulf ports, but the work moved ponderously. In 1646 a royal Spanish engineer, Jacques de Beste, was sent from Puerto Rico to the Gulf of Mexico to undertake survey work for coastal defenses. At Campeche, he found the coast "completely defenseless." He erected a parapeted fort with traverses arranged so that artillery and musket fire could be directed to prevent an enemy landing. The work of Beste and his successors, however, failed to protect Campeche in its time of need. Beste went on to Veracruz Nueva (Veracruz at its present site, having been moved in 1599–1600 from the second location five leagues up the coast), where San Juan de Ulúa's fortifications had undergone almost continuous development ever since the Hawkins episode of 1568.

In the war with England following the 1648 Peace of Westphalia, Spain lost Jamaica. The first permanent annexation by another European power of an integral part of Spanish America was a severe blow. France, meanwhile, came into possession of western Hispaniola and Tortuga Island (Ile de Tortue) off the northern coast. Spain's rivals had advanced a step farther into the once exclusive Spanish realm, enhancing their access to the Gulf of Mexico as well as the western Caribbean. In combination with their other insular possessions, these new bases harbored the wartime privateers and bred the buccaneers. They fostered the piracy that was rampant in the West Indies and the Gulf for the remainder of the seventeenth century.

All manner of renegades—desperate men who acknowledged no political allegiance—came to roost among the islands to take up piratical pursuits. They found the woods and savannas populated with feral swine and cattle, bred from those of the early settlers, and these animals provided a convenient livelihood. The renegades cured meat by the *boucan* (smoking) process and thus came to be known in the French idiom as *boucaniers*. As their activities expanded into piracy, the word was anglicized as "Buccaneer." Conversely, the English equivalent, "freebooter," became *flibustier* in French and rebounded back into English as "filibuster." Each term, of course has its Spanish equivalent: *bucanero* and *filibustero*.

A peace, of sorts, between Spain and England followed the ascension of Charles II, of the Stuart line, to the English throne in 1660. There was some question in English minds as to whether the peace extended to the New World; privateers were permitted to continue their operations in hope that Spain would accede to English demands for free trade among her colonies. While Yucatán officials shuffled about surveying the province's defensive needs in response to a royal *cédula*, an English fleet led by Captain Christopher Myngs of the Royal Navy aimed a crippling blow at San Francisco de Campeche. Early in 1663, Myngs sailed from Jamaica with twelve ships and fifteen hundred men, bound for the Gulf of Mexico. A month later, on February 9, he landed his troops a league and a half from Campeche and marched along hidden paths into the town. Even though the contiguous, flat-roofed stone houses might, in Myngs's opinion, have been defended like a fortress, the townspeople yielded readily. The invaders met stiffer resistance at the Castillo de Santa Cruz, and Myngs himself was thrice wounded. But the fort was taken and demolished, part of the town burned, and fourteen Spanish vessels seized.

Campeche's problem extended to the entire peninsula, vulnerable on the east coast as well as the west. Within a decade the privateers—inching closer and closer to outright piracy—would ravage the Gulf coast from the Boca de Conil to the Río de Alvarado. The focus of their operations was the Laguna de Términos, stretching out behind the Isla del Carmen and offering an abundance of fish, turtle meat, and *palo de tinta*, the so-called Campeche wood with commercial applications for dyes.

In January 1665 three English privateer captains, Morris, Jackman, and Henry Morgan, disembarked 107 men at the Río de Grijalva and, with native guides, set about exploring the country. After tramping through some 300 miles of inland territory, they sacked Villahermosa, 12 leagues from the coast. Returning to the river mouth, they found their ships held by 300 Spaniards, whose attack they withstood to escape in canoes and barks.

When Sir Thomas Lynch came out to Jamaica in 1670 as the British lieutenant governor, he carried orders to revoke all privateering commissions, settle the sea rovers in more peaceful pursuits, and grant pardons for past offenses. Word of such plans, unfortunately, preceded him by more than two years. The buccaneers already had escaped governmental authority; they had no intention of returning to it. In late May, 1669, all the privateer ships in Jamaican ports quietly weighed anchor and put to sea. Two vessels made for the coast near Havana to rob passing ships and pick up what plunder they could find on shore. Eight headed west to the Caymans, where they split up, five making sail for the Mosquito Coast of Honduras and three for the Yucatán Channel and the Gulf of Mexico. The empty anchorages around British Jamaica signified their intent: they would lurk among the Caribbean islands or along the Gulf's desolate coastal stretches, continuing their time-honored custom of rapacity until the colonial officials came to their senses.

Vacillation of official French and English policy—the respective crowns in peacetime could not endorse their activities yet dared not offend them—often left the status of the buccaneers in doubt. Were they corsairs, or privateers—implying that they were licensed—or outright pirates? To their victims it made no difference; by any name they had a foul smell.

SOURCES AND NOTES

French pirates, remember, sacked and burned Havana in 1539, just before Juan de Añasco arrived to begin preparations for Soto's Florida campaign. The *flibustiers* had planned to attack the Indies fleet but evidently were frustrated in that design. Charles de la Roncière (*Histoire de la Marine Française*, 4:587) offers the 1558 episode as the first instance of a strike against the fleet inside the Gulf.

The English privateering voyages are treated in documents contained in two different works published by the Hakluyt Society: Kenneth R. Andrews, *English Privateering Voyages to the West Indies, 1588–1595*, and Irene A. Wright, *Further English Voyages to Spanish America, 1583–1594.* John Twitt's account is in Richard Hakluyt, *The Principal Navigations, Voyages, Traffiques & Discoveries of the English Nation*, 10:184–90.

The Background

The social, political, and economic forces bearing on these endeavors are assessed by John Lynch (*Spain under the Habsburgs*, vol. 2). Lynch deals with conditions in Spain at the beginning of Philip III's reign in a chapter entitled

"The Hispanic World of 1600" (pp. 1–13). The plague epidemic he describes, occurring at the start of the seventeenth century, was repeated in Seville at midcentury, according to a newspaper feature I came across in that city ("La Sevilla de Ayer," *Andalucía*, May 2, 1979). Ships from the Far East reintroduced the bacillus with the result that the population center of two hundred thousand persons was reduced by two-thirds.

Lesley Byrd Simpson ("Mexico's Forgotten Century," in Howard F. Cline, ed., *Latin American History*, 2:500–506) and Charles Gibson and Benjamin Keen ("Trends of United States Studies in Latin American History," ibid., 539) appraise Spanish colonial endeavor in the sixteenth century.

The Pirate's View

The considerable geographical and hydrographical knowledge accumulated by foreign intruders in the Gulf is brought out by William Dampier (*Dampier's Voyages*, 2:117–61). Dampier discusses his own piratical forays into the Gulf, 1675–76, treated in the next chapter.

Dampier describes (pp. 193–96) the relationship between "privateering" and the pursuits of logwood cutting and cow killing. "The logwood Trade," he says (p. 155), "had its origin in the decay of Privateering. Had it not been for the great care of the Spaniards in stocking the West-Indies with Hogs and Bullocks, the Privateers must have starved." He also describes Tabasco during this period, noting that Spanish ships came up the Río de Tabasco (Grijalva) to discharge their cargoes of European goods at "Villa de Mosa" and load cacao and "sylvester," or hides and tallow. The freebooters quite naturally found their way up the river. Dampier credits two attempts on Villahermosa by a Captain Nevil, who succeeded the second time in taking it. On another occasion (p. 207) a Captain Hewet, with two hundred men, took Villahermosa and planned to proceed to Tacotalpa but was repulsed at "Estapo" (Astapa on present-day maps).

Campeche's Woes

Juan Juárez Moreno (*Piratas y corsarios en Veracruz y Campeche*) relates the Campeche raids more completely and in greater detail, including a raid led by Diego Mulato (Diego Grillo, a renegade from Havana) and Pie de Palo (Jol) in August, 1633, involving Hollanders, Englishmen, and Frenchmen (pp. 12–18); a raid by Edward Mansfield and twelve hundred men in February 1663 (p. 24); and another shortly thereafter led by Christopher Innis (see also pp. 26–29).

Documents dealing with Campeche raids fill a fat *legajo* in AGI, Mexico 1006. Here appears Joseph Brenan's "Proposición que el Cappn Joseph Brenan de Bertiz hace a V.M. sobre fortificación del puerto de San Francisco de Campeche"; Melchior de la Rosa's "Testimonio de la información hecha sobre la entrada del enemigo Ynglés in Campeche," June 9, 1663; and a number of other items related to defense. Jacques de Beste's "Ynforme" is in AGI, Mexico 92, ramo 3. In this connection, see the printed documents in "Ocupación de la Isla de Terminos por los Ingleses, 1658–1717."

The Dutch and the Gulf

Piet Heyn's raid is related by Petrus Johannes Blok in *History of the People of the Netherlands*, 4:36–37; and Irene A. Wright, "The Dutch and Cuba, 1609–1643," 614–15. Philip IV's reaction is given by Lynch (*Spain*, 2:75). Wright also discusses the Dutch plan for establishing a colony at Matanzas, details Ibarra's battle with Pie de Palo's Dutch fleet, and relates the later episodes in which Jol was involved.

Valuable as background but lacking specific information pertaining to the Gulf of Mexico is Engel Sluiter's "Dutch-Spanish Rivalry in the Caribbean Area, 1594–1609."

The aftermath of the Ibarra-Jol battle, as told by the English sea captain, and a version of the battle itself appear in a 1638 printed copy in AHN (Diversos 337): "Relación verdadera de la refriega que tuvieron nuestros galeones de la plata en el Cabo de San Antón, con catorze navíos de Olanda, de que era general Pie de Palo."

Cristóbal Montoya, in his account of Antonio de la Plaza's encounter with "enemy" ships at the Río de Alvarado and Roca Partida, does not specifically identify the enemy as Dutch but implies it by his later mention of "olandeses" in another connection. His "Relación de todo lo sucedido en estas provincias de la Nueva España, desde la formación de la Armada Real de Barlovento, despacho de flota, y sucesso della, hasta la salida deste primer aviso del año de 1642" (printed copy) is in AHN, Diversos 344. His purpose was to show that the Armada de Barlovento, recently revived, was cost-effective as an instrument for protecting the colonies against enemy maritime forces.

The Buccaneers Generally

C. H. Haring (*The Buccaneers in the West Indies in the XVII Century*) offers a general survey of the seventeenth-century sea rovers. See also Weddle, "The Buccaneers," in *Wilderness Manhunt*, 34–45.

The "spirit of the age" statement is in Thomas Gage, *The English American*, 4.

Palo de Tinta

The tree producing the dyewood was the *coaba*, a mahogany with very hard, almost black wood, according to Absalón de la Cruz L., an agronomy student at the University of Campeche whom I met on my tour of the Yucatán peninsula in April, 1980. Stands of the timber were virtually eliminated by the logwood cutters in present Campeche state, although it still grows in considerable numbers in Quintana Roo and Tabasco. Cruz drew a distinction between the *coaba* and the *caoba*, also a mahogany which, having softer wood, is more widely used in furniture-making. See Dampier's description of the dyewood (*Voyages*, 2:159–60).

--··❧ CHAPTER 21 ❧··--

The Bloody Buccaneers:
Harbingers of Change, 1669–85

HEADING west from the Caymans in the spring of 1669 were a frigate
and two brigantines, all heavily armed and flying the British flag. Of the
three captains—one English, the other two Dutch—two had taken
part in Henry Morgan's sack of Portobelo the previous June. They had
missed Morgan's raid on Maracaibo earlier in 1669—when he destroyed the feeble Armada de Barlovento—only because they were
engaged at the time in bloody slaughter at Cumaná. By name, these
captains were Bran (or Brand), the Englishman; Roque, described
in Spanish documents as a Dutch native of Brazil; and Juanes Ycles
de Cot.

The only one of the three to win prominence in the annals of piracy is Roque, known by the pseudonym Roche Brasiliano. This rogue,
says John Esquemeling, the pirate-turned-author, was noted for roasting his Spanish captives alive, reflecting not only his brutal nature but
also a bitter hatred born of a previous experience at Campeche.

The three westering ships, after clearing the Yucatán Channel
into the Gulf, coasted Yucatán toward the Laguna de Términos, their
eyes peeled for plunder. For two or three weeks they hung about San
Francisco de Campeche, seizing two men and their cargo of salt at the
Campeche salines. Then Roque's men went ashore to rob a village
three leagues down the coast, and two of his men were killed by the
villagers. Ycles, meantime, sacked the church at nearby Lerma, where
Brand's frigate seized a flour-laden vessel from Havana.

The pirates spent two months at the Laguna de Términos, in company with other poachers, laying in turtle meat. Roque's brigantine
was careened, while Ycles loaded up with dyewood. Such activities
represented the practical side of piracy; when there were no ships to

raid, and prospects for plunder in the coastal towns were not appealing, there was profit in more prosaic pursuits. Conversely, piracy often served as a diversion for some whose ordinary occupations were cutting logwood, butchering wild cattle, or salvaging sunken vessels. In the process, they came to know the Gulf of Mexico and its coves and bays better than the Spaniards themselves.

Growing restless, Brand and Roque at last sailed up the coast to look for prizes. Roque, in his smaller ship, carrying oars as well as sail, searched the coast for *chinchorros*—small fishing boats—needed for navigating the shallow waters of the Laguna de Términos. Brand's frigate took her stance off Campeche, while Roque hauled up at Las Bocas, four leagues south. The brigantine's crew seized three fishermen and their gear. Roque, spotting a timid man among them, tormented him until he learned what he wanted to know: a ship from Veracruz, bringing a new governor, was due in Campeche shortly. Roque rubbed his hands in anticipation.

The Campechanos, meanwhile, sighted the strange vessels, and pirate jitters born of their previous afflictions set in. Three armed ships went out on December 18 to chase the marauders away but failed to find them before a norther forced Roque to claw off the shore and make for open water. Beating his way northeast, he doubled the northwest point of Yucatán against a stiffening wind. The small ship, unmanageable in the heavy sea, was driven upon the Chicxulub beach, a thin strip of barrier sand just east of the present town of Progreso.

The Venezuelan Indian Juan Carreño, one of those seized four months previously at the Campeche salines, took advantage of the pirates' preoccupation with salvaging effects from the ship; he stole away into the woods. At a nearby coastal watchtower, he found two native sentries who guided him to Mérida, whence a mounted troop was sent to investigate the pirate landing.

The pirates, in the act of burying their tools and artillery, took flight at the Spaniards' approach, eluding their pursuers by crossing the lagoon to the mainland in an Indian canoe. Only two men who failed to make it into the craft were captured: one an English cripple, "Juan Boc," a native of the island of Nevis, who had lost both his legs to frostbite in New England four winters previously; the other, a helmsman called "Juan Yon"—John Young—of uncertain nativity and Dutch upbringing, who had formed the pirates' rearguard.

Taken to Mérida, these two and Carreño were interrogated by the provincial governor. Thus was revealed the role of Roque and Brand— as well as Young and four or five others of Roque's crew—in the sack of Portobelo and Cumaná; the self-deployment of the pirate vessels from Jamaica to avoid having their commissions revoked; the freebooters' general mode of operations and their activities on the Campeche coast; and the general makeup of the Jamaican pirate fleet.

Dr. Fructos Delgado, the governor, probed for some sign that Carreño had been the marauders' willing accomplice rather than their victim. The Indian acquitted himself well: Roque's interest in him had been that he was a salvage diver; when no salvage site was found, the pirate captain made him his cook. Concerning Roque, Carreño knew only that, on a previous Campeche raid, he had been taken prisoner and sent to Spain.

To interrogate Boc and Young, Delgado used an English inter- preter named Richard Lewis (which the Spanish scribe rendered first as Luis Ricardo, then as Ricardo Luis). Young, now thirty, had literally grown up in piracy; he claimed twenty years as a buccaneer, freely acknowledged his part in the Portobelo affair with an Irish captain named Gunn, and revealed that Roque's lost brigantine was a Spanish prize from that episode. He denied having been involved in a recent attack on Florida. Even though he was certain that his captors meant to execute him, he agreed to show them where the artillery was buried.

Roque's crew, thirty-four to forty men, according to the various accounts, contained six Englishmen; the rest were Hollanders. Brand's eighty-man crew was English except for two captive Negroes and a renegade Spaniard who had joined willingly in the sack of Portobelo and Cumaná. Boc, having sailed previously with a French captain named Merlan, had joined Roque eight months before. Besides the three ships, there had been three barks or *piraguas* at the Laguna de Téminos engaged in cutting logwood, an activity only slightly less of- fensive to Spanish officials than piracy.

Young made no effort to conceal his lifelong career as a sea raider against the Spaniards, or the fact that the Jamaican ships were out to plunder any vessels or coastal settlements offering pleasing prospects. Indeed, he equivocated on only one point: his religion. Claiming at first to be a Catholic, he later admitted that he was a Protestant.

The ultimate fate of Young and Boc does not appear. Roque and the rest of his crew eluded the Spaniards. Following Young's directions, Spanish soldiers went back to the Chicxulub beach and retrieved the buried artillery: a bronze cannon bearing the arms of Philip II, two bronze swivel guns, and sixty-odd iron balls. The ordnance was taken to Mérida and installed in the fortress.

The pirate host's probing of the Gulf's recesses—seeking ways to afflict the Spaniards and enrich themselves—goaded the Spaniards to new voyages, searching out the coastline for interlopers. The declarations given at Mérida disclose the method of the pirates' operations; Pablo de Hita Salazar, in command at Veracruz a few years later, reveals their extent. In 1674 Hita noted, "For six years the English nation has occupied on the coast of Campeche [Yucatán] the places of Cabo Catoche; La Ascensión; Bocas de Conil; the islands of Cozumel; and the Laguna de Términos, cutting dyewood and trading with Hollanders who come to Puerto Real." They were plundering the land, supplying the Spanish or Indian inhabitants illicitly with European goods, and inciting the Campeche and Tabasco natives to defiance of Spanish authority. A dozen foreign ships came each month to those places, and the number of intruders more or less permanently settled was placed as high as two thousand; they relied for protection on "three or four corsairs who run these coasts, putting into the mouth of the Río de Tabasco in some *piraguas* or canoes, which they make from large trees . . . with capacity of up to thirty men. They come to the Río de Tonalá and the Isla de Santa Ana and proceed to the province of Agualulcos." Some had come even to the Río de Coatzacoalcos, committing acts of unbelievable audacity.

The viceroy, Marqués de Manzera, the previous year had sent Mateo Alonso de Vidobro with a small armada to run the southern Gulf shore and chastise the interlopers. Sailing from Veracruz with four vessels, Vidobro dropped down to the Coatzacoalcos but failed to find the poachers. At the Barra de Santa Ana, he drove a boatload of pirates ashore and burned their craft, leaving the freebooters stranded in the wilderness.

Almost by the time Vidobro returned to Veracruz, news came of more pirate troubles at Campeche. He sailed again in late August 1673, this time with three heavily armed ships and a sloop and three hundred infantrymen, from the San Juan de Ulúa fortress, to run the coast from Veracruz to Campeche. At Xicalango three enemy *piraguas* came out to reconnoiter the approaching armada but, on sizing up its force, beat a hasty retreat to a shore position. Pursuing in launches, the Spaniards burned their huts and boats, killing one man and wounding several. Deprived of further success by the jungle, they sailed on to the Laguna de Términos, in the mouth of which lay a small ship that promptly made off into the lagoon. Proceeding toward Campeche, they jumped a *piragua* manned by a mixed crew of Englishmen, Frenchmen, and Indians. A gathering storm frustrated the chase. While awaiting better weather at Campeche, Vidobro benefited from a stroke of luck when a Dutch crew approached the port with a recent prize; she was the brigantine that had eluded him at the Laguna de Términos. The pirate captain, taken utterly by surprise, yielded readily. Vidobro's armada took ship and crew to Veracruz, putting a happy ending on the sixty-five-day voyage.

The Dutch captives swelled the population of the Veracruz jail, already full to overflowing with pirates from the Gulf's far corners. The Dutch captain, John Lucas, turned state's evidence, giving an account of all the buccaneers operating against Spain in the Gulf and Caribbean and the prizes they had taken. There was a bit of news of Captain Roque—here called "Roche Inglés"—who was still on the loose; also of Diego Grillo, the renegade mulatto from Havana, still ranging the Caribbean from Havana to Cartagena.

From Lucas's testimony, Hita drew up a tabular listing of French and English positions in the Indies. The French held eleven islands with 33,800 inhabitants; the English, nine with 51,400. The other pirates in the prison verified Lucas's account, and advantages were seen in pressing the Dutch captain into Spanish service. He thus escaped the garrote that was the likely fate of his fellow jailbirds.

Vidobro's voyages failed to curtail the foreigners' operations on the Campeche-Tabasco coast. No longer content with coastal raiding, they were sailing up the rivers to strike places like Villahermosa, Tacotalpa, and Acayuca, plundering and burning villages along the way. The logwood cutters were denuding the jungle flatlands of valuable hardwood and shooting cattle to load their ships with meat and hides. When summer rains curbed such activities by flooding the marshy coast, they careened their ships on the remote beaches as boldly as if in their home ports; they pillaged neighboring haciendas and robbed village churches of their sacred ornaments. The list of atrocities went on and on.

These troublous times in the Gulf are chronicled from the English point of view by William Dampier. That inveterate sea rover made voyages in 1675 and 1676 from Jamaica to the Laguna de Términos, where 250 men, mostly Englishmen, were cutting dyewood. On his second voyage Dampier decided to stay and work with the woodcutters; from that sojourn comes his unparalleled description of their lifestyle.

On Saturdays this hardbitten crew forsook its wearing labor to go hunting for cattle. In June, 1676, this routine was broken by a storm that laid waste the logwood camps and spoiled provisions. The men were forced to "range about" for their sustenance, scouring the coast from the Isla de Trist (Isla del Carmen) to the Río Alvarado. Visiting all the rivers, as Dampier tells it, they "made many Descents into the Country among the Villages there, where we got Indian Corn to eat with the Beef, and other Flesh that we got by the way, or Manatee and Turtle."

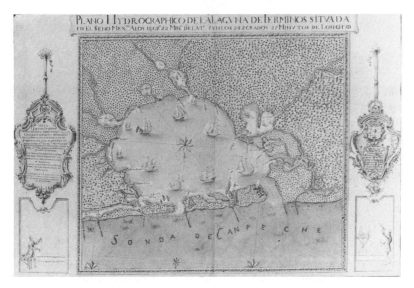

Fig. 13. Laguna de Términos, hangout of pirates and logwood cutters. Courtesy Museo Naval.

The adventure culminated in an assault on the town of Alvarado. In two barks, each with thirty men, the freebooters negotiated the shoaly river mouth where Pedro de Alvarado had sprung the bottom of his ship in 1518. For five hours they laid siege to the bastion atop the hill to the left of the channel entrance. Eleven of the attackers were slain before the defenders yielded after sundown. In the interim the townspeople carried away all their valuables in small boats.

Next day the invaders scoured the town for provisions. After killing and salting thirty beeves, they availed themselves of salted fish, corn, and poultry for their larders and, for their amusement, brilliantly hued tame parrots of which Dampier says "there was scarce a Man but what sent aboard one or two."

Their pilfering was cut short the second day when seven ships of the Armada de Barlovento from Veracruz, sailing large before a west wind, took shape out of the rainy morning. The two barks, still loaded with logwood, barely had time to get out over the bar before the *almiranta, Toro,* brought her ten guns to bear, and seventy musketeers on each of the other vessels began pouring out fire from bullhide barricades. Once clear of the bar, the buccaneers jettisoned their logwood as *Toro* bore down on their quarter. Maneuvering to windward while the larger ships struggled against the current, the pirates slipped away. Voyaging back to Trist, they searched the bays for "munjack," the tarry substance washed up by the sea in lumps of three to thirty pounds, the likes of which Soto's men had used to caulk their leaky brigantines on the northern Gulf shore in 1543.

Depredations on the Spanish coastal towns continued throughout the decade. The Laguna de Términos was known as a veritable nest of pirates and poachers, yet the armada seemed powerless to drive them out. The situation was galvanized somewhat when, at three o'clock the morning of July 10, 1678, 160 English and French freebooters based at the lagoon fell upon long-suffering Campeche.

The subaltern and five soldiers who stood guard in the plaza were overcome without a shot fired. No warning sounded to arouse the sleeping town. Seizing the *castillo,* the marauders divided themselves into squads to sack the houses, attacking the Spaniards in their beds; then the government buildings, which housed not only important official correspondence but also 4,027 marks of silver on deposit from Panama and another 2,300 pesos for the military payroll. The *sargento mayor* and a captain of the presidio were taken captives, as were members of the local *cabildo* and many citizens' families. The captives also included some Indians and numerous mulatto women, without regard for whether they were free or slave, to be sold at the Laguna de Términos and sent to Jamaica and other English and French possessions.

Later in the day, a Spanish ship approaching the port saw the smoke of burning houses and turned off for Veracruz to sound the alarm. The viceroy, Archbishop Payo Enríquez Afán de Rivera, sent a small ship to reconnoiter the coast. Fearing an Indian revolt, he later dispatched a hundred soldiers to beef up Campeche's defenses. In the painful post mortem, there were complaints of the poor state of the town's guard, allegations of military mismanagement, and suggestions that the invaders had been aided by a local Judas. The Veracruz governor, Sancho Fernández de Angulo y Sandoval, alibied to the king for not having dislodged the foreigners from the Laguna de Términos, alleging foot-dragging by the viceroy.

Meanwhile, piracy was spreading across the Gulf; no longer was the Laguna de Términos the freebooters' only refuge, as the cadre of cutthroats extended itself along the northern Gulf shore. The pirates and their Spanish counterparts—those who engaged in contraband trading or raiding among the colonies—were building a familiarity with the Gulf that was woefully lacking among legitimate Spanish maritime elements.

During the 1670s the Spanish freebooters, often with licenses from local governors, waged a brutal, unofficial war on English shipping. They justified their piratical acts with claims that their victims were carrying logwood from Honduras or Yucatán, contraband for any but Spanish vessels. Their role, though of greater importance than has been ascribed, was in truth largely defensive. The motley pirate host of diverse nationalities held the initiative.

From 1672 to 1678, during France's war with the Netherlands, most of the depredations on the Spanish colonies stemmed from the English. In the Caribbean, France sicced her *flibustiers* on the Dutch, thereby bringing the West India Company to ruin. That conflict ended, the French corsairs again focused on the Spanish colonies, and piracy rose to new heights of infamy.

When, in 1675, Pablo de Hita Salazar left his post at Veracruz to govern Florida, he may have felt a sense of relief. The new assignment, however, offered as many problems as the old one. Since English colonists had landed at the mouth of the Ashley River of South Carolina in 1670, they had presented a growing menace to Spanish control over the Florida Indians. The early threat was from inland traders, but the sea rovers soon added to the pressure.

Hita, reading the signs, reopened the longstanding issue of defending the port of Apalache. The Crown responded to Hita's plan, instructing him by two royal *cédulas*, 1676 and 1677, to take steps toward fortifying the location but failing to provide the means. Before he could act, French and English pirates sailed quietly into the defenseless estuary, killed a number of Indians, and captured two missionaries and the corporal of the guard. The raiders made off with the loaded frigate used to supply San Agustín.

About the same time, in June, 1677, buccaneers surprised Juan de la Rosa in the mouth of the "Puerto de San Martín" (Suwannee River) and captured his loaded vessel. The pirate ship, one of those that had

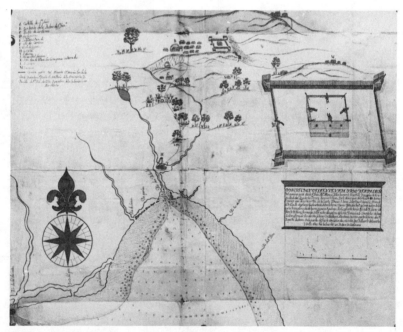

Fig. 14. San Marcos de Apalache, 1706. Courtesy AGI.

menaced San Agustín in the past, hung about the Florida coast all summer, prowling the Bahama Channel and the eastern Gulf of Mexico.

Hita perceived the danger in the pirates' growing familiarity with the coast; they could not help realizing its fertility and potential abundance. Should they avail themselves of a Gulf port, they would be in position to harass the Spanish fleets and rob the treasure galleons.

Considering the long stretch of unoccupied coast west of Apalache, he pondered the problem of defending it against increasingly obvious and multiple threats. His appeal, joined with a memorial taken to Spain by Fray Juan Moreno, was underscored by the pirate raids. His efforts at last bore fruit. The Junta General de las Indias, on October 12, 1677, enforced by a royal *cédula*, instructed him to choose a site for fortifications and submit a specific plan, cost estimate, and area map. He was ordered also to report on the feasibility of opening a road between San Agustín and Mexico, the distances and Indian tribes involved, and how the project might be made to pay for itself. Hita embarked on the endeavor with "all the earnestness I have been able to muster."

His map (not in evidence) extended to the province of Mauvila (Mobila) and beyond. It showed the places between Apalache and Apalachicola that offered settlement possibilities. The distance from San Agustín to Mexico, the governor advised, had been estimated at "little more than three hundred leagues." To extend the Florida settlements to join those of Mexico, he proposed a thorough exploration of the intervening coast. With Apalache fortified, a brigantine manned by thirty men should be outfitted there to run the coast toward Tampico, sounding the rivers and bays. Thus the possibility of opening a road could be assessed more accurately.

But then Hita sounded the death knell for his own plan. The king had asked for ideas on how the project might be carried out without expense to the Crown, expecting that he would leap at the opportunity to conquer and settle this wilderness as Narváez, Soto, and Menéndez had done. But Hita, having confronted the realities of the Florida frontier for three years while noting the failures and frustrations of more than a century, was not buying. "I find no means whatsoever that it can be so," he responded, "because these provinces collect no tribute as New Spain does." Florida enjoyed no income from its produce. The families so often requested—from Yucatán or the Canaries, to raise cotton and grain—had never come. Yet if the Crown could see its way clear to ask the royal officials at Havana to outfit the ship, Hita offered, the project still might be carried out; once settled, the whole coast could benefit from prosperous farms and limitless natural resources.

A note appended to the document by the Council of the Indies reveals that "this same report and plan" had been sent to the New Spain viceroy, but for the present no expenses were to be supplied. Once again the Crown turned its back on a proposal that might have altered its destiny. But by this time, with the inept Hapsburg rule at its nadir, the forces of decline were overpowering.

As Hita ended his five years as Florida governor in 1680, to be succeeded by Juan Márquez Cabrera, the English were pressing the jurisdiction from San Jorge to Mobila. Allying themselves with the enemy Indians and supplying them with firearms, Hita advised, they threatened Spanish control over the mission converts. In the coming decades his apprehension would be well justified.

Hardly was the wooden fort of San Marcos de Apalache completed when pirates struck a second time and burned it to the ground. The freebooters sailed stealthily into the river in the predawn of March 20, 1682, seized a merchant vessel from Havana, and captured the fort's meager garrison. The rapacious sea rovers, both French and English and some 400 strong, had established a base on the Anclote Keys, near present Tarpon Springs, Florida. Repeatedly, they raided ships plying from Apalache to Havana and those en route from Veracruz and Tierra Firme to Spain. During the first half of 1682, they captured seven Spanish vessels and raided Tomás Méndez Márquez's hacienda up the Suwannee River.

The record of pirate activity on the northern Gulf shore is sketchy. Yet the scattered, fragmentary sources leave no doubt that the period's most knowledgeable pilots of this particular coast were among the French pirates harboring in western Hispaniola (present Haiti). It was they who would provide the hydrographical information utilized in the first serious effort by one of Spain's principal rivals to plant a colony in the Gulf of Mexico.

In the spring of 1683 a pirate from Saint-Domingue (French Santo Domingo) named Du Chesne ran the northern Gulf coast as far west as Tampico, where his rowdies went ashore to commit their customary rape and pillage. Few details are at hand on either the voyage or the attack; but the venture of this professional gave rise a year later to another by a bunch of amateurs. The latter group ran afoul of the Armada de Barlovento, the resolve of which had been steeled in the interim by the rape of Veracruz.

The Veracruz raid was the most flagrant of all the pirate atrocities yet committed in the Gulf. Having set a high-water mark of daring and cruelty, it is the one best remembered and most often told. It marked the entry into the Gulf, as far as definite knowledge goes, of two of the most dreaded and feared cutthroats of all the buccaneer fleets: Michel de Grammont, a Frenchman, and Laurens de Graff, probably of Netherlands origin. Graff is still held by some authorities to have been a renegade Spanish mulatto whose rightful name was Lorenzo Jácome, more popularly known as Lorencillo. He is said to have changed his allegiance to serve under both English and French flags. The Spaniards reserved a special hatred for such turncoats, whose expert knowledge gave the pirates a key to the Spanish possessions, and "Lorencillo" was the most hated and most feared of them all. The name, synonymous with piracy, was linked to many atrocious deeds in which he had no part. Mexican historians even yet attribute to him the two Tampico raids, 1683 and 1684, neither of which was his doing. Yet whenever unidentified sails appeared off the Mexican coast, the colonists were wont to whisper with awe and dread the hated name, "Lorencillo."

The Veracruz raiders, comprising one thousand men on eight ships, were from Saint-Domingue, principally the island cesspool, Petit Goâve. Besides Grammont and Graff, the captains included Nicholas Van Horn and three other Hollanders, two Englishmen, and one other Frenchman. Crowding most of the men into two vessels, they stole into the port before dawn on May 18, 1683, and seized the poorly guarded fortress of San Juan de Ulúa. Taking the sleeping town completely by surprise, they captured 150 of the leading citizens and held them for ransom. The rest of the townspeople, of all ages and both sexes, were herded into the parish church. The buccaneers then roamed the streets, breaking into each house and taking every item of value. It is said that Lorencillo, not satisfied with the loot, placed a barrel of powder in the church and threatened to blow up the edifice with all the people in it unless they delivered their hidden valuables.

For almost four days the people were kept imprisoned without food, jammed together so tightly they could not sleep, wallowing in their own excrement. Some 300 died.

While the rape of the city was in progress, the fleet from Spain, a dozen sail or more, hove into view. The pirates hastened their withdrawal to the Isla de Sacrificios, within sight of the town, to await delivery of ransoms. Van Horn and Lorencillo crossed swords over division of the spoils, and Van Horn was nicked on the wrist. He died of gangrene two weeks later.

Aboard the incoming ships were twenty-four Franciscan priests, destined to establish the missionary college of Santa Cruz de Querétaro and to carry the gospel north into Texas. Going ashore in the devastated town, they found their services needed immediately. The maimed and dying lay unattended—by one cleric's account—while the living moaned in anguish at the loss of their young women, borne away by the pirates to satisfy their lust, then to be sold into slavery. The missionaries consoled and confessed the living and administered final rites and proper burial to the dead.

By the time news of the attack reached the capital on May 21, it was almost over. A wealthy *encomendero* and *corregidor* of Mexico, Fernando Altamirano de Velasco Legazpi y Castilla, Conde de Santiago Catimaya, gathered with lightning speed a force of two thousand men. They marched from Mexico on May 24, not knowing that the pirates already had sailed away to the remote islands of the Caribbean to count their loot, swill their rum, and plan their next strike.

Lorencillo is still remembered in Veracruz; on the waterfront near the Hotel Mar y Tierra is a bistro that bears his name and the subscription, "since 1683." He was remembered, too, the very next spring, when a pirate fleet lay becalmed in Veracruz waters for four days awaiting a favorable wind to carry it again upon the town. It finally withdrew. Ironically, Graff was not involved. He had declined a part in the operation, which was headed by his partner-in-crime, Grammont.

Lorencillo's dreaded name again was on Spanish lips when a few days after the Veracruz sighting, in late April, 1684, a different band of pirates went ashore at Tampico. This time the Armada de Barlovento under General Andrés Ochoa de Zárate closed in on the port and captured a small frigate and a sloop with 104 men; 26 Hollanders, a Spaniard, 3 Negroes, 4 Florida Indians, and 70 Englishmen. The record consists of testimony taken from 14 of the foremost leaders, who later were condemned to die by the garrote. The fate of the others is not known. At least one, a pilot called "Juan Poule" (John Poole), entered Spanish service. By his special knowledge of the ports and bays of the northern Gulf, he was able to render valuable aid to Spanish explorers for several years. He also served as an interpreter in the interrogation of English prisoners. English defectors to the Spanish cause, identifiable by the phonetics of their names, were as common as Spanish to the English. The interpreter for interrogating the Tampico prisoners, for example, was an *alférez* called Juan de Lenzi—probably John Lindsay; he was standing by while General Ochoa questioned the one Spanish renegade among the captives. Francisco de los Reyes, native of Sanlúcar de Barrameda, may not have been a pirate, but he certainly had got himself mixed up with the wrong crowd: the assortment of Dutch and English adventurers who called themselves Presbyterians. Asked what a Presbyterian was, Reyes said he did not know. For the interrogators, Lenzi offered his own explanation. A Presbyterian, he said, was the same as a corsair. Reyes was to die with his companions.

Only half a dozen or so of the 104 men had previously followed a course of piracy. The expedition had begun as a quest for sunken treasure, and circumstances or bad company had led them to the plight they were in. But all had been sea wanderers of a sort, perhaps borderline pirates, until this venture carried them over the edge. Their assorted backgrounds, before they had come together in the Bahamas seven months previously, reflect the curious maritime life of the seventeenth century. They exemplify a particular type of seafarer that was quite common.

Reyes, age thirty, had been captured by a French privateer eight or nine years before and kept in servitude three years while the ship raided Dutch vessels in the Caribbean. Finally put ashore in New England, he lived in "Yarca"—New York—another five years before escaping to sign on *Isabella*, the 40-ton frigate captained by Samuel Juanes (Johns), at Providence (in the Bahamas).

Johns, himself now a prisoner in the Veracruz jail, was from Boston. A New Englander by birth, he had been to Barbados and gone turtling around Little Cayman. In Providence he found the 55-ton sloop *Mariante*, and the pilot Ricardo Quetre (Richard Carter) laid out his get-rich-quick scheme for salvaging sunken treasure in the Mimbres Cays.

Carter, as it developed, had been a prisoner in the French pirate fleet of Captain Du Chesne, from Saint-Dominigue, when it sacked Tampico the previous year. When the silver he promised failed to turn up at Los Mimbres, he offered an alternative: a sunken treasure ship in a certain bay in latitude 27° (28° in Johns's statement), marked by a floating cask, of which he had heard in Tampico. The two small ships made their way into the Gulf by the Florida Straits and sailed up the west side of the peninsula.

Johns testified that the four Florida Indians they carried as divers had been given him by the English governor at Providence. Yet he admitted having burned San Marcos de Apalache, after four or five men he had sent ashore were attacked by natives and two of them killed: "For this reason, all those on the ships went ashore and burned the village."

Sailing west through the Gulf, the would-be salvagers came to the bay they sought, but the cask could not be found. Johns's frigate, sailing into the lagoon several leagues, encountered some Indians, and members of the crew tried in vain to convey by signs what they were looking for. From later developments, it is known that the bay was Matagorda, on the Texas coast, and the Indians were Karankawan. The treasure hunters missed finding a place in history by approximately a year; had their venture come that much later, they might have encountered the French colonists landed there in February, 1685, by the Sieur de la Salle.

Failing in their quest at Matagorda Bay, the venturers dropped down to 25° and searched another, probably the Laguna Madre where it opens behind the Boca de San Rafael some distance south of the Río Grande. Supplies dwindled and starvation threatened. Again, Richard Carter offered a solution. Tampico, he recalled, was just down the coast; it was a defenseless Indian village, where they could obtain everything needed. Driven by hunger, the others followed his lead.

The precise sequence thereafter is obscured by the dissembling of the deponents, each trying to save his own skin. Yet it is clear that the vessels anchored before the town late in April, and most of the men went ashore in a manner bearing all the earmarks of piracy. One old pirate, name not given, drowned while making the landing. The invaders rounded up the townspeople, robbed them of their valuables, and herded them into the church, from which they took the sacred vessels and ornaments. The spoils were divided among the men. No harm was intended, they claimed; the capture was only to assure that they got the supplies they needed. But at some point a squad of men fired their muskets into a motte and killed a local citizen.

The Armada de Barlovento at the time was anchored at Veracruz. When General Ochoa received word of the raid on May 4, he made sail immediately, arriving on the scene three days later to catch the salvagers-turned-pirates redhanded. On June 5 at Veracruz, he began interrogating the leaders to establish their guilt and send them to the garrote.

It was a motley crew that gave testimony. Some had been involved in earlier brushes with the Spaniards. John Tudor, for example, had been captured at the Laguna de Términos by "Castro's ship," brought to Veracruz, and sent to Cádiz before being returned to his native England. The Hall brothers, John and Steven, had been sailing in the Bahama Channel—on an earlier salvage expedition to Los Mimbres—when they were captured by a ship from Havana. Impressed into the Armada de Barlovento, they jumped ship at Curaçao and escaped to Jamaica and thence to Providence. Pressed for any knowledge of the 1683 Veracruz raid, they offered one fact: while they were in Providence, a pirate ship brought in prisoners taken in that affair to be sold as slaves; three days later the governor learned about it and chased the vessel away.

It was common knowledge that two members of the salvage expedition had taken part in the Veracruz strike. One was the man drowned at Tampico; the other was James Harleston, a native of County Cork, Ireland. Harleston himself offered no denial. In the crew of a Captain Daniels, he had received 800 pesos as his share of the loot. When the ship was lost later in a Caribbean storm, Harleston was saved by a ship bound for Virginia, whence he sailed for Providence and joined the treasure hunters.

Several deponents indicated four others as known pirates: Richard Reed, Thomas Beck, one Alexander, and Steven Ibens. Reed, who admitted having sailed as a pirate for nine of his thirty-two years, was typical of the lot. As a buccaneer he had prowled about Campeche and the Laguna de Términos, and had taken prizes off Cartagena and Caracas. But while readily implicating himself, he claimed no knowledge of other pirates in the group. None admitted knowing anything at all about Lorencillo.

Various ones sought to alibi the raid or themselves, but there was one key witness against them: a free Negro named Cristóbal de Campos, who had been seized by pirates on the Río de Tlacotalpán (near present Alvarado, Veracruz) eight years previously, in the 1676 raid described by William Dampier. Still a prisoner on the salvage expedition, Campos had suffered considerable abuse. He now had his day in court. As the Spaniards paraded the pirate leaders before him, he destroyed, one by one, their pleas of innocence. On June 9 the death sentence was pronounced against the 14. They were conducted through the Veracruz streets on pack mules while a crier chanted the nature of their crime and punishment, and thence to the marina, where the garrote awaited them. At the last minute nine of the "heretics" accepted the Catholic faith and were returned to the jail to be baptized and confessed; their sentences were carried out later—with one exception. As John Markham, twenty-two-year-old Barbados native, was about to have the cord tightened around his neck, a priest intervened. "Then all the priests present, like the religious and clerics, came forth and lifted up the said Juan Marcan and carried him toward the college of the Company of Jesus." The guards were powerless to interfere with the ecclesiastics. "On the other eight the sentence was executed, the garrote applied until they were naturally dead."

The other prisoners were spared only because of a royal *cédula* of February, 1684, stipulating that captive pirates should be sent to Spain. Viceregal officials had considered the matter and ruled that the captains and principal leaders might be executed, the rest kept in fetters until passage was available. More than three years later, the remaining Tampico pirates still had not arrived in Spain. Charles II asked the new viceroy, Monclova, to advise him of their disposition; if they were still in Mexico, he should do with them "what is provided by the latest decrees." The final outcome is not known.

The Negro Campos was restored to freedom. Two black slaves from one of the ships were sold at auction with the vessels, artillery, and rigging.

In the meantime, one other pirate raid with far-reaching consequences stood in the offing. Pirates or privateers had raided virtually every Gulf coast settlement of significance and some with hardly any importance at all. In the previous decade, freebooters of one stripe or another had sacked Alvarado, Campeche, Veracruz, Apalache, and Tampico, not to mention the lesser Tabasco towns between Coatzacoalcos and the Laguna de Términos. Campeche's turn had come up again. From its new affliction came word of developments that would influence the Gulf's future into eternity.

In the spring of 1685 the pilot major of the Indies, Admiral Gaspar de Palacios, on a voyage to salvage a treasure cargo lost on the Caribbean banks, was driven by storm into the Yucatán Channel. Seeking shelter behind Cabo Catoche, the Spanish ship stumbled upon eight pirate vessels at anchor. The buccaneers hoisted sail and gave chase. Palacios, crowding on every inch of canvas, ran west into the Gulf, escaping at nightfall to make port on June 24 at Campeche and give warning. He then proceeded to Veracruz and dispatched news to Viceroy Paredes on July 2.

On July 6 some 750 pirates led by Grammont and Graff landed at Campeche and overran the town, while another 550 men stood by on twenty-three ships. Angered that almost everything of value had been sent off to the inland wilds, the raiders vented their wrath in a fifty-seven-day orgy. They burned the fort and took 200 prisoners, 9 of whom were hanged. When help came at last from Veracruz, the Spanish governor marched up the coast with 350 men to lay an ambush for Grammont's cutthroats, killing many. The freebooters, their mission a signal failure, began their withdrawal.

Lorencillo, the pirate prototype, sailed from Campeche on September 3, coasting northward. Beyond the point, sails appeared; General Ochoa's armada closed with booming cannon, answered in kind from the pirate fleet. Missiles tore into Lorencillo's rigging. The armada overhauled and boarded a pirate vessel, a Spanish prize properly called *Nuestra Señora de Regla*. A pirate sloop burst into flames, and Spanish ships gathered in her crew. Closing fast on Lorencillo's command ship, Ochoa's crew suffered a terrible accident that thwarted total victory: a cannon exploded, killing three gunners and maiming another five. In the moment of confusion, Laurens de Graff—his contribution to Spain's woes still not finished—righted his vessel and slipped from Ochoa's grasp.

Even so, the Armada de Barlovento counted one enemy ship destroyed and another captured, with 120 prisoners. It was the interrogation of these captives that altered Spanish priorities, touching off a new wave of discovery, exploration, and settlement continuing well into the next century. Among them were six men who had embarked on the path of piracy by an interesting route: having sailed from France with a colonizing expedition headed by the Sieur de La Salle, bound for the Gulf of Mexico, they jumped ship at Petit Goâve. By this time, the Spaniards concluded, the French must be well settled on a river called Micipipi, wherever that might be, in prime position for harassing the Spanish colonies.

For a century, Spanish energies for extending exploration around the Gulf had been siphoned off by other concerns. Foreign rivals and voracious pirates moved into the void. For years the intruders, the pirates especially, had held all the aces: superior intelligence, larger forces and faster ships, and more intimate knowledge of the hidden bays and inlets offering refuge—plus the capacity to instill fear.

The poachers had no authority from, and often no loyalty to, any government; despite their outlawry, the Gulf of Mexico had effectively remained a Spanish sea, unblemished by any legitimate colony of another European nation. But the buccaneers—notably those seized following the Campeche raid—were harbingers of change. The challenge posed by the La Salle invasion was clear; the intrusion brought to sharp focus Spain's neglect in preserving the Gulf's inner sanctum, and the dearth of her knowledge concerning the unguarded coasts. If the threat was to be eliminated, exploration of the northern shore—having long lain in limbo—must be resumed with urgency.

The hour was late. Spain thenceforth must share her pretended realm and admit a partner to the enterprise of discovery. It was a narrow choice, as devout Spaniards were wont to view it, between French Catholic and English heretic. The rebirth of reconnaissance was French inspired, and it was the French who would help to nurture it. Never again would the Gulf of Mexico be so exclusively a Spanish sea.

If one would weep for the injustice done Spain, let him remember that she had her choices, which were duly exercised. If he would fault her for choosing unwisely, let him consider that none of her rivals, given the same options, would have chosen differently.

The Discovery, in a practical sense, had opened another world all too vast for any one nation to cope with; there was hardly a chance, even at the outset, that all the New World could become Spanish; that Spain alone could explore, conquer, and defend it against all comers.

Spain's practical choices, though fixed by accident, are the same ones she would have made had she possessed all the facts. What nation, for example, would have turned its back on the riches of Mexico and Peru in favor of settling a wide expanse of forest and plain offering scant evidence of any great wealth? Such has been the choice of the ages, by men and nations: instant rewards in preference to lasting benefits for posterity. The eventual loss by Spain of the territories she had discovered may represent a miscarriage of justice. Yet the clock cannot be turned back; old wrongs cannot be put right by new ones.

Was there, after all, justice in Spain's sense of having been divinely chosen for her role of stewardship? Any attempt to assess the nature of that "calling" can lead to theological quicksand. Yet it seems clear that Iberia's conditioning for the task was unique, its geographical position advantageous, its spirit willing. Perhaps the difficulty lay in the interpretation of the call, if such it was. The failing was not peculiarly Spanish but simply human; man's pride has obscured his vision from time immemorial.

Was the sacred trust betrayed? Catholic historians, at least, have not been prone to see it so. Possibly the spread of Catholicism in the New World *was* the fulfillment of the charge. Yet the holy task surely was meant to transcend the elimination of human sacrifice and other barbaric practices among the "heathens" and the extension of the gospel in mere numbers of converts. The beam in the Spaniard's eye was the same as the one afflicting all mankind: he bowed to two masters, God and gold. The syndrome should be easily recognizable, for it is everywhere in evidence today. The warning sounds grow louder and louder; in the hesitancy of its choice between the two, humanity stands to find itself with neither.

SOURCES AND NOTES

Two pirates-turned-author broaden the picture of Spain's warfare with the pirates in the Gulf that is available from documents: John Esquemeling (*The Buccaneers of America*) and William Dampier (*Voyages*). While the two complement each other, Dampier's account must be considered the more valuable. Esquemeling tends to romanticize events and personages, giving grounds for suspicion that he harkened too much to lively tales told in pirate hangouts while the rum was flowing freely. His account of "Roche Brasiliano's" shipwreck episode, for example (p. 70), not only has it misplaced but also attributes to the pirates a valorous and victorious stand against the Spaniards that is nowise borne out by the formal depositions taken in Mérida.

Dampier (2:155–56) relates graphically the transition from privateer to pirate. The privateers, having lived by plundering the Spaniards in wartime, were "put to their shifts" when peace was made. They must either give up their sea roving or go into the Bay of Campeche for logwood. Finding wood-cutting a dry business, many took to hunting but still missed the challenge of privateering. They therefore made sallies among the "Indian towns" to plunder and bring away women "to serve them at their huts," sending the husbands to be sold in Jamaica. The usual fate of the pirates and poachers was to be captured and taken to Mexico and sold into servitude themselves. It was not his business, Dampier allows, to determine how right or wrong the English were in taking logwood from Spanish possessions.

The Roque Affair

The record of this episode is essentially complete in a single document: Fructos Delgado, "Información sacada de los prisoneros del naufragio de la fragata del Capitán Roque," Mérida de Yucatán, Dec. 29, 1669 (AGI, Mexico 559). It includes the testimony of "Juan Yon," "Juan Boc," and the Indian Juan Carreño. Seldom is such a document so complete within itself. Whether or not Esquemeling's assessment of Roque's brutality is correct, his reputation for such was known to the Spanish interrogators, who asked Young if it were true that Roque never gave quarter to his Spanish captives. Young, of course, denied it. The two pirate-authors enlarge the picture in several respects:

The Campeche Salines: Dampier (2:144–45) locates the salt works 20 leagues north of the town. When the salt coagulated in May or June, he says, the Spaniards sent Indians to rake it ashore and gather it into a great pyramid; then grass and weeds were burned on top to make the salt form a crust to protect it from weathering.

The salt was loaded on barks destined for ports around the Gulf. The salt harbor was often visited by English logwood cutters en route to the Laguna de Términos, and any Spanish vessel found there was likely to be seized, her Indian crewmen sold into slavery. The Jamaica governors were unaware of such doings; Spaniards dared not complain, for they were wont to take any English ship caught "in these parts," even those bound for England with sugar from Jamaica. The ships were sold at Havana, their crews "imprisoned without redress."

The watchtowers: several like the one to which Carreño fled were situated along the coast north of Mérida, from Dzilam to Sisal, says Dampier (2:118). "Some built from the Ground with Timber, others only little Cages placed on a Tree, big enough for one or two Men to sit in, with a Ladder to go up and down." They were manned by Indians from nearby villages.

Piraguas: the term can mean either a dugout canoe, or a sailing vessel of shallow draft, equipped with oars. The latter, being highly maneuverable, says Esquemeling (*Buccaneers*, 89), was the craft most often used by pirates of the Indies; it was capable of gaining the advantage over the large and cumbersome ships of the Spanish fleet by coming in so close that the larger vessel's guns could not be lowered enough to fire directly upon it. Additionally, it could dart into shallow bays where warships of the Armada de Barlovento could not pursue. The Spaniards adapted this type of vessel to coastal exploration in 1686, when seeking La Salle's colony.

Spanish Countermeasures

Pablo de Hita Salazar's 1674 report from Veracruz ("Relación de las noticias de enemigos franceses y ingleses que corren esta costa") is in AGI, Mexico 559. Summarizing the enemy activity, it relates Vidobro's voyages and the disposition of the Dutch prisoners, and contains the tabular summary of French and English positions in the West Indies. The report is dated just a year before Dampier's first venture into the Gulf and two years before the incident at Alvarado that he relates.

The 1678 Campeche raid and the Spanish reaction to it are treated in a number of documents in AGI, Mexico 1010: Pedro Enríquez de Noboa to the Crown, Campeche, July 27; Payo Enríquez Afán de Rivera, "Carta del Virrey de Nueva España dando cuenta del saco de Campeche," Mexico, Dec. 28; Gonzalo Borrallo Cantú to the Conde de Medellín, Campeche, Dec. 28; and Sancho Fernández de Angulo y Sandoval to the Crown, Nueva Veracruz, Aug. 16.

An example of the Spanish freebooter raiding English shipping is found in the "Testimonios" of Diego de Castro and Jorge Nicolás given at Havana, Jan. 2, 1686, concerning operations of Juan Corso's galley (AGI, Mexico 616, University of Texas transcripts).

Hita and Florida

The documentation is profuse, much of it in AGI, Santo Domingo 839: Pablo de Hita Salazar to the queen, San Agustín, Aug. 24, 1675; Philip II, *real cédula* to Hita, June 20, 1776; Hita to the king (concerning the Apalache port), Sept. 6, 1677; "Da quenta a V.M. de la entrada que hizo un pirata francés y inglés en el puerto de San Marcos," Sept. 6, 1677; Report of Junta, Oct. 12, 1677; royal *cédula* to Hita, Nov. 5, 1677; Hita to the king, San Agustín, Nov. 10, 1678.

Manuel de la Cendoya (to the Crown, San Agustín, Nov. 6, 1671, ibid., no. 14) had urged fortification of the port and extolled the assets of Apalache from the standpoint of productivity and defense; he urged importation of Canary Islanders to settle it. Hita took up the settlement plan in his letter to the queen of June 15, 1675, modifying it with the suggestion that Indian weavers

410   *The Building Rivalry*

be brought from Campeche to utilize cotton grown in Florida (Reding, "Plans for Colonization and Defense").

See also the testimony of Juan de la Rosa in Domingo de Leturiondo, "Visita de las provincias de Timuqua y Apalache hecha por comisión del Señor don Pablo de Hita Salazar," San Agustín, Nov. 29, 1677 (Stetson Collection from AGI, microfilm reel 14); Hita to the king, San Agustín, May 14, 1680 (in Serrano y Saenz, *Documentos históricos*, 216–19); Joseph Fernández de Córdova to the Crown, Havana, July 8, 1682, and "Autos del saqueo de Apalache," Havana, July 5, 1682 (Stetson Collection, microfilm reel 16); and Mark F. Boyd, "The Fortifications at San Marcos de Apalache."

Hita (in his letter to the king of Nov. 10, 1678) says he had heard of a pilot at Tampico who had explored the coast as far as the Río de Magdalena— probably meaning the Río Grande in this instance—and found it with a deep channel 70 leagues inland. The reports, he says, placed the Magdalena 80 leagues from Bahía (Río) del Espíritu Santo, and Espíritu Santo 90 leagues from Apalache (present St. Mark's).

All this discussion concerning the opening of a road between Florida and Mexico, interestingly enough, occurred prior to the royal *cédula* of Dec. 10, 1678, in which the Crown took note of the treasonable activities of Diego de Peñalosa in Paris. Peñalosa, former Spanish governor of New Mexico, was attempting to interest Louis XIV in a scheme to conquer for France the provinces of Quivira and Teguayo (AGI, Mexico 616, University of Texas transcripts). It is generally held that the subsequent proposals of the Sieur de la Salle for invading Mexico had their basis in Peñalosa's plan.

The Veracruz Raid

Concerning deeds attributed to "Lorencillo" that were not actually his, see Velasco y Mendoza, *Repoblación de Tampico*, 188, 191; Joaquín Meade, *Documentos inéditos*, 81. Meade heads one document, which makes no mention of this particular pirate, "Sack of Tampico by Lorencillo."

Dampier (*Voyages*, 2:221) says Veracruz "was taken by the Privateers about the Year 85 under the Conduct of one John Russel an old Logwood-Cutter that had formerly been taken by the Spaniards and sent to Mexico; where . . . he escaped to La Vera Cruz; and afterwards managed this Expedition." So far, I have not been able to reconcile this statement with the 1683 raid or a later one.

This episode, mentioned in summary in numerous places, tends to be distorted or presented sketchily. I know of no definitive account, in Spanish or English. J. Ignacio Rubio Mañé (*Introducción al estudio de los virreyes de Nueva España, 1535–1746*, 2:118–24) reviews the various accounts. He notes that "only the Negro men and women, free and slave," were taken by the pirates, who later attempted to ransom them at Coatzacoalcos.

The attempt from Mexico to relieve Veracruz is told by the Conde de

Santiago in a report to the Crown, Mexico, July 26, 1683 (AGI, Mexico 91, ramo 3).

The Tampico Raids

The naval commander conducting La Salle to the Gulf (Taneguy Le Gallois de Beaujeu), reporting to the Marquis de Seignelay, tells of meeting the pirate captain Du Chesne in Petit Goâve and learning of his sack of Tampico (Pierre Margry, ed., *Découvertes et établissements des Français dans l'ouest et dans le sud de l'Amérique septentrionale*, 2 : 488–89).

The 1684 raid is recorded in "Testimonio de las declaraciones que hicieron los piratas de los que cojió la armada Real de Barlobento en el robo de Tampico y sentencia que se les dió," Veracruz, June 5, 1684; and "Testimonio de los autos del remate de las dos embarcasiones y dos negros que apresó la Real Armada de Barlobento en Tampico," May 27, 1684 (AGI, Mexico 560, ramo 1).

Mention of the English defector Juan Poule, or John Poole, is found in several Spanish documents. Juan Enríquez Barroto, in his diary of the Rivas-Iriarte voyage of 1686–87 (BRP, manuscript 2667), tells of his part in that voyage and his previous visit to Matagorda Bay with the Tampico pirates. (I have translated the Enríquez Barroto diary, for which publication is planned eventually in a volume with other translated documents pertaining to the La Salle episode.) Related to that voyage also was "Castro's ship," a Spanish privateer, by which the Englishman John Tudor had been taken prisoner. The galley of Pedro de Castro and Juan Corso was lost on the northern Gulf shore, and Enríquez Barroto tells of finding two of the crewmen among the Atákapa Indians of Louisiana. One of them was an Apalachino taken in a pirate raid at San Marcos de Apalache and left at Tampico, where "six years" previously he had been impressed by Castro as his interpreter. The "Testimonios" of Diego de Castro and Jorge Nicolás detail the ship's operations. See Weddle, *Wilderness Manhunt*, 42–45.

Concerning disposition of the Tampico pirates, see the royal *cédula* of Nov. 20, 1687, in Meade, *Documentos inéditos*, 84–85.

Campeche, 1685

Admiral Gaspar de Palacios reports on this affair (to Pedro de Oreytia y Vergara, Nov. 17, 1685, in AGI, Mexico 616 (University of Texas transcripts). See Weddle, *Wilderness Manhunt*, 5–7.

The information on La Salle is in Denis Thomas, "Declaración de Dionicio Thomas," also in AGI, Mexico 616, summarized in *Wilderness Manhunt*, 8–13.

In Sharper Focus . . .
The Conclusions

THE history of New World discovery is filled with what-ifs and maybes. Yet even with bits of positive evidence to suggest pre-Columbian landings in North America, the first discoverer for practical purposes remains Christopher Columbus. Columbus found no more than the continent's outlying islands before jumping off to Central and South America, however; believing to his death that his *nuevo mundo* actually was a part of Asia, he left much of the discovery task unfulfilled.

With spurious claimants discredited, it was Juan Ponce de León, so far as the record goes, who in 1513 made the first post-1492 discovery of the North American mainland, and he who first carried exploration into the Gulf of Mexico. Taking Sebastián de Ocampo's discovery of the Gulf one step farther, Ponce pushed wider the door to the Spanish Sea. Thereafter, the Gulf became the conduit for discovery, exploration, and settlement of the continent, unrivaled as such for years to come—the Atlantic coastal voyages and search for a northern strait notwithstanding.

Exploration was a continuing concern of the various European powers until near the end of the colonial period. This work extends only to 1685, a year that marks the beginning of great change within the Spanish Sea. The Frenchman La Salle's attempt to settle inside the Gulf brought into focus the longstanding Spanish neglect of the northern Gulf shore and gave rise to new concerns, which will be treated in a subsequent volume extending this study to the Louisiana Purchase (1803).

No work such as this could be accomplished in a lifetime without building on the efforts of countless scholars that have preceded it. Great is my debt to that vanguard of historians who tracked down, transcribed or translated, and published the original explorers' accounts that are the indispensable components of this narrative. If those pioneer researchers should be faulted, it is for being better compilers than interpreters—for occasionally being uncritical in their judgments. Yet reassessment is possible now only because their work can be viewed from a distance. Their greatest source of error lay, after all, in being first: when a significant discovery was made, immediate interpretation was required, often when there was little basis for comparison at hand.

Bit by bit, the pieces have fallen into place, yet no one has taken the pains to lay them all out side by side and consider them together. Without critical reassessment, the original errors have become ingrained and compounded in monographic studies reaching for convenient background, as well as in surveys too broad to be precise yet too specific to avoid the pitfalls.

While the interpretative capacity of the pioneer researchers was limited by a lack of comparative data, historians generally have been poor geographers and navigators. They often have been guilty of accepting primitive data at face value, of failing to make allowances for crude navigational techniques and map interpretations that do nothing more than reflect the geographical ignorance of their time. On such faulty bases, conclusions have been drawn that can be disproved with nothing more than a modern sea chart or map and a pair of dividers.

Add to these factors the proclivity, especially among writers of state and local histories, for provincialism. History is no respecter of political boundaries, and historians attempting to confine themselves to such limits assume a built-in source of distortion. One-shot local histories are probably responsible for spreading more myths than any other kind, with university professors writing solely for professional advancement running a close second.

Thus, the history of discovery and exploration has been afflicted by these three shortcomings: (1) a lack of comprehensive modern studies to assimilate and compare all the known data; (2) inaccurate maps and explorer accounts, based on the limited geographical knowledge and inadequate navigational techniques of the period; and (3) provincialism or myopia by the interpreters.

In essence, all these factors may be summed up in one: the selective viewing of the parts without a fair consideration of their relationship to the whole.

As to the present effort, there is no claim of personal infallibility, no pretense that the writer is the sole possessor of truth. Rather, an attempt is made to offer—from consideration of evidence that still is often obscure—the conclusions that seem most reasonable. They begin with the first hypothetical representation of the Gulf of Mexico before its actual discovery.

The Gulf before 1508

The notion that the Juan de la Cosa who drafted under date of 1500 a map showing Cuba as an island was different from *Santa María*'s master on the first Columbian voyage and the chartmaker on the second should be discarded; likewise the idea that the map was drawn later—or begun in 1500 and completed later. The basis for La Cosa's and other mapmakers' conceptualization of an insular Cuba before the proof cannot be fully known, but it is the judgment here that it was in part hypothetical and in part information from the island natives. While the possibility still exists that some unrecorded voyage provided the fact, the proof has not been forthcoming.

The mere absence of mention of Amerigo Vespucci's purported 1497 voyage by any other source seems reason enough for rejecting it, although there are plenty of other reasons. (Sebastian Cabot, with his claim of having run the Atlantic coast south as far as Florida—in whatever context that name is taken—belongs in a class with Vespucci.)

Vicente Yáñez Pinzón reached the western end of Cuba in 1508, probably ahead of Ocampo. The oft-stated conclusion that he did so in 1499 represents a misreading of the source.

The Florida Landings

Confusion surrounding the various Florida landings, beginning with that of Ponce de León in 1513, is more or less typical of the confusion afflicting the subject of discovery in the Gulf as a whole. A hiatus occurs in the only extant account of Ponce's voyage, from May 15 to May 23. Most of that time seems to have been spent getting around the Florida Keys from a position calculated as east of Upper Matecumbe Key. The missing lines have produced wholesale confusion among the expedition's interpreters. Five of those usually most relied upon draw five different conclusions as to the site of his landing and his fight with the Indians on the west side of the peninsula. Each chooses a different starting place to take him up the west coast to various landings, from Charlotte Harbor to Pensacola Bay. Those extending his voyage the farthest do so on the basis of the 1519 Alvarez de Pineda map sketch, yet the extent of Ponce's discoveries credited on the sketch cannot be reconciled with the account published by Herrera. The voyagers had proceeded cautiously, feeling their way along the unknown coast and anchoring at night. To have reached the top of the peninsula and returned in the time allotted, they would have had to crowd on full sail and cast caution to the winds. The notation on the Alvarez map sketch must be judged in error.

There are, in fact, a number of indications that Ponce did not even ascend as far as Charlotte Harbor, the most generally accepted landing place. In 1517, Antón de Alaminos, who had been Ponce's chief pilot, guided the remnants of Hernández de Córdoba's luckless voyage to the very bay visited by Ponce. After taking on water and fighting the Indians early in the day, the voyagers set sail for Havana, sighting the keys before nightfall and negotiating the passage inside the Marquesas that evening. How far might they have come in, say, half a day's sail? Certainly not from Charlotte Harbor. Cape Sable, in fact, was a good day's sail from the Marquesas under ordinary circumstances; only the voyagers' dire plight and a fair wind could account for their making it in less.

Ponce's bay, says the sixteenth-century cosmographer Juan López de Velasco, was two or three leagues from Punta Muspa (Cape Sable) and twelve from "Bahía de Tampa." But this Tampa Bay was not the one presently known by that name; more likely, it was Charlotte Harbor, the northern limit of Calusa territory, also defined by the notable castaway Escalante Fontaneda as "Tanpa." The bay of Ponce's fight with the Calusa and that of Pedro Menéndez de Avilés's 1566 settlement of San Antonio were the same, generally indicated as being between 25° and 26° latitude. The Ponce de Leon Bay of present-day maps may not be far off.

Menéndez's second outpost on the west side of the Florida peninsula was at Tocobaga, generally conceded to be on Old Tampa Bay, an offshoot of Tampa Bay proper. Yet López de Velasco separates it from sixteenth-century Tampa by 33 leagues. The cosmographer also asserts that on his second voyage Ponce returned to the bay visited on his first, and there received his fatal wounds. Efforts to extend the second voyage to Apalache or Pensacola bays, therefore, should be disregarded.

Recent claims that Ponce proceeded from Florida to a 1513 discovery of Yucatán must be rejected on grounds that the distance is too great for the time. He could not have made a landfall west of Cabo Catoche from the Dry Tortugas in two days. Sailing against the considerable current, the ships initially would have been set toward Cuba, which undoubtedly is where they landed and found European artifacts.

Ponce's voyages represent only the beginning of the confusion over Florida's historical geography. Miruelo's bay, for example, originated with the pilot of the 1528 Narváez expedition, not from any 1516 landing inside the Gulf by his uncle. Narváez evidently landed in the Tampa Bay vicinity, and his pilot finally found the bay he had visited on a previous voyage—probably with Alvarez de Pineda—close at hand. The name Bahía de Miruelo, it now seems obvious, was originally applied to present Tampa Bay.

The finding of a Narváez castaway by Soto's men most often leads to the assumption that Narváez and Soto landed at the same bay. It must be remembered, however, that Juan Ortiz was lost not from Narváez's main force but from a ship that had been to Havana and was feeling its way along the Florida coast looking for the troop. Evidence that Soto's landing place was different from Narváez's is found in records of the Cáncer *entrada* a few years later. Cáncer's ship, according to the latitude given, had been a little north of present Tampa Bay before turning about and sailing south eight days, looking for the bay itself. Within that time, from latitude 28°, it surely passed Tampa Bay and came to one farther south, where a castaway from one of Soto's vessels made his appearance. Aside from the length of Cáncer's southward voyage, the difficulties experienced by both his ship and Soto's vessels in finding a suitable anchorage indicate that they landed at Charlotte Harbor, not Tampa Bay.

Yucatán and New Spain

Key to the first four discovery voyages into the Gulf of Mexico was the pilot Antón de Alaminos, whose various achievements have often been recorded separately, without any attempt at consolidation. Let us briefly put together what is known of him. Alaminos was born at Palos about 1482 and sailed with Columbus on the fourth voyage. Being then twenty years old, he was not, as is often said, a ship's boy but well on his way to becoming a full-fledged pilot. On that occasion he witnessed Columbus's reluctance to sail with the powerful Caribbean current into unknown waters, lest his return become impossible, and the Admiral's decision was to influence his own choice on at least two important occasions: when sailing north on the eastern Florida coast with Ponce, 1513, and when ascending the Veracruz coast with Grijalva five years later.

As chief pilot of Ponce's first voyage, Alaminos discovered the Bahama Channel, the Gulf Stream, and the island of Bímini. He evidently had no involvement either in Ponce's 1516 Carib campaign or, certainly, his 1521 return to Florida. Alaminos appeared in Cuba just before the Hernández de Córdoba voyage sailed, signed on as its chief pilot, and apparently influenced its purpose toward the discovery of new lands rather than merely the quest of Indian slaves. As the bloody, thirst-crazed remnant sailed homeward following the rout at Champotón, he directed the course to Ponce's bay on the Florida coast, where they might take on water and catch a favorable wind for Cuba. He was seriously wounded in a battle with the Calusa Indians at the watering place.

His presence on the 1518 Grijalva voyage to extend Hernández's discoveries was considered so crucial that departure was delayed to allow his wounds to heal. As chief pilot on this third voyage into the Gulf, he explored the Yucatán peninsula on both east and west and concluded that the Bay of Ascensión (Chetumal) and the Laguna de Términos were joined and that the territory was an island.

Henry R. Wagner attributes to Alaminos the account of this voyage given by Fernández de Oviedo, but if that is the case, the noted *cronista* was grossly unappreciative; he takes occasion to castigate Alaminos in print for his petulance, as well as for his faulty conclusions.

Bernal Díaz del Castillo credits Alaminos with suggesting to Francisco de Garay the expedition that he dispatched the following year under Alvarez de Pineda to reconnoiter the northern Gulf shore, while he himself sailed with Cortés. (He could not have made both voyages, as Morison—in *Southern Voyages*, 516–17—says he did, because they overlapped.) It was Alaminos who conducted the voyage under Francisco de Montejo's command to find a suitable site for Cortés's first settlement on the Mexican coast; it was he who piloted Cortés's proctors to Spain, with the first shipment of Aztec treasure, on a previously unknown course through the Straits of Florida and the Bahama Channel.

Such an achievement, however, did not win Cortés's undying gratitude. Alaminos was back in New Spain in time to give testimony in the 1522 hearing concerning Cristóbal de Tapia's visit. Shortly thereafter, he and some of the other pilots who had served Hernández and Grijalva were ostracized by Cortés and returned to Spain. Nothing more is heard of the Gulf's pilot of discovery. While Díaz relates that Alaminos's son, also named Antón, took part in the Conquest, the record is silent as to his achievements.

Juan de Grijalva, like Diego Velázquez, was a native of Cuéllar. Past equivocation on whether or not he was Velázquez's kinsman should now be put to rest, for we have the testimony of another kinsman that he was Don Diego's nephew. From his various appearances after the 1518 voyage—with Velázquez at the start of Narváez's voyage to Mexico in 1520; with Vasco Porcallo, putting down the uprising at Sancti Spíritus in 1522; and at Santo Domingo with Las Casas late in 1523—suggest the likelihood that it was he who in 1523 conducted Garay's ships to Pánuco, rather than someone else with the same name.

The extent of Grijalva's 1518 exploration has generally been cut short on the eastern end and alternately curtailed and lengthened on the west. Bahía de Ascensión on the eastern Yucatán coast has been misplaced by almost 2° (120 nautical miles). The error, like the one responsible for misplacing the Cáncer expedition's final landing place in Florida, stems from a failure to account for several days' sailing time. The choice of Chetumal Bay as the Bahía de Ascensión renders more reasonable Alaminos's latitude of 17° and his conclusion that the bay joined the Laguna de Términos, making Yucatán an island.

From San Juan de Ulúa, Grijalva sailed north four days. Since it was summer, with favorable wind and current and with deep water almost to the shore, he was able to reach Cabo Rojo—the "great cape" described by Bernal Díaz del Castillo. He did not, as Morison asserts (*Southern Voyages*, 514), proceed to "a point north of the Pánuco

River." Nor can the Río de Canoas of his voyage be identified with the Río de Tamesí, as suggested elsewhere. Such erroneous conclusions have arisen in part from confusion of "the borders of Pánuco province" with the river of that name. The border, though somewhat indefinite, was farther south.

The Alvarez de Pineda map sketch is in error in its designation of the limit of the discovery made for Velázquez, as it is in that of Ponce de León. The sketch places Grijalva's turning point too far south.

A slight involvement in nautical archeology, plus the realization that some of both Cortés's and Narváez's ships were scuttled in the Villa Rica cove, led to my on-site investigation not only of Villa Rica but of other Cortés-related sites along the Veracruz coast. Villa Rica today is only a fishing camp, but the anchorage is just as it is described in the historic accounts. Towering above it, the loaflike Bernal Grande Peak stands guard over Quiahuitzlan's tomblike structures, doubtless the tip of an archaeological iceberg. Down the coast a few miles is Cempoala (Zempoala), the subject of extensive excavation and restoration following the 1890 rediscovery, but the thoroughness of the archeology comes to question as one encounters local urchins peddling bits of Totonac figurines picked up on the grounds.

At Antigua, the second site of Veracruz, the magnificent old ruin known locally as the "Casa de Cortés" gave rise to initial excitement, then disappointment with the realization that it probably had nothing to do with Cortés at all. The conqueror's house, and the church at which he gave thanks for his deliverance from the hazardous journey to Honduras, were both at Medellín, south of the present-day city of Veracruz. At Medellín I found, if local lore is to be trusted, the foundation of the real Cortés house, possibly important from an archeological standpoint. Interest in such a subject, however, still is lacking in Mexico, where the plethora of pre-Columbian sites enjoys a decided preference.

The Northern Gulf Shore

From Ponce's bay in Florida to Cabo Rojo in Veracruz state, Alvarez de Pineda was the first European to glimpse the Gulf shore. Yet nothing is known of the man, and confusion surrounds his exploits.

The extent of his exploration is often abbreviated, said to be from the Pensacola Bay vicinity to Tampico. In reality, it encompassed the whole coast from the Florida Keys to Villa Rica, some thirty-five miles north of present Veracruz.

Much in question has been the identity of the river he ascended twenty leagues on his return voyage to spend forty days careening his ships. It was the Mississippi, which appears on his map sketch as the Río del Espíritu Santo, says one group of interpreters, failing to note that the Mississippi was discovered during the first part of his voyage; the Río Grande, called Las Palmas, says another, maintaining that Garay, in following up this voyage four years later, landed there also.

Others focus on the identity of the Río del Espíritu Santo, denying the Mississippi in favor of Mobile, Galveston, or Matagorda bays. But the Mississippi it truly was. Despite the confusion, the answers to the other questions are fairly clear: the river of Alvarez's forty-day sojourn and later settlement was neither the Mississippi nor the Río Grande but the Pánuco. Alvarez, in fact, may never have left the Pánuco but remained there to begin a settlement while his ships sailed back to Jamaica in the charge of another. Diego de Camargo—usually credited with commanding the enterprise—returned to the Pánuco with supplies early the following year and found Alvarez de Pineda under attack. Alvarez and many others were slain, and Camargo hauled off for Villa Rica, which he may have seen from the sea the previous year as a member of Alvarez de Pineda's crew.

When Garay attempted in 1523 to renew the settlement, he landed by mistake at the first considerable river north of the Pánuco, and named it the Río de las Palmas. The Río Grande? Most assuredly not. López de Gómara (1552) identifies this river as being thirty leagues north of the Pánuco: the Soto la Marina.

Ever since Buckingham Smith first published his flawed translation of Cabeza de Vaca's *Relación* in 1851, the course of Cabeza's travels has been the subject of widely diverse interpretations, surpassing even those concerning Narváez's first landing place and the location of the Bay of Horses. From the landing near Tampa Bay, the expedition came to the desperate plight that brought on the boat-building enterprise on upper Ochlockonee Bay. The boats, after spending a week trying to get out of the swamp, emerged into St. George Sound and began their voyage westward. Smith himself finally ruled out his initial conclusion that Cabeza's boat was cast ashore east of Mobile Bay and that he and his three companions trekked north through Tennessee and then west through Arkansas and Oklahoma—but other hypotheses almost as wild arose to take its place. Such route interpretations usually have been made without the Fernández de Oviedo account, said to have been taken jointly from Cabeza and Dorantes. It expands considerably upon the narrative of Cabeza alone. We find, for example, that Narváez, often said to have been swept seaward by the Mississippi River current and never heard from again, actually reached Matagorda Bay. It becomes apparent also that all the surviving castaways followed a coastal route past Matagorda Bay, and one boat was well down the Tamaulipas coast before it met its end. Cabeza and his three companions, after their escape from the Indians, continued southward, and the river they crossed "fifteen leagues from the sea" was the Río Grande. The mountains that "ran from the direction of the North Sea"—meaning the Atlantic, or the unnamed Gulf of Mexico—were those of Nuevo León, not the hills of Texas's Central Mineral Region. The identification of the river "as wide as the Guadalquivir at Seville" with the Colorado should be terminated forever, as should the route ascribed to Cabeza through central Texas.

The "De Soto Map" of Alonso de Santa Cruz lends credence to the southern route for Cabeza, for it obviously drew information from sources other than Soto. It does have implications for establishing Soto's route, in names of Indian tribes identifiable with those mentioned by the Soto chroniclers. The route through Georgia and Alabama is important because of its influence on later explorations. An arm of the Luna *entrada*, including some of the men who had marched with Soto, followed a section of it, in reverse, through Alabama in 1560. Menéndez de Avilés sent expeditions from Santa Elena, seeking the road to New Spain, along Soto's route in 1566–67. Evidence has been adduced that the Spanish soldiers discovered in the Georgia gold country the precious metals that Soto, so eager in the quest, had walked over unseeing.

Moscoso, in his attempt to lead Soto's men to Mexico by land, probably reached the Trinity River in southeastern Texas. In that region he is said to have been joined by an Indian girl who had belonged to one of Vázquez de Coronado's men; left behnd by her captor, she had crossed Texas to form "a pesonal link between the explorations of

Coronado and the men of De Soto" (Bolton, *Coronado*, 356). Be that as it may, the two expeditions never came closer to each other than several hundred miles. Moscoso and his followers, however, most probably reached the area through which Cabeza de Vaca had traveled as a trader among the East Texas Indians.

Conjecture has often provided the Indian and early colonial background for popular histories. A journey from Tampico to peninsular Florida that was never made, for example, has been ascribed to Father Andrés de Olmos. To Alvarez de Pineda have been attributed territorial descriptions that are not of record, as well as his mythical ascent of the Río Grande (and the Mississippi River). Some of the myths might now be supplanted with the actual facts. Besides the Florida landings that are well known, and excluding shipwrecks, there were four known overland expeditions or landings in the Texas coastal region in the sixteenth century: (1) the combined land and sea expedition to salvage the treasure from the 1554 shipwrecks off Padre Island, conducted by Angel de Villafañe and García de Escalante Alvarado; (2) the 1558 landing at Matagorda Bay of Guido de Lavazares (Las Bazares), who formally claimed this bay and its environs for the king of Spain well over a century before La Salle claimed it for France; (3) the transcontinental trek of three Englishmen put ashore in Tamaulipas by John Hawkins, 1568; and (4) the 1572 Indian campaign and reconnaissance of Luis de Carvajal. With the exception of the first, details of these are disappointingly few, but such is often the case.

Carvajal, who has not yet found his way into the standard Texas histories, may yet prove a missing link. Though his contributions were far less than he claimed, his deeds lie at the roots of a significant portion of early history touching Texas and New Mexico, as well as the northern Mexican states.

Where Was Florida?

Few geographical names have contributed as much confusion as the word "Florida," the sixteenth-century application of which was vastly different from that of today. Ponce de León, finding the peninsula, took it for an island. Alvarez de Pineda proved that it was attached to an extensive mainland, and the "island of Florida" became the "continent of Florida." Even the colonials occasionally seem to have been confused as to the area designated by the name in its broader context. The southern boundary was regarded as the Río de las Palmas (Soto la Marina), although some (for example, Pedro Menéndez) sought to extend it all the way to the Pánuco. Up the Atlantic seaboard, Florida, by Spanish definition, ran to latitude 50°, or the discovery conceded the Cabots, which was Newfoundland or Tierra Nueva—until it was curtailed by other European claims.

Still, the ambiguity of the term gives rise to questions and misconceptions. For example, López de Gómara relates that in 1524, Cortés sent ships to explore the coast "between Pánuco and Florida," to look for a strait. Does he mean only that section of coast between the Pánuco and the Soto la Marina?

Royal concessions to both Narváez and Soto clearly encompassed the region "from the Río de las Palmas to Florida." But, when the three ships were wrecked off Texas's Padre Island in 1554, the location was reported as being "on the coast of Florida near the Río de las Palmas at 26½ degrees." The early histories, and some not so early, have taken that to mean *peninsular* Florida. When remains of the ships were found in the 1960s, there was much confusion to be cleared up.

The same kind of uncertainty has surrounded Fray Andrés de Olmos's journey "to the borders of Florida" to seek mission converts. Olmos went only to the Río de las Palmas of Tamaulipas, the ancient homeland of the Olive Indians he recruited.

And where did Hawkins, after getting shot up at San Juan de Ulúa, lighten his ship of its extra human burden? "On the Gulf coast of Florida," says Morison (*Northern Voyages*, 467), without elucidation. The late historian thus halves the epic journey of the three men who walked from near Tampico to Nova Scotia.

To the sixteenth-century Spaniards, Florida was adjacent to Mexico, a concept suggesting that the two provinces ought to be linked by communication routes. The failure so to join them is accounted for by an unfathomable contemporary ignorance of the geography involved. Numerous proposals and plans for forming the linkage died aborning, and the geographical confusion that thwarted them prevailed until the late seventeenth century. After Carvajal's time, the coastal stretch from Pánuco to Apalache lay in limbo, scarcely trod by Europeans save for the pirates and privateers who, taking over during the interim as the Gulf's principal explorers, occasionally sheltered in its remote bays and coves. Only the threat of foreign invasion rekindled Spanish interest in the region, and by then it was too late. During the next century Spain had to pay an exorbitant price for her failure to open the much discussed road to join the Florida colony with New Spain's northernmost settlements.

It has been the aim of this study to stimulate interest in reopening discovery and exploration as an area for historical investigation—at least to the extent that writers and teachers will stop repeating the old myths and cease taking for granted the "old reliable" versions that should have been outmoded long ago. To this end, a new concern for historical cartography is advocated, that the early maps might be better understood, thereby enhancing the capacity for understanding the documentary sources.

These steps accomplished, the teaching of North American history should gain a new perspective. Colonial studies should be given a reorientation that no longer accords back-door treatment to the Gulf of Mexico.

Glossary

adelantado: title given founders and early governors of new Spanish colonies

alcaide: governor of a castle or fort; jailer or warden

alcalde mayor: the chief executive of a district administered from a principal town, with both political and judicial authority

alcalde ordinario: an officer of municipal authority, specifically a magistrate

alférez: military rank equating with second lieutenant or ensign; subaltern

alguacil mayor: chief constable

almiranta: the admiral's flagship, second command vessel of the fleet to the *capitana*

Armada de Barlovento: "The Windward Squadron," or fleet of armed ships assigned to protect the Spanish colonies in the Gulf of Mexico and the Caribbean, directed principally against privateers and pirates

asiento: a word of many meanings, used herein to designate a particular kind of contract

audiencia: an administrative and judicial tribunal presided over by the viceroy (if sited in the capital of the viceroyalty) or the provincial governor

bark (*barca*): a small ship of the type used for fishing; not to be confused with *barco*, a word applied to every floating craft or whatever size or purpose

bohío: Indian house or lodge; an Arawak word often applied also to native dwellings in other localities

brigantine (*bergantín*): a small two-masted vessel with a square sail *cabildo*: municipal council; also the building in which the council met

cabo: as used herein, cape or headland

cacique: Indian chief

cacicazgo: the territory ruled by a *cacique*, especially Mayan

capitana: flagship of the fleet's captain-general, the primary command vessel

capitulación: a contract, especially between the Spanish Crown and the organizer of an expedition for discovery, conquest, or colonization

caravel (*carabela*): originally, a small coastal trading ship of Mediterranean design and no more than sixty or seventy *toneladas* and seventy to eighty feet overall length; in the Spanish Indies trade, the term encompassed a variety of types and sizes of vessels

carta: chart or map; also letter

castellano: a gold coin weighing one-fiftieth of a mark

castillo: castle or fortress

cédula: decree, especially from the Crown

cenote: a deep underground water reservoir, especially the natural sinks of Yucatán that provided access to groundwater

chichimeca, or *chichimeco*: a generic term derived from the more primitive, nomadic natives of Nueva Galicia, the Chichimecs, and applied to any of the more primitive and hostile nomads, as distinguished from the advanced, sedentary natives of central and southern Mexico

chinchorro: a fishing boat used in the Americas; also a fishing net; also an Indian hammock

contador: accountant, treasurer

corregidor: chief magistrate, originally of Spanish towns; after 1531, the Spanish official in an Indian town, with the duty of protecting the natives and fostering their welfare while exercising political and judicial authority

cronista: chronicler, correspondent

doctrina: an Indian parish centered on a mission church, conducted by a priest and administered by a *corregidor*; term applied especially in the Florida mission field

encomendero: the holder of an *encomienda*

encomienda: land and inhabiting Indians granted to a Spanish colonist *entrada*: entry, here specifically the entry of a Spanish force into an unsettled or unexplored area

fiscal: a Crown attorney who in the viceroyalty was an important member of the viceroy's council

flibustier: pirate, freebooter, buccaneer, filibuster; privateer

fray: friar; member of a mendicant order

frigate (*fragata*): a war vessel, usually square rigged

galizabra: a ship with lateen sails, adapted from the Levant trade

galleon (*galeón*): a large sailing ship of revolutionary design developed in the mid-sixteenth century: 250- to 500-ton capacity

gobernación: government district or province under the jurisdiction of a governor

guanín: a copper-gold alloy; base gold

league: a distance measurement used differently by different nationalities; Spanish land league approximately 2.63 statute miles; marine league, 3.43 nautical miles

macana: a wooden weapon edged with flint or obsidian, used by the Indians of Mexico and Peru: originally an agricultural tool of the island Arawaks, among whom the word originated

maestre de campo: field commander (not to be confused with the military rank of *mariscal de campo*, or "field marshal")

maravedí: the smallest Spanish monetary unit in use in the sixteenth century; 32 to the *real*, 272 to the one-ounce silver peso

mestizo(a): the offspring of mixed parentage, Spanish and Indian; half-blood

mozo: young man; *el mozo*, "the younger," used after a man's name when it was the same as his father's (or uncle's)

nao: ship or vessel with decks and sails

navío: a ship, especially a large one; man-of-war

oidor: a judge of the *audiencia*

palo de tinta: wood especially valued in the production of natural dyes

peso de oro: a gold coin or monetary unit valued at 450 *maravedís* (as opposed to the silver peso, worth 272 *maravedís*)

pinnace (*pinaza*): a light craft with oars and sail; a ship's boat, often towed by a sailing ship rather than being carried on board

piragua: dugout canoe; also shallow-draft sailing vessel equipped with oars *puerto*: port or harbor; haven

punta: point

regidor: alderman or councilman

regimiento: government; town council; also military regiment, or nautical rule book

relación: report, account

repartimiento: division; here, specifically the division of Indians among their conquerors as forced laborers

requerimiento: notification; request; injunction

residencia: the process of reviewing a colonial official's conduct in office, done at the end of his term, in which anyone with a grievance might come forth and complain

sargento mayor: a military rank corresponding to major

shallop (*chalupa*): longboat

tierra despoblada: unsettled region

tierra incógnita: unexplored region

tonelada: used to express the carrying capacity of a ship in terms of wine tuns

urca: a ship of the hooker type, pink-built and sloop-rigged; storeship

vecino: a citizen or permanent resident of a place; neighbor

veedor: overseer or inspector; the Crown representative on an expedition of discovery or conquest charged with seeing that the royal treasury got its share of any proceeds

visita: an official visit or inspection; as applied to a missionary endeavor, a congregation or parish served by a visiting priest

Bibliography

Archival Material

Archivo General de Indias, Seville (AGI):
  Audiencia de Mexico, legajos 19, 68, 91, 92, 95, 98, 99, 100, 101, 104, 105, 108, 110, 168, 257, 323, 559, 560, 1006, 1010.
  Audiencia de Santo Domingo, legajos 9, 11, 15, 49, 77, 99, 115, 129, 177, 225, 232, 839.
  Contaduría, legajo 941.
  Contratación, legajo 2490.
  Escribanía de Cámara, legajos 155, 156.
  Indiferente General, legajos 421 (libros 12, 13), 1203, 1205, 1378, 1383A, 1383B, 1384.
  Patronato Real, legajos 19, 23, 51, 54, 55, 57, 60, 61, 63, 69, 78A, 83, 178, 179, 183, 184, 265, 267.
Archivo Histórico Nacional, Madrid (AHN): Sección Diversos, legajos 74, 201, 203, 337, 344.
Archivo Protocolos de Sevilla (APS): Libros de 1508–20, 1525, 1580.
Biblioteca Nacional, Madrid (BN): Manuscript 7119.
Biblioteca del Real Palacio, Madrid (BRP): Manuscripts 2667, 2861.
British Museum, London:
  Additional manuscript 28,189 (copy in Southwest Mission Research Library, Our Lady of the Lake University, San Antonio, Texas).
Museo Naval, Madrid (MN): Manuscript volume 1764, documents 21, 23.
Real Academia de Historia, Madrid (RAH): Colección Muñoz, A/103, A/112–15.
Stetson Collection, University of Florida, Gainesville (microfilm from AGI).
University of Texas Library Archives, Austin (transcripts from AGI).

Published Material

Alessio Robles, Vito. *Coahuila y Texas en la época colonial*. Mexico City: Editorial Cultura, 1938.
Altolaguirre y Duvale, Angel de. *Descubrimiento y conquista de Mexico*. Madrid: Salvat Editores, S.A., 1954.

Andrews, Kenneth R. *English Privateering Voyages to the West Indies, 1588–1595*. Cambridge, Eng.: Hakluyt Society, 1959.

Anglería, Pedro Mártir de (Peter Martyr). *Décadas del Nuevo Mundo*. Translated from the Latin by D. Joaquín Torres Asensio. Buenos Aires: Editorial Bajel, 1944.

"¿A qué rio dió Juan de Grijalva el nombre de Canoas?" *Boletín de la Sociedad de Geografía y Estadística de la República Mexicana, segunda época* 1 (1869): 467–71.

Arnade, Charles W. *Florida on Trial, 1593–1602*. Coral Gables, Fla.: Univ. of Miami Press, 1959.

Arnold, J. Barto, III, and Robert S. Weddle. *The Nautical Archeology of Padre Island: The Spanish Shipwrecks of 1554*. New York: Academic Press, 1978.

Bailey, Ben P., Jr. *Border Lands Sketchbook / Libro de Bosquejos Fronterizos*. Spanish text, translated by Channing Horner and Louise Bailey Horner. Waco, Tex.: Texian Press, 1976.

Ballesteros Beretta, Antonio. *La marina cántabra de Juan de la Cosa*. Santander, Spain: Diputación Provincial, 1954.

Barcia Carballido y Zúñiga, Andrés González de. *Barcia's Chronological History of the Continent of Florida*. Translated by Anthony Kerrigan. Gainesville: Univ. Presses of Florida, 1951.

Barreiro-Meiro, Roberto. *Juan de la Cosa y su doble personalidad*. Madrid: Instituto Histórico de la Marina, 1970.

———. *Puerto Rico, La Aguada, Ponce de León, Etc.* Madrid: Instituto Histórico de la Marina, 1977.

———. "Vespucio y Levillier." *Revista General de Marina* 175 (Oct. 1968): 351–68.

Barrientos, Bartolomé. *Pedro Menéndez de Avilés, Founder of Florida*. Translated by Anthony Kerrigan, with facsimile reproduction of original Spanish edition. Gainesville: Univ. Presses of Florida, 1965.

Benavides, Alonso de. *Benavides' Memorial of 1630*. Translated by Peter P. Forrestal. Washington, D.C.: Academy of American Franciscan History, 1954.

———. *The Memorial of Fray Alonso de Benavides, 1630*. Translated by Mrs. Edward E. Ayer. Albuquerque, N.M.: Horn and Wallace, 1965.

Bertrand, Louis, and Charles Petrie. *The History of Spain from Musulmans to Franco*. New York: Collier Books, 1971.

Berwick, Maria del Rosario Falcó y Osorio (Le Duquesa de Berwick y de Alba). *Autógrafos de Colón y papeles de América*. Madrid, 1892.

Bishop, Morris. *The Odyssey of Cabeza de Vaca*. New York: Century, 1933.

Blok, Petrus Johannes. *History of the People of the Netherlands*. 5 vols. Translated by Oscar A. Bierstadt and R. Putnam. New York: Putnam, 1898–1912.

Bolton, Herbert Eugene. *Coronado: Knight of Pueblos and Plains*. Albuquerque: Univ. of New Mexico Press, 1949.

———, ed. *Spanish Exploration in the Southwest*. New York: Scribner, 1908. Reprint. New York: Barnes and Noble, 1963.

Bourne, Edward Gaylord. *Spain in America: 1450–1580*. New York: Harper, 1904.

———, ed. *Narratives of the Career of Hernando de Soto in the Conquest of Florida*. 2 vols. New York: Allerton, 1922. Reprint. New York: AMS Press, 1973.

Boyd, Mark F. "The Fortifications at San Marcos de Apalache." *Florida Historical Quarterly* 15, no. 1 (July, 1936): 3–34.

———, trans. "Enumeration of Florida Spanish Missions in 1675." *Florida Historical Quarterly* 27, no. 2 (Oct. 1948): 181–88.

Bricker, Charles. *Landmarks of Mapmaking: An Illustrated Survey of Maps and Mapmakers*. New York: Thomas Y. Crowell, 1976.

Bullen, Ripley P. "The Southern Limit of Timucua Territory." *Florida Historical Quarterly* 47, no. 4 (April, 1969): 413–19.

Burrage, Henry S. *Early English and French Voyages, Chiefly from Hakluyt*. New York: Scribner, 1906. Reprint. New York: Barnes and Noble, 1967.

Burstyn, Harold L. "Theories of Winds and Ocean Currents from the Discoveries to the End of the Seventeenth Century." *Terrae Incognitae* 3 (1971): 7–31.

Bushnell, Amy. "'That Demonic Game': The Campaign to Stop Indian *Pelota* Playing in Spanish Florida, 1675–1684." *The Americas* 35, no. 1 (July, 1978): 1–19.

Cabeza de Vaca, Alvar Núñez. *The Journey of Alvar Nuñez Cabeza de Vaca and His Companions from Florida to the Pacific, 1528–1536*. Translated by Fanny Bandelier. New York: Barnes, 1905. Reprint. Chicago: Río Grande Press, 1964.

———. *Relación de los naufragios y comentarios de Alvar Núñez Cabeza de Vaca*. Madrid: Librería General de Victoriano Suárez, 1906.

Cartas de Indias. 3 vols. Biblioteca de autores españoles, vols. 264–66. Madrid: Ministerio de Fomento, 1877. Reprint. Madrid: Ediciones Atlas, 1914.

Castañeda, Carlos Eduardo. *Our Catholic Heritage in Texas*. 7 vols. Austin: Von Boeckman–Jones, 1936–50.

Cervantes de Salazar, Francisco. *Crónica de la Nueva España*. Madrid: Hispanic Society of America, 1914.

Chamberlain, Robert S. *The Conquest and Colonization of Yucatán, 1517–1550*. Washington, D.C.: Carnegie Institution, 1948. Reprint. New York: Octagon Books, 1966.

———. "Discovery of the Bahama Channel." *Tequesta* 8 (1948): 109–16.

———. "The Spanish Treasure Fleet of 1551." *American Neptune* 6, no. 4 (1946): 241–52.

Chatelain, Verne E. *The Defenses of Spanish Florida: 1565–1763*. Washington, D.C.: Carnegie Institution, 1941.

Chavez, Angelico. *Coronado's Friars*. Washington, D.C.: Academy of American Franciscan History, 1968.

Chipman, Donald E. *Nuño de Guzmán and the Province of Pánuco in New Spain, 1518–1533.* Glendale, Calif. Arthur H. Clark, 1967.

Cline, Howard F., ed. *Latin American History: Essays on Its Study and Teaching, 1898–1965.* 2 vols. Austin: Univ. of Texas Press, 1967.

Coastal Environments, Inc. *Cultural Resources Evaluation of the Northern Gulf of Mexico Continental Shelf.* 3 vols. Washington, D.C.: National Park Service, 1977.

Colección de documentos inéditos para la historia de Ibero-America (CDI-IA) 4 vols., extended to 14 under title of *Colección de documentos inéditos para la historia de Hispano-America.* Madrid: Editorial Ibero-Africano-Americano, 1927–35.

Colección de documentos inéditos para la historia de España (CDIE), 112 volumes. Madrid: Viuda de Calera, 1842–95.

Colección de documentos inéditos relativos al descubrimiento, conquista y organización de las antiguas posesiones españolas en América y Oceanía (CDI). 42 vols. Madrid: José María Pérez, 1864–84.

Colección de documentos inéditos relativos al descubrimiento, conquista y organización de las antiguas posesiones españolas de ultramar. (CDU) 25 vols. Madrid: Real Academia de la Historia, 1885–1932.

Connor, Jeanette Thurber, trans. and ed. *Colonial Records of Spanish Florida.* 2 vols. Deland, Fla.: Florida State Historical Society, 1925, 1930.

Cortés, Hernán. *Cartas de relación.* Mexico City: Editorial Porrúa, 1973.

Cortés, Hernando. *Five Letters, 1519–1526.* Translated by J. Bayard Morris. London, 1928. Reprint, New York: W. W. Norton, 1962.

Covián Martínez, Vidal. *Cronología histórica de Tampico, Ciudad Madera y Altamira, Tam. y de la expropiación petrolero.* 2 vols. Ciudad Victoria, Tamaulipas: Ediciones Siglo XX, 1969.

Cumming, W. P.; R. A. Skelton; and D. B. Quinn. *The Discovery of North America.* New York: American Heritage Press, 1972.

Dampier, William. *Dampier's Voyages: Consisting of a New Voyage Round the World, Two Voyages to Campeachey, a Discourse on Winds, a Voyage to New Holland, and a Vindication in Answer to the Commercial Relation of William Funnell.* Edited by John Masefield. 2 vols. London: E. Grant Richards, 1906.

Davenport, Harbert, ed. "The Expedition of Pánfilo de Narváez by Gonzalo Fernández Oviedo y Valdez," *Southwestern Historical Quarterly* 27, nos. 2–4 (Oct., 1923; Jan., April, 1924): 120–39, 217–41, 276–304; and 28, nos. 1–2 (July, Oct., 1924): 56–74, 122–63.

Dávila Padilla, Agustín. *Historia de la fundación y discurso de la provincia de Santiago de Mexico, de la Orden de Predicadores, por las vidas de sus varones insignes, y casos notables de Nueva España.* Madrid: Pedro Madrigal, 1596.

Davis, T. Frederick. "Juan Ponce de León's Voyages to Florida." *Florida Historical Quarterly* 14, no. 1 (July, 1935): 5–70.

De Golyer, Everette Lee. *Across Aboriginal America: The Journey of Three Englishmen across Texas in 1568.* El Paso, Tex.: Peripatetic Press, 1947.

Delanglez, Jean. *El Rio del Espíritu Santo: An Essay on the Cartography of the Gulf Coast and the Adjacent Territory during the Sixteenth and Seventeenth Centuries.* New York: United States Catholic Historical Society, 1945.

Díaz del Castillo, Bernal. *Historia verdadera de la conquista de la Nueva España.* 2 vols. Mexico City: Editorial Porrúa, 1955.

———. *The True History of the Conquest of New Spain.* 5 vols. Translated by Alfred Percival Maudslay. London: Hakluyt Society, 1912.

Dorantes de Carranza, Baltasar. *Sumaria relación de las cosas de Nueva España, con noticias de los descendientes legítimos de los conquistadores y primeras pobladores españoles.* Mexico City: Museo Nacional, 1902.

Duaine, Carl L. *Caverns of Oblivion.* Corpus Christi, Tex.: privately printed, 1971.

Ekholm, Gordon F. *Excavations at Tampico and Pánuco in the Huasteca, Mexico.* New York: American Museum of Natural History, 1944.

Escalante Fontaneda, Hernando de. *Memoir of D.° d'Escalante Fontaneda, Respecting Florida.* Translated by Buckingham Smith. Washington, D.C.: 1854. Revision and republication, ed. David O. True. Miami: Univ. of Miami and Historical Association of Southern Florida, 1944.

Espinosa, Isidro Félix de. *Crónica de los colegios de propaganda fide de la Nueva España.* 1746. New ed., with notes and introduction by Lino G. Canedo. Washington, D.C.: Academy of American Franciscan History, 1964.

Esquemeling, John. *The Buccaneers of America.* New York: Dover, 1967.

Fehrenbach, T. R. *Fire and Blood: A History of Mexico.* New York: Macmillan, 1973.

Fernández de Navarrete, Martín. *Biblioteca Marítima Española.* 2 vols. Madrid: Viuda de Calero, 1851.

———. *Colección de documentos y manuscriptos compilados por Fernández de Navarrete.* Nendeln, Lichtenstein: Kraus-Thomson, 1971.

———. *Collección de los viages y descubrimientos que hicieron por mar los españoles desde fines del siglo XV, con varios documentos inéditos concernientes á la historia de la marina castellana y de los establecimientos españoles en Indias.* 5 vols. Madrid, 1825–37. Reprint. Buenos Aires: Editorial Guarania, 1945.

Fernández de Oviedo y Valdés, Gonzalo. *Historia general y natural de las Indias, islas y Tierra-Firme del Mar Océano.* 14 vols. Asunción del Paraguay: Editorial Guarania, 1944.

Fiske, John. *Discovery of America.* 2 vols. Boston: Houghton, Mifflin, 1892.

French, B. F. *Historical Collections of Louisiana and Florida, Including Translations of Original Manuscripts Relating to Their Discovery.* 2d ser., 1527–1702. New York: Albert Mason, 1875.

Gage, Thomas. *The English American: A New Survey of the West Indies, 1648.* London: George Routledge, 1928. Reprint. 1946.

Galtsoff, Paul S. "Historical Sketch of the Explorations in the Gulf of Mexico." In *Gulf of Mexico: Its Origin, Waters, and Marine Life.* United States Fish and Wildlife Service Fishery Bulletin 80. Washington, D.C.: Government Printing Office, 1954.

Gannon, Michael V. *The Cross in the Sand: The Early Catholic Church in Florida, 1513–1870.* Gainesville: Univ. Presses of Florida, 1965.

García Icazbalceta, D. I. *Obras de D. I. García Icazbalceta.* 10 vols. Mexico City: V. Agueros, 1896–99.

Gardiner, C. Harvey. *Naval Power in the Conquest of Mexico.* Austin: Univ. of Texas Press, 1956.

Geiger, Maynard. *The Franciscan Conquest of Florida (1573–1618).* Washington, D.C.: Catholic University of America, 1937.

Gross, Edward. *Warrior of the Sun.* New York: Dell, 1980.

Guzmán, Nuño de. "Memoria de los servicios que había hecho Nuño de Guzmán desde que fue nombrado gobernador de Pánuco en 1525." In *Crónicas de la conquista del reino de Nueva Galicia,* vol. 1. Guadalajara: Instituto Jalisciense de Antropología e Historia, 1960.

Hakluyt, Richard. *The Principal Navigations, Voyages, Traffiques & Discoveries of the English Nation.* 12 vols. Glasgow, Scotland: James MacLehose and Sons, 1903–1905.

———. *The Principall Navigations of the English Nation.* 1589. 2 vols. London: Cambridge Univ. Press, 1965.

Hallenbeck, Cleve. *Alvar Núñez Cabeza de Vaca: The Journey and Route of the First European to Cross the Continent of North America, 1534–1536.* 1940. Reprint. Port Washington, N. Y.: Kennikat Press, 1971.

Hamilton, Peter J. *Colonial Mobile.* Boston: Houghton, Mifflin, 1897. Reprint. University: Univ. of Alabama Press, 1976.

———. "Was Mobile Bay the Bay of Spiritu Santo?" Alabama Historical Society, Transactions: 1899–1903, vol. 4, reprint no. 3 (Montgomery, 1904), 73–93.

Hammond, Norman. "Unearthing the Oldest Known Maya." *National Geographic* 162, no. 1 (July, 1982): 126–40.

Hampden, John, ed. *The Tudor Venturers.* London: Folio Society, 1970.

Haring, C. H. *The Buccaneers in the West Indies in the XVII Century.* London: Methuen, 1910. Reprint. Hamden, Conn.: Archon Books, 1966.

Harrisse, Henry. *The Discovery of North America: A Critical, Documentary, and Historic Investigation, with an Essay on the Early Cartography of the New World.* London and Paris, 1892. Amsterdam: N. Israel, 1961.

Herrera y Tordesillas, Antonio de. *Historia general de los hechos de los castellanos, en las islas y Tierra-firme de el Mar Océano.* 10 vols. Buenos Aires: Editorial Guarania, 1944.

Historic New Orleans Collection. *Degrees of Discovery: From New World to New Orleans* (exhibition catalog). N.p., n.d.

Hodge, Frederick W., and T. H. Lewis, eds. *Spanish Explorers in the Southern United States, 1528–1543.* New York: Scribner, 1907.

Hollon, W. Eugene. *The Southwest: Old and New.* New York: Knopf, 1961. Reprint. Lincoln: Univ. of Nebraska Press, 1968.

Horgan, Paul. *Great River: The Rio Grande in North American History.* 2 vols. New York: Holt, Rinehart and Winston, 1954.

Hoyo, Eugenio del. *Historia del Nuevo Reino de León (1577–1723).* 2 vols. Monterrey: Instituto Tecnológico y de Estudios Superiores de Monterrey, 1972.

Irving, Washington. *The Life and Voyages of Christopher Columbus, to which are added those of His Companions.* 3 vols. New York: Putnam, 1849.

Johnson, J. G. "The Spaniards in Northern Georgia during the Sixteenth Century." *Georgia Historical Quarterly* 9 (1925): 157–68.

Johnson, William Weber. *Cortés.* Boston: Little, Brown, 1975.

Johnson, Willis Fletcher. *The History of Cuba.* 5 vols. New York: B. F. Buck, 1920.

Juárez Moreno, Juan. *Piratas y corsarios en Veracruz y Campeche.* Seville: Escuela de Estudios Hispano-Americanos, 1972.

La Fay, Howard. "The Maya: Children of Time." *National Geographic* 148, no. 6 (Dec. 1975): 729–66.

Landa, Diego de. *See* Tozzer, Alfred M.

Lanning, John Tate. *The Spanish Missions of Georgia.* Chapel Hill: Univ. of North Carolina Press, 1935.

La Roncière, Charles German Marie Bourel de. *Histoire de la Marine Française.* 5 vols. Paris: Librairie Plon E. Plon, 1899.

Las Casas, Bartolomé de. *The Devastation of the Indies: A Brief Account.* Translated by Herma Briffault. New York: Seabury Press, 1974.

———. *Bartolomé de las Casas: A Selection of His Writings.* Translated and edited by George Sanderlin. New York: Knopf, 1971.

———. *History of the Indies.* Translated and edited by Andrée Collard. New York: Harper and Row, 1971.

"La Sevilla de Ayer." *Andalucía* (Seville), May 2, 1979.

Lawson, Edward W. *The Discovery of Florida and Its Discoverer, Juan Ponce de León.* St. Augustine, Fla., 1946.

León, Alonso de; Juan Bautista Chapa; and Fernando Sánchez de Zamora. *Historia de Nuevo León.* Monterrey: Centro de Estudios Humanísticos de la Universidad de Nuevo León, 1961.

Levillier, Roberto. *América la bien llamada.* 2 vols. Buenos Aires: Editorial Guillermo Kraft, 1948.

Lewis, T. H. "The Chroniclers of De Soto's Expedition." *Publications of the Mississippi Historical Society* 7 (1903): 379–87.

———. "Route of De Soto's Expedition from Talipacana to Huhasene." *Publications of the Mississippi Historical Society* 6 (1902): 449–67.

Liebman, Seymour B., ed. *The Enlightened: The Writings of Luis de Carvajal el Mozo.* Coral Gables, Fla.: Univ. of Miami Press, 1967.

436 *Bibliography*

López de Gómara, Francisco. *Cortés: The Life of the Conqueror.* Translated and edited by Lesley Byrd Simpson. Berkeley: Univ. of California Press, 1966.

———. *Historia general de las Indias.* 1552. Madrid: Espasa-Calpe, 1932.

López de Velasco, Juan. *Geographía y descripción universal de las Indias* (1574). Biblioteca de autores españoles, vol. 248. 1894. New edition. Madrid: Ediciones Atlas, 1971.

Lowery, Woodbury. *The Spanish Settlements within the Present Limits of Florida, 1562–1574.* New York: Putnam, 1905.

———. *The Spanish Settlements within the Present Limits of the United States, 1513–1561.* New York: Putnam, 1901.

Luxán. *See* Pérez de Luxán, Diego.

Lynch, John. *Spain under the Habsburgs.* 2. vols. New York: Oxford Univ. Press, 1969.

Lyon, Eugene. *The Enterprise of Florida: Pedro Menéndez de Avilés and the Spanish Conquest of 1565–1568.* Gainesville: Univ. Presses of Florida, 1976.

Margry, Pierre, ed. *Découvertes et établissements des français dans l'ouest et dans le sud de l'Amérique septentrionale.* 6 vols. Paris: D. Jouaust, 1876–86.

Martyr, Peter. *See* Anglería, Pedro Mártir de.

Maynard, Theodore. *De Soto and the Conquistadores.* New York: Longmans, Green, 1930.

Meade, Joaquín, ed. *Documentos inéditos para la historia de Tampico: siglos XVI y XVII.* Mexico City: José Porrúa e Hijos, 1939.

———. "El adelantado Francisco de Garay." *Boletín de la Sociedad Mexicana de Geografía y Estadística* 58, no. 2 (April, 1947): 405–29.

Medina, José Toribio. *Juan Díaz de Solís: Estudio histórico.* 2 vols. Santiago de Chile: Impreso en casa del autor, 1897.

Mendieta, Gerónimo de. *Historia eclesiástica indiana.* Mexico City, 1870. Reprint, ed. Joaquín García Icazbalceta. Mexico City: Editorial Porrúa, 1971.

Mexico. *Los Judíos en la Nueva Espana.* Vol. 20. in *Publicaciones del Archivo de la Nación.* 1932.

Millares Carlo, Agustín. Indice y extractos de los protocolos del Archivo de Notarías de Mexico, D.F. 3 vols. Mexico City: El Colegio de Mexico, Centro de estudios históricos, 1945.

Morison, Samuel Eliot. *Admiral of the Ocean Sea: A Life of Christopher Columbus.* Boston: Little, Brown, 1942.

———. *The European Discovery of America: The Northern Voyages, A.D. 500–1600.* New York: Oxford Univ. Press, 1971.

———. *The European Discovery of America: The Southern Voyages, A.D. 1492–1616.* New York: Oxford Univ. Press, 1974.

———. *Portuguese Voyages to America in the Fifteenth Century.* Cambridge, Mass.: Harvard Historical Monographs, no. 15, 1940. Reprint. New York: Octagon Books, 1965.

Murga Sanz, Vicente. *Juan Ponce de León: Fundador y primer gobernador del pueblo Puertorriqueño, descubridor de la Florida y del estrecho de las Bahamas*. San Juan: Ediciones de la Universidad de Puerto Rico, 1959.

Newcomb, W. W., Jr. *The Indians of Texas from Prehistoric to Modern Times*. Austin: Univ. of Texas Press, 1961.

Nunn, George E. *Geographical Conceptions of Columbus: A Critical Consideration of Four Problems*. New York: American Geographical Society, 1924.

"Ocupación de la Isla de Términos por los Ingleses, 1658–1717." *Boletín del Archivo General de la Nación* 24, no. 2 (1953).

O'Daniel, V. F. *Dominicans in Early Florida*. New York: United States Catholic Historical Society, 1930.

Oré, Luis Jerónimo de. *Relación histórica de la Florida, escrita en el siglo XVII*. 2 vols. Edited by Atanasio López. Madrid: Librería General de Victoriano Suárez, 1931, 1933.

Orozco y Berra, Juan. *Apuntes sobre Cayo Arenas*. Mexico City: Sociedad de Geografía y Estadística, 1886.

Parkman, Francis. *Pioneers of France in the New World*. Boston: Little, Brown, 1865.

Parry, J. H. *The Age of Reconnaissance*. New York: New American Library, 1964.

Paso y Troncoso, Francisco del. *Epistolario de Nueva España*. 16 vols. Mexico: J. Porrúa e hijos, 1939–42.

———. *Las ruinas de Cempoala y del templo del Tajín*. Mexico City: Arqueología Mexicana, 1912.

Pérez Cabrera, José Manuel. *En Torno del bojeo de Cuba*. Havana: privately printed, 1941.

Pérez de Luxán, Diego. *Expedition into New Mexico Made by Antonio de Espejo, 1582–1583*. Translated and edited by George Peter Hammond and Agapito Rey. Los Angeles: Quivira Society, 1929. Reprint. New York: Arno Press, 1967.

Peter Martyr. *See* Anglería, Pedro Mártir de.

Pichardo, José Antonio. *Pichardo's Treatise on the Limits of Louisiana and Texas*. 4 vols. Translated by Charles Wilson Hackett, Charmion Clair Shelby, and Mary Ruth Splawn; edited and annotated by Charles Wilson Hackett. Austin: Univ. of Texas Press, 1931–34.

Pike, Ruth. *Enterprise and Adventure: The Genoese in Seville and the Opening of the New World*. Ithaca, N.Y.: Cornell Univ. Press, 1966.

Prescott, William Hickling. *History of the Conquest of Mexico*. 1843. New York: Book League of America, 1934.

Priestley, Herbert Ingram, trans. and ed. *The Luna Papers: Documents Relating to the Expedition of Don Tristan de Luna y Arellano for the Conquest of La Florida in 1559–1561*. 2 vols. 1928. Reprint. New York: Books for Libraries Press, 1971.

"Probanza sobre las causas que se dieron a la suplicación de las provisiones del veedor Cristóbal de Tapia, que se hizo por parte del capitán Hernando

Cortés." *Boletín del Archivo General de la Nación* 9, no. 2 (1938): 183–235.

Puente y Olea, Manuel de la. *Los trabajos geográficos de la Casa de Contratación.* Seville: Escuela Tipográfica, Librería Salesianas, 1900.

Reding, Katherine, trans. and ed. "Plans for the Colonization and Defense of Apalache, 1675." *Georgia Historical Quarterly* (1925): 169–76.

Reyes Flores, Candelario. *Apuntes para la historia de Tamaulipas en los siglos XVI y XVII.* Mexico City: privately printed, 1944.

Roel, Santiago. *Nuevo León—Apuntes históricos.* 2 vols. Monterrey: Talleres linotipo gráficos del estado, 1938.

Roukema, Edzer. "A Discovery of Yucatán prior to 1503." *Imago Mundi* 13 (1956): 30–38.

Rovirosa, José N. de. *Ensayo histórico sobre el Río de Grijalva.* Mexico City: Secretaría de Fomento, 1897.

Rubio Mañé, J. Ignacio, ed. *Archivo de la historia de Yucatán, Campeche y Tabasco.* 3 vols. Mexico City: Aldina, Robredo y Rosell, 1942.

———. "Fin de los días de don Tristán de Luna y Arellano, genearca de los mariscales de Castilla en Mexico, año de 1573." *Boletín del Archivo General de la Nación,* 2d. ser., vol. 8, combined nos. 1–2 (1967): 19–21.

———. *Introducción al estudio de los virreyes de Nueva España 1535–1746.* 4 vols. Mexico City: Universidad Nacional Autónoma de Mexico, 1959.

Ruidíaz y Caravia, Eugenio. *La Florida: Su conquista y colonización por Pedro Menéndez de Avilés.* 2 vols. Madrid: Hijos de J. A. García, 1893.

Rújula y de Ochotorena, José de, and Antonio del Solar y Taboada. *Francisco de Montejo y los adelantados de Yucatán.* Badajoz, Spain: Ediciones Arqueros, 1931.

Samonte, Mariano G. *Doña Marina, "La Malinche."* Mexico City: privately printed, 1969.

Sauer, Carl Ortwin. *The Early Spanish Main.* Berkeley: Univ. of California Press, 1969.

Schell, Rolfe F. *De Soto Didn't Land at Tampa.* Fort Myers Beach, Fla.: Island Press, 1966.

Scholes, France V., and Eleanor B. Adams. *Documentos para la historia del Mexico colonial.* Mexico: José Porrúa e Hijos, 1956.

Scholes, France V., and Ralph L. Roys. *The Maya Chontal Indians of Acalán-Tixchel.* Norman: Univ. of Oklahoma Press, 1968.

Scholes, Walter Vinton. *The Diego Ramírez Visita.* Columbia: Univ. of Missouri, 1946.

Seckinger, Ron L. "Observations on the Origin and Date of a Seventeenth-Century Florida Map." *Florida Historical Quarterly* 43, no. 4 (April, 1965): 385–87.

Serrano y Saenz, Manuel, ed. *Documentos históricos de la Florida y Luisiana, siglos XVI al XVIII.* Madrid: Librería General de Victoriano Suárez, 1913.

Sluiter, Engel. "Dutch-Spanish Rivalry in the Caribbean Area, 1594–1609." *Hispanic American Historical Review* 28, no. 2 (May, 1948): 165–96.

Smith, Thomas Buckingham, ed. *Colección de varios documentos para la historia de la Florida y tierras adyacentes.* Vol. 1 (there is no vol. 2). London: Trübner, 1857.

————, ed. *Narratives of De Soto in the Conquest of Florida.* 1866. Gainesville, Fla.: Palmetto Books, 1968.

————, trans. *Relation of Alvar Núñez Cabeça de Vaca.* New York: privately printed, 1871. Reprint. Ann Arbor, Mich.: University Microfilms, 1966.

Solar y Taboada, Antonio del, and José de Rújula y de Ochotorena. *El adelantado Hernando de Soto. Breves noticias, nuevos documentos para su biografía y relación de los que le acompañaron a la Florida.* Badajoz, Spain: Ediciones Arqueros, 1929.

Stephens, John L. *Incidents of Travel in Central America, Chiapas, and Yucatán.* 2 vols. New York: Dover, 1969.

Suárez Peralta, Juan. *Tratado del descubrimiento de las Indias.* 1589. Mexico City: Secretaría de Educación Publica, 1949.

Tebeau, Charlton W. *A History of Florida.* Coral Gables, Fla.: Univ. of Miami Press, 1971.

Tió, Aurelio. "Historia del descubrimiento de la Florida y Bímeni ó Yucatán." Número conmemorativo del cuadrigentisexagésimo aniversario del descubrimiento de la Florida y Yucatán, 1513–1973, *Boletín de la Academia Puertorriqueña de la Historia* 2, no. 8 (June 30, 1972): 7–267.

————. *Nuevas fuentes para la historia de Puerto Rico (Documentos inéditos o poco conocidos cuyos originales se encuentran en el Archivo General de Indias en la ciudad de Sevilla, España).* San Germán: Ediciones de la Universidad Interamericana de Puerto Rico, 1961.

Toro, Alfonso. *La familia Carvajal: Estudio histórico sobre los judíos y la Inquisición de la Nueva España en el siglo XVI.* 2 vols. Mexico City: Editorial Patria, 1944.

Toussaint, Manuel. *La conquista de Pánuco.* Mexico City: Edición de el Colegio Nacional, 1948.

Tozzer, Alfred M., ed. *Landa's Relación de las Cosas de Yucatán.* Cambridge, Mass.: Peabody Museum of Archeology and Ethnology, 1941. Reprint. New York: Kraus Reprint Corp. 1966.

Trueba, Alfonso. *Retablo Franciscano: Los Padres Bernardo de Sahagún, Andrés de Olmos, Diego de Olarte, Juan de San Miguel y Francisco Lorenzo.* Mexico City: Editorial Campeador, 1955.

United States De Soto Expedition Commission. *Final Report of the United States De Soto Expedition Commission.* 76th Cong., 1st sess.; H. Doc. 71. Washington, D.C.: Government Printing Office, 1939.

Vargas Ugarte, Rubén. *Los Mártires de la Florida, 1566–1572.* Lima, Peru: A. Castañeda, Vicario General, 1940.

Vega, Garcilaso de la. *The Florida of the Inca.* Translated by John Varner and Jeannette Varner. Austin: Univ. of Texas Press, 1951.

————. *Royal Commentaries of the Incas.* 2 vols. Translated by Harold V. Livermore. Austin: Univ. of Texas Press, 1966.

Velasco y Mendoza, Luis, ed. *Repoblación de Tampico: Documentos compilados, con disertación por Luis Velasco y Mendoza*. Mexico City: Manuel León Sánchez, 1942.

Wagner, Henry R. *The Discovery of New Spain in 1518 by Juan de Grijalva*. Berkeley, Calif. Cortés Society, 1942.

————. *The Discovery of Yucatán by Francisco Hernández de Córdoba*. Berkeley, Calif.: Cortés Society, 1942.

————. *The Rise of Fernando Cortés*. Berkeley, Calif.: Cortés Society, 1944.

————. *The Spanish Southwest, 1542–1794*. 2 vols. Los Angeles: Quivira Society, 1967. Reprint. New York: Arno Press, 1967.

Weddle, Robert S. *Wilderness Manhunt: The Spanish Search for La Salle*. Austin: Univ. of Texas Press, 1973.

Wenhold, Lucy L., trans. "A 17th Century Letter of Gabriel Díaz Vara Calderón, Bishop of Cuba, Describing the Indians and Indian Missions of Florida." *Smithsonian Miscellaneous Collections* 95, no. 16 (Nov. 20, 1936): 1–15.

Winsor, Justin, ed. *Narrative and Critical History of America*. 8 vols. Boston: Houghton, Mifflin, 1884–89.

Wright, Irene A. "The Dutch and Cuba, 1609–1643." *Hispanic American Historical Review*, 4, no. 4 (Nov. 1921): 597–634.

————. *Further English Voyages to Spanish America, 1583–1594*. London: Hakluyt Society (2d ser., no. 99), 1951.

————. *Spanish Documents concerning English Voyages to the Caribbean 1527–1568*. London: Hakluyt Society (2d ser., no. 62), 1928.

Index

Florida Keys, 39, 42–43, 46, 291–92, 378
Florin, Juan, 132
Follet's Island, 194, 196, 206
Fort Caroline, 289–91, 315, 316
Fountain of Youth, 38–39, 40
freebooters, Spanish, 395. *See also* pirates
and privateers
Freeport, (Tex.), 196
French, 274, 334, 406
Fuentes, ———, 237, 238, 239, 240, 243

Gage, Thomas, 381–82, 386
Gallegos, Baltasar de, 170, 179, 217, 219,
222
Galveston Island, 194, 206
Gamboa, Sebastián, 269, 279
Garay, Francisco de: and Alaminos, 107,
417; and Alvarez de Pineda, 99–102;
background of, 97; and Cortés, 91–92,
102, 141; death of, 142; and Díaz de
Aux, 106; finances of, 97, 106; granted
Amichel, 101; and Grijalva, 418; and
Jamaica, 98–99, 106; overland march
of, 133, 145; at Pánuco, 133, 135,
138–39; ships of, 98, 106; sources on,
143; territories of, 126, 131, 132, 420;
voyage of, 130
García, Diego, 211
García, Fray Juan, 235, 237, 238, 241
García Bravo, Alonso, 108
García de Sepúlveda, Jacinto, 352
Gayón, Gonzalo, 259–60, 264, 266, 267,
277, 278, 282, 289, 316
Gaytán, Juan, 230
Genoese merchant-bankers, 76–77, 97,
106
Genovés, Francisco, 316
Gentleman of Elvas, 216, 227
Georgia, 218, 324, 327, 421
Gibson, Charles, 385
Gilbert, John, 305
Goddard, Anthony, 301, 303
Godoy, Diego de, 67
gold: Alvarez de Pineda and, 96; Bena-
vides on, 355; in burials, 74; among
Calusa, 317; Cortés and, 112–13; in
Cuba, 28, 55; Garay and, 97; gifts of,
88, 89, 113, 166; Grijalva and, 71–72;
in Hispaniola, 23; Mayan, 58–59, 63; in

New Spain, 156; Pardo and, 327–29;
Ponce and, 45; Sandoval and, 122; sent
to emperor, 99, 131; in shipwrecks,
246; Soto and, 218, 220; source of,
323–24; stories of, 63; in Tabasco, 88;
among Timucuas, 188; Velázquez and,
32, 73
Golfo de Nueva España. *See* Gulf of
Mexico
Gómara, Francisco López de. *See* López
de Gómara, Francisco
Gómera (Canary Islands), 211
Gómez, Gonzalo, 13
González, Alonso, 57, 58
González, Gil, 130
González de Avila, Gil, 150–51, 153
González de Nájera, Pedro, 128
Graff, Laurens de (Lorencillo), 399–400,
405, 410
Grammont, Michel de, 399, 400, 405
Gran Cairo, 58
Grenville, Sir Richard, 373
Grijalva, Juan de: and Alaminos, 68, 70,
73, 417; at Cabo Rojo, 74; at Cam-
peche, 69–70; and Cortés, 137–38; in
Cuban conquest, 27; death of, 141; dis-
covers Cayo Arenas, 76; expelled from
Pánuco, 141; after 1518, 145; and
Garay, 130, 133; and natives, 71–72;
orders of, 67; at Potonchán, 75; return
of, 83; search for, 76, 81–82; ships of,
66–67; sources on, 77–78; and Váz-
quez de Ayllón, 128; and Velázquez,
63, 66, 83; voyage of, 67–76, 418–19
Grillo, Diego (Diego Mulato), 385, 392
Guadalupe River (Tex.), 198, 199
Guale (Ga.), 358, 359
Guaniguanico (Cuba), 117
Guatari, 326, 327
Guatemala, 234, 235
Guaxutla (Huejutla, Hidalgo), 336
Guerrero, Francisco, 343
Guerrero, Gonzalo, 86–87, 169, 175, 177
Guevara, Ladrón de, 260
Gulf of California, 154
Gulf of Mexico: access to, 382; and Al-
aminos, 416–17; as conduit for discov-
ery, 14, 412; corsairs in, 372, 380, 384,
395, 397; defenses of, 382; discovery

Salazar, Eugenio de, 343, 344
Salazar, Fray Domingo de, 271
Salazar, Gonzalo de, 211, 299
Salazar de Martel, Pedro de, 345
salt trade, 174, 304, 309, 408
Sámano, Juan de, 115, 124
San Agustín (Fla.), 293–94, 315, 373, 396, 397
San Antonio (Fla.), 318, 319, 320, 321, 415
Sánchez Calabrés, Antón, 164
Sánchez de Aguilar, Gonzalo, 268, 271
Sandoval, Gonzalo de, 119, 121–22, 123, 142, 151, 154, 155
San Felipe (Fla.), 316
San Francisco (Nuevo León), 351
San Francisco de Potano (Fla.), 359
San Jerónimo friars, 66
San Juan (Pardo's fort), 326
San Juan de Ulúa (Veracruz): Cáncer at, 237; Cortés at, 88; fortification of, 310–11, 313; and Hawkins, 298–300; named, 73; Narváez at, 113, 118; and pirates, 287, 399; as port, 113, 149, 161; Villafañe at, 275
Sanlúcar de Barrameda (Spain), 156, 165, 211, 295, 308, 341, 380–81
San Luis, Fray Pedro de, 339
San Luis (Monterrey), 344
San Luis de Apalache (Tallahassee), 249, 365
San Marcos, Mission, 365, 366
San Marcos de Apalache, 364, 367, 398, 402, 409, 411. *See also* Apalache (province)
San Mateo, 315, 319
San Mateo River. *See* St. John's River
San Miguel (Huasteca), 344
San Nicolás, Mission (Fla.), 365, 366
Santa Bárbara (Nueva Vizcaya), 341
Santa Cruz, Alonso de, 232, 233, 421
Santa Cruz de Querétaro, 400
Santa Cruz de Sabacola, Mission (Fla.), 364, 365
Santa Elena, 260, 268, 274, 275, 276, 277–78, 279, 280, 316, 325–28
Santa María, Fray Domingo de, 251, 262
Santa María de la Victoria (Tabasco), 88, 117, 171, 177, 179

Santa María de los Remedios. *See* Yucatán
Santa María de Ochuse, 266–67, 269, 271, 273, 276. *See also* Ochuse; Pensacola Bay; Polonza
Santana, Captain, 236
Santander, Pedro de, 255–57, 263–64
Santiago de Cuba, 57, 67, 211, 229
Santiago de los Valles, 158
Santiesteban del Puerto, 131–35, 157. *See also* Pánuco (settlement)
Sarasota Bay (Fla.), 205
Sarmiento, Fray Diego, 252
Sauer, Carl Ortwin, 36
Sauz, Mateo del, 265, 268, 269, 271–72, 275, 276, 280, 281, 328
Schell, Rolfe F., 231
Segura de la Frontera (Mexico), 120
Seno Mexicano, 279, 381. *See* Gulf of Mexico
Serpa, Diego de la, 130
Seville (Spain): Cáncer in, 249; Carvajal in, 334; Casa de Contratación in, 5, 149, 294; Cortés's proctors in, 115; English in, 294, 297, 308; Garay in, 98; Indian towns likened to, 68, 73; Ocampo in, 33; and plague, 385; Soto and, 210, 225; and Vespucci, 16
shipbuilding, 115, 192, 205, 221–22, 269, 370
ships: of Alvarez de Pineda, 99; of Cáncer, 237; of Carvajal, 341; and Cortés, 83, 84, 91, 94, 128, 418; Cuenca's, 153; of 1554 fleet, 246, 255; and Garay, 98, 106, 130; of Grijalva, 66–67; Guzmán's, 156, 157; and Hawkins, 291, 297, 298, 299–300; of Hernández de Córdoba, 56, 57; of Lavazares, 257, 259; of logwood cutters, 390; of Luna, 260, 262; and Menéndez, 316; Montejo and, 165–66, 169; of Narváez, 117, 119; of Pinzón-Díaz de Solis, 20; *piraguas* as, 409; of Ponce de León, 40; privateers and, 374, 388, 400, 401–402; revolution in, 5; salvage of, 248; of Santa Elena expeditions, 274, 277; scarcity of, 131; and Soto, 211, 224; of treasure fleets, 374; Velázquez and, 115
shipwrecks: at Cabo San Anton, 25; captives from, 332; off Carlos Bay, 362;